Contested Terrains and Constructed Categories

CONTESTED TERRAINS AND CONSTRUCTED CATEGORIES

Contemporary Africa in Focus

edited by

George Clement Bond
Teachers College, Columbia University

and

Nigel C. Gibson
Emerson College

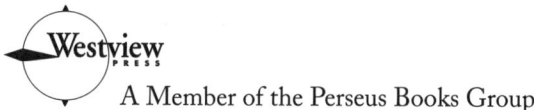

A Member of the Perseus Books Group

All rights reserved. Printed in the United States of America. No part of this publication may be reproduced or transmitted in any form or by any means, electronic or mechanical, including photocopy, recording, or any information storage and retrieval system, without permission in writing from the publisher.

Copyright © 2002 by Westview Press, a member of The Perseus Books Group

Westview Press books are available at special discounts for bulk purchases in the United States by corporations, institutions, and other organizations. For more information, please contact the Special Markets Department at The Perseus Books Group, 11 Cambridge Center, Cambridge MA 02142, or call (617) 252-5298.

Published in 2002 in the United States of America by Westview Press, 5500 Central Avenue, Boulder, Colorado 80301-2877, and in the United Kingdom by Westview Press, 12 Hid's Copse Road, Cumnor Hill, Oxford OX2 9JJ

Find us on the World Wide Web at www.westviewpress.com.

A Cataloging-in-Publication Data record is available at the Library of Congress

ISBN 0-8133-3678-3 (HC) and 0-8133-3974-X (pbk)

The paper used in this publication meets the requirements of the American National Standard for Permanence of Paper for Printed Library Materials Z39.48-1984.

10 9 8 7 6 5 4 3 2 1

In Memory of Claude Ake and William A. Shack

Contents

Illustrations — xiii
Acronyms — xiv
Preface — xv

    Introduction: African Studies in Contention,
    George Clement Bond and Nigel C. Gibson — 1

Part One
Challenging Modes of Thinking: Making Maps and Mapping History

1. "So Geographers in Africa Maps with Savage Pictures Fill Their Gaps": Representing Africa on Maps, Mohamed Mbodj — 37

    History of Mapmaking, 38
    Development of Scientific Cartography, 43
    Cartography Becomes Geography, 46
    Role of Maps in European Expansion, 47
    Accuracy in Size Versus Accuracy in Distance, 52
    Conclusion, 57

2. The Challenges of Writing African Economic History, Paul Tiyambe Zeleza — 59

    Introduction, 59
    Spatial and Temporal Scales, 60
    Themes and Theories, 65
    Comparisons and Connections, 72
    Conclusion, 83

Part Two
Contested Categories: Economy, Politics, and Society

3   Structural Adjustment, Sayre P. Schatz   87

The Failure of Structural Adjustment, 87
The Ideological Marketing Operation, 95
The Success of World Bank Spin, 99
Conclusion: Developmental Activism, 100

4   Poverty Profile in Sub-Saharan Africa: The Challenge
    of Addressing an Elusive Problem, Oliver S. Saasa   105

Introduction, 105
Main Causes of Persisting Poverty, 109
Measuring Prevalence of Poverty, 112
Conclusion, 115

5   Civil Society, Pluralism, Goldilocks, and Other Fairy Tales in
    Africa, Irving Leonard Markovitz   117

Introduction, 117
Conflicting Conceptions of Civil Society, 121
Africa Growth and Opportunity Act, 130
International Banking, Capitalist Development,
   the Asian Crisis, and Africa, 132
The Construction of Civil Society in Senegal: A Case Study—
   The Senegalese-Mauritanian Conflict, 134
Pogroms, "Restructuration," and Civil Society, 136
Conclusion: Cruel Democracy and Cruel Capitalism, 142

6   Beyond the State and Civil Society: Labor Movements and
    Economic Adjustment in African Transitions—South Africa
    and Nigeria Compared, Franco Barchiesi   145

Neoliberal Adjustment as a Challenge for
   African Labor in Transition, 145
African Transitions and "Transition Studies":
   Constraining the Space of Labor, 147
The Nigerian Labor Movement, Militarized Economic Adjustment,
   and the Uncertainties of Transition, 151
Labor in the South African Democratic Transition:
   The Challenge of Subordinate Incorporation, 160
Conclusion, 170

7   Silencing Power: Mapping the Social Terrain in Post-
    Apartheid South Africa, Kate Crehan   173

    Development as Discourse, 174
    The Space of the NGO, 175
    The Virtuous Community, 177
    NGOs in South Africa: From Struggle to Development, 181
    Working with the "Community," 182
    *Community as Historical Precipitate and Community
       as Interest Group,* 189
    Conclusion, 192

8   Negotiating Identity in Post-Settlement South Africa:
    Ethnicity, Class, and Race in a Regional Frame,
    Edward Ramsamy   195

    Introduction, 195
    *Group Identity and the National Liberation Struggle
       in South Africa,* 197
    The Politics of Zulu Nationalism, 200
    The National Question and the Indian Community, 204
    Conclusion, 209

9   Negotiable Property: Making Claims on Land
    and History in Asante, 1896–1996, Sara Berry   213

    Property as Exclusion, 215
    *Pushing on a String? Property Rights Reform and
       African Realities,* 217
    Negotiable Property in Asante, 220
    Property as Participation? 226
    Beyond Familiar Fictions, 230

PART THREE
Violence of the Word/Violence Against the Body

10 Mapping Africa's Presences: Merleau-Ponty, Mannoni,
    and the Malagasy Massacre of 1947 in Frantz Fanon's
    Black Skin White Masks, Nigel C. Gibson   235

    *Beyond Manicheanism: Merleau-Ponty and the
       Lived Experience of the Black,* 236
    *The Triple Person: Merleau-Ponty's Intersubjectivity and Sartre's
       Manicheanism,* 238

Outside the Psychoanalytic Office: Fanon and Mannoni, 243
1947: 100,000 Massacred, 249
Mannoni's Dreams and Fanon's Reality, 254

11 Contesting Terrains Over a Massacre: The Case of Wiriyamu, Mustafah Dhada 259

The Walls of Aching Silence, 259
Wiriyamu: Genesis, 265
Essentialism Defined, 267
Binaries, Values, and Attributions at Work, 269
The Grateful—and the Dead, 274

12 Negotiating Postwar Identities: Child Soldiers in Mozambique and Angola, Alcinda Honwana 277

Introduction, 277
Child Soldiers: A Worldwide Phenomenon, 280
Child Soldiers in Post-Colonial Conflicts in Africa, 280
Notions and Discourses About Childhood, 281
Experiencing War and Violence, 283
"Being in the War": Initiation to Violence and Terror, 287
The Quest for Reconciliation and Healing, 292
Conclusion, 298

13 Sex and the Politics of Space in Colonial Zimbabwe: The Story of Chibheura (Open Your Legs) Exams, Lynette Jackson 299

The Politics of Space, 300
The Politics of Sexuality, 310
The Politics of Memory, 312

14 Girls, Sex, and the Dangers of Urban Schooling in Coastal Madagascar, Lesley A. Sharp 321

Introduction, 321
Urban Danger and Scholastic Failure, 323
Girls in Town: An Independent Sister, 327
Worldly Diversions, 328
The Immorality of Play: Ny Soma, 337
SIDA and Sexual Danger, 339
Conclusion: Girls, Sex, and Urban Danger, 344

15 The Moving Frontier of AIDS in Uganda: Contexts, Texts, and
    Concepts, George Clement Bond and Joan Vincent   345

   Introduction, 345
   The Moving Frontier: The Contextualization of a Pandemic, 348
   AIDS: Civil War and Violence, 352
   Cultural or Intellectual Maps, 355
   The Uganda Districts Speak Out, 360
   Conclusion, 362

16 Contested Claims and Individual Bodies, Meredeth Turshen   365

   Epidemic Disease, 367
   Population Growth, 368
   Endemic Wars, 371
   Health and Political Violence, 373
   Gendered Violence, 375

Notes   379
References   407
Contributors   459
Index   463

Illustrations

Tables

3.1	Change in Real Gross National Product in Sub-Saharan Africa	89
3.2	Economic Growth of Reform-Performance Groups in Sub-Saharan Africa	92
3.3	Growth-Performance Rankings of Countries Listed by Reform Performance Rankings	94
3.4	Reform Performance of Growth Groups	95
3.5	Changes in Economic Policy Compared to Changes in Economic Growth, Contrariety Test, 1981–1986 and 1987–1991	96
3.6	Growth of Domestic Product in Sub-Saharan Africa	99
4.1	Prevalence of Poverty in Selected Countries of Sub-Saharan Africa, 1989–1994	107
4.2	Human Development Indicators by Country	108
4.3	Ranking of Countries by Incidence of Poverty and GDP per Capita	109

Figures

10.1 Banania Breakfast Food adverts	240

Maps

Map of Africa	xxii
Map of Mozambique	278
Map of Angola	279
Map of Uganda	346

Acronyms

ANC	African National Conference
ECA	Economic Commission for Africa
FAO	Food and Agriculture Organization (United Nations)
GDP	Gross Domestic Product
IMF	International Monetary Fund
ILO	International Labour Organization
NGO	nongovernmental organization
NIC	Natal Indian Congress
OAU	Organization of African Unity
SA	structural adjustment
SAP	structural adjustment programs
UNAIDS	[Joint] United Nations [Programme on HIV]/AIDS
UNCTAD	United Nations Conference on Trade and Development
UNDP	United Nations Development Fund
UNESCO	United Nations Economic, Scientific, and Cultural Organization
UNICEF	United Nations International Children's Emergency Fund
USAID	United States Agency for International Development

Preface

Background

Most of the essays in this volume, *Contested Terrain and Constructed Categories*, were first presented as invited lectures to advanced undergraduate and graduate students at Columbia University. The lectures were part of a series of multi-disciplinary seminars developed at the Institute of African Studies (IAS) within the School of International and Public Affairs (SIPA). The seminars were taught at Teachers College, Columbia University, and funded from the IAS's Department of Education National Resource Center grant. They were part of the effort to disseminate information about Africa within the university system and to provide critical markers for exploring the construction and application of knowledge.

The students, who were drawn from SIPA, the Graduate School of Arts and Sciences, Columbia College, and Teachers College, represented the academic disciplines of anthropology, comparative literature, economics, history and political science. They were also from professional schools and programs oriented toward education, development, health, law, social and public policy, and urban planning. The seminars were chaired by the Director of IAS, a social anthropologist, and the Assistant Director, a political scientist, with the faculty members of the IAS being the core speakers. Presentations were made by Professors Lee Baker, Linda Beck, Lynette Jackson, Winston James, Brian Larkin, Anthony Marx, Peter Marcuse, Mohamed Mbodj, Sayre Schatz, Lesley Sharp, Gayatri Spivak, Marcia Wright and Joan Vincent.

The idea for the seminars grew out of the interests of a lively body of students who wanted to relate their disciplinary and technical training to the empirical problems confronting Africa and the "developing countries" of the "Third World", designations that both the instructors and the students found pejorative and limiting. In our planning we discovered that these designations, and others like them such as "North and South" and "center and periphery", were imprecise and intellectually constraining. They confused social conditions and social theory with geography and location and provided a tenuous basis for comparative analysis. They also obscured the concatenations of historical and social processes, complex economic and political linkages, and the differences within regions and the similarities between them. They shed little light, for example, on the relation of theory to practice, explanation to reality, modes of exploitation to patterns of development, and power to representation.

Students expressed a wide range of topical interests and were dissatisfied with the state of knowledge in area studies. They contributed to designing seminars that reflected their interests and sought to push the boundaries of their fields of inquiry. The conceptualizations of Africa, African studies, and academic disciplines were taken as problematic. Thus, the very circumstances of organizing the seminars brought into play a multi-disciplinary perspective that highlighted basic controversies within and between disciplines and challenged their entrenched paradigms, especially as they related to Africa. The invited lecturers confirmed our suspicion that Africa and African studies were contested domains as were the principal academic disciplines and the analytic categories that they used in characterizing Africa. The dominant emphasis was on the construction of knowledge and its application in representing "Africa" and its problems.

Consistent with this orientation, we as editors have sought to retain a wide range of themes and not to limit the volume's focus to a single topic within African studies. Instead the volume attempts to preserve the broad perspective of intellectual inquiry that framed the seminars. Thus, it includes a variety of topics. The chapters may be read on their own. And yet, there are basic themes such as the relation of power to knowledge, the criteria of selection and presentation, and the consequences of applying particular theoretical paradigms that flow through the chapters. The chapters probe the social conditions within Africa and relate them to the way in which they have been represented within the academic disciplines. The terrain is sometimes complex. Thus, we encourage readers to read the introduction. It attempts to place the chapters in a broader context, set out common themes, and provide the general framework for exploring the volume.

African Studies: A Brief Historical Note

The study of Africa in the United States has always been a contested terrain, one littered with hidden land mines, sometimes obscured by strategic and personal interests, collective misrepresentation and diversions, and historical fabrications. There is no one "Africa" or history of "African" studies. There are a series of interwoven images and accounts representing dominant and minority renditions and interpretations and the perspective of the author. "Africa" is both an idea and a reality and the attempts to represent it are informed by the theoretical orientations and pragmatic purposes of those who study and write about it. "Africa" has been an integral part of America's historical development, it has been an essential ingredient in the making of American public culture and an important element in framing the rights and entitlements of ethnic and academic "communities" and associations.

Although African studies has never been the sole preserve of the academy, nonetheless academics have claimed it. They have played an important role in shaping African images and as master builders, they have had a vested interest in maintaining the intellectual contours and parameters of African studies and the manner of its investigation. They have usually approached Africa from the vantage point of their disciplinary training. The study of Africa has, thus, been subjected to the dominant theoretical paradigms of the historic moment. These paradigms have framed the selection of empirical data and their representation in texts. They have left their mark on the development of African Studies.

"African Studies", as a formal endeavor based within major research institutions, has experienced many transformations. In her book, *African Studies in the United States: A Perspective* (1996), Jane Guyer identifies two main waves, with each wave being intimately related to the international and social conditions of the times. The first wave begins after the Second World War in the early 1950s. It is part of the United States government's response to the gradual collapse of European colonial rule, the beginning of the "cold war" between the United States and the Soviet Union and the government's concern with developing area studies and regional specialists. The primary purpose of African studies was, thus, to train diplomats, scholars and practitioners and to increase the United States' knowledge of Africa. The two main centers were at Northwestern University (1948) under Melville J. Herskovits, a Columbia-trained cultural anthropologist who taught at Princeton, and at Boston University (1953) under William Brown, a sociologist who was teaching at Howard University. Although Howard University's center of African studies was founded in 1953, it was never as well funded as the centers at either Boston or Northwestern. These two centers were the recipients of generous government and private foundation grants and attracted faculty and students from a variety of disciplinary backgrounds.

During this initial phase, at least at Boston University, the study of Africa was charged with intellectual and political excitement. The faculty was stellar. The program brought together scholars such as Jeffrey Butler, Elizabeth Colson, George Dalton, Adelaide Cromwell Hill, Daniel McCall, Carl Rosberg and Ruth Schacter from a variety of disciplines. The students included future distinguished academics and activists such as Norman Bennett, James Forman, Irving L. Markovitz, and Aristide Zolberg . Their discussions of Africa extended to their peers at Harvard such as James Coleman and Martin L. Kilson, students of Government professor Rupert Emerson. Exchanges occurred between African studies centers. For example, during the late 1950s, Eduardo Mondlane, FRELIMO's first president, completed a Ph.D. at Northwestern and spent a year at Boston University's program in African Studies. His innovative theoretical insights and pragmatic political understandings of colonial domination and African resistance movements influenced his colleagues in African studies and the social sciences, especially anthropologists at Boston, Northwestern, and Columbia Universities.

A community of scholars was in the making, one that transcended disciplinary boundaries. Among most of these scholars there was the general understanding that Africa provided the context for exploring theoretical problems. The particular problematic defined the unit of analysis, and the delineation of a set of interrelated propositions was constrained neither by geographic nor political boundaries. Functionalist, structuralist, and Marxist paradigms competed for the attention of students.

In the mid–1950s, Gray Cowan, a political scientist at Columbia, assembled a group of distinguished scholars that included Gwendolyn Carter, E. Franklin Frazier, William Hance, and Melville J. Herskovits to discuss the state of African studies. From this meeting of senior academics the African Studies Association was founded in 1957. In 1959, Columbia established its own Institute of African Studies.

As part of the academy with its own professional association, African Studies gradually became an exclusive club, removed from the popular debates within minority intellectual traditions, accountable primarily to the disciplines and evaluated by its contribution to the dominant theoretical paradigms. By the late 1960s, as a field of endeavor, it had become domesticated, reflecting the patterns of social differentiation that marked academia and American society. It was during this period that black Americans and African scholars led protests at the African Studies Association meetings in Toronto. It was also the period that the African Heritage Association was founded and held its first national meeting at Howard University in Washington, D. C.

The second phase in African studies encompassed much of the next few decades, and the conditions that produced it have persisted into the present. It has reflected the monumental tasks confronting independent African countries in dealing with problems of governance, development, population growth, growing international debt, poverty, war, natural disasters, and the imposition of the policies of the World Bank and other international organizations. The period has been one marked by the decline in funding of African Studies in the United States and a diminished interest of students about Africa. From the early 1970s until the present, Africa has been neither a major government nor academic priority.

However, even during these decades of declining resources and neglect, there was a proliferation in the domains of inquiry in African Studies, especially in the humanities. But two themes tended to dominate others, the problems of development and governance. This emphasis brought about a division between basic research and research directed toward the problems of development and governance and the more technical fields. The people of Africa were confronting real problems that were thought to be amenable to technical solutions. Much of the research became driven by the pragmatic interests of international non-governmental organizations (NGOs) framed within nonspecific, transposable research designs that were thought to be appropriate to any "Third World" social setting.

The division between basic and technically oriented research produced a healthy tension, but it has also had the potential for fragmenting and compartmentalizing African Studies into narrowly focused specialties. Many of the earlier hallmarks that characterized basic research and area studies such as extended field work and an in-depth knowledge of a region's language, history, and culture, were set aside for short-term periods of investigation. Moreover, the innovative critical orientation of the first phase were being submerged by the magnitude of the problems confronting the people of Africa and the responses to them by governments and international organizations. Much of African Studies was loosing its sharp, critical, radical edge, that is, its concern with exploring the roots and criteria of knowledge and the mechanisms of its application. It became more a domain for imposing policies than a field of independent research. Africa was experiencing a new mode of domination.

During this second phase, African Studies programs grew in number, as did the number of African scholars within the American academy. African scholars were themselves divided along the two paths of basic and technically oriented research. Within most African universities the possibility to pursue research at all was intimately linked to government and NGO-funded research projects. However, no matter what their particular research orientation, African scholars brought with them a critical perspective. They have subjected the dominant theoretical paradigms of the academy to careful scrutiny as well as those of the grounded theories of practitioners. They have added a new element to African Studies.

African Studies is entering a new phase. With the collapse of the Soviet Union and the demise of the "cold war", the continued viability of "Area studies" or "Regional studies" is being challenged. African Studies, often on the periphery of regional studies, may not be able to maintain its present integrity within the new configuration of "global" alliances, technological innovations, and global studies. Confronted by the pressures of this new environment, the old arguments, tensions, and cleavages have surfaced and manifested themselves in complicated ways. As a field of inquiry it has undergone scrutiny in a number of journal articles (see for example, *A Quarterly Journal of Opinion (1995); African Studies Review* (1996); and *Africa Today* (1997)); and books: Robert Bates et al.(ed.), *Africa and the Disciplines* (1993); Jane Guyer et al., *African Studies in the United States* (1996); and Mark Pires et al., *Investing in Return* (1999).

The present volume reflects the tensions and new directions in African studies. In many respects, it combines the two phases, representing the critical appraisal of entrenched paradigms and the range of conditions confronted by African governments and ordinary people. Thus, it follows a path across a broad landscape that includes a critique of the techniques of manufacturing Africa's geography, African economic historiography, World Bank policies, measures of poverty, community and ethnicity, the nature of being and becoming, and conditions of violence and health. It illustrates the expectations of a body of students from the academic disciplines and professional schools for both basic and technically oriented research. The students wanted to explore the criteria of knowledge, the reasons for presenting Africa in one way and not another, and the basis for applying one set of formulations instead of another. This expectation brought them directly into the highly contested terrain of constructed categories and images within African Studies. It encompassed "social facts" about Africa and also their significance for bodies of theory and social policies.

Acknowledgments

This volume is the product of the efforts, generosity, and goodwill of a large number of people. It represents a selection of papers presented over a period of four semesters between 1998 and 2000 in the seminar series as well as at a mini-conference that included most of the contributors. We were unable to include many of the issues developed in the seminars and the fine papers presented by colleagues such as Professors Anthony Kwame Appiah, Linda Heywood, Paul Landau, Ricardo Laremont and John Middleton. Our hope is to have a companion volume that focuses on religion, philosophy, and identity in Africa.

We would like to express our appreciation to all the participants in these seminars and to the U. S. Department of Education for funding them through Columbia University's IAS National Resource Center grant. We are especially grateful to Ms. Karla Verbryck Block of the Department of Education. We owe a strong intellectual debt to the students who participated in the seminars and especially to that core who helped to design them. Thus, we wish to acknowledge the contributions of Sika Awoonor, Kevin Dwyer, Stephen D'Allessandro, Kevin Gross, Michael Leonard, Timothy Mangin, Angela Ndinga-Muvumbo, Michelle Sieff, Michelle Trudeau, and Paulette Young. Ms. Marlyse Rand, the IAS administrative assistant, did invaluable work in making the seminars possible. We also wish to thank Alison Bond, Jonathan Bond, Sarah Bond, Aidan Gibson and Kate Josephson for their generosity. We are grateful to Mr. Karl Yambert, Ms. Barbara Greer and other members of the staff at Westview Press for their unstinting efforts in the production of this volume.

George Clement Bond
New York City

Nigel C. Gibson
Boston

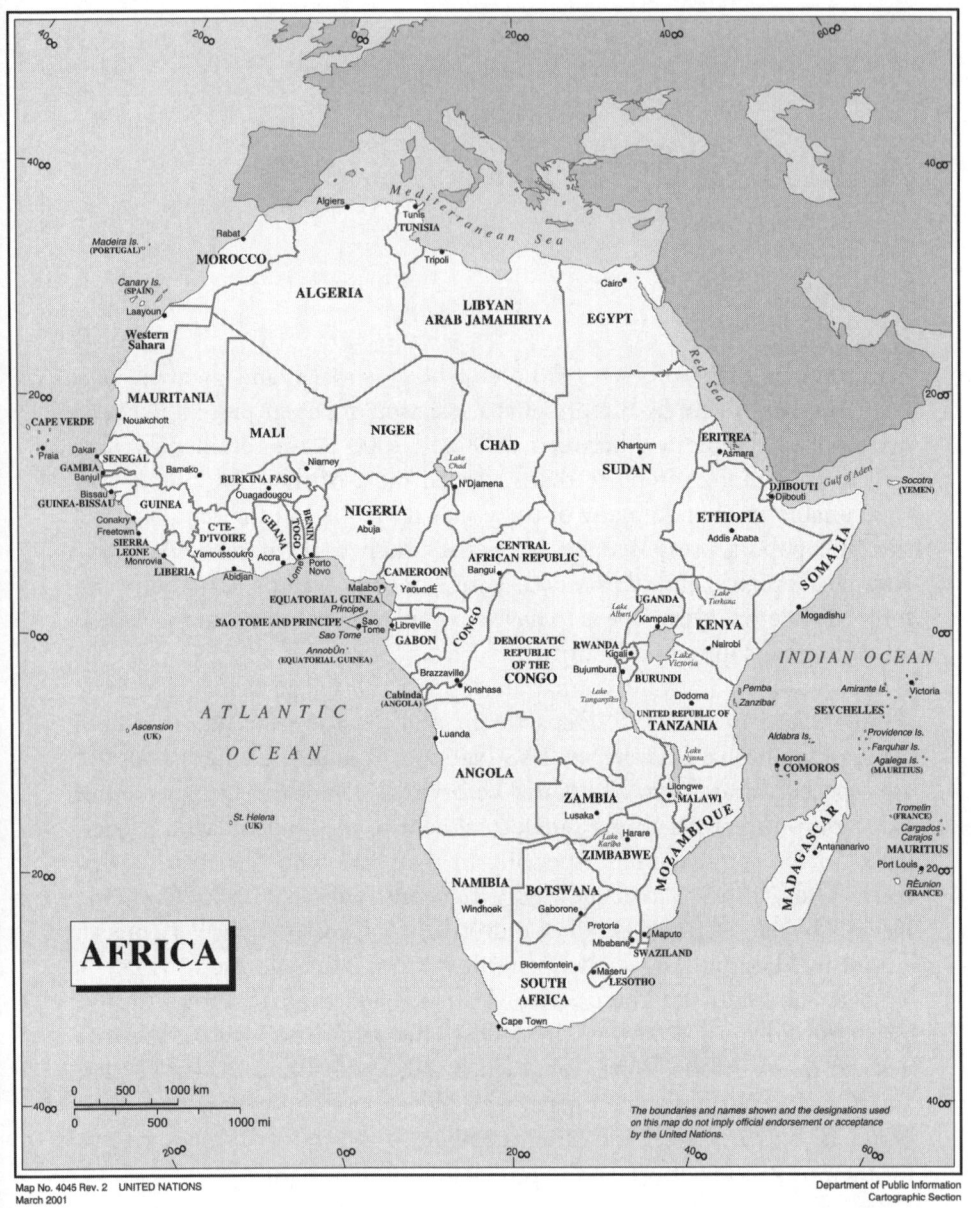

Map of Africa, Map No. 4045 R.2, UN Cartographic Section. Permission granted by the United Nations.

Introduction

African Studies in Contention

GEORGE CLEMENT BOND AND NIGEL C. GIBSON

Contested Terrains and Constructed Categories: Contemporary Africa in Focus brings together intellectuals from a variety of fields, backgrounds, generations, and continents to deepen and reinvigorate the theoretical integrity of African studies. In every chapter, case studies and ethnographic materials, drawn from such regions as Angola, Ghana, Madagascar, Mozambique, Nigeria, Senegal, South Africa, Uganda, Zambia, and Zimbabwe, demonstrate the application of theory to concrete situations as well as the constructed and contested character of intellectual exploration.

The approaches taken in this volume are heterodox, and readers will discover methodological tensions. Case studies present a nuanced view of Africa, but *Contested Terrains* is also a challenge. What remains important is not simply to reveal the underlying contested terrains of knowledge. Instead of counterposing methodological approaches, the chapters work as a series of constructions and deconstructions. This double process of putting Africa in focus challenges its mapping geographically and intellectually. Historically, Africa's borders have always been porous, and the "African diaspora" can be traced back to the beginning of human existence. Epistemologically, the ways in which Africa, its people, and its history have been mapped express subtle worldviews. The chapters in this volume can be read in a variety of different modes, and "Africa" can be approached in a multifaceted manner.

Post-Colonial African Studies

Contested Terrains reflects the current theoretical and empirical debates *in* African studies that have engaged "Africanists" and African scholars since the collapse of European colonial rule. The debates center on three key questions: Which scholars are best qualified and entitled to describe the daily lives of African peoples? Which theoretical paradigms may best explain the economic, political, and social conditions of Africa? Should African studies include the entire continent or regions south of the Sahara? Controversies over geography, entitlement, the production of knowledge, and representation are part of the very history of African studies itself, especially in the United States.

Post-colonial African scholars have infused purely intellectual paradigms with a marked concern for the mundane and practical techniques involved in producing knowledge (see Chapter 1), eliminating intellectual dependency (Appiah, 1992: 228; Hountondji, 1992: 238–248), and exploring principles for constructing different modes of thought and new societies (Ake, 1996). Three positions can be distinguished related to a critique *of* African studies. The first, cultural autonomy, refers to the position that Africans should create space for their own development. It is proposed by Oyekan Owomoyela, that the primary task of representing the real Africa must fall to African scholars because in the past Africanists purporting to have the best interests of Africans at heart have perpetuated "notions of an Africa that never was" (Owomoyela, 1994: 1–2). The second position, advocating an intellectual synthesis, seeks to retain the collaborative efforts of African and Western scholars. Michael Chege argues that the

> real gains—in Africa and the West—could be made by more forthright and critical engagements of the dominant ideas generated on both sides of the Atlantic against one quintessential yardstick. This is best realized through a more intensified, empirically grounded debate . . . between both groups and the wider social science community. (Chege, 1997: 134)

The third position is that of political praxis. Mahmood Mamdani adds a further degree of complexity to the relationship between the African scholar and his or her attempt to control the production of knowledge. He points to a peculiar irony: "[T]o gain access to resources which would enable more than an artisanal perspective, such a scholar has to connect, directly or indirectly, with the very centres of wealth and power whose critique must be the springboard of any transformative knowledge. The effect is to discipline and shape the very process of knowledge production." He goes on to say that "when not anchored in popular struggles whether in Africa or at home, the Africanist tends to succumb to the pressure of institutional ideologies" (Mamdani, 1990: 7). Thus, escape appears to be through struggle and praxis (Mamdani, 1990: 11), putting the "displaced African" (Appiah, 1992: 228) scholar into even more of a bind. Living in the overseas metropolitan centers of wealth, power, and knowledge has its own benefits and comforts, but it also has heavy constraints. Distance may deprive one of firsthand research experiences. It may also mute the effects of a critical voice and the ability to assess the personal experiences and public sentiments of the common people, both rural peasants and urban workers. Engagement in African affairs is from afar.

However, one may argue that the production of critical transformative knowledges is itself a form of struggle, praxis, and engagement at a fundamental level, especially when it occurs within the metropole. This is the position of the "post-colonial critic" (Spivak, 1990) attempting to create a "counter-knowledge." The mushrooming of "marginality studies" in the United States in the 1990s has been the source of further divisions in which the estranged "post-colonial intellectual" abroad has to re-confront the problem of their own agency (see Chapters 10 and 11). The philosopher Emmanuel Eze argues that when he refers to "post-colonial" the word *post* should be under erasure or in brackets: It "serves as a signal and pointer to the (in many parts of Africa) unfulfilled dreams of the independence achievements of the 1960s. . . . The brackets are to be opened, but only as far as the lived actuality of the peoples and the lands formerly occupied by European imperial powers can suggest, or confirm, in some meaningful ways, the sense of the words 'post.'" (Eze 1997: 14, 342). In this view of post-colonial scholarship there is less concern with the search for an authentic Africa than with the hybrid nature of the philosophical questions rooted in the everyday.

With the collapse of European colonial rule and the immediate post-colonial regimes that replaced it, the debates have become more pervasive and intense. Lodged within academic institutions in Europe and the United States, African universities, and research organizations such as the Council for the Development of Social Science Research in Africa (CODESRIA) in Dakar, they have become an accepted, if not an expected, part of African studies. They are now part of the common discourse of those scholars who have sought to revise the field's basic terrain. The very premises of well-established academic paradigms are being rigorously explored and their formulations thoroughly contested. It has become increasingly apparent that Africa has been framed in constructed categories stemming from its colonial history of conquest and subjugation. For example, "tribal" groups were created by native and district commissioners, and well-established indigenous "national" identities were dismissed by colonial authorities and sometimes even by anthropologists. Africans themselves often accepted the categories of colonial rule. An example is the "Hamitic hypothesis." The hypothesis categorizes the Tutsi as being not only "foreigners" but also of a genetically different "race" than other Rwandans. It also provides interesting instances of the construction, imposition, and manipulation of racial ideologies by European colonizers and African rulers alike. According to Peter Uvin, "the notion that the difference between Hutu and Tutsi is a racial one probably dates from the colonial period" although "the images of social and moral differentiation in all likelihood predate colonization" (1998: 31). The distinction was first used in the pre-colonial period as an ideology of conquest; then during the colonial period for entitlement and privilege; and finally, in the years following independence, for the systematic extermination of actual, imagined, and fabricated "enemies."

During the post-colonial period African political elites have constructed their own categories based on the dominant ideologies of "nationalism" (Mkandawire, 1997: 18–19) and "development," which support the interests of the elites and the policies of international organizations such as the World Bank and the International Monetary Fund (IMF) (Ake, 1996: 7; Mkandawire, 1997: 20–24; see Chapters 2, 3, and 4). African governments have readily accepted and encouraged technical solutions for what have often been basically social and political problems (Ferguson, 1990). African ruling elites have rarely been held accountable to the people they rule, and national democratic institutions and procedures may not be securely implanted in the social fabric (Bratton & van de Walle, 1992: 52–54). As Mkandawire points out, ideologies of nationalism and development may serve the interests of the elites and not always those of the common folk. The primary role of the intellectual may be critic and gadfly, contesting the political and social terrain of dominant explanatory paradigms (see Chapters 2 and 16) and the claims of government agencies, political elites, and international organizations.

An Orienting Frame

Contested Terrains finds its intellectual pedigree in the idea of hegemony developed by the Italian Marxist Antonio Gramsci and in French intellectual Michel Foucault's understanding of the intimate relation of power and the production of knowledge. Hegemony can be conceived of as processes of political, economic, and social consensus involving an interplay of force and consent and implying a struggle or contestation in a number of different spheres of society at the same time.

Hegemony, the pervasive ideational constructions of the dominant group, is by definition contested and never absolute. In Gramsci's formulation, "the intellectuals are the dominant group's 'deputies' exercising the subaltern functions of social hegemony and political government" (Gramsci, 1971: 12). They understand the operation of the "state" and its apparatus of domination. They are positioned at almost every level of society and serve to diffuse the hegemony of the ruling class and the state. Because they perform "organizational and connective functions" in society and the state, they have the potential for power. Moreover, their relation to the main productive mode is mediated, and thus they are not integrated into the system of social classes. They occupy an autonomous space in the social order, and in their capacity as thinkers they engage in the production of knowledge. They may become involved in counter-hegemonic activities, de-anchoring dominant paradigms of knowledge from their historical base. Both the paradigms and the historical moment may be subjected to careful scrutiny.

Gramsci could not have foreseen the degree of potential autonomy, or perhaps pseudo-autonomy, that the present-day scholar would attain in this era of global transport. Although keeping in mind Mamdani's caveat, post-colonial scholars have an unprecedented opportunity to shift their local functional involvement. They may exit one situation and enter another, retaining their critical productive capacities (Hirschman, 1982: 64–65). They have the opportunity to be master critics of hegemonic bodies of knowledge as well as master builders.

The contributors to this volume recognize that dominant knowledge is a product of power but also that knowledge is itself a form of power. They are aware of the hegemonic sway of the recent European colonial past and that it has created a cluster of subjugated knowledges that contain the multifaceted histories of the conquered and colonized, the stories of individuals and collectivities. Through the efforts of post-colonial scholarship this body of subjugated knowledges is being brought to the fore and introduced into the main currents of intellectual thought. It affords a broader and deeper perspective on the nature of history and the experiences of the common people. At times it may challenge the way in which Africa has been understood and represented. It may begin to take the measure of the explanatory power of dominant paradigms, including even those currently being generated by post-colonial scholars. The history of African studies in the United States is itself an example of the struggles of entitlement in the production of knowledge, with minority voices being channeled to the periphery.

In this book "Africa" is approached from a global perspective while also being embedded in local knowledge. We recognize that Africa, African intellectuals, and African studies are constructed and contested domains. For example, there is no one "African studies," nor is African studies simply a product of postwar area studies. To speak of the field in the United States today one must take into account the important role played by African intellectuals such as James Aggrey, Frederic Dube, Kwame Nkrumah, Nandi Azikiwe, Hastings Banda, and Eduardo Mondlane. They, like many other Africans, studied and worked in the United States and actively contributed to the construction of knowledge about Africa.

The influence of the African scholars of the first half of the twentieth century has been extensive. They were on intimate terms with the publishers and editors of religious and secular journals such as *The Star of Zion* (Bishop George Clinton Clement) and the *Crisis* (W. E. B. Du Bois). They knew and worked with the distinguished members of the National Negro Academy and the American Society for African Culture (AMSAC). AMSAC was established in 1956 with the full support and participation of Alioune Diop, the Senegalese intellectual who founded *Présence Africaine* (Davis, 1958: 1–8). These "displaced African" intellectuals were part of regional and international networks that included leading authorities on Africa in the United States, the Caribbean, England, and France (see Chapter 10).

The question of contestation and construction turns on the dialectics of power, history, structure, and agency in the production of knowledge.

Africa in Focus

Historical Configurations

Africa, a continent of more than 11,700,000 square miles with a population of some 800 million people, has been one of the primary sources of Western European and American wealth. For more than five centuries Europe and the Americas have benefited from African labor and exploited its natural resources. And yet, since the fifteenth century Africa has been depicted as peripheral and marginal to the modern world and its peoples, viewed as contributing little to its economic, political, and cultural development.

Africa and its peoples, however, have been an essential part of the making of the modern world. They were linked with the economies of the Middle East, India, Europe, and the Americas through the slave trade, the extraction of natural resources, and the expansion of capitalism. The relation of Africa to Europe reflected interdependent economic and social processes that created a complex history of commercial and political domination. As Zeleza points out (see Chapter 2), these linkages may not conform to the usual periodicity of European temporal impositions, pre-colonial, colonial, and post-colonial. They reflect fundamental forces that have pulled in the direction of regional and global integration. The past and present rhetoric of Africa's marginality has concealed how deeply it has been implicated in the development of the contemporary modern world.

Two examples will suffice to demonstrate this fact. Within the historical configuration of Europe's and America's developing modernity, Africa has served as a reservoir of cheap labor and natural resources. The consequences of extracting these resources have been marked by extended periods of major social upheavals but also of order. Philip Curtin (1969) estimates that from the beginning of the fifteenth to the end of the nineteenth century approximately 10 million African slaves were brought to the Americas. Although J. E. Inikori (1976) has criticized this figure as being at the low end of the range, both he and Curtin would agree on the social disruption that this magnitude of persistent forced population displacement had on African societies.

The history of slavery is one of regional violence and international trade. It set the stage for European colonial expansion in the nineteenth century, the making of empires, and the accumulation of vast individual and corporate fortunes. Almost all of the African continent experienced European colonial rule from the end of the nineteenth century to the middle of the twentieth century. The main colonial powers—England, France, Belgium, Portugal, Germany, and Spain—imposed authoritarian forms of governance. Africans became subjects in European empires.

The 1885 conference of Berlin, which established European colonial boundaries in Africa, is the second example of the important role of Africa in the development of the modern world. It brought into being new political territories. These territories were imperial holdings, lacking the sovereignty associated with independent states. As colonies they were administered from the metropole. They were integrated into international commercial systems that relied heavily on the extraction of their raw materials and the sale of processed goods in their markets.

With conquest European states confronted the problem of governing vast African territories. One mode of governance was "indirect rule." In his general survey of the different procedures employed in organizing the system of native administration in British colonial Africa, Lord Hailey, perhaps the most important surveyor of British colonial rule, identifies two types of territories. The first was those territories that used agencies deriving "their authority entirely from statutory enactment or from appointment as executive instruments of the Administration." The second group employed agencies that brought "to the service of the Administration an authority derived from their traditional status in their community" (1951: 9). The first came to be described as *direct rule,* the second as *indirect rule.*

Achille Mbembe points to two essential features of post-colonial state power, which, one may suggest, also apply to the imposition of colonial rule. First, through its administrative and bureaucratic practices the state attempts to create a world of meanings all its own that governs the logic of all other meanings within society. Second, the state attempts "to institutionalize its world of meanings as a 'socio-historical world,' and to make that world fully real" (1992: 2). Colonial governments confronted a formidable task in seeking to create bureaucratic structures and worlds of meaning through which they could govern diverse peoples without relying on the "systematic application of pain" or resorting to the massive punitive apparatus of their empires. As imperial productions they neither had the full properties of modern states nor existed in a global world organized on modern state principles (Wallerstein, 1997: 97).

Colonial administrators confronted the daunting task of having to rule people from different cultural and linguistic backgrounds, many of whom belonged to acephalous societies with complex political forms based on, for example, age grade and lineage systems. These forms, like "indigenous" state structures, were either incorporated or destroyed during the colonial period. Africans were brought into new commercial and political affiliations. They became taxpayers, small commercial farmers, migrant laborers, and wage earners. They organized "independent" churches, trade unions, and political parties. They developed new ideologies and struggled to gain independence. In the years immediately following the Second World War, they began to accomplish the goal of independence.

With the collapse of European empires and their colonial governments, former colonial territories confronted the formidable problems of constructing viable state structures, ranging from working through the conceptual and practical issues of sovereignty to defining the relationship of individuals and collectivities to the state and their rights in property and land. But even with independence the basic commercial and economic relationships were not fundamentally changed.

Structured toward the colonial metropole, post-colonial regimes inherited "states" that had little capacity or autonomy. Julius Nyerere's remark that "the British Empire left us a country with 85 per cent illiteracy, two engineers and 12 doctors" is true for most of post-colonial Africa. Although they had been transformed from imperial holdings into states, the African states remained tied into the world economy. As an integral part of the global system, the countries in Africa may be seen as being at the base of an economic hierarchy, with exploitation of their raw materials occurring as much in intraregional as in international terms. Although the immediate post-colonial period saw hopes pinned to state-centered national development, during the 1990s much was said about the crisis of governance in Africa and the "collapsed state" (Zartman, 1995). The context for this multinational collapse is the end of the Cold War, policies of economic liberalization, and a global capitalism that has penetrated deeper into the African continent than ever before.

Contemporary Context

Structural adjustment has been an attempt to come to grips with the economic and political problems confronting African states. But after two decades of structural adjustment, even where there has been economic growth and World Bank predictions are problematic (see Chapter 3), it has become clear that growth alone does not guarantee reduction of poverty and political "stability." In fact, structural adjustment has produced adverse social conditions severely affecting the social structure of the "core poor" countries. The African continent contains most of the world's poorest nations, so the problem is a significant one.

Structural adjustment was first developed in the mid-1970s. Influenced by University of Chicago economists, the authoritarian Pinochet regime in Chile instituted a monetarist neoliberal economic program that had become a global World Bank policy by 1980.

In the 1980s welfare states in the advanced capitalist nations were dismantled and workers' wages (in terms of both net pay and benefits) were cut. New global competitiveness and global integration have been based as much on new technology and "post-Fordist" production techniques as on lowering wages and increasing the length of the working day. The collapse of Soviet communism and the "privatization" of Chinese communism illustrate the same phenomena. In Russia, for example, economic liberalization quickened the collapse of the already decrepit welfare system, with devastating effects on the living standards of workers and the old; life expectancy was substantially decreased.

Does the World Bank's Africa Structural Adjustment Program (including its latest reform guise; see Chapter 4) simply mirror these policies? From the point of view of privatization and neoliberal economic programs, the answer is yes. Yet even if the playing field were level—which it is not—and Africa's economies were powerful—which they are not—Thatcher and Reagan, or for that matter, Blair and Bush or even Putin are not subject to the same political strictures as "developing countries." Policies might be determined by the world economy and comparative advantage, but in terms of political power the African nations exist in a different league.

In one sense, an African "homegrown" structural adjustment is nothing but the internalization of global structural adjustment. Yet having 28 of the 41 "less-developed countries" means that the standard of life on the African continent, compared with every other continent, is particularly poor.[1]

As a continent confronting the challenges of development, Africa affords a laboratory in which to analyze political ideas and economic and social processes taking place globally. Modernizers still believe that Africa can develop efficient capitalistic economies like the "Asian tigers." Other analysts see postmodern Africa as the object of exploitation following at best a path of "uneven development," partly as a result of globalization and partly as a legacy of late colonialism. Even if one considers "the African state criminalized," as some postmodernists, such as Jean-François Bayart (see Bayart, Ellis, and Hibou, 1999), do, or so thoroughly privatized that it is a "warlord" state (cf. Reno, 1998), states in Africa are operating within the confines of a global capitalism that is "weakening" national state structures everywhere. If it took Europe hundreds of years and decades of war and violence to develop the modern state form, is present-day Africa, plagued by war and dislocation, simply echoing that bloody development of the modern European state as a process of "organized crime," as Charles Tilly (1990) has put it? The historical context is now quite different from the one that produced the European state.

Africa is a subordinate partner in a global system with distinctive development problems. Privatization and liberalization have not undermined unproductive clients nor encouraged new states along the lines of how they supposedly developed in Europe, that is, a model of a new middle class allied to the power of the state. Instead, the recent period has seen state rulers using both formal and informal commercial activities to manage competing elites, often at the expense of formal state structures. These types of rulers, who are not confined to Africa, have also been surprisingly adept at manipulating the World Bank and other international organizations.

The conceptual shift from "state" to "civil society" as the new hope for development and democracy reinvents the modernization paradigm of the 1950s, namely that Africa will follow the European/American model. It was thought that nongovernmental organizations (NGOs) would bolster "civil society" and create an "enabling environment" that would recognize the "supremacy of society over the state" (Hyden, 1988: 150). Instead of placing all hopes on development through the state, NGOs are now serving "broader ends, notably the goal of greater diversity and plurality in society." The NGO would "form part of the process toward recreating civil society in Africa and thus the initiation of new mechanisms of government" (Hyden, 1988: 150).

The shift from state-centered to society-centered development paradigms obscures class analysis, patron/client relationships, and the manner in which "civil society" is a conceptual grab bag ranging from venture capitalists and smugglers to missionaries and sincere human rights advocates. The loosening of financial regulations for speculation is performed under the cover of the "NGO," another amorphous concept of anything that is not governmental. NGOs are mostly undemocratic, accountable to head offices that are often in New York or Brussels, Paris, or London, not to the local people. Advised by African intellectuals in the metropole, the NGOs often remain distant from the local people.

The Aim of This Volume

This volume considers the idea of contestation from two main perspectives. The first illuminates how interests are politically, economically, and ideologically constructed in already existing terrains; the second analyzes the ways in which dominant ideologies become organic and are mapped in society and on the human body. We seek to understand the ways in which the terms of debate, be it in the context of technology and geography (see Chapter 1), "civil society" and "community" (see Chapters 5 and 7), property and history (see Chapters 2 and 9), or knowledge and corporeality (see Chapters 11 and 14), are part of the process by which hegemony is constructed.

Part 1 scrutinizes the very physical construction of Africa. Starting from the mapping of Africa geographically, historically, and economically, the section ends by questioning the terms of Africa's growth and poverty. In Part 2 the questioning continues, with an emphasis on contesting constructed categories such as "civil society," "community," and "ethnicity." Although focusing on South Africa in a comparative frame, the discussion is in no sense limited to that region. Underlying some of the debates are issues such as modernity and development, urban versus rural, and governance and accountability in an international frame. In Part 3 the issue of the construction of knowledge is seen through the control of individual bodies and viewed in terms of meta-discourses on subjects such as disease and health and violence and war. Most of the chapters in this volume consider contemporary Africa, but there is no dividing line drawn between the colonial and post-colonial.

Part 1, Challenging Modes of Thinking:
Making Maps and Mapping History

An underlying theme of this volume is to explore dominant views and to foster constructive debate about African studies. In his discussion of maps in

Chapter 1, Mohamed Mbodj recognizes the hegemony of representations contained in the technology of replication, and in his chapter Paul Zeleza provides a counter-hegemonic perspective constructed through a careful analysis of African economic history.

Mbodj's chapter, "So Geographers in Africa Maps with Savage Pictures Fill Their Gaps," deals with the history of mapmaking in the context of the power of knowledge. In what appears to be the most mundane of technical activities, he reveals worlds of intrigue, purpose, direction, and social and political impositions. The techniques appear to order the world of thought, yet the very technique itself is an expression of human thought and social will. Maps are products of their time and place, reflections of the social order that produced them. They are thus powerful cultural statements that seek to control human actions and destinies.

Mbodj takes us through different forms of maps and their purposes. He distinguishes between mental and technical maps. The distinction brings forward a central problem in the social sciences related to the particularity of events situated in a localized context and the abstraction from them for comparative purposes. Mental maps involve making sense of local space and ordering it, whereas technical maps involve "reproducing maps without any links with the described land." The former process relates the production to the event itself and does not specify the rules governing it and the mechanisms of its transposition into some other form. The crucial issue is not solely the technology but the meaning contained in the transposition and the manner in which it purports to represent reality. Africa, as the source of cheap labor and raw materials, has been presented by imperial cartographers in various forms, none of which have been technically accurate or particularly complimentary. The maps are themselves a geography of imperial power and cultural biases related to dominating colonial territories.

Little has changed in the technologies of mapmaking in post-colonial Africa. European and American cartographers continue to control the production of maps. They have technologies that are not readily accessible to African institutions and countries. These technologies are an indication of wealth, and the inability of African countries to afford the necessary equipment places them at a marked disadvantage in realizing many of their own goals. They do not have the remote sensing devices that would enable them to predict crop yields or natural events such as rainfall and droughts. Because most African countries are agrarian, with 70 percent of the population living in rural areas, there is usually at least one other partner in their economic planning. Modern African countries are mainly the consumers of technical knowledge and not its producers. They are by necessity thrust into the global system and must rely on its technology and international organizations such as the World Bank and the National Oceanographic and Atmospheric Administration (NOAA) for the distribution of vital information.

In "The Challenges of Writing African Economic History" (Chapter 2), Paul Zeleza provides an overview of the traditions and establishes the context for discussing Africa's economic history from the fifteenth to the twentieth centuries. He does so in a self-conscious and self-reflexive mode. His goal is to "recast Africa's spatial realities and processes; to reclaim the continent from Eurocentric cognitive and cartographic mapping." Zeleza insists that the separation of Africa into two, above and below the Sahara, is "untenable," but "no less problematic is the construction of regions as coherent historical units." For example, he asks, when did West Africa become West Africa?

To avoid the confusion of regional historical units and the basis on which they are created—colonial cartography, geographical contiguity, and historical interconnection—Zeleza argues for a different approach that qualifies regional configurations with demonstrable historical affinities: Mozambique might have been part of East African economic history in the nineteenth century, but labor migration makes it part of the economic history of Southern Africa in the twentieth. Zeleza's project is to articulate a subjugated, submerged, integrated history of Africa. The historian, he says, plies his or her trade by constructing from "bits and pieces of available evidence" Africa's economic history. But rather than celebrate a fragment, Zeleza resists the postmodern turn, positing instead the creation of a new synthesis. Being marginal does not mean being unaffected, and African economic history must situate Africa as an integral part of worldwide empires, comparisons, and conjunctures. But this should not mean that the scholar from Africa looks to or comes to the elite universities in the West for knowledge. Zeleza wants to collapse the "North/South" dichotomy, seeing hierarchies and exploitation cutting across a number of levels while encouraging collaboration and exchanges among the "less-developed countries."

Although both Mbodj and Zeleza chart Africa in the discourses of geography, history, and economics, another context for the study of Africa today lies in the relationship of these bodies of knowledge to the apparent neoliberal economic perspectives promoted in World Bank and IMF structural adjustment programs (in their guise of "traditional reform"; see Chapter 4 Saasa).

Part 2, Contested Categories: Economy, Politics, and Society

Part 2 moves from the historical and macro-economic to the politics of knowledge and its practical application and effects. The ways in which these categories are employed have a direct effect on, and are themselves created by, policy decisions of international organizations, governments, and NGOs. The chapters in this section scrutinize social policies; the use of statistics; and categories such as "poverty," "civil society," "the state," "community," and "ethnic identity," explicating the social terrains on which these hegemonic categories are constructed.

In Chapter 3, "Structural Adjustment," Sayre Schatz offers a critical approach for analyzing this terrain. He carries out a careful analysis of the World Bank's data in its own terms; in doing so, he undermines the World Bank's claims about the success of structural adjustment in Africa. As the old adage says, one can lie with statistics. What is more, by reducing African realities to numbers one objectifies and dehumanizes the people and the social conditions in which they live. Schatz's main point is to document the failure of structural adjustment. He notes two phases of economic development in Africa, one from 1950 to 1977 of continuous modest economic growth, and a second, the period since 1978, which has seen deterioration and crisis. He argues that the decline began as structural adjustment policies were imposed.

In "Poverty Profile in Sub-Saharan Africa: The Challenge of Addressing an Evasive Problem" (Chapter 4), Oliver Saasa argues that the very indices we use to measure poverty are problematic and have to be rethought if the issue is going to be addressed seriously. In the African context, the majority of the poor live in rural areas, and 145 million people, or about half the population of sub-Saharan Africa, are affected by poverty. In this context, the case of Zambia is instructive. According to the World Bank, as reported in the United Nations publication *African Recovery*, "Zambia's privatization programme has been among the most successful in Africa" (Harsch, 2000: 17). But successful privatization has not meant a reduction in poverty.

In the late 1980s the Kaunda government in Zambia attempted a homegrown structural adjustment supported by the Trade Union Congress. After its failure, the newly elected Chiluba government embarked on a harsh program of reform that included a state of emergency and disempowerment of the trade unions. During this restructuring, even when the country had a positive growth rate of 7.5 percent, unemployment increased. Underemployment and unemployment are strongly correlated with poverty, Saasa adds, which in turn is positively correlated to crime rates and the capacity for effective governance.

The slow realization that their policies have had a negative effect on poverty reduction has prompted the IMF and World Bank to propose a new initiative focusing on poverty reduction. Yet can the nature, severity, and magnitude of poverty in sub-Saharan Africa be fully appreciated and understood using current tools of quantification? Saasa proposes new tools and indices, defining poverty from a number of different perspectives, such as the Human Development Index, a composite of longevity, knowledge, and standard of living, which has engendered other indices related to gender and human poverty. These indices offer a much better alternative to Gross National Product (GNP) as a measure because income and resource inequalities will block the alleviation of poverty. Per capita income is a misleading indicator of poverty. In countries such as South Africa, Namibia, and Botswana, which have high per capita income, a high proportion of the population continues to live in "absolute poverty," that is, under $1 a day. A thorough rethinking of poverty indices means contesting what constitutes the poverty line. In Zambia the poverty line is fixed at a "basic food" level, which is set at an abstract vegetarian diet and minimum caloric requirements. It is a level so "basic" that it does not fully factor in shelter, education, clothing, footwear, and clothing. Saasa concludes that a fully human conceptualization of poverty, one that takes the needs of the human being as its root, is demanded if policy priorities are to be created for its eradication.

The other chapters in Part 2 explore the relationship of international organizations, the state, and society. They focus on the collaboration of elites and the rights of and over labor, identity, and property. These relationships are particularly pertinent for post-apartheid South Africa, where its economics, politics, and ideology (see Chapters 5–8) are products of a contested and negotiated settlement between the apartheid National Party and the anti-apartheid African National Congress (ANC).

In "Civil Society, Pluralism, Goldilocks, and Other Fairy Tales in Africa" (Chapter 5), Leonard Markovitz points out that ideological consensus is built on the power of dominant social and economic groups. In the South African case these "groups," including the ANC government, have embraced neoliberalism. Although the ANC's process of ideological change, from the Freedom Charter of 1955, proclaiming nationalization and redistribution to the pro-capitalist Growth Employment and Redistribution (GEAR) of 1996, often appears preordained, the chapters on South Africa demonstrate that this ideological shift is highly contested. Indeed, the very ideology of "TINA"—Margaret Thatcher's famous statement that "There Is No Alternative" to a neoliberal economy and a "popular authoritarian" anti-welfare but centralist state (see Hall, 1988: 150–160)—is under scrutiny.

Markovitz's attempt to enlighten us about "civil society" is directed not so much at conservatives as at radicals who uncritically embrace the term. The South African case provides a rich example of how the discourse of civil society and transition to democracy has played a role in setting the agenda of debate. Markovitz argues that the "establishment" notion of civil society promotes "democracy lite" (or what some political scientists call "polyarchy") for its own instrumentalist reasons. The meanings of "the people" and "civil society" are conditioned by dominant economic powers and international lending agencies such as the World Bank and the IMF, which "do not hesitate to intervene in domestic politics." Such conditioning is felt not only by nations but also by NGOs and Organizations of Civil Society (OCSs), which in the post-apartheid era are forced to shift from a liberation discourse to the pragmatics of a cost/benefit emphasis on outputs demanded by the funding authorities. Behind the construction of NGO, OCSs, privatization, and liberalization discourses is the "real" world of increasing inequalities of income and concentration of wealth in the "globalized economy,"[2] inequalities that find their most extreme form in Africa.

The very terrain of South Africa's "homegrown structural adjustment," as Franco Barchiesi puts it in Chapter 6, built on the legacy of apartheid, is in need of contestation. Post-apartheid South Africa emerged at the very time when the world has witnessed increasing inequalities. In South Africa, despite the growth of a sizable black middle class, the GINI curve coefficients (a measurement of income inequality) (see Chapter 4 for a discussion of GINI coefficients and poverty reduction) have not changed with the end of apartheid. Thus we should ask: What exactly constitutes a genuinely post-apartheid regime? The ANC government has made conscious policy choices. It has had the capacity to mold the future.

Is such an examination simply moving us to a different terrain? If the classical Hegelian idea of civil society is a hodgepodge of contradictory interests, the Marxian move from this noisy sphere is not to the production of ideas but to the conception of labor so often left out of the literature on the transition to democracy. Barchiesi notes that unlike the mainstream transition studies model, the trade union movement in South Africa, the Congress of South African Trade Unions (COSATU), played an enormously important role as an opposition organization during the late 1980s and early 1990s when other organizations were banned. But what did the unions get in return? Many economic demands, from land redistribution to job creation, have remained unrealized. In "Beyond the State and Civil Society: Labor Movements and Economic Adjustment in African Transitions—South Africa and Nigeria Compared," Barchiesi places "labor" and social stratification at the core of his analysis of civil society. Social science transition studies, he argues, emphasize labor's subordination to neoliberal policies as a trade-off for democratic rights. At best, as a component of civil society, labor's multidimensionality as a movement and organization, in production and outside of it, is relativized within an undifferentiated set of community-based organizations.

Nigeria and South Africa provide Barchiesi with a comparative approach to the relationship between democratization and neoliberalism. In both countries the idea of civil society is unable to account for labor's role in political change. In Nigeria the regime's authoritarianism found an elective affinity with IMF and World Bank prescriptions, making labor a target of state repression and/or co-optation. In South Africa the transition was judged to be a success, with labor playing an important role, which Barchiesi claims reveals the limitations of the paradigms preferred by transition studies.

South Africa, opines Barchiesi, challenges transition studies for three reasons: First, organized labor was decisive in overcoming apartheid; second, labor is the "major driving force of the transition and post-transition phase"; and third, and more important, "the rise of neoliberal hegemony in South Africa was less dependent on economic crisis and external constraints imposed by international financial institutions, and more a matter of contestation and internal strategy choices." Particularly fascinating are the tensions created by labor's institutionalization within the post-apartheid political system, which has meant not simply a compromise around such issues as wages or job security but also an ideological acquiescence to the discourse of democracy "lite" (see Gibson, 2001).

The subsuming of COSATU's ideological independence to a multiclass "civil society" headed by the ANC ignored powerful oppositional interests in the workplace and the townships. A radical shift occurred between the ANC as social movement and the ANC as government. Despite its previous commitment to social and economic justice, by the late 1990s the ANC government no longer spoke of redistribution but rather "fiscal discipline," "labor productivity," "international competitiveness," and "export promotion." Just as the realization of the Freedom Charter as the basis of the post-apartheid society (which was historically the transitional program for anti-apartheid intellectuals inside and outside South Africa) has now become visionary, labor's compromise with the ANC government has been further and further narrowed to alleviating the effects of its policies rather than determining them. The discourse has not only shifted, the space for dialogue has narrowed. Ideological hegemony and political power depend on constricting, marginalizing, and silencing other voices.

In "Silencing Power: Mapping the Social Terrain in Post-Apartheid South Africa" (Chapter 7), Kate Crehan argues that we apprehend the world through established social categories and that these categories are constructed in contested terrains. Thus, categories and their inventory of terms can be understood in different ways even if they appear to have the same meaning. As part of the dialectics of social life, even established social categories are constantly being challenged (Murphy, 1971). The meaning of concepts such as community are subject to negotiation and transformation. *Community* is a term that everyone seems to accept and understand. Supposedly, it evokes the same cluster of meanings.

Crehan's analysis demonstrates not only that categories are products of particular historical situations but also that words can shift their meaning, be "floating signifiers" (as some might put it) in different social contexts. Sometimes neologisms are created to signify something new, but the word *community* has a long history of ambiguity. A woolly, and "warmly persuasive word," as Raymond Williams puts it (1983: 75–76), it harks back to a time before capitalism, to "organic" solidarities in Durkheim's sense. Associated with "tradition" and with an unreflected humanism, *community* is a highly problematic term in political discourse.

The process of "naming," which is one aspect of the construction of categories, is also contested. As Crehan sees it, naming associates a certain set of meanings even if those meanings appear quite arbitrary or contradictory to the name or signifier. Naming is related to power, yet naming alone cannot change social structures.

Contesting categories and constructing new intellectual terrains are important to rethinking social formations. We are not, however, naive idealists. We are interested in the dialectic of knowledge and power, of words and their meanings not separated from the social realities in which they are spoken. But naming also silences. This is particularly apparent in the South African case, where the rhetorical legacy of "the struggle" and "development" is used to fragment oppositional demands. The stretching of the discourse of liberation to enforce pro-business economic policies is a legacy of the contested terrains of the last decade. It indicates a problem. It is far from clear that the idea of "African Renaissance" has the capacity to grab and hold the imagination and silence opposition. Instead, it must rely on processes of co-optation and compromise.

Crehan uses a Gramscian conception of "intellectual," understood as a social function, to discuss the interconnections between the production of knowledge and the production of reception, seeing how an individual's own experience of meaning is central to the hegemonic process. She calls this a process of experiencing the hegemony of social maps. Central to accepting one meaning is the lack of alternative maps, or what might be called alternative ways of naming. These alternatives are not available because the dominant maps are hegemonic. In other words, the constructed categories are an end product, a terrain now rewritten as if there is no alternative (TINA). It is a double bind. To question the "certainty" of TINA we have to reassess the very "openings" created by the movements against apartheid, as symptoms not of crisis in the "interregnum" (Gramsci, 1971: 276) but of fields and processes of contestation. Crehan offers one possible retrospective with her analysis of the shifting terrains of the meaning of the word *community*.

Although NGOs might be thought to inhabit a terrain outside the state and free enterprise, they are embedded in the discourse of development. The term *community* is basic to their universe. What is fascinating about Crehan's analysis of three NGOs in South Africa is that two of them use the term *marginalized* alongside the term *community*. This modification of community further narrows and in a sense "marginalizes" the objects of discourse. Crehan takes us from labor to those socially excluded (Byrne, 1999). These are not "working-class communities," "youth communities," or "black communities" that could develop a consciousness for themselves. Instead, the marginalized self-consciousness is by definition nonessential and fragmented. The goal is not empowering the marginal qua marginals but ending their marginality so that they enter another community. In this sense, the marginalized are similar to a sack of potatoes: They are unable to develop a counter-hegemonic consciousness or discourse.

Concentrating on ethnic identity in post-settlement South Africa in Chapter 8, "Negotiating Identity in Post-Settlement South Africa," Edward Ramsamy shows the interconnection of two principles of the anti-apartheid movement, redistribution and non-racialism. The post-apartheid inability to deliver on these two principles, he argues, seriously undermines the ability to create a South African national identity. He wonders how long the spirit of goodwill in post-apartheid South Africa can remain alongside a growing sense of disillusionment among the underprivileged. Will the spirit of goodwill associated with Mandela be available to Mbeki? The terrains of economy and ethnicity, so neatly finessed by Mandela, could become more explicitly contested under Mbeki.

With Ramsamy the question of the future South Africa becomes a contested terrain not simply from the pragmatic decisions that resulted from the negotiation process but in its very principle of reversing the structural legacies of apartheid-based ethnic categories and economic inequalities. The challenge of liberation was to rechart the apartheid ethnic map on the physical terrain of a new South Africa. Ramsamy finds that on this score, the post-apartheid regime has fallen short of its goal.

The regional map of South Africa, argues Ramsamy, bears a strong similarity to the National Party's own regional plan of 1982, with the unity of the Eastern Cape, the bulwark of the National Party's "Coloured" vote, and the territorial integrity of KwaZulu Natal. Ethnicities are the maps of post-apartheid South

Africa just as they had been earlier, but now, Ramsamy adds, the ANC vies to be their representatives. This puts the ANC in a bind. Rather than challenging Buthelezi directly, the ANC has attempted to undermine his hold over "Zuluness." Most critically, the ethnic terms of apartheid have been contested but remain exploited by ethnic entrepreneurs. While Indian politicians ferment fear of the black masses are being encouraged by overtures to "Africanization," Winnie Mandela, Ramsamy notes, espouses an old anti-Indian trope. In short, while ethnicities are constructed, they are lived through. Negotiating this contradiction expresses a central problem of contesting the terrain of constructed categories.

Are the problems of post-apartheid South Africa unique, or do they replicate those of other African independence movements which, on taking over power, were unable to extricate themselves from the structures and discourses of the old regime? Ramsamy reminds us of the pitfalls of national consciousness where an elite does not genuinely want to reorder society. Could the South African anti-apartheid elite reorder society? Did it create a homegrown structural adjustment, or was it pushed away from a genuine redistribution that would attempt to rebalance and redraw the social and economic map of apartheid? Perhaps South Africa provides the best opportunity to see the development of a "productive" African bourgeoisie. Yet this will be confined to the urban areas while the rural areas remain largely marked by the legacy of apartheid and the struggle over land.

One pressing issue that has had profound consequences for post-colonial Africa is land. For Zimbabwe the question goes back to the beginnings of colonial expropriation in the 1890s and was the raison d'etre for the anti-colonial liberation movement. In South Africa, where the issue may have even deeper social consequences, it predates apartheid by 35 years (i.e., 1913). As the Zimbabwean situation has shown, the landless are black, but not all large landowners are white. It is a problem, therefore, that illuminates the politics of economics. If democracy is to develop, and if it is to be rooted in property, the issue of land redistribution and the power of the chiefs over land remain crucial problems and are far from unique, as demonstrated in Sara Berry's chapter on land claims in Ghana (Chapter 9).

Berry's "Negotiable Property: Making Claims on Land and History in Asante," moves into the heart of one of the most complex, controversial, and contested domains in recent African history and politics, claims over land and its use. The claims relate authority to power, legality to legitimacy, identity to gender, ethnicity and citizenship, and the rights of the state to those of corporate units. In the primarily agrarian societies of Africa, land brings into play each one of these relationships in structuring the past and the present. Their configuration is never fully predictable, especially in attempting to forecast the future. Rights in land have often been treated as an essential feature of the political order; without them one may be excluded from the political community and subjected to the decisions of the propertied or landed, as has been the case in Zimbabwe and South Africa. They involve the state in the claims of local people and the local people in the affairs of the state; at another level, they have become an essential element in the argument over the conditions for "sustained and sustainable economic development."

The debate over property reforms has brought the World Bank, the IMF, and other international organizations directly into the everyday life of the average farmer and agrarian worker. The primary focus is on the relation between property rights and productivity. Although fully aware of this focus, Berry argues for a broader approach, one that treats property as a field of social and political as well as economic interactions. In this simple, elegant formulation she restores the integrity of a well-established academic research approach to the study of African land tenure with all its complex relationships. She does not stop there but points to functionalist assumptions of stability, the persistence of predetermined rules according to which people pursued land claims. Instead of accepting this position, she argues for the view that property is "an ongoing social process in which claims are shaped by people's understanding of the past as well as the present." Although power does not precede the creation of wealth, nonetheless wealth is informed and influenced by it.

Berry's argument restores the debate about the relation of power and wealth and the extent to which property relations are fixed and govern claims to land and the right to use and alienate it. Here the problem is not only one of contested terrains but also of the ability of practitioners and social scientists to understand the meaning of local or indigenous categories. In the dialectics of conquest, new categories were constructed based on the assumption of power by colonial governments.

Ghana, then the Gold Coast, and the Ashanti peoples belonged to Lord Hailey's second group of British territories. As a shrewd administrator and observer, Hailey recognized that both history and custom were in the making and that that which was often treated as indigenous was a recent invention. Although he argued that most political or administrative institutions had not retained their character, he thought that "native Africa" was far more conservative in "its respect for the customary law regulating matrimonial relations or the holding of land" (Hailey, 1951: 10). As Sara Berry's chapter illustrates, territorial affiliation and rights to land are issues that have engaged both colonial and post-colonial governments. They involve the rights of citizenship and those of ownership as well as the complex processes of incorporating diverse political and social units.

Together with scholars such as Elizabeth Colson (1971), Martin Chanock (1985), and Mahmood Mamdani (1996), Berry explores the colonial order based on indirect rule, with its recognition of native authorities and customary law and practice. Her chapter probes Mbembe's two features of state power not only within the context of the post-colony but also as a vital aspect of the colonial project. Within the colonial order, custom was invented and enshrined within a stable temporal domain insulated from change; it was part of the apparatus used in attempting to orchestrate the logic of meanings in different domains as well as to embed local histories in the historical narratives suited to colonial domination. But the reality was quite different from the colonial construction.

Berry's Ashanti case study refutes the view of the conservative "native Africa" and, as do T. O. Ranger (1996) and Frederick Cooper (1996, 1997), she demonstrates the fluidity of "customary practice and law," especially with respect to land holdings. Moreover, Berry explores the iconology of symbolic representations of social positions in their relation to power and wealth. Thus, even during the colonial era the domain of customary practice formed a fluid social field marked by experimentation, negotiation, manipulation, and the production of new strategic relationships. In other words, custom was not king but rather there to be used, and through use, transformed.

Berry's careful empirical analysis of land issues in Ashanti over a hundred-year span provides her with a sweep that transcends temporal demarcations and enables her to identify behavioral and processual interactions not as static but as negotiated and transformative. Her study has done what Ranger advocates: "attacked colonial societies with postcolonial problematics and methods" and "come up with a very different picture of colonial practices—a picture that has very many similarities to and connections with postcolonial Africa" (Ranger 1996: 273).

The chapter challenges, on the one hand, the pragmatic propositions set out by the World Bank related to property rights reforms and productivity and, on the other hand, the intellectual post-colonial characterizations of the colonial period. It helps to clarify the limitations of technical bureaucratic solutions to social problems and the constructed images of post-colonial intellectuals and scholars in their assessment of the past and the present. It reveals the manner in which knowledge is constructed and also the ways in which average persons negotiate the realities of their own particular circumstances.

Part 3, Violence of the Word/Violence Against the Body

From what we have discussed thus far, it is apparent that, as Mbodj has so eloquently pointed out in his analysis of mapmaking, what at first appears to be a simple construction of objects upon closer scrutiny expresses a subtle world of complex meanings. The mapping of the social world carries with it a more demanding set of requirements in that the physical map is no more than an expression of the social. Social thought and analysis form the crux of both endeavors.

Nigel Gibson's chapter, "Mapping Africa's Presences: Merleau-Ponty, Mannoni, and the Malagasy Massacre of 1947 in Frantz Fanon's *Black Skin White Masks*" (Chapter 10), raises many significant questions related to the mapping of Africa's mental geography and its colonial domain. The construction of the colonial "state" and its "socio-historical world" was as much a part of the metropole as it was of the colonies. Features of this situation still obtain, as portrayed in the struggle to invent an Africa suited to the purposes of special interests and the vision of individual scholars. Although there appear to be similarities, the goals and mechanisms of the special interests and the scholars are fundamentally different. European countries were constructing colonial empires and a hegemonic order that would enable them to rule with the minimum use of force and resources.

The chapter turns to the complexities of intellectual history and explores the situation of intellectuals of African descent as theoreticians and activists in the metropole and the colonies and the manner in which they related to the colonial order in Africa. The focus of the exposition is Frantz Fanon, a Martinican who, while studying in Lyon, discovered himself and the black world in the years immediately following the Second World War. These were years of recovery and political ferment during which French intellectuals joined with Africans and persons of African descent to protest French colonial policies (Mouralis, 1992: 3).

In 1947, the year Fanon arrived in Paris, *Présence Africaine* was founded by Alioune Diop, a French-educated West African scholar. As V. Y. Mudimbe observes, "around him and his journal, one finds some of the most prestigious French intellectuals at that time: Albert Camus, Andre Gide, Michel Leiris, Theodore Monod, Emmanuel Mounier, Jean-Paul Sartre (1992: xvii). *Présence Africaine* was to become more than just a journal; it was almost a social movement, bringing together scholars from Africa, the Americas, the Caribbean, and Europe. The founding of the journal marked a rise in anticolonial thought and activity in France. Although Fanon was not at the center of *Présence Africaine*, his experiences in France proved to be transformative, projecting him into a career of analyzing the psychology of colonization while contributing to the anti-colonialist and nationalist struggles of Algeria and the Gold Coast (Ghana). For Fanon, colonial Africa formed a single, expansive territory in which the realities of oppression and subjugation established a commonality of being and resistance. Arbitrarily constructed geographical boundaries did not limit his engagement in praxis.

Gibson explores Fanon's transformations and his arguments with Octave Mannoni over the nature of colonial rule and the consequences of colonial governance. Violence provided the central denouement of any possible intellectual rapprochement. How would one explain the effects of violence on the colonizer and the colonized? How could one account for the slaughter of 100,000 Malagasy by the French in 1947?

The central issue is whether colonial rule *results in* the dependency of the colonized or dependency *is the reason for* colonization. The former position provides the basis for immediate independence and the latter for a gradual process of careful tutelage, even then with an uncertain result. Whereas Mannoni's ideas fitted into the cultural logic and meanings of colonial domination, Fanon's views served to promote the goals of African nationalist movements. The lines were being clearly drawn between the conservative rhetoric of colonial domination and the emergent properties of a future radical post-colonial discourse. But the debate between Fanon and Mannoni in fact did little to explain or prepare scholars for the potential of mass violence in the post-colonial years. For them it was enough to understand the violent struggles of the colonial era.

In Chapter 11, "Against a Wall of Aching Silence: Contesting Terrains Over a Massacre?," Mustafah Dhada returns us to the general problems set out by Mbodj and Zeleza, the challenge of mapping the geographies of knowledge, human experiences, and social processes "to reclaim the continent from Eurocentric cognitive and cartographic mapping" (see Chapter 2). The task is daunting, especially considering the dominant empiricist legacies of mainstream social analysis.

To move into the abyss that mass violence generates and to understand the manner in which it is apprehended, Dhada transforms himself into both the subject and the object of his investigation. His account exemplifies many of the philosophical issues raised by Gibson in his discussion of Fanon and Maurice Merleau-Ponty, especially with respect to the understanding that the body cannot be either separated or divorced from the world as experienced. The initial framing of his chapter, a personal reaction to the Wiriyamu massacre in Mozambique, positions him within the militant literary tradition of social critics such as Fedor Dostoevski and Chinua Achebe. Social transformations situate their central characters at the very periphery of, if not outside, contested social orders. As Dhada learns of this particularly nasty massacre, he too, as if a character in a novel, becomes a man outside of society, involved in the social life of neither the metropole nor the colony. A moving force in his presentation is his attempt to reduce his personal alienation induced by violent acts committed against the other (ultimately himself the colonized subject), to reconstitute his lived-in experiences and restore himself as intellectual and activist. Gibson concludes that it is only through the experiences of the Algerian revolution that Fanon finally transforms the notion of "being among one's own" as one defined by "the other." Reflecting while in exile about a massacre in the country of his birth, Dhada undergoes a similar transformative experience.

Both Dhada and Gibson rely on published texts as the basis for their exegesis. Within the confines of the media, Dhada uses the English press, specifically *The Times of London*, as his main source of information about the massacre in Mozambique, his country of origin. From his reading of *The Times* he explores the politics of representation. He calculates the frequency and quality of the press reports and notes the silences and omissions of the Portuguese colonial government in their acknowledgments of the event. He also recognizes the unfolding of the offstage dramas of cultural imperialism and brings them to bear in his effort to understand the accountability of colonial governments. As Edward Said (1993) so correctly points out, the unstated structures of power and wealth must be brought into textual analysis or, as he puts it, "representation itself has been characterized as keeping the subordinate subordinate, the inferior inferior" (1993: 80).

Dhada becomes the voice of the dead, representing the villagers of Wiriyamu who were exterminated by Portuguese paratroopers in 1972 during the last stages of the Portuguese government's war against the Front for the Liberation of Mozambique (FRELIMO) and the Mozambique people. No one stood trial for the Wiriyamu massacre; there were no moratoriums. Dhada speaks for the memory of the colonized dead. While he recognizes, like Lynette Jackson (see Chapter 13), the complex, selective nature of memory. Unlike Jackson, he has to rely on the written text far removed from the actual event. For him there is both temporal and spatial distance, yet he is galvanized by a shared colonial identity. Dhada memorializes the silenced voices of his compatriots by bringing them into the present.

For the purposes of discovery and establishing some degree of veracity from accounts of highly charged events, Dhada puts forward a series of interpretive concepts based on different forms of essentialism. The thrust of the chapter is not only an intersubjective description of a massacre but also a methodological exploration in interpretive analysis. The main problem is how one may apprehend and represent the domain of violence, with all its subtle and intangible complexities. The problem is a real one for social scientists who prefer to consider their endeavors something more than journalism. It is a matter of meaning and understanding.

In "Negotiating Postwar Identities: Child Soldiers in Mozambique and Angola" (Chapter 12), Alcinda Honwana brings us directly into the domain of violence and its human instruments, child soldiers. She excludes herself as an object of analysis and focuses on Angolan and Mozambican children's experiences with war. She argues that "the issue of child soldiers ... has to be understood in the context of the crisis of the post-colonial state in Africa." Framed in this manner, her exposition could lead in one of two directions: the investigation of the post-colonial state or the situation of children and the problems of social reproduction and development. To our benefit, Honwana has chosen to focus on the latter and the mechanics of reintegrating children into the social fabric of ordinary community life. She does not, however, dismiss the former and provides a brief discussion of the crisis of the post-colonial African state.

Africa is marked by major violent conflicts. They may be of the magnitude and intensity found in Rwanda, in which up to 1 million Tutsi and 50,000 Hutu were killed during a 100-day period, or an extended cumulative conflagration as found in the Sudan. Children, women, and the elderly are the ones most seriously affected during periods of major violence and the ones most vulnerable once it subsides. But, as Honwana demonstrates, children may not only be the victims of war but also its combatants. It is estimated that 6,000 children under the age of 15 fought in Liberia's civil war (Flieschman & Whitman, 1994: 2), 3,000 in Uganda's National Resistance Army (Goodwin-Gill & Cohn, 1994: 34), 9,000 in Angola, and approximately 8,000 for Mozambique's RENAMO (Goodwin-Gill & Cohn, 1994:138). Yet one must be careful not to become too involved with numbers because the combatants were themselves often victims forced into service.

Honwana explores the different mechanisms and processes used to recruit children into rebel groups in Angola and Mozambique. Once in these groups, they are disciplined in such a manner as to remove them from their former social affiliations. They are expected to assume a new social persona. They are transformed into persons who stand outside their former societies and communities, subject neither to their rules of behavior nor their social relationships. Once the conflagration has ended the main issue is how to remove them from a culture based on violence and terror and reintegrate them into community life.

The problem is a basic one on two counts. First, it has become increasingly prevalent in African societies. In many instances, the potential productive capacities of a generation have been temporarily diverted into destructive activities or permanently lost. If the views of the Red Cross and Red Crescent Movement are correct, "children who have participated in hostilities are often marked for life, mentally, morally and physically" (Goodwin-Gill & Cohn, 1994: 4). They form an unpredictable element in the social order, with the experience and skills to take up and use arms in an effective manner. Second, the problems of reintegration are intimately related to understanding the social mechanisms by which behaviors may be changed. The behavioral argument is important because it is thought by some to be at the crux of limiting the spread of diseases such as HIV/AIDS and social conflagrations. But Honwana takes the argument one step further. She views the problem of child soldiers as a feature of the crisis of state politics stemming from struggles over power, resources, and identity. The state is itself a contested terrain that assumes a vital role in the production of social violence.

In Chapter 13, "The Story of Chibheura (Open Your Legs) Exams," Lynette Jackson explores more subtle forms of violence expressed in the Southern Rhodesia (Zimbabwe) colonial government's concern with the spread of sexuality transmitted diseases (STD) and the medical health of women. The colonial government sought to control access to physical and social space by regulating the movement of men and women from the rural into the urban areas. One way of doing this was through the inspection of African women for sexually transmitted diseases, a practice known as *Chibheura* (open your legs). To reside in an urban area women had to submit to this mandatory examination on a regular basis. Thus, one of the most fundamental human spaces was open to government scrutiny.

African women were the recipients of the most intrusive form of regulatory activities. Lacking in power, they were the least feared by the colonial government and the most vulnerable of its subjects. Their vulnerability stemmed from the fact that they were African and that they were women. The British had conquered both the Shona and the Ndebele. Although essential for agricultural production and social reproduction, they were legally and economically jural minors subordinate to men, a status supported by the British.

For the colonial government, the place of African women was in the countryside, tending to domestic agricultural production. Women were counted neither as part of the public domain nor as potential urban wage earners. They did not stay in the countryside, and to remain in urban areas they had to be examined. Colonial health officers, as well as many African men, saw them as key vectors in spreading sexually transmitted diseases infecting laboring men. The colonial government and African men could not accept independent African women moving freely in the urban areas; they were viewed as matter out of place and thus posing a danger to the social order (Douglas, 1966). As they moved from the domestic constraints of the countryside, they had to be redefined, and part of that redefinition was to inspect their bodies and thereby regulate their sexuality. Independent, self-supporting urban women reflected upon the inability of both the colonial government and

African men to control African women. The basic issue was one of maintaining both colonial and indigenous structures of authority.

The colonial order of Southern Rhodesia was constructed on a well-defined social hierarchy in which whites regulated the affairs of blacks and men the activities of women. Southern Rhodesia was a society constructed on racial segregation. Europeans lived in the cities or on large commercial farms and Africans in the townships and reserves. The colonial government feared its inability to regulate movement into colonial and colonized spaces. This fear was intensified by the underlying ideologies of conquest which, on the one hand, viewed the African as a simple creature of nature waiting to be civilized, and on the other hand as a savage, uncontrollable force within it constituting a potential threat to European supremacy and civilization. Women were key icons in the symbolic construction of conquest and colonial authority. Purity and moral supremacy lay in the laps of European women, and the impurities of social diseases were attributed to the unregulated activities of African women.

Fortunately, Jackson was able to interview women who had undergone the experience of *Chibheura*. There is the play of memory in which the women speak for themselves, preserving that which they consider to be important. But memory is situationally triggered, and the inventory of past experiences is conditioned by understandings of the present. The past is brought into the present, revealing the indignities that township women experienced. And yet, for many women it was just the nature of the times. As Jackson observes of one of her informants, "Madzingirwa saw the exams as simply how things were, as part of the banalities of life under colonialism." Thus, the exposition is multifaceted and complex, with historical texts confronting the lived experience of human memories. There is the external world of colonial domination and the experiential world of the colonized. The colonial situation assumes a human face in the accounts of these African women. Jackson's brilliant exposition and sophisticated interpretation of *Chibheura* is a welcome contribution to the analysis of race relations in colonial and post-colonial societies (Day, 1972) and the logic of their cultural constructions.

It is here that one may return to Mbembe's understanding of state power, but not in his terms as a post-colonial construction. There are basic principles of state governance that transcend the periodicity of regimes. This periodicity is not a matter of pre-colonial, colonial, or post-colonial, as both Mbembe and Zeleza assert and we agree, but the exercising of state power, the expression of a form of government that is manifestly oriented toward subjugation.

There is another element that one often associates with conquest and that Jackson's chapter makes clear: the construction of identities based in the ideology of racial differences. State power operates along and reinforces the lines of cleavage framed as conqueror and conquered, ruler and subjugated, citizen and subject, European and African.

The manifestation and manipulation of state power in this fashion has been clearly observed in both colonial and post-colonial governments. Socially constructed categories may serve as mere markers, but those who they designate may not remain constant. They may be used as a basis for social action. Rwanda is perhaps the most striking and informative example: The justification for exterminating about one million people was framed within the ideology of conquest and the categories of race. As Leonard Markovitz (see Chapter 5) and Anthony Marx (1998) have pointed out, scapegoating is a powerful political instrument. The focus may assume a variety of forms such as race, gender, "alien" cultures, and those suffering from incurable diseases.

Leslie Sharp's discussion in Chapter 14 of the lives of school girls in Ambanja, a town in the northwest of Madagascar, brings together many themes raised in this section. It serves as a strong reminder of the importance of the mundane and that individuals accept conditions as part of the banalities of everyday life. However, that which appears to be mundane and banal is fraught with meaning and hazards. Consistent with the subtext of other chapters, Sharp is concerned with providing the schoolgirls of her study "a means to articulate the true nature of their lives and their own collective experiences." Many authors in this volume have sought to represent the lived experiences of the social actor and to reduce the distance between themselves and their informants without losing sight of the focus of the study itself. (For a discussion of this matter see Geertz, 1968; Rosaldo, 1989; and Bond & Gilliam, 1994). There is a rapprochement between the social analyst and the social actor. It is one thing to work with texts and quite another to work with living people, yet in the final analysis the endeavor is much the same. The observed social reality is reduced into text.

The chapter's primary focus is on independent schoolgirls, their efforts to pursue an education, and the dangers they confront. The theme is the movement of young girls from the countryside into the town of Ambanja to advance their studies and prepare themselves for wage employment. In the town they are stereotyped and thought to be receptive to its numerous corrupting diversions, such as video cinemas, discotheques, and the foreign cultures they exemplify. The townspeople think that they may even succumb to prostitution and drugs.

Sharp's research reveals that none of this is true. The rural girls are from poor backgrounds and do not have the means to partake of these diversions. Instead, schoolgirls who can engage in these activities are the daughters of the middle and upper elites. But even they do so infrequently. There is, however, a fear among their parents of the corrupting affects of foreign public cultures as portrayed in the cinema and the discotheques. In the absence of parental guidance, naive rural girls become the object of their fears. They are the ones thought to be more easily seduced by the images represented in the foreign commercial media.

Sharp recognizes that there are at least two contending moral forces operating within Malagasy society. One is indigenous and manifests itself in public festivities and individual activities surrounding royal ritual events. Individual and collective behaviors are marked by their permissiveness and the absence of strong social constraints. They tend to have much in common with the stereotypical behaviors associated with discotheques. The second is derived from the colonial period and the Malagasy Post-colonial socialist regime that came into power.

During the last 30 years of the twentieth century Malagasy experienced fundamental political and economic changes, moving from French colonial rule into a socialist regime that emphasized a strict nationalist moral order. In 1993, the socialist government fell and was replaced by a government that embraced capitalism, an open market economy, and private land tenure. Policies of Malagasization were discontinued and French was restored as the language of instruction in schools. The policy of isolationism was discontinued. The country was open to commercial media and foreign popular cultures that represented moral images that were permissive, emphasizing individual action and entrepreneurial success. In this constructed permissive world individual desires had ceased to be constrained in the ritual bounds of festive occasions. Naive young girls from the countryside, the domain of the "provincial," were projected as being at the locus of two moral orders, the one ritual and "traditional" and the other "foreign" and modern, both emphasizing the unconstrained permissive desires of the individual. Thus, Ambanja was a contested social field of several moral configurations. Although it is tempting to postulate an elective affinity between ideologies of individualism and the state's emphasis on capitalism and private enterprises, one must resist this direction of intellectual exploration. Instead, Sharp's chapter turns to pressing issues of a different and practical kind, the relation of permissive behavior to the spread of sexually transmitted diseases, such as HIV/AIDS, among Malagasy and African youth.

The focus on youth and AIDS has been and will be the center of attention for African governments and international NGOs for some time to come. Some 24.5 million Africans are HIV positive, and the second UNAIDS comprehensive report on the AIDS pandemic estimates that about half of all youth 15 years old in the 16 hardest-hit African countries will die (Altman, 2000) from the disease. There is no known medical cure. African governments and NGOs have relied on epidemiologists and social scientists to map the medical and social geography of the disease (Bond & Vincent, 1997a: 85–99). They have sought to develop appropriate instructional materials such as posters and comic books to inform the general public about AIDS and to curb practices related to its transmission. In both Uganda and Madagascar these forms of public materials were primarily oriented toward the perils of urban life, a fitting initial orientation because AIDS has been most pronounced in the urban areas. However, as any contagious disease will, it has gradually spread into the rural areas with ever-increasing rates of infection.

The course of the disease and effective preventive measures have always been problematic, especially in African countries marked by a recent history of civil strife and population displacements. With an estimated annual rate of infection at 4 million in 1999, the deadly consequences of the pandemic have now outstripped those of war. The recent UNAIDS report points out that "in 1998, 200,000 Africans died in war but more than 2 million died of AIDS. AIDS has become a full blown development crisis" (UNAIDS, 2000: 21). The magnitude of the epidemic poses serious problems for African governments and the policies of international organizations such as the World Bank and the IMF concerned with African economic development.

Uganda is one of the few success stories in the attempt to control the spread of AIDS. Through its early recognition of AIDS as a central health and social problem, it has "brought its estimated prevalence rate down to around 8% from a peak of close to 14% in the early 1990s with strong preventive campaigns" (UNAIDS, 2000: 9). But the story of AIDS in Uganda is more complicated than these figures represent.

In "The Moving Frontier of AIDS in Uganda" (Chapter 15), George Clement Bond and Joan Vincent trace the progression of the HIV/AIDS epidemic in Uganda through time and space, exploring the contours of its physical and intellectual geography. Their argument is that the epidemic is not solely a biomedical problem rooted in behavioral practices. For them, a more powerful understanding of the epidemic is gained by analyzing it within the context of Uganda's historical configurations and political circumstances.

The chapter's main theme is that research based on the study of specific localities is frequently used as a basis for generalizing about the conditions of entire regions and countries. However, the generalizations often obscure political and social complexities as well as important differences in the phases of the disease's progression. AIDS research in Uganda, the first African country to open itself to AIDS research, has been primarily in the south, yet the findings are often used to represent the entire country. The unsettled situation in the north has precluded extensive research.

The chapter is a cautionary account of representations and misrepresentations, involving the construction of powerful texts, research reports, and the stories of journalists. These texts not only contribute to our knowledge about the disease, they also help to shape public policies, social practices, and public opinion. Thus, they should not be taken lightly. Instead, they should receive careful scrutiny and, like the disease itself, they should be framed and analyzed within the immediate context of their production.

In the pandemic that has drawn an array of international scholars, researchers, practitioners, and organizations into its deadly wake, the importance of local circumstances is sometimes neglected. The plight of the weak and vulnerable, women, children, orphans, the elderly, and refugees is often set aside. The context of the AIDS epidemic has frequently included widespread social violence, limiting the possibilities and localities for systematic inquiry. It has also included natural disasters such as droughts and famines. The convergence of these different social and natural events not only has provided the context for the HIV/AIDS epidemic but also has been the source of devastating "Complex Emergencies" that have drawn heavily on the scarce resources of African governments and international organizations. When the epidemic is combined with civil strife and natural disasters such as droughts and famines, it becomes a formidable force in African history, with the potential of reshaping fundamental economic, political, and social relationships.

In "Contested Claims and Individual Bodies" (Chapter 16), Meredeth Turshen illustrates what it means to be a responsible scholar concerned with praxis. In much the same manner as Bond and Vincent, she is concerned with the linkages among the social, medical, and physical. She turns her attention to one of the main features of African studies, the epistemological and theoretical basis of research and policy and the manner in which they affect the lives of ordinary people. She focuses on the interrelationships of epidemic diseases, population growth, and endemic wars on a continental scale, paying close attention to the impact of political and structural violence on health. Through a series of fundamental questions, she returns us to the central contested domains and constructed categories employed in other chapters. She sets the stage for her discussion of health with questions such as "Does personal behavior explain illness and does education hold the key to better health? Or, do rapid population growth, a poor environment, and poverty account for ill health, and does sustainable development . . . hold the prescription for longevity" and political stability?

Turshen probes the logical and philosophical arguments commonly used to explain conditions in Africa as well as the claims and policies put forward by international organizations such as the World Bank and the World Heath Organization and African regimes as appropriate corrective measures to solve a particular problem. The reasons given for pursuing a specific policy related to controlling population growth are often based on the misreading of African history and false assumptions, obscuring the complexities of serial progressions and convergent interactions.

The chapter also points to the absence of responsibility and accountability and poses the question, who pays the price for failed projects and false claims? The shortcomings of many explanations is that they focus on a behavioral paradigm, blaming the failure of a specific project on the behavior of individual Africans. "The common depiction of AIDS as a personal, behavioral, and medical issue," observes Turshen, "allows the state to project its responsibility for public health onto individuals" and for international organizations to suggest that "African sexuality is abnormal." With this type of behavioral paradigm the state and international organizations cease to be accountable. Unwittingly, they engage in a subtle form of collusion, accepting technical solutions to problems that are basically political and require fundamental social and economic changes. Thus we return to a central focus of this volume: Technical discourses elide other discourses. The technical solutions may become aspects of domination, often contributing to basic political conditions. In writing about Rwanda and the international donor community, Uvin makes the following observation:

> Unfortunately, the development aid system is not simply ineffective, unsustainable, limited, and uncertain in its impact. It contributes to the processes of structural violence in many ways. It does so directly through its own behavior, whether unintended (as in the case of growing income inequality and land concentration) or intended (as in the condescending attitude toward poor people). It does so indirectly, by strengthening systems of exclusion and elite building through massive financial transfers, accompanied by self imposed political and social blindness. (1998: 143)

When the proposed projects fail it is the people who pay, as they did in Rwanda, for the "false claims of the international community" and national government.

Conclusion

One of the main purposes of this book is to suggest that, in various ways, intellectuals and international organizations represent and frame the social and human condition of African peoples. However, average Africans are not only the recipients of their descriptive representations, their analytic paradigms, and their pragmatic technical solutions; they are themselves actors and participants in the construction of their own histories and social realities. The realities are often harsh and unforgiving and can only be understood by exploring the mechanisms of domination, the poetics and politics of resistance, and the search for an immediate solution to some pressing problem. In other words, there is an actual landscape, a physical terrain of thought and emotion in which people live their lives and confront the problems of daily life as well as the multitude of complex social upheavals exemplified in acts of violence, warfare, and disease. These experiences are differentially inscribed in the lives of intellectuals, on the bodies of ordinary people, in the texts of reports, in the cultural productions of youth, and in the complex situations of the historical moment. It is a multifaceted and layered terrain of experience, structure, and discourse, which we hope in some way has been expressed not only in the individual chapters but also in the totality that makes the project of contesting terrains an ongoing one.

PART ONE

Challenging Modes
of Thinking: Making Maps
and Mapping History

1
"So Geographers in Africa Maps with Savage Pictures Fill Their Gaps"

Representing Africa on Maps

MOHAMED MBODJ
Manhattanville College

Postmodernism and post-colonialism are among the major themes in current humanities studies, especially when they are concerned with defining the identities of non-Western societies and their representation. Both themes have been theorized by linguists, philosophers, and literary critics, all often engaged in discussion by historians. The main emphasis has been on the study of the production of discourses and representation of colonized societies. From a different but convergent path, historians have also been preoccupied with evaluating texts as sources and have long been interested in the study of the production of identity and its historical representation.

Beyond the persistent relative imbalance between the analysis of internally and externally produced representations of colonized societies, and in addition to Philip Curtin's pioneering work (Curtin, 1964), historians have produced many interesting works on the history of identity and representation of Africa in Europe (Cohen, 1980; Schneider, 1982; MacKenzie, 1984). But most have not adequately addressed the crucial question of the basis of elaboration of such representations, dealing rather with their manifestation. This is because they often relied on literary sources expressive of high culture, as did Curtin and W. B. Cohen; W. H. Schneider used the popular press but limited himself to a 30-year period (1870–1900). J. M. MacKenzie covered a wider period (1880–1960) and a much more comprehensive scope. These authors were also primarily interested in debunking racism, scientific or religious, official or popular, open or covert, thus privileging art and prose. All assumed a diffusionist schema of culture and ideas, Schneider and MacKenzie less than the others. It is surprising how few studies there are based on the analysis of two major technical tools in the process of the production of discourses and images, the alphabet (writing) and the map. The case of African studies is compelling because Africa and Africans have suffered the most from the production of negative descriptions and images through the never-ending domination of foreign-produced materials. This chapter argues that more attention should be paid to the elaboration and the results of the representation of Africa on maps because they have played a major role in shaping perceptions of the continent from the outside. I also discuss how such representation and perception changed during three different periods, especially how they were internalized, rigidified, and reified by African elites and states in the last period.

History of Mapmaking

There is no clear indication of the origins of mapmaking or writing, but research points to an independent evolution among different peoples. Evidence found to date shows that they developed earliest in China and Mesopotamia. Africa is usually depicted as a continent that only recently began to write and to produce maps, and then only under foreign influence. In other words, before the coming of Arabs and Europeans, there was no original African writing system or mapmaking experience. Many parts of Africa had to wait until the late nineteenth century to appear systematically on maps and/or to adopt a unifying script.

Looking at the Asante of Ghana, Ivor Wilks argued that they lacked cartographic skills and therefore had to resort to "mental mapping" (1993: 189–214). The Asante combined time, distance, landscape, stress of the environment, religious beliefs, and cultural factors to devise a mental map of their country. They determined that one month (an Asante month equals 42 days) was needed to travel from one end of their empire to the other. The capital, Kumasi, was at the center of a circle, putting the longest travel time from the city at 21 days. The mental map fulfilled a practical purpose by providing a timetable within which administrative decisions could be taken and executed. This may also explain the lasting determination with which the Asante defended their control over the coastal territories that lay within those limits.

However, there is a difference between making sense of space and ordering it (as in mental maps).

The process of ordering space is sometimes associated with the capacity to make maps of surroundings (like a cadastre) or of symbolic areas (like the Luba "map") and the ability to make and reproduce maps without any direct physical links to the area described. The first ability exists in almost all societies, whereas the second is limited to the so-called more advanced societies in Europe or the West. D. Wood makes a decisive distinction between "mapping" and "mapmaking" (1992: 32–34). He marks a sharp difference between two kinds of societies. On the one hand, the West is "map-immersed"; people frequently consult and produce maps and see them as part of their everyday life. In the West, the task of mapmaking has become highly technical and professionalized. On the other hand, in the rest of the world maps are only occasionally made, consulted, or reproduced. Systematizing his observation of map usage and mapmaking, Wood concludes that some societies (those in the West) are "bigger" and more "developed" than others. He argues that growth, increasing hierarchies, and modernization of the state constitute the decisive factors (Wood, 1992: 42–43). There are several objections to these conclusions. First, Wood seems to subscribe to a linear or positivist approach to history, in which societies evolve from the "primitive" to the "complex." Second, whose "modernization," what kind of "modernity," and what "decisive" moment is he referring to? Third, it is debatable how much curiosity (scientific or amateur, individual or collective) and greed (political or economic) have contributed to the historic drive to fill in the "blanks" on the maps.[1]

Maps and alphabets share two characteristics. They are both coded, and the decoding is accessible to anyone who has the opportunity and the willingness to learn the signs. The decoding processes differ, however. A map displays its decoding key through the title and the legend. With an alphabet, one can arrange the order and relation of the letters or characters, thus conveying a meaning. It is obvious that the diffusion of literacy has made reading maps and deciphering writing easier. Writing is generally considered an act of creation of early humankind,[2] whereas maps seem to have had a connection to the secretive domains of royalty and the military. They were, and often remain, part of the domain of strategic intelligence gathering and of economic exploitation. Yoro Fall asserts that not only were maps inaccessible to many, they also sometimes included false information to induce erroneous conclusions in the minds of unauthorized readers (Fall, 1986).

Although Africa is not known as a producer of maps, there are nonetheless coded records of data one could refer to as "maps." It is obvious that such signs could be found in many shapes and on a multitude of media, such as staffs, body scarifications, and cloth. Sometimes the style and the medium are strikingly close to those found in Western mapmaking. For example, the Luba of Central Africa devised a system of abstract signs painted on wall murals that one could easily interpret as "codified maps." However, only Luban initiates at a very advanced level could actually learn to decipher the code. The signs represent both the Luba sacral and real territories, such as lakes, rivers, and abodes of spirits, and chiefs' capitals figure on the paintings. These signs provided Lubans with knowledge about their spiritual or religious world as well as the coinciding political realm (Nooter, 1990). The geographical bearing of the Luba map was less important than its religious and political significance. A decision is made based on age and status rather than being made by an individual, as in the West (an author, a king, or a military commander). The kind of power provided through this access was more symbolic than material. This is especially true when the symbolism of the Luba "map" is compared to the overwhelmingly utilitarian aspects of Western maps. One could argue that the emphasis on the local in the Luba "map" is in opposition to the claim of universality of the Western map.

When referring to maps, we should make a distinction between commonly found representations of itineraries (route maps) or cadastres and topographic projections (for which the term *map* is usually reserved). It is logical to assume that all societies know the geographical relation of their surroundings and that many people with no Western or Islamic education keep in their memories sketches of itineraries (or "route maps") and cadastres that they can use when needed. It seems that the ancient Egyptians did not get beyond this first stage of mapmaking. Norman Thrower (1996: 13–15) estimates that they used two diverging types of "maps," the itinerary or cadastre type and a speculative, cosmological one similar to the Luba "map" in essence and use. The Arabs, however, were the first to draw and to use maps in Africa, beginning in the eleventh to twelfth centuries (Thrower, 1996: 45–50). The absence of cartography in Africa prior to the coming of Islam is usually explained in terms of the limitations or choices of so-called non-literate societies and also by the absence of necessary social conditions (Hunt, 1994). Richard Pankhurst mentions the existence of schematic geographical representations in eighteenth-century Ethiopian manuscripts (Pankhurst, 1989). In one of the most comprehensive surveys on the question, Jeffrey Stone remarks:

> [I]t seems unlikely that the map as an artifact was totally absent in the sub-Saharan states from Mali and Songhai to Bornu and south to Asante and Benin, from the Islamic societies of northeast Africa, or from the Bantu-speaking states of central, east and southern Africa. (Stone, 1995: 6)

To prove his point, Stone mentions a map shown to Clapperton by the Sultan of Sokoto in 1826 (Stone, 1995: 7), but he does not elaborate on this evidence. Stone finally concludes that "the earliest hard-copy maps of Africa known in any significant numbers" were only found in Western and Islamic cultures (Stone, 1995: 9).

Mapmaking addresses a series of formidable challenges that can be summarized in a few questions. How does one put a round or curved object like the Earth on a flat sheet? How does the mapmaker account for the distortion created in distance and size by his or her perspective from that location; in other words, how can the mapmaker put in correct proportion two objects when one is closer? Mapmakers' responses to these questions are projections, which have always been inadequate. Indeed, a heated debate continues to the present day (Peters, 1983; Thrower, 1996; Wood, 1992).

Map projection is the transfer of the features of the Earth's surface or those of another spherical body onto a flat sheet of paper. Only a globe can represent surface features correctly with reference to area, shape, scale, and direction. The projection of a globe onto a flat map always causes some distortion. A grid of two intersecting systems of lines corresponding to parallels and meridians must be drawn on a plane surface. Some projections (equidistant) aim to keep correct distances in all directions from the center of the map. Others show areas (equal-area) or shapes (conformal) equal to those on the globe of the same scale. Projections are cylindrical, conical, or azimuthal. Most of the methods and techniques of map projection belong to the field of mathematics. Just as early cartographers stressed empiricism, it is generally accepted that ultimate progress in "science" will make more advanced mathematical and theoretical tools available.

A second problem, the accuracy of the represented data, is less serious, because gaps can be filled through the accumulation and verification of knowledge over time. However, this solution largely depends on the relationship between the map and reality. Is a map the product of the cartographer's own conception of reality or its source? What about the authority or customer who ordered the production of the map? Of course, these questions were more crucial before the age of modern mass scholarly publishing. But it remains true even today that prejudice and ignorance usually combine with social attitudes and cultural values to influence the mapmaker's view of the world, especially those parts of the world supposedly "unknown," "strange," or less valued. The character Marlow in Joseph Conrad's *The Heart of Darkness* is a good illustration of this phenomenon. Marlow is attracted by the necessity to explore "blank areas" on the maps of Africa, Australia, or South America, which eventually lead to their colonization by his nemesis.

A third and perhaps more peripheral question is the explanation or decoding and readability of maps. During the course of the development of Western mapmaking, maps have become less verbose and less explicit. Gradually, the scale and the title have replaced the abundant and colorful. During the eighteenth century norms and conventions established by scholars began to prevail in the West and had become almost universally validated by the second half of the nineteenth century. Maps now are readable by almost any literate individual with a minimal knowledge of scale and orientation indicators. In addition, the computer age is quickly making available large databases (allowing for military and economic limitations) to almost every computer user, who in turn can produce any map conceived of, when wanted, and wherever located.

The history of mapmaking is intrinsically dominated by European historiography, and it centers heavily on Western history. Therefore, I consider that the periodization proposed in 1926 by Joseph Conrad is still valid in large part, although it needs further elaboration for the twentieth century.[3] Conrad proposed three distinct phases (1926: 1–31). In the first period, which lasted into the 1700s and which he labeled the "fabulous phase," circumstantial and extravagant speculation mixed ancient and medieval phantasmagoria with speculative representations of non-European worlds. Religious preoccupation and sensationalism abounded, and honest ignorance was hard to accept. The second phase, the 1700s–1800s, was one of "geography militant." This was the period of systematic compiling by arduous artisans and scholars, later joined by explorers filling in the "blank" spaces on the map by gathering on site the necessary data while at the same time verifying the accuracy of the existing maps. When there was a lack of data, the area was left blank, void of any information, thus inviting further work. Following the then-dominant positivist ambiance, ignorance was considered to be only temporary because human genius would ultimately uncover every inch of the Earth. However, this expected discovery had two aspects. On the one hand was the wrong kind of exploration, incited by more or less avowed but nevertheless economic and political ambitions, which Conrad deplored.[4] On the other hand was the search for scientific truth, nurtured by noble explorers motivated by disinterested faith, which trend Conrad admired and identified with.[5] The last period, "geography triumphant," from the early twentieth century to the present, is a direct product of the earlier trend toward scientific exploration. This is the time of the final triumph of the scientific idea, the progress of the human spirit or civilization. It is also a period of triumph for the map that Conrad could not have envisaged. Not only has almost every inch of the Earth been discovered, but it has become possible to map beneath it, beneath the sea, and beyond the planet as well. Another sign of the triumph of the map is how it encapsulates and defines the existence of dozens of states Conrad would have considered unlikely to emerge.

Development of Scientific Cartography

The beginning of scientific cartography in Europe is usually attributed to the ancient Greeks. The Greeks were deeply interested in Africa as both a source and an object of knowledge. For example, the continent occupies a major place in the writings of Herodotus in the fifth century B.C. Herodotus identified three different "races" (Libyans, Ethiopians, and Atlantians) subdivided into 16 groups. He depicted the East Coast of Africa terminating around the Horn and located the sources of the Nile River in the western part of the continent. He mentioned features that would have been considered "negative" by the ancient Greeks, such as "dog-headed men and the headless peoples that have their eyes in their breasts . . . and the wild men and women"; Amazons; vegetarian habits; a gynecocracy; and strange customs such as initiation, body scarifications, and sacrifices. However, he also described elements that were probably considered "positive" or would at least have elicited sympathy, such as Pygmies, clean peoples, devoted parents, and orderly and peaceful communities.

It is now widely accepted among scholars that the ancient Greeks' concept of "otherness" was based on a reverse mirroring of their own self-image, so one should be cautious of accepting their views as the product of real testimony or experience (Hartog, 1980). Valentin Mudimbe, among others, sees in the ancient Greeks' concept of "other" the birth of "a science of barbarians" reserved to Africa (Mudimbe, 1994: 71–104). When post-medieval Europeans rediscovered the ancient Greeks' texts, they adopted them as verified truths. Descriptions by authors such as Herodotus and Pliny the Elder were repeated again and again, well into the nineteenth century, with the "barbarians" then becoming "savages." What began more as a characterization of strange peoples, however degraded, eventually became the basis of modern race prejudice.

The ancient Greeks generally used the name "Libya" for the African continent. In the first century B.C. the Romans were the first to use the name "Africa," extending that appellation beyond ancient Carthage's territorial limits (Mudimbe, 1994: 72).

The Greek Ptolemy was the first to draw a series of world maps depicting Africa, in the second century B.C. He worked from Alexandria in Seleucid, Egypt, which at the time had the largest and most sophisticated library in the world. Ptolemy introduced some major innovations to argue that Earth was a sphere and could be divided into a series of concave parallels and meridians. He also used a rigorous geometrical design and avoided images. In his celebrated maps, Africa is correctly extended to the west and to the south, a series of large lakes is recorded as the source of the Nile, and so forth. However, another major river with features almost identical to the Nile is drawn running east to west. Apparently, whenever he was short of information, Ptolemy advanced theoretical conceptions. For example, southeast Africa and southwest Asia are linked by an enigmatic "Terra Incognita" locking in the Indian Ocean.

For over 1,500 years, Arabs, Europeans, and Chinese reproduced Ptolemy's maps, often altering them slightly to suit their needs.[6] In Europe, religion and imaginative iconography, especially from around the time of the Crusades, influenced mapmaking, which was generally performed by the scholars of the time, the monks. On the one hand, for example, from the twelfth century until at least the late sixteenth century, Prester John's mythical Christian kingdom figured on maps, located south of the Nile River basin. On the other hand, as early as the mid-twelfth century, a major step had been achieved by the famous Moroccan and Arab traveler al-Idrisi. Al-Idrisi's atlas showed Ptolemy's influence and was superior by far to any contemporary European maps. The maps accompanied his famous *The Book of Roger*, published in 1154. The maps avoided all graphic dimensions, thus approaching as much as possible a purely geographical style. Al-Idrisi put Arabia at the center and gave many details about Europe, Asia, and North Africa. Africa was represented without a link with southwest Asia, leaving the Indian Ocean open-ended.

At the beginning of the European Renaissance Ptolemy's work as preserved by the Arabs and the Chinese was rediscovered. A fierce commercial, religious, and political competition among European nations and princes stimulated a great demand for new maps. As Western Europe developed, the geographical focus of Western cartography shifted from the Mediterranean Sea before the 1500s to Africa, South Asia, and later America after the 1500s. Many cartographers, especially in Portugal, started to inscribe their national colors and coats of arms on areas of the world they claimed were under their domination. Spain and other aspiring European powers followed suit. Navigational charts and colored shields and flags coexisted on these maps, which were shown in courts or exchanged as gifts between royalties. A map made in 1375 by the Catalan Abraham Cresques was offered by the king of Aragon to the king of France in 1380. The celebrated map put Timbuktu and Gao at approximately the right places. More important, it figured a seated king of Mali dressed in magnificent

Muslim garb and holding a golden nugget, suggesting immense wealth, which in turn triggered or accompanied a rush to the western coast of Africa and later to the circumnavigation of the world. The map also figured the famous priest-king Prester John reigning over an African Christian kingdom.[7] By the late 1400s, the invention of movable type had enabled the development of many centers of map production. By the late sixteenth century, first the Dutch, then the Germans and the French, had taken over the lead in mapmakng from the Portuguese and the Spaniards. By then, mapmaking had become a prestigious activity of professional technicians and scholars. However, religious influence and imaginative iconography continued to influence mapmaking for two more centuries.

The first map devoted only to Africa was published in Milan in 1508 (Stone, 1997: xix). Soon thereafter, entire atlases of Africa were printed. Sailors became the main users of maps, and they were also the main providers of new information. They used new instruments, such as the sextant, the compass, and the measuring chain, and over time their measurements became more precise. By the early 1500s, many advances in geographical knowledge were reflected on the maps of Africa. For example, the previously landlocked Indian Ocean was replaced by an open-ended space, and the Cape of Good Hope was figured clearly; the general shape of West Africa was well rendered; and Muslim or African rulers were acknowledged south of the Sahara. At the same time, however, the interior of the continent continued to have imprecise names, large rivers ran straight west to east or north to south, and so forth; some maps even identified a "Paradise" in Africa (previously located in Asia).

In the sixteenth and seventeenth centuries, two trends of mapmaking predominated, one for the purpose of navigation, the other for the wider audience of princes, courts, scholars, and publicists. Sailors preferred maps with distances and navigational directions. They were especially interested in knowing the itineraries from one port to another. These maps, or portulans, were printed mostly in black and white. For the wider audience, however, colored images and drawings adorned the maps. The didactical purpose of the display is obvious in that case. Big animals, costumes, cities, and kings were the favorite themes. Images of strange peoples were juxtaposed with biblical episodes and ancient myths. On many maps, the size of Prester John's Empire, variably called Abyssinia or Ethiopia, was grossly exaggerated, extending almost to the Atlantic and south to the Great Lakes. This depiction remained on maps well into the eighteenth century (Wallis & Middleton, 1987: 47). Exaggeration and ignorance combined to discredit more and more what was frequently relegated to entertainment. The famous British author Jonathan Swift summed up the general skepticism of the educated elite about maps:

*So Geographers in Africa-Maps
With Savage-Pictures fill their Gaps;
And o'er unhabitable Downs
Placed Elephants for want of Towns.*
(Swift, On Poetry—A Rhapsody, *1733, verses 177–180*)

Cartography Becomes Geography

Beginning in the 1700s, the images inscribed or inserted in maps became less abundant and were relegated to the title-piece and the legend, and geographical and topographical details prevailed. The commercial production of maps increased through general atlases and works of description and travel. The British entered the field of map publishing and, along with the French, they began to dominate it. There was also a strong German tradition. During this period, the shape of the African continent was finally ascertained, although gross errors remained in the courses of some rivers (the Niger being the most obvious case) and in the shape of some of the larger lakes. Regional atlases of Africa also began to be produced at this time. Missionaries who started to settle in Africa helped to refine some of the details of the African interior. For example, in the early eighteenth century the Jesuits provided a great deal of information about Ethiopia. By the end of the eighteenth century, cartographers had become an integral part of the new academic world emerging at modern universities in northern Europe. An author's creativity, imagination, social attitudes, and cultural values began to play a much smaller role, and more scientific techniques were developed. In 1749, the French cartographer Jean Baptiste d'Anville inaugurated an important new standard by deciding to leave blank uncharted areas while deleting all speculative features. The cartographer became a geographer.

Before d'Anville, the Fleming Gerhard Kramer (1512–1594), more widely known as Mercator, had been an isolated precursor of this new trend. Appointed in 1552 to the chair of cosmography at the University of Duisburg, Germany, Mercator became the most innovative cartographer since Ptolemy. In 1568 he published the first map using the projection that bears his name, although his great atlas (1585–1594) was only published after his death. Mercator was the first to draw a map as a mathematical exercise with the desired end of providing an accurate representation of distances. He was not interested in visual appeal but in the effective utility of the map. Mercator noticed that the plane-chart ignored the sphericity of the Earth by not rendering the diminishing value of longitude toward the poles. To address this problem, he designed a technique to render both latitude and longitude with a constant ratio, thus making navigation with instruments more accurate. However, Mercator's focus on distance led him to neglect both the relative and real sizes of land masses, so that areas closer to the poles tended to have significantly disproportionate sizes. He also perpetuated many factual errors, such as placing the source of the Nile River too far to the west and south on the African continent.

Role of Maps in European Expansion

I would argue that the map was decisive in Europe's expansion from the fifteenth century onward. Maps played an obvious role in the planning and charting of European expansion and also served as a powerful tool of propaganda, either as an autonomous display or incorporated in another kind of publication. Thus, the map was a kind of incentive to European imperialism long before becoming a tool of propaganda and popularization of it. It played a considerable role, perhaps more than the printed word, especially before the popularization of photography in the late nineteenth century. The map by itself could inform a much larger audience than the printed word before the advent of universal education and of the popular press, and it played an important illustrative role as a companion when inserted in publications. One can generally evaluate the important role played by Enlightenment essayists such as Rousseau, explorers such as Mungo Park or René Caillé, popular writers such as Pierre Loti in France or Rudyard Kipling in England, and propagandists such as Leroy-Beaulieu in France or Cecil Rhodes in England, in promoting colonial adventure and conquest. But it is equally crucial to evaluate how a pro-colonial popular public opinion and conventional wisdom were created and sustained in Europe. Historians to date have only explored the roles of books and the penny press. Perhaps the study of historical maps had suffered from the fear of dwelling on the worst kind of determinism, geographic determinism. This is especially true after the Second World War, when, as a discipline, history tried very hard to be part of social sciences, a view explicitly held by Marxism and its avatars.

In the nineteenth century, almost all decorative artifacts disappeared from maps, and coloring was used to indicate different political entities or territorial claims. Nineteenth-century travelers and explorers helped to fill in the gaps and to define the shape of the interior. In addition to numerous maritime instruments, travelers used new instruments like the artificial horizon and the chronometer. Commercial ventures and powerful learned societies funded many explorers' endeavors. Maps became an intrinsic part of newspapers articles and books, especially in magazines, travelers' accounts, and exotic novels. The popular diffusion of this literature helped to attract the layperson's curiosity, as typified by the character Marlow in *The Heart of Darkness:*

> Now when I was just a little chap I had a passion for maps. I would look for hours at South America, or Africa, or Australia, and lose myself in all the glories of exploration. At that time there were many blank spaces on the earth, and when I saw one that looked particularly inviting on a map (but they all look like that) I would put my finger on it and say, When I grow up I will go there. . . . But there was one yet—the biggest, the most blank, so to speak—that I had a hankering after. (Conrad, 1995: 21–22)

Napoleon I was the first modern head of state to systematize mapping and mapmaking and to give it a high priority in all his military and administrative endeavors in Europe and elsewhere. He even proposed his services to Persia. Napoleon's campaign in Egypt remains the perfect archetype of how science and the military were entwined in the nineteenth century. One can safely say that tens of thousands of maps were produced under Napoleon's auspices.[8] At the same time, slowly but inexorably, from the early 1800s onwards, maps appeared on classroom walls and in school textbooks as mass public education became increasingly the norm. These maps helped incorporate in the psyche of students and citizens the shape of the newly acquired nation and that of their neighbors or enemies. France, again, was the leader in this trend. For example, the French published the first complete national atlas in 1847.[9] They were also the first to publish a map specifically designed for schools, at the high school (college in France) in this case.[10] To impregnate children's minds with nationalist values is a common thread in every state's policy, and one can easily conceive how some among these children would be inspired to go to Africa. Joseph Conrad recounts how his imagination was captured in his native Poland, an experience he later transposed as Marlow's in *The Heart of Darkness*:

> It was in 1868, when nine years old or thereabouts, that while looking at a map of Africa of the time and putting my finger on the blank space then representing the unsolved mystery of that continent, I said to myself with absolute assurance and a amazing audacity which are no longer in my character now:
> "When I grow up I shall go *there.*"
> And of course I thought no more about it till after a quarter of a century or so an opportunity offered to go there. . . . I did go there: *there* being the region of Stanley Falls which in '68 was the blankest of blank spaces on the earth's figured surface. (Conrad, 1995: x)

France's aggressive approach was soon followed by its imperialist competitors such as Germany, England, Russia, and Italy.[11] Maps also helped to unify many of Europe's new nations linguistically by creating and spreading an official and compulsory toponymy. From the 1780s to the 1950s, the teaching of history in Europe developed into an intense form of patriotic indoctrination in which maps were considered a vital tool. Conventional colors were adopted for the various rival imperial powers. In France, the chosen colors were pink for France and its possessions, green for Portugal, white for the last "unexplored areas," and so forth.

Maps were also part of the imperialist toolbox, first and foremost by providing a direct basis for territorial claims and political negotiations. For many Europeans, their own mastering of maps was a clear indication of their superiority and representative of their civilizing mission, while providing a justification to the most infatuated for calling themselves "discoverers." And of course, these self-declared "discoverers" felt entitled to claim property rights over their "discoveries." By identifying and defining some part of Africa as a discovery of their own world, Europe, they could then define its occupants as foster children. For example, in the 1870s one of these "discoverers," described his interaction with local people in Africa in the following way:

> The guides were never able to name a place until close to it, and had very little conception of the lay of the land they had coasted many times. Local knowledge is wonderfully good, but they seem incapable of grasping anything like a general idea.
>
> They stared at my map and thought it a most wonderful performance; and when I said that people in England would know the shape and size of Tanganyika, and the names and situation of rivers and villages by means of it, I am inclined to fancy they thought me a magician. (Cameron, 1877: 284)

After 1850, the topography on Western maps of Africa became almost error free, especially after all major waterways were charted. Indications about the topography, especially rivers and elevations, became abundant, as well as names of ethnic groups, states, and localities. The 1884–1885 Berlin conference defined the general rules of occupation of Africa by Europe, requiring effective occupation along with documented claims. As a consequence maps became essential in public and diplomatic territorial disputes. The publication or use of certain maps could attest to a particular political viewpoint or claim. Direct occupation and conquest necessitated a large scale and detailed mapping of the continent. On the drawing board, boundaries became an essential element of national representation. The distinction between official and non-official ("working") maps became fundamental. Colors and illustrations disappeared in favor of more numerical and statistical data.[12] Specialized army personnel took over mapmaking from travelers and other amateurs. Their access to new survey tools such as aerial photography provided a decisive instrument. Army maps, especially the popular 1:50,000, were used as sketches one could fill in to suit particular or local interests.

Benedict Anderson believes that the process of filling the "box" is fundamental to the establishment of a colony, which is the seed of a future independent nation: "Triangulation by triangulation, war by war, treaty by treaty, the alignment of map and power proceeded" (Anderson, 1991: 127). However, the colonial map was no longer the scientific abstraction of reality, as maps were generally believed to be in Europe after the Renaissance. It was rather a reality in "project," a virtual reality to put to work effectively. To support his point, Benedict Anderson cites Thongchai Winichakul, a Thai historian reflecting on the history of the mapping of his country:

> A map merely represents something which already exists objectively "there." In the history I have described, this relationship was reversed. A map anticipated spatial reality, not vice versa. In other words, a map was a model for, rather than a model of, what it purported to represent.... It had become a real instrument to concretize projections on the earth's surface. A map was now necessary for the new administrative mechanisms and for the troops to back up their claims. (Anderson, 1992: 173–17)

After the colonial boundaries were set in the late 1890s and early 1900s, censuses, tax lists, administrative units, and so forth would fill in the topography of the map. Maps were used extensively during the colonial era. Settlers, missionaries, and the military needed them to assess the territorial scope of their authority, to legitimate their power, and to organize the exploitation of both human and natural resources. Maps were also used as symbols of modernity and European superiority as they became standard issue for colonial administrators, soldiers, and missionaries. Geological surveys, censuses, court decisions, administrative tours, and public works projects were crucial to displaying authority. During the twentieth century, one of the most systematic uses of maps was in the colonial school system and in the popular propaganda tools evident in colonial fairs and exhibitions.

The late nineteenth and early twentieth centuries saw large European cities organize regular colonial fairs and exhibitions that drew large crowds[13] eager for exotic sensations and willing to discover the scope of their nation's glory through its colonial achievements. Some of these exhibitions were itinerant, increasing their propagandizing effect. Maps were a regular feature in such manifestations. Above all, they helped to locate various colonies in relation to the metropoles and other colonies. They also had a pernicious effect through the juxtaposition of the imperial powers and their possessions on the same maps. On these maps the small size of France, Great Britain, and other imperialist nations, especially when compared to the much larger size of their possessions, fed a sense of chauvinism and national destiny. These map displays became a requisite along with colorful representations of colonial subjects, monuments, and landscapes. In addition, the maps often helped to lend a degree of credibility to the often exaggerated drawings and paintings they accompanied. They also helped to territorialize colonial dreams, thus lending those dreams a hint of feasibility.

The same kind of maps found their way into a variety of publications, even the scholarly ones. Many historical atlases of the world published until recently do not have maps of Africa for any historical period before the 1400s, especially when ancient Egypt was not considered part of the continent. In these atlases, the first map to figure Africa is regularly the world map of European navigations or "discoveries" or, slightly better, the map of Muslim conquests in North Africa. In other words, Africans just did not exist until outsiders, preferably Europeans, brought them into the world. Subsequent maps dealt overwhelmingly with Europe's presence in Africa through the slave trade, the conquest, the post–World War I changes, and the achievement of independence in the 1950s and 1960s.

Maps placed on the walls along with other imperial images were a regular feature in most Western schools during the twentieth century. MacKenzie cites a student in the 1920s describing his rural English classroom as

> steeped in officially sanctioned nationalism. The world map was red for the Empire and dull brown for the rest, with Australia and Canada vastly exaggerated in size by Mercator's projection. The Greenwich meridian placed London at the centre of the world. (MacKenzie, 1984: 193)

Such maps were a standard item in European colonies also, especially in the French colonies, where personnel were trained under the same Jacobinist ideology as were their counterparts in France. The same mural maps were displayed in Europe and in Africa, and the indoctrination process was quite similar. Until the late 1960s, most French schools in Africa still used wall maps with large pink areas delimiting the French Empire.[14] The terminology attached to imperial maps reflects a political desire for extended space and was associated with visual expressions of this desire. For example, to describe their territorial extension, the French used "La plus grande France (The Largest France)" before World War II and "La France des 100 millions d'habitants (The 100 million inhabitants France)" after 1945. Africans and Europeans, subjects and citizens, all students were invited to revere the same values, although these values did not apply equally to all. Maps played a crucial role in this process, not only by making exotic places familiar (in both directions) but also by creating the perception of a territorial continuity that could be translated into claims for political unity and effective loyalty.[15] The sense of homogeneity of a colonial territory is also suggested by the strong visual effect created by the color assigned to that territory, usually a very sharp one. The full effect was attained in the post-colonial era.

Accuracy in Size Versus Accuracy in Distance

The attainment of political independence in Africa has not brought much change either in the purposes or the meanings of maps. Mapmaking remains controlled by Europeans and North Americans. The strategic domination of the West is extended by the new costly techniques, such as remote sensing and computer-driven processes, both techniques still not readily accessible to most African institutions or countries.[16] Mapmakers are no longer confined to what the human eye can see. They can now map where no human may ever go, such as distant planets or beneath deep sea waters. They can also map areas once occupied by humans and now buried. The new techniques are more precise than ever and enable mapmakers to update their output on a continuous basis. They also allow the production of maps tailored to individual needs and at will. The crucial importance of maps remains, but economic interests tend to overshadow politics. Maps are used not just to assess current reality but also to predict future crops, which in turn allows entities to control cereal or commodities markets. The sale of maps to countries, companies, and institutions has become a big industry, especially by France and the United States. Moreover, the current age of international tourism and expanded cultural interaction has created a new type of map designed to attract or sell travel or to educate children. Colors abound on such maps. On these maps, Africa is presented as a land of exotic big animals such as elephants, lions, and zebras.

The shock wave following the independence of former Asian and African countries has started numerous debates about the fairness of their treatment. Moreover, the objectivity of almost every mathematics-based science is no longer accepted as unequivocal fact. Mapmaking is among the fields where such dispute has flourished. Specifically, the old debate about the choice between accuracy in distance and accuracy in size has resurfaced. Some authors have argued that the choice of putting distance first, which has dominated mapmaking since the inception of the Mercator projection, tends to exaggerate Northern Europe's size vis-à-vis the tropical latitudes. The vantage point from the north looks at the world through Northern European eyes, with Africa and Asia crouching at Europe's feet. Thus, Mercator projection-based maps are more detrimental to Africa than to any other continent (Peters, 1983). This technique of projection has served Europe's sense of superiority. During the colonial era, it conveyed a sense of destiny by showing small European powers reigning over large blocks of Africa and Asia. With independence, many blocks were broken into much smaller pieces. The Mercator projection then showed European countries as "normal" in size.

However, a more sensitive and scientific approach is to represent the relative real size of the different continents and countries. The German historian Arno Peters (1983 and 1989) has been the most systematic in denouncing the "Eurocentrism" of the Mercator projection. He has attacked the assumed political neutrality of cartographers and geographers under the cover of the hard sciences.[17] To replace the Mercator projection, in the late 1960s and early 1970s he developed what he sees as an objective and egalitarian technique of projection, dubbed "the Peters projection."[18]

Regardless of which projection is used in mapmaking, the African continent is still much larger than imperialist Europe. What is more interesting is that the scientific and neutral standings of maps are increasingly being challenged (Vujakovic, 1989; Black, 1997; Thrower, 1996). Thus, it appears that even sophisticated, mathematically based techniques do not allow us to escape the crucial questions: What is represented? By whom? How? When? Cartographers were and are a strategic element in state agencies and processes, and they exhibit the underlying values of their own societies.

When African countries became independent in the 1960s, they broke away from the colonial federations or ensembles. The large pink or blue areas under French, British, or Belgian domination have been replaced by dozens of pieces, each with a distinctive color. By creating a "jigsaw" effect, color detaches countries from their context, thus abstracting them from their neighbors and allowing them to stand distinctively on their own. On such a basis, one could even defend improbable territorial claims.[19] The "jigsaw" effect thus creates another opportunity for chauvinism to enter people's minds. Another important effect is the portability of the "jigsaw piece," a phenomenon Benedict Anderson calls "map-as-logo" (1991: 175). Maps are now just abstracted shapes that can be reproduced infinitely on any available medium, thus providing a powerful emblem for local nationalism, a rallying point easily recognized by everybody. A country's map gets into its people's psyche the same way a logo does, using subliminal power. In the context of the intense propaganda that followed the African countries gaining their independence, this could be decisive by inculcating strong adherence to the nation-state along with a flag, a national anthem, and an independence day (Mbodj, 1999). A very powerful effect of the modern map of Africa is to create a basis of power for the nationalist elite who took over after the colonizers' departure. Nurtured by colonial schools, the elite had internalized the colonial map. They could now claim a space identified as their own. The territory defined on the modern map that was previously occupied by the Europeans became theirs to take in their own hands, on their own terms. They are the legitimate inheritors of title deeds; they were taught that ownership of the land is the primordial basis of civilization. Therefore, as was the case in capitalist Europe, the deeds were sacred and indisputable by outsiders, and those who questioned them from within were bound to be considered traitors.

Today, the map of Africa is dominated by the intangibility of the colonial borders agreed upon as a fundamental principle by the Organization of African Unity (OAU) in 1963. These borders are to be preserved at all costs despite many internal and external challenges (Touval, 1972). The model of the state implanted in Africa is of one exerting power uniformly over a given area. It derives from the eighteenth- and nineteenth-century European nation-states (Davidson, 1992). The European model is centered on the control of land and land-based resources. Borders could follow straight lines and be materialized by markers. On the other hand, most pre-colonial African political entities were based on the control of human labor. In this conception, states are generally constituted by flexible political centers surrounded by provinces whose boundary lines tend to fade gradually into neighboring political entities. Therefore, the borders based on that model could not be drawn in straight lines. Today's map of Africa has been arbitrated by imperial history as it has adopted the European model of states. This explains in part why the OAU recognized it as a "fact product" of history in the 1960s. That outsiders should decide the border of a country is a phenomenon not particular to Africa, as numerous examples throughout history and well into the twentieth century demonstrate, even in Europe (Belgium, almost all of Central and Eastern Europe, Israel, etc.). Yet many argue that today's map is arbitrary because the divisions it inscribes produce conflict that seems unneeded, and that many African people find the divisions and juxtapositions of the current map artificial, inconvenient, disruptive, threatening, or oppressive (Kodjo, 1985: 230; Asiwaju, 1990). Of course, it could be argued that such events are not caused as much by where the lines are drawn as by how states treat people within them.

It is legitimate to ask how historical forces have generated the current political map of Africa and to ask if a better map could be produced that would be more beneficial for Africa. But to redraw the map of Africa is a fairly dubious proposition and would not resolve many current borders disputes, which are generally just an extension of internal problems. In fact, any redrawn map would have the same character because it would arbitrate among claims and even bases for making claims. The process would be based on power rather than ideals. Post-colonial mapmaking would be just as arbitrary as colonial mapmaking, just an exercise of power, opening all sorts of questions about who would and who should have what sort of influence in such a project. The legitimacy problems of many African governments raise questions about who should negotiate each country's place on the map. Considering their overall poor performance, it is doubtful that these governments would do a good job.

One of the few deliberate attempts to redraw the African map in the twentieth century, the controversial creation of ethnic homelands by South African Europeans under the regime of apartheid, is illustrative. The project, like many ideas for redrawing Africa's map, was based on the unverified premises that ethnic groups are strictly and easily identifiable as natural groupings in separate areas, that they are desired by their members as the most relevant political unit, and that they are linguistically homogenous. Among other flaws, the project ignored the fact that many pre-colonial polities harbored different languages and cultural groups, and that ethnicity is in many places a product of colonialism through the reification of cultural difference and the creation of standardized written languages. A map of Africa based on ethnicity would show a myriad of ethnic groups, with the likely effect of depicting Africans as living in many tiny "tribes," unable to be coherent and self-sustainable, therefore suggesting the need for some ordering or tutelage (from the West?).

If redrawing Africa's map consists of getting rid of the few colonized spots like the Spanish enclaves in Morocco, or the French La Réunion, then one could argue that it follows the general course of African history. Even if the right to self-determination is a political standard of current international relations, the changes would be difficult to come by. However, there have been recent changes in the map of Africa: The Eritrea-Ethiopia example has shown that the OAU principles on boundaries are only general guidelines. South Africa has finally returned Walvis Bay to Namibia, and various borders have been redrawn, even if only slightly (Senegal-Gambia, Namibia-South Africa, etc.). But many boundaries remain contested, and conflicts abound and are likely to erupt in violent confrontations. Some well-known examples are the conflicts between Somalia and Ethiopia, Cameroon and Nigeria, and

Mali and Burkina. When military action fails to redraw the map, which is usually the case, the recourse is some kind of international arbitrage or court decision, which invariably confirms the colonial borders. After all, today's international law was born from the Western tradition, where maps play a decisive role. The only available maps are the imperial ones, the same that have been seen as the cause of the conflict. Even where success has been acknowledged, reversals could happen. An example is provided by the recent border war between Eritrea and Ethiopia, two states that had agreed to separate amicably in 1993. In that case, which colonial map should prevail in delimiting the border was at question: the Italian map of 1890 or 1936, or the British map of 1941? What about the changes made by Ethiopian governors in the following 50 years (Khadiagala, 1999: 45)? In all cases, the maps invoked were those of the same reviled imperialists.

The same phenomenon can be found in other situations. For example, many autonomists or independence movements use the colonial maps to support their quest for self-determination. One illustrative case is the Casamance in southern Senegal. The Casamance independence movement argues that the area was first united by the Portuguese occupation before the French in the late nineteenth century, and that under the French they enjoy a separate status different from that of Senegal. Among the proofs they offer are colonial maps drawn by the French, hence their demand that a French archivist do the research to produce them. The French archivist did not confirm their position, but many of them still believe that the maps they need exist. Obviously, such maps would have corresponded to the Portuguese explorations (and a partial occupation later) of the Casamance River.

It is paradoxical that the separatists insist on using the maps produced by the same colonial entity that handed power over to the Senegalese state in the 1960s, thus creating the problem they seek to redress. One would have expected the Casamance independence movement (MFDC) to use the Portuguese initial exploration and occupation of part of the area in a more systematic way, notably by using maps drawn at that time. However, the deliberate use of French maps and documents can be explained. First, the Portuguese never occupied the whole course of the Casamance River, and by putting their claim under such an umbrella the independence movement risks igniting Guinea-Bissau's ambition to inherit Portugal's possessions. The second reason is that France, as a major power, has the means to promote and sustain any new territorial arrangement. A third reason may be that most of the separatists were French trained (even via Senegal) and thus are familiar with the colonial maps they want to redraw. Here again, the colonial map is the centerpiece of a sovereignty claim.

Conclusion

Africa is depicted as a continent that began only recently to produce maps, doing so only under foreign influence. Coded records of data that one could refer to as "maps," like the "Luba" map, are of restricted circulation. Western maps have acquired wide circulation and have become the universal standard of maps. These maps will not depict Africa in the best light or promote actions beneficial to the continent. In fact, Africa has suffered many kinds of mistreatment from Western mapmakers. The first is crude misrepresentation. The Greeks were the first, depicting Africa as a strange and wild land, the epitome of "non-Greekness," of "otherness." For more than 15 centuries these maps were reproduced, often being altered to suit particular needs, the wild images continuing to adorn them. Some of these images represented demeaning entertainment; others were designed to fool rivals. Such maps lasted well into the eighteenth century. Aiming at producing maps on a scientific basis, in the sixteenth century Mercator proposed a projection destined to keep correct distances in all directions. But he sacrificed accuracy about landmass, reducing Africa's size vis-à-vis Europe, making its conquest more conceivable. A second category of mistreatment was inciting an assault on Africa, and it derived from Mercator's habit of leaving blank areas uncharted by Europeans, areas about which imagination ran wild. The blank areas attracted those with a desire to fill them in by exploration, then by conquest. For some time maps suggested both Africa's backwardness and its availability. They converged in helping to form a favorable atmosphere for an imperialist and missionary movement in the nineteenth century. Little by little, many speculative images disappeared from maps, and color was used primarily to indicate different political entities or territorial claims. Now an intrinsic part of news media, books, and popular exhibitions, maps were also part of the imperialist toolbox, providing a direct basis for territorial claims and colonial administration. A third mistreatment of Africa by maps is their role in the indoctrination of African elites who cannot conceive of their future outside of the limits marked there. Before and after independence was gained, the most systematic use of maps was in the colonial schools, where the indoctrination process put the country's map into the people's psyche. With the colonial map, African elites inherited a "real world," but the intangibility of the colonial borders agreed upon by the OAU in 1963 has prevented many attempts to redraw it. In other words, for the new states, the colonial map is the unique basis for future international relations, while it is also the indisputable basis for national unity.

Previously we asked, "Is a map the product of the cartographer's own conception of reality or its source?" The answer is, "It's both!" Consider two different sides in a paradigm. For example, if the cartographer's side is imperial Europe, today's recipients are the African state and its elite. Europeans, and even Africans, have drawn maps they believe in so much that they constitute a basis for action and a conceptual framework for both internal and external relations. The Africa on the map for the Greeks, the modern Europeans, and the Africans is a product of historical processes, but at the same time it represents a reality to protect, a project to realize, and the basis for future relations.

2

The Challenges of Writing African Economic History

PAUL TIYAMBE ZELEZA
*Professor of History and African Studies,
Director, Center for African Studies
University of Illinois at Urbana-Champaign*

Introduction

In the late 1980s, I embarked on a rather ambitious project: to write an economic history of Africa. Looking back, it is clear I had little idea of the albatross I had hung around my neck. What was envisaged as one volume soon turned into two, covering the nineteenth and twentieth centuries, respectively. I had expected the volume about the nineteenth century, which I knew little about, to be the most difficult to write. It turned out to be much easier than the one on the twentieth century, which I am still writing. This self-imposed sentence of intellectual hard labor has given me some time, not only to temper the intellectual enthusiasms of youth, but also to reflect on the paradigms, practices, and even politics of producing African economic history. I share with you in this chapter the challenges of writing African economic history. What are the contents and components of such a history, its social and spatial scales, its concepts and theories, its narrative structure and rhetoric?

The chapter is divided into three parts. No attempt is made to offer an overview of African economic historiography, a subject adequately dealt with in the introduction to volume 1 of *A Modern Economic History of Africa* (Zeleza, 1993) and in a series of chapters in *Manufacturing African Studies and Crises* (Zeleza, 1997a). Instead I present personal and theoretical reflections on the challenges of writing an economic history of Africa that is integrated in thematic, spatial, and temporal terms. It is an argument for an inclusive methodology, for interdisciplinary, multidisciplinary analysis. The first section examines the challenges of spatial and temporal scales. The second looks at themes and theories. The third focuses on the challenges of drawing intra- and intercontinental comparisons and connections. Throughout the questions of narrative structure, analytical language, and rhetoric are raised.

Spatial and Temporal Scales

History is about human activities located in space and time. The spatial contours of African history are quite problematic. Hegel's ghost still casts a pall over Africa's historical geography and epistemological identity, as Olufemi Taiwo (1998) has recently argued. The excision of North Africa into the imperial cartography of the "Near" or "Middle" East turned Africa into the "Dark Continent," the ultimate other of white Western civilization. The sub-Saharan Africa of African studies was born and bred by Hegel's descendants. African economic history did not escape Hegel's ghost; the grand generalizations made about Africa's economic past were mostly about "sub-Saharan Africa," "Africa south of the Sahara," "black Africa," "tropical Africa," or "equatorial Africa" (Munro, 1976; Konczacki & Konczacki, 1977; Freund, 1984, Austen, 1987). That was one inspiration for embarking on my project: to recast Africa's spatial realities and processes and to reclaim the continent from Eurocentric cognitive and cartographic mapping.

Reviews of the existing literature showed that in its spatial scope African economic history, despite its avant-garde pretensions, is in fact behind the older political and general histories as represented by the two major collections of current significant knowledge in African history, the Cambridge and UNESCO series (each in eight thick volumes), as well as the introductory texts by P. D. Curtin et al. (1995), R. July (1995), J. Iliffe (1995), and E. Isichei (1997), in which Africa is treated as a single, albeit highly differentiated, historical unit. In a sense, I was simply trying to expand the geographical horizons of African economic history to encompass the continent as a whole, as had been done in the general histories. But those wedded to the Hegelian schema were not impressed, insisting that North Africa, in the words of one reviewer, can "be legitimately viewed as more a part of the Mediterranean or Middle Eastern worlds than of a rarefied Africa" (Allen, 1997: 190). Surely continental Africa is as "real" as the "West" or the "Third World" about which much has been written. Another reviewer accused me of basing myself "upon the dubious authority of Martin Bernal's *Black Athena*" (Austen, 1995: 142). All I can say is that I hadn't read Bernal by the time I conceived the project, although I had read the Cambridge and UNESCO series and the other general histories mentioned above that had appeared by the late 1980s. And certainly I had read Diop, Dubois, and Davidson. But in the canon wars of the American academy Bernal had to be my inspiration; my intellectual biography had to be trivialized.

Africa, like all civilizational spaces, such as Europe, Asia, or the Americas, is of course constructed. The same is true of concoctions such as the "West," the "East," or the "Third World." They are imagined communities, to borrow Benedict Anderson's (1991) term. As with the imagining of the modern nation we have to ask, whose imaginings predominated in the invention and reinvention of the civilizational community, and why? How did the contestations in the imaginings simultaneously contribute to and constrain the imagining that was possible and affect its investment in the construction of the community? How are the imaginings given spatial and social content and cohesion? What are the internal ties that bind and also the external ties that separate? In other words, as a social construction of a spatial entity Africa has boundaries but has never lived in bounded isolation. The fact that North Africa had links with Europe does not make it any less a part of African history any more than Southern Europe is any less a part of European history because it had links with North Africa.

The separation of Africa into two, Africa above and below the Sahara, is based on the untenable assumptions that there are no cultural similarities between societies in the two Africas and that societies in each are relatively homogeneous. One only has to compare the Hausa and the Zulu to see the falsity of these assumptions: Historically and culturally the Hausa have more in common with societies to the north than with those in southern Africa, unless of course the issue is skin pigmentation. The common tendency to make "Africa" conterminous with "sub-Saharan Africa" or with one or two regions, countries, polities, societies, and economies bespeaks intellectual laziness at best and Eurocentric oversimplification at worst. I still believe, as I stated in the introduction to volume 1 of *A Modern Economic History of Africa*, that "generalisations that purport to be referring to 'Africa' must be abstracted from a reading of African history as a whole, rather than partial accounts of regions segmented according to rather dubious geographical or racial considerations."

The spatial units whose landscapes historians fill with human drama are almost invariably differentiated by the undulations of uneven development. The challenge for the historian is to capture, or rather construct, the connections from the bits and pieces of available evidence. The patterns and processes of intra- and inter-regional integration ebb and flow, often unpredictably. An integrated economic history of Africa must show the existence of intracontinental linkages. It is tempting but futile to see such linkages in terms of North Africa and sub-Saharan Africa or Africa's current geopolitical regions: North, West, East, Central, and Southern. Rather, the linkages must be seen in terms of interactions among particular societies, cultures, commodities, classes, ecologies, happenings, ideologies, and movements at specific moments. Obviously the intensity and importance of such linkages have changed over time.

No less problematic is the construction of regions as coherent historical units. When did West Africa become West Africa? When did Southern Africa or North Africa become distinct regions? What is East Africa or Central Africa? In anglophone circles "Central Africa" often refers to the former British Central Africa, comprising Malawi, Zambia, and Zimbabwe. In the geopolitical context of modern Africa, Central Africa consists of the region from Cameroon and the Central African Republic to Zaire, whereas Malawi, Zambia, and Zimbabwe belong to Southern Africa. Similarly, East Africa is usually confined to the former British-ruled territories of Kenya, Tanzania, and Uganda, excluding Somalia, Ethiopia, Burundi, and Rwanda. Sudan tends to find itself in a limbo, unsure whether it is a part of eastern or northern Africa. In short, there is confusion as to whether the definition of regional historical units should be based on colonial cartography, geographical contiguity, contemporary regional boundaries, or historical interconnections. My approach has been to qualify contemporary regional configurations with demonstrable historical affinities. For example, in the nineteenth century Mozambique had more trading links with East Africa, but in the twentieth century these have gravitated to South Africa, so that it makes sense to treat Mozambique as part of East African economic history in the nineteenth century and of Southern Africa in the twentieth.

Geographical categories and configurations reflect historically changing reality, so they change their meaning and sometimes even become obsolete (Timár, 1992). Regions, like nations and civilizations, need their historians and inventions of collective regional memories, mentalities, and mythologies (Nandy, 1995; Wurgaft, 1995). Following in the footsteps of the political and social historians, such as J. F. A. Ajayi and M. Crowder (1976) and J. B. Webster and A. A. Boahen (1967), A. G. Hopkins (1973) brilliantly charted an integrated West African regional economic history. No similar history has yet been produced for Africa's other regions, although not for lack of trying. R. M. A. Zwanenberg and A. King (1975) wrote a tentative text on a truncated East Africa; Z. A. Konczacki, J. L. Parpart, and T. M. Shaw (1990–1992) compiled two volumes of uneven contributions on the economic history of Southern Africa; and C. Issawi (1982) came up with an economic history of the Middle East and North Africa. Amorphous Central Africa is still awaiting its regional economic history, although an excellent two-volume general economic history has been produced on the region (Birmingham & Martin, 1985). It appears to be easier to write continental and regional economic histories for the nineteenth century than for the twentieth because the relative paucity of data allows the historical imagination to roam more freely. Also, in the nineteenth century the modern nation-state had yet to impose its hallowed, even if hollow, managerial and manipulative will on its hapless subjects. For the twentieth century, one has to factor in dozens of "national economies" in addition to multitudes of micro-studies.

Continental historians largely face the same problems as world historians. They must aspire to be Isaiah Berlin's hedgehogs, great system builders or holists, rather than foxes, those who relish detail and particularity. The contemporary academic enterprise, including history, seems to prefer the foxes, which is a tribute both to the explosion of research and researchers and the intellectual de-skilling of our modern academic factories. Continental and world historians need synthetic vision or imagination, because without it "one cannot write global history, because otherwise one is lost in a morass of details, many of them accidentally preserved, and incompletely codified" (Abu-Lughod, 1995: 91). Historians, who love to dig painstakingly for archival gems, "ordinarily leave the grand syntheses and master narratives," bemoans Philip Pomper, "to sociologists, anthropologists, and philosophers, and either applaud or heckle from the sidelines." Unlike their colleagues "who focus more narrowly and use all relevant primary as well as secondary sources, practitioners of world history rely heavily upon secondary sources" (1995: 2). Reliance on secondary sources seems a violation of the rituals of the historian's craft, and world historians and their cousins, continental historians, are often dismissed as academic popularizers. The postmodernist fulminations against holistic and systemic paradigms has reinforced the assault against syntheses. The irony is that as historians focus on ever-narrower topics and the cultural theorists chant their post-something cacophonies, we need syntheses more than ever to make sense of the possibilities and pitfalls of globalization.

Periodization is a vexing problem for the hedgehog historians who have to find connections, patterns, and systems in the data covering a diverse range of societies. Periodization is essential to historical explanation and coherence. It contextualizes events and processes, giving them their meaning and importance, and conditions our images of the past; generates many of the theories and abstractions that sustain historical discourse; and defines the protocols of scholarly production and turf among historians. It is the essence of historicity. But periodization is difficult to construct; it is, in Ged Martin's poignant metaphor, "a perennial quicksand: the plots of history are rarely sufficiently tidy to run from starting pistol to melodramatic final act" (1995: 769).

African history in general, let alone African economic history, has yet to find a satisfactory periodization. The tripartite division of African history into pre-colonial, colonial, and post-colonial not only mimics the increasingly sterile periodization of European history into ancient, medieval, and modern, it also gives epistemological authority to the colonial as the conjunctural pivot around which African history spins. There is a tendency in many books and courses to give each of these periods, especially the first two, equal treatment in terms of coverage. It does not make much sense to compare the vast stretch of historical time from the beginnings of human society to the nineteenth century with the colonial period (which in much of Africa lasted no more than 70 years, less than the life span of my great grandfather, who preceded and outlived British colonial rule in Malawi) and the independence period, which is only four decades old. As I have argued in *Manufacturing African Studies and Crises*, "this subtly reinforces the view that dynamic movement in African history started with colonialism, that the multitude of generations that lived before the Berlin Conference were preparing for this great moment" (Zeleza, 1997a: 153).

It is such considerations that made me decide against using the term *pre-colonial* in the title or descriptive analyses of volume 1 of *A Modern Economic History of Africa*, because nineteenth-century Africa was a complex collection of autonomous and colonial economies, connected in complex and contradictory ways, and with varying degrees of intensity and immediacy, to an expanding global capitalist economy. It is for the same reason that I have increasingly developed an aversion to the term *post-colonial*, in both its temporal and postmodernist guise. For how long are we going to be post-colonial, for eternity? What lies beyond the post, the end (Zeleza, 1997b)?

How, then, does one periodize an economic history of Africa? As William Green reminds us,

> [T]he identification of period frontiers has generally taken two forms. One focuses on a coincidence of forces, the other on a leading sector. The coincidental approach identifies the convergence of numerous important developments at a single moment in history.... The leading-sector approach concentrates on one overwhelming source of change that exercises decisive pulling power on all others.... Both concepts identify major happenings. Both demand the application of organic theories of change. (1995: 102)

For world history, various versions of commercial, world systems, and ecological theories compete for explanatory power. Fernand Braudel suggested alternative ways of looking at historical time, dividing it into three levels: the longue durée, extending over centuries in which the parameters and rhythms of human existence in a region remain unchanged; the moyenne durée, from 50 years to a century long, characterized by the dominance of a particular economic cycle or power; and the courte durée, that is, moments of temporary dislocation (Hufton, 1986).

These theories have sometimes been conflated with the pre-colonial/colonial/post-colonial periodization of African history. The challenge for a plausible intra- and transcontinental periodization—and plausibility is all we can really hope for—involves not only identifying shared experiences among the regions involved but also demonstrating the importance of the shared experience in transforming each region's history. A compelling periodization has yet to be produced for African history in general and economic history in particular. For my study, I took the easy way out, dividing it into two centuries, the nineteenth and the twentieth. But even such a periodization is not free from the messy twists and turns of history, which do not respect calendar years. When does the nineteenth century begin and end? I tried to contextualize developments in the nineteenth century by tracing them to earlier times, and frequently the narrative spilled over into the early years of the twentieth century.

Themes and Theories

Conditioning and complementing the spatial and temporal constructions as organizational anchors for historical writing are the thematic and theoretical considerations. I sought to broaden the thematic scope and interrogate the theoretical models of African economic historiography. "Thematically, in most of the literature," I noted in the introductory chapter to volume 1 of *A Modern Economic History of Africa*, "there is undue emphasis on trade and exchange systems, especially external trade, rather than on the history of production, which would tell us far more about the dynamics of economic, social and political change" (Zeleza, 1993: 2-3). I was interested in more than analyzing the production of commodities, in the broader cultures and contexts of production, especially the demographic and ecological dimensions and class and gender dynamics. In short, I wanted an economic history that integrated environmental, social, and political history, informed by theory that, to quote A. G. Hopkins. "illuminates reality rather than obscures it," and that allows "Africans to speak for themselves without being subordinated to mis-translations of alien observers" (1973: 41). My aim was to show how Africans produced and reproduced their material lives, an endeavor that went beyond the narrow calculations of economic models.

It seemed to me that none of the prevailing dominant approaches to African economic history was capable by itself of guiding and structuring the multiple stories I wanted to tell. The teleological tales of modernization theory, with its evolutionary assumptions and irreconcilable dualisms of "traditional-modern" societies, "subsistence-market" economies, and "formal-informal" sectors, seemed particularly uninformative. African economic history has been dominated by three main paradigms: neoclassical, dependency, and Marxist. Each of these offers partial, and sometimes misleading, analyses of the process and content of economic change and development in Africa. The first two have little to say about pre-nineteenth-century African economic history, apart from offering myths and stereotypes, because their concepts and models are derived from, and are intended to analyze, the operations of capitalism or relations between advanced capitalist and dependent capitalist formations.

The strengths and weaknesses of the dependency and Marxist perspectives are discussed in greater detail in volume 1 of *A Modern Economic History of Africa* and in *Manufacturing African Studies and Crises*, so a few brief remarks will suffice here. The key concepts of the dependency approach, such as "incorporation," "unequal exchange," "development of underdevelopment," and "center-periphery," have tended to emphasize external economic linkages and to ignore internal processes. In fact, like its purported nemesis, neoclassical economics, the dependency approach had far more to say about exchange relations than about production processes. Studies written from the dependency perspective have little to say about Africa's economic history before the continent's "incorporation" into the world capitalist system, apart from idealized images of "auto-centric" and "self-sustaining" development. From the moment of Africa's incorporation, dated to the sixteenth century with the onset of the Atlantic slave trade, African history, like the history of other so-called Third World regions, is often frozen into an unrelenting saga of deepening underdevelopment. It cannot be denied, however, that the dependency approach has produced works that have illuminated our understanding of Africa's external economic relations since the sixteenth century.

Marxist economic historians have given more prominence to internal production processes and relations, including class struggle. But some have been in a hurry to force African societies into ill-fitting Marxian modes of production and stages of historical growth: "primitive communism," "slavery," "feudalism," or the "Asiatic mode of production." Others have sought to construct their own Marxian modes, such as the "tributary" and "lineage" modes of production, which have pronounced biases toward mechanisms of surplus appropriation but are weak on the analysis of the actual organization and control of the labor process, especially, the mobilization and use of the productive resources themselves. For the colonial period, modes of production were seen to be articulating everywhere, before fatigue from intellectual overkill led to the abandonment of the concept of articulation of modes of production. The collapse of "actually existing socialism" in Europe and Africa led to a crisis of faith among erstwhile Marxist scholars. But the Marxist approach retains impressive explanatory power to elucidate the political economy and historical sociology of African economic change.

The three approaches constituted a paradigmatic patchwork that was known as "development theory." The start of the 1990s marked an important watershed in African and global economic and political history that was still unfolding when volume 1 of my book was completed. The dimensions of the changes in economic, political, and epistemological terms have become clearer since. We seem to have entered a period of paradigmatic crisis; recovery is not yet in sight. Specifically, it appears that development theory, which dominated African economic analysis and policy prescription, has unraveled. The implications for African research and the continent's development prospects are profound. Africa had been central to the emergence of developmentalism as a discursive formation and a social project and the subsequent invention of the "Third World."

Developmentalism emerged after the Second World War following the discovery and problematization of poverty and backwardness in Africa, Asia, and Latin America. It was fueled by four forces: the modernization demands of African and Asian nationalist movements, the antidependency struggles of Latin American revolutionaries and reformists, the anticapitalist revolt and rhetoric of the expanding socialist bloc and movements, and the neo-colonialist designs of the former imperial powers and the postwar multilateral agencies.[1] In short, development theory emerged in the contexts of decolonization, the Cold War, and the long postwar boom as a guide for colonial and ex-colonial states to accelerate national economic growth. Not surprisingly given such complex and contradictory origins, developmentalism encompassed and articulated diverse positions, ranging from the modernization prescriptions inspired by neoclassical economic texts and institutions, to dependency critiques of modernization theory and calls for a new international economic order, to socialist condemnation of Western capitalist domination and invocations of noncapitalist paths of development.

The 1960s and early 1970s were the heyday of development theory in its various guises; it dominated policy and research in, and on, Africa and other "developing" regions. The policymakers optimistically drew detailed development plans, packaged in the appropriate ideological flavor of each regime and its godfathers in Washington or Moscow, to be implemented by benevolent states and financed by export earnings and foreign aid. For their part, academic researchers chronicled the patterns, processes, and problems of development, in the process of which they opened new areas of inquiry on the dynamics of social, political, and economic change, as well as other topics previously ignored by colonial ideologues. To be sure, the various schools of development theory had different analytical and prescriptive emphases. But they all shared the belief that development was sacred and universally desirable and possible, and that the state had a role to play in its realization. Critics have argued that development became such a powerful ideology that wanton acts of political disenfranchisement, economic destitution, social dislocation, and environmental devastation were often rationalized as the price of its future benefits (Rahnema & Bawtree, 1997). In Joseph Ki-Zerbo's memorable phrase, it imposed the mantra of: "Silence! We Are Developing!" (1997: 88).

Development theory began to fall from its ideological pedestal in the 1970s and 1980s thanks to internal and external critiques and profound transformations in the world political economy. On the left were the dismissive attacks of the dependency and neo-Marxist writers; from the right came the combative claims by re-energized neoliberals about the inimitable development benefits of unrestricted markets. Joining these critics were postmodernists railing against "metanarratives" and positivism, feminists attacking gender biases in development theory and practice and demanding the incorporation of women in development (Scott, 1995; Elson, 1995; Gordon, 1996), and environmentalists talking about sustainable development. In the meantime, Keynsianism and the welfare state were being abandoned in the West; the Soviet bloc was falling apart, thereby delegitimizing socialism as a viable means of overcoming the problems of underdevelopment; the gap between the rich and poor countries was widening despite decades of developmentalist intervention; the Third World itself was splintering and disappearing as the newly industrialized countries (NICs) escaped from its ranks, leaving the rest submerged in debts and structural adjustment programs; and the possibilities of national economies and national economic planning were being swept away by the roaring tide of globalization. Development theory appeared to have lost its raison d'etre. It had reached an impasse (Booth, 1993; Sklair, 1988; Vandergeest & Buttel, 1988; Mouzelis, 1988; Toye, 1987). Michael Edwards (1989, 1993) went so far as to proclaim "the irrelevance of development studies" for real people in the real world.

Although some social scientists abandoned development research altogether and invested their intellectual energies elsewhere or joined the neoliberal bandwagon, many continued conducting local studies unattached to any overarching development theory, fortified by the belief that it was no longer possible, or desirable, to construct such a theory. The proponents of "post-development," indeed, argued that it was imperative to eschew the functionalist, teleological, and reductionist generalizations of development theory and focus on the voices, visions, and experiences of ordinary people in their struggles to create more humane and sustainable ways of living (Rahnema & Bawtree, 1997). What is not often clear, however, is whether the "ordinary people" for whom the post-developmentalists claim to speak don't want economic modernization. It may not be that economic modernization is a universal goal, as Francis Fukuyama (1995) believes it is, especially in its neoliberal guise, but the restive masses in the South certainly want better lives; they are still struggling for development and democracy, for modernist goals, not postmodernist fantasies (Mkandawire, 1995, 1998; Schuurman, 1993a).

Proposals to get "beyond the impasse," to use the title of Frans Schuurman's (1993b) book, have proliferated in recent years. F. Buttel and P. McMichael (1991) urge that explaining diversity, not homogeneity, within the Third World should become the new research focus. David Booth, who did much to popularize the idea that development theory had reached an impasse because it had aspired to excessive explanatory power, agrees: "[T]he field of social development research has already been reconstituted on new, more productive and more challenging lines. What is common to the new directions in which research is moving is the attention being given—at macro, meso and micro levels—to the investigation and explanation of diversity" (1993: 68). Schuurman finds that explanation inadequate and has added the theme of inequality: "inequality of access to power, to resources, to a human existence—in short, inequality in emancipation" (1993b: 30).

Also unimpressed is Colin Leys, an unrepentant advocate of the old, neo-Marxist political economy. He accuses Booth and his colleagues of idealism for assuming that "new development theory will emerge autogenetically from the accumulating volume and density of all this work . . . the construction of a new theory of development is necessarily a political task, involving political choices about whom (what social forces) the theory is for, to accomplish what ends and in what contexts" (1997). Leys is also critical of what he calls the "eclecticism as usual in the development community" (1997: 29), as well as the pessimism of the revisionist globalism of dependency theory as articulated by Andre Gunder Frank (1991) and the limited explanatory power of the rational choice theories of the new institutional economists represented by Douglas North and the so-called new political economy of Robert Bates (1981, 1987, 1989). According to Leys, rational choice theory harbors explanatory ambitions that are too big for its concepts and tends to suffer from a contrived separation between institutions and ideology, from reductionism and an inability to explain how institutions emerge or change, and from a propensity to take some aspect of reality that can be modeled as the determinative or key one. Commenting specifically on Bates's work on African agriculture, Leys finds it "not particularly persuasive" (1997: 94). Leys himself does not offer an alternative new theory of development, except to point out that it is necessary to have a theory of capitalism on a global scale, and on the basis of such a general theory "new development theories at a lower level of abstraction can then be formulated" (Leys, 1997: 44).

The difficulties of constructing a new general theory of development persuaded some to search for and polish other existing theories. There were those who sought refuge in the French regulation school, or the actor-oriented approach, or post-imperialism. The regulation approach seeks to explain development in terms of the specific combination and conjunction of what the "regime of accumulation" and "mode of regulation" within a particular country and the country's position in the international economy, an approach that seems to allow more precise historical comparative research (Aglietta, 1982; de Vroey, 1984; Lipietz, 1984; Jessop, 1989; Zeleza, 1997b: chapter 13). The actor-oriented approach is interested in the interface between the macro level and the individual actor and how the two interact with and transform each other, the assumption being that individual actors, which include corporations, the state bureaucracy, and other institutions, have a range of options and access to a variety of discourses that can influence their behavior even where the structural conditions and types of external impulses are relatively constant (Long, 1990; Slater, 1990, 1993). The post-imperialists believe that the operations of international capitalism involve complex and mutually beneficial relations between the developed and developing countries and their respective bourgeoisies (Becker & Sklar, 1987; Frieden, 1987).

As they awaited a general theory, progressive development researchers turned to a refurbished triad of analytical hope and social commitment: "equity, democracy, and sustainability" (Moore, 1995: 2; see also Schmitz, 1995). Many others chronicled the sins or blessings of neoliberalism imposing its neoclassical economic will on the global economy and Africa. Even its diehard critics were forced to take the discipline of neoclassical economics seriously, if only to critique it and the effects of its doctrines, implemented with uncompromising zeal through structural adjustment programs (SAPs), on African countries.

African studies and societies have had a checkered relationship with neoclassical doctrines and prescriptions. By the time African economic history came on the scene in the 1960s and 1970s, neoclassical economists were worshipping at the altar of technique, mathematical modeling, and deductive reasoning; their topical concerns had contracted and they spoke in the suffocating language of pseudo-physics, in the mistaken belief, to quote Robert Solow, a concerned guru, "that the laws of economics are like the laws of physics: exactly the same everywhere on earth and at every moment since Hector was a pup. But the part of economics that is independent of history and social context is not only small but dull" (1997: 56). Economics drifted away from the other social sciences and avoided the humanities like the plague. Economists basked in their scientific pretensions, oblivious to the real world beyond their formalistic theories, spurious precision, and sterile stylizations (Onimode, 1985; Mayer, 1993; Mkandawire, 1996).

Historians, including economic historians, with feet in both camps, increasingly shied away from economics. A pithy observation by the British economic historian D. C. Coleman accurately reflects historians' disenchantment with neoclassical economics:

> It is by no means clear what are the relevant, or at any rate useful, bits of economic theory. Economists come and go, usually in happy ignorance of history, and so do their theories. . . . Furthermore, the historical economic phenomena to be examined have no existence independent of the social, political, cultural, religious and physical environment in which they occurred. (1985: 23)

Africanist economic historians felt particularly estranged. Not only did few of them have formal training in economics, as Patrick Manning (1989, 1996) has observed—a feature apparently shared with British economic historians (Minchinton, 1988)—but the pressure of Africa's developmentalist challenges proved too strong to withstand the apparent indulgence of econometric modeling.

But even economic historians who maintained fidelity to neoclassical economics were doubtful of its historical explanatory power. Douglas North, the Nobel Prize-winning economic historian, wrote:

> Neoclassical economics . . . may account very well for the performance of an economy at a moment of time, or with comparative statistics, contrasts in the performance of an economy over time; but it does not and cannot explain the dynamics of change. The source of changes in an economy over time is structural change in the parameters held constant by the economist—technology,

population, property rights, and government control over resources. Changes in political-economic organization and its consequent effects are basic to theorising about all these sources of structural change. (1981: 57)

However, there is hope, we are told. David Kreps assures us that economists have begun to broaden the issues they examine, and that "as a result of increasing access to both experimental and field-based data, pressure from important constituencies, and the desire to have something new to work on, the canonical principles are under attack in our nearest estimation of high temples—journals such as *Econometrica*, the *Journal of Political Economy*, and the *American Economic Review*" (1997: 60). Renewed confidence that dialogue between economists and historians is possible is articulated forcefully by Thomas Rawski et al. (1996). With the rise of feminist economics, the new institutional economics, and environmental economics, questions long ignored in orthodox neoclassical economics can now be raised and answers attempted.

Comparisons and Connections

African economic history should not be examined in isolation from other parts of the world contextually and conceptually. Therefore, in addition to drawing intracontinental comparisons, it is instructive to compare Africa's experiences with the rest of the world, to integrate Africa into the mainstream of world history. Africa's colonization at the end of the nineteenth century was part of the global process of the "New Imperialism." But it is understood that the economics of imperialism in each region even within Africa exhibited quite specific processes. Similarly, during the course of the twentieth century Africa was deeply immersed, for better or worse, in global economic transformations, notwithstanding the popular rhetoric of Africa's marginality. Being marginal does not mean one is unaffected by or does not have an effect on developments of whatever is conceived as the mainstream, as is clear from feminist studies of women's alleged marginality. The rhetoric of marginality may actually serve to conceal how deeply involved the mainstream and the marginal are with each other.

For the twentieth century, there are three levels of comparison and conjunctures of connection into which African economic historiography has been inserted, the eras and matrices of colonialism, developmentalism, and globalization. The first level seeks to analyze the economic implications for Africa of colonialism and imperialism as international systems; the second centers on Africa's incorporation, in discursive and developmentalist terms, into the Third World, which coincided with decolonization and the immediate post-independence era; and the third examines Africa's contemporary encounters with globalization, the supposedly brave new world generated by the dynamics, technologies, and consciousness of what David Harvey (1989) calls "time-space compression" and Anthony Giddens (1990) calls "time-space distantiation," and which is characterized by the growth of a new global economic, political, and cultural order. African economic historians have to theorize these three levels as historical processes and discourses.

The need to analyze Africa in a comparative colonial context lies in the fact that African colonies belonged to worldwide empires, so they formed part of a complex, shifting international system of economies and political relationships. This requires the African economic historian to analyze African colonial economies in the contexts of the global empires of the various European imperial powers, which were in turn integrated at the core of an evolving world capitalist system. In short, African economic history during the colonial period cannot be understood entirely from within; it must be articulated with imperial and global economic trends and dynamics. The same is true of other colonized regions, such as India (Perlin, 1998). Colonialism allows African historians to delve into two types of comparative relationships: South-South and North-South. African historiography has much to gain from, and contribute to, the historiography of other colonized regions. For example, there have been reverberations—fruitful intellectual conversations—between African and Latin American studies, spawned by dependency theory, and between Africa and Asia, engendered by the notions of resistance and subaltern agency (Manning, 1974; Cooper et al., 1993; Cooper, 1994).

The South-North nexus allows, indeed requires, African historians to engage and intervene in various debates in imperial and European historiography. One of the most heated is over the "balance sheet of empire," about the benefits and costs of empire for the imperial powers and the colonies. From the imperial viewpoint, it centers on calculating capital flows from the metropoles and the returns on that capital, defense and trade expenditures, and transfers through loans and subsidies. Many imperial historians conclude that the empire represented a severe drain on Britain's and France's national resources, without matching return, even if some businesses, industries, sectors, and elites may have benefited at certain times (Duignan & Gann, 1969–1975; Davis & Huttenback, 1986; Phillips, 1989; Fieldhouse, 1986, 1991). Mindful of the malady of "decimal dementia" (Porter, 1988: 686), African economic historians must critique, at each level, the statistical and conceptual bases of the imperial historians' narrow and unimaginative accounting, not by repeating the story from the citadels of empire but by telling it from the trenches of the colonized peasants, workers, and capitalists and deciphering the complex connections between these multiple worlds and the dynamics of their reproduction.

After independence Africa graduated into an epistemological and empirical part of the "developing world" or the "Third World" or the "South." Consequently, its post-colonial economic fortunes and history came to be prescribed and analyzed through the prism of development theory. As argued earlier, the construction and reconstruction of development theory was influenced as much by developments in Africa as by those in other regions of "the South." This is to suggest that development theory and studies contain implicit comparative perspectives that have both illuminated and distorted the economic histories and trajectories of African countries. The apparent current impasse in development theory offers an opportunity to sort the wheat of explanatory possibilities from the chaff of superficial comparisons. Unencumbered by a homogenizing and dichotomizing theoretical construct, it becomes feasible to compare specific sectors, or countries, or regions in "the South" as well as "the North." In my view, the challenge for development theory is not to splinter "the South" into more worlds—Third, Fourth, Fifth, as Samir Amin (1997) proposes—but to dissolve the very duality of North and South, to conceptualize economic hierarchies and exploitation as much in spatial and international terms as in social and intranational terms.

Proponents of globalization, the third level and conjuncture of analysis, seek to dissolve national and regional particularities and narratives of difference and exploitation. In this sense, their analytical and prescriptive vision is the flip side of world system theory, which also saw the world as a single integrated unit, but one subject to the laws of capitalist development and exploitation, not the assumed benefits of the invisible market. To its supporters globalization is celebrated as inevitable and progressive, whereas its detractors attack it for reinforcing global economic inequalities, political disenfranchisement, and environmental degradation. Debates on globalization have centered on how to characterize and date it and delineating its dynamics and trajectory. Globalization is seen variously as implying the growth of a new global economic, political, and cultural order. Those who focus on its economic dimensions emphasize the development of a new international division of labor. The components of economic globalization are, however, in serious dispute. Conventionally, three key economic indicators are used to demonstrate the increasing globalization of the world economy: the expansion and spread of world trade, foreign direct investment through multinational corporations, and international capital flows and their unprecedented pattern of integration. The historical record, however, paints a far more complicated picture, that current patterns of global economic integration and capital and commodity flows are not unprecedented (Mittelman, 1996; Hoogvelt, 1997; Zeleza, 2001). The evidence for the emergence of a new global political and military order is even less compelling. Few now talk confidently of former U.S. President Bush's "New World Order," proclaimed in the heady days immediately following the collapse of the Berlin Wall in 1989, and fewer believe in Francis Fukuyama's (1992) hasty declaration that history had ended. Dating globalization has proved particularly vexing.

But even the skeptics who tend to regard globalization as a polite way of saying imperialism, or the world capitalist system, or Western modernization in these neoliberal times, often admit that the world has entered a new phase in the historical process of world capitalist development. It is argued that the new era began to emerge following the collapse of the Fordist model of production and social welfare in the industrialized "North," the demise of Sovietism in the East and national liberation in "the South," and the realignment of regional politics and social systems (Amin, 1997). So the debate has increasingly become about the causes and consequences of the transformations encapsulated by the term *globalization*. Globalization should be understood as a process, the trajectory of which is continuous, uncertain, and unpredictable, not the culmination of some predetermined phenomenon. As such, it is premature to talk of a global economy, or global society, although there are ever-growing and thickening circuits of globalization.

It is often said that there are at least three new elements in the world system: the disappearance of the autocentered nation-state committed to national development; the evaporation of the old divide between the industrialized centers and nonindustrialized peripheries; and the emergence of new dimensions of integration and polarization based on technological, financial, ecological, media, and military monopolies. It has become common to posit the thesis that the so-called Third World and the cleavages between the developed and underdeveloped countries have decomposed. This thesis seems to mistake an intensive regime of Third World exploitation through debt peonage, launched since the late 1970s, for the structural irrelevance of these countries. If they were that irrelevant perhaps they would have been left alone.

When it comes to Africa, the argument is often advanced that globalization's interest in the continent is exclusion and the containment of anarchy (Hoogvelt, 1997: chapter 8). This smacks of familiar Afropessimism and echoes the pervasive Western moral condemnation of "the South," especially Africa, which "is linked to a retrospective vindication of colonialism," as Frank Furedi (1997: 78) has argued so persuasively. This lends credence to Tade

Aina's contention that much of the discourse on globalization is Eurocentric in that it privileges "a particular positioning or understanding which undervalues, ignores or rejects non-European, non-Northern visions and knowledge. Backed by the very global power being studied, these discourses succeed in imposing on the rest of the world, particularly the South, their outlines of the visions and imaginations of the globe" (1996: 18–23). Consequently, contemporary issues of Western intervention in the former Third World are ignored, just as struggles against, and alternatives to, the neoliberal global agenda are often dismissed out of hand, based on the TINA doctrine, that there is no alternative.

In Africa, Aina contends, instead of celebrating globalization there should be greater attention paid to the inequality, unevenness, and injustice of the new world order; the effects of economic restructuring embodied in structural adjustment programs on Africa's possibilities for development; and the social, economic, political, and gender implications and consequences of the global restructuring of capital through the SAPs. In "the North" globalization discourse tends to be equally elitist in that it ignores the resistance and oppositional narrative of numerous social groups and movements, such as labor, that have been affected negatively by globalization (Glenn Adler, 1996). This is to suggest that African economic historians need to interrogate globalization both as a discourse and a process and critically examine the historical and contemporary manifestations of the processes it encompasses, their impact on Africa, and Africa's impact on them.

All this points to the need to connect African economic history to other regional and global economic histories. The other level of comparison is at the methodological level. How does Africa's economic history compare with that of other regions in the way it is conducted? Anthony Hopkins, one of the doyens of African economic history, has argued that Africanist economic historians use a generous definition of economic history, one that embraces anthropology and political history as well as economics, which can be attributed to "the youthfulness of the subject, the fortunate failure of any one school of thought to impose its dominance, and the diversity of evidence" (1973: 41). What is interesting is that economic historians of other regions and older historiographical traditions appear to be moving in the Africanist direction. Readings on European economic history suggest growing interest in reconnecting economic and social history, indeed, in integrating economic, social, and political history (Daunton, 1985; Coats, 1985; Feldman, 1986). T. C. Barker, a British economic historian, recalls that before econometric history spread from the United States in the 1960s and specialization led to fragmentation of the discipline, "few people then doubted that economic history included social history" (1985: 25). Now the discipline seems to be returning to some of its roots and using new sources, including oral ones, that "can fill many gaps and much enrich our understanding of ordinary folk's social conditions and personal priorities, so often distorted by the writings of leaders and activists" (Barker, 1985: 27).

In an extensive review and prognosis of European economic and social history, Charles Tilly et al. proclaim:

> As we peer into the futures of economic and social history, our most general message is quite simple: *it is time to de-economize economic history and re-economize social history.* The de-economization of economic history should include the analysis of rights, power, coercion, state action, and related "institutional" factors; it does not entail the abandonment of economic analysis, but its broadening from a single-minded application of free-market models. The re-economization of social history should include new treatments of the interdependence among different forms of production and reproduction, both material, biological, and social. It should challenge the surprising recent tendency either to treat the three as separate spheres or to reduce all of them to artifacts of discourse. In this limited but crucial sense, we call for the revival of materialist social and economic history (emphasis in original). (1991: 647)

That this advice may be catching on can be seen in studies on topics that previously incorporated little social history. For example, in examining the second industrial revolution or the rise of science-based industry, dated from the late nineteenth century to the 1930s, James Hull emphasizes the need for broad analytical strokes: "A study of the second industrial revolution in all its aspects must include not just economic history, but business and labour history and the history of science and technology as well as the history of education and sociology of knowledge, to name only the most obvious candidates. Thus it provides a splendid focus for interdisciplinary studies" (1996: 207). Similarly, as William Hubbard informs us, the study of European inflation during and after the First World War, which was previously dominated by monetary economists and "treated simply as a technical phenomenon of monetary policy with few links to its social and political setting," is now seen "as the outcome of complex bargaining between economic, social, political, and even ideological interests" (1990: 554–555). Research has shifted "from the study of the monetary theorists of the time toward the investigation of the social and political determinants of the decision-making process" (1990: 555).

The winds of change seem to be blowing even to the United States, where economic models have had the strongest hold on economic history. In a major intervention on the development of the U.S. economy during the late nineteenth century when corporate capitalism rose to prominence, James Livingston makes a compelling argument for bringing social analysis into U.S. economic history:

> At a higher level of argument it . . . follows that economic events are explicable only by reference to the social relations within which they appear—by reference, that is, to historically specific contexts of production and exchange. . . . We can see that the social and cultural context of economic change is not what the new economic historians have assumed it to be—an "exogenous factor" that can safely be ignored in building quantitative models of economic behavior and growth. (1987: 71)

As in Europe, specific topics in U.S. economic history that were previously confined to narrow, technical analyses seem to be increasingly subjected to wider social exploration. For example, Larry Schweikart (1991) demonstrates in a masterly historiographical survey of U.S. commercial banking that for a long time money and banks were seen as something special that did not behave as other commodities and institutions did:

> Since the 1970s, however, a new generation of banking historians, business historians, and monetary historians has challenged this analytical framework or abandoned it altogether. Among the new issues they have raised are the historical function of money; the role of regulation itself has played in affecting the market; the significance of public psychology as a unique element of banking and bank panics; and the sociology of bankers and banking. These scholars have reinterpreted nearly every episode in American banking history. (Schweikart, 1991: 607)

Similar trends are apparent in Asian economic historiography. In Southeast Asia, Thomas Lindblad informs us, there is growing interest in a comparative intra-Asian perspective—that "was certainly not present in previous years" (1995: 167)—focusing, predictably for a region that until recently enjoyed rapid economic growth, on the causes and consequences of growth. Writing on China, Philip Huang (1991) contends that Chinese social and economic historians are searching for new and relevant paradigms, divorced from Western neoclassical models and communist models, both of which were based on simplistic dualisms and shared a vision of the benefits of commercialization. The challenge is to overcome the dualistic models—commercialization without development, segmented natural economy and integrated markets, expansion of the public realm without the development of civic power, legal formalism without liberalism, structure and agency, and so forth—through which Chinese economic history has been analyzed and "to establish the theoretical autonomy of Chinese studies, not with the exclusivism and isolation of the old sinological studies, but in creative ways that would relate Chinese experience to the rest of the world" (Huang, 1991: 335–336).

Clearly, African economic historians are preoccupied with many of the same questions that confront economic historians of other regions. In an extensive review of volume 1 of *A Modern Economic History of Africa*, Patrick Manning (1996) raises the question of the relative isolation of African economic history in two senses: first, from the new economic history in North America centered on quantitative analysis and formal testing of hypotheses based on neoclassical theory; and second, from economic policy on the continent itself. The expansion of the contours of economic history in "the North" beyond neoclassical models implies that the isolation of African economic history from other regional economic histories may not be as wide as Manning assumed. What remains true, however, is that historians from different regions do not read each other's work as often as they should even when they work on the same themes and topics and use similar theories and methodologies. It is important for economic historians from different regions to be aware of each other's work to sharpen the analysis of their own societies and promote comparative analysis. But if it is to be fruitful, the exchange has to be in both directions. All too often economic historians of Africa and other regions in "the South" are expected to know the research trends and theories emanating in "the North," whereas the latter hardly pay attention to their counterparts in "the South." Such asymmetrical and hierarchical intellectual relations are of course not confined to economic history, but pervade the entire gamut of cultural, political, and economic relations between "the North" and "the South," as I have argued elsewhere (Zeleza, 1997).

One of the major challenges of doing comparative economic history at whatever level—regional, continental, or global—centers on the problem of data. Quantitative and qualitative data are extremely uneven across time and space. Yet such information is essential for the determination of trends. The amount of data that Africa economic historians have been able to build up in a few short decades is nothing short of phenomenal. But much more needs to be done, even for the twentieth century. The problems of data are not confined to "the South" as is often assumed. As Thomas Rawski admonishes: "Indeed, we should abandon the notion, dispensed by glib doctors of economics on the evening news, that precise and accurate economic data exist even for advanced economies that employ veritable armies of specialized economic statisticians. Consider relatively simple concepts, neglecting the thorny complexities of 'national product' or 'capital stock.' What is the rate of unemployment? The answer is based on questions asked a (presumably representative) sample of respondents" (1996: 30). This is a reminder that quantitative data are often beset with gaps and flaws involving both concepts and measurement.

Economic historians are all too familiar with debates centered around different interpretations of quantitative data. A typical example is the controversy between N. F. R. Crafts (1995) and David Landes (1995) over why it was Britain, not France, that produced the inventions and innovations that led to the Industrial Revolution, when the two countries appear to have had comparable growth rates of output. The debate cannot be resolved simply by relying on numbers, but by examining a whole range of other social, cultural, institutional, and political factors that, combined and cumulatively, determined that it was Britain rather than France that inaugurated the Industrial Revolution. In our own times, comparative labor data provide a cautionary tale on the uses and abuses of statistics. There is something seriously wrong when figures show that Pakistan, for example, has a lower rate of unemployment than the United Kingdom because only a select aspect of unemployment is measured: that of total lack of work and the existence of unemployment insurance and other public relief schemes that can be tracked statistically. In other words, in the developing countries the unemployed are often swept under the rug of the "informal sector" and the statistical invisibility of generalized poverty, just as unremunerated household work, mostly performed by women, is not counted in the employment statistics (see ILO, 1995: chapter 1).

Much of the data on African economies, including information produced in the glossy reports of the international and continental financial institutions and economic agencies, is based on estimates, some of them quite rough. Describing Africa's agrarian crisis in the early 1980s, Philip Raikes (1988) shows that no less than 75 percent of all cereal production figures produced by FAO for 1982 were based, wholly or in part, on "estimates" that were no better than guesswork. No wonder the FAO made frequent revisions in its "estimates" from year to year. Indeed, using those very figures over a long period, the African performance did not vary significantly from the world average. Between 1970 and 1990, for example, African food production, excluding Egypt, Libya, South Africa, and Sudan, rose by 50 percent, as compared to a world average of about 58 percent. Comments Thandika Mkandawire sardonically: "If one took into account official figures of food production and food imports and matched those against population growth in Africa, the continued existence of large parts of Africa would simply be inexplicable"

(1987: 15). It is difficult to estimate food production in Africa because most of it comes from small peasant farms, the vast majority of which are not covered by any system of registration or reporting. Moreover, primacy in the food production statistics is given to cereals, reflecting the consumption patterns in "the North," rather than to tubers and other crops consumed widely in various parts of Africa.

Indeed, it is not always clear which "Africa" is being referred to. Each of the major institutions that covers Africa, such as the World Bank and the various United Nations agencies, including the United Nations Conference on Trade and Development (UNCTAD), the United Nations Development Fund (UNDP), and the Economic Commission for Africa (ECA), produces its own statistics, using very divergent methodologies. There is no unanimity even on the same country. These groups' definition of what constitutes "Africa" in their coverage also varies. For the World Bank "Africa" is an abbreviation for sub-Saharan Africa, and until recently it excluded South Africa and Namibia, as well as North Africa, which is often appended to low and middle income Europe and the Middle East. UNCTAD and the ECA, on the other hand, usually cover the continent as a whole. Generalizations about Africa depend on which "Africa" is being covered. For example, according to UNCTAD (1988: 38, 1989: 4), average annual growth rates of real GDP in its Africa were 5.6 percent in the 1961–1972 period and 2.7 percent from 1973 to 1985. In the World Bank's "Africa" the average annual growth rate was 6.1 percent in the 1965–1973 period, 3.2 percent from 1973 to 1980, and –0.5 between 1980 and 1985 (World Bank, 1989: 147, 1990: 161). Interestingly, in its 1990 report the World Bank's estimates for the earlier periods are revised downwards, to 5.9 percent for the 1965–1973 period and 2.7 percent for 1973 through 1980. It would not be going too far to argue that the data these organizations produce in their elegant annual reports are nothing more than estimates, some of them very crude.

These statistics exclude the informal sector, which by its very nature is not part of the national accounts. From all indications, this sector grew rapidly in the 1980s partly in response to the crisis of the formal sector itself, which was exacerbated by the SAPs. Interestingly, it was not until 1993 at the ILO-sponsored Fifteenth International Conference of Labour Statisticians that a resolution was passed specifying the criteria for a statistical definition of the informal sector and making recommendations on the design, content, and conduct of informal sector surveys (see ILO, 1995: 21–23). Another criticism of the conventional statistical comparisons, as indicated earlier, is that they do not take into account women's work, which tends to be concentrated in unremunerated or informal sector activities, or the environmental costs of natural resource depletion. In response to these critiques national statistical agencies and the United Nations Statistical Commission have been trying to devise new statistical measurements of national accounts that include women's and environmental income accounting.

Including women's work and environmental costs can have a varied impact on GDP figures: The former tends to increase them, whereas the latter often decrease them. For example, Alex Winter-Nelson (1995a, 1995b) has demonstrated that accounting for natural resource depletion, incurred through mineral exports, in 18 African countries indicates different patterns of growth—usually lower—than those suggested by standard GDP figures. On the other hand, incorporating women's unremunerated work in national accounts, Martha Macdonald cautions, "does not alter the fact that the work is unpaid, and it may convey a false message of recognition. While feminist researchers will certainly be able to use these data, they can also be used to support anti-feminist initiatives. There is suspicion about why measuring this unpaid output is suddenly popular. It may be part of a search for better numbers by nation states" (1995: 171). Although efforts to improve current measurements of national accounts are long overdue, if they are to be useful for historians old data must also be reconfigured as far as possible.

If measuring growth in one country is not easy, trying to quantify income differences between countries is even more problematic. Most measurements are based on exchange rate conversions, which, as critics have pointed out, distort the actual purchasing power. Given the fact that the conversions are based on the currencies of the rich countries, which tend to fluctuate less and depreciate less precipitously than those of the poor countries, exchange rate conversions tend to overstate the wealth of the rich countries and the poverty of the poor countries (Kuznets, 1972; Heston, 1973; Kravis et al., 1975; Morris, 1979; Summers & Heston, 1984; Ward, 1985). Comparisons based on purchasing power parity yield quite different results in national rankings. Data from the International Comparison Project, launched by the United Nations in 1968 and still continuing, show that the "real" GDP per capita produced with a purchasing power parity index (RGDP/PCs) of the developed countries "averages $1,878 less than the exchange-rate converted GNP/PCs, whereas the non-developed countries' RGDP/PCs are approximately $870 dollars higher on the average" Passé-Smith, 1993: 11).

It is well known that per capita income averages tell us little about the patterns of wealth distribution and the nature of economic and social life in a society. The fact that the per capita income in the United States in 1990 was 5,889 percent higher than in Kenya does not mean of course that the "average" American lived that much better off than the "average" Kenyan. If the comparative statistics that are bandied about were to be believed, the vast majority of Africans and other people from "the South" should have long since died. It was partly in response to these inadequacies that the UNDP launched the Human Development Index, a more realistic measure of human development than mere GDP per capita. The HDI measures life expectancy; adult literacy; school enrollments; real GDP based on purchasing power parity; gender-related development and empowerment; employment; trends in economic performance; and other indicators of income distribution and access to such resources as health services, safe water, sanitation, food, and political and economic participation. The annual *Human Development Reports* have consistently demonstrated that rankings by HDI do not always match income rankings. For example, in 1993 37 countries were higher or lower by their HDI ranking than by per capita income. Also, some countries fall in the category of high human development despite modest per capita incomes, and vice versa. It is quite clear that there have been remarkable improvements in global and regional HDI since 1960, including in Africa, although the improvements have come faster in some regions than others. Of course enormous challenges still remain (UNDP, 1990–1998).

Conclusion

The fetish for national accounts, growth rates, and per capita indices should not be allowed to displace questions of differentiation and distribution or conceal the complex social and spatial dimensions of Africa's, or any region's, economic performance. It is certainly inaccurate to date the beginnings of the African economic crisis to 1960, the year of African independence, as has become fashionable in revisionist Africanist circles, which smacks of nothing but an apologia for colonialism. Measurements like the HDI provide more meaningful historical analyses of individual countries' economic performance and a basis for drawing international comparisons. The role of the economic historian, however, is not simply to rank countries according to whatever hierarchical scheme is fashionable, but to explain the processes of economic transformation in specific societies or countries or comparatively, or for particular sectors or moments, and how these processes intersect with and influence and, simultaneously, are influenced by changing social, cultural, political, and environmental forces and factors. Even the poor have economic lives. How they live and reproduce those lives should be no less interesting and intriguing for the economic historian than it is to analyze how the rich do it.

This is the task I set myself: to explain the development of African economies over two centuries using a broad and inclusive interdisciplinary methodology that would allow me to unravel the complex and sometimes contradictory, but always captivating, patterns and processes by which diverse communities of African men and women, over several generations, produced and reproduced their material lives, in response to their needs and the changing definition of those needs, as conditioned by their intricate linkages to national, regional, and global markets and forces, and the challenges of their changing environments and histories of social relations, negotiations, and struggles. Through these theoretical media I seek to tell a story, or rather stories, of African economic history from within without losing sight of the external influences. Africa, like the other continents, has experienced the long, complicated, and tumultuous twentieth century in its own ways and is an integral part of the human story as a whole. It is in both Africa's specificity and its globality that the joy of writing African economic history ultimately lies.

PART TWO

Contested Categories:
Economy, Politics, and Society

3
Structural Adjustment

SAYRE P. SCHATZ
Temple University, Columbia University

This chapter considers the effects of structural adjustment (SA) on the state and the common people in Africa. Structural adjustment has failed, and the World Bank has done its best to hide that failure. The Bank is in a position, however, to act much more constructively.

Structural adjustment is a package of policies, initiated in the late 1970s by the governments of the United States, the United Kingdom, and other countries that were moving from government economic activism to market enthusiasm, and carried on by the World Bank and the International Monetary Fund (IMF), under the lead of the World Bank.

The term *structural adjustment* (SA) is used here in a broad sense. There really is no single set of measures. Moreover, though intertwined, the policies of its two chief implementers, the World Bank and the IMF, have never been identical. Policies (particularly those of the World Bank) have also changed over time and have varied among countries. Still, it is accurate to characterize SA as macro- and micro-economic neoliberalism or *laissez-faireism*, a tendency to move insofar as is feasible toward a policy of laissez-faire. It is marked by an enthusiasm for markets that often approaches market dogmatism. This chapter shows that SA has failed;[1] dissects the World Bank's efforts to disguise that failure; and presents a case for an alternate orientation, developmental activism (DA).

The Failure of Structural Adjustment

Although no charge of failure (or claim of success) can ever be "proven," I believe the case for failure of SA is convincing. To support this position I examine the statistics of African economic *growth*, briefly depict the *worsened state of poverty* of sub-Saharan Africa after two decades of SA, and scrutinize the World Bank's major defense of SA and its proclamation of success.

Africa's Great Economic Reversal

An erroneous perception prevails that African economies have experienced continuous stagnation or worse since the mid-twentieth-century power shift to Africans. The common view, accepted even by many Africanist scholars,[2] is exemplified by a front page article in the *New York Times* in 1998, which incorrectly states that currently, for the first time, Africa's growth rate has been lifted above its rate of population increase, and describes sub-Saharan African economic performance in the late 1970s as characterized mostly by economic disaster (French, 1998).

These statements about African economic performance embody two major misconceptions: that Africa's period of government-activist capitalism, starting with the phasing out of colonial rule in the early 1950s and cresting in the late 1970s, was an abysmal failure characterized by atrocious economic performance; and that World Bank-IMF-donor country pressure on sub-Saharan Africa for government minimalism, which began to have an effect in the late 1970s, engendered gradual economic improvement that finally bore fruit in a 1997 rise in per capita income.

In fact, African economic development since 1950 has gone through two phases. The first, 1950 to 1977, was *not* one of stagnation or retrogression; it was one of continuous albeit modest economic growth and development.[3] Performance, although considered less than satisfactory, was by no means poor. Standards of living improved on average and a significant degree of modernization took place.

For sub-Saharan Africa as a whole, the annual economic growth rate was 3.7 percent during the 1950s, 4.3 percent in the 1960s, and 4.2 percent from 1970 to 1977. In the low-income sector, sub-Saharan Africa's[4] economic growth was 3.0 percent during the 1950s, 3.8 percent during the 1960s, and 3.3 percent from 1970 to 1978.[5] In middle-income sub-Saharan Africa, the growth rate was 4.9 percent in the 1950s and 1960s and 6.4 percent from 1970 to 1976. Real income per capita rose for both low- and middle-income sub-Saharan Africa (see Table 3.1).

Broader indicators of well-being also reflect a long phase of limited but positive economic development. From 1950 onward, sub-Saharan Africa experienced decreasing crude death rates, population per physician, and infant and child mortality, as well as increasing life expectancy, primary and sec-

TABLE 3.1   Change in Real Gross National Product in Sub-Saharan Africa

Period	Average Annual Change in GNP (percent)	Change in GNP per Capita
1950s	3.70	increase
1960s	4.30	increase
1970–1977	4.20	increase
1977–1984	1.80	decrease
1984–1990	1.70	decrease

SOURCE: World Bank, *World Tables*, 3d ed., *Volume 1: Economic Data* (Baltimore: Johns Hopkins University Press, 1983); World Bank, *Sub-Saharan Africa: From Crisis to Sustainable Growth* (Washington, DC: World Bank, 1989), 221 table 1.

ondary school enrollment rates, literacy rates, per capita rates of energy consumption, radio receiver possession, and newspaper circulation. Calorie supply per capita was constant, and higher than in South Asia.

The second phase, since 1978, has been one of deterioration and crisis. Economic growth in sub-Saharan Africa fell off sharply—to 1.8 percent annually (1977–1984) and 1.7 percent annually (1980–1990)—and more severely in the low-income than the middle-income African economies. The reversal initiated a 20-year period of miserable economic performance (hardly dented by a recent mild improvement) characterized by declining average real income. Throughout the 1980s and up to 1994, gross national product per capita for sub-Saharan Africa as a whole fell at an average rate of 1.1 percent per annum (*Africa Recovery*, 1996). By 1995, African economic performance was showing small signs of improving; aggregate real income may have increased, although not enough to reverse the slide in per capita income.

To recapitulate, from 1950 to 1977, during the period of government economic activism, economic growth rates—the highest ever achieved in sub-Saharan Africa—exceeded population increases and average real income rose steadily. This economic growth culminated in 1977, when real income per capita reached its highest-ever level, just about at the time when government activism also peaked. It was only during the second phase, as SA was phasing in during the late 1970s, that economic performance became truly atrocious and a long period of economic decline began (See Table 3.1).

It is important to note that global factors (as distinguished from domestic policies) were a major cause of the Great Economic Reversal in sub-Saharan Africa (and of the deterioration in many other developing nations).[6] A 20-year world economic slowdown pinched poor countries in many ways: curtailment of export volumes as world trade slowed; substantial terms-of-trade deterioration; sharp increases in real interest rates for debtor countries; reductions in the availability of foreign credits; sudden cuts for many countries, especially in Africa, in the availability of foreign credits or concessionary loans; two important recessions; acceleration of inflation; and the collapse of the post-World War II international payments system.

Nevertheless, Africa's Great Economic Reversal was more than merely a temporary downturn. It suggests that the shift from DA to SA has been an important cause of Africa's lackluster performance since 1978. In this chapter I support this interpretation using data on the present poverty of sub-Saharan Africa, by analyzing the specious nature of the World Bank defense of SA, and indirectly by stating the case for the superiority of DA (Sachs, 1996; see Schatz, 1996).[7]

The Economic Backwardness of Sub-Saharan Africa[8]

After almost 20 years of decline, Africa's poverty is appalling. The data make it clear that SA has at the least failed to prevent economic catastrophe.[9] Thirty-seven of the 43 sub-Saharan African countries (86 percent) fall into the World Bank's lowest income category.[10] Three-fifths of the world's 63 lowest-income countries are in sub-Saharan Africa.

Sub-Saharan Africa's long slide in real income (gross domestic product per capita) contrasts poorly with the performance of other low-income countries. Between 1965 and 1996, Africa's real per capita income declined at an annual average rate of 0.2 percent per annum. This compares to an annual increase of 3.1 percent for the entire low-income country group. With such a growth-rate divergence, hypothetical African and other low-income countries starting with equal per capita incomes would soon differ sharply; after 22 years the income of the other low-income countries would be twice that of the African country.[11] In striking contrast to sub-Saharan Africa, the East Asia and Pacific area group achieved an annual increase of 5.5 percent during that period.[12]

The structure of the sub-Saharan African economies is backward. For example, manufacturing contributed only 15 percent of the region's gross domestic product (GDP) in 1996, much less than agriculture's contribution of 24 percent. For all low-income economies, including sub-Saharan Africa, manufacturing contributes 25 percent, almost on a parity with the 27 percent for agriculture. Manufacturing export data are available for only a few African countries. For Nigeria, one of the continent's major economic powers, such exports amount (officially) to the round figure of zero (in 1996).

Gross domestic investment in sub-Saharan Africa (including that of foreign-owned firms) fell from 23 percent to 15 percent of GDP between 1980 and 1996, whereas for all low-income countries it went up from 27 to 31 percent of GDP. Gross investment for 1980–1990 actually fell by 3.7 percent per annum, while the entire low-income group (including sub-Saharan Africa) experienced an annual increase of 6.7 percent. The East-Asia and Pacific region's annual investment growth was 8.6 percent for 1980–1990 and an astounding 13.3 percent for 1990–1996.

Quality-of-life indicators are also unfavorable. Life expectancies in sub-Saharan Africa are the lowest in the world. For males at birth in 1996, it was 51 years; for females, it was 54 years. For the entire low-income group, life expectancies were 62 and 64, and for high-income countries they were 74 and 81. Adult illiteracy rates for males and females were 34 percent and 53 percent for sub-Saharan Africa and 24 percent and 45 percent for the entire low-income country group.

Specious Denial of Failure

Even more telling evidence of SA failure than the data presented in the preceding sections is the jerry-built nature of the best defense the World Bank could construct for SA. The World Bank has strenuously denied that sub-Saharan Africa's poor economic performance is in any way attributable to SA. To the contrary, in innumerable statements and publications it has repeatedly proclaimed success.

A climaxing statement was the World Bank's highly publicized and widely quoted study, *Adjustment in Africa: Reforms, Results, and the Road Ahead* (1994) (*AIA*). In its quest for vindication, the World Bank, bolstered by a superabundance of data, tables, and other scholarly paraphernalia, claims to demonstrate the efficacy of SA.

According to the study, the data show a clear and positive relationship between the two variables: (1) implementation of the macro economic reform package urged by the World Bank[13] (*reform performance*) and (2) the change in the GDP per capita growth rate between 1981–1986 and 1987–1991 (*growth performance*). The World Bank claims that, on average, the better a country's reform performance (as rated by the World Bank study), the better its growth performance. The almost universally cited showpiece finding is that the best reform performance group of sub-Saharan African countries raised the economic growth rate by a median of 1.8 percent (stated as almost 2 percentage points); the group of countries with more moderate reform performance raised the growth rate by 1.5 percent, and the group of countries that experienced negative reform performance (policy deterioration) suffered a growth rate decline of 2.6 percentage points[14] (see Table 3.2).

TABLE 3.2   Economic Growth of Reform-Performance Groups in Sub-Saharan Africa

AIA Reform Performance Groups	Median Growth Performance	Schatz Reform Performance Groups	Median Growth Performance
large improvement (6 countries)	1.80%	best (6 countries)	1.80%
small improvement (9 countries)	1.50%	other above average (7 countries)	-0.10%
deterioration (11 countries)	-2.60%	other below average (9 countries)	2.50%
		worst (4 countries)	-3.80%

SOURCE: World Bank, *Adjustment in Africa: Reforms, Results, and the Road Ahead* (New York: Oxford University Press, 1994, 4–5 cols. (1) & (2); 138, 260–261, cols. (3) & (4).

Careful scrutiny of the World Bank *AIA* data, using *AIA* definitions, shows that the *AIA* data fail to support its thesis and that in fact, to the degree that the data provide support for any hypothesis, it is for the *contrary* one: that implementation of the macro-economic reform package (i.e., positive reform performance) has actually retarded economic growth.

Four Criticisms of the AIA

I present four criticisms of the *AIA* findings in this section. I first judge the efficacy of SA just as *AIA* did, by examining the growth performance associated with each level of reform performance (criticisms 1–3).

Criticism 1: Growth by reform performance groups. *AIA* employs a three-part grouping of countries by reform performance: those that experienced a large improvement in macro-economic policy (6 countries); those that had smaller improvements (9 countries); and those experiencing policy deterioration (11 countries). The large bottom group encompasses seven nations with moderate reform deterioration and, equally important, also the four worst cases. This classification submerges essential information.

The results are strikingly different if we set up a more symmetrical four-part classification: (1) best, that is, *AIA*'s large improvement or top group; (2) other above average; (3) other below average (excluding those in the worst group); and (4) worst, the bottom group of policy transgressors (with six, seven, nine, and four countries respectively).

Confounding results emerge under the four-part classification. The best growth performance was achieved by the other below-average reform performance group. The median growth improvement of that group (the third of four) was 2.5 percent—a performance 39 percent better than that of the top reform performance group, which attained a median growth improvement of 1.8 percent (see Table 3.2). The fact that the below-average reform performers had the best growth performance directly contradicts the major finding of *AIA* (World Bank, 1994: 4).[15] A similar contradiction is demonstrated in a different manner in criticism 2.

Criticism 2: growth, country by country. A country-by-country comparison bypasses the classification issue, thereby avoiding debate about the merits of different country groupings. In this test, I rank the 26 countries by reform performance (as scored by the World Bank) and note the growth performance of each nation (see Table 3.3). The same anomalous result emerges: Most of the below-average reform performers, excluding the four at the very bottom, achieved above-average growth performance. Of the nine countries ranked fourteenth to twenty-second in reform performance, six had superior growth performance, ranking first, third, fifth, seventh, eleventh, and twelfth[16] on this criterion. Moreover, when we exclude the four countries in the worst reform performance group, four of the seven other countries with negative reform performance scores had positive growth performance grades. Once again we see a strong linkage between below-average reform performance and superior growth performance, a linkage that was obscured by the *AIA* procedure.

Criticism 3: reform performance test. Consider the relationship between reform performance and growth by reversing it. Instead of grouping the 26 countries by reform performance and examining each group's median growth performance, I group the countries according to growth performance and examine each group's median reform performance score. My groups here are countries with large improvements in growth (A), small improvements (B), small declines (C), and large declines (D).

Again, the results confound *AIA* (see Table 3.4). The best growth group, A, has only the third-best median reform performance score. Inferior growth groups B and C are better reform performers than group A (and equal to one another). The relationship between reform performance and growth is the *opposite* of that claimed by *AIA*.

Criticism 4: the contrariety test. In the course of assessing overall macro-economic policy, *AIA* generated separate evaluations of each component of reform performance, assigning separate reform performance grades for policies

TABLE 3.3 Growth-Performance Rankings of Countries Listed by Reform-Performance Rankings

Reform Performance Ranking	Growth Performance Ranking
Ghana	4
Tanzania	5–6
Gambia	17
Burkina Faso	20
Nigeria	2
Zimbabwe	14
Madagascar	9
Malawi	8
Burundi	18
Kenya	10
Mali	19
Mauritania	15
Senegal	16
Niger	7
Uganda	3
Benin	24
Central African Republic	21–22
Rwanda	26
Sierra-Leone	5–6
Togo	11
Zambia	12–13
Mozambique	1
Congo	25
Côte d'Ivoire	23
Cameroon	21–22
Gabon	12–13

Notes:
(1) Reform performance scores of countries listed 4–6 are equal to one another, as are those of countries listed 7–8, 9–13, 16–20, and 25–26.
(2) Growth performance scores of countries marked 5–6 are equal to one another, as are those of countries ranked 12–13 and 21–22.
SOURCE: World Bank, *Adjustment in Africa: Reforms, Results, and the Road Ahead* (New York: Oxford University Press, 1994), 138, 261.

regarding seigniorage, inflation, overall monetary policy,[17] fiscal policy, and exchange rate policy. Making use of the *AIA* grades, I conducted a contrariety test. For each of the 26 countries included in the study, I asked whether the actual change in economic growth was consonant with or contrary to the change expected as a result of the reform performance. Does favorable reform performance correlate positively with enhanced growth, or is there contrariety, that is, negative correlation?

Again, *AIA*'s data contradict its conclusions. The change in economic growth was usually the opposite of that which the reform was supposed to

TABLE 3.4 Reform Performance of Growth Groups

Growth Group	Median Reform Performance Grade
A. large increases in growth, +2.5% or more, 7 countries	+0.3
B. small increases in growth, +0.1% to 2.4%, 7 countries	+0.5
C. small decreases in growth, -0.1% to -2.4%, 6 countries	+0.5
D. large decreases in growth, -2.5% and down, 6 countries	-0.5

SOURCE: World Bank, *Adjustment in Africa: Reforms, Results, and the Road Ahead* (New York: Oxford University Press, 1994).

produce. I examine each of the five reform performance components in turn below. (See Table 3.5.)

In nine of the 13 relevant countries[18] graded for seigniorage (69 percent) the outcome was contrary; that is, improved reform performance was accompanied by deterioration in growth or the converse. Only four displayed positive results. Contrariety regarding inflation is slightly more pronounced. Economic growth and inflation reform performance (assessed primarily by changes in budget deficit size) changed inversely for 16 of the 22 relevant countries; that is, in 73 percent of the cases, good marks for improving anti-inflation policies were associated with growth slowdowns or vice versa. The overall monetary policy record is no better: 17 (74 percent) of the 23 relevant countries experienced contrary outcomes.

For fiscal policy the evidence is inconclusive. Contrariety appears in virtually half (10 of 22) of the cases. The only category for which the results are clearly (and strongly) positive is exchange rate policy, where contrariety is rare. However, the significance of this positivity is murky. Sub-Saharan Africa countries did move away from complete control over imports and foreign exchange but nevertheless continued an active government role; thus the changes fell far short of the laissez-faireism (complete convertibility of current accounts) proposed by the World Bank and IMF. The results therefore provide support equally for reformed government activism and for World Bank-recommended government minimalism.

The Ideological Marketing Operation

The breakdown of the World Bank's proclamation of SA success brings us face to face with the issue of bias.

TABLE 3.5 Changes in Economic Policy Compared to Changes in Economic Growth, Contrariety Test, 1981–1986 and 1987–1991

Countries	Economic Growth (%)	Seigniorage Score	Seigniorage Test	Inflation Score	Inflation Test	Overall Monetary Policy Score	Overall Monetary Policy Test	Fiscal Policy Score	Fiscal Policy Test	Exchange Rate Policy Score	Exchange Rate Policy Test
Benin	-3.1	-2	P	1	C	-0.5	P	2	C	-2	P
Burkina Faso	-1.7	1	C	1	C	1	C	3	C	-1	P
Burundi	-0.9	n.a.		0		0		0		1.5	C
Cameroon	-12.5	0		1	C	0.5	C	-3	P	-2	P
Central African Rep.	-2.6	1	C	2	C	1.5	C	-2	P	0	
Congo	-4.9	0		1	C	0.5	C	-2	P	-1	P
Côte d'Ivoire	-2.6	1	C	1	C	1	C	-3	P	-2	P
Gabon	0.9	0		1	P	0.5	P	-3	P	-2	P
The Gambia	-0.8	0		1	C	0.5	C	2	C	1	C
Ghana	3.7	1	P	2	P	1.5	P	2	P	3	P
Kenya	1.5	0		0		0		0		1.5	P
Madagascar	1.6	0		1	P	0.5	P	0		2	P
Malawi	2.2	0		-1	C	-0.5	C	2	P	1	P
Mali	-1.6	2	C	1	C	1.5	C	-1	C	-1	P
Mauritania	-0.1	0		1	C	0.5	C	1	C	0	
Mozambique	7.6	n.a.		-3	C	-3	C	1	C	3	P
Niger	2.5	1	P	1	P	1	P	2	P	-1	P
Nigeria	7	-1	C	-1	C	-1	C	-1	P	3	P
Rwanda	-5.5	0		0		0		1	P	0.5	P
Senega	-0.6	1	C	2	C	1.5	C	2	C	-2	P
Sierra Leone						-1.5	C	-1	P	0	
Tanzania	2.9	-2	C	1	P	-0.5	C	2	P	3	P
Togo	1.4	2	P	1	P	1.5	P	-1	C	-1	C
Uganda	4.3	n.a.		-2	C	-2	C	0		2.5	P
Zambia	0.9	-1	C	-3	C	-2	C	1	P	0	
Zimbabwe	0.7	-1	C	0		-0.5	C	1	P	2.5	P
Summation		4P 9C			6P		6P		12P		19P

Pressures and Opportunities for Bias

When Lance Taylor characterized the World Bank research and publication effort as a multi-million-dollar ideological marketing operation disguised as research, he was hardly being hyperbolic.[19] When preparing its major publications, there are powerful pressures on the World Bank to come up with its own version of correctness, that is, findings that support its major policy orientations; there are abundant opportunities to do this, and the consequent result is that sophistry is common.[20]

The pressures to present findings supportive of basic World Bank policies are powerful. As *The Economist* remarked about SA, the Bank desperately needs to see success. (1994: 24). It is difficult to imagine that the Bank, a heavyweight, world-scale political institution, would publish a major report on the basis of the work of staff economists stating that its long-standing policies are fundamentally erroneous. The very articles of agreement that established the World Bank and IMF—committing them to a liberal, market-oriented orientation—constitute a pressure to claim success for such approaches (Helleiner, 1990).[21]

Consider "The Case of the Reissued Study," an instance of Bank pressures on its professional staff that happened to come to public attention. A World Bank econometrician published a study in 1992 called "Why Structural Adjustment Has Not Succeeded in Sub-Saharan Africa." The Bank retrieved it from the printer, reissued it (in a form that had limited circulation) with a less controversial title, and pointed out that the analysis was flawed anyway (*Economist*, 1994: 22).[22]

Opportunities for bias. These also abound in studies of major issues such as AIA[23] and require the participating staff to select from huge masses of often unreliable data;[24] to set up the classifications; to decide what information to use and what to ignore; to arrange, manipulate, and interpret the data;[25] and often to make highly subjective judgments,[26] such as those involved in assigning AIA's crucial reform performance scores.

Often major World Bank publications are exercises in advocacy, supporting a predetermined position. Following are examples of a few specific devices employed in such publications: the disappearing of information, playing with numbers, concealing through classification, and playing with words.

- *The disappearing of information:* Information that proved troublesome for the thesis sometimes simply disappeared. For example, in each of the three policy areas—seigniorage, inflation and overall monetary policy—there was absolute silence regarding the striking contrariety between reform performance and growth performance. The underlying data had been calculated; the reform performance-growth performance relationships were crucial; there was no way the authors could have failed to check these relationships. If they had been supportive, they surely would have been featured in the report.[27] However, the reform performance scores were confined to a table in the appendix, whereas information on growth performance was presented in a text table 120 pages earlier. Only the most diligent research-oriented reader could have uncovered the contrariety.[28]

- *Playing with numbers:* The World Bank has also supported its brief for SA by manipulating African economic growth data. To my knowledge, the World Bank has never publicly presented those data[29] in what appears to be an obvious form, one that allows the reader to see Africa's Great Economic Reversal, illustrated in Table 3.1 and columns 3 and 4 of Table 3.6. Instead, presentation consistently takes the form shown in the first two columns of Table 3.6.

Such a format has a dual effect: It conceals a relatively satisfactory performance record during the period of government economic activism and at the same time softens the record of poor performance under SA. It thereby lends support to a World Bank version of African economic history, a story of government interference gradually squandering the economic opportunities available when African countries became independent.

- *Concealing through classification:* Classification can be a powerful tool. It has already been pointed out that *AIA*'s three-part grouping of countries showed a positive relationship between reform performance and growth performance, whereas my four-part grouping showed at best no relationship and even suggested a negative relationship. The reader will wonder, of course, just where the bias lies. The country-by-country analysis provides the clincher, because it avoids classification problems entirely. That analysis showed that the best growth performers came predominantly from the below-average reform performers. It is inconceivable that the *AIA* team did not do a country-by-country reckoning, but no sign of this appeared in the report.
- *Playing with words:* The report offers careful formulations that are not blatantly false but are crafted to give an erroneous impression. Thus, despite the striking 74 percent contrariety of the relationship between monetary policy and growth, *AIA* devised an artful formula-

TABLE 3.6 Growth of Domestic Product in Sub-Saharan Africa

Period	World Bank Average Change per Annum Aggregate (percent)	Per Capita (percent)	Period	Schatz Average Change per Annum Aggregate (percent)	Per Capita (percent)
1965–1973	5.90	2.90	1950s	3.70	increase
1973–1980	2.50	0.10	1960s	4.30	increase
1980–1987	0.50	-2.80	1970–1977	4.20	increase
			1977–1984	1.80	decrease
			1984–1990	1.70	decrease

SOURCE: World Bank, *World Tables*, 3rd ed., *Volume 1, Economic Data* (Baltimore: Johns Hopkins University Press, 1983); World Bank, *Sub-Saharan Africa: From Crisis to Sustainable Growth* (Washington, DC: World Bank, 1989), 221, table 1.

tion, headed "Monetary Policy Mostly on Track," that gave just the opposite impression.

Major publications on World Bank policy appear to be governed by a tacit three-part rule: Whatever happens, devise a way to claim success; describe the success with a striking sound bite, a short vivid paragraph that catches the attention of the media and thereby the public; and convince yourself that the interpretation is valid.

The Success of World Bank Spin

World Bank spin has been largely successful. The biased nature of its major reports usually encounters little mainstream challenge. There are several reasons for this: the stature of the Bank; the scope of its massive research operations with access to government personnel and data all over the world; the instant presumption of soundness and authority accorded to its utterances by the major media; its continual flow of handsomely produced reports; the reiteration year after year of the same themes; and, not least, the persuasiveness of its showpiece presentations of often manipulated statistical data.[30]

Challenge is minimized also because Bank economic publications—frequently in excruciating detail, difficult to plow through, and stupefyingly boring—are rarely read carefully. Most people read only the overview or summary. The major reports put off most scholars, let alone journalists and government personnel. Even development economists rarely undertake the intensive scrutiny required to make independent judgments. In matters of African economic development, as a consequence, the World Bank's voice has been dominant, shaping even emotionally resistant African opinion.

Conclusion: Developmental Activism

I have said that SA has failed; its effects on the state and the common people of Africa have been predominantly negative. Theoretically, however, one cannot evaluate a course of action without considering its opportunity cost. This refers to the alternative foregone, more particularly to the outcome of the measures that would otherwise have been undertaken. Conceptually, then, one can say that SA has failed only if actual African economic performance fell short of that which would have occurred if the World Bank had pursued a different course.

The opportunity cost criterion is problematic. The development that would otherwise have occurred—a counterfactual proposition—is not knowable. Assessing opportunity cost is inevitably an exercise in speculation. Another problem is that there are, of course, many alternatives to SA.

However, it is useful to make one's best judgment of an alternate course of action. I consider here—and only in general terms—only the most likely alternative. This brings us to the case for DA. In a limited sense, DA can be seen as the opposite of SA. They both assume a capitalist market economy, but where the latter involves a laissez-faireist inclination, the former involves a propensity to rely on government economic activism.

Following is my six-point case for DA:

1. Sub-Saharan Africa's economic record was better during its DA phase than during its subsequent SA phase.
2. DA has shown itself to be a successful strategy elsewhere.
3. Despite their deficiencies, African governments do have *some* capacity for carrying out constructive DA.
4. By redirecting its efforts, the World Bank can significantly encourage, enable, and accelerate successful DA.[31]
5. The World Bank reorientation may interact synergistically with positive African forces.
6. Improvement, once underway, may proceed cumulatively.

There remains one major portion of my case for DA. It involves a broader argument that requires extensive development[32] that is beyond the scope of this chapter.

Economic progress in sub-Saharan Africa has been limited by describable development-impeding conditions, primarily by an adverse economic environment and secondarily by entrepreneurial deficiencies in experience, education, and familiarity with modern procedures and technologies. These conditions cause a paucity of profitable investment opportunities. The crucial policy issue is the appositeness of the proposed development process, that is, its suitability for dealing with the impeding conditions. It is my contention that SA is not apposite. Its exaggerated reliance on the market is frustrated by the developmental inadequacy of that market. That inadequacy can only be compensated for by DA.

Economic growth. Support for a DA orientation is provided by sub-Saharan Africa's overall growth record during the second half of the twentieth century: modest economic achievement during the period of the old government activism up to 1977 and markedly poorer economic performance during the subsequent laissez-fairest period of SA.

DA's record elsewhere. DA has been successful in other parts of the world. East Asia's activist strategy, although marred by corruption, has worked, even if it has not proven to be a miraculous shield against crises. In the past quarter century, the more rapidly developing countries typically had activist governments, often with even more extensive roles than generally thought (Sachs, 1996; Amsden, 1997). Although conditions in various countries and regions differ, experience in the rest of the world is not irrelevant. This brings us to a critical question: Are *African* governments capable of carrying out an effective program of DA?

Capability of African governments. African governments have frequently done considerable economic harm. In my own work on African economies, including a 17-month in-government stint advising on Nigeria's Third National Development Plan, I encountered incompetence, aimlessness, simple obstructiveness, and utter uselessness. I have seen petty and huge wastes of funds and have been aware of substantial corruption. Many of my writings have been strongly critical. However, I have also seen competent and honest personnel and governance. Within African governments, there are islands of probity and capability that could contribute to a cumulative process of economic development.

This extant capability is generally underestimated. A self-reinforcing skepticism prevails about government in sub-Saharan Africa; having something favorable to say is considered naive. In general, it is not what scholars are about. Good governance usually goes unreported and therefore unnoticed. If described, the reports are often not believed. I first encountered this skepticism (initially in Nigeria and subsequently in the United States) when presenting the findings of my intensive study of the Federal Loans Board of Nigeria, which because of its particular circumstances was one of these islands of economically based decision making in a sea of political and personal manipulation.[33]

Moreover, some of the deficiencies of African governments are iatrogenic disorders.[34] Significant administrative-political difficulties have been caused by SA itself. World Bank economists have described a basic dilemma in Africa: In curtailing the role of the state, SA demoralized the civil service and impaired government capabilities. Governance by decree and from the top down inhibited local-level mobilization and individual initiative. African countries have been subject to a kind of economic receivership, with the policies of many African nations decided in a seemingly endless series of meetings with the IMF, the World Bank, donors, and creditors (Sachs, 1996). Consequently, economic reform faces enormous obstacles (World Bank, 1994: 427–428).

Despite the prevailing skepticism, the literature abounds with examples of effective government functioning in sub-Saharan Africa. In her study of 29 government bodies functioning well in overall environments of poor government performance (in six countries, including Ghana, Central African Republic, Morocco, and Tanzania), Merilee Grindle found effective government operations even in dauntingly unfavorable contexts (Grindle, 1997).

Although African scholars tend to be among the most vehement critics of their own governments, most nevertheless believe that laissez-faireism is an inadequate mode for developing Africa, that blanket judgments of African governments' economic fecklessness are overstated,[35] and that development in sub-Saharan Africa requires productive government intervention in the economies. Most see a developmental state as a linchpin.[36]

The World Bank also, although it has been highly critical of government economic activism and remains skeptical of African government capability, nevertheless finds room for some optimism. This is implicit in the development-promoting programs the Bank sponsors jointly with African governments, and it is stated explicitly in its *World Development Report 1997*.

In that report, the Bank publicly revisits the developmental role of government. It does continue to emphasize the market; the central economic role of the state is to do those things that allow markets to flourish. Nevertheless, the report recognizes that state intervention can sometimes improve outcomes: "Well-designed regulatory systems can help societies influence market outcomes for public ends; and when markets are underdeveloped, the state can sometimes reduce coordination problems and gaps in information and encourage market development" (World Bank, 1997b: 1–7). It also recognizes "activist industrial policy [pursued] successfully; the demonstrated utility of various mechanisms to spur the growth of markets in . . . early stages of development and of a variety of mechanisms for market enhancement, including sometimes interventions [that] were quite elaborate" (World Bank, 1997b: 1–7). And it speaks benignly of economies of countries such as China, Korea, and Taiwan, "[which] opted not to give top priority to privatization, but to allow the private sector to develop around the state sector" (World Bank, 1997b: 1–7).

Positive role for the World Bank. Given the limited capability of African governments, an external boost is needed. The World Bank is capable of providing such a boost. Given the failure of SA, however, the Bank's orientation must change. Considering the Bank's rather friendly revisitation of the role of government, it may not be quixotic to propose a change from past one-sided advocacy of laissez-faireism to accepting the need for some degree of DA in Africa and undertaking to make it more effective.

The president of the World Bank has stated that "[W]hat we as a development community can do is help countries—by providing financing, yes; but even more important, by providing knowledge and lessons learned about the challenges and how to address them" (Wolfensohn, 1999). The Bank could help African countries by undertaking a two-part effort. First, it could devote a significant portion of its enormous research capabilities (including its incomparable access to government and other sources of information) to worldwide studies of DA measures that have worked (as well as promising policies that have failed but that might be successfully modified). The purpose would be to develop programs, tactics, and strategies that could be successfully adapted to African conditions. World Bank and African personnel could work together on this.[37]

Second, the Bank could help to implement agreed-upon policies. Implementation is what conditionality is all about; it could be promoted much as before, but hopefully on a more cooperative basis.

Synergy. Although an African renaissance is yet to come, positive forces in civil society and better leadership may strengthen the African contribution to the development process. Leaders with a greater interest in national development and reduced focus on unlimited personal enrichment are emerging. Repelled by Africa's present pauper-and-supplicant status, by the perception that they count for little in world decision-making councils, and by a sense that World Bank–IMF conditionality is a form of neo-colonialism, the new leaders, abetted by progressive civil society forces, may pursue economic development more effectively.

Government personnel are also likely to contribute more effectively. Participation in what is perceived as a cooperative and effective development effort is likely to raise morale. Good morale characterized Grindle's government bodies that functioned well although surrounded by poor government performance. They were distinguished by healthy organizational cultures, emphasizing commitment to organizational goals, a strong sense of professionalism, a stress on efficiency, a sense of elitism, commitment to hard work, a strong sense of mission, some autonomy in personnel matters, and high expectations regarding employee performance (Grindle, 1997).

Cumulative forces. Finally, economic development tends to be a cumulative process (Sklar, 1987). This is attested to by the fondness development economists have had for concepts such as vicious and virtuous circles, balanced growth, the big push, takeoff into self-sustaining growth, and linkage effects.[38] It creates its own energy as it proceeds.

4

Poverty Profile in Sub-Saharan Africa

The Challenge of Addressing an Elusive Problem

OLIVER S. SAASA
University of Zambia

Introduction[1]

The majority of people in sub-Saharan Africa today suffer from weak purchasing power, homelessness, and insufficient access to basic social services and necessities such as education, health, food, and clean water. Three major problems principally continue to afflict Africa: poverty, unemployment, and vulnerability. These three problems, however, are largely manifestations of a single phenomenon, exclusion:

Poverty is exclusion from the economic development process.
Unemployment implies exclusion from the economy.
Vulnerability is a product of exclusion from social safety nets and social security systems.

Poverty can therefore be defined in the African context as lack of access to income, employment opportunities, and normal internal entitlements by the citizens to such things as freely determined consumption of goods and services, shelter, and other basic needs of life, including education and the prevention of diseases.

Although a number of poverty-reducing programs are being implemented in almost all sub-Saharan African countries, they have had little impact, and experiences with poverty-reduction program that have been implemented in many countries do not provide evidence of actual poverty reduction. The current debate regarding the failure of poverty reduction policies and programs is gaining strong support among development economists, policymakers, and practitioners. Many are increasingly being led to the conclusion that the World Bank's adjustment operations during the 1990s have at best had a limited impact on current poverty in these countries and at worst have contributed to an increase in poverty. The aggressive implementation of structural adjustment programs (SAP) in the 1990s has compounded the situation.

Presently, poverty in sub-Saharan African countries touches almost 145 million people, or about half of the population of the region. These people have entered the new millennium living under severely dehumanizing conditions. Because the overwhelming share of the population of the region is rural, rural poverty accounts for about 83 percent of total poverty in this part of the world. The prevalence of poverty by country is shown in Table 4.1.

As shown in Table 4.1, the people of most countries of the region are living on less than $1 per day. The range is from 85 percent in Zambia to 24 percent in South Africa. Table 4.1 also shows that large numbers of people in both urban and rural areas live below the national poverty line. The total percent ranges from 70 in Madagascar to 19 in Seychelles. In Burundi, the percentages were 66 for the urban and 58 for the rural population; in Ethiopia, 32 and 34 percent; in Madagascar, 47 and 77 percent; and in Zambia, 46 and 88 percent.

Another noteworthy phenomenon in the eastern and southern African regions is that annual per capita income has been established to be a misleading indicator of poverty. Although countries with a low annual per capita income tend to have a high portion of the population living below the poverty line, the opposite is not true. In other words, in a number of countries with relatively high per capita income, such as South Africa, Namibia, and Botswana, the major share of the population still lives in absolute poverty, at income levels of below U.S. $1 per day per capita. Thus, there is little correlation between the level of relative national economic affluence and the magnitude and severity of poverty in these countries. In the countries for which dollar poverty data are available, nearly half of the populations have per capita incomes of less than U.S. $1 per day. The percentage of the population living on less than U.S. $1 per capita per day is highest in Zambia (85 percent), Madagascar (72 percent), and Uganda (69 percent), whereas in the Republic of South Africa (RSA) it is less than 25 percent. In the majority of these countries, 40–50 percent of the population is living below the national poverty line.

TABLE 4.1 Prevalence of Poverty in Selected Countries of Sub-Saharan Africa, 1989–1994

Country	Percent of Population Living on Less Than U.S. $1 per Capita Day	Percent of Population Living Below National Poverty Line
Botswana	35	NA
Burundi	NA	60
Eritrea	NA	69
Ethiopia	34	34
Kenya	50	42
Lesotho	50	49
Madagascar	72	70
Malawi	42	54
Mauritius	NA	11
Mozambique	NA	71
Namibia	NA	67
Rwanda	46	54
Seychelles	NA	19
South Africa	24	NA
Tanzania	51	40
Uganda	69	55
Zambia	8 5	68
Zimbabwe	41	61

SOURCE: UNDP 1997.

The percentage of the population in this region living below national poverty lines averages 57 percent for rural areas and 26 percent for urban areas. Countries with the highest poverty at the national level are Madagascar (70 percent), Eritrea (69 percent), Zambia (68 percent), Namibia (67 percent), Zimbabwe (61 percent), Burundi (60 percent), Uganda (55 percent), and Malawi and Rwanda (both 54 percent). Those with the lowest percentage of the population living below the national poverty line are Mauritius (11 percent) and Seychelles (19 percent).

Poverty is largely a rural phenomenon in sub-Saharan Africa. In the 18 countries in the region where the majority of poor people are rural, the incidence of poverty is highest among small farmers, herders, and fishermen. Smallholder agriculture is by far the main source of income and livelihood for the poor. Subsistence farmers are much more likely to be over-represented among the poor and ultra-poor than households whose main income source is wage employment outside the agricultural sector. Within the agricultural sector, subsistence farmers are poorer than cash crop farmers, who in turn are poorer than households with regular off-farm employment. In

TABLE 4.2 Human Development Indicators by Country

Country	Life Expectancy at Birth[a] Years		Infant Mortality per 1,000[a]	Adult Illiteracy (Percent of Population)[b]		Access to Safe Water (Percent of Population)[b]	Human Development Index 1995[c]	Capita 1997 (Atlas Method) USD[a]
	M	F		M	F			
Angola	45	48	124	44	71	32	0.344	260
Botswana	50	53	56	19	40	93	0.678	3 310
Burundi	45	48	97	51	77	52	0.241	140
Comoro Islands	58	61	67	36	50	53	0.411	400
Eritrea	54	56	64	–	–	22	0.275	230
Ethiopia	48	51	109	54	75	25	0.252	110
Kenya	57	60	57	14	30	53	0.463	340
Lesotho	57	60	74	19	38	62	0.469	680
Madagascar	57	60	88	40	68	34	0.348	250
Malawi	43	43	133	28	58	47	0.334	210
Mauritius	68	75	17	13	21	98	0.833	3 870
Mozambique	44	46	123	42	77	63	0.281	140
Namibia	55	57	61	22	26	57	0.644	2 110
Rwanda	39	42	129	30	48	79	0.187	210
Seychelles	68	75	18	17	14	–	0.845	6 910
South Africa	62	68	49	18	18	99	0.717	3 210
Swaziland	75	82	67	22	24	60	0.597	1 520
Tanzania	49	52	86	21	43	66	0.358	210
Uganda	43	43	99	26	50	46	0.340	330
Zambia	44	45	112	14	29	38	0.378	370
Zimbabwe	55	47	56	10	20	79	0.507	720

[a]World Bank 1999 Development Indicators. CDROM (data for 1996).
[b]UNICEF Country Statistics website (updated 1998).
[c]UNDP Human Development Index (1998 Human Development Report UNDP, 1998).

Zambia, for example, 89 percent of the poor either work in semi-subsistence agriculture or engage in casual labor on other people's farms in exchange for food. Tables 4.2 and 4.3 show the face of poverty in the eastern and southern Africa region.

Table 4.2 presents a range of measures used by the World Bank and the United Nations Development Programme as indicators to assess the standard of living in various countries. The indicators range from life expectancy at birth to annual per capita income as indicated in U.S. dollars. The table shows that the standard of living for peoples of countries such as Angola and Zambia is particularly for all indicators. In Angola the life expectancy at birth is 45 years for men and 48 years for women, the rate of infant mortality is 124 out of 1,000, and the annual per capita income is $260. In contrast, the people of Botswana are in a much better position, with a life expectancy at birth of 50 years for men and 53 years for women, a rate of infant mortality of 56 out of 1,000, and an annual per capita income of $3,310.

TABLE 4.3   Ranking of Countries by Incidence of Poverty and GDP per Capita

Poverty Incidence			GDP per Capita, 1997		
Percent	Country	Rank	$US	Country	Rank
93	Rwanda	1	110	Ethiopia	1
90	Malawi	2	140	Burundi	2
88	Zambia	3	140	Mozambique	3
83	Eritrea	4	210	Malawi	4
77	Madagascar	5	210	Rwanda	5
75	Zimbabwe	6	210	Tanzania	6
70	Namibia	7	230	Eritrea	7
69	Mozambique	8	250	Madagascar	8
65	Angola	9	260	Angola	9
58	Burundi	10	330	Uganda	10
57	Uganda	11	340	Kenya	11
55	Botswana	12	370	Zambia	12
54	Lesotho	13	680	Lesotho	13
50	Swaziland	14	720	Zimbabwe	14
50	Tanzania	15	1,520	Swaziland	15
46	Kenya	16	2,110	Namibia	16
34	Ethiopia	17	3,310	Botswana	17
19	Seychelles	18	3,870	Mauritius	18
12	Mauritius	19	6,910	Seychelles	19

SOURCE: World Bank, 1999.

Main Causes of Persisting Poverty

Many assessments have identified the following main causes of poverty in Africa:

- An unsupportive policy environment and weak implementation capacity, as expressed in both the content of the countries' externally initiated economic reform programs and these programs' evident failure to integrate poverty-reducing elements into their operations.
- The failure of economic reforms to lead to robust and sustainable economic growth. The low level of economic growth in Africa has resulted in significant suppression of the productive sectors' output.
- Budgetary allocation patterns in many countries that have been biased against properly targeted and poverty-focused interventions that are pro-poor.
- Poor access to real assets due to, among other things, unfavorable land ownership laws and an unsupportive land tenure system that has worsened the productivity of the majority of the poor who depend on agriculture as the main source of their livelihood.

A serious obstacle to reducing mass absolute poverty in recent decades in Africa has been economic stagnation and decline. Economic growth can be a powerful means to eradicate poverty. A redistributive strategy that is undertaken under conditions of weak economic growth cannot be conducive to sustainable poverty reduction. Public welfare programs that are not founded on a strong economic base are unlikely to succeed no matter how committed the political leadership is to the improvement of social welfare, particularly if external assistance is not forthcoming to fill the funding gap. Economic growth can also raise the productivity and incomes of poor people, expanding opportunities and choices. Sustained national gross domestic product (GDP) growth, combined with rising wages and productivity, accounts for much of the "East Asian Miracle." Having no economic growth is almost entirely bad for poor people. Without economic growth, it is almost never possible to reduce "income poverty," and even advances against other aspects of human poverty, such as illiteracy or child mortality, cannot be sustained without economic growth.

Statistics on economic growth and employment in many countries suggest that the two need not be strongly correlated. Work by the United Nations Development Fund (UNDP) shows that employment growth worldwide has consistently lagged behind output growth since 1975. The Zambian case is instructive. During the restructuring period in that country, 1993 was the only year in which the country had a positive growth rate, 7.5 percent. In that same year, employment fell by 25,000, nearly 5 percent of those in employment. This demonstrates that policies and conditions that stimulate growth need not necessarily increase employment. A country must design policies aimed at directly creating productive employment. The lack of a clear-cut policy on employment promotion in Zambia is one of the main drawbacks of the country's policy regime vis-à-vis poverty reduction.

But whereas economic growth and employment may not necessarily go hand in hand, poverty and unemployment are strongly correlated. Having a significant proportion of the population be unemployed or underemployed, as is the case in Zambia today, has a telling effect on the productive capacity of the economy. To the extent that unemployment, especially if prevalent among the young, is positively correlated with the crime rate, it reduces the capacity for effective governance. Because it mars the enabling environment for investment or forces the channeling of higher levels of resources toward containment of crime, unemployment reduces the country's capacity for sustained economic growth.

Against this background, it is evident that although economic growth is important, it is not sufficient for poverty reduction. Although sustained growth is imperative for poverty reduction, rising inequality has serious adverse effects that dampen the efficacy of growth in realizing the desired goal of poverty reduction. This fact contradicts the long-standing belief that redistributive considerations often conflict with growth considerations. It is increasingly becoming apparent that redistributive policies do matter for reducing poverty and that growth and equity are not necessarily conflictual. The United Nations Conference on Trade and Development (UNCTAD)'s *Trade and Development Report* (1997) warns of the adverse consequences of unchecked inequality.

This growing realization challenges both the wisdom of the 1970s, which placed a high premium on redistributional measures at the expense of growth considerations, and the major focus of the 1980s on growth while relegating equity to the backseat. Emerging wisdom, particularly in the context of the current debate about the social dimension of adjustment, questions the assumption that distribution must be allowed to worsen, in the interest of economic growth, before it gets better. The concept of broad-based growth has emerged as an alternative way of recognizing the importance of growth with redistribution in any meaningful approach to poverty reduction. Most important is the fact that economic growth does contribute to poverty reduction, but there are still losers from the adjustments that growth requires. Economic growth explains only about half of poverty reduction. The rest depends on good policy to harness the growth dividends for poverty reduction.

In the light of earlier limited success of their African growth approaches through SAP, the International Monetary Fund (IMF) and the World Bank and member countries are presently proposing an enhanced framework for poverty reduction that is intended to make country-level actions and those of development partners more effective in achieving sustained poverty reduction. To support this development, the IMF and the World Bank have initiated a Poverty Reduction Growth Facility (which replaces the Enhanced Structural Adjustment Facility) through which country-led economic growth and poverty-reduction strategies will be supported.

The country-led strategies would be presented by countries in a document to be known as the Poverty Reduction Strategy Paper (PRSP), which, among other things, will promulgate long-term goals for key poverty reduction targets and the macro-economic, structural, and institutional framework for achieving those goals. The PRSP is expected to become a key instrument for a country's relations with the donor community and the Bretton Woods Institutions. These institutions in their lending operations and assistance strategies to concerned countries will first endorse their PRSPs. The PRSP would provide a basis for IMF and World Bank concessional lending to the country as well as debt relief under the Heavily Indebted Poor Countries (HIPC) Initiative. The implications for the African countries are that to access assistance under the Poverty Reduction Growth Facility, a PRSP, which is country-driven and broad-based, has to be prepared. Uganda and Tanzania have already completed their PRSPs, and Zambia launched the process to develop its paper in June 2000.

Expenditures on poverty-reducing interventions have been given little priority in the average African government's budget despite the general recognition that growth alone through the "trickle down" and multiplier effects is not sufficient and can only be an indirect and, quite often, slow manner of addressing the growing problem of poverty on the continent. It has also been acknowledged (as the rationale for preparing the IMF and World Bank PRSPs in African countries implies) that the growth-promoting measures of the standard IMF–World Bank approved SAPs have produced adverse social dimensions that have come to bear heavily especially on the "core poor." The indirect approach through growth stimulation should therefore be complemented by measures designed to protect the growing number of the poor from the adverse effects of economic reforms.

Measuring Prevalence of Poverty

Current Tools

It is increasingly being questioned by the authors of publications such as the UNDP Human Development Reports whether the nature, magnitude, and severity of poverty in sub-Saharan Africa can be fully appreciated and understood using the current tools of quantification. The difficulties encountered in the World Bank's current efforts to assist developing countries in Africa to develop poverty-reduction strategies that reflect the specific realities of these countries underlies the growing recognition that new tools and indices have to be developed to better understand this phenomenon. Without a proper diagnosis of the problem, the interventions that ultimately are prescribed will continue to have little bearing on the reduction of poverty itself.

Encyclopaedia Britannica defines poverty as "the state of one who lacks a usual or socially acceptable amount of money or material possessions." Welfare economists define poverty as consumption per household member or per adult equivalent below an accepted poverty line. Consumption (expenditure plus the imputed value of home production) is taken as a proxy for "income." In the human resource development field, poverty is defined by the Human Development Index (HDI), which is based on life expectancy, infant mortality, nutrition, literacy, primary school enrollment of girls and boys, and population with access to safe drinking water. For the purposes of measurement, these human dimensions are expressed by the following variables: the index of life expectancy at birth; the educational index, measured by a combination of adult literacy and the rate of attendance in primary, secondary, and higher education taken together; and standard of life, as measured by real per capita GDP (converted to dollars using purchasing power parities—PPP). In short, the HDI is a composite of three basic components of human development: longevity, knowledge, and standard of living.[2]

Because the concept of human development is much broader than the HDI shows, the UNDP Human Development Reports (HDRs) have been constructing more specific and disaggregated indices that include a Gender-Related Development Index (GDI), introduced in the 1995 HDR, which uses the same variables as the HDI, with a few differences. The GDI adjusts the average achievement of each country in terms of life expectancy, educational level, and income, in accordance with the disparity in the achievements of women and of men. The greater the disparity in basic human development, the lower will be the GDI of a country, compared with its HDI.

The Gender Empowerment Measure (GEM), was also introduced in the 1995 HDR. It measures the inequality between the sexes in key areas of economic and political participation and decision making. The GEM uses variables constructed explicitly to measure the relative acquisition of power by men and women in political and economic activity (e.g., percentage of women in the national legislature, percentage of women in administrative and managerial positions, women's share of professional and technical jobs). Unlike the GDI, the GEM reveals inequalities in terms of opportunities in selected areas.

The Human Poverty Index (HPI) is another tool, this one introduced in the 1997 HDR. It includes, in a composite measure, several characteristics of deprivation to reach an overall judgment about the extent of poverty in any given community. It concentrates on deprivation in three essential areas of human life, already reflected in the HDI: longevity (i.e., survival—vulnerability to death at a relatively early age); knowledge (exclusion from the world of reading and communication); and decent living standard (in terms of overall economic provisioning). In the 1998 HDR, the HPI has been subdivided into two indices: HPI–1, is used to measure poverty in developing countries, and HPI–2, employed to measure poverty in developed countries.

In the quantification of poverty intensity/gravity at the national level, aggregate statistics in one of the Sub-Saharan African countries, Zambia, where over 73 percent of the people are considered to be poor, have adopted the following measures:

Absolute poverty. This measure constructs a poverty line based on a fixed expenditure or consumption level. Absolute measures assume that poverty exists when individuals or households are not able to acquire a specific level of consumption.

Relative poverty. Relative poverty describes an individual or group's wealth relative to that of other individuals in the group under study. Relative poverty lines are usually set as a percentage of average income or expenditure of the group. Very often two-thirds of the mean expenditure per capita has been used as the poverty line. This implies that all persons or households whose consumption falls below the threshold are considered poor.

Extreme poverty. Households with per adult equivalent expenditures of a specified income level or below are considered to be in extreme poverty. The consumption of such household members is considered insufficient to meet even the basic required daily food intake.

Poverty depth or gap. The average gap or distance between the income of the poor and the poverty line is the poverty depth. More specifically, it is the extent to which the incomes of the poor lie below the poverty line.

Poverty incidence. Also referred to as the head count ratio, poverty incidence is defined as the fraction of the population below the poverty line, that is, the proportion of people in the total population whose consumption fell below $$n$ per adult equivalent in a year.

Analysis of Current Tools

It is clear that, although it has some limitations, the HDI offers a better alternative to the GNP for measuring the relative socioeconomic status of countries in sub-Saharan Africa in general and the eastern and southern African countries in particular. It enables people and their governments to evaluate progress over time and to determine priorities for policy intervention. It also permits instructive comparisons of the experiences of different countries.

However, it is misleading to refer to a single HDI for a country with great inequality because national averages can conceal much. The best solution would be to create separate HDIs for the most significant groups, by gender, for example, or by income group, geographical region, race, or ethnic group. Separate HDIs would reveal a more detailed profile of human deprivation in each country, and disaggregated HDIs are already being attempted for countries with sufficient data.

It is equally noteworthy that, for rural people in the average African country, per capita consumption in money terms is only one of many aspects of poverty. Since the onset of the SAP in Zambia, for example, the country has continued to suffer from alarming and unprecedented levels of poverty. Unfortunately, available measurements of poverty and income distribution derived from them are both inadequate and inappropriate. For example, with respect to income distribution in Zambia, the poverty incidence indicator as reported by that country's Central Statistical Office (CSO) uses the proportion of the population below the "poverty line," which is determined as the amount of monthly income required to purchase basic food to meet the minimum caloric requirement for a family of six. In 1991, using this quantification tool, the percentage of population below the established poverty line was 69.7 percent; it had soared to 73.8 percent by 1993. But the situation, in reality, is worse than that because the "food basket" used is abstract, based on a vegetarian diet. Indeed, in recognition of this fact, CSO itself points out that "the food basket used to arrive at the poverty lines . . . is very modest and based on a predominantly vegetarian list of food. It is based on the minimal caloric requirements. If meat, chicken, and fish were added to the food basket, the cost would go up by a large margin" (Zambia CSO 1999).

It is clear that the indices used in the quantification process have ultimately determined the statistical figures that emerge, and if care is not exercised at this stage, national policies and strategies/interventions adopted will continue to be founded on incorrect representation of the problem being addressed. In the Zambian case, it is also worth observing that the measurement of poverty has not fully factored in such basic needs of the people as shelter, education, health care, lighting, clothing, footwear, and transport. If these were also taken into account, the poverty level would worsen to well over 90 percent.

Care must be exercised in statistical quantification of phenomena as complex as poverty. There is always the danger that, in our quest to be scientific and technical, we will reduce to quantifiable indicators matters such as "poverty" that are so deeply human that they cannot be translated into mere numbers. This recognition, however, does not question the value of quantification and the importance of economic growth indicators in getting a clear picture of the magnitude and severity of poverty.

Conclusion

This chapter has acknowledged that economic growth can be a powerful means to eradicate poverty and that positive GDP growth rates are important in this regard because GDP can raise the productivity and incomes of poor people, expanding opportunities and choices in a variety of ways. Sustained national GDP growth, combined with rising wages and productivity, was an important part of the historic ascent from poverty in the industrial countries and in the past 30 years in such countries as China, Indonesia, and Malaysia, which have dramatically reduced poverty in income and other critical dimensions.

But these successes contrast with present realities in sub-Saharan Africa. In too many countries, growth has failed to reduce poverty, either because it has been too slow or stagnant or because its quality and structure have been insufficiently pro-poor. Thus, although economic growth is important for poverty reduction, it is evidently not sufficient by itself. Economic growth does contribute to poverty reduction, but there are still losers from the adjustments that growth requires. And economic growth accounts for only about half of poverty reduction. The rest depends on good policy to harness that growth. Having no economic growth is almost entirely bad for poor people. Without economic growth, it is almost never possible to reduce income poverty, and even advances against other aspects of human poverty, such as illiteracy or child mortality, cannot be sustained without economic growth. Economic growth contributes most to poverty reduction when it expands the employment, productivity, and wages of poor people—and when public resources are spent to promote human development.

Another important condition is initial equality. Income poverty is reduced more quickly where equality is greater. Recent studies have estimated that an annual per capita GDP growth of 10 percent would reduce the incidence of income poverty by 30 percent in relatively egalitarian societies, with a Gini coefficient[3] of 0.25, and by only 10 percent in less equal societies, with a Gini coefficient of 0.50. Indeed, growth does not help poverty reduction when big chunks of GDP go out of the country in public spending that neither advances human development nor benefits the poor, such as to pay international debt or purchase weapons.

Another way of seeing how growth affects poverty is to consider the growth elasticity of poverty reduction. The higher the elasticity, the better—the more each percentage point of growth will reduce poverty. Countries in sub-Saharan Africa and Latin America and the Caribbean have some of the lowest elasticities: 0.2 in Zambia, 0.8 in Senegal, 0.7 in Guatemala and Honduras, and 0.9 in Brazil and Panama. At the other end of the scale is East Asia, where the elasticities tend to be well above 2: Indonesia, 2.8, Malaysia, 3.4, and rural China, 3.0.

The key elements of a pro-poor growth strategy naturally depend on the situation in each country. But for all countries an essential precondition is to make poverty eradication a priority objective of the national development strategy.

5

Civil Society, Pluralism, Goldilocks, and Other Fairy Tales in Africa

IRVING LEONARD MARKOVITZ
*Queens College and the Graduate Center
of the City University, New York*

Introduction*

Both capitalism and democracy are constructed of cruel processes accomplished less by constitutional lawyers in sacrosanct temples of higher learning than by sausage makers in the shadow of the slaughterhouse. Pogroms in Senegal in 1989 and their aftermath illustrate some of the complexities in understanding civil society in Africa, in theory and in the real world. One cannot understand what happened in this small African country without understanding a global environment dominated by superpowers, especially the United States; international lending agencies, including the World Bank; and

---

*For critical but encouraging readings of this chapter, I am indebted first and foremost to my closest colleague and home counsel, Ruth Markovitz; to Nigel Gibson and George C. Bond for their sympathetic editing and for having always included me in the Columbia Africanist community; and to Ali Jimale Ahmed, John R. Bowman, Michael A. Krasner, Peter Liberman, Solomon Resnik, Burton M. Zwiebach, William K. Tabb, Howard H. Lentner, Jeffrey C. Issac, Nelson Kasfir, Ronald Kassimir, Irene L. Gendzier, Francois Pierre-Louis, J. Patrice McSherry, Jonathan Markovitz, Richard Franke, William S. Miles, Cheryl Payer, Lesley Sharp, Tom Karis, Herbert S. Lewis, Alem Habtu, Amy S. Patterson, and Kenneth Paul Erickson who have cautioned, corrected, chastised, cajoled, and warned against onomatopoeia.

117

intellectual currents of thought such as establishment civil society theory that provide legitimacy to these institutional endeavors.

Every society contains many conflicting elements. Those elements of civil society that come to the fore in any historical period are those most aligned with dominant social and economic forces—if those establishment interests properly understand that environment and take the appropriate actions. The argument of this chapter is that establishment interests and their intellectual allies do in fact have this understanding and that they are effectively acting upon it. The objective of these dominant forces is stable, predictable, and effective—for their purposes—government. The cheapest way to achieve this end in the modern era is through "mild democracy." "Democracy lite," like "lite beer," which smells and looks like beer but has no body, is but a shadow of the real thing. Institutions of participation promise that "the people" or "civil society" can do anything that they want. The reality is that these democracies come circumscribed by "conditionalities," reinforced by international actors, superpowers, and lending agencies that do not hesitate to intervene in domestic politics. Various establishment civil society theorists may differ among themselves about the amount of time that will be necessary for the trickle down process to benefit the people, but they share the common perception that capitalism and democracy are universal goods, that is, good for all people at all times. The reality is that stark disparities between rich and poor in global opportunity have grown greater. In the words of the United Nations *Human Development Report of 1999*, "The past decade has shown increasing concentration of income, resources and wealth among people, corporations and countries" (United Nations, 1999: 3). Although it may be hard for most middle-class Americans to believe, the harsh reality is that the conditions of life of most people in the world will worsen, not improve, in their and our lifetimes. This chapter analyzes these phenomena and examines the African Growth and Opportunity Law, passed by the U.S. Congress in 1998, and the reaction of the World Bank to the 1997–1998 world financial crisis to illustrate the nature of the "cruel capitalism" and "cruel democracy" advanced by their proponents.

Unrealistic conceptions of civil society fostered by U.S. social scientists have provided justification for politicians demanding from African nations "civil societies" compatible with their own neoliberal economic objectives. The African Growth and Opportunity Act made this connection explicit by calling for increased trade and investment "for those countries in sub-Saharan Africa attempting to build civil societies." The advocates of free enterprise who wrote the African Growth and Opportunity Act trade bill included a major section on civil society. To envisage a "proper" type of civil society as the ramparts and trenches, in Antonio Gramsci's (1971) vivid image, for *their* ideal society is a necessity. Civil society can appeal for the sacrifices needed from ordinary folk in the interests of future development, the sacrifices needed for "the long run." Civil society, like procedural democracy itself, provides cheap and effective mechanisms and solutions for problems of social conflict. Establishment views of civil society emphasize the individual and autonomy, competition and opportunity, risk and the future; they thereby shield those who command governments and economic resources by seeming to offer universal access to wealth and power. If individuals fail to succeed, the fault lies in themselves, not in the social system or in economic arrangements. The remedy is also available: to try and try again through the established institutions of elections and the marketplace. Civil society helps people learn to yield to the inevitable frustrations and pain demanded by governments who want the discontented to know that they are morally as well as legally obligated to accept the standards of the day—the governments' standards—and to not go marching in the streets. This chapter does not argue that everyone who uses the concept of civil society necessarily supports the pro-business policies reflected in the African Growth and Opportunity Act. The way in which the term *civil society* has been mystified or misunderstood, however, has facilitated the co-optation of many who would otherwise be in opposition.

Advocates who are politically dissimilar use the term *civil society*. Radical images of civil society serve as an ideal against which to measure the deficiencies of existing regimes. Conservatives contemplate a cornucopia from an unfettered corporate capitalism. Establishment liberal images of civil society function as ideological constraints against fundamental changes of control and seek to prevent the sudden intrusion of a mass-based politics. This chapter concentrates on the political and economic functions of establishment-liberal civil society theory because it is the most misunderstood version and the most pernicious in its consequences.

Western political analysts have provided detailed statements about the types of regimes they consider to embody democratic ideals (Diamond, 1997: 3–23; Chazan, 1992: 279–308). Their positions are based on ideological preconceptions. They do not advance African public interests, but instead promote agendas for the creation of Western-friendly governments putting forth civil society as the foundation for a new "Goldilocks" world. The "Goldilocks" economy, like the ideal porridge that was not too hot and not too cold but just right, will have just the right amount of growth so that all social interests benefit. Too much growth is destabilizing; too much inflation, too extravagant rises in wages, or too aggressive a working class are unbalancing. The "Goldilocks" society will also have just the right amount of democracy. Too much democracy is no good because it threatens stability. Too much participation whets the appetite for social changes (Huntington, 1968; Lipset,

1983). This apparently reasonable quest for moderation in all things turns out to be the newest version of the "trickle down," "don't rock the boat," "patience is its own reward" theory. However, the sudden drop in the stock markets during the summer of 1998 made even Francis Fukuyama question his belief in the "end of ideology" (quoted in Kristof, 1998c: sec. 4, 1). Current financial difficulties in Asia, Latin America, and Russia—and their accompanying social misery—have raised new doubts about the effectiveness and legitimacy of laissez-faire market policies.

The changing emphasis on the relations between state and society analyzed by several waves of social science literature compounds these ideological difficulties. My impression of the recent literature on civil society suggests that we have, in a relatively brief period of time, experienced three different approaches. The first emphasized the rise of civil society, especially in Eastern Europe, and spoke of civil society against the state; the second envisaged a "precarious balance" between state and society; and the third approach, advanced in this chapter, maintains that it is misleading to refer to either "the state" or "civil society"; instead, one must distinguish elements in both state and civil society and empirically examine the terms and conditions of their interrelations (Markovitz, 1998: 21–53). This view recognizes that the formation of civil society is not always benign. Social interests claw their way into the structures of the state, extending and expanding the basic institutions of power. The state is never above the fray; political leadership always has its own interests. An understanding of civil society requires specific attention to the processes—the centralization of institutions and the concentration of bureaucratic authority—that embody and strengthen power.

Pluralism and pluralist assumptions about society lie at the heart of most of the Western Africanists' assumptions about civil society. Yet pluralism has never succeeded as a satisfactory theoretical explanation for the causes of democracy in Western, advanced industrial societies. It is even less successful when applied to issues of civil society in African cases. Although pluralist theorists claim the *Federalist Papers* as a foundation, the *Federalist* authors clearly believed that some factions rated more highly than others. They had a sense of priorities in their understanding of which interests were crucial and why. Their understanding of civil society clearly differed from that of our contemporaries. They privileged property interests and sought to bring those they considered crucial into the state; struggled to incorporate civil society into constitutionally determined organizational niches; and saw state and society as integrated, not "precariously balanced."

Whereas in other publications I have dealt with the views of the *Federalist* authors and constitution making, as well as with the integrated nature of state and civil society, this chapter focuses on the difficulties of applying pluralist theory to African cases and attempts to demonstrate the ideological affinity of pluralism to neoliberal economics and political policy (Markovitz, 1999). I again draw on aspects of the ethnic clashes of 1989 in Senegal between Senegalese and people of Mauritanian descent to illustrate some of these propositions, particularly the ability of existing establishments to buy the support of the disenfranchised by gradually incorporating them into the electoral rolls and by extending a social contract in the form of a broadened set of education and business arrangements. The link between democracy and civil society emerges as more problematic than pluralist theory would have us believe.

The civil society of establishment pluralism (defined below) leads to a focus on bird-watchers, choral societies, bowling leagues, parent-teacher associations, and athletic clubs, and leaves us ill prepared to understand the calamitous effects of whirlwind capitalism. Establishment civil society discourse directs our attention equally to burial societies, singing groups, and giant conglomerates. We lose concentration on multinational corporations and labor unions, on the poor, and the on the victims of a frequently rapacious capitalism (Putnam, 1993).

This chapter illustrates how the power of elites or ruling classes interacts with the power of significant non-elites, or *lumpen* or workers, to create new institutions of government. Sometimes these institutions restrain rather than enable social groups from participating as citizens. Coercion and compulsion abet in defining the nature of democracy. In considering the making of democracy, it often proves more apt to use the language of constraint and exclusion, of victims and scapegoating, than the liberal voice of pluralism and participation. Structural adjustment and neoliberalism require weakening, dismantling, and/or incorporating many of the social interests—organizations of labor and of the poor—that liberal and compassionate proponents wish to see advanced. Because they fail to see how this language masks the pursuit of objectives antithetical to their goals, these proponents of reform use the same language of "civil society" as do advocates of the status quo. They do not recognize that the analysis embedded in this language produces a misreading of the political realities.

Conflicting Conceptions of Civil Society

Pro-Democracy Advocates of Civil Society

This chapter raises basic issues about the practical and political consequences of establishment uses of "civil society," but it does not intend to be dismissive of the democratic and liberating thrust of courageous intellectuals who have wielded the concept of civil society against overbearing regimes. I welcome "a political liberalism that is indispensable to any meaningful conception of human freedom," and I agree that "the rule of law, political pluralism, parliamentary reform, the creation of a legally independent sphere of associations, etc., are promoting genuinely important values and institutions."[1] Too often, however, defenders of establishment interests have used the vision of "civil society" to justify anti-democratic interests and to divert attention from the substantive beneficiaries of stultifying economic policies. The "hermeneutic dimension" of this chapter is to argue that "the historical discourse" now underway about African political development has in many ways potentially negative effects. Rather than shedding light on the difficulties of African development, the terms of this new discourse make it more difficult to answer the classic political science questions of who gets what, when, where, how, and why. To illuminate these propositions, I consider in turn conservative, radical, and liberal-establishment views of civil society, with an exemplar of each approach, paying most attention to the liberal-establishment perspective as the most important for my analytical purposes.

The Conservative View of Civil Society:
The Unity of Civil Society and Capitalism Revisited

Most Africanists would be uncomfortable with an unabashedly conservative view of civil society. Michael Novak (1997), in *The Fire of Invention: Civil Society and the Future of the Corporation*, goes much farther than the liberal pluralists in his arguments about the business basis of civil society. Novak offers "some reflections on the history and distinctive nature of the business corporation, as a primary institution of democracy (second only to religion) . . . and as the major material institution of civil society"(1997: 20). The United States taught the world that "the social question" that wracked the nineteenth century could be dissolved by "universal upward mobility"(1997: 17). Corporate leaders "raise the poor out of poverty and offer unparalleled opportunities for the development of human talents"; they "animate civil society": "These two significant achievements, raising up the poor and energizing civil society, provide powerful moral claims for business corporations"(1997: 119). From the days of the *Federalist Papers* to today, Novak contends, business interests have maintained the foundations of peace and promoted comity in society (1997: 42). Civil society, capitalism, and democracy are not only plaited inexorably together, but this is a matter not for apology but for proud proclamation. Overall then, according to this conservative perspective, not only are business associations part of civil society—unlike those liberal pluralists who would vanquish them from our consideration—but they are at the foundation of our democracies, responsible for our liberties, and the source of our civility. Not everybody would agree.

Radical Civil Society

What many progressive observers have in mind when they use the term *civil society* is described eloquently by C. Douglas Lummis:

> Unlike mass society, civil society is not a herd but a multiplicity of diverse groups and organizations, formal and informal, of people acting together for a variety of purposes, some political, some cultural, some economic. . . . Civil society provides space for public discourse, for the development of public values and public language, for the formation of the public self [the citizen], a space separate from the formal political sphere dominated by state power and political parties that aim to control that power. . . . Civil society does not demand freedom, but generates it. This, at least, is the radical image of civil society, and it is powerful and persuasive. (Lummis, 1996: 31; Cohen & Arato, 1992)

This view of people from every social order working together, not merely in harmony but helpfully, is very appealing. The generation of freedom, the creating of a fountainhead of liberty, the endowing of every creature with its own space, the flowering not merely of the individual but of the person—all are radical expectations, but not romantic. However, Lummis goes on to delineate radical civil society from establishment civil society:

> But a problem with the civil-society notion is that it is not that easy to distinguish from the dreary old model of liberal pluralism. It must be remembered that in the United States such social scientists as Robert Dahl, Seymour Martin Lipset, and Daniel Bell were developing their own "post-Marxist" political theory back in the Cold-War 1950s. According to this notion, democracy is best achieved and liberty best preserved in a society in which competition takes place not between classes but between a multiplicity of interest groups—precisely the kind of society, it turned out, that had been (allegedly) achieved in the liberal capitalist countries, and especially in the United States. (1996: 31)

Seymour Lipset could then say that democracy, as defined above, "is the good society itself in operation," and Daniel Bell could argue that with the appearance of liberal-capitalism, world political development had reached its conclusion and ideologies were no longer needed. Lummis declared that: "The emergence of the new civil-society discourse has enabled Bell, who saw his *End of Ideology* become the laughingstock of the ideological 1960s and 1970s, to come back in the 1980s and boast that "the United States has been the complete *civil society* . . . perhaps the only one in political history" (1996: 31–32). For Lummis, this clearly will not do. He hopes to achieve the maximum possible space for the person to develop in harmony with as much community as possible in the face of overbearing bureaucracies and institutions of gigantic capitalism and states insatiable for power. He develops his own low-scale, modest notions of participatory democracy. Lummis's aspirations may be arguably utopian, but I suspect that his vision is what many progressives have in mind when they speak of civil society. What I have called "establishment civil society" differs fundamentally from this vision in its objectives, values, strategies, and constituencies.

Establishment Civil Society: The Enterprise Pluralism of Larry Diamond

When I describe "establishment civil society," I do not mean that the authors of this way of looking at the world, serious scholars like Larry Diamond,[2] are or aspire to be members of the "establishment." Nor do I mean that they consciously advocate conservative policies as does Michael Novak (1997), whose blatant capitalist apologia they might find distasteful. Nevertheless, their ideas and mode of analysis work to serve establishment interests. I am interested in the political function of those ideas within the framework of the sociology of knowledge. Mainstream proponents of civil society offer much that appears to be a reasonable liberal agenda but that on close inspection is closer to Novak's position. How should one characterize this latest literature on civil society? Judgments about civil society in Africa by mainstream social scientists are not always categories of analysis that they have discovered through hard empirical work. They are not always scientific findings that come from objective undertakings through hardheaded technical investigations. They are not facts that emerge from the hard bed of social reality.

Larry Diamond's work as an example of this approach is important because he enables us to clearly see the dissimilarity between these conflicting visions, the establishment and the radical view of civil society (Diamond, 1997: 2–23; see also Diamond, 1994). I find Diamond's definition of civil society problematic. He has used his definition to criticize political interests that have invoked his distrust or suspicion, such as the African National Congress, and to try to convince African populations of the necessities of painful neoliberal laws and programs. His argument is that the consolidation, normalization, or regularization of democratic politics "requires, most of all, political institutionalization—building up stable, efficacious, and enduring political parties and state structures." Vital for these purposes is "a vigorous and autonomous civil society" (1997: 4). According to Diamond:

> Civil society is the realm of organized social life that is voluntary, self-generating, (largely) self-supporting, autonomous from the state, and bound by a legal order

or set of shared rules. It is distinct from "society" in general in that it involves citizens acting collectively in a public sphere to express their interests and ideas, achieve mutual goals, make demands on the state, and hold state officials accountable. Voluntary collective action within the public sphere takes place in competitive ideological markets; civil society, thus, implies notions of partialness, pluralism, and competition. Organizations that seek to monopolize a sphere of collective life (in the sense of denying the legitimacy of competing groups) or to envelop totally the lives of their members are, thus, not part of civil society. Civil society also excludes the private dimensions of individual and family life, the inward-looking activities of parochial groups, the profit-making enterprise of individual business firms, and political efforts to take control of the state. Actors in civil society recognize the principles of state authority and the rule of law, and need the protection of these in reality to prosper and be secure. (1997: 4)

This definition is laden with good words and phrases: *voluntary, autonomous, self-supporting, shared rules, citizens acting collectively, rule of law, pluralism*. These good ideas, however, march in the service of "political institutionalization," that is, for the purpose of establishing governments and creating order for known purposes and foretold results. Diamond's conception of civil society either is tautological or assumes the existence of an ongoing already structured society, when it is precisely the existence of a legitimate order that is in question. He sets boundaries and commands social interests, like a pet dog, to stay within them.

Diamond tells us nothing about who "organized social life," about why and whether membership in civil society must be "voluntary," about why civil society must be "autonomous from the state," or about where all these requirements came from. By assuming (or requiring) that civil society be bound by a legal order and shared rules, Diamond starts out with what he purports to be establishing, the existence of democracy. But he never asks who established the rules, or by what process. Who is to say that only "citizens" are to be members of civil society? What about non-citizens? Foreigners? Riff-raff? Lumpen? What if social interests don't want to hold state officials accountable and make demands on the state, but desire to overthrow the state and establish new institutions and offices? Diamond's framing of the purview of civil society makes it impossible to even envision the eventuality of societal interests that are already in the state and part and parcel of the state. He never defines *competitive ideological markets*, explains what enables them to exist, or tells us what happens if they are not there. He assumes that they are the norm, yet one could well argue that a true marketplace of ideas has rarely existed in any society. The contention that "civil society thus implies notions of partialness, pluralism and competition" (1997: 4) builds his preconceptions into his alleged objective observations. His ends are desirable, but they cannot be simply assumed into a definition of civil society.

In failing to attempt to answer the hard questions, and by the terms of his definitions, Diamond translates his preferences into preconditions for civil society: "*Organizations that seek to monopolize a sphere of collective life (in the sense of denying the legitimacy of competing groups) or to envelop totally the lives of their members are, thus, not part of civil society*" (4; emphasis added) Of course, we do not want totalitarians in civil society. We want the dock workers of Gdansk, not the Communist Party. Diamond continues in this arbitrary vein when he says that "civil society also excludes the private dimensions of individual and family life"—a point strongly objected to by many of those currently working on feminist and family issues, such as Aili Mari Tripp (1998) —as well as when he objects to "the inward-looking activities of parochial groups" (Diamond, 1997: 4).

Unlike Novak, Diamond forsakes, or rather deliberately leaves out of his conception of civil society, profit-making enterprises, corporations, and business interests. He also excludes any group "involved in political efforts to take control of the state" because by definition, civil society is separate from the state. He distinguishes between "civil society" and "political society," but does so in the same arbitrary manner. When he declares that "actors in civil society recognize the principles of state authority and the rule of law" (1997: 5), we can certainly hope that they do, but what guarantee does Diamond have that they will, and why should they? Diamond has offered us his personal desires and democratic good wishes, a lot of political philosophy, and very little empirical observation. This is a lovely wish list, an ideal portrait extending Frank Capra's Washington to the rest of the world, a land of political pixies and Peter Pan leaders escaping the clutches of peg-legged pirates. These measured conditions only happen when one enters into the fairy woods. Diamond's is the testimony of a pluralist, but it contributes little to our understanding of what is happening in Africa.

In large measure, Diamond's contentions recapitulate the basic perceptions and contentions of classic U.S. pluralist theory. In his effort to apply these propositions to Africa and to the African context, Diamond shares and repeats the difficulties inherent in this theoretical approach. This includes its ideological and political biases, biases that are today congruent with a neoliberalism with which I would beg to differ.

Pluralism offers five propositions about democratic society: (1) Society is divided into interest groups; (2) these groups conflict with each other; (3) every interest is a potential group that can be mobilized; (4) individuals may belong to multiple groups, and this will mitigate conflict; and (5) groups abide by the "rules of the game." This theory does not differentiate among groups in any qualitative way. It does recognize differences in size, finances, organization, and so forth, but these are always matters of degree and not of kind. Pluralism also leaves unexplained the origins of the rules of the game. Consider, for example, the following statement:

> Since the early 1980s, it has become increasingly apparent that the impetus for political renewal and resistance to authoritarian domination in Africa has come from students, the churches, professional associations, women's groups, trade unions, human rights organizations, producer groups, intellectuals, journalists, and informal networks that are either autonomous from the state or struggling to break free from its control. (1997: 6)

This sounds good. However, Diamond lumps all sorts of groups together without trying to distinguish among them in terms of their power or effectiveness. We may well remember the actions of brave churchmen in Kenya or Uganda in opposing arbitrary governments. We may also think of far more powerful churches in civil society in Germany and elsewhere in Europe that did little to thwart totalitarian regimes (Bohlen, 1998). To provide what is little more than a laundry list of those who have raised their voices is no substitute for a hard analysis of who and what counts under which circumstances. Stephen N. Ndegwa (1996), for example, in *The Two Faces of Civil Society*, claims evidence "that strikes at the heart of the thesis that civil society organizations such as NGOs necessarily invest their resources in support of democratization efforts" (1996: 1). He questions the "notion that generic civil society is uniformly progressive in challenging the African state and in advancing democratization" (1996: 3). He argues that it depends a lot on whether the leadership "chooses to commit its resources to a progressive political agenda" and declares that "this evidence of the 'two faces' of civil society strikes at the heart of the thesis that civil society organizations such as NGOs necessarily invest their resources in support of democratization efforts" (1996: 1).

Proponents of civil society like Novak and Diamond trace their intellectual antecedents back to the *Federalist Papers*. The *Federalist* authors, however, distinguished between factions and recognized the importance, above all, of those interests that were rooted in "property." James Madison, in *Federalist 10*, linked the elements of civil society to basic economic forces in society, that is, to those factions that maintained liberty because their members struggled so hard that they were willing to die for their preservation. Madison, too, informs us of basic facts about society. He might not like them, but these unpleasant findings are the building blocks of society. One does not have to be a Marxist to understand that state and society are intrinsically intertwined. Diamond also tells us that society will contain lots of different groups, and that they will conflict with each other. He does not share the hardheaded analyzing of the *Federalist* authors, however, when he moralizes that:

> First, the goals and methods of groups in civil society, especially organized associations, must be compatible with the practice of democratic politics. The chances for stable democracy significantly improve if civil society does not contain maximalist, uncompromising interest groups or groups with anti-democratic goals and methods. To the extent that these groups seek to displace the state or other competitors, *they may not qualify* [my emphasis added] as constituent elements of civil society at all, but their presence in society can do much damage to the aspirations of democratic forces in civil society. Maximalist interest groups are more likely to bring down repression from the state that may have a broad and indiscriminate character, affecting the core of civil society, . . . [so that] it is, therefore, vital that intellectuals and civil society activists not disparage parties or the state or the whole messy process of politics, per se—in a way that would discourage such political development. (1997: 10)

Where does this position come from? If political activists do criticize or otherwise disparage the state, and the state then turns on them and becomes increasingly authoritarian, that is obviously the fault of the nasty critics. Diamond contends that participation in his preferred organizations provides the experience, training, information, and confidence that will be the foundations of democratic societies. People will learn how to live together better and develop the virtues of tolerance and cooperation.

Neither a willingness nor an ability to participate in politics, however, seem to have been lacking among Africans or among many other peoples threatened and overwhelmed by despotic regimes. In *The Anthropology of Anger* Celestin Monga declares that "the quest for freedom in Africa is deeply entrenched" (1996:). He contends that "[f]or several decades, the rules of the political game and the social game (concerning power, status, wealth, and domination) were unilaterally determined by Africa's authoritarian states, and people feigned to accept those rules when in fact they constantly adjusted their behavior to escape domination and to circumvent the most coercive strictures" (1996: 26). Monga warns us that we should not ignore "the silent struggle by men and women of all social classes from the beginning of the colonial era" (Monga, 1996: 26; Scott, 1990: 199). Diamond is neither telling us anything new nor pointing to whether some interests are more important than others in determining the limitations and effective constraints on government. His prescriptions are adamant but not based on any observations of why and how civil society actually works to restrain tyranny.

Civil Society and Neoliberalism

Diamond returns to the link between civil society and neoliberal economic policies. He enables us to see clearly and understand the direct connection between his version of popular participation and capitalist development. What, in the final analysis, is the purpose of civil society? Considering the case of South Africa he tells us:

> A democratically elected government in a new South Africa will face a formidable dilemma. To produce real and sustainable economic growth, it will need to allow exchange rates and possibly real wages to fall. It will need to increase taxes but not so much as to destroy incentives to invest and produce. It must demand payment of rents and rates while resisting pressures to overspend the country into hopeless debt or hyperinflation. Such policies for long-term growth will be difficult to square with expectations for massive, immediate, and rapid material progress. Organizations and media in civil society must help a new government to level with the people, share with them the dilemma, and preempt, to some extent, the surge of populism. Policies for economic reform, growth, and redistribution forged through such a broad societal dialogue will be more sustainable than those negotiated secretly by a narrow stratum of corporatist elites. (1997: 18)

No wonder civil society—and democratic regimes—are so important. They legitimate; they take the heat; they make the unbearable more tolerable. Diamond spells out what the proponents of the Africa trade bill merely assumed: that civil society would pacify workers when African governments accommodated domestic and international corporate interests in lowering wages. Civil society, through the calm and reasonable nature of its membership, will stand in the way of "the surge" of a resentful "populism." The wisdom of civil society will make palatable tax policies that take from the poor and middle class and allow the rich to accumulate great wealth so they can better invest in those industries that we know are coming. It is much better that civil society do all of these things than "a narrow stratum of corporatist elites." No wonder establishment liberals love civil society. Diamond details the connections between establishment civil society and the buttressing of neoliberal reforms. We might again differ over whether either "more structural economic reforms—privatization, trade and financial liberalization" or "economic stabilization policies" are implemented in Third World countries as a result of democratic processes. It is striking, however, that Diamond argues that a major function of civil society is to rally support for their implementation, and that he feels that those neoliberal reforms "appear to be more sustainable and far-reaching (or, in many post-Communist countries, feasible only) when they are pursued through the democratic process" (1997: 9). This co-joining of civil society and what in the circumstances of less-developing countries must be called "neoliberal" economic reforms of retrenchment and restructuration, characterizes U.S. government efforts as well as the establishment civil society ideology. The suspicion that the South African National Congress (and the South African government) have shown toward the African Growth and Opportunity Act of the U.S. government, which embodies the establishment-pluralist concept of civil society and neoliberal-based economic growth, should not be surprising.

Africa Growth and Opportunity Act

The Africa Growth and Opportunity Act was a serious, apparently well-intentioned effort by the Clinton administration "to lead Africa into the twenty-first century." Philip Crane (R-Illinois) introduced the African Growth and Opportunity Bill, which passed the House. Senator Richard Lugar (R-Indiana) introduced a similar measure in the Senate (S 778), and in July it became part of the proposed Trade and Tariff Act of 1998 (S 2400). In this bill the U.S. government allegedly sought to advance democracy and to strengthen civil society. One aspect of the bill that is striking is the direct and strong emphasis on the connection between civil society and capitalism. The correlation between neoliberal economic policies and a type of democracy conducive to established interests is manifest.

The section of the bill entitled "Democratization and Conflict Resolution Capabilities" promises "(A) to promote democratization, good governance, and strong civil societies in sub-Saharan Africa"; and "(B) to strengthen conflict resolution capabilities of governmental, intergovernmental, and nongovernmental entities in sub-Saharan Africa." At the same time, the bill establishes at great length the necessity for African governments to do everything possible to advance private enterprise, both domestic and foreign, under penalty of extreme sanctions. It requires the president of the United States to specify that the country has established, or is making continual progress toward establishing, a market-based economy. The bill called for joint ventures with African and U.S. investors, the protection of intellectual property rights, and guarantees against expropriation and other property protections. It required nations to reduce "high" import and corporate taxes. It also demanded that African governments spend less, that they pledge themselves to "controlling government consumption," and that they "minimize government intervention in the market such as price controls and subsidies." In determining whether a sub-Saharan African country was eligible for support, the U.S. president would take into account the lowering of tariffs and how far along the African country had proceeded in its program of privatization (African Growth and Opportunity Act sections 1–6). In a nicely balanced provision, the bill declared that "Investments in human resources, development, and implementation of free market policies, including policies to liberalize agricultural markets and improve food security, and the support for the rule of law and democratic governance should continue to be encouraged and enhanced on a bilateral and regional basis." Free markets and freedom, liberalization and liberty, the rule of law and the rule of the market are the basis of civil society and "democratic governance"—democracy as the U.S. government would have it.[3]

President Clinton's allies rushed to defend the bill, but not everyone shared these sentiments. Many recognized that the commitments required by the bill advanced not African but multinational corporate interests. Some thought that although the bill's promoters spoke of assisting Africans, African-Americans, and women, the primary group targeted for assistance was the multinationals who control Africa's trade and access to rich markets.

Randall Robinson of TransAfrica denounced the act on the grounds that it would allow foreign corporations to buy African assets, especially government corporations, at extremely low prices and it would allow them to exploit low-priced African wage-labor. Robinson (1998) went as far as to declare: "This bill nakedly and unqualifiedly promotes the interests of American business. It should be called the African re-colonization act." Despite the positive sentiments expressed by anti-ANC parliamentarians, the South African government reacted very strongly against the bill.[4] Nelson Mandela said of the Trade Bill: "This is a matter over which we have serious reservations, this legislation. To us, it is not acceptable. But, nevertheless we accept each other's integrity and we are discussing the matter in that spirit" (Apple, 1998). South Africans feared that the trade bill would compromise the sovereignty of African governments by opening U.S. markets completely only to those countries that the United States judged to have sufficiently advanced political and economic reform. This could penalize governments that did not follow a path approved by the International Monetary Fund (IMF). Moreover, the singling out of half a dozen or more countries for special treatment would further exacerbate the already exceedingly difficult efforts to achieve some form of African unity. Finally, South African leaders worried that the trade bill would strengthen the power of the multinational corporations at the expense of the fledgling African economies (Apple, 1998). Their fears certainly do not seem outlandish given the record of the international banking agencies in financing African development. Not surprisingly, they do not appear comforted by the renewed emphasis placed by the head of the World Bank on working in partnership with "civil society."[5]

International Banking, Capitalist Development, the Asian Crisis, and Africa

In his speech to the 1998 Annual Meeting of the World Bank and the International Monetary Fund in Washington, D.C., World Bank Group President James D. Wolfensohn, reacting to the Asian financial crisis of 1998, argued that the financial turmoil could not be solved by stabilization measures alone. He announced that the World Bank was moving toward a new "total" approach to its development work, one that would move the Bank "beyond projects" and, "in partnership with governments and *civil society*, including the private sector, to rigorously pursue the social and structural priorities needed to champion sustainable development" (Wolfensohn 1999; emphasis added). He stressed that poverty reduction was the heart of the Bank's mission. He warned that "if we do not have the capacity to deal with social emergencies, if we do not have longer-term plans for solid institutions, if we do not have greater equity and social justice, there will be no political stability and without political stability no amount of money put together in financial packages will give us financial stability" (Wolfensohn, 1999). Wolfensohn added that the human crisis is not confined to East Asia or Russia. From sub-Saharan Africa, where 250 million people still live in abject poverty, to Bangladesh, "the human pain of poverty is all around us." Thus, Wolfensohn said, the World Bank is experimenting with a new development framework which, "in partnership with governments, parliaments, and civil society," is intended to move the Bank "beyond projects" and toward a more balanced pursuit of sustainable development (Wolfensohn, 1999). This is a far cry from IMF and U.S. treasury prescriptions of belt-tightening and higher interest rates.

One must wonder why it took so long to develop this laudable concern with direct aid to empower the poor, and what the World Bank means by "civil society." Nonetheless, two points are clear: (1) The World Bank recognizes that something direct and immediate must be done about the social costs of development, an improvement over the programs of the IMF and the U.S. government, which insist on a long-term policy of growth at any price, with benefits to the poor coming through a "trickle down" process; and (2) the Bank explicitly acknowledges that "capitalist miracles" may not be forthcoming, capitalist development may in fact be reversible, and masses of the population may suffer irremediable losses.

The 1998 Asian financial crisis memorably demonstrated that capitalist development was not uni-directional, that economic forces could dwarf all others, and that class still mattered. Not surprisingly, economic catastrophe produced turmoil and tore asunder the social contract. Precariously positioned politicians lost power. Although all elements in society declined, those with the least suffered the most. The most telling categories of social analysis were not those of "civil society" but of class. Ethnicity and race certainly counted as economic discontent threw up new, sometimes demagogic, leaders who often sought scapegoats in their quest for solutions. These currents of global capitalism swirled into Africa and brought to a halt a promising economic upturn. Africa's poor suffered disproportionately.

The World Bank's fiscal 1997 *Annual Report* was optimistic about 1998 and the future: "For the third year in a row, the average Sub-Saharan African country experienced positive per capita economic growth in 1997. This, combined with improved economic policies and increased political openness, has created greater opportunity for development" (1997). In 1997 the economy of the average African country grew 4.6 percent, slightly lower than in 1996 (4.8 percent). Some 37 countries registered positive per capita growth in 1997, and 21 of them grew at 5 percent and more. Exports expanded roughly twice as fast as gross domestic product in recent years, and lower fiscal deficits and inflation also boosted growth (World Bank, 1998b). Although in fiscal 1998 the Bank claimed to have "worked closely with African clients to support them in efforts to improve social services and infrastructure" and that "special attention was given to human development" (World Bank, 1998b), when the crunch came, it is hard to see how the poor benefited. The Bank did, however, provide a $100 million adjustment credit to Senegal to support power company privatization and petroleum sector liberalization. It also helped as many as 18 African countries privatize telecommunications by the end of 1998 (McNeil, 1998).

A subsequent study, *Global Economic Prospect 1998/99*, greatly dampened the optimism of only a few months previously (World Bank, 1998a). Dipak Dasgupta, the lead author of the report and principal economist at the World Bank, declared that: "The crisis has revealed just how little social protection there was for the poor in East Asia once the regional economy ran into serious trouble" (1998a: 111). In its most dramatic statement, the report states: "*Economic crisis hurt poor and rich. The poor, however, are much less able to respond to a non-diversifiable risk like a recession*" (emphasis added; see also Kristof 1998a)[6]. Capital markets are imperfect: "*Thus, crisis and recessions may result in irreversible damage to the poor: malnutrition or death from starvation (in extreme cases) and lower schooling levels*" (World Bank, 1998a: 111). There is no question that, as the report puts it: "Both poverty and inequality increased in Sub-Saharan Africa during most episodes of economic crises and attempted adjustment" (World Bank, 1998a: 111. See also Demery & Squire, 1996: 39–59). For international bankers and the bright, young technicians associated with them, the discovery that the poor are more at risk of health and life than the rich during times of great economic crisis, as well as encountering the lasting effects of malnutrition, seems to have come as a shock.

The virtually unchallenged U.S. government position is that unfettered capitalism generates untold wealth as well as greater freedom, new job opportunities, and democracy. Some, however, have described it as "no more than a slick reincarnation of the unfettered capitalism of the 19th century, using new technology to atomize societies, isolate the poor and advance a new ideology of exploitation upheld by an ever-wealthier, on-line global oligarchy" (Cohen, 1998).

The World Bank, a majority of the U.S. Congress, and the U.S. Treasury agree that if economic development is to succeed, if development is to be "firmly based and historically grounded," they must consult with civil society. The World Bank has declared that it would work with "governments and civil society." A "regular review" with governments and civil society was necessary to monitor progress on its structural agenda. President Wolfensohn attested that the World Bank was experimenting with a new development framework that "in partnership with governments, parliaments, and civil society" would move the institution "beyond projects" and toward a more balanced pursuit of sustainable development. What the World Bank means by civil society, however, may not provide solace to Africa's poor. A Senegalese example illuminates these issues in sometimes unexpected ways.

The Construction of Civil Society in Senegal: A Case Study—The Senegalese-Mauritanian Conflict

The United States Agency for International Development (USAID) provided the financing and technical assistance to construct a series of dams on the Senegal River, the natural boundary between Senegal and Mauritania. Irrigation of the river's floodlands added enormous value to previously marginal areas that had been suitable only for occasional sparse grazing.[7] Bitter conflict grew rapidly between landlords and the landless, pastoralists and agrarians, Senegalese and Mauritanians. Suddenly, nomads who had for generations taken their flocks wherever they could find fodder without any eye to invisible borders came up against the modern state in the form of soldiers with AK-47s.

Maurs had lived in Senegal for generations. In a country of some 8 million people, the Maurs were a highly visible, tiny minority because they provided most of 10,000–30,000 small retail outlets that provisioned most of the country. The "boutiques" of the Maurs, ubiquitous in every neighborhood, generally consisted of unpainted wooden stalls with tin roofs that occupied a few square meters. The Maurs lived in their shops. They sold rice and oil, cigarettes by the piece, and basic daily necessities. They gave credit and charged interest, worked long hours and were always available, and kept to themselves and intra-married. They provided essential services to their neighborhoods. In many basic ways, they functioned like the Asians in East Africa, the Lebanese in parts of West Africa, and the Jews in Eastern Europe. Like others who were absolutely vital to their communities, they were deeply hated.

When in April 1989 Mauritanian soldiers killed several Senegalese nomads on the border, all hell broke loose. Rumors about the killing of Maurs in Senegal and of Senegalese in Mauritania traveled at unbelievable speed. Mobs went on the rampage in both countries. Tales of "white Maurs" sending their black "slaves" to kill black Senegalese particularly infuriated Senegalese nationals.[8] In Senegal, mobs rose in fury to attack and kill Maurs. Tens of thousands of Maurs fled their homes. Maurs who had lived all of their lives in Senegal had to flee to Mauritania. The Senegalese government provided belated protection. They put the Maurs into secured camps, then expedited their transition to Mauritania ("Senegal-Mauritanie," 1989; "Les Actes Infamants," 1989; "De La Republique Islamique," 1989; "Et Quoi Demaine?" 1989; French, 1996). Senegalese from a wide social spectrum expressed their astonishment at how "the Senegalese" had behaved. These Senegalese could not understand or get over the violence. They expressed their bewilderment—and, especially persons of some status, their fear. If such boiling rage could lurk so undetected under a surface calm, who was safe?

This was not the end of the story. The mob consisted in the main of unemployed youth. The official unemployment rate in Senegal ran close to 20 percent; the real rate in some neighborhoods must have been 50 percent or even higher; nobody really knew. The government had succumbed to severe pressure from the World Bank, the IMF, and the United States to cut back on state programs and expenditures, particularly state employment. Under what had become President Diouf's byline, *"Moins d'etat, mieux d'etat,"* his administration drastically cut back the number of government employees and announced even more severe cuts to come. With the double pressure of rising prices for basic needs and declining prices for Senegal's chief export, peanuts, life had become increasingly burdensome and even unbearable.

All that was needed was a spark, and the shots fired in Mauritania provided it. However, the trail of powder did not stop at Senegal's borders; it clearly led overseas. Everything in Senegal, from the price of peanuts and fertilizer, rice and cloth, to the number of people on the state's payroll, was in large measure determined, indirectly and ever more frequently directly, by the forces of international capitalism. These were not abstract forces. Like Banquo's ghost, they had a name; but they were not ethereal.

The government's response to the riots illuminated the nature both of civil society and of state-building and confirmed that no sharp distinction exists between state and society. It illustrated a process that the French decades ago called the "encadrement" of the population and that U.S. social scientists have more recently labeled "embeddedness" (Evans, 1995). It demonstrated the heavy weight of capitalism on political as well as economic advancement in Africa and provided insight into the repressive as well as the progressive nature of parliamentary-style democracy. The Senegalese state did not merely restrain the rioters, although, using its French-trained and -equipped military and police forces, it did do that. It marshaled all the forces at its command to co-opt the rioters, seeking to make them into entrepreneurs. Government officials adopted a policy of placing the "Senegalese" into the positions of the Mauritanians. They aspired to make them into small businesspeople by incorporating them into the proper structures. The rioters were to be "encadred," embedded into a framework for development.

At first, the government's plans were greeted with a great deal of skepticism and even derision. The "Senegalese," the Senegalese said, would not work hard like the Maurs. They would not expend the necessary hundreds of hours a month, live in such modest quarters, and have the discipline to save and to sacrifice on the one hand and refrain from giving away their earnings to relatives and marabouts on the other hand. Nevertheless, the government decided to make an all-out effort. It set up a special office in the administration to oversee the project, calling on experts in private enterprise for advice. It drew on both the formal and informal sectors. Higher education participated through special business programs, including a special master's degree. The banks provided financing; international corporations provided links to overseas goods and markets; USAID and the French aid agencies gave grants and special training (see, e.g., Zarour, 1989; McKenzie, 1989). The world beamed in on this effort, and it paid off. The threatened vacuum in the distribution system of vital goods left by the exiled Maurs did not materialize. Senegalese jumped in and quickly took their place. These newly "socially mobilized" members of civil society entered the state structure as they became politically relevant ("Commerce de Detail," 1989).

Pogroms, "Restructuration," and Civil Society

French planners had for long contended that the major difficulty of capitalist development in Senegal was the lack of "encadrement" (structures for development, from the French *cadre*, framework). From an African and Senegalese nationalist perspective, however, the major problem of structuration was that although the economy was very organized, the arrangements that were in place were inhospitable to indigenous capitalist growth. Those institutions were designed to prevent industrialization and to guarantee, to put the matter crudely, that the French would have enough oil in which to fry their *pommes frites*. On the one hand, the organization of *la traite* (the peanut trade) provided subsidized prices for peanuts that were above the world market price. On the other hand, from the time of the first establishment of the great colonial commercial companies, Senegalese farmers became ensnared in a vicious debt trap. The farmers had to perpetually borrow at outrageously high rates of interest on the next year's harvest to pay for the seed, tools, and fertilizer necessary for the current year's food and production. For almost all of Senegal's farmers, the accumulation of capital was virtually impossible. Little wonder that Senegal's agriculture was not amenable to innovation, diversification, or very rapid growth. The same French companies that bought Senegalese farmers' peanuts and then exported them to France with very little processing or manufacturing also sold the farmers everything from soap to sewing machines to bicycles. The companies imported their manufactured goods from abroad, especially from France. To engage in manufacturing in Senegal was not only not necessary but contrary to their interest as established international merchants. Under colonialism, therefore, the French established the basic structures of the import-export trade. Independent Senegalese governments ratified these structures and they have endured almost down to the present. These are the roots of the difficulties of indigenous capitalist development (Markovitz, 1969/1970, 1976: 1–18).

The informal sector, popular academic images notwithstanding, has never existed completely separate from the formal sector (Desoto, 1989). Ultimately, the formal sector is the source of all types of goods and products, particularly imported goods including foodstuffs, but more obviously manufactured goods from televisions to word processors. The informal sector ultimately relies on the formal sector for currency and banking—not necessarily the smallest traders, but the *operateurs* at the top of the pyramids of exchange or at the pivotal points of trading and distribution networks. The informal network is, of course, far from informal in the sense of being casual or disorganized. It is organized into chains of production and distribution. The movement of large amounts of credit and of cash ultimately requires using the resources of "establishment" institutions, including banks, the agencies of communication and transportation—including the mails, the telephone and telex, roads, ships, and airplanes—and other government services. Here again are functional relations that clearly manifest that state and civil society are interrelated.

Businesspeople in the informal sector, however, maintain as low a profile as possible to prevent the capture of their resources and organization by unfriendly interests. At the least, they seek to suffer as little damage as possible from the predators that threaten to engulf them. In the communities of rural

Senegal, in the villages and small towns, even in the "native quarters" of large cities such as Dakar, the streets are not paved; the children do not go to school; and electricity, running water, and drainage do not enter the houses of most of the people. No wonder most of these "citizens" see the police, the inspectors, and the tax collectors as parasitic visitors from another world, one with which they are nevertheless inextricably interconnected.

In 1989, when confronted by the looming crisis of the pogroms, the government turned easily to leading elements in the informal sector. Lamine Diagne, for example, was one of the keys to the Senegalese governments' solution of the crisis. When during the course of doing research on Senegalese entrepreneurs[9] I asked a well-placed Senegalese friend if I could interview the most important Senegalese customers of one of the largest banks in Senegal, I ended up at a two-story cement block building the size of a double storefront in the center of the Medina. Lamine Diagne lived in his office behind the store. He slept on a ragged mattress and had no refrigerator, television, or air conditioner. He had not been to college. Mr. Diagne was one of the largest wholesalers in Senegal. His network of *demi-grossists* covered the country. Maurs had been among his most important customers. He sold to them, as to everybody else, on credit. When I asked if he had been much affected by the anti-Mauritanian demonstrations and looting, he showed me the signed chits of "his" Maurs detailing losses of tens of millions of francophone francs. What would he do? "Continue." This was what business was all about. He was confident that business would continue and that he would recover his losses.

Lamine Diagne advised the government about the creation of the *magasins Temoins* (modest-sized, all purpose general stores). The government intended that these more substantial enterprises would take the place of the more numerous but less provident stalls of the Maurs. Lamine Diagne was willing to incorporate "Senegalese" into his circuits. He would "train" them (although "train" was not a word in his vocabulary). He had no doubt that Senegalese could and would quickly take the place of the Maurs and that the country would suffer no problems of distribution or loss of services. A year later his prediction turned out to be completely accurate.

Linking State and Civil Society:
The Magasins Temoins *and Senegalese Entrepreneurs*

In 1990 the then-head of the *magasins Temoins*, Aboubacar Fall, who was also a *chef de cabinet* of the Ministry of Commerce, talked about the origins of the program, about why it was absolutely essential, and about how the conflict with the Maurs had stimulated its success:

The magasins Témoins is a very simple operation that was designed to place young Senegalese who had acquired the mastery of a Western language, the capacity to have their own business. Senegal is one of the rare countries in Africa where the aggregate of commerce was dominated by three ethnic groups until 1989: the French controlled all of industry and big business such as supermarkets and other things; the Lebanese who, historically speaking were the auxiliaries of the French who brought them here during colonization and who occupied the position of intermediaries between the industrialists, the big businessmen, and who were also large importers. The third group was the Mauritanians. After the events of the last year, they all left. We said that if we don't take the lead, we must begin to aid the Senegalese to become at least a factor in the commercial circuits because the Senegalese would represent less than five to ten percent of the Senegalese commercial networks. We would have been the only country to be like that.[10]

The *magasins Temoins*, therefore, according to Mr. Fall, was a program in the national interest, something that the country needed. With the proper work ethic and the right attitudes, these stores could become very successful. As the head of this government-sponsored program, Fall chose the *operateurs*. What were his criteria? Certainly nothing political. He could not use political favoritism, because then the stores would fail, and he would be responsible. What he looked for were indications of responsibility and aggressiveness. He reported, for example, that he inquired very carefully into a candidate's family situation because, he said, the larger the family, the greater the chances were of someone becoming sick and of other tragedies, and why should he multiply his risks?

These rationalizing, profit-seeking attitudes and behaviors, characteristic of government employees such as Aboubacar Fall and of a small but growing number of merchants such as the new owners of the *magasins Temoins*, were also evident at the highest levels of Senegalese corporate life. We would expect to find an ease of movement between persons in top positions in government, the administration, and business in as small a country as Senegal, with its limited resources and great scarcity. The hierarchical structure of Senegal's traditional society and religious organization further promotes those tendencies. Reinforcing informal networks of "friends," frequently of similar age, cut across the business-government divide.

When the head of IBM Senegal was loaned to the government to oversee a special program to aid unemployment, it was simply, as in the United States, an act of generous good citizenship. When pro-business, university-educated Senegalese in both the private and public sectors created associations, clubs, or other types of formal organizations to develop a network of contacts in key government policy-making positions, administration executive positions, and entrepreneurial corporate positions, this seemed like a natural development given the character of the times. They sought to consolidate and to expand their enterprises, to have access to special information, and to be within reach of decisionmakers. They intended to invest and to take advantage of special opportunities both as individuals and as a corporation. Networks such as these also aided in the incorporation of civil society into the state and the solving of the Senegalese-Mauritanian crisis.

Networking and the New, Pro-Business Ideology

Nothing more dramatically illustrates the change in the dominant ideology in Senegal from various forms of socialism to the clear hegemony of capitalist values than the thinking of university students. Once wholly disdainful of business, students now compete earnestly to gain their degrees in business administration. Having once dreamt of attaining lifelong positions in the administration, students now look for their heroes in the J. R. Ewings of *Dallas*. At the time of the Senegalese-Mauritanian conflict, these new aspirations found a payoff in new networks of stores and small business enterprises such as *boulangeries* bringing together university graduates in formidable organizations that took the place of the Maurs and furthered the government's pursuit of free enterprise.

These events, networks, and ideologies strengthened the construction of civil society and thickened the ties with the state. As Mr. Diouf, a university advanced degree holder who became head of one association of small businessmen, told me:

> In the past, most students wanted to become *fonctionnaires* when one wished to be respected.... One had to be in the administration in order to be in the swing of things, to be seen as doing well. And so, there was the myth of "the administration" that had been inculcated in us. Business was for the others, for the Mauritanians, the Libano-Syrians. They had a tradition of doing business but we didn't. One had to go to school and then one entered the Administration. Now, the administration has had its problems in paying the *fonctionnaires*. Now the youth see their future as becoming part of the economic network. We have become *opérateurs économiques*, though we hadn't studied for it.[11]

Mr. Diouf linked these changing attitudes among "the Senegalese" toward business with the Mauritanian pogroms. He clarified how changing mind-sets and new opportunities merged: "After the Mauritanian affair [*l'évène-ment de la Mauritanie*], all the Mauritanians had been repatriated and there was a sector which was empty. Therefore, it was suddenly necessary, to immediately immerse oneself into commerce."[12]

Mr. Diouf went on to say that

> These University graduates who have gone into business have each created their own corporations. However, instead of each of these corporations going off to labor in their own corner, everybody has awakened to the need to become organized. So all of these companies, 30, 40 or 50 companies must work together because there are problems that we must face together, and we have to wake up to the fact that we have these problems. For example, the raw materials are expensive. Must we always continue to buy from our existing providers or can we make use of our own power? Moreover, it is at this level that we can get together to go to the United States. And actually, at the present moment, we are awaiting a container from Oakland, because we have been to Oakland, to the Fleischman yeast factory where we met the head of the business there and immediately entered into contracts with them. And so, at the present moment, we are expecting a container of yeast from Fleischman which is coming from the United States. Therefore, we no longer have to buy from the vendor here who sells us very expensive yeast. So, we try to manage our production problems ourselves. Everything that enters into the making of bread, we must try as far as possible to import, and then to sell to our members, and then plow back the profits into our organization. And so that is the way that it is with the organization of *maîtrisards boulanger* which has organized all of the *maîtrisards* who are in the bakery business.[13]

Particularly interesting are Mr. Diouf's comments about the international factors that go into a loaf of bread in Senegal. USAID treated members of this bakers' association to a trip to the United States that seems to have paid off, at least for the Fleischman Corporation.

Incorporating these newly aspirant bourgeois into administrative and economic structures paid off in a number of ways. Above all, it was cheap. These originally dissident social members did not add to the public payroll. They were helped to become competitors with great expectations but no guarantees. The state thus obtained maximum leverage for the dollars (or francs) that it did invest. If these new "friends" of the government—or of the dominant political party that clearly called the tune—were to fail, then it was the fault of the "entrepreneurs" themselves, of, as they say in Senegal, the *operateurs*. They had been given the opportunity. They could not come back and blame the government. This was a good deal better than the old days when the largesse that the government gave out not only was expensive but constantly had to be renewed. The virtues of classic capitalism were *en plein operation.*

Everyone involved also got a shot of superpatriotism and nationalism. They could all thank their lucky stars that they were Senegalese—unlike the Maurs, most of whom had never seen Mauritania. Unlike the Maurs, they were privileged to participate in elections. Out of this crisis there emerged, somewhat paradoxically, a reinforced state and civil society.

Conclusion: Cruel Democracy and Cruel Capitalism

Civil society, like democracy, capitalism, and pluralism, is not an unmixed blessing. This chapter has argued that state and civil society are not precariously balanced but rather intertwine. It has pointed to the confusion that arises from the three different versions—liberal, radical, and conservative—of the concept of civil society and maintained that although even the radical conceptions of civil society might be utopian, the failure to distinguish among them creates special difficulties because of the unexpected liberal-establishment uses of civil society, frequently as an ideology in defense of capitalist interests. Establishment liberals think civil society can be constructed—and they are the ones to do it—in such a way as to foster global capitalist development; create conditions for free access to all markets for global corporations; and aid the development of indigenous entrepreneurs through low taxes for corporations, limited social programs, minimum government employment, no subsidies for food or lodging, cheap education, paltry health expenditures, mean wages, and generous grants for business efforts.

The World Bank programs and the East Asian crisis illustrate that unrestricted capitalism does not necessarily benefit African development, either in the short or long run, a contention that today runs against the conventional wisdom. The African trade act sets forth the supporting policies and mechanism for the strengthened civil society that would bolster unfettered capitalist development. Most people in the "less-industrialized countries" do not benefit, have not benefited, and will not benefit in their lifetimes or in the lifetimes of their children from capitalist expansion. A small portion of the population, the organizational bourgeoisie, has accrued the advantages. Trickle down benefits to middle-class elements have been ephemeral and easily diminished. Rampant capitalism has pushed people into cities where they are unable to earn their daily bread; it has eventuated in episodic famines as well as less-visible but more invidious daily privations. Some of us experienced the shock of the discovery of hunger in "the other America" in the 1960s. What must it be like in other parts of the world at a cruder stage of development?

What right do we have to be surprised at the "depraved" poverty of those suffering from an out-of-control capitalism?

What happened in Senegal was not simply the creation of new businesspeople who are or who remain "autonomous," succeeding or failing on their own merits. Their autonomy is contained within an international and national framework that both supports and limits the liberty of interests in civil society. This "autonomy" is useful because it is cheap, turns responsibility inward, places blame for failure and injustices on individuals and the individual and not on the system, and, as technology becomes more complex, decentralizes decision making and increases productivity.

In Nazi Germany, under conditions of war and economic depression, with a different set of establishment political and ideological objectives, the government sought to deny independence to all organizations and to incorporate them into the Nazi movement. Civil society did not have to "cave in" to this ruling class; for the most part, it was not a question of compulsion. Many of the major civil society interests willingly and enthusiastically supported the goals of the regime, including genocidal programs. These interests included all the major professional associations of lawyers, physicians, and engineers, as well as most religious dominations. Some claim that "civil society" rallied and strengthened in Germany after the war because of disastrous conditions, and that the disaster was not the Nazi regime but rather the defeat in war and the Allied occupation. However, I contend that in Germany, like elsewhere, it is not disaster that gives rise to an independent civil society. Every society contains a plethora of interests of every possible concern. This was the basis of hope for radical opponents of establishment society such as Gramsci, who had faith that opposition to repressive institutions might one day succeed. This is the hope today of many humanists and radical critics. The question, however, is which elements in civil society will succeed and under what conditions. This chapter gives credit to establishment-liberals, the World Bank, and the authors of the Africa Trade and Development Act for understanding this basic fact better than some well-intentioned advocates of social change.

A critical but sympathetic reader of this chapter has asked: "Aside from the fact that it originated in a pogrom, what do you think of the consequences of the Senegalese developments that you analyze? Isn't it a good thing that Senegalese students are turning from wanting to be bureaucrats to wanting to be businessmen? Isn't it a good thing that more Senegalese are no longer mystified by low-level commerce? Isn't it better that university students turn to baking bread than that they be unemployed regurgitaters of half-baked semiotic theories? Are you claiming that the result—civil society—is okay, but that the means—pogroms—were bad?" These are good and fair questions. Do the answers depend only on one's perspective? Maurs are not happy.

Not all Senegalese are pleased, either. Opportunists exist everywhere. Ordinary people also "merely" take advantage of what is thrown their way. However, it is important to note that many Senegalese defended Maurs. They did so during the heat of the pogroms; they continue to do so today. The case study spells out how pogroms occurred; how specific government, social, and international agents, banks, the UN, NGOs, international lending agencies, and educational institutions all participated.

Skeptics have doubted that violent explosions fueled by illiterate, unemployed *lumpen* can add to the construction of democracy, or even that disorganized have-nots are part of civil society. Establishment civil society theorists like Larry Diamond would certainly deny their legitimacy. "Legitimacy," however, is not the issue. What cannot be denied is the fact of their existence. Is it possible that pogroms may contribute to the growth of civil society in African states as a result of the economic exclusion of alien minorities? We may not like this prospect any more than we would like to admit that the expulsion of German Jews might well have facilitated the consolidation of civil society in Nazi Germany. However, the answer in both cases is clearly yes. Were these terrible developments in any sense "necessary" or "inevitable?" No! Did they happen? Unfortunately, yes.

This chapter in its pursuit of the meaning of civil society has pointed to a cruel democracy[14] as well as to a cruel capitalism, both considerably less desirable than the establishment civil society proponents would have us believe. The surprising developments in Senegal produced a result that strengthened civil society. I do not claim that that was a "good" thing; I claim that it was a bothersome fact. To think otherwise is to believe in fairytales. This should really come as no surprise.[15] Dominant classes have always included in their arsenal of weapons race and scapegoats to sell out minorities in the interests of protecting their own political power. In the process, states and nations develop and mature. American mythology tells us that the "blood of patriots watered the tree of liberty," but a lot of innocent bodies have cemented the foundations of democracy. The construction of civil society has been part of this process.

6

Beyond the State and Civil Society

Labor Movements and Economic Adjustment in African Transitions— South Africa and Nigeria Compared

FRANCO BARCHIESI
University of the Witwatersrand

Neoliberal Adjustment as a Challenge for African Labor in Transition

This chapter assesses and analyzes organized labor's adaptation and resistance in democratic transitions under policies of free market economic adjustment in the cases of Nigeria and South Africa. Within the generally problematic nature of relationships between African democratization and neoliberalism, South Africa and Nigeria can be seen as two opposites of a continuum. In the former case the democratic electoral transition was successful, labor played a decisive role in popular mobilization, and its influence is now increasingly institutionalized in the political system and in structures of social mediation. In Nigeria, on the other hand, a long-standing tradition of military rule, aborted democratic transitions, and the uncertainty surrounding the current shift to multi-party democracy have seen labor's role targeted by state repression or co-optation. Here an authoritarian political system was encouraged by the convergence of prescriptions from the International Monetary Fund (IMF) and World Bank with strategies for the self-reproduction of domestic elites. The usefulness of a comparative study of these two cases resides precisely in its combination of diversity of trajectories and emerging common problems.

145

Processes of political transition in Africa during the 1990s have raised rich and diversified intellectual debates on the role and articulation of "civil society" in different trajectories of democratic politics. At the same time, the role of organized labor is related by these debates to opportunities and constraints deriving, respectively, from relations with other sociopolitical actors and from structural adjustment programs (SAPs) sponsored by international financial institutions as vehicles of a rising neoliberal hegemony in economic policy making and development discourse. "Labor" has emerged in this scenario as a complex and stratified subject, affected by multiple determinants of organization and collective identity, whose impacts on specific aspects of transition politics are responsible for diverse and even contradictory outcomes. Conversely, the various levels that constitute labor as a sociopolitical actor are influenced in different ways by SAPs and related policies, which not only prove to be limiting and repressive factors but also provide routes for new approaches to organization and alliances. In particular, this chapter examines the impact of structural adjustment on labor taken as a set of formal organizations and as a social movement capable of relating with broader processes of identity construction and social mobilization.

The peculiarities of the processes of class formation in Africa and the political potential of its formally employed waged population (Freund, 1988) indicate recurrent patterns of weak unionization, attempts at co-optation by the powers of the day, and, generally, a comparatively limited numerical weight of the wage-employed workforce. However, Africa's location in global markets and policies of structural adjustment cannot be dealt with as a coherent whole presided over by the undifferentiated heading of "neoliberalism." Rather, a variety of neoliberalisms can be traced in Africa that provide a much more useful framework of analysis for challenges facing labor movements. Finally, the impact of SA programs on labor is characterized by the relative importance of labor movements and organizations vis-à-vis other sectors of the "civil society" in various countries during phases of transition and cannot be assumed to be static and ahistorical. From one perspective, labor's strength modifies approaches and strategies adopted by international institutions and their national sponsors, thus contributing to the differentiation, and the contradictions, internal to neoliberalism. However, from the other side, neoliberal policies themselves recursively modify the nature of "civil society" and its potential for resistance. Dynamics of popular radicalization are mediated by factors not reducible to the impact of SAPs. Studies of African labor have emphasized the participation of workers in oppositional progressive and/or nationalist alliances, the leverage this provided for labor's influence in transition policies, the nature of party systems and their inclusion of working class interests, and the relationships between organized labor and other associational forms (ethnic, regional, religious).

Critical analyses of economic adjustment have stressed how worsening social and economic conditions due to SAPs in many African countries are responsible, to a large extent, for processes of radicalization of the urban working class (Walton & Seddon, 1994). This radicalization is produced by curbs on spending in social services; public sector wage freezes and downsizing; the removal of subsidies for primary production, usually coupled with currency devaluations that shrink purchasing power; the liberalization of barriers to foreign competition, which leads to job losses in the private sector; the privatization of state assets with accompanying increases in the price of goods and services; and the promotion of primary or low value-added export, which encourages labor flexibility and compression of wage costs (Simon et al., 1995). Political democratization under a neoliberal ideological hegemony often identifies organized labor as a "special interest" adverse to economic efficiency. Therefore, market-oriented economic reforms require sacrifices and trade-offs to workers, with potential demobilizing consequences in terms of marginalization and even repression (Przeworski et al., 1995: 56–57). Conversely, political authoritarianism displays, even in the presence of formally democratic institutions, a high degree of functionality to the kind of economic liberalization advocated by SAPs. As a result, some analyses regard the struggle for democracy and the struggle against SAPs as complementary (Beckman, 1993). Finally, a satisfactory discussion of the relations between adjustment and democracy requires a conceptual clarification and a preliminary critical assessment of problems related to the notion of "transition."

African Transitions and "Transition Studies": Constraining the Space of Labor

The analysis of social actors in African democratic transitions has been influenced recently by paradigms heavily indebted to notions of democratization borrowed from the political sciences. *Democracy* assumes here the meaning of multilateral acceptance of formal frameworks and procedures to enable opposing political forces to compete in elections and to alternate in government. Important in this respect are the dissemination of beliefs and values conducive to democracy, the need for social compromises (Przeworski, 1991; Diamond, Linz & Lipset, 1995), and the preservation of a capitalist system and a free market economy (O'Donnell, Schmitter & Whitehead, 1986). The role of the "civil society" is codified as enforcing and scrutinizing state accountability, and the party system is charged with the incorporation of different interests and the emasculation of potentially anti-systemic forces. Labor is explicitly mentioned in this regard mainly to warn readers of the potentially disruptive outcomes of its "radicalism" and in praise of organizational pragmatism and attitudes to compromise (Valenzuela, 1989). These preoccupations are present in writers supporting "corporatist" solutions to the problems of transition. The containment of social conflict requires a system of interest intermediation around institutionalized multilateral negotiations involving state, capital, and labor (Lehmbruch, 1979). As a corollary, organized labor's "visible" role in sociopolitical processes is identified almost exclusively with trade union organizations as part of institutionalized systems of tripartite bargaining and regulation (Crouch, 1979). This scheme often amounts to a substantial neglect of labor's relevance in broader social dynamics of opposition (Collier & Mahoney, 1997). The same authors also seem to maintain that private capital is fundamentally committed to democracy, which is made coincident with the free market as an embodiment of economic rationality.

The African context departs significantly from conventional views of the relationships between social and political aspects of democratization that confine labor movements to the role of purely institutionalized actors in transitional structures and arrangements. African labor responds to a social movement politics that articulates meanings of political change around much broader practices and demands about the satisfaction of basic needs, defense of human rights, social citizenship, employment protection, removal of abusive and discriminatory practices at the workplace level, and expansion of worker control at the point of production (Von Freyhold, 1987; Benjamin & Turner, 1992). The neglect of interactions of labor's dimensions as movement and as organization allows the political transition paradigm to downplay non-institutional dimensions and implications of labor's role in political change.

More recent scholarly developments have focused on labor not only as an institutional actor but also as a component of "civil society," as the articulation, through institutional and non-institutional channels, of interests and patterns of organized collective action. An optimist reading views an "awakening" of civil society as a factor conducive to democratization (Bratton, 1989; Riley & Parfitt, 1994: 167–170). These views find resonance in the neoliberal emphasis on the expansion of civil society as reduction of state intervention and of the alleged "privileges" of urban-based working-class "elites" (World Bank, 1989). At the same time, they relativize the importance of labor inside an undifferentiated set of community-based associations, informal networks, and ethnic or religious groups.

A more critical view emphasizes how relations between civil society and democracy are mediated by power, conflict, and resistance and affected by continuous state intervention in societal dynamics (Fatton, 1995). Even a formally democratic and pluralist state can retain options for repression and manipulation (Ekeh, 1992), which are paradoxically exercised precisely on the most activist and organizationally articulated structures (such as unions, civic groups, and student groups). Informal resistance and solidarity by subordinate, not formally associated groups could hardly be grasped by "optimist" definitions of "civil society" if the formal democratization of the state is not their main priority (Lemarchand, 1992). Moreover, behind the formal adherence to democratic motifs often lie informal patterns of subordination linked to personalization of politics, class, ethnicity, religion, gender, and language. Finally, formal associations often marginalize large sections of society, such as the rural poor (Holmquist, Weaver & Ford, 1994). Far from expressing a distance from the state, overt or covert access to state power is still a valuable asset for competing social groups, and the state potential for repression is not necessarily "weakened" by SAPs (Herbst, 1990). These limitations and ambiguities in the associations' political potential can significantly reduce their available options, and they "codify" the discourse of democracy around themes of probity and efficiency, neglecting issues of social transformation, justice, equality, and solidarity. Insofar as they reflect predominant political styles, these groups can also be regarded as vehicles for individual and group self-promotion.

Crucial issues in these debates concern the possibility for organizations of civil society to open up a "constitutionalized" democratic space inside the state, the democratic nature of such organizations, and their ability to represent demands for universal civil and political rights (Beckman, 1993). From labor's point of view, the question of the constitutionalization of a democratic space under neoliberalism is inseparable from defining political alliances able to have an impact on policy outcomes in the distribution of resources. "Constitutionalization" is an ambiguous concept: African states often addressed this question by recognizing an institutional space for labor through corporatism, monopoly unionism, or some degrees of consultation, even if this was not accompanied by real workers' power in defining wages, social security, and creating jobs (Hashim, 1994). The conjunction of structural adjustment with the absence of strong traditions of collective bargaining and social compacts greatly contributes to these contradictions. Moreover, deindustrialization, retrenchments, and the decentralization of wage bargaining hamper the development of unions' sociopolitical strategies at a national level (Simutanyi, 1996). In particular, corporatist arrangements to legitimize the representation of collective interests are undermined by the neoliberal restructuring of public spending and state intervention (Wood, 1992). Neoliberalism arguably creates those "new configurations of social relations" and "new conditions of rule" that Michael Hardt (1995: 34) identifies as responsible for the decline of a paradigm of civil society based on entrenched mechanisms and structures for representing interests. On the other hand, working-class identities are increasingly rearticulated along strategies of survival in front of a fragmentation of the labor market due to retrenchments, public sector downsizing, decentralization of production, subcontracting, informalization of work, and unequal access of men and women to waged occupations. These strategies imply new organizational relations across the mobile borders separating formal and informal labor, factory work and homework, the workplace and the household, and production and reproduction of social labor (Dalla Costa & Dalla Costa, 1993). The decline of civil society linked to neoliberalism faces labor movements in SAP-affected countries with a choice between state-led options for constitutionalization that are severely constrained and new networks of social cooperation and resistance against neoliberalism that are, at best, tentatively explored by pro-democracy social movements.

In Africa SAPs provide opportunities for alliances between labor and community organizations and movements (Kester & Sidibe', 1997), triggered by increasing prices in essential commodities, degradation of services, corruption, and enrichment of political elites. The role of the state as a major employer in most African countries further politicizes labor relations, and the dislocation of many waged workers into the informal sector, smuggling, and starvation on the land reinforce labor-community ties and support networks. This can also be an expression of unions' weakness on the economic front in their traditional role as defenders of workers' rights and interests. The crisis of state incorporation of the unions often revives preexisting traditions and methods of grassroots resistance. This may prop up a new demand for organizational accountability and legitimacy, but it also clashes in many countries (Ghana, Zambia, Nigeria, Zimbabwe) with the unions' exclusion from economic decision making, thus radicalizing cycles of protest-repression that delegitimize the authoritarian order (Raftopoulos, 1992).

Contrary to the conventional wisdom of the "transition theory," the weakness of the unions qua unions in SAP-affected Africa often militates against institutionalization and incorporation, whereas their links with social movements, based on dynamics that are often fluid, unpredictable, and difficult to institutionalize, reinforce their democratizing potential. In these cases struggles can easily cross the border between workplace and non-workplace issues or lead to a politicization of wage bargaining and industrial relations due to labor's alliance with other social subjects. However, the increased likelihood of intragroup and leadership rivalries; personalization of power; and ethnic, religious, language, or associational cleavages in alliances between unions and movements can make this scenario unstable. Localized alliances of worker and popular militancy can trigger labor mobilization far more effectively than the homogeneous spread of union organizing across regions and countries (Cohen, Gutkind & Copans, 1978). These observations confirm a conceptual distinction between labor as a social movement and as formal organizations that is the basis of the following cases.

The Nigerian Labor Movement, Militarized Economic Adjustment, and the Uncertainties of Transition

Class Politics Without Class?

The intervention of international financial institutions in the Nigerian debt crisis has contributed since the 1980s to the restructuring of state-society relations in the direction of an authoritarian rollback and containment of prodemocracy forces. In this scenario, Nigerian labor is unevenly affected at both the centralized and industry levels. The Nigerian post-independence state's hegemony has been historically undermined by hollow development plans, the frequent resort to violence to contain popular pressures, the inefficiency of institutions, political instability, massive wastefulness, and corruption (Ihonvbere & Shaw, 1988: 50). Modernization was implemented by sectional interests that, competing for scarce resources, found in the access to the state the most effective way to accumulate power and status. The state could then formalize a complex regulatory function in the political and economic sphere on the basis of patron-client relationships, which promoted the rise of a "political class" without visible links to class politics (Joseph, 1984; Ohiorhenuan, 1989).

The politicization of labor relations, in this scenario, depended on the social contradictions created by the central distributional role of the state in development projects. State support for internal accumulation substantially discouraged direct productive investment and contrasted with strategies to promote a domestic industrial bourgeoisie. This contrast was reinforced, rather than solved, by subsequent state attempts to indigenize local production (Biersteker, 1987). The limited nature of proletarianization in Nigeria, a widespread social exclusion, and the role of the authoritarian state as the repository of the development discourse and as the most important employer prevented a meaningful system of collective bargaining. This allowed worker resistance to politicize bargaining beyond the limited sphere of "industrial relations." Therefore, the labor movement's social and political leverage often addressed the economic weakness of labor organizations. Moreover, the absence of a Nigerian workers' party generally prevented labor political mobilization from taking the form of homogenous electoral participation (Cohen,

1974: 147–150), thus reinforcing the political potential of the union movement, while the construction of ethnicity as a vehicle to mobilize patronage networks gave political life a distinctively "ethno-clientelist" flavor.

The rise of the "political class" was a product of capitalist modernization and differentiation, and access to political power developed configurations of specific economic interests in competition with other class groups. Cross-ethnic and cross-regional alliances were occasionally formed to preserve the equilibrium of the system against working-class inter-ethnic mobilization, as was the case in the 1964 general strike (Diamond, 1983). The definition of class politics in Nigeria was clarified, after the militarization of political life following the 1966 coup, by the emergence of new elites in the climate of the 1970s post–civil war reconstruction and in the campaign for the "indigenization" of production. Compared to the traditional ones in the immediate post-independence period, such elites were less dependent on the land and more connected to the modernization of the economy and the political system under the aegis of state-led developmentalism (Graf, 1986: 109). The Nigerian class formation of the first two post-independence decades showed a meaningful urban working-class opposition to elite-sponsored developmental projects, even if the main actors of such opposition lacked a real unity (Momoh, 1996a). This seems to validate Akwetey's (1996) emphasis on the continuities of labor movements' resistance to explain anti-SAP protests in the 1980s. However, grassroots worker activism formed at the same time an uneasy relationship with the trajectory of Nigerian labor organizations.

Oil Boom, State-Led Development, and Shifting Labor Regimes

The limited extent of proletarianization in Nigeria and the continuing relevance of the state as a major employer weakened a union movement already heavily dependent on state sanction. Moreover, workers were made vulnerable to the ideological appeal of development, with its implications of containment of labor militancy. Finally, wages and working conditions set for the public sector usually provided the guidelines for the entire economy. Workers' demands to improve minimum standards could easily transcend into a direct confrontation with the state. The coincidence of these factors undermined the unions' role as institutions of social mediation and compromise. Moreover, unions were not allied to any strong nationalist party, and business, which competed for favor and patronage from all the main parties, usually regarded organized labor as an unnecessary interference (Otobo, 1992: 90). The ineffectiveness of the unions in this sphere led to fundamental grassroots diffidence toward union leadership, which added to the unions' distance from the political system.

Even if workers were loath to participate continuously in union affairs, they nonetheless expressed a highly self-conscious identity and a heightened political perception of industrial conflict (Cohen, 1974: 79–80, 141). The first post-independence period witnessed a gap between union organization and dynamics of identity and opposition in the workplace. As an indication of this gap, highly dispersed local industrial affiliates or non-affiliated "house unions" showed a great degree of independence and radicalism in relation to union centers themselves, especially in the most internationalized sectors of the economy and in "estates" owned by "expatriate" capitalists (Peace, 1979; Ihonvbere, 1992). Working-class identification was facilitated by the closeness of union officials to the rank and file in the same production process. In these enclaves, the most militant sections of the Nigerian workforce displayed a remarkable awareness of the links of workplace issues and problems in their residential locations. However, these localized experiences proved to be a weak source of resistance when, after a civil war and faced with spiraling inflation, the government intervened directly to restrict the right to strike (Decree 53 of 1970) and to force the house unions' unification and incorporation inside new industrial unions (Peace, 1979: 124–126).

At the same time, the developmental effort following the 1970s "oil boom" and the subsequent phase of industrialization made industrial peace an imperative for the state. Tumultuous transformations were at the heart of such dynamics. The emerging elites enriched by the oil boom combined old methods of self-promotion, such as corruption associated with the release of import licenses and over-priced sale of goods by the "marketing boards," with their new status of intermediaries of foreign investment flows (Obi, 1997). The urban working class, engulfed by waves of migrants expelled from the countryside, was hit by the impoverishment caused by inflation, the decline of living standards, the degradation of social services, and the abuses of the "political class" (Otobo, 1992: 82–83; Okolie, 1995). These factors led to rising resentment that culminated in episodes such as the 1971–1972 cost-of-living riots. Departing from its previous approach favorable to union fragmentation and emasculation, the government became more orientated toward institutionalizing labor organizations (Fashoyin, 1980: 97–102), which were restructured to allow for some industry-wide collective bargaining (Etukudo, 1977: 110) in what the regime named "guided democracy." In the process, the National Labor Congress (NLC) was reconstituted in 1978 as the only recognized central labor organization after three years of state repression against the most radical sectors in its ranks following the dissolution of the just-founded NLC in 1975 (Otobo, 1992: 94–95). The new union federation was charged with defending the "true" interests of the workers as defined by the state, which reserved to itself the right to write the unions' constitutions. The 1978 "labor pact" introduced state-backed union funding in exchange for the new unitary union body's role in enforcing wage restraint and industrial discipline.

The government could use this framework of state-led "paternalist corporatism" (Andrae & Beckman, 1998: 272) to contain anti-SAP working-class protests during the 1980s. However, even if this increased the degree of control by state bureaucrats and technicians over the central union body, it was not sufficient to turn local and industry-based unions into mere tools to be used against militant pressures from below. The unfulfilled promises of development and the decay of independent sources for rural subsistence combined with state intervention in local unions' affairs to trigger worker militancy and the politicization of the workplace that already existed in the pre-SAP decade. At the same time, corporatism "Nigerian-style" proved to be in contradiction to the government's stated aims. It tried to promote the unions as agents of industrial stabilization and modernization, but in so doing it also provided workers' self-organized activism with new avenues for resistance, which were then channeled to demand collective bargaining provisions, standard working conditions, and workplace legality. However, as Gunilla Andrae and Bjorn Beckman (1998) convincingly argue, only where such processes of self-organization from below were already advanced (such as in some private sectors like the textile industry) were the unions able to exploit the contradictions of the institutional framework and to resist the state's adoption of a more repressive attitude. In other cases (for example the public sector), where the state could more easily contain grassroots activism, the unions' militant potential was substantially disrupted.

When structural adjustment came to Nigeria, many established unions were already facing the alternative of being radicalized by their own grassroots or being isolated and incorporated into the structures of the state. The attempt to demobilize worker militancy was crucial to implement SAPs in Nigeria in the 1980s. Repression of labor provided the necessary continuity for the shift in economic orientation from "indigenized" developmentalism to neoliberalism. On this basis, the regime could define the policies imposed by the IMF and the World Bank as technical and non-ideological matters, excluded from the unions' agendas. Opposition to SAPs inside the NLC was then easily labeled as contrary to the "true" interests of the workers. As a result, in response to heightened worker resistance to IMF-inspired measures, the regime could resort to unprecedented levels of repression. This targeted united struggles by workers, students, and women engaged in micro- and macro-levels of confrontation and in strategies for survival throughout the social body. The role of the state in restructuring the internal class composition through SAPs became a terrain of renewed contestation (Otobo, 1992: 119).

Militarized Economic Adjustment and the Uncertainties of Political Transition

The embrace of structural adjustment by the Nigerian state during the 1980s was not linear and uncontroversial (Okome, 1997). The Shagari civilian administration's (1979–1983) neoliberal Economic Stabilization Act of 1982 maintained a nominal commitment to the public ownership of social services. At the same time, the exhaustion of the oil boom had left in its wake spiraling inflation, huge debt, and a balance-of-payment crisis, and the widespread corruption contributed to the government's legitimation crisis (Othman, 1984). The military regime of General Babangida came eventually to adhere entirely to IMF prescriptions in 1986. General Buhari's administration (1983–1985), which had ousted Shagari with a coup, had in fact resisted the devaluation of the naira (the national currency), the removal of state oil price subsidies, and a widespread privatization. A crisis in relations with the IMF followed, even though Buhari accepted other substantial points of the IMF program, such as the reduction in public expenditure and employment and wage cuts enforced using the unilateral determination of industrial wages by the local governments, the so-called Imo formula (Otobo, 1992: 86–87). In 1986 Babangida, who had ousted Buhari with a further coup, chose a SAP that fully aligned the country with the IMF agenda in the name of the "national economic emergency" as a conscious point of departure from previous regimes. As a consequence, currency devaluation, large-scale privatization, and the reduction of the oil subsidy were fully endorsed (Olukoshi, 1989; Anunobi, 1992: 243–270; Adejumobi, 1995; Osaghae, 1998: 196–207). On the other hand, the Emergency Powers Decree 22 of 1985 marked a significant discontinuity from earlier attempts to institutionalize forms of corporatist decision making by placing in the president's hands full powers to implement the SAP and to "correct distortions in the nation's economy" (Obi, 1997: 30). Manufacturing was undercut by the consequences of economic austerity, the deterioration of the terms of trade, and currency breakdown. Restructuring and retrenchments heavily affected the industrial working class (Bangura, 1987). Many workers were plunged into the pool of informal labor and undetected occupations. Although this reinforced the links between working-class and impoverished rural and urban communities, it also confined these relations to mere survival strategies through self-exploitation in multiple low-income occupations. At the same time, ethnic and religious networks often provided more stable links of solidarity than the unions, which were also undermined by familial, ethnic, and regional bonds, and by work avoidance and informal strategies of resistance and survival at the workplace level (Mustapha, 1991; Oloyede, 1992). The unions' stalemate translated a more general crisis of the civil society into a decline, brought about by neoliberalism, of identities that were previously only precariously constitutionalized.

The crisis of civil society did not imply a disappearance of resistance. Even if prospects for a state-led institutionalization and "constitutionalization" of waged labor were deteriorating, the control of the working class by the authoritarian regime was far from being stable. Although the decentralization of survival strategies in the informal economy and multiple occupations weakened the formal union organizations, it also diminished the amount of time devoted by workers to their jobs, favoring their escape from wage labor (Mustapha, 1991). The worsening prospects for the productivity pacts and worker cooperation that were required by the employers entered a contradiction with authoritarianism and neoliberalism. Relations between government and unions were then strained as a result of resurgent worker struggles, spurred on by anti-SAP riots. In 1988 the NLC was temporarily banned to isolate labor organizations from the widespread popular protest. The limited corporatist arrangement that followed the 1975–1978 "restructuring" of the unions was then replaced by directly exclusionary and repressive regulation linked to market liberalization (Otobo, 1992: 92–123; Fashoyin, 1990).

The SAP, as a project to discipline the working class through repression and precariousness and to manage the contradictions in the class composition created by industrial modernization, did not prevent the politicization of worker resistance. Workers' survival strategies in the informal sector met the plight of the urban poor facing deteriorating living standards and the breakdown of social services. These grievances combined with those of workers who had to sustain relatives in the depleted rural areas (Nnoli, 1993). As a result, worker opposition to SAP became a catalyst to reject an authoritarian and corrupt regime and oppose Babangida's goal of using SAP to usher in a political transition based on the recomposition of elites around the project of economic liberalization (Momoh, 1996b). Furthermore, as in the 1970s, the factories became the foci of new forms of social antagonism, which ultimately had important effects on the radicalization of industrial unions. On the other hand, the combined impacts of neoliberalism and social dislocation on workplaces and communities did not help to translate the new sense of mass militancy into clearly discernible alternative democratic programs. Workers displayed their massive political potential mainly in everyday demands for wages and working conditions, which Jimi Adesina (1992) calls "militant economism." The networks of informal social cooperation, knowledge, and resistance formed in this way are not easily captured by conventional views on the "awakening of the civil society" as an igniting factor for state democratization. This problem was evident for organized labor; while the unions were engaged in mainly defensive shop-floor battles to defend existing employment levels, worker strategies of escape from wage labor toward farming or more or less legal forms of self-employment weakened even those strategies (Bangura & Beckman, 1991: 150). This seems to indicate a worker rationality that privileged an option of "exit" from an organized civil society whose "voice" was thwarted and for which spaces of negotiations with the state where denied. Moreover, the resort to hidden strategies of resistance, based on informal activities and "unconstitutionalized" identities, could also be rooted in diffidence toward the leadership (Lemarchand, 1992) of both the state and the unions.

In 1989, a limited political opening saw the institutionalization by the military of a competition between two "approved" parties for the presidential elections of June 1993. The coup with which, on November 7, 1994, General Abacha ousted the interim government installed by the military after its annulment of the 1993 elections, overturned this timid beginning of political change. Widespread protests discredited the political system entirely, bringing into the streets students, professionals, public employees, human rights associations, and trade unions opposed to authoritarianism and structural adjustment. However, the lack of articulation of a clear political democratic alternative operated in favor of the status quo. Sections of the peasantry and business could make common cause with labor in their opposition to the SAP, demanding, respectively, the reintroduction of agricultural subsidies and a new developmental policy to revive the domestic industrial base, but this did not amount to a structured convergence of interests for the transition (Babawale et al., 1996), confirming the shortcomings of the Nigerian "civil society." Democratic organizations were significantly divided along ethnic, regional, and religious lines. A tradition, inaugurated by Babangida, of co-opting critical intellectuals inside government-sponsored structures heightened the leadership crisis of national organizations of the democratic movement (Momoh, 1996b), and no mass support could be built by the two parties admitted to the annulled elections, given their nature as creatures of the regime. The winner of the elections, Moshood Abiola, a wealthy businessman with a past of close association with the Shagari regime, could hardly be a catalyst for popular mobilization. The leadership of the two parties either substantially accepted the coup, chose to bargain with the regime, or, as Abiola did, appealed to foreign condemnation instead of mobilizing an internal mass opposition (Lewis, 1994).

However, the demonstrations following Abiola's arrest showed some capacity on the part of grassroots opposition to transcend religious, ethnic, and regional divisions (Mustapha, 1998). The crisis of the organs of civil society did not imply a decline in resistance by movements for change. From this point of view, the popular strategy of "exit" did not, as Henry Bienen and Jeffrey Herbst (1996) assume, necessarily lead to the retreat of any possible alternative. After July 1994, upsurges of grassroots worker militancy revitalized to some extent the democratic movement. The decay of tertiary education encouraged the militant Academic Staff Union of Universities (ASUU) to challenge the intellectuals' consent to authoritarian rule, and important strikes hit the oil industry. Two unions in particular, NUPENG (organizing blue-collar workers) and PENGASSAN (recruiting clerical and staff members), came to the forefront of worker mobilization with an explicit political agenda aimed at ending authoritarianism. Eventually, the NLC itself was forced to support the oil workers' strike with a call for national industrial action that, even if it was immediately revoked, prompted workers to strike spontaneously for six weeks before surrendering to state violence, the arrest of union leaders, and economic hardships (Isaacs, 1995). The struggle in the oil industry connected with the mobilization of minorities affected by the combination of impoverishment and environmental degradation, as in the case of the Ogoni in the oil-rich Niger Delta. The Abacha regime responded with further repression, including bans and detentions of unionists, and the execution of Ogoni leaders, most notably the writer Ken-Saro Wiwa. As Terisa Turner (1997) notices, the conjunction of the oil workers' struggle and the mobilization for indigenous and environmental rights helped local coalitions, which opened new opportunities for the democratic opposition. Crucial to these alliances was the realization of how the authoritarian regime was functional to a neoliberal project of commodification of collective resources, land, and mineral rights. This process affects in different and interrelated ways a plurality of actors (women, farmworkers, minorities, and waged workers), thereby defining the issue of community control of local assets as pivotal in building new democratic spaces at the local level.

These oppositional "spaces" still confront the challenge of articulating new foundations for movements at a national level. In any case, they seem to indicate a continuing relevance of grassroots activism in deepening the regime's lack of legitimacy, which often starkly contrasted with the extremely poor state of formal organizations (Ihonvbere & Shaw, 1998: 144). Abacha's plans for a new "guided" transition to civilian rule, scheduled for 1998, were disrupted by his sudden death, which followed the popular outrage due to the death in jail of Moshood Abiola in May 1998. The Abacha regime had just entered into fresh negotiations with the World Bank and the IMF for a Medium Term Program, which would review the existing SAP in view of the 1998 budget. The regime's commitment to the objectives of the SAP was confirmed: A target of 1.6 percent debt-to-GDP ratio in 1998 (down from 7.9 percent in 1994) was premised on further devaluation, public sector downsizing, and privatization (National Economic Intelligence Committee,

1996). The new military administration, led by General Abdulsalam Abubakar, was then charged with completing the "guided" political transition in the continuity of socioeconomic orientations. The approval by the military, of the political parties for the general elections of February 27, 1999, was the first step in the process that led to the rise of General Olusegun Obasanjo to the presidency and of his People's Democratic Party (PDP) to the parliamentary majority.

However, several uncertainties still mar the prospects of the Nigerian transition to multi-partyism. The transition developed in a context in which the military regime did not disclose the details of the new constitution and with most of the emergency regulations still in place. Moreover, the new political dispensation raises new, weighty questions concerning its effective capacity to relate to social forces and pro-democracy movements. The southeastern regions, the most militant and oppressed under the military, have largely not been represented in the top echelons of the two contending political forces, the PDP and the coalition between the All People's Party (APP) and the Alliance for Democracy (AD). This confirms feelings of exclusion and alienation from national politics, already widespread among these populations. In addition, the two candidates for the presidential elections symbolize different faces of a past that greatly contributed to the current predicament of the working class and popular opposition. Obasanjo, as the military ruler in the 1976–1979 period, promoted a federal constitutional reform that, together with his 1978 Land Use Decree, contributed to centralizing land allocation and oil rents in the hands of the state. This mechanism was then used by subsequent dictators to expropriate local communities, especially in the southeast, and to bind local elites to the regime (Osaghae, 1998: 94). Obasanjo's opponent, Olu Falae, supported by an extremely heterogeneous APP-AD coalition that included both former pro-Abacha politicians and opponents with a background in the democratic movement, had been the minister of finance under Babangida and one of the leading strategists in the introduction of the SAP.

The place of labor under the new political order will be affected by the combination of new opportunities deriving from the establishment of multiparty rule and new strains resulting from the continuity in the country's socioeconomic options. The situation at present appears uncertain. The workers' direct exposure to the effects of the SAP encouraged their militancy; however, if organized labor remains unable to influence the political sphere, it will also be weakened in its shopfloor opposition to restructuring and retrenchments (Bangura, 1987: 185; Bangura & Beckman, 1991: 150–151). As Adesina (1992) notes, the processes of construction of workers' identity and subjectivity are essential to explain their political potential. The subjectivity of

Nigerian workers responds to multiple and to some extent contradictory appeals. Visions of class opposition inside the workplace can be reinforced by the ethos of symbolic communities beyond the point of production. However, even if this combination potentially contains elements of resistant morality and rationality, it is also constantly permeated by the regime's development discourse. This can obscure labor-capital opposition while legitimating popular claims for fairness and equality. Moreover, when the discourse of development presents waged workers as a privileged stratum, it forces them to search for broadly based alliances. On the other hand, as June Nash (1979: 9–10) explains, the vulnerability of workers' family lives generated by economic uncertainty can contradict workplace solidarity if the employers retain an unfettered power to hire and fire. If this is not clarified in labor-community alliances, the contradiction between family and work is an impediment on militant action. Labor's place in the post-military Nigerian dispensation will depend on how it will represent and organize the complex multiplicity of its determinants, roles, and connections across the entire social fabric (workplace, household, and informal sector). A project aimed at the emergence of civil society as an institutionalized actor for negotiated change is limited without an analysis of non-institutional relationships able to address the inadequacies of the neoliberal state.

Labor in the South African Democratic Transition: The Challenge of Subordinate Incorporation

"Homegrown Structural Adjustment"

The Nigerian case suggests that explanations based on institutional transitions and the reemergence of civil society are inadequate to explain labor's role in African processes of social and political change. The former reduce labor to a set of organizational behaviors and mechanisms compatible with state restructuring. On the other hand, although the notion of civil society is decisively and adversely affected by neoliberalism, its resumption oversimplifies the specific dynamics of conflict and militancy through which the neoliberalism-authoritarianism nexus is challenged. The following discussion of the South African transition supports this conclusion.

The South African case is starkly different from the Nigerian one. In the first place, South Africa successfully moved to a democratic representative political system, and the contribution of organized labor in overcoming apartheid was decisive. Second, labor has been a major driving force in the transitional and post-transitional phases, due to the formal electoral and programmatic alliance of the biggest union federation, the Congress of South

African Trade Union (COSATU), with the leading party in government, the African National Congress (ANC), and with the South African Communist Party (SACP). Third, the rise of a neoliberal hegemony in South Africa was less dependent on economic crisis and the external constraints imposed by international financial institutions, being more a matter of contestation and internal strategic choices involving state and capital. However, these differences do not rule out similarities in the impact of neoliberalism and its pressures for a subordinate institutionalization of labor.

As an important peculiarity in African decolonization and democratization, the labor movement in South Africa played a decisive part in the political transition (Mamdani, 1996a). The trade union organizations built since the struggles of the first half of the 1970s combined the representation of a new class composition centered on a stable urban African proletariat with a strong workplace identity nurtured in a culture of worker control, autonomy, internal democracy, and accountability (Friedman, 1987; Kraak, 1993). COSATU's adoption of broader political agendas for democratic change and social reform was influenced by a shift in grassroots perceptions in the union movement. At the beginning of the 1980s worker struggles over wages, working conditions, and workers' rights became inseparable from popular demands for improved living conditions, democracy, and the end of apartheid. This new awareness was stimulated by a resumption of social movement politics around civics, youth, churches, and student associations.

As a result, closer organizational relations were defined between COSATU (founded in 1985), the domestic opposition, and the exiled liberation movements. The synthesis of workplace and community struggles contributed during the 1980s to a growing politicization of industrial relations. At the same time the unions could offer their strong and broad-based organizational structures as a resource for the internal political opposition. They provided the entire democratic movement with an example that emphasized participation, democracy, and organization building, which shaped the political style of the anti-apartheid resistance. This role was reinforced during the repeated states of emergency that at the end of the 1980s disrupted the overt activities of many organizations. COSATU then became the main oppositional actor in the political sphere, in overt substitution to the banned structures (Webster & Von Holdt, 1991). The role of the South African unions inside social movements for democracy was then politically clarified and institutionally recognized. In 1989 COSATU adopted as its political platform the ANC's Freedom Charter, a document combining the demand for democracy and equal civil and political rights with welfare provisions, nationalization, and redistribution of strategic assets. This anticipated the formation of the "Tripartite Alliance" between COSATU, ANC, and SACP after the "unbanning" of the two political organizations in February 1990 (Baskin, 1991). The Alliance later led COSATU to second candidates in the ANC lists for the 1994 democratic elections.

The relevance of the unions as pivotal actors of social and political opposition through the combination of workplace-related demands and the direct challenge to the apartheid regime has been defined as "political unionism" or "social movement unionism" (Webster, 1988). This notion substantially enlarged a concept of labor as confined to factory waged employment, and it encompasses resistance at the level of both factory and community. For some analysts, "social movement unionism" in South Africa combined at the level of strategies and programs a remarkable pragmatism and flexibility with radicalism and mobilization (Adler, Maller & Webster, 1992). This has been evidenced since the late 1970s by the capacity of the workers' organizations to adjust to reforms in the industrial relations system. Whereas the state aimed to use some official recognition and organizational rights to gain a more effective control over worker struggles, the unions used those spaces to consolidate their presence in the factories and to gain legal protection. This presence was strengthened by workplace negotiations with the employers, which reinforced the unions' bargaining status in exchange for their acceptance of commonly agreed problem-solving procedures.

The transition meant new areas of institutional responsibilities for the unions. In particular, many COSATU affiliates were involved in workplace negotiations for the restructuring of the organization of work and production. Union organizations demanded, with mixed success, a place in sectoral-level negotiations over industrial policy, restructuring, and competitiveness. Finally, COSATU was recognized as a player in centralized tripartite national negotiations with capital and government over macro-economic policy, social reconstruction, employment standards, and restructuring of the labor market.

The institutional location of South African labor introduces a further discontinuity with the Nigerian case. South African organized labor not only ignited the transition but acted as a driving force for it. This translated into labor's contribution to changes to the Labor Relations Act (LRA); its influence on the ANC's policies, such as the Reconstruction and Development Program (RDP); and the strengthening of collective bargaining. It also involved the unions' participation alongside state and business in national tripartite forums on social and economic policy making, after the launch in 1995 of the National Economic Development and Labor Council (NEDLAC). A very influential appraisal of labor's role was provided by Glenn Adler and Eddie Webster (1995). Building on the capacity of the unions to strategically combine militancy, autonomy, and pragmatism, they capture the unions' contribution to the transition under the heading of "radical reform." In opposition to conventional theories of democratic transitions, their argument is that South African labor's radical programs and mobilization interacted with, rather than being marginalized by, pact-making processes involving reformers in the old regime and moderates in the opposition. Union radicalism therefore contains some potential for sociopolitical change to be achieved through the acceptance of institutionalized class compromise.

However, this view suffers from various limitations, and it ends up sharing many of the basic assumptions of mainstream theories. In particular, for Adler and Webster, labor's chances in the transition depend on prospects of institutionalization of the unions' influence or, as I call it, *constitutionalization* of wage labor inside the post-transitional dispensation. On the other hand, this argument recognizes that labor's hegemony in processes of mass mobilization has been replaced by the hegemony of the ANC in government as a force shaping the pace of social and economic transformation. It also acknowledges that the ANC represents various constituencies and is subject to multiple pressures from powerful economic actors linked to multinational capital and international financial institutions. It is questionable whether the acknowledgment of labor's organizational strength and capacity for mass organization is sufficient to solve the problems that arise from these contradictions. The emphasis on institutionalized mediation advanced by labor leadership often does not coincide with rank-and-file radicalism and militancy. The ANC's growing alignment with a free market paradigm based on fiscal discipline and labor market flexibility is signaling a progressive narrowing of institutional options for the unions. Sakhela Buhlungu (1996) argues that the rise of the unions' "influence" in government has in many ways contrasted with their loss of independent "power." Factors that facilitate such an outcome are the exodus of experienced union leaders to political positions in the ANC and government and the growing involvement of COSATU in economic activities such as union investment funds. The rising importance of the latter indicates an integration of labor in a changing South African business landscape, for which traditional mechanisms of grassroots control are proving inadequate (Naidoo, 1997). Workers' opposition to the 1995 LRA (Von Holdt, 1995) and to the 1995 three-year automobile industry agreement (Bohmke & Desai 1996), or to the privatization of public municipal services (Van Driel, 1998), confirms the strains suffered by a purely institution-based understanding of labor's role and outcomes in the transition.

The rise of a free market hegemony in South African policy making depends largely on strategic choices of domestic economic and political actors, rather than on external conditionalities. Defined by Patrick Bond (1998) as "homegrown structural adjustment," this dynamic contrasts markedly with the SAP process discussed in the Nigerian case. In fact, the democratic South African state combines the promotion of the country's position in global markets with social compacts through institutionalized negotiations to provide legitimacy, social control, and the promotion of grassroots cooperation and demobilization. Although it coexisted uneasily in the RDP with the promotion of domestic demand and basic needs, the neoliberal orientation has become predominant in post-RDP policy documents (Adelzadeh, 1996: 43–45), especially the 1996 Growth Employment and Redistribution (GEAR) strategy (Department of Finance, 1996). GEAR maintained a vague commitment to job creation, which was, conversely, made dependent on fiscal discipline, public spending restraint (a 3 percent deficit-to-GDP ratio by year 2000, with further expansion conditional upon the by now highly unlikely growth rate of 6.1 percent), export promotion, and privatization. Moreover, although redistribution was made dependent on economic growth, the growth potential of redistribution was ignored, and a tight monetary policy was privileged over an inward-looking industrial strategy and the expansion of domestic demand (National Institute for Economic Policy, 1996, 1999). Finally, GEAR's recommendations for labor market flexibility echoed positions (Nattrass & Seekings, 1996) supporting a two-tier labor market, the deregulation of certain categories of semi- and unskilled employment, and the exemption of small businesses from collective bargaining provisions in the new labor legislation. On the other hand, the International Labor Organization (1996, 1999) notes that the South African labor market is already extremely flexible, characterized by significant wage gaps between sectors, by the expansion of atypical employment—including subcontracting, outsourcing, and casualization—and by employers' evasion of implementing basic employment standards (Standing, 1997).

Phil Eidelberg (1997) notes that COSATU's radicalism was effective when the apartheid state was weakened by international isolation, but it became constrained by the new democratic institutions in a context of economic liberalization and transnational capital's support for the ANC government. In particular, South African unions now must face the challenge of representing changes in class composition due to shifts in work organization, technology, and labor markets. This points at the general problem, discussed in the Nigerian case, of the crisis of the institutionalization of social actors in "structurally adjusted" Africa. The South African "homegrown structural adjustment" translated organized labor's central role in the transitional phase into labor's powerlessness in the face of a neoliberal agenda after the transition. The following sections analyze the emergence of this powerlessness in two specific areas.

Industrial Relations, Social Policy Making, and the Marginalization of Labor

The 1995 LRA emphasizes the creation of a conflict-free workplace environment (Du Toit, 1997). To this end, the act does not enforce a statutory duty for capital and labor to bargain. It tries instead to institutionalize workplace labor relations through "workplace forums" for consultation and joint decision making (a distinction not always clear in the act) over "non distributive issues" (retrenchments, productivity, technology, and work organization). On these issues the possibility of industrial action is substantially reduced. Distributive and "collective bargaining" issues (wages and working conditions) are delegated to centralized bargaining in national, regional, or sectoral bargaining councils. The government's accompanying documents (Ministerial Legal Task Team, 1995) give the LRA responsibilities normally well beyond a piece of labor legislation. These directly link the new LRA to the need to promote industrial peace as a means to boost domestic and international business confidence.

It has been convincingly argued (Etkind, 1995; Klerck, 1998) that this dispensation can substantially reduce rank-and-file bargaining power, especially in the weakest and least-competitive sectors, at the same time isolating centralized negotiations from the grass roots of unions. The new act also seems compatible with a diversification of bargaining levels that takes into account the needs of smaller companies, which is actually encouraged by the Department of Labor's emphasis on "regulated flexibility." This prioritizes the firm's market performance over the institutionalization of "productivity pacts" with unions as the crucial determinant of workers' remuneration.

South African proponents of worker participation and "co-determination" (Adler, 2000), from this point of view, must face an uncomfortable reality. Exercises of worker participation are often reported as being instrumental to elicit worker commitment in processes of unilateral restructuring to cut production costs (Kraak, 1996; Buhlungu, 1996). This end is totally compatible with "management-by-stress" techniques well known in international research (Parker & Slaughter, 1990). Supporting a model of codetermination as increasing worker power premised on the unions' commitment to productivity and competitiveness is particularly problematic in most South African industries. Global pressures are used to reinforce worker compliance through capital-intensive automation, employment flexibility, and work intensification, which make "codeterminist" strategies the target of workers' rejection as avenues of "sweetheart" unionism (Barchiesi, 1998). In general, the promotion of workplace cooperation does not seem able to redress the balance of power at the point of production and to affect the power of capital in restructuring processes.

Moreover, such processes are affecting the structure of the working class outside the workplace as well, following the neoliberal advocacy for the deregulation of labor markets. Industrial restructuring is witnessing the rise of forms of "atypical" employment, especially in the most labor-intensive sectors (mining, retail, construction, and clothing), where most new jobs are created through subcontracting, part-time work, labor-brokering, homework, and temporary employment (Kenny & Bezuidenhout, 1999). These processes of "casualization" are combined with trade liberalization and intensified competition as formidable pressures on historical bases of union support, and they provide capital with cost-cutting advantages to "produce for the formal sector according to formal sector standards, under 'informal' sector conditions" (Theron, 1996: 9). At the same time, unprotected, unstable, and exploitative jobs proliferate for an increasingly vulnerable, and largely female, workforce. Combining aspects of self-employment with the subordination to the factory hierarchy, these processes envisage the extension of capitalist command over the territory through loose networks of relations that partially use the "atypicals'" and homeworkers' desire for self-management of time as a vehicle to increase working time and labor flexibility. The separation of the union organizations from potential bases of support and their inability to influence broad social dynamics have also increased (Rees, 1997). The rising heterogeneity and fragmentation in forms of employment, combined with labor's weakness in the workplace, adversely affect the organizational cohesiveness and the collective solidarity of South African labor. Therefore, the possibility that the institutionalization of labor organizations—sought by the democratic political system—can deliver progressive outcomes is seriously questioned by social processes that are an integral part of "homegrown structural adjustment."

These conclusions are confirmed by looking at the unions' performance in tripartite structures at the national level. In particular, NEDLAC is an institution based on consent on economic policy making, social reconstruction, and labor market restructuring. Its four "chambers" include representatives from government, business, labor, and the "civil society." NEDLAC's mandate is to reach agreements on proposed socioeconomic legislation, giving it a strong legitimacy from stakeholders (Maree, 1998). This path was theorized (Baskin, 1993) as opening the possibility for a "democratic-corporatist" compact that would enable a labor-led political transition. This is echoed in NEDLAC's official position:

> NEDLAC is a vehicle for the *social partners to mobilise their constituencies* into an effective joint strategy for social and economic transformation. . . . We have reached a moment wherein *the leadership of each constituency is willing* to consider the possibility of making short-term trade-offs and of mobilising our collective

resources in order to create a longer-term outcome which will deliver employment, economic growth and uplift the living standard of all.... *There is no other alternative* open to South Africa except to seek a meaningful social partnership. (National Economic Development and Labor Council, 1995: 3; emphasis in original)

It has been observed (Heller, 1995) that in societies characterized by apparent inequalities corporatist solutions can be a conservative alternative to redistributive policies, which would otherwise encourage radical expectations and a militant rhetoric counterproductive to "development." Recent studies on economic reform in Latin America (Gibson, 1997; Weyland, 1996) show that corporatist structures, rather than authoritarian ones, can be the most conducive to neoliberal reforms in countries ruled by parties that, like the ANC in South Africa, are supported by multiple constituencies and legitimated by a non-class developmental discourse. In these countries, the populist rhetoric on the "needs of the very poor" provides an effective tool for the ruling party to mobilize "peripheral" constituencies (rural, unemployed) to constrain demands and militancy from their own "metropolitan" bases of support (primarily organized labor). The conclusion from these cases seems to be that neoliberalism and neo-corporatism do not constitute clearly discernible alternatives in processes of societal bargaining. These observations lead to a further series of problems in the South African case. First is the unresolved dualism of NEDLAC, which is defined as both a consultative body and a decision-making institution. This allows business to sidestep NEDLAC through bilateral contacts with government and decentralized negotiations with labor (Pretorius, 1996). Uncertainties in NEDLAC's mandate also make it possible for the policy-making role of the government on socioeconomic issues to define and constrain the mandate of the tripartite body. This goes to the advantage of those government departments that, more in tune with neoliberal approaches, are able to discipline the policies of the state around the need to "adapt" to global realities. It is on this basis that the Department of Finance could introduce GEAR as "non-negotiable," in exception to NEDLAC's mandate.

Moreover, labor's contribution to democratization can easily be defined in terms of sacrifices to uplift the "more disadvantaged" in a technocratic mode of decision making. The potentially adverse consequences such a situation carries for labor emerge from a discussion document published in circles close to the current president, Thabo Mbeki:

Proceeding from the objective reality of the place and role of private capital ... which exists independent of our subjective wishes, the correct strategic decision the democratic movement must take is that the democratic state must establish a dialectical relationship with private capital as a social partner for development and social progress.... This is meant to describe a complex, contradictory, co-operative and dynamic relationship, many of whose elements are formed or decided at the international level. What is certain is that there is a need for co-existence and co-operation between the democratic state and private capital in order to address social development. (African National Congress, 1996: 10–11)

On the part of labor the document

emphasises the centrality of the continuing and special role of the progressive trade union movement and its leadership to the mobilization of black workers to understand and adhere to the broader objectives of the process of democratic transformation, in their own interest. The instinct towards "economism" on the part of the ordinary workers has to be confronted through the positioning of the legitimate material demands and expectations of these workers within the wider context of the defense of the democratic gains as represented by the establishment of the democratic state. (African National Congress, 1996: 2)

The similarities to the discourse of subaltern institutionalization of labor in Nigeria are striking. Although the state recognizes the role of capital as a partner in dealing with "international" dynamics, the role of labor is to mobilize its constituency inside a state-defined modernization project for the "true interests" (to recall the analogous formulation used by the Nigerian government) of the working class. On the other hand, it is the "objectives of the process of democratic transformation" as "represented by the democratic state," rather than unions' independence and accountability to their members, that will determine these interests. Very few of these interests are specified, except that the struggle for better wages and working conditions, as an "instinct towards economism," must be "confronted" by undefined "legitimate" demands and expectations. In addition, although labor is required to sacrifice its immediate instincts, not much of a similar call is made on capital. Once again, institutionalization of labor in a context of neoliberal hegemony provides a call for demobilization.

COSATU's response to the discussion document recognizes that in many instances the transition has been led not by its alliance with the ANC but by "the old bureaucracy, business advisers, economists from the Reserve Bank, the World Bank, etc." (Congress of South African Trade Unions, 1996: 6), and that demobilization and demoralization of the rank and file followed, whereas the democratic state has been "confined to limited areas of governance" (1996: 8). The union federation does not question the institutionalization of its alliance with the ANC and the pressures for labor subordination arising inside it. The federation's adoption of a pragmatic approach to "flexible independence" (September Commission, 1997: 31–32) advocates electoral pacts with the ANC that include COSATU's "top priorities" as a condition for maintaining the alliance in place in case a common political program—prevented by COSATU's opposition to GEAR—does not emerge.

Labor's criticism of the alliance is particularly echoed in many COSATU affiliates, which are distant from top-level tripartite bargaining and whose members directly face economic restructuring, downsizing, retrenchments, and outsourcing. In the case of municipal workers' campaigns against privatization of local public services, for example, grassroots criticism also touched the increasing subordination of COSATU, reinforced by corporatist tripartite bargaining. In particular, a wide perception exists among unions that, if labor cannot shape decisive macro-economic and industrial policy orientations, there is little point in taking part in NEDLAC structures that are largely confined to details (Marais, 1998: 230–234).

Labor's political and policy role in democratic South Africa is conducive to what Steven Gelb (1998) defines as a "mixed" model. This would combine a strong central power holding the prerogative to insulate "non-negotiable" general principles of macro-economic policy from societal bargaining, with an emphasis on market forces in the intermediation of different interests. "Tripartite bargaining" would then be confined to the technical ways in which to implement those principles. As noted for the Nigerian case, a neo-liberal economic framework faces labor with a stark alternative: to accept institutionalization and sell that very framework to its constituency or face marginalization. The functioning of NEDLAC in this scenario can hardly be defined as a labor-led process of change. As Leo Panitch (1996) argues, rather than responding to an optimist view of "democratic corporatism," NEDLAC operates according to the same logic of state-led union subordination that gave corporatism a "bad name" among trade unions all over the world.

Here the similarities between South Africa and Nigeria are clearer. In both cases the institutionalization of labor has proved functional to the alignment of those countries to neoliberalism. Of course, the respective state institutions approached labor movements in different contexts and through completely different means, via direct intervention of a military dictatorship in Nigeria and through recognizing labor's decisive role in democratization in South Africa. However, it appears that the hegemony of neoliberalism faces both labor movements with the same alternative: being institutionalized in a subordinate position or being marginalized and therefore invisible. As Barry

Gills, Joel Rocamora, and Richard Wilson, in their analysis of four countries, put it:

> The onset of formal representative government changes the conditions under which labor and other popular movements must operate. The pattern emerging ... can be summed up under the headings "mobilization and realignment." (1993: 23)

Although mobilization is necessary to create a political space for the transition, the forces of civil society that are mobilized are soon after "peripheralized" from the centers of power by the realignment of ruling social coalitions around narrow formal democracy and conservative economic and social policies. In this way, the visibility of labor in social mobilization is obliterated and democratization becomes little more than a strategy of containment and legitimacy for various forms of structural adjustment (Hippler, 1995).

Conclusion

The impact of labor on the two cases discussed can be defined as ultimately ambivalent. In both countries labor as a movement had a strong influence on struggles for democracy, based on a capacity to mobilize rank-and-file constituencies inside broader anti-authoritarian struggles. The picture is more problematic if the role of labor institutionalization is considered. In the Nigerian case the failures of the democratic transition were facilitated by the capacity of military regimes to institutionalize trade unions and to intervene in their internal life. This was mainly achieved under a neoliberal SAP. Its adverse social consequences mobilized a broad range of social grievances around workplace organizations. However, the distance between these dynamics of resistance, unions, and parties decisively weakened the chances of Nigerian pro-democracy forces. In South Africa, unions strongly committed to grassroots democracy and worker control mobilized social movements' demands for change. However, during and after the transition this was equally challenged by the rise of a neoliberal hegemony in the form of "homegrown structural adjustment." Institutionalization rapidly turned from an achievement of the past unions' role into a disciplining and demobilizing device.

Comparative analyses of organized labor's position in relatively democratic and relatively authoritarian political systems have shown (Candland, 1995) that a democratic dispensation may reinforce labor's influence on policy outcomes. However, in the context of neoliberalism such an influence tends to leave space for labor's subaltern institutionalization and growing separation from grassroots constituencies and processes. In both cases examined in this chapter, differences in political-institutional outcomes did not prevent an important convergence of trends in weakening labor's influence. As Abdul Mustapha (1991) emphasizes, structural adjustment implies either the incorporation or the dismantling of the associations of labor and civil society, as well as the realignment of state institutions. This led in Nigeria to increasing forms of exclusion, survivalism, and precariousness of life chances, whereas in South Africa it facilitated the separation of organized labor from broader social dynamics of resistance and its subaltern institutionalization in corporatist structures incapable of progressive social deals. Both trajectories confirm an unresolved dilemma for organized labor, that of finding a political response to neoliberalism that is able to counter subaltern institutionalization through innovative relations with differentiated, autonomous forms of everyday resistance.

7

Silencing Power

Mapping the Social Terrain in Post-Apartheid South Africa

KATE CREHAN
College of Staten Island, City University of New York

Ideas and opinions are not spontaneously "born" in each individual brain: they have had a centre of formation, of irradiation, of dissemination, of persuasion.

(Gramsci, 1971: 192)

No social environment ever confronts its individual members with a single, homogeneous set of categories. There are always competing ways of seeing the world that involve different ways of naming the relationships within it. These names do not, however, all carry the same weight and authority. In any given time and place there are certain names that are, to a greater or lesser extent, hegemonic (to use the Gramscian term); in that time and place they seem simply to name reality as it is. Their hegemony is defined, in part, by the degree to which they are able to silence other ways of naming and mapping the world.

This chapter draws on Antonio Gramsci's writings on intellectuals and the production of knowledge. For Gramsci intellectuals are defined primarily not by the intellectual activities they engage in but by the nature of the social relationships within which that activity is carried out.[1] Intellectuals are those whose *business* it is to produce knowledge, to name the features of the social landscape, whether they do this in the groves of academe, government think tanks, the editorial columns of newspapers, or any of the other socially recognized sources of "knowledge." Gramsci also stresses, however, that the authoritative, socially recognized maps of society are not produced solely by intellectuals. In this chapter I focus, through a particular case study, on how individuals experience the hegemony of the social maps they are given; how even though their own attempts to use those maps may call them into question, as long as alternative maps are not readily available, simply jettisoning them is difficult. As I have stressed, hegemony is defined in part by its ability to prevent those alternative maps being drawn.

This chapter examines the use of one basic term, *community*, in the specific context of South Africa, looking both at the associations it carries with it and the implications of using it to map the social landscape. The data come primarily from a series of interviews carried out in 1997 with 18 individuals in four land and housing NGOs based in the Western Cape. The interviews centered on three basic terms in the contemporary NGO lexicon: *community, empowerment,* and *participation*. The aim was to tease out some of the assumptions, many of them implicit rather than explicit, bound up in these three terms, and to explore certain tensions between the inescapable associations these words carry with them and the actual social realities they are called upon to name. All the interviews were conducted jointly by a former employee of one of the NGOs, Julia Shapiro, and myself. Consequently I refer throughout to "our" interviews and what our interviewees told "us." I also make use of the publications of the following NGOs: the Surplus People Project (SPP), Umzamo, Development Action Group (DAG), and the Centre for Rural Legal Studies (CRLS).

Development as Discourse

Outside the relatively small world of Africanist scholars the basic lens through which African social realities are viewed and their contours mapped tends to be a discourse of "development." One of the hegemonic commonplaces of the contemporary world is that the world is divided into two fundamental categories: the "developed" countries and the "developing" countries (the currently preferred term for "underdeveloped"). Bound up in this simple binary opposition is an assumption that whatever it is that ails the "developing" world—that these countries, particularly the African ones, *are* ailing is taken for granted—the problem is ultimately one of a lack of "development." Whether this is seen as a simple failure to develop or as some form of blocked development, due perhaps to the inequities of various world systems or perhaps to the "developing" countries' own pathological institutions, the ultimate problem has already been defined by the terms of the opposition itself. However much debate there may be about causes and reasons, from this vantage point the ultimate problem remains that "development" is not taking place as it should. Underpinning the basic notion of development is a very old teleology whereby it is assumed that all societies—with the possible exception of those that have already arrived—are headed, albeit at different rates, toward some future and more desirable state, the essential characteristics of which are already known. The ostensible purpose of the huge, worldwide development industry is in some general sense the facilitation of this journey.

My point here is not that the opposition of developed to developing is simply wrong. Clearly, at some very general level, this approach does capture certain undeniable differences and inequalities, but how useful is this way of framing the analysis of particular social formations and their history? The problem, as I see it, is that this way of naming those differences and inequalities tends to preempt and close off analysis instead of opening it up. Rather than exploring the actual trajectories of social formations in all their complexity and contradiction, following the twisting and turning of their historical development wherever it may lead, the richness of these trajectories is jammed into a rigid teleological template. There may be different assessments of the mileposts along the way, but that the ultimate destination is that of "being developed" (however that is defined) remains an unspoken assumption underpinning development discourse. At any one time there tends to be an agreed-upon vocabulary that runs through the literature produced by the development industry in which is defined what it is that development initiatives are supposedly doing, or should be doing, to move individuals, groups, and/or societies closer to the glittering prize of "development." These are terms that it is not felt necessary to define, the assumption being that their meaning is self-evident. This essay focuses on the role played by one such term, *community*, in the "development interventions" of one of the most ubiquitous players on the development stage in the contemporary world: the non-governmental organization (NGO).

The Space of the NGO

During the 1980s and 1990s the NGO became an ever more prominent player in the "development" arena. According to Ian Gary:

> Worldwide, more than US$7 billion is channelled through NGOs, equivalent to 16 per cent of bilateral aid flows, with most official aid agencies giving 10 per cent or more of their aid money to NGOs. . . . During the 1980s funding to NGOs grew at five times the rate of official development assistance overall. (1996: 149)

But what exactly are NGOs? NGO is clearly a very heterogeneous category that has been given numerous different definitions. These range from David Korten's succinct "any organization that is both nongovernmental and nonprofit is generally considered to be an NGO" (1990: 95) to Eve Sandberg's more expansive "minimalist definition," on which she says "many observers can agree":

> that NGOs are legal, not-for-profit organizations that include a community-based, voluntary character, and that pursue humanitarian, developmental, environmental, or relief activities, and/or that deliver social (welfare, health care, educational training—including management and technical training) services. (1994: 28)[2]

As both Korten's and Sandberg's definitions indicate, the NGO is thought of as inhabiting a terrain outside both the realm of the state and that of the ordinary profit-driven world of the market and free enterprise. Sandberg's defining activities and services are very much the kind that the free market, left to itself, seems notably reluctant to undertake. And whereas in the past many policymakers and academic theorists would have looked to the state to provide these kinds of welfare services and to undertake necessary infrastructural projects, it is a brave soul these days who would champion the strong developmentalist state. International bodies such as the World Bank and the International Monetary Fund (IMF) tend to be highly distrustful of the state, and especially perhaps of the post-colonial African state. At the same time, these powerful international bodies increasingly play a policing role, insisting, for example, that countries impose structural adjustment programs (SAPs) and in general keeping a watchful eye that the countries of "the South" do not stray from the straight and narrow path laid down by the needs of capitalist accumulation. The distrust of the state coupled with the faith in market forces has helped to open up an ever-increasing expanse of human need for which there seems little remedy: Private enterprise will not venture here; the state should not. It is this space that tends to be the province of the NGO, and it is the expansion of this space that lies behind the mushrooming of NGOs in the 1980s and 1990s. It is important to note, however, that the NGOs' separation from both state and market is a lot tidier in the case of the NGO as an *imagined* category than it is when the linkages between particular state institutions and actually existing NGOs or their empirical links to market forces are examined carefully. For example, according to Marcusson: "On average, a third of NGO funds stem from government sources" (1996: 406).[3]

The Virtuous Community

To describe and understand the social realities in which they intervene, NGOs, like everyone else, cannot but use the names and concepts of their historical time and place. In an earlier time, for example, the prism through which Africans were most commonly seen by colonial states and "experts" of various kinds was that of the "tribe."[4] This term tended to be seen by the colonial officials and anthropologists who used it as no more than the naming of a simple fact, but in reality it framed colonial societies in very particular ways as, for example, when tensions between black miners and their employers were defined as problems of "detribalization" rather than as, say, struggles between capital and labor. Nowadays the term *community* seems as ubiquitous as *tribe* used to be. As *tribe* was in the colonial era, *community* is a term whose meaning is assumed to be so self-evident as not to need explicit definition. Precisely because of its taken-for-granted, commonsense nature, it is worth teasing out some of the unspoken assumptions it carries with it.

The following passage in a 1989 World Bank document condenses much of the contemporary zeitgeist of the international development world:

> Many basic services ... are best managed at the local level—even the village level—with the central agencies providing only technical advice and specialised inputs. The aims should be to empower ordinary people to take charge of their lives, to make communities more responsible for their development, and to make governments listen to their people. (World Bank, 1989, quoted in Thomas, 1992: 133)

"Ordinary people," this passage tells us, are to be "empowered" "to take charge of their lives," to become "more responsible for their development," and "to make governments listen to their people." Leaving aside the thought that those who are able to achieve all this are probably rather *extra*ordinary people, what I want to draw attention to is how the community here is defined as an entity that should, and by implication can, take responsibility for its own "development."

For NGOs working in the field of "development," *community*, whether they like it or not, is a basic term in the language universe they inhabit. It is a term their funders expect, and even demand, to see in mission statements and funding proposals. As a way of naming a significant dimension of the reality within which they work, the concept of community is inescapable. In South Africa the term *community* also carries—for reasons I discuss later in this chapter—a particular political resonance. The mission statements of three of the NGOs in the case study (SPP, DAG, and Umzamo) illustrate the centrality of *community* as the basic entity toward which the efforts of the NGO are seen as directed.

The SPP mission statement begins as follows:

> Assist and empower landless, dispossessed and homeless *communities* to take forward their struggles for land rights, land claims, housing, and democratic forms of local and regional government.
>
> Assist *communities* to engage in a participatory developmental process. (Surplus People Project, 1995: 3; emphasis added)

The DAG mission statement defines its partners as "marginalised *communities* with an average household income of less than R2,000.00 per month, living in Cape Town and the surrounding peri-urban areas" (Development Action Group, 1996; emphasis added); Umzamo describes itself as a "*Community* Based Development Agency" working with "*communities* in marginalised areas of the Western Cape" (Umzamo, n.d.; emphasis added). But what exactly is a community, and what are the consequences of seeing particular groups of people through the prism of community?

To begin with the most general associations of *community*, Raymond Williams, in his indispensable *Keywords*, draws attention to how the term *community* in English was from an early period used to refer both to "actual social groups," such as the people of a particular district, and to "a particular quality of relationship," such as a sense of common identity. Often, however, these two senses bleed into one another, so that a community becomes understood as an actual social group bound together by a particular quality of relationship. This blurring is one of the reasons *community* is such a slippery term. A second point made by Williams is the overwhelmingly positive connotations of community. It is always a "warmly persuasive word" and "unlike all other terms of social organisations (state, nation, society, etc.) it seems never to be used unfavourably, and never to be given any positive opposing or distinguishing term" (Williams, 1983: 75–76).

Part of the baggage the term *community* carries with it is this roseate glow: communities are good, unlike, for example, the state. There is also the idea of community as an older, organic, human form of social organization that was supplanted by the impersonal and bleak social relations characteristic of the modern industrial world—the *Gemeinschaft* and *Gesellschaft* of Tönnies. This use of *community* makes it stand for all that is *not* characteristic of capitalism and the market. Communities are intimate and small; they are founded on affective ties between people, not the cash nexus. This way of thinking about community tends to produce a dichotomy between the community, with its warm, human values, within which the profit motive is absent, and the heartless market in which there is nothing but a relentless search for profit. In an African context this dichotomy can easily translate into the warm, human community of "traditional" African values being opposed to the harsh anomie of modernity and the market.

In addition to its general, widely shared associations, community also tends to develop in the course of the specific histories of particular places, with added local nuances; in South Africa also *community* comes freighted with its own particular historical baggage. Underpinning South African history from the earliest years of Dutch settlement is a struggle over land and other resources. The apartheid system was, among other things, the culmination of the long history of relentless, if uneven and interrupted, displacement of black Africans by Dutch (then Afrikaans) and English-speaking settlers. The racialized struggle for land was always at the heart of apartheid ideology. The struggle over resources, however, was not only between whites and blacks, it also involved struggles between blacks themselves and, very importantly, between Afrikaans-speaking whites and the entrenched power of the English-speaking elite. The Afrikaners' sense of marginalization and exclusion found expression in the National Party, which after its 1948 election victory instituted the policy of apartheid. To base government policy *openly* on racial exclusion, however, played increasingly badly in the postwar international arena, and consequently the apartheid regime resorted to various euphemisms for race. *Community* was one of the most popular of these, and official categories that were clearly racial were commonly designated "communities": the Indian community, the coloured community, the black community, and the white community. As Robert Thornton and Mamphela Ramphele have stressed, the apartheid government was always "especially adept at co-opting international jargon to justify the pursuit of its long-standing policy of 'divide and rule'" (1988: 32), and the government was quick to seize on such fashionable concepts as "community development" and "community participation." One example of this was in 1961 when "the name 'Community Development' was given to the department concerned with the development of white (mainly Afrikaans-speaking) 'communities,' and the removal of all others from areas designated as 'white' under the Group Areas Act" (Thornton & Ramphele, 1988: 32–33).

From its earliest days the National Party drew heavily on the language and images of nineteenth-century nationalism; distinct peoples bound together by blood and culture, rooted in distinct territories, and so forth. In this context the language of community slid easily into a rhetoric justifying, on the basis of some vague notion of self-determination, "separate development" for all the so-called separate communities. As a minority themselves, albeit a dominant one, many Afrikaners were very conscious of the need to defend "their" culture, not only against the black majority but also against the powerful English-speaking whites. This sense of being a beleaguered "community" fighting for its cultural life was something that many Afrikaner organizations, including the National Party, used to mobilize their constituency.

The notion of "community" was also used by those trying to mobilize against the apartheid regime. Whatever the rhetoric of "separate development," the practice of apartheid involved the forced and often violent removal of hundreds of thousands of overwhelmingly black and coloured[5] South Africans. These removals centered both on getting rid of whole communities (in the sense of particular groups of people located in particular geographical areas) and tidying up existing racially mixed communities (again those living in a particular area) so as to make them racially homogeneous. As a result, opposition to the apartheid state often assumed the form of struggles by embattled communities against removal—struggles fought out in the name of a particular community. In addition, the iniquities of life under apartheid for black South Africans, who had to battle even to maintain their status as South Africans, let alone provide themselves and their families with a livable existence, tended to weld existing black settlements into communities of struggle—even if the united front presented to the apartheid state concealed all kinds of cleavages. The popularization of *community* as an oppositional term was, according to Thornton and Ramphele, the result of the Black Consciousness Movement of the 1970s (of which Ramphele was one of the founders), which used the term *communities* "to refer to wide sociopolitical groups like 'black community' (which included all those classified as African, coloured, and Indian) or, even more loosely, '*the* community' to describe residential entities such as the townships" (Thornton & Ramphele, 1988: 35, emphasis in original). Certainly the term *community* came to have a particular political meaning in progressive circles in South Africa. As one of our interviewees put it when explaining why her organization would continue to use the word *community* even though she and others found it problematic, "[I]t has . . . I suppose progressive political connotations—it's a term that is ours."

At the same time, at the other end of the political spectrum the term retained its popularity among Afrikaner groups. In short, once again the term *community* could be seen as signifying everything that was both good and authentic, and as such a name that virtually all South Africans, whatever their political stance, wanted to claim for *their* political endeavor.

NGOs in South Africa: From Struggle to Development

NGOs in apartheid South Africa were shaped in important ways by that country's political realities, occupying a space carved out by both the international pariah status of the official government and that government's attempts to outlaw virtually any expression of opposition to it by blacks. This could not but be a highly politicized space, in which virtually any attempt to alleviate the miserable conditions endured by the black majority inevitably became a form of political opposition to the regime. In the 1980s it was also the space into which almost all financial and other support by foreign donors was channeled, because even the most conservative of organizations or states was reluctant to provide open support to such a discredited regime. In general the South African NGOs of the 1980s can be seen as characterized by their politicization and a general awareness that whatever their specific project, it was locked into a larger political struggle.

Another important characteristic of the South African NGO world, related both to the high level of organization among oppositional groups (not only in spite of, but also in part because of, the harshness of state repression) and the existence of large numbers of educated, professional whites opposed to the regime, was that this was a world dominated by local South Africans (white and black, but with an over-representation of white professionals) rather than expatriate experts. SPP, DAG, and CRLS are all examples of this pattern. Umzamo is different only in that black hostel dwellers themselves played a dominant role in the organization from its creation.

Founded to fight apartheid, until the period of negotiation and transition to the "new" South Africa, the relationship of NGOs like SPP, DAG, and Umzamo to the state was one of simple opposition. Funded primarily by foreign donors, their concern was to help those living in black communities to assert their right, denied by the state, to decent living conditions free from the threat of forced removal. There was never any doubt that such NGOs were part of a wider struggle to wrest power away from a racially based state. With the ending of apartheid and the transition to a new ANC-dominated government, the relationship of such NGOs to the state necessarily became much more complicated. On the one hand, the new state seemed to represent what many had been fighting for, and indeed many NGO people moved rapidly into new positions in national and local government. On the other hand, although South Africa in 1997 was a very different place from the South Africa in which SPP, DAG, and Umzamo were founded, it was also not the South Africa of the first heady, post-apartheid days. All the NGOs in the case study, in common with virtually every other South African NGO, were undergoing fundamental changes. All had to rethink their role in the context of the new South Africa, including their relationship to the post-apartheid state.

An example of this shifting relationship was President Mandela's sharp criticism of the NGO sector in his 1997 address to the 50th Conference of the African National Congress, in which he said, among other things:

> We must also refer to sections of the non-governmental sector which seek to assert that the distinguishing feature of a genuine organisation of civil society is to be a critical "watchdog" over our movement, both inside and outside of government. Pretending to represent an independent and popular view, supposedly obviously legitimated by the fact that they are described as non-governmental organisations, these NGO's also work to corrode the influence of the movement [i.e., the broad democratic movement that the ANC sees itself as embodying]. (African National Congress, 1997: 11)

South African NGOs had to cope with a steady hemorrhaging of personnel as individuals left for jobs in government (both local and national) and the private sector. At the same time, much of the foreign funding previously available to organizations opposing apartheid dried up or was subject to much more stringent conditions; value for money had to be demonstrated in a way that it never was in the old days of struggle. The needs that the NGOs were set up to address, however, were still there; a new non-racial South African state had been achieved, but the basic living conditions of the vast majority of those at the bottom of the economic heap had changed little. At the level of rhetoric the state might be championing the goals of land redistribution, affordable housing, and the like (see African National Congress, 1994: 22–28), but its commitment in practice to the principles of free enterprise and its reliance on the private sector made the realization of these goals unlikely. As a way of summing up their changed environment, those within the South African NGO world in 1997 often referred to a shift from the era of struggle to the era of development, a formulation that assumes South Africa's problems are indeed best characterized by the term *development*.

Working with the "Community"

As I have stressed, *community* is a term that the NGOs I looked at had little choice but to use. The language of "community development," "community participation," and "community empowerment," it would seem, was the way to win funders' hearts and open their wallets. In addition, in the South African context with its history of dispossessed communities, redressing this legacy in the field of land and housing could not but engage the injustices that have been suffered by "communities," and the struggle against apartheid lent the notion of community a very specific romantic glow. Nonetheless, virtually all of those we interviewed[6] were to varying degrees uncomfortable with the term *community*. For example, one person replied in response to a question about its usefulness: "No, I don't think it is a useful term. I think I'm finding more and more it's not a useful term. That it . . . it masks all sort of differences within different groups of people." Another, commenting on how such differences can fracture a community, remarked that "from my experience you have . . . a community while you're fighting, but the *minute* you add any resource—you haven't got a community anymore." Much of the discomfort with the term had to do with the disjuncture between the idea of community and the messy realities of actually existing communities, and it is this thread on which I want to focus here. On the one hand, there is the name "community," which comes wreathed with all the positive associations I have discussed; on the other, there is the refractory, often conflict-ridden reality within which NGO fieldworkers were operating. As one of our interviewees put it:

> I discovered at first hand how loosely the term community can be used. . . . Just to give you an idea, the village that the project was centred in had a population of about . . . 11,000 people, within about a three kilometre radius of the village and probably 35, 000 people within say, a ten kilometre radius. And the notion of community was just nonsense, in those circumstances. [There were] all sorts of different class within the community, groupings [with] different agendas, different religious groupings, even sort of different sub-ethnic groupings.

Later on in the same interview this person added:

> People are involved in day-to-day survival strategies. People . . . are essentially competing with each other. I think the notion of rural communities dancing around the maypole is you know. It's not like that. Certainly, I didn't see a great deal of sort of general co-operation between the people—I think they accept competition as reality.

For our interviewees the "community" existed not only as an undeniable reality—communities *had* been dispossessed, and it was their organization's goal to improve the lot of those communities—but also as some kind of platonic ideal that seemed to have little to do with the fractious and shifting realities with which they had to deal on a day-to-day basis. All too often, although the outlines of "the community" might seem clear enough at a distance, close up they had a frustrating tendency to dissolve into messy incoherence. Given the discomfort of so many of our interviewees with the term *community*, one might be tempted to ask why they did not simply jettison it. The problem here—and this is where the notion of hegemony can be useful—is that, quite apart from the very real pressure of funders, "community" was too much a part of the social reality within which they worked. It is only through the process of attaching names to the social landscape—such as community, class, and tribe—that the landscape is ordered and made intelligible. All of us when we look at the social world cannot but see it in terms of the preexisting categories that our particular social world has given us. This world is, as it were, always already named, and what we see as possible, impossible, desirable, inevitable, and so forth is crucially dependent on those names. As individuals it is difficult for us to abandon the categories that make the world intelligible to us. Any such renaming—at least as regards the fundamental categories—has to be a social process whereby a whole group is able to find a new, and to it more accurate, way of naming the world it sees. An effective renaming depends on a group having the power to impose its new account of reality.

In the course of the struggle against apartheid the term *community*, as Thornton and Ramphele stress, became a key political entity for both left and right. All those we interviewed had, as had their organizations, a strong identification with the opposition to apartheid. In practice what this often meant was the defense of black "communities." The person quoted above who said, "it's a term that is ours," undoubtedly spoke for many. Another spoke about the particular appeal the term could have for *white* South Africans:

> I think one of the reasons why . . . this term [community] became a catch-all phrase . . . was because it was a euphemism, a substitute for . . . black . . . people . . . and . . . I think the reason why was because . . . , because of the emotive value of the word. You know, it suggests rallying together, it conjures up images of warmth, and strength, and togetherness. . . . However I . . . I think that . . . white professionals working in NGOs, or white lefties, the reason why this was such an attractive term for *them* was because to a great extent they had lost their community. At that time by being, merely by being white lefties they were outside their communities. . . . This new term of "the community" was very attractive because maybe they could also be part of that community. But I think that . . . black people knew very well that the reality was that they were not part of that community.

Another important point made here is the way that "community" in South Africa became a kind of euphemism for black people; this was the entity on behalf of which the struggle against apartheid was being waged. Abandoning the term *community*, therefore, involves more than simply dropping a label that seems not to fit; it can almost feel like a denial of the struggle itself.

Community is also an inescapable part of the social landscape in which the Cape Town NGOs operated. Community remains in post-apartheid South Africa, as it was under apartheid, an official category. Communities have a very concrete existence in the legal framework of the state. It is communities, for example, that in the post-apartheid era can make claims for land restitution and land redistribution. NGOs like SPP or the CRLS, which work with communities involved in land restitution claims, have no choice but to work with "communities," however problematic this may be. And problematic it certainly is. As one person put it:

> There's such a variety of tenure needs within this grouping that is called "a community" and one of the main problems is that the Department of Land Affairs[7] is seeing them as a unified community, with one type of tenure need, to the extent that they are wanting to move all of them together from their disparate land holdings and current accommodation, to one piece of land on the outskirts of the town, and force them to be "a community."

Implicit in this kind of official categorization is an assumption that all the various members of a "community" share a set of common economic needs, whereas in reality this may not go much beyond a general desire to reclaim the land from which they were dispossessed. During the apartheid years a struggle waged around a general aim of repossession could be an effective way of mobilizing support and, since the land was not in fact about to be repossessed, questions about the precise forms of land tenure, what land should be used for, and so forth could be safely ignored. But when land repossession became, at least for some,[8] a reality, such questions had to be addressed, and inevitably this began to undermine the cozy illusion of the homogenous and harmonious community, as the following comment illustrates. After stressing his organization's long history of working in a particular area in which land was on the point of being returned, this NGO worker went on to say:

> But even there, who are we actually working with? We were working with Land Committees, historically. I would think that when a Land Committee says "the community wants this," or, "the community wants that," there's probably a fair

amount of truth in that. . . . But it's really based on kind of issues of national pride, . . . I mean nobody's really stopped to think, I think, what the land's going to be . . . what they're going to *do* with the land once they get it back. The question is, "our land was taken away from us, now we want it back." There's no guarantee that the Land Committee . . . does represent all of the interests of all the people. Certainly, the gender question would arise. About whether the women would really like the land back, or would they rather like housing? You know?

More generally, under apartheid all blacks were, to a large extent, welded into a single community of suffering, excluded by their racial categorization from any but the most menial of jobs or the most low-level of other economic opportunities. With the ending of apartheid people are no longer excluded from economic opportunities on the basis of race; those black South Africans who are in a position to take advantage of the new opportunities opening up are free to do so, but their interests are likely to be increasingly divergent from the many blacks who, because of their lack of relevant skills, capital, or whatever, again find themselves excluded, albeit no longer on racial grounds. In other words, various class differences, which remained embryonic under apartheid, are opening up larger and larger fissures in the old communities of struggle. Fractures, which were always there but which seemed insignificant compared with the overwhelming need to present a united front to the racist state, are increasingly more difficult to ignore. The old forms of community organization seem inadequate to the demands of the new economic and political order. As one person worried, "A committee that has been established . . . for a sort of a 'struggle' purpose . . . is not necessarily the appropriate committee to be deciding what should be done with the land at a subsequent stage."

Many of those we interviewed stressed the inescapably fractious nature of the communities with which they worked, and one of the perceived key fault lines was gender. The problems people ran into with gender illustrate some of the problems arising from the issues of heterogeneity within communities in general. Although the difficulties and hardships of life in South Africa's poorer "communities" may have fallen upon both men and women, their precise effects and the ways in which they were experienced were often systematically different for women and for men. A number of our interviewees talked about the gender differences within "communities" and their implications for NGOs trying to work with them. One of our interviewees, whom I shall call A, gave us a practical example. At the time he was working for a farmers' co-operative. The cooperative, which was made up of men, was very keen to get a tractor. A was personally convinced that this was not a good idea, foreseeing all kinds of technical problems, such as how the group could manage to maintain a tractor. He was reluctant to impose his view, however, and eventually a secondhand tractor was bought. At first there were indeed many of the technical problems that A had feared, but these were solved and finally the tractor started working. Then, however,

> a totally unanticipated problem arose, which I'd never thought about for a second. The women, historically, did the weeding and all the watering and all the rest of it. Now, up until then, the women had been weeding and watering perhaps twenty hectares. Now, all of a sudden, the tractor ploughed 400 hectares. ... And the same number of women had to weed and water ... eighty times or whatever the fact was, as much land. And it, it *incredibly* increased the pressure on them. Without really offering them any significant advantage ... the women just wound up with a bigger problem and no more power.

Presumably this increased workload did not come as such a surprise to the women involved, which raises the question of who gets to speak for "the community" in the arenas where such decisions are made. Women, it is clear, tend not to be given this role, but even among men there can be big differences in terms of power and status; it seems safe to assume that those who are entrusted with articulating a community's needs and aspirations are not likely to be the least powerful. In South Africa and in much of the rest of Africa, it is often taken for granted that the proper spokespeople for any "community" are older men who are well established locally, and it is the way they see their interests that tends to be given prominence, with women and younger men frequently being left out in the cold.[9]

Even when there is a genuine effort to identify women's needs, establishing what these are is not always easy, as another person stressed in talking about her experience of trying to find out what women want:

> These things need, I believe now, a lot of disaggregation. Obviously, in many places it's a place to live. ... And then the next, the next things [are] ... a creche, a clinic ... and then there are a list of things. They're social services in a way, that are particularly relevant to women. Now ... I've begun to think that ... those things—if one were to work with women around those things—need so much disaggregation, because that [a creche] was one of the things identified in this community. In fact there were about five people who were child-minders. Now, were they saying that that isn't good enough, that they want a building? Were they saying they want to be free so they can go out to work? *Is* there work? Were they saying, ja, you know: "We see in the white suburbs creches, so we want one of those as well." So every need that they identified to me, needs *mas-*

sive disaggregation. Is it like a fashion or is it that we want to be in competition with the child-minders? Is it, "I don't think the child-minders do it well enough—can we improve this?" Is it, *I* want, "you know, to make an income in a creche"? So you're talking about six women and oh, they want, "we've identified a creche." Is that because they think they'll get an income every month if they have it? . . . I don't trust those needs, that are being identified like that. I don't trust them. I'm sure they have a kernel but we've never . . . disaggregated enough to find out what is the kernel? Maybe the kernel is as simple as they want something *better* for their children—right from the word go?

Of course this argument does not apply only in the case of women. Men also articulate their desires in the light of what they think legitimate, appropriate, possible, and so forth. All of us articulate our desires within both a dense network of real and imagined constraints and an equally dense network of positive pressures pushing us toward what our particular time and place inculcate in us as what we are supposed to want. Even when those desires are ones we are told we should resist, the very fact that it is assumed that we will have these forbidden or antisocial desires helps to shape the landscape of desire. However much we may feel we know what we want, our desires have always arisen in a specific economic, political, and social context.

Another more general point that came up in the context of a discussion of gender was the enormous, and difficult to explain, variation there can be between places regarding who in fact gets to be a political spokesperson. The following quote is from a discussion of the differences among three apparently rather similar "communities" regarding the political role of women. All three areas mentioned here are rural and poor. All could fairly be described as conservative and strongly religious, and at first sight an outsider would probably be struck more by their similarities than by any differences.

> At X. There is a community Trust. So that's a kind of a new organization, . . . and . . . we had a very high turn-out of voters. And they voted in a trust which has 50/50 men and women, with *no* pushing and shoving. I mean that was how it fell, they chose people who they felt could do the [work]. Whereas if you do the same with one of these old places like Y, I mean, it's an old reserve area. There's much more discrimination against women. . . . But . . . , I still don't know why, but it varies enormously, I mean, in Z, which is also another old reserve area, the women play a *very* powerful role and, nearly in everything, they seem to be in the majority. They always take the lead. . . . Why? . . . I mean, I just, I can't understand it. The only thing that is that one is Catholic, where the women are so strong. And the other isn't Catholic. Whether that's got anything to do with it?

It's the only difference that I can really—it's just extraordinary... In Y, where ... there are women's organizations that have been going for ages and when it was this local government election, there was a big push to try and get women into local government and ... mostly it was men who nominated women, but they wouldn't stand ... even though they were nominated, they wouldn't accept nominations and so on. It's extraordinary. Whereas in the, in Z, there are a whole lot of women on the council. I just, I really can't understand why!

This variability is particularly important to stress in the context of gender because once the significance of gender is recognized "women" are all too often treated as an undifferentiated category. One of our interviewees cited above emphasized that "one cannot make assumptions about 'the community'"; similarly, one cannot make assumptions about "women."

Community as Historical Precipitate and Community as Interest Group

As I have stressed, those we interviewed seemed generally agreed that the term *community*, with its romantic haze, often seemed to have little to do with the protean and fractious realities with which they deal, and yet it was a term they felt they could not abandon. So how, in practice, did they approach these untidy realities? Running through a number of our interviews—and quite often within a single interview—were two rather different ways of thinking about the realities standing behind the name *community*. One of these focused on how collectivities defined as communities—whether by outsiders, themselves, or both—are the products of particular and, in the South African context often fiercely contested, histories. From this perspective, communities are essentially precipitates of the past. The second way of thinking about communities was to see them rather as groups which, explicitly or implicitly—community "in itself" or "for itself"—have interests in common or share some goal. The first of these two understandings, a sense of "community" as something resulting from shared historical experience, is illustrated by the following two descriptions, by two individuals within the same NGO, of a "community" that had been removed from their land and, at the time of our interview, was in the process of getting that land back. I shall call the community Missiondorp.

It was thirty four years ago that they left the land, so many of the Missiondorpers were not born yet. But they still have ..., they will become part of 'the

community.' They still have that historical experience, that understanding that
... that links me to that person over there.
    We [can] take an example of Missiondorp, which is a restitution case.
... Now there's no doubt, although that group of people haven't been together
for twenty years—they originally ... were removed from a place. They *were* a
community in the easiest sense of the word and they had that common thread:
that's where they came from.

One implication of thinking about communities in this way is to ask how a
given collectivity has become a community, in what sense it *is* a community,
and in whose eyes it is a community. These questions can only be answered by
careful empirical research into a community's specific history and the larger
histories within which it is located. This understanding of "community" accepts the sprawling, untidy, and contradictory reality of "communities" but
leaves us with the problem of how such incoherence can be seen as the active
subject of its own self-conscious history. Given that NGOs are in the business of producing change, changes moreover that are seen as being in the interest of "the community," as in the mission statements of SPP and DAG
quoted above, it is not surprising that many of our interviewees also tended to
define communities as some kind of interest groups. The first of the two people quoted above, whom I shall call B, also said this about Missiondorp:

[A community is] a group of people identifying that "we want that piece of
land," whether it's restitution or ... redistribution, whatever. And then you can
identify the community. And that community is inclusive of—and they themselves think of it in that way, I think—men, women, ... children. The various
levels of authority and right, rights and that sort of thing that then happens
within that community, doesn't mean that everybody has equal rights. But you
are all part of that community. If you are part of the group that are wanting land.
I think that becomes "the community."

At a certain point B explicitly denied that a shared past is enough to create
a community:

With the Missiondorp, for example, they were scattered, ... throughout the
Western Cape. They're not a community any more. They're a group of people
who have ... a common past experience, historical experience . They have to
recreate their community. But they all talk about "the community." And, in a
sense, I think the "community" is a group of people that identify with something

and that are in daily or weekly or monthly contact around that thing. Parts of the Missiondorp group of people are a community. So they live together, they've common struggles around day-to-day kind of aspects. Increasingly, the fight for the land which is over there and which is our common experience from the past, increasingly that is making people . . . *become* a community.

We all tend to use the same terms to mean different things in different contexts, particularly in the case of such large and shapeless concepts as "community," but when these different meanings collide with one another it can produce problems. For example, B described how in Missiondorp the Land Commission's mechanisms of land restitution, with their carefully demarcated rules of who is and is not entitled to benefit, collided with a far looser sense of community simply as shared past:

People lived there [Missiondorp] until 1962. They were then thrown out. Before then, people had left the land. . . . It was a mission station. And they had left it as a result of a fight with a minister or . . . to look for better options elsewhere. It's an incredibly difficult thing for the committee now, I mean it's happening right at this minute, where I'm saying to them, "your Constitution says: 'Missiondorpers are those that were removed.' But on your list of applicants to be part of "the community" you've got a whole lot of people who left beforehand." Now, they themselves, the committee, has said that they're not Missiondorpers. They're not, they don't have a right to be beneficiaries. But they can't enforce it. They can't get themselves to do this because those people who remained part of "the community," they have a right to return, from a moral point of view. From a legal point of view, they don't. So there is a situation there where you've got "the community" but you've also got another section which is . . . part but not really part. And I think [that] will become part, eventually.

This collision of meanings also points to the divergence there can be between such a community's own moral universe and hegemonies governing in the wider world of the state and NGOs.

South Africa's bitter and violent history has helped to blur the distinction between community as historical precipitate and community as interest group. In the face of the long history of state onslaughts on black South Africans, communities have tended to be brought into being as communities of struggle, united by their common need to defend themselves and their right to land. One person described this particular history, and the kind of communities it has brought into being, as follows:

For me community in many ways has been on as a debate ... since the 80s.
... We would refer to a group of people as a community and we very quickly
said, ... this is rubbish ... especially in urban centres, where this group of people might have been together for a few *months* and even if they'd been together
for a some years, they would've come together for various reasons, been *thrown*
together. They haven't sort of *chosen* to be together. ... Nevertheless, they did
have a common ... articulation of something. They had nowhere to stay and
they were as a *group* articulating that and so they did have to constitute themselves and I think they recognized that. ... Each time I need to define [what]
I'm specifically talking about. ... For me, it can be the community of people
that are *landless*—I mean it has a common thread in it.

Another of our interviewees thought that community, especially in the context of NGO work in post-apartheid South Africa, should be defined in
terms of a particular group of people who have explicitly committed themselves to a shared goal.

Let me end my account of NGO workers' confrontations with *community*
with this tentative suggestion for a re-imagining of the notion of "community":

My preference of defining community would be ... a group of people who have
a common interest in achieving a commonly held goal, which doesn't necessarily
coincide with a geographical ... line around a group of households....

I would prefer ... to see [the NGO] getting into more proactive projects
where they actually virtually advertise amongst ... the people that we have a ...
knowledge of or access to—and say, "right, we're starting a project in ... District
Six! ... Put your name on the list, and become part of that community if you
want to." Rather than constantly having to deal with a group of people who are
defined as a community just because they're there.

Conclusion

I hope the various examples I have given of NGO fieldworkers' struggles with
the concept of community have shown something of how a hegemonic term
such as *community*, although not determining how particular social realities
are mapped and understood, does nonetheless exert a strong shaping influence on how those realities appear to those whose business it is to intervene
in them. It is very difficult, it seems, to banish completely the roseate aura
that clings so persistently to the notion of community, even though, as I have

argued, *community* as a name tells us nothing about the relationships existing within any specific place designated as a community. It also tells us nothing about, and indeed tends to deflect our attention away from, the ways in which those living in a particular place are tied into larger political and economic realities. If we want to understand actual places at actual moments in history, as well as the relationships within them, it is necessary to engage in empirical investigation. This empirical investigation, however, must be—and this brings us back to Gramsci and the way knowledge is produced—informed by both the theoretical knowledge produced by intellectuals and the practical experience of those attempting to use the knowledge produced by intellectuals.

An empirical mapping of social realities that brings together theory and practical experience is especially necessary in post-apartheid South Africa, first because of the way in which the old racially based contours of social differentiation are shifting—although in complicated ways always shot through with the heavy racial legacy of the past—in favor of the more straightforwardly economic inequalities of any modern capitalist economy. It may be, for example, that categories such as employed, unemployed, landlord, and backyard tenant, which are not bounded within the geographical confines of a particular community, are more useful ways of naming and mapping out the often confused contours of power that South African NGOs confront. Second, the interrogation of the theoretical paradigms by local experience is crucial if the particularities of South African history and contemporary realities are not to be forced into the various ready-made and hegemonic maps generated not out of South African, or even African, histories but, most likely, out of European or North American ones.

The cozy embrace of community can too easily obscure real inequalities and conflicts of interest existing both within it and across its imagined boundaries. All too often community as a name is not merely silent about the inequalities and power differentials there may be within the "community" and between the "community" and the wider society, it also actively denies them. Mapping South Africa's social landscape as a series of "communities" can indeed be a way of silencing the realities of power.

8
Negotiating Identity in Post-Settlement South Africa
Ethnicity, Class, and Race in a Regional Frame

EDWARD RAMSAMY
Rutgers University

Introduction*

The transformation of South Africa from an apartheid state to a non-racial democracy is undoubtedly a complex process.[1] In addition to developing economic policies to reverse centuries of separate and unequal development, one of the major challenges facing the new South African state is forging a sense of national unity to overcome the legacy of deep racial division. The current transition in South Africa has been characterized by a rhetoric of reconciliation. However, the new political order faces the daunting task of how "yesterday's perpetrators and victims—today's survivors" confront the problem of

---

*I am indebted to Professors Betty Govinden of the University of Durban-Westville and Brij Maharaj of the University of Natal, Pietermaritzburg, as well as to Ms. Sylvia Gounden and Ms. Anushuya Gounden, who kindly sent me many articles I required from South Africa. Ms. Kavitha Ramsamy and Ms. Anitha Ramachandran read an earlier draft meticulously and offered insightful suggestions, for which I am indeed grateful; any remaining errors and omissions are completely mine. A note of thanks also goes to Professor Walton R. Johnson of Rutgers University, who introduced me to the Institute of African Studies at Columbia.

building "new and common identities" in a post-settlement South Africa (Mamdani, 1996a: 3).

A key tenet of apartheid policy was to encourage particularist consciousness among Indians, Coloureds, and the various African ethnic groups, following the old Roman maxim *divide et impera*—"divide and rule"—while simultaneously discouraging intergroup contact. Yet the history of resistance to apartheid reveals a strong tradition of cooperation among the different groups in spite of the state's attempt at racial fragmentation (Frederikse, 1990; Reddy, 1991). The spirit of unity was certainly evident at the 50th Conference of the African National Conference (ANC) in December 1997, when Kader Asmal, a South African of Indian ancestry, received the second highest number of votes from an African majority of delegates in an election for the ANC's national executive committee. In fact, four Indians were among the top 10 democratically elected members of the ANC's national executive committee, which may augur well for the ecumenical potential of South Africa in dealing with ethnic and cultural differences. However, it is disturbing, that in recent times, latent but rising ethno-nationalistic sentiments within each community are increasingly interrupting the long-standing tradition of racial solidarity against apartheid. For example, the non-racial ANC encountered significant problems in garnering the Indian and Coloured votes, in spite of these communities' previous identification with the broader African struggle, and in dealing with the volatility of Afrikaner and Zulu nationalism. The ANC lost an estimated 65 to 70 percent of the Indian and Coloured electorate to the National Party and lost the province of KwaZulu-Natal to Buthelezi's Inkatha Freedom Party in the first democratic elections. With respect to the Indian and Coloured votes, a clearly disappointed Nelson Mandela said after the elections:

> In the Indian and Coloured areas you find that as much as seventy percent of the population voted against an African government. They decided to vote to be part of a minority and not the majority. They decided to be part of a past which had divided us, created conflict, hostility, instead of being part of the future. . . . We have had the most difficult task in the government of National Unity because of the fact that the Indian and Coloured communities have identified themselves with the oppressors, and have created problems for me in promoting a spirit of reconciliation and the building of a nation which will be the joint activity of all South Africans.[2]

Sections within the ANC realize that minority anxieties and ethno-nationalism pose a threat to the vision of an inclusive and united South Africa. Still, in an effort to foster inclusiveness, Mandela and current president Thabo Mbeki campaign for a spirit of reconciliation. In this vein, Archbishop Tutu's (1994) exuberant definition of South Africa as the "Rainbow Nation" has also been embraced by Mandela and others in the ANC leadership as a unifying point of identification.

This chapter focuses on four issues related to the challenges of nation-building in South Africa. The first section is an overview of the ANC's shifting position on the national question, paying particular attention to the ANC's stance before and after its unbanning in 1990. The next two parts examine the challenges Zulu nationalism poses to the new political order in South Africa and the politics of ethno-nationalism among the Indian community. The concluding section highlights the dual challenge South Africa faces: overcoming socioeconomic inequality and building a collective sense of nationhood.

Group Identity and the National Liberation Struggle in South Africa

The white ruling classes of South Africa imposed an exclusive nationalism that marginalized from the body politic the indigenous Africans and other non-whites, whose political, economic, and social rights were restricted to protect white economic privilege and political power from non-white democratic demands (Magubane, 1996; Marks & Trapido, 1987). Consequently, social movements fighting white minority rule contested the restricted white definition of South African nationhood, and each advanced alternative images of a national community that contrasted with those of the other movements (Marx, 1993). The ANC and other groups ideologically committed to the Freedom Charter (commonly referred to as the Charterists) stressed the principle of non-racialism and emphasized the need for unified national coalitions to achieve their political and economic goals.[3] In its formative years, the ANC believed that the different national groups in South Africa could carry out the struggle against apartheid by maintaining separate, racially defined organizational bases. This view was subsequently replaced by a commitment to non-racialism, and the ANC opened its doors to all South Africans who were committed to its philosophy. Charterist organizations rejected the ethnic nationalism promoted by the state as well as the Africanist conceptions of nationalism that included only indigenous peoples. The activists belonging to this tradition generally highlighted the common interests of all peoples, relegated ethnicity and other cultural differences to the private sphere, and advanced a self-defined "imagined community" of the South African nation, "united by the experience of history, shared ideas and a sense of destiny" (Marx, 1992: 15). However, the ANC, in spite of its non-racialism, still recognized and gave tacit approval to ethnically based organizations like the Natal Indian Congress (Ramsamy, 1996; Singh & Vawda, 1988).

Other resistance movements such as the Black Consciousness Movement (BCM) and the Pan African Congress have advanced alternative positions on the national question (Davies, O'Meara & Dlamini, 1988; Frederickson, 1995; Murray, 1995; Walters, 1993). However, the ANC's Charterist position began to dominate popular opposition to apartheid in the 1980s. With the ANC's overwhelming electoral victory in 1994 and 1999, the Charterist position has emerged as the major axis of contestation pertaining to the national question.

Prior to the 1994 elections the ANC broadly defined the national question in terms of ending white minority rule, ending the Bantustan policy, and the political unification and integration of the country to create a single South African nation (Jordan, 1988). In addition to overcoming the racial and ethnic divisions of the apartheid era, the national liberation struggle in South Africa, as elsewhere in the developing world, looked forward to a more equitable development path upon independence. The ANC reiterated on many occasions that the transformation would entail more than just flag independence. It is ironic that Joe Slovo, a central figure in negotiating crucial compromise clauses with the white government in the recent transition, had once written that

> [i]t is inconceivable for liberation to have any meaning without a return of the wealth of the land to the people as a whole. It is, therefore a fundamental feature of our strategy that victory must embrace more than formal political democracy. To allow existing economic forces to retain their interests intact is to feed the root of racial supremacy and does not represent even a shadow of liberation.[4]

These sentiments were popularized during the insurrections of the 1980s. The major liberation movements in South Africa, including the ANC, had begun to articulate a radical reconstruction policy in the 1960s and 1970s, inspired by revolutionary Marxism and socialist ideologies. Rob Nixon (1992) argues that the anti-apartheid struggle became wedded to socialism and revolution during the populist insurrections of 1976–1977 and 1984–1986. Statements from the Freedom Charter such as "the banks and monopoly industry shall be transferred to the ownership of the people as a whole; . . . all people shall have the right to live where they choose, [and] to be decently housed," implied that an ANC-led government would follow a radical reconstructionist path once it came to power.

Following Mandela's release from prison, opposition movements shifted from a politics of confrontation to one of negotiation and incorporation. Due to various national and international constraints, the current ANC-led government has opted for a pragmatic development path, abandoning the socialist principles and radical ideologies it espoused during its years in exile. After its historic electoral victory, the ANC focused more on national reconciliation and nation-building, trying to find "a place for everyone" in the "new" South Africa. Echoing Tutu's metaphor of a "Rainbow Nation," Mandela stressed in his inauguration speech that "we shall build a society in which all South Africans, both black and white, will be able to walk tall, . . . a rainbow nation at peace with itself and the world."[5] Mandela has repeatedly gone to great lengths to stress the principle of reconciliation: "I love each one of you—of all races. I sincerely wish the pockets of my shirts were big enough to put all of you in. I regard you as my children and grandchildren, every one of you."[6]

Mandela's gesture of wearing a Springbok rugby jersey when South Africa won the 1995 rugby World Cup was enthusiastically accepted even by white South Africans, especially Afrikaners who passionately follow the sport. Adam (1996: 7) points out that with such an inclusive style and rhetoric, Mandela is admired even by some of his former enemies. Eugene de Kock, killer-commander of an aberrant police force, praised Mandela as "the most important figure after Jesus Christ." Even the 93-year-old Betsie Verwoerd welcomed Mandela when he visited her in Orania. [7] His apparent lack of bitterness has "symbolically exonerated whites from the sins of apartheid," according to Adam (1996: 8).

However, in light of the gross socioeconomic inequalities in South Africa and the ANC's own former rhetoric of radicalism, it remains to be seen how long the spirit of goodwill and reconciliation will be maintained. Mandela seems to believe in a Pareto optimal solution to the economic and political crisis in South Africa, in which resources could be allocated in a manner so that the conditions of the poorest will be improved without worsening the conditions of the affluent. This means addressing the serious disparity between blacks and whites without affecting the high standard of living enjoyed by white South Africans. Although the transition in South Africa clearly has enjoyed broad popular support, there is a growing sense of disillusionment among the lower socioeconomic classes, who have not benefited tangibly and materially from the transition. Africans constitute 76 percent of South Africa's 37.9 million people, whereas whites make up only 12 percent, but 95 percent of poor South Africans are African. The average white earns more than nine times the income of the average African, and unemployment rates are 4 percent for whites but 40 percent for Africans.[8] A further problem is that whites as a group are still reserved about Mandela despite his repeated overtures toward them and his demonstrated commitment to reconciliation rather than revenge in spite of his 27-year imprisonment. A recent Markinor opinion poll showed that Democratic Party leader Tony Leon was far more popular among whites than Mandela. A clearly annoyed black newspaper editorial asked whites: "Have those who voted for Leon suddenly forgotten President Mandela's olive branch to those who incarcerated him and ruined this country's economy and political and social fibre?"[9]

These realities have caused the ANC to occasionally abandon its rhetoric of national reconciliation and highlight the serious racial inequalities that characterize the "Rainbow Nation." At the ANC national conference in 1997, Mandela chastised white South Africans for failing to participate in the economic and social transformation of the country. President Thabo Mbeki argued that far from being a Rainbow Nation, South Africa is "still divided into two nations: one of relatively rich whites and another larger nation of the black poor." He went on to warn that "we are faced with the danger of a mounting rage to which we must respond seriously."[10] The task of reconciling these two nations is daunting indeed. Although a small segment of the black population has benefited from the transition, the economic disparities are likely to cause serious fractures and make the goal of unity increasingly elusive. The racial/class disparity is one of the most serious issues facing the new black government, and it has been compounded by the politics of ethno-nationalism.

The Politics of Zulu Nationalism

Chief Mangosuthu Gatsha Buthelezi and his Inkatha Freedom Party (IFP) pose one of the most serious challenges to the ANC in its quest for a non-ethnic political future for South Africa. In the mid-1980s, the conflict between the ANC and Inkatha in parts of Natal escalated into a small-scale civil war. Interestingly, the conflict between the two parties has been frequently and incorrectly represented in ethnic terms. An article in the *Johannesburg Star* stated that "it is nonsense to think that one could isolate political divisions from ethnic divisions." Another article in *Spear of the Nation* also examined the conflict through the lens of ethnicity and argued that "the fierce fighting between Xhosas and Zulus [is] deeply rooted in the past, particularly in the proud warrior history of the Zulu nation" (Taylor, 1991: 4). Such descriptions are inaccurate because they conflate two different conflicts. The *inter-ethnic* tensions are mostly confined to migrant workers' hostels, whereas the far more serious violence in Natal, in which some 30,000 people have died since the mid-1980s, is largely an *intra-ethnic* ideological conflict among Zulus. Heribert Adam, Federick Van Syl Slabbert, and Kogila Moodley (1997: 126) situate the conflict within three larger, overlapping sociocultural struggles: modernity versus traditionalism, traditional versus modern democratic legitimacy, and urban insiders versus rural outsiders. The conflict originated in the early 1980s when Inkatha tried to incorporate several urban townships under its authority to strengthen its weak urban base. Inkatha was pushed farther to the right of the political spectrum as movements like the United Democratic Front (UDF) assumed the center stage of oppositional politics. With the assistance of the apartheid state, Buthelezi's Inkatha movement increasingly resorted to terror tactics to solidify its weakening position (Marè & Hamilton, 1987; Sutcliffe & Wellings, 1988).

The unbanning of the ANC, PAC, and the South African Communist Party (SACP) in February 1990 fundamentally altered the terrain of South African politics for Buthelezi. Once regarded as the ruling classes' "great white hope," Buthelezi was marginalized from the national and international scene as Nelson Mandela's ANC assumed center stage. Buthelezi also felt alienated from the transition process as the NP and ANC made a number of bilateral deals. The end of apartheid spelled the demise of the homeland system and with it Inkatha's access to institutionalized power, funds, and means of coercion. As a consequence, Inkatha attempted to reinvent itself. Despite its rhetoric of an inclusive pan-Africanism, Inkatha was essentially a Zulu political organization. In an effort to keep up with political transformation in South Africa, Inkatha attempted to transform itself into a broader-based political party by changing its name to the Inkatha Freedom Party (IFP) and opening itself up to all races. Senzo Mfayela, chair of IFP local government election campaigns, explained the transformation as follows:

> [W]e thought, as a party in 1990, after de Klerk's speech and the release of Mandela, politics had changed dramatically in South Africa. It was no more a case of fighting against apartheid. That was gone. So we entered a new phase of politics where we had an open political market and were now moving away from protest politics to the politics of building one South Africa that includes everybody. (Jung, 1996: 48)

While the IFP was attempting to broaden its base, it simultaneously evoked images of Zulu nationalism to strengthen its position in the negotiation process. Buthelezi refused to participate in CODESA because the Zulu monarch, King Goodwill Zwelithini, was not represented at the talks.[11] Through the transition process and beyond, Buthelezi continued to be "the most insistent entrepreneur of politicised Zulu identity" (Campbell et al., 1995: 289). In his speeches, he underlined the history of Zulu resistance to British colonialism and repeatedly accused the ANC of engaging in a campaign to "eliminate KwaZulu entirely from the new South Africa." "Can we tolerate the great Zulu nation being brought to its knees?" he asked. "We are born Zulu South Africans and we will die Zulu South Africans, and we have a historic responsibility to make our Zulu contribution to the emergence of a new, just, free, and prosperous South Africa. For this we will die."[12] Nixon argues that Buthelezi's manipulation of Zulu identity is a "neo-genetic attempt at shielding [his] ethnic organization against competing claims of historical identities" (1993: 16).

The ANC experienced a great deal of difficulty in articulating a clear policy toward Buthelezi and his Zulu nationalist politics. Prior to its unbanning in 1990, the ANC tried to isolate Buthelezi, criticizing his ethno-nationalism and collaboration with the NP. In a highly critical book Mzala (1988) of the ANC's research department portrays Buthelezi as an opportunistic fraud who willingly cooperated with the white ruling classes and subverted African interests in his own quest for power. John Saul, a Canadian activist/intellectual and ANC sympathizer, called Buthelezi "a hired tool of the security services" (1991: 16). The ANC's instinct was to sideline Buthelezi because his advocacy of Zulu nationalism ran contrary to its own commitment to non-racialism. However, in contrast to the prevailing ANC view on Inkatha at the time, Mandela adopted a tone of reconciliation in his first public speech on the conflict in Natal, just two weeks after his release from prison. Although ANC sympathizers had long blamed Inkatha for the conflict, Mandela said that the responsibility must be shared: "We have reached a stage where none of the parties can be regarded as right or wrong. Each carries a painful legacy of the past few years."[13] Mandela drew his first jeers and boos from an audience since his release on February 12, 1990, when he praised Inkatha for demanding that the ANC be legalized. "While there are fundamental differences between us, Inkatha has spurned the government's attempts to entice it into a separate negotiated settlement. This stand of Inkatha has contributed in no small measure to making it difficult for the regime to implement successive schemes designed to perpetuate minority rule." The crowd responded disapprovingly when Mandela said, "We extend a hand of peace to Inkatha and hope that it might one day be possible for us to share a platform with its leader, Chief Mangosuthu Gatsha Buthelezi."[14]

At first, the ANC's leadership in exile did not respond favourably to Mandela's conciliatory gestures toward Inkatha. A proposed meeting between Mandela and Buthelezi was unilaterally canceled by the ANC, and the two sides met only in late September 1990 after an escalation of the violence.[15] The political wisdom of isolating Inkatha, in light of the increasing violence, was increasingly questioned by many within and outside the ANC. Herbert Vilakazi (1991) argued in the left-leaning publication *Work in Progress* that the ANC had made a strategic error in trying to isolate Inkatha. Furthermore, the ANC's contradictory policies and double standards toward the homelands exacerbated the situation. At the same time that Buthelezi's Bantustan regime was vilified by the ANC, other ANC-aligned Bantustans, like the Transkei, were embraced. The ANC's own unprincipled and contradictory position thus reinforced and legitimated the ethnic suspicions of Zulus who supported Buthelezi (Adam & Moodley, 1993).

In light of these realities, the ANC altered its position on non-racialism and tried to appropriate symbols of Zuluness and Zulu culture for its own political purposes. In the early 1990s, when the violence in Natal reached staggering heights, the NP considered banning the carrying of weapons (mainly spears and shields) in public. The IFP protested, arguing that the Zulus had a right to carry their "cultural weapons" and that a restriction on traditional weapons "would stifle the cultural expression of the Zulus" (Jung, 1996: 48). After initially opposing the IFP on the issue of "cultural weapons," the ANC changed its position to challenge Buthelezi's construction of Zuluness and his appropriation of Zulu culture and symbols. S'bu Ndebele, an ANC member of the provincial legislature, put it as follows:

> Finally I made a decision and it caused quite a stir within the ANC even. I said "we are also Zulus, we also have the right to carry traditional weapons." And I said that to the people, because . . . we don't have the right to tell any Zulu not to carry those weapons. . . . It was at Inanda. There were about 60 000 or 70 000 people there . . . carrying anything that could vaguely be called a traditional weapon. They had spears, clubs, everything. . . . And we were using the same slogans about Zuluness and about the King, and Shaka. We were using the same slogans. (Jung, 1996: 49)

In response, Buthelezi alleged that his Inkatha movement was the sole guardian of Zulu culture, and the ANC then attempted to subvert this claim by illustrating that Zulu history was an integral part of the ANC's legacy. The memory of Albert Luthuli, the Nobel laureate and Zulu leader of the ANC, was frequently evoked by the ANC to counteract claims that it was predominantly a Xhosa movement.

In this manner, the ANC conceded to the potential power of ethnic mobilization around Zulu identity. However, the ANC's dialogue with Inkatha and its challenge to the IFP's monopoly of Zulu symbols had mixed results. On the one hand, the conferences between the ANC and IFP did help in lowering the levels of violence; South Africa, and indeed the world, breathed a sigh of relief when Buthelezi made a last-minute decision to call off a potentially calamitous boycott of the 1994 elections.[16] The IFP went on to win the provincial election with 50.3 percent of the vote, contrary to expectations and opinion polls. Anthony Lemon contends that Inkatha's electoral victory in KwaZulu-Natal "was effectively a negotiated outcome following substantial evidence of electoral malpractice in the region" (1996: 111). The IFP is now part of the national government, with Buthelezi occupying the important cabinet position of Minister of Home Affairs. He has also acted as president occasionally during Mandela's visits abroad. There is even repeated speculation about a merger between the ANC and the IFP with the hope that it will bring about peace in KwaZulu-Natal. On the other hand, cooperation at the top does not automatically translate into stability on the ground. People's memories, sentiments, and grievances do not fade easily. Also, local leaders and warlords may not relinquish fiefdoms carved out during 20 years of bitter conflict just because political elites are striking deals in conference halls.

The National Question and the Indian Community

Indians constitute just 3 percent of the South African population. Approximately 80 percent of Indians live in KwaZulu-Natal and are mainly concentrated in and around the Durban metropolitan region, which gives them considerable voice in this area despite their small numbers nationally but also complicates the already volatile ethno-class tensions in the province (Desai & Maharaj, 1996). Indians are sandwiched between the powerful and affluent white minority and the disadvantaged African majority. The apartheid state has frequently exploited this vulnerability and fueled tensions between the African majority and the Indian minority (Bhana, 1991; Maharaj, 1992; Padayachee, Vawda & Tichmann, 1985; Pahad, 1988). There were sporadic instances of violent conflict between Indians and Africans. However, the absence of continued racial violence attests to the success of past political movements in building inter-ethnic coalitions in spite of the divisive strategy of the apartheid state, the middleman position of Indians in the racial pecking order, and segments of the Indian merchant class that have a reputation for exploiting poor Africans (Adam & Moodley, 1986; Bhana, 1997; Moodley, 1980; Reddy, 1986). Nevertheless, without the political or economic power of the whites or the numerical security of the Africans, Indians have often found themselves in a precarious position politically, fearing both white and African domination. Perceiving themselves to be politically and culturally encroached upon by both whites and Africans, Indians have retreated into a kind of "cultural narcissism" when faced with hostility (Adam & Moodley, 1986: 37). Their reservations about an African government, for example, were evident in Indian voting choices in the 1994 democratic elections. In an effort to survive in South Africa, Indians have practiced a contradictory politics, whether it is in expressing solidarity with the African majority, in withdrawing into forms of cultural nationalism and isolationism, or in voting against the ANC.

When the first democratic elections were held in 1994, it was expected that Indians would overwhelmingly support the ANC, given their disfranchisement under white rule. Natal Indian Congress activist and social historian Yunus Carrim predicted that most Indians would vote for the ANC:

> It would seem that the history of the Indian people, their past political engagement, their subordinate position under white minority rule and the virulent anti-Indianism of the NP in the past, would constitute an important foundation for the ANC to win significant support among Indians.[17]

Contrary to this expectation, however, many Indians voted for de Klerk's National Party. The method of polling used in the national elections made it difficult to ascertain exactly how specific ethnic/racial groups voted because the results were reported in terms of provincial totals. Consequently, Indian voting patterns had to be gauged from opinion polls. Andrew Reynolds estimates that approximately 65 to 70 percent of Indians and Coloureds voted for the NP (1994: 192). The NP received approximately one-tenth of the Natal vote and depended heavily on Indian supporters. Furthermore, a significant number of Indian voters in Chatsworth in Natal remained loyal to the tri-cameral parliament politician Amichand Rajbansi, who gave his Minority Party its only seat in parliament. A similar trend was observed in the Western Cape, where the Coloured population also voted for the NP. Z. Erasmus and E. Pieterse (1997) put forth the following reasons for the Indian and Coloured voting pattern: Coloured people share a language and religious affiliation with white people, they are racist in their attitude toward Africans and anti-ANC, they suffer from slave mentality and are psychologically damaged, and they have to unshackle themselves from their ideological chains. Although there may be some truth in these "explanations" of the Indian and Coloured vote, they decontextualize and dehistoricize the choices made by the Indian and Coloured communities given the contradictory political and cultural circumstances these communities face.

First of all, in attempting to reach beyond its traditional white constituency, the NP tried to manipulate the fears of the Indian community. In an aggressive election campaign, some NP officials reportedly spread rumors that Africans would soon seize Indian homes.[18] On his campaign trail, de Klerk repeatedly stated that the Indians had been intimidated by ANC supporters, not NP supporters, and that their homes were under threat.[19] The National Party campaign successfully tapped into existing economic and racial insecurities in the Indian and Coloured communities; for example, the invasion by neighboring African squatters of vacant low-income Indian homes in Cato Manor, Durban, substantiated the community's fear of retributive actions by the Africans.[20] Many saw these events as indicative of future measures to dispossess them of their hard-earned gains. During its election campaign, the ANC tried to allay Indian fears about their property rights, but people remained skeptical because of the ANC's inability to take action during the invasion.[21]

Second, although there are a number of Indians in the hierarchy of the ANC, the frequent rejection of Indian identity by Indian ANC activists has also contributed to the community's misgivings about the ANC. After historically demoting ethnicity in favor of the umbrella ideology of non-racialism, the ANC now finds itself in a quandary, unsure about how to respond to the power of ethnic identification in the Indian and Coloured communities as well as among Africans as exemplified by Zulu nationalism.

Third, the symbolic "Africanization" of the ANC, as exemplified in its overtures to the Zulus, has made it difficult for the ANC to gain the support of Indians, many of whom fear African political and cultural domination in a post-settlement era (Adam & Moodley, 1993). In an attempt to woo the Indian vote, the ANC named two tri-cameral politicians, J. N. Reddy and D. S. Rajah, as candidates, giving them priority over NIC leaders George Sewpershad and Ismail Meer. The NIC protested, claiming that it was hypocritical for their organization to campaign for the same individuals they protested against during the tri-cameral elections. Reddy and Rajah were subsequently dropped from the ticket.[22]

Fourth, generational differences also played a role in the political choices made by the Indian community. The trauma of the Indian-African riot of 1949 remains embedded in the folk history of the older generation, creating a sense of mistrust and doom. The poorest sections of the Indian community bore the brunt of the upheaval because of their greater proximity to the African poor in outlying slum areas. Surveys indicate that the Indian poor feel greater fear of the possible negative repercussions of the recent changes than do more affluent Indians. Bill Freund (1995) estimates that the ANC's share of the Indian vote, 25 percent, came from younger, more educated, middle-class Indians. This leads to the fifth element, that class factors were also important in determining the Indian vote.

The final major factor influencing Indian attitudes toward the new order is the factional warfare between the ANC and Inkatha in KwaZulu-Natal, where 80 percent of the Indian population lives. Indian support for the ANC would have antagonized Buthelezi's Inkatha movement. The Indian community itself was frequently threatened with violence by Buthelezi when Indian activists and politicians openly criticized his politics. When Fatima Meer, a veteran NIC member, asserted in a public forum in 1976 that Buthelezi was not a credible leader and that the real black leaders were on Robben Island, her statement was raised in the KwaZulu legislature as a case of Indians insulting African leaders, and open threats of a repetition of the 1949 race riots were made. A year later, when Buthelezi was invited to address a meeting at the University of Durban–Westville, Indian students protested that he was a government stooge, and again Buthelezi responded with threats of "another 1949." He threatened Indians again in 1990 when African and Indian students prevented him from addressing a public forum at the University of Durban–Westville. The boycott by the Indians of the tri-cameral system in 1984 suggests that they are more likely to support African causes if Buthelezi and other oppositional movements agree with each other on an issue. When Inkatha and the UDF both campaigned for a boycott of the tri-cameral elections, Indians expressed their most forceful commitment to a politics of non-racialism. Therefore, tensions between Inkatha and the ANC during the national elections of 1994 undoubtedly played a role in the Indian community's support for the National Party.

The persistence of group identification within the Indian community is an example of defensive nationalism, which ought to be understood as a product of the social and cultural reproduction of the community as it is situated within apartheid and the global sociopolitical and economic order. Culturally, Indians are generally endogamous and have a strong extended family system. The cohesiveness of the community is also maintained through a network of associations and institutions, including religious bodies, schools, welfare organizations, management committees, and business groups. These organizations play crucial roles in group reproduction and reinforce identity through their teachings and everyday practices (Moodley, 1980). In the current period, Indians perceive that their economic, cultural, and religious rights may be crushed by African majority rule and therefore feel compelled to assert group identity more vehemently than in the past. It is clear that the implications of the current reform initiatives for the Indian community are the most important factor in influencing Indian political choices at present. For example, unskilled Indian workers fear African competition. Professionals and students tend to be less apprehensive but express concern that affirmative action programs and Africanization will inhibit their upward mobility in the new order.

At the 1991 National Convention of the ANC, Mandela acknowledged that the ANC will have to take the power of ethnic mobilization into greater consideration: "We must ask ourselves frankly why this is so. . . . [We have to] confront the real issue that these national minorities might have fears about the future. . . . The ordinary man, no matter to what population group he belongs, must look at our structures [ANC structures] and say that "I, as a Coloured man, am represented. I have got Allan Boesak there whom I can trust. And an Indian must also be able to say: There is Kathrada—I am represented."[23] Mandela's invitation to Indian actress Shabana Azmi to campaign for the ANC in the Indian community also reflects his acknowledgment of "Indian consciousness."[24]

Mandela's sensitivity toward the power of ethnic mobilization met with opposition from political movements to the left of the ANC and from certain members of the ANC alliance. Neville Alexander of the Workers' Organization for Socialist Action (WOSA) charged that the ANC's notion of ethnic representation is analogous to the National Party's policy of separate development.[25] The ANC's attempt to build a governmental leadership core representative of the diverse ethnic/racial groups in South Africa was thwarted by a number of controversies, beginning with the removal of Indian John Samuel from the position of Director General of Education. Although Samuel headed the ANC's Strategic Management Committee and designed its education policy, certain individuals within the ANC caucus felt that it was inappropriate for an Indian to head the education department in the new South Africa. They argued that John Samuel lacked the "credentials" to advance African educational interests and that his directorship would portray the ANC as being insufficiently sensitive to African needs in the new order.[26] When a faked confidential memorandum alleging a plot to remove Nelson Mandela as president of the ANC was circulated in 1992, Indians were the first to be suspected (Parekh, 1993). Finally, Cyril Ramaphosa, who was once seen as Mandela's successor, was identified by critics as a member of an "Indian-dominated cabal" alleged to control the party. These critics included Peter Mokaba, past president of the ANC Youth League, and Winnie Mandela, both of whom recognized that Africanization has enormous popular appeal.[27] Winnie Mandela reiterated at the Truth and Reconciliation Commission (TRC) hearings that an Indian cabal was responsible for her predicament.[28] Her contention that the UDF's 1989 statement distancing itself from her was also the work of an Indian cabal is another example of expedient racial sniping, which can only defeat the cause of national reconciliation and generate more tensions between Indians and Africans. The bigotry inherent in her reference to Murphy Morobe as "Murphy Patel" sends a loud signal that Indians can be conveniently scapegoated by ambitious politicians for the woes of the nation.[29] Although Winnie's argument that the ANC government has neglected poor Africans is true, her accusation that Indians are somehow responsible for that and her own current predicament is a brand of reactionary nationalism that will not only hurt Indians but also derail the quest for a just socioeconomic order in South Africa.

Conclusion

Post-settlement South Africa faces the twin challenges of overcoming the obstacles of socioeconomic inequality while building a collective sense of nationhood in a society that continues to be deeply divided along ethnic and racial lines. These challenges are intertwined. National solidarity cannot be nurtured or sustained in a climate of acute economic disparities when large segments of the population have not yet benefited from the changes. In addition to the structural limitations faced by the ANC in restructuring the economy equitably, there is the growing danger of expedient politicians igniting reactionary populist nationalism to rouse their constituents. Such tactics have historically provided an escape hatch for ruling elites seeking to evade popular demands for social justice, to marginalize political opponents (mainly left-wing critics), and to attribute socioeconomic problems to visible but less powerful groups. The exclusive *leitmotif* of the growing rhetoric of "Africanization" threatens to undermine the ANC's commitment to a democratic and inclusive political order. In a paper delivered at a special ANC parliamentary caucus on the national question, ANC member of parliament Wally Serote writes about Africans:

> [T]heir being indigenous to South Africa, their being in the majority and most important, their being the most oppressed group in the country, dictates to and seeks a special positioning for them within the liberation process and the resolution of the National Question. (Serote, 1997)

Serote goes on to argue that "the liberation movement is overwhelmingly African both in numbers and content, and that it is the African vote which has established the initial stages of the democratic South Africa, whose base is a democratic culture" (Serote, 1997). Peter Mokaba, deputy minister of Environmental Affairs and Tourism, calls for unity and empowerment of Africans first:

> [T]he need to consolidate power in our country must first and foremost entail the imperative of consolidating our power base. On the basis of that strength we must move to consolidate the Black power base. . . . If 60% of the 62% that voted the ANC into power is African, why is it that the percentages of other national groups in the leadership structures is more than their contribution to the democratic vote? (Mokaba, 1997)

The increasing appeal of Africanization to segments of the ANC's leadership and membership can be understood partly as the need for restoring self-worth after years of economic and psychological battery under apartheid as well as a general response to the degradation of African humanity in Western thought and practice historically. Africanization as cultural resistance is an important element in the struggle of marginalized populations to assert their identities and historical agency. In this context, according to Stuart Hall, cultural nationalism may be understood as "the source of the production of new subjectivity" (Hall, 1993). Edward Said also feels that "for those of us emerging from marginality and persecution, nationalism is a necessary thing: a long-deferred and denied identity that needs to come out into the open and take its place among other identities" (1991: 16). However, as the euphoria of liberation dies, the bitter lesson of the decolonization process is that national elites employ the same divisive techniques used by former colonial rulers to guarantee their privileges and maintain their power base. As Fanon (1968) ever so perceptively observed in his classic *Wretched of the Earth*, unless national consciousness, at its moment of success, is transformed into a genuine desire and quest to re-order society on a more equitable basis, there is always the risk of extending the old order. National elites, Fanon warned, can easily become co-opted agents of the former colonial elite by reconstituting the hierarchies and divisions of the old order and placing themselves at the helm.

Anthony Appiah notes that some forms of cultural nationalism, like the brand championed by Mokaba and others in the South African case, are misguided because they "propose as a basis for common action the illusion that black people are fundamentally allied by nature" (1992: 176). The pitfall of Mokaba's racial reasoning is that it obscures the complexities of region, class, gender, historical, and social differences within unitary categories such as race and ethnicity. The form of Africanization promoted by Mokaba, Serote, and others will not alter the fundamental relations of power in South Africa, which already has one of the most unequal distributions of income in the world. In 1991, the poorest 40 percent of the households in South Africa earned just 4 percent of the total income of South Africans. The richest 10 percent earned more than 50 percent of the income. Black professionals, skilled workers, and entrepreneurs benefited most from the erosion of apartheid. The richest 20 percent of the black households increased real average incomes by almost 40 percent during 1991, making them the most upwardly mobile group. Although class still overlaps with race in South Africa, the divide is more complicated than it was during the apartheid years. In 1975, less than 10 percent of the richest 20 percent of the households were black. By 1991, this figure had risen to 26 percent.[30] Three years after the election of the ANC government, black conglomerates controlled 10 percent of market capitalization in the Johannesburg stock exchange (Adam, 1998).

The ANC's deputy minister of Trade and Industry, Phumzile Mlambo-Nguka, has said that "Black business men should not be shy to say they want to become filthy rich."[31] Supporting this line of thinking, Peter Mokaba believes that the failures of capitalism have nothing to do with profit seeking by a privileged few, but rather with the fact that "distribution and allocation have been mismanaged.... The minor problem with capitalism has been that the markets are unable to read any signals from the poor and therefore fail to respond to them."[32] As head of the ANC's Youth League, Mokaba was once the very acme of radicalism, criticizing Mandela's reconciliatory overtures to whites and chanting along with Winnie Mandela, "Kill the boer, kill the farmer" (Bell, 1998). This former champion of economic justice is now an advocate for an American Reagan-style trickle down economics. For Mokaba, "the super-exploitation of black workers in South Africa, pioneered by the mining houses, with the compound system, pass laws, and racial organization of production, was just mismanaged distribution" (Nzimande & Cronin, 1997: 2). However, to shield themselves from the class warfare that inevitably results from the free play of market forces, expedient politicians like Mokaba could deflect the conflict along ethnic lines by blaming relatively powerless "middleman" minorities for socioeconomic inequalities rather than examining their own policy choices. A further complication is that because the ANC's support base is primarily urban workers, rural poverty is often overlooked or ignored, thereby giving rural-based parties like Inkatha the opportunity to politicize ethnicity.

The new government of national unity undoubtedly faces enormous challenges as it attempts to unify a highly fractured society dealing with many contending ideologies. Some factions within the ANC have begun to realize that a sense of common nationalism can be embraced only by accepting the cultural diversity in South Africa despite the fact that "diversity" was used historically as a euphemism for apartheid. Cultural diversity need not be tantamount to legitimating the old apartheid order if it is used to foster mutual recognition and a joint uplifting of self and other. Cultural ethnicity becomes a problem only when it is transformed into an economic and political ethnicity intended to give particular groups power and leverage over others, as in the case of apartheid. Non-racialism need not imply colorblindness, as observed by Adam: "Non-racialism merely holds out the promise that the state will not recognize or tolerate race as a public and legal criterion of exclusion" (1995: 473). Therefore, non-racialism does not and ought not to imply that ethnicity is an insignificant arena of struggle in post-apartheid South Africa. In the spirit of reconciliation, the Rainbow Nation of South Africa must come to terms with racial and ethnic difference as well as socioeconomic inequality.

9
Negotiable Property
Making Claims on Land and History in Asante, 1896–1996

SARA BERRY
Johns Hopkins University

Throughout the twentieth century, land has been a contested terrain in Africa, both in a literal sense and as a central focus of struggles over legitimacy, authority, and identity. In countries such as Kenya and South Africa, where European settlers claimed hugely disproportionate amounts of land, the land issue became a central symbol of colonial domination and anti-colonial struggles, as well as competition for a crucial economic resource. Elsewhere, claims on land featured prominently in debates over the meaning of custom and its place in the regulation of economic and social life under colonial rule. Africans' access to land affected the supply of labor, the production of goods for local use or export, and colonial regimes' ability to raise revenue. In addition, disputes over land ownership and use presented an ongoing challenge to colonial authorities' ability to adjudicate conflict and maintain order.

The land question receded after 1945, as official and scholarly attention shifted from colonial control to economic development and, by the late 1950s, preparations for independence. Except in Kenya, where land remained at the forefront of the political agenda during and after "Mau Mau," the problem was not how to allocate Africa's "abundant" supplies of land but how to increase the rate of capital formation. Following the continent-wide crises of the 1970s, however, land reemerged in debates over economic reform, not

213

as a newly "scarce" factor of production but as a symptom of the "failure" of African states and institutions to avert economic instability and/or promote sustainable development. Arguing that "free markets cannot be expected to produce efficient and sustainable results when property rights are not clearly defined, complete, enforced, and transferable" (World Bank, 1996c: 19), the World Bank and others insisted that property rights reform is a necessary condition for sustained and sustainable economic development in the long run and pressured African governments to revise their laws and administrative and judicial practices accordingly.

The case for property rights reform has both revived older doctrines about the historical importance of property in defining conditions for the production and distribution of wealth[1] and narrowed the scope of scholarly and official debate over land and development in Africa. In contrast to late colonial schemes such as Kenya's Swynnerton Plan in Kenya, which advocated land reform as much for political as for economic reasons, recent policy debates have focused primarily on relations between property rights and productivity. In keeping with its programmatic mandate, policy-oriented research has also focused on describing the present and projecting the future benefits of reform. The importance of property rights in the history of capitalist development is taken for granted, and the history of land claims in Africa is inferred from the timelessness of custom.

In this chapter I argue for a broader approach, one that treats property not simply as a condition of capitalist accumulation but rather as a field of social and political as well as economic interaction. Drawing on a case study of colonial and post-colonial Asante, I attempt to place contemporary debates over land and property in historical perspective. In examining changes in the way people have made and exercised claims on land in Asante, I have come to question both the argument that African land tenure arrangements are in transition from one stable "regime" of property rights to another and the widely held assumption that property is primarily a relation of power, which people exercise over things according to predetermined rules. I argue that it is more realistic to view property as an ongoing social process in which claims are shaped by people's understanding of the past as well as the present, and the exercise of power does not precede the creation of wealth but rather informs and is influenced by it.

In the colonial period, struggles over property in Asante were as much about the scope and constitution of authority as about the creation and appropriation of wealth. In their initial efforts to gain control over the region, British officials articulated an interpretation of "customary" tenure that linked ownership of land to the structure of chiefly authority. This official "invention of tradition" helped to set the terms in which claims on land were made and contested but did not control the subsequent course of land acquisition and use. Contrary to the colonizers' intentions, appeals to custom neither avoided conflict nor shielded Asante from the disruptions of modernity. Land emerged early in the colonial period as a focus of ongoing struggle and debate, in which the pursuit of economic advantage was closely intertwined with contests over the scope and structure of power in the colonial order. Debates over property and power drew on and informed competing interpretations of custom and historical precedent, stimulating further debates over the past and its relevance to the present. Configurations of power and economic opportunity have changed, of course, since independence, but the debates continue, helping to shape the possibilities of political participation and control over wealth and inviting us to reconsider the historical relationships between them.

Property as Exclusion

Weakened by global market crises, drought, ambitious development programs, and simple mismanagement, by the early 1980s most African economies were stagnant or in decline, and their governments were deeply in debt at home and abroad. In exchange for emergency aid and structural adjustment loans, one African government after another acceded to its creditors' demands for policy reform, adopting policy packages designed to stabilize the economy and lay a secure foundation for future development. In the short run, the price of financial stability was contraction: sharp cutbacks in imports and government spending, followed by declining income and employment. To prepare the way for market-oriented growth in the long run, governments were urged to deregulate and privatize their economies, dismantling price and exchange controls; selling off state-owned assets and enterprises;[2] and replacing "customary" systems of tenure with rights of private ownership defined by law, enforced by the courts, and registered by the state.[3]

The standard argument for property rights reform is that clear title to a piece of land or other valuable asset gives the titleholder the opportunity and the incentive to use resources productively and preserve their value over time. By empowering property holders to exclude others from access to resources, well-defined property rights allow them to capture the benefits of resource use or realize their present value by transferring them to others. Because property holders also have a vested interest in maintaining and/or increasing the value of their property as long as they hold onto it, well-defined property rights are said to encourage investment and guard against resource depletion.

In cases where resources are used in ways that benefit the owner, but impose costs on others, registration of title facilitates regulation by making it easier to hold property owners responsible for the consequences of their actions.

The power of exclusion, which lies at the heart of this conception of property and its role in history, may be deployed in many different ways. The right to exclude other people may refer to specific uses of a thing rather than the thing itself; for example, a person may own the right to cultivate a piece of land and exclude others from doing so but may not be entitled to use it in other ways, such as gathering fruit from naturally occurring trees. In Western property law, ownership of an asset usually conveys the right to alienate it, but in many parts of Africa this is not the case, particularly with respect to land. Ownership, or the power to exclude others, may be vested in groups rather than individuals, in which case resource use depends in part on the internal organization or governance of the collectivity in question. If people get along, they may manage resources more effectively together than they would individually. The "tragedy of the commons" is by no means an inevitable consequence of collective ownership (Bassett, 1993; Bromley, 1989; Galaty, 1993; McCay & Acheson, 1987; Ostrom, 1990).

Property, then, is a relation of power that people exercise over others in respect of things. This does not mean, of course, that individuals should resort to coercion to translate their "rights" into effective control. On the contrary, liberal theory usually assumes that property holders' powers of exclusion are both conferred and guaranteed by a governing body, such as the state, whose powers are defined and exercised independently of the production and circulation of wealth.[4] In a market economy, wealth derived from the use of property will be used to acquire more property but not to influence the definition and enforcement of property rights, and agents of the state do not use their power to appropriate wealth.[5] Thus, arguments for the power of property rights assume that the production and circulation of wealth are both predicated on the exercise of power and separated from it. This paradox is not resolved simply by postulating an institutional or statutory distinction between different types of power holders—property owners versus bureaucrats, say, or elected officials. According to the logic of self-interest, property holders have just as much incentive to trade material goods for influence as for other material goods, and officials are not likely to be indifferent to wealth (Bates, 1981, 1983, 1989; Sandbrook, 1986). In short, the argument that clearly defined property rights are a necessary condition for sustainable development assumes that institutions both foster self-interest and suppress it.[6]

The case for the power of property rights also rests on methodological individualism, arguing, in effect, that resource use in the aggregate is the result of decisions made independently by many social agents. Property rights promote progress by improving the quality of individual decision making. By reducing uncertainty about the terms and extent of their power over material resources, well-defined property rights improve resource allocation by increasing decisionmakers' access to information. In addition, the power to exclude others from access to one's property allows people to detach decisions about resource use from social obligations that might interfere with their exclusive enjoyment of the resulting gains. Exclusion "frees" property holders from having to take other people's interests into account in deciding how to use the things they own—and analysts from having to think about the wider social context in which property rights are transacted. In a market system, where limited forms of access are precisely specified and paid for and the underlying contracts are universally and impartially enforced, property holders' decisions are unencumbered by personal or other social pressures and obligations. By the same token, the social consequences of property rights do not depend on who exercises them or who feels their effects.

In reality, of course, property rights must be enforced to be effective, and agencies of enforcement do not float, like heads of hydroponic lettuce, rootless and unconnected to the societies they are supposed to discipline. Whether rules and mechanisms of enforcement are agreed upon—products of a social contract between the governing and the governed—or imposed by the former on the latter, the process by which they come into being is likely to affect the way in which they are exercised. In either case, further change is likely: Agreements are always subject to (re)negotiation, and impositions are likely to be contested. Over time, the way in which property rights are defined and exercised depends as much on ongoing processes of negotiation and struggle and the social relationships that shape them as on discrete acts of legislation or unilateral enforcement by the state. Property is less a relation of power that defines the conditions under which wealth and knowledge may be produced and circulated than part of a social process in which people make wealth, power, and knowledge, although not exactly as they please.

Pushing on a String? Property Rights Reform and African Realities

Property rights reform was not invented in Africa by the architects of structural adjustment (SAP). At the time of independence, many governments took steps to modify or abolish customary tenure. In Kenya, for example, registration of individual titles was initiated by the colonial regime in the wake of the Mau Mau rebellion and continued after independence. In many francophone countries, land-to-the-tiller laws were enacted soon after independence. Implementation of these statutes was uneven, however, and their effects seldom conformed to lawmakers' intentions. In Kenya, for example, although the law provides that "registration extinguishes all prior claims," local courts and land boards often continued to respect them (Okoth-Ogendo, 1986; Haugerud, 1989; Mackenzie, 1989; Ensminger, 1996). Similarly, where governments have opted to preserve "customary" tenure or introduce more formal systems of collective ownership, there is often little resemblance between statutory principles and practices on the ground. In Zimbabwe's Communal Areas, for example, claims to actual parcels of land are held (and often contested) by farmers and traders, fathers and sons, schoolteachers and traditional healers, long-term residents and recent immigrants under a variety of informal arrangements, and are administered by chiefs, headmen, and bureaucrats whose respective areas of authority are themselves subject to contention (Ranger, 1993a; Cheater, 1990; Nyambara, 1999; Hughes, 1999). Similarly, Nigeria's Land Use Act of 1978, which nationalized land ownership in the name of private development, frequently served in practice to intensify land conflict and the proliferation of claims (Francis, 1984; Omotola, 1983).

The limited effects of recent legislation reflect, in part, the ongoing dynamics of practice. If colonial regimes did not succeed in redrawing the map of African land rights according to their own specifications, their efforts did provoke widespread debate. Under the aegis of indirect rule, interpretations of custom proliferated, not only in officials' encounters with their African "subjects" but also in their debates with one another over strategies of governance, and among Africans struggling to come to terms with the colonial order. Such debates were reflected, if not always acknowledged, in much of the ethnographic research on African peoples and cultures that accompanied, and abetted, the colonial project and subsequent critiques of the colonial project itself (see, e.g., Asad, 1973; Fabian, 1983; Kuklick, 1994; Stocking, 1984). In recent years, a number of scholars have taken up Elizabeth Colson's point that "custom" in colonial Africa was not traditional (Colson, 1971), going further to suggest that much of it was invented by European missionaries, officials, and settlers to facilitate and justify their own domination.[7] This argument has been revised, in turn, to take account of the limits and contradictions as well as the power of colonial rule. Modifying his own earlier analysis, T. O. Ranger has suggested that custom was negotiated rather than simply invented, and others have elaborated on the point, showing that the invention of custom was not a one-way street but rather an arena of contestation, in which colonial regimes disrupted Africans' lives but did not fully control them, and Africans engaged actively and purposefully in constructing and interpreting the colonial encounter (Ranger 1993b).[8]

Among advocates of "property rights reform" in Africa, reactions to the fluidity of custom range from enthusiasm to dismay. Some writers have simply ignored the issue, preferring to work with images of traditional institutions and practices as stable, bounded systems that functioned effectively in the past but cannot cope with the modern world (Cleaver & Schreiber, 1994; Ensminger, 1997). Others insist that ambiguous rules and negotiable practices are counterproductive, impeding social progress by undermining people's ability to make well-informed decisions.[9] A third group of scholars maintains that although custom has neither "broken down" nor spread confusion, it has often been manipulated to concentrate wealth and resources in the hands of the rich and powerful. They cite numerous instances in which socially advantaged people—men, elders, and salaried and/or educated workers—have expanded their rights over land at the expense of women, youth, the illiterate, and the poor, or communities have found their access to resources blocked or undermined by commercial interests, international organizations, or the state.[10] Others have pointed out that socially disadvantaged people have not always acquiesced in their own dispossession. Women, strangers, and landless laborers have also invoked or challenged "custom" or availed themselves of changing market conditions to strengthen their bargaining position and access to resources (Carney, 1988; Mackenzie, 1989; Slater-Thomas, 1985; von Bulow, 1992). Commentators may disagree about who benefits from the manipulation of custom, but they tend to agree that actual patterns of land access differ, sometimes substantially, from those delineated in the statute books.

There is also growing agreement that if tenure arrangements continue to elude statutory definition, this is not because African property rights are inherently resistant to change, but because they have changed in their own way. Cultural ecologists argue, for example, that social arrangements through which people gain access to and use resources have adapted to changing population densities, market conditions, and political circumstances (see, e.g., Biebuyck, 1963; Netting, 1968, 1993). Land rights, if not land itself, have become increasingly commercialized in response to population pressure and rising demand (Bassett & Crummey, 1993; Downs & Reyna, 1988). One recent set of studies, sponsored by the World Bank, found little evidence that titling has had a significant impact on agricultural improvements or yields in Africa. To explain this "counterintuitive result," the authors argued that property rights had evolved spontaneously toward de facto privatization, so that where titling had occurred, it was redundant.[11] In contrast, a number of recent studies by anthropologists point out that commercialization is often accompanied by struggles over access and authority, in which the meanings of land, claims on land, and the social idioms and relationships through which claims are negotiated have also changed, in diverse, sometimes ambiguous, ways. How contested meanings shape actual patterns of land access and control remains less clear, in part because of the ineluctable nature of the evidence (Shipton & Goheen, 1992; Rose, 1994).

An exceptionally rich picture of the dynamics of struggles over land, authority, and meaning is provided in Pauline Peters's study of land and water rights in the Kgatleng district of southern Botswana (Peters, 1994; see also Bassett & Crummey, 1993; Haugerud, 1989; Mackenzie, 1993; Carney & Watts, 1990). Cattlemen who formed syndicates to maintain boreholes and organize access to them had to cope with competing claims on access to "their" water points and surrounding pastures, and their own divided loyalties among the claimants. Hoping to resolve some of these tensions and strengthen incentives for investment and commercialization of livestock management, the United States Agency for International Development (USAID) urged the government to fence portions of the range threatened by overgrazing. Syndicate members stood to benefit from fences, which would strengthen their ability to limit others' access to their boreholes and surrounding pasture, but they could also lose if fences constrained their ability to move their herds in case of drought or fire. Faced with conflicting loyalties and ambiguous interests, cattle owners neither built fences nor rejected them but continued to debate the issue while negotiating multiple claims on water and pasture on a case-by-case basis. In other words, Peters (1994) argues, enclosure is neither a socially disembedded process nor one that necessarily contributes to the clarification of property rights.

Negotiable Property in Asante

Since the British annexed Asante to the Gold Coast Colony at the beginning of the twentieth century, claims on land have been closely linked to debates over power and wealth.[12] From the outset, colonial officials sought to co-opt traditional systems of governance into the apparatus of colonial rule, practicing indirect rule de facto well before it was instituted de jure in 1935. To strengthen the foundations of indirect rule by backing chiefs' authority and ensuring their financial viability, colonial administrators endorsed an interpretation of Asante "custom" that held that land ownership was vested in the stools.[13] Their backing ensured that this interpretation figured prominently in the ensuing struggles as land values rose under the combined impact of growing agricultural and extractive exports and urban construction. The colonial state was not strong enough to redefine land tenure single-handedly, but its policies ensured that claims on property were linked to ongoing debates not only over the content of customary law but also over the respective rights and responsibilities of colonial officials, chiefs, and commoners under indirect rule.

These debates have continued, in one form or another, under successive regimes that have governed Ghana since independence. Kwame Nkrumah proposed sweeping legal reforms of property ownership and chiefly prerogatives but, in the end, let "customary" rights alone. Eager to cultivate the support of locally influential citizens, including "traditional rulers," and to avoid potential unrest, subsequent regimes have not challenged this precept directly, preferring to extend the state's claims over resources deemed vital to the national interest (such as minerals and timber) rather than stage a frontal assault on "customary" claims to land itself (Ghana, 1962; compare Ghana, 1992).

In addition to changes in political structures and economic opportunities, claims on property and patterns of resource use in Asante have been shaped by social relationships among claimants and users. As a number of scholars (myself included) have argued, access to resources has often been linked, in African societies, to membership in social networks (Berry, 1985, 1993). This did not mean that access to land was "open" or unregulated, or that it followed automatically from particular social identities.[14] Allegiance to a chief does not, for example, give a "subject" automatic access to a part of the stool's land, nor does membership in a descent group guarantee protection from landlessness. In practice, identity and property are interdependent and mutable. Both are products of debate and contestation over who may legitimately exercise claims on and/or authority over whom, rather than ascribed qualities or fixed rules, detached from social practice. Such debates did not precede the constitution and deployment of wealth and power in Asante, during or after the colonial period; rather, as I argue below, they have been integral to the processes through which wealth and power are produced.

When British forces occupied Asante in 1896, their first concern was to secure control of the region by dismantling what was left of the once-powerful Asante state. Prempeh I, the reigning Asantehene, was deported, together with a number of his relatives and supporters, and British officers signed treaties with several prominent provincial chiefs, recognizing their autonomy from the erstwhile monarchy in exchange for professions of loyalty to the British crown. Five years later, following a rebellion led by the queen mother of Ejisu, Britain annexed Asante to the Gold Coast Colony and established a civilian administration in the region. Although the monarchy was formally disbanded, the colonial regime was anxious to capitalize on established forms of social order and sought, wherever possible, to uphold chiefly authority and incorporate customary law into the apparatus of colonial rule. Indeed, the regime hoped that chiefs would assume not only administrative but also financial responsibility for maintaining order and mobilizing labor for road work and other "public" projects in their respective jurisdictions.

With these objectives in mind, colonial administrators turned at an early stage to the question of customary rights to land. Alarmed by previous experience in the Gold Coast Colony, where the proliferation of land sales in the late nineteenth century was accompanied by a rising tide of litigation (Asante, 1975; Gocking, 1994; Sutton, 1984; Kyerematen, 1971; Busia, 1951; Fortes, 1948), officials hoped to nip this process in the bud, while strengthening the fiscal and political position of Asante chiefs, by appealing to "custom." Anticipating the argument later applied throughout Britain's possessions in West Africa, the administration declared that land belonged to "the community"—represented by its head, the stool—and therefore could not be alienated.[15]

Historically, it is doubtful that this was the case. Wealthy and influential individuals acquired rights over both land and people in pre-colonial Asante and exchanged them for money, often to defray debts to the state (McCaskie, 1984). Land values rose during the early years of the British occupation, pushed up by the growth of export production (cocoa, minerals, wild rubber, and timber), urban construction, and the expanding domestic market. In Asante, as in the Gold Coast Colony, chiefs initially sought to capitalize on economic expansion by selling portions of their land. As colonial officials began to insist that this was contrary to custom, however, chiefs did not put up much resistance. There were other ways to appropriate rising land values. By the early 1910s, chiefs and commissioners had reached a working consensus on the principles of "customary" tenure. Chiefs were entitled to receive a share of any valuable object derived from their land (e.g., fish, game, minerals, timber). They could also collect "tribute" from strangers who wanted to farm on stool lands (particularly those who planted cocoa and other permanent crops) and receive payments (equivalent to prevailing market prices) for allocating long-term rights to individuals who wanted to put up buildings or other permanent structures. In contrast to Annette Weiner's concept of inalienable possessions as objects "so imbued with the intrinsic and ineffable identities of their owners" that they cannot be given away, in Asante land became an "inalienable possession" by colonial fiat (cf. Weiner, 1992), and chiefs and commissioners collaborated to institutionalize rent-seeking in the name of custom (Berry, 1998).

But rent-seeking involved more than a simple exercise of colonial hegemony or the misallocation of resources. If they hoped that inalienability would protect stool lands from dispute and prevent chiefs from squandering their subjects' wealth, British officials were soon disappointed. Far from reducing the frequency of land disputes, the administration's commitment to upholding "custom" simply shifted the focus of dispute from land sales to chiefly jurisdiction and the interpretation of custom. As chiefs took every opportunity to turn their prerogatives into profit, their efforts and their suitability for office were vigorously contested throughout the colonial period—and remain a subject of lively, sometimes rancorous debate today.

Custom was a bone of contention in Asante not only because it was used to justify surplus appropriation but also because "custom" itself embraced contradictory meanings. Custom is routinely framed as timeless—its authority deriving "from time immemorial"—but it is also firmly rooted in historical precedent. In debating claims to land, whether in casual conversation or in formal pleadings before the courts, Asantes continually invoke the past. Tales of origin and descent, migration and settlement, courtship and betrayal are recounted and reworked in the course of contemporary disputes over boundaries and titles. Many of these stories are linked to the early history of the Asante state, and their influence has not receded over time. In the closing years of the twentieth century, sizable tracts of land in metropolitan Kumase and its environs were under litigation in cases that turned, inter alia, on conflicting interpretations of Osei Tutu's conquests (circa 1700) and their role in defining the Asantehene's rights over land.[16]

In the context of struggles over property and power, debates over custom have flourished, causing proliferation of interpretations rather than consolidating them. Colonial administrators tried repeatedly to compile a definitive version of Asante custom, only to revise it as new accounts were put forth and old ones challenged.[17] Since independence, successive regimes have passed numerous laws relegating chiefs to ceremonial functions and limiting the legal force of customary rules and practices, yet evidence suggests that neither the codification of statutory and customary law nor the proliferation of written documents has produced consensus on the facts of Asante history or their relevance to contemporary claims on property. Far from converging toward a single hegemonic narrative, both written and oral accounts of Asante history have proliferated, stimulating rather than stifling debate and contributing to the ongoing reinterpretation of tradition. Some voices are, of course, heard and attended to more often than others, but silence does not necessarily produce oblivion.

Since pre-colonial times, literacy and orality have provided complementary rather than competing modes of historical transmission and interpretation in Asante. Written documents and oral testimony are both accepted in Ghanaian courts, of course, and their meanings are debated by lawyers, academics, and ordinary citizens, orally as well as in writing. Evidence presented in support of land claims is also drawn from many sources. At the National Archives in Kumase, academic researchers are regularly outnumbered by litigants seeking evidence to use in court. In conversations with litigants I have been shown copies of documents—old court judgments, official correspondence, works by professional historians and ethnographers—that give conflicting accounts of "relevant" historical events. Asked how they expected to build a case on contradictory evidence, my interlocutors suggested cheerfully that if the court didn't like one version, perhaps it would prefer another.[18] The result, I would argue, is not just an expanding but increasingly consistent and definitive body of law and precedent, but an ongoing process of social and discursive interaction in which claims on property work not to separate the production of wealth and the use of resources from the constitution and exercise of power and social relationships but rather to link them together in ways that are historically distinctive rather than simply dysfunctional.

Whether written or oral, all historical productions are selective: For every tale that is told, others go unheard. Silence is often read as a sign of powerlessness, silencing as an instrument of exclusion, and those who are silenced as invisible and forgotten. In the context of struggles over property and power in Asante, however, this is not necessarily so. Not only does oral history continue to be spoken, and heard, in the corridors of power as well as the courtyards of ordinary citizens, but silence itself can be an act of social engagement. Oral history is performative: Just as knowledge of the past is transmitted through interaction between raconteur and audience, so withholding historical knowledge also presupposes an audience.

In 1993–1994, I followed a case in the High Court involving a disputed tract of land in Duase, a village on the outskirts of Kumase, where the process of suburbanization was well underway. The dispute began in the mid-1970s, when a local merchant announced plans to build a small garment factory in Duase on land belonging to his kinsman. Hoping to share in the rents generated by industrial development, several people contested the kinsman's claim to ownership. In the deteriorating economic conditions of the late 1970s, the entrepreneur was unable to carry out his project, but the land question was not forgotten. On more than one occasion, neighbors came to blows, accusing one another of planting or uprooting crops on the disputed site without permission. When Jerry Rawlings came to power for the second time, in 1981, he launched a nationwide campaign to bring justice to the people by instituting impromptu administrative tribunals or "people's courts" to settle outstanding disputes. A local administrator conducted a brief hearing on the land dispute in Duase and issued a report, but his ruling was subsequently repudiated by the disputants. By the early 1990s, structural adjustment loans and reviving exports had touched off a construction boom in and around Kumase, and claimants to the disputed site decided to take their case to court.

I first learned of the Duase case during an exploratory visit to the High Court and decided to follow its progress, attending court whenever the case was scheduled and interviewing litigants, lawyers, and witnesses outside of court. Because the entrepreneur's kinsman's claim to the disputed land was based on his position as custodian of a local shrine, a key point at issue in the trial was the historical question of how the shrine had come to this particular village. One of the plaintiffs' star witnesses, a member of the Kumase Traditional Council whose own stool shared a boundary with Duase, gave a vivid account of the case. The shrine, he explained, which was named for its resident deity, Tano Kwabena, had been captured in a battle between Asante and Dormaa (in Brong-Ahafo) "in the time of Osei Tutu," and subsequently traveled from place to place. As the chief approached the climax of his story, he paused for effect. "How," he exclaimed in ringing tones, "did Tano Kwabena get to Duase? Did he *walk*?" The question was purely rhetorical, of course; relying on his "audience" of one clueless foreign researcher to supply the obvious answer ("of course not, he was *carried*"), the chief left it unspoken and proceeded calmly with the rest of his tale.

As the Duase case unfolded before a public audience in court, a more significant "silence" emerged. Despairing of eliciting conclusive testimony from the litigants' witnesses, the judge finally issued a subpoena summoning the Asantehene to testify in court as to the true history of Tano Kwabena's travels. Delighted at the prospect of hearing testimony from such an august witness, I hurried to court on the appointed day, only to be disappointed when, instead of Otumfuo, a palace official appeared to offer excuses and request a postponement. As the same scene was replayed, at two- to three-week intervals, during the remainder of my stay in Ghana, my chagrin slowly gave way to comprehension. By refusing to testify, the Asantehene was controlling the "outcome" of the case. If the judge finally gave up and ruled on the case without benefit of the Asantehene's testimony, the decision could always be challenged retroactively on the grounds that the court did not have adequate knowledge of the relevant history.[19] Thus, the Asantehene could withhold his knowledge from the court, but the power of his silence depended on its being publicly displayed in a crowded courtroom. If no one knew that history had been withheld, its absence would not matter.

More than once in the course of my fieldwork I was reminded that the power of history depends on the audience as well as the historian.[20] Several times, an informant would refer to his or her family's history as "our secrets," then proceed to recount exploits in detail to me and anyone else who happened to be listening. Secrecy was invoked not to silence the past but to demonstrate the speaker's power to impart significant information. Asked to comment on such narratives, a friend thought for a moment, then explained that "history is a 'secret' because it can affect you." Whether a narrator proceeded to tell the story or, like the Asantehene, declined to testify, was less important than letting other people know that he or she *could* tell it if he or she wished.

Sometimes the power of history is enacted, rather than spoken or implied. In 1994, I lived for two months in Kumawu, a rural town about 50 kilometers northeast of Kumase, collecting stories about the history of the stool, the town, its residents, and their lands. On one occasion, after a long and vivid recital of his forebears' exploits (including their descent from the sky to settle at Kumawu), one of the town chiefs suggested that we visit his ancestral shrine. The shrine was located in the bush about half a mile from town, and we walked there accompanied by his family elders, my research assistant, and a small throng of curious children. On the way, we passed a settlement recently established on the outskirts of Kumawu by members of a small Christian community who had decided to separate themselves from the rest of the town. Known locally as the Gyedifoɔ ("believers"), the Christians had built their town (*kurom*) on land donated by my informant, and some were renting farm plots from him as well. It was late afternoon when we passed, and many of the Gyedifoɔ were standing about, having just returned from their farms. As the chief exchanged greetings with his tenants, they witnessed our procession to pay homage to a sacred icon of their landlord's ancestral rights. Like the Asantehene's "refusal" to testify in Kumase High Court, our impromptu pilgrimage demonstrated the chief's keen appreciation of the importance of audience to the production of history.

Property as Participation?

The argument that property rights are (or ought to be) increasingly individualized is part of a broader paradigm of modernity in which persons are constructed as autonomous individuals whose actions are driven by self-interest rather than molded by social position or group identity, and social processes are driven by individual action. Self-realization is both a means and an end of social progress. By empowering individuals to exclude others from access to particular things, "well-defined" property rights release them from social entanglements and obligations that might inhibit their ability to use resources in their own interest, as measured by market conditions. Whether these conditions are, or ought to be, met in contemporary Africa is the subject of much popular as well as academic discussion. In a recent study of land tenure and agricultural productivity in several African countries, the authors argued that the highest degree of tenure security was enjoyed by farmers who said they could transfer their land without consulting anyone first (Migot-Adholla, 1991; Bruce & Migot-Adholla, 1994). Such scholarly endorsements of the progressive power of unconstrained individualism find a ready counterpart in popular discourse, which lauds individual enterprise and laments the contemporary decline in people's concern for community and kin (Barber et al., 1997).

At the same time, however, there is plenty of academic and popular discussion that leans the other way, questioning whether the disentangled individual of post-enlightenment modernity has completely taken over African social practices and understandings (Riesman, 1986; Jackson & Karp, 1990; Gyekye, 1997). Similarly, the literature on wealth-in-people raises questions about how African understandings of personhood and the value of people compare with Western concepts of individualism, and whether culturally specific understanding of personal capacity shapes social practices in distinctive ways. Akan cosmology is not particularly fatalistic; individuals have agency and can exercise it in both helpful and harmful ways (see, e.g., Gyekye, 1987; Wiredu, 1996; McCaskie, 1995; Arens & Karp, 1989). Belief in witchcraft, for example, assigns considerable power to individuals' ability to influence the fortunes of others; reports of the continued salience of witchcraft in contemporary Africa, as a practice and a system of explanation, abound in both popular media and ethnographic literature (Geschiere, 1992; Geschiere & Fisiy, 1994; Crehan, 1997a; Comaroff & Comaroff, 1993). But the idea of witchcraft also makes it clear that individual agency does not determine social outcomes. People act, with good or evil intent, but the social efficacy of their actions depends not only on their own capacities but also on their access to sources of power that lie beyond individual control.

In Asante, it is widely believed that access to spiritual power is crucial to the social efficacy of individual action. In a recent article, Akyeampong and Obeng argue suggestively that the importance of spiritual power in Akan understanding of the world places limits on the power of the state (as well as of individuals) to control other people and events:

Onyame (the Supreme Being) . . . created a universe impregnated with his power . . . and individuals and groups that successfully tapped into this power source translated this access into authority. . . . Authority . . . could be monopolized, but access to power (Twi: *tumi:*, "the ability to bring about change") was available to anyone who knew how to make use of Onyame's powerful universe for good or evil. (Akyeampong and Obeng 1995: 483)

Their argument parallels Caroline Bledsoe's illuminating discussion of child fostering and education in Sierra Leone, where children are taught that there is "no success without struggle" (Bledsoe, 1990). No matter how talented a child may be, or how hard he or she studies, Bledsoe explains, Sierra Leoneans believe that education will not lead to future success unless the child also earns "blessings" by demonstrating proper respect for divinity and his or her social superiors. However laudable, or culpable, a person's actions may be in their own right, their effectiveness depends on earning the support of others.

In the case of property, such arguments suggest that making rules for the definition and transfer of property rights is only part of the story. To make and exercise claims on property effectively, it is important to develop and sustain relations with other people and with the gods.[21] Like persons, social relationships are made as well as born. An individual may be born into a descent group, a religious order, a community, or an occupation, but his or her position and influence within any particular social group are not fixed but negotiable, advancing or attenuating according to the energy, skill, and resources he or she "invests" in cultivating them. Carefully cultivated, social relationships may enhance people's access to wealth and knowledge and, even if they fail—because of conflict or a decline in other people's fortunes—people are more likely to seek new or alternative social ties than attempt to go it alone.[22] From this perspective, it is ironic that the World Bank study cited previously insists that the right to transfer property without anyone's approval is the highest form of "tenure security" in Africa.[23]

Cultivating social relationships resembles the accumulation of social capital—or wealth-in-people—but is not exactly the same (cf. Bourdieu, 1977; Miers & Kopytoff, 1977; Bledsoe, 1980; Putnam, 1993; Widner & Mundt, 1998). Concepts such as "human capital," "social capital," and "wealth-in-people" treat people's skills and relationships as analytically comparable to things—convertible, in Bourdieu's formulation, to "economic capital" and amenable to exclusive control. "The endless reconversion of economic capital into symbolic capital [occurs] at the cost of a wastage of social energy which is the condition for the permanence of domination" (Bourdieu, 1977: 195). In a recent critique, Jane Guyer used ethnographic evidence from equatorial

Africa to suggest that wealth-in-people derives not simply from labor power but also from knowledge, creativity, even idiosyncrasy. The concept of capital accumulation, with its implications of additivity and control, is antithetical, she argues, to the spontaneity and originality of creative endeavor and the "value" of uniqueness, which figure so importantly in cultural representations and practices across the region. Realizing the "wealth" that springs from individual creativity is a matter of bringing together people's unique talents in synergistic, often improvisatory, ways, rather than multiplying the number of human subjects (or possessions) at the disposal of particular agents. Creating wealth-in-people depends on a capacity to inspire rather than to control and is better described, Guyer suggests, as a process of "composition" rather than of "accumulation" (Guyer, 1993; Guyer & Eno Belinga, 1995).

One issue that it seems to me is not fully addressed in Guyer's stimulating discussion is the question of social relationships, patterns of human interaction that not only are improvisational but also construct and invoke claims and obligations, linking people through time, however partially and variably. Her critique equates accumulation to the acquisition of property—rights of ownership, or the power to exclude and (therefore) to control—as this concept is used in both liberal and Marxist political economy.[24] However, if accumulation is seen as a process of cultivating (or investing in) social relationships as well as things—relationships that are both negotiable and necessary to the effective exercise of claims on things and people—the concept accommodates the simultaneous fluidity and materiality of human interactions, as well as the centrality of people to Africans' understandings of "wealth." Such a redefinition enables us to understand property as a process, or more precisely as a set of interacting processes, in which people make and exercise claims on things, such as land, in the course of negotiating claims to power and knowledge, and vice versa.[25]

If historical knowledge and social relationships are negotiable, produced and reproduced through social interaction, they are neither static nor unambiguously exclusionary. In describing history as "a[n open] secret," Asantes dramatize the tension between exclusion and inclusion that lies at the heart of both social relationships and the power of history. The very act of publicly withholding historical information includes the audience in producing it. In Asante, as we have seen, self-appointed guardians of history withhold knowledge (invoke secrecy) not to consign events of the past to oblivion but to remind people of the power of history and its guardians in the present.[26] By claiming the power to silence the past, such assertions make the production of history into a social process, one in which audience participation is integral to the historian's effect, and silence is not so much a sign of the unthinkable, or even an act of unilateral suppression, as a tactic that enables as it seeks to control.

Like history, the process of making claims on property in Asante is a participatory one. Property, and the social relationships that sustain and effectuate it, are not simply exclusionary. People may postpone or evade others' demands to enjoy their time and money privately, but they rarely repudiate outright the relationships that give rise to requests for assistance. Property rights are established not through discrete decisions but rather through a continuous interplay between exclusion and inclusion, which invites people to participate because it is ongoing. The tension between inclusion and exclusion is evident in a wide range of social interactions in Asante, from casual conversations to major events. In ordinary conversation, for example, people avoid direct refusal, declining an unwanted offer with a polite "it's all right" rather than a straightforward "no thank you." Similarly, at funerals—probably the most conspicuous and time-consuming of Akan social rituals—histories of a deceased person's relationships with kin and affines, friends and neighbors, colleagues and co-religionists are reenacted and reinterpreted in complex dramas of personal, ritual, and financial participation, as the dead are mourned and buried and the disposition of their property is negotiated.[27]

In describing property in Asante as negotiable—socially and conceptually, as well as commercially—I am not suggesting that negotiability constitutes an underlying attribute of economic life there, but that property itself is an ongoing process, rather than a set of rules and a record of their application. During my fieldwork in Kumawu, a long-standing dispute over a portion of the stool's boundary was scheduled for judgment in the Superior Court in Accra.[28] As the anticipated date approached, tension mounted, especially among villagers in the disputed territory who had long faced competing demands for tribute and allegiance from the contesting stools. Toward the end of my stay, I had an opportunity to discuss the case with the Kumawuhene, and asked him what effect the court's ruling would have. Whichever way the Superior Court ruled, he explained, the losing party would appeal, so that a final outcome was probably several years away. "But," I persisted, "the Supreme Court will decide the case eventually. Suppose they rule in favor of Kumawu: What will happen then?" "Oh," the chief replied genially, "then we'll have to sit down [with representatives of the other stool] and negotiate!"

Beyond Familiar Fictions

To those accustomed to think of decisive action as the basis of social progress, such stories appear to confirm the most pessimistic assessments of African prospects for sustained economic development and political reform. In social analyses predicated on methodological individualism and the heuristic importance of equilibrium conditions, negotiations are viewed as, at best, a means to an end: They may enable people to make better decisions by expanding their access to relevant information, but the "payoff" occurs only after the negotiations are finished. Ongoing, open-ended negotiability, on the other hand, leads to confusion, inaction, and social stagnation. I suggest that this picture is too stark. In Asante, negotiability certainly hasn't prevented the commercialization of land rights or blocked investment in mines, tree crops, houses, stores, or workshops. (If it has discouraged some foreign investors, not everyone would see this as an unmitigated misfortune.) Indeed, by promoting participatory patterns of claiming and contesting wealth and power, ongoing, inconclusive negotiations over land have also shaped, and to some extent limited, the state's ability to define conditions of accumulation or control ordinary people's lives.[29]

The logic of negotiability did not, of course, determine the course of Ghanaian history in the twentieth century—but neither did the logic of structural adjustment. Politics in Ghana work through a dense web of social networks and participatory claims on property and power that extend from the local level to the upper echelons of the state, in contrast to Nigeria, where oil wealth and military rule have severed the state's dependence on and responsiveness to the productive energies and needs of ordinary people. In Nigeria, the military regime has obtained a lock on power, and relative isolation from the grass roots, through a combination of oil—which gives the ruling elite a monopoly on wealth independent of the labor and resources of most of the population—and the ruinously centrifugal dynamic of sectional competition and fragmentation that has destabilized each of Nigeria's civilian regimes, giving the military repeated opportunities to retake power and to use it in increasingly authoritarian ways. In Ghana, by contrast, attempts by both military and civilian regimes to impose policies and programs from above have so far been diluted by the multiplicity and vitality of networks by which power and resources are mobilized, contested, and rechanneled at all levels of society. Wealth and power are not equally distributed in Ghana, by any means, but they are actively debated and pursued at all levels. Rawlings's victory at the polls in 1996, for example, should not obscure the fact that a number of parliamentarians were also unseated at the nomination stage by constituents demanding that the National Democratic Congress (NDC) field new candidates in place of those who had "done nothing" during their first term in office. The relative openness of Ghanaian politics stems not from a greater degree of negotiability in Ghanaian political culture but from a different conjuncture between processes of political mobilization and control of wealth at different levels of social interaction.

Certainly the "rent-seeking state" has not withered away in the time of structural adjustment, in Ghana or anywhere else. One has only to tune in briefly to debates in Washington over campaign finance to be reminded that academic moralizing over the separation of wealth and power has as little to do with the realities of economic growth and governance in the United States as it does in Ghana. It is not the separation of wealth and power, but the way in which they interact, that makes history.

The story of Asante—where history makes property, and vice versa—not only illuminates this point, but offers insights into how wealth and power interact, and with what effects. The "story" of property in Asante has been made up of innumerable daily dramas of contestation, the significance of which lies not in their long-run convergence toward de facto privatization but rather in the fact that they keep going and, in doing so, have helped to construct the particular dynamic of participatory inequality that constitutes the *longue duree* of Ghanaian political and economic history.

The Asante story also suggests that the question for comparative social analysis is not how to bring down the curtain on these daily dramas by separating wealth and power once and for all, so that economic progress may proceed "free" from the "distorting" effects of power and ambiguities of ongoing negotiation. Rather, it invites us to move beyond familiar fictions of markets and states in which the consumer, or civil society, is sovereign, to understand how wealth and power interact by observing how people make claims on property and one another and how the process of making claims has moved ideas forward and shaped possibilities of economic and political participation in different historical contexts.

PART THREE

Violence of the Word/ Violence Against the Body

10
Mapping Africa's Presences
Merleau-Ponty, Mannoni, and the Malagasy Massacre of 1947 in Frantz Fanon's Black Skin White Masks

NIGEL C. GIBSON*
Emerson College

This chapter explores Frantz Fanon's critique of Octave Mannoni's *Psychologie de colonization* as an aspect of the postwar debate about African decolonization and independence among West Indian, African, and French intellectuals, especially around the journal *Présence Africaine*. The chapter includes a discussion of the theoretical framework for Fanon's approach to Mannoni, found in Fanon's critique of psychological models, and his engagement with the existentialist philosophers Jean-Paul Sartre and Maurice Merleau-Ponty.

Founded in 1947, when demonstrations and rebellions against French and British colonial rule were taking place in Africa, *Présence Africaine* (edited by Alioune Diop and including articles in its first two issues by Sartre, Wright, Jacques Rabémananjara, Gwendolyn Brooks, and Leopold Senghor) brought the African presence into the very center of French civilization, as illustrated by the titles of articles in the first issue: "Présence noir" by Sartre and "Présence africaine" by Naville. The "presence" was the lived present, that is, a dialectical present that put the West on trial. *Présence Africaine* represented

---
*My thanks to Lesley Sharp for some last-minute answers to questions about Madagascar and to Kate Josephson for discussion of psychology, psychiatry, and psychoanalysis. Any errors, of course, are mine.

became a new kind of postwar anti-colonial African studies and Paris in 1947 a "place where the African writers belonged, because the city was, from then on, one of the theaters in which the political and cultural future of Africa was being prepared" (Mouralis, 1992: 4). By establishing itself in Paris, alongside Sartre and Merleau-Ponty's *Les Temps Modernes*, *Présence Africaine* avoided marginalization, becoming part of the postwar liberation intellectual milieu and also, through a constant interaction across the borders of the black world, avoided exile.

In the French constitution of 1946, colonialism disappeared, to be replaced by a new union of citizenship and parliamentary representation and the end of forced labor and the colonial education system. Yet the reality of this union was made clear in Madagascar a year later. The price of challenging the French union was 100,000 deaths. Although by no means simply an apology for colonialism, Octave Mannoni's *Psychologie de colonization*, published in 1950, represented the old liberal French civilizing attitude toward Africa, putting the blame for the massacre on the Malagasy's inherently dependent consciousness. Representing the new postwar activist African studies embodied in *Présence Africaine*, Frantz Fanon, who had arrived in France in 1947,[1] tore apart Mannoni's thesis. The revolt in Madagascar, rather than an expression of dependency, as Mannoni would have it, was a source of unity and inspiration for the continent.

Beyond Manicheanism: Merleau-Ponty and the Lived Experience of the Black

According to Simone deBeauvoir, Fanon attended Merleau-Ponty's philosophy classes in Lyon.[2] In 1947 Merleau-Ponty had just published *Humanism and Terror*.[3] Having participated in Alexandre Kojève's Hegel seminars in the mid-1930s and already studied Marx's *1844 Essays* and Lukacs's *History and Class Consciousness* (reflected in his 1948 collection *Sense and Non-Sense*),[4] Merleau-Ponty was knowledgeable about Marx and Hegelian dialectics. Sartre recognized Merleau-Ponty's acumen and made him political editor of *Les Temps*.

In 1947 Merleau-Ponty still believed in proletarian revolution and, according to Sartre, argued that the class struggle unmasked could be found in the 1947 massacre and the continuing forced labor in Madagascar: "Our colonies are—*mutatis mutandis*—our slave labor camps" (Sartre, 1965: 185).[5] Fanon, like so many around *Présence Africaine*, was already an engaged intellectual when he attended Merleau-Ponty's lectures in 1947–1948.

Black Skin White Masks, published in 1952, is an eclectic work with references to philosophy, politics, literature, psychoanalysis, film, and popular culture; combined with what seems like an authorial and autobiographical "I," it can create in the reader a certain disorientation. Nevertheless, *Black Skin* represents both Fanon's profound ability to synthesize an enormous range of scholarship and his working through existential phenomenology. His use of the first person "I" should be considered akin to that employed by Sartre in *Being and Nothingness* (1943) or Merleau-Ponty in *The Phenomenology of Perception* (1945). Even at his moment of great personal anger at Sartre in *Black Skin*, when he accuses him of a betrayal, Fanon's point is a philosophical one. Fanon's methodology in *Black Skin*, as it is in *The Wretched of the Earth*, is a fairly simple one, reflecting the Manicheanism of colonial society. In *Black Skin*, the attribute of color, namely black and white, becomes the lens through which social relations and theories of the time period are judged. The simplicity of his approach is illustrated in his description of the "lived experience" of the black who, in a Manichean fashion, "has two dimensions." This is not W. E. B. Dubois's double consciousness, but rather two ways of being, "one with his fellows, the other with the white man." In other words, blacks behave differently among whites than among blacks. This identity and difference is not ontological but a product of colonial relations. Among whites, the black experiences no intersubjectivity, no reciprocity. The black is simply an object among other objects. Why is this? How does it happen? These are two questions Fanon asks that express his deep immersion in a humanist standpoint.

The literal translation of the important chapter 5 of *Black Skin White Masks*, "L'experience Vécue du Noir," as "the lived experience of the black," clearly indicates the influence of Merleau-Ponty.[6] The lived experience as a "body-subject" facing the world explicates how colonial racism has affected the corporeal existence of the colonized black and presented "him" with "difficulties in the development of his bodily schema" (1967a 110).[7] The idea of "lived experience" alerts us to Fanon's appreciation of the differences in the existentialism of Sartre and Merleau-Ponty. For example, where Sartre argued that the fundamental struggle between individual consciousnesses creates social relations, for Merleau-Ponty it is the social nature of consciousness that creates the possibility of conflict. The methodological emphasis on the social is repeated in Fanon's critique of Mannoni as well as in the introduction to *Black Skin*, where Fanon states that his method will be sociodiagnostic, putting emphasis on the *social* basis of *non*-recognition in an anti-black racist society.

Fanon opens "L'experience du Vécue Noir" with a statement that ontology alone does not "permit us to understand the being of the black man." This is because there is not really a black being or essence (1967a: 110). At the same time there is the experience of being black, a dialectic of *physical being* and *situation*, which Merleau-Ponty describes as body in a spatiality of situation, or as Fanon puts it, "a definitive structuring of the self and of the world." It is definitive, Fanon adds, because "it creates a real dialectic between my body and the world" (1967a: 111).

The situation is different when saturated by color. Where for Merleau-Ponty "the body image is finally a way of stating that my body is in-the-world" (1962: 101), for Fanon there are times when the black is not in the world but "locked into his body" (1967a: 225). Where for Merleau-Ponty, "one's body is the third term . . . as far as spatiality is concerned" (1962: 101), for Fanon the fact that the black "must be black *in relation* to the white" means that the consciousness of body for the person of color is not only a "third person consciousness" but a person triply split.

The Triple Person: Merleau-Ponty's Intersubjectivity and Sartre's Manicheanism

The Black is aiming for the universal, but on the screen his Black essence, his Black "nature," is kept intact: always a servant/always obsequious and smiling me never steal, me never lie/eternally "y' a bon banania."

Fanon

When "the Black man is among his own" (which assumes a certain level of equality and recognition of identity and difference), Fanon argues, Merleau-Ponty's conception of intersubjectivity appears correct, yet in a colonial society "every ontology is made unattainable" (Fanon, 1967a: 109). There is a tension because the relation of being and other is determined by the absolute of color and is thus *inauthentic*.

In a racist society where the image of whiteness has been powerfully internalized, Sartre's notion of the objectifying power of the gaze, his conflictual and dualistic philosophy, appears a powerful explanatory tool to understand the causes and effects of the statement: "Mama, see the Black (Nègre)! I am frightened!" (1967a: 112). Driven back, as it were, into "race," an ontology based on mutual reciprocity is, by definition, sealed off. Although the existence of the black is dependent on the white, "the Black man has no ontological resistance in the eyes of the white man" (1967a: 110).

Although it is true that for Fanon, as for Sartre, existence precedes essence, the black's existence is defined by the essence of blackness. (In Manichean terms the black is equated with being evil and lazy and is associated with bestiality and the biological.) The black's being is reduced to a corporeal malediction. The body has been snatched away and in its place is put a "racial epidermal schema." Thus, in contrast to what Merleau-Ponty describes as being aware of the body as a "third person,"[8] Fanon replies, my body is "a triple person.... It was not that I was finding febrile coordinates in the world. I existed triply. I occupied space" (1967a: 112). Blacks are not simply individual actors responsible for themselves, they are responsible for their race (culture) and their ancestors (history). Quite a load. But on top of that there is the racist caricature, the smiling Negro, like Uncle Ben, who says, "Sho' enough good eating." In France there was the smiling Senegalese on the popular breakfast cereal Banania, saying, "Ya' bon." (See Figure 10.1)

From the perspective of "the Black," Sartre's proposal of an absolute freedom in *Being and Nothingness*, projecting a consciousness that can tear through inferiority complexes that have structured one's life, as an act of sheer will, appears eminently concrete. In the Manichean world of colonialism that Fanon depicts, the very fact that Sartre allows no other perspective and no need to quibble about shades of gray, is a plus. On the other hand, Merleau-Ponty's perspective that the lived body cannot be divorced from the world as experienced complicates things. These relationships are, according to Merleau-Ponty, "the third term between the for-itself and the in-itself" that Sartre lacks (1962: 122). For Merleau-Ponty, freedom is rooted in the world and mediated through the body. The body appears to limit the possibility of freedom but actually makes such a possibility concrete in that it is in relation to other bodies and thus freedom, and the limits to freedom are confirmed through intersubjective relations. Freedom is a social act, not simply an act of individual will (itself a product of social relations), just as values are socially constructed and thus changing and changeable. Where the social world is crucial to Merleau-Ponty's conceptualization of freedom and intersubjectivity, for Sartre all intersubjective relations are the same: "[T]he essence of relations between consciousnesses is not *Mitsein*, but conflict" (Sartre, 1957: 555). Sartre's expression "Hell is other people" reflects this alienation. On the other hand, Merleau-Ponty views the relationship between ourselves and other people as already a result of intersubjectivity. Relationships might be alienated. Indeed, the truth of the hell of other people is understanding that the perceiving subject is already an interrelation of subject and object, body and mind, and is already "open" to other bodies and minds.

The fact that consciousness is mediated by lived experience in a social environment does not mean that *mutual* recognition exists. In his reading of Hegel's master/slave dialectic, for example, Merleau-Ponty sees the necessity of the struggle for recognition to get beyond "unilateral recognition" (quoted in Whiteside, 1988: 88). Unlike Kojève, and indeed Sartre, who makes unilateralism an ontological principle, Merleau-Ponty recognizes the dialectical character of Hegel's master/slave conflict. The conflict is a *moment that must*

Figure 10.1   Banania Breakfast Food. An assortment of tins; the original is the farthest left.

Source: www.ucad.fr/pub/virt/mp/banania. Charles Lam Markmann, the translator of *Peau Noire, Masques Blancs* into English, translates *Banania* as "eating," but it actually refers to a breakfast drink made from banana flour, cocoa, and sugar. The Banania tin carries a picture of a smiling African with the caption "Y'a bon" (an interpretation of African French for "C'est bon"). Banania was launched in 1917 with a Senegalese soldier spooning Banania into his mouth. Interestingly, the frightening savage soldier had become a sympathetic figure during the war. Over the years the smiling full figure of a Senegalese militia man sitting on a box had lost his legs and arms, and by 1980 he had become a caricature with his head transformed into the B of Banania. The Banania figure was unique in that it began as a real picture. In the United States "Sho' good eatin'" immediately refers to the "comfortable stereotype" of Aunt Jemima, Uncle Ben, Uncle Remus or the Cream of Wheat chef.

be experienced (indeed, the drama of the *Phenomenology* is the drama of consciousness of experience). At the same time, the goal of "mutual recognition" is given content by the drama that consciousness experiences in getting there.

Adding Color

One's experience of the body is part and parcel of one's experience of the world, argues Merleau-Ponty. This is no doubt true for the black who, "walled in by color," has two different experiences of one's body and one's being in the world. When race is added to the dialectic, however, the dialectic seems to fall apart and is replaced by a dualism that looks remarkably like Sartre's ontology: two different species, the black and the white. In the colonial world, the administration very often is associated with the army and is thus correctly perceived as part of a system that functions as a police force. In

1947 one was literally "face to face" with the torturers. In *The Wretched* Fanon writes of the cycle of dehumanization of the tortured and torturer in Algeria (1968: 249–258; 1967c: 64–73), but in Madagascar the dynamic takes another twist. The Senegalese militia who are ordered to carry out torture become the absolute Other associated with fear and African (black) blackness, which at one and the same time reinforces and problematizes Manicheanism.

In the Manichean colonial world there are no choices, only a series of double binds. If blacks renounce their bodies as products of their internalization of the gaze of the other—in other words, the third (who in this case is white)—one is forced into bad faith (see Gordon, 1995) either by creating a solipsistic community before consciousness or creating a make-believe world of assimilated colorless angels (Fanon, 1968: 218). In such a bind, how does one become conscious of oneself and in doing so change the world? Merleau-Ponty had understood this flaw in Sartre's philosophy as a closed dialectic. Rather than an individual consciousness that results from the gaze of the other and that always resists intersubjectivity, Merleau-Ponty's grounding of consciousness in the social world offers a way out.

"Sartre's error lies in his exclusive focus on intellectual projects to the neglect of the *existential* project," opines Monika Langer (1989: 144, emphasis added), a judgment repeated by Fanon, who declared in "Orphée Noir" that Sartre had intellectualized the experience of being black but had forgotten the black's experiential suffering. Sartre had forgotten that "the Black suffers in his body quite differently from the white man" (1967a: 138). Although Fanon had almost essentialized the difference between the body experience of the black and the white, it was grounded in a social context and was the result of a lived experience, not an ontological flaw: One is not born black but becomes black, to paraphrase Simone de Beauvoir.

Fanon's response to Sartre's "Orphée Noir," shouting at him "in the paroxysm of my being and my fury" (1967a: 138), was broadcast in another ontological register. Fanon was reminding Sartre that in terms of the movement dialectical negativity, "a consciousness committed to experience is ignorant, has to be ignorant, of the essences and the determinations of its being" (1967a: 134). The dialectic for Fanon, like Merleau-Ponty, remained "open-ended," not predetermined. On the other hand, Sartre, the existentialist, had jumped over experience. As Margaret Whitford puts it, Sartre's philosophy is "more of an essentialism than an existentialism, since Sartre's categories are not derived from experience" but are in fact cut off from experience (Whitford, 1982: 146).

Although Fanon questions the possibility of reciprocity in Hegel's master/-slave dialectic when color was added, he rejects Sartre's radical dichotomy between being-for-self and being-for-others. Fanon, the existentialist, reminds Sartre of the lived situation, "the white man is not only The Other but also the master, whether real or imaginary" (1967a: 138n). In other words, there is a power relation, making it appear that Sartre's radical dichotomy between oneself and others, which he posits as an absolute, seem correct. On first blush this may appear to be a useful way of thinking about Fanon as a Sartrean, but Fanon's position is purely contextual whereas Sartre precludes one's *ever* experiencing the other as intersubjective and reciprocal, seeing it as an expression of inauthenticity and bad faith.[9]

The idea of mutual intersubjectivity is not possible in Sartre's existentialism. Fanon, on the other hand, like Merleau-Ponty, believes in the possibility of mutual recognition (1967a: 109). This is not simply a Christian utopia or ethical ought but an expression of Fanon's "untidy dialectic." Yet working out the steps of how to get from black consciousness to mutual recognition remains problematic. Because recognition is closed off by the Other (who is white), Fanon is "driven back" into race. He makes reference to black consciousness but notes that it doesn't change the situation:

> The few working-class people whom I have had the chance to know in Paris never took it on themselves to pose the problem of the discovery of a Negro past. They knew they were black and they knew they had to struggle. (1967a: 224)

In other words, as Merleau-Ponty says of lived experience, "the world is not what I think but what I live through" (1964b: 144). Consciousness is not what I think but what I am able to do. What I am able to do thus grounds consciousness and how I think, but it is not a wall. For Fanon, cognition is essential for creating the world.

Ways of Being

When Fanon writes of the blacks "among one's own," he assumes an Other to "one's own," determined by the reality, image, or internalization of the Other *qua* white. Fanon speaks of two ways of being: "one with his fellows, the other with the white man." Among blacks there are "normal," or perhaps "authentic" (to use a Sartrean term), ways of being, Fanon argues—a truthful consciousness of the situation and all that that entails. But how could this be? How might one know that the other—who appears as one's own—is in fact authentically so and vice versa?

The ideal of "among one's own" is a place where consciousness of the body in the world is "subject/object," in the Merleau-Pontyan sense, and is not "solely a negating activity" as it is for the black in the colonial world. Fanon's engagement with the Hegelian dialectic in *Black Skin* (whose basis he argues is mutual reciprocity) does not provide him with an answer. The addictive of color halts the dialectic. The black slave looks to the white master; the master simply laughs at the consciousness of the slave. There is no way out.

In the colonial situation this notion of "among one's own" is always already shot through with contradictions. Even if we add the class perspective of Fanon's conclusion to *Black Skin* and operate in a binary of colonized citizen and subject, the black worker or peasant exists in a system that already complicates being among one's own. When enforced from above, "being among one's own" corresponds with "separate development," "Association," "Bantu Homelands" and "customary law." But when developed from below, by blacks, "being among one's own" means black consciousness.

Fanon believed that getting beyond the vicious cycle of dependency and inferiority was connected to a new humanism rather than narrowly racial national consciousness. At the same time this new humanism is a result of the dialectic of black consciousness; of an equality of cultures. This tricky problematic is key to Fanon's critique of Mannoni where the conception of lived experience is employed. However limited, it is by the very Manicheanism that Fanon seeks to avoid, it provides us with an interesting and problematical view of Fanon's early engagement with African independence.

Outside the Psychoanalytic Office: Fanon and Mannoni

This book sets out to describe colonial situations as primarily the results of misunderstanding, of mutual incomprehension.

Mannoni

Chapter four of *Black Skin*, "The So-Called Dependency Complex of Colonized Peoples," represents an attempt to apply ideas of being and existence to an African situation through a critique of Octave Mannoni's *Prospero and Caliban: The Psychology of Colonialization* (1948, 1990). Even more openly than Sartre, who had in "Orphée Noir" equated black consciousness with "nature and immanence," Mannoni rejected the possibility of independence for Africans, denouncing the 1947 demonstrations in Madagascar as an irrational act of an abandoned psyche. Mannoni's book, in fact, has much to say about *his* psyche. At the time of writing, Mannoni claimed that he was more interested in his own psychological makeup than in the "psychology of the subjects under observation" who, he said, "presented a less complex problem" (1990). It was his Madagascar experiences, he claimed, that cured his obsessional neurosis (see

Roudinesco, 1990: 234) and it was this self-understanding that was "an essential preliminary for all research in the sphere of colonial affairs" (Mannoni, 1990: 5, 34).

Interviewed by Elisabeth Roudinesco for her book *Jacques Lacan & Co.*, Mannoni reported that he spent 20 years in Madagascar from 1925 to 1945 "as an ethnologist and director general of the information service" (the two trades often went together) (1990: 234). Two years later he interrupted his psychoanalytic studies and his analysis with Jacques Lacan in Paris and returned to Madagascar. His return coincided with an anti-colonial rebellion that resulted in the brutal massacre of 100,000 Malagasies by French troops. For Mannoni the rebellion tore aside a veil and, he said, "for a brief moment a burst of dazzling light enabled one to verify the series of intuitions one had not dared to believe in" (Mannoni, 1990: 6). The series of intuitions were developed into a psychology of colonization that could explain Malagasy life and the dynamics of the rebellion. In short, his thesis was that the colonizer overcompensated for an inferiority complex that was the result of feelings of abandonment, and the colonized, mired in a dependency complex, were prone to feelings of abandonment by the colonial father figure.

Mannoni wasn't the only one for whom African colonial experiences were therapeutic. In Lord Lugard's case it was a failed love affair that put his African colonial adventure into motion. He dropped out of the army (the best place for people like him, he had thought) and tried to snuff out his burning desire by becoming a fireman. Seeing Zanzibar on a map he decided to go there. Although denied a chance to join the Italian campaign to invade Ethiopia, he was lucky enough to come across Rider Haggard's *The Witch's Head*. The hero, who "crossed in love," seeks adventure in central Africa, spoke directly to Lugard. Reading the book on the boat to Zanzibar feeling that he was going mad, Lugard gave up religion and "struggled with self-destruction"; "still in a pathological mental state Lugard reached the scene of his first African adventure" (Perham, 1958: 69, 105).

From Mannoni's point of view Lugard was a marvelous example of a type of inferiority complex, and Fanon welcomed Mannoni's attempt to understand the colonial dynamic psychoanalytically. Here was a man, it seemed, working in the same area as himself. A few essays by Mannoni had whet Fanon's appetite, and he was thinking of writing to Mannoni to find out more about his views when he was working on *Black Skin*. Particularly arresting and new was submitting the colonizer's behavior to psychoanalytic inquiry.

However, when Mannoni's book was published Fanon was disappointed and subjected it to harsh criticism. What he had taken to be shared conclusions about dependency[10] were, it turned out, based on very different notions of human subjectivity, a different analysis of the roots of colonialism and racism, and ultimately different ideas about what constitutes being and existence.

Fanon's critique of Mannoni is very general; as he has little to say about life in Madagascar. Lacking the necessary empirical knowledge, he does not criticize Mannoni's ethnographic observations[11] and makes no claims about indigenous life, the possible meanings of, for example, about ancestor worship.[12] What does Fanon know about the Malagasy spirit worlds? These kinds of details are of little concern; Fanon's theoretical position is very much like that of many of the first generation of *Présence Africaine* militants.[13]

The crucial difference between them was the differentiation between being and existence: Fanon argued that dependency was a *result* of colonial rule whereas for Mannoni it was the Malagasy's very being to be colonized. According to Mannoni, the European easily became revered by the Malagasy and took the place of ancestors. The colonized are not made dependent because they are colonized but are colonized because they are dependent. In fact the colonized "unconsciously expected—even desired" such a development (Mannoni, 1990: 86):

> To my mind there is no doubting the fact that colonization has always required the existence of the need for dependence. Not all peoples can be colonized: only those who experience *this need*. (1990: 85)

When Fanon read passages like this he said he felt "turned upside down."

According to Mannoni, European colonialism unleashes rather than creates the different psychologies of the colonizer and the colonized. These archetypes find their true personalities in the colonies. Amazingly all parties fall into their allotted place, says Fanon sarcastically, "Prospero or Caliban": "It is obvious that the white man acts in obedience to an authority complex, a leadership complex, while the Malagasy obeys a dependency complex. Everyone is satisfied" (Fanon, 1967a: 99).

What Mannoni had forgotten, insists Fanon, is the lived reality of the Malagasy. Fanon repeats this over and over even if he knows little about the details of everyday life and employs a Martinican negritude poet to describe reality. Lived experience is not only detailed empirical knowledge. And it is Aimé Césaire's negritude poetry that provides Fanon with the most powerful examples of racist dehumanization, experience of life, and grinding poverty of the colonies. In contrast to Mannoni's psychoanalytic types and his claim that "colonial exploitation is not the same as other forms of exploitation and colonial racism is different from other kinds of racism" (Mannoni, 1990: 27),

Fanon insists that there are not different types of racism. Is one form of racism better than another? From the point of view of experience, Fanon says, all forms of exploitation resemble each other because each is applied against the same "'object': man." The problem of racism is not that of blacks living among whites but of systematic exploitation. The similarity among racisms is dehumanization. The existential point is the existence of personhood. In other words, the appearance of colonialism marks the fragmentation of Malagasy intersubjectivity, which is in fact a multicultural identity developed over hundreds of years of interactions between various peoples, of being, in other words "among one's own."

For Fanon, lived experience is far from solipsistic, and the Malagasy are not "sealed" in their own customs. Customs are always in the process of being invented or reinvented. It is the colonial regime that attempts to render them inert. Fanon argues that the Malagasy have ceased to exist in their Malagasy-hood since the time of General Gallieni's slaughter of innocents in 1905 (1967a: 94). This dating of colonization might create problems because it ignores the processes of internal differentiation and external relations with colonial powers from the early nineteenth century onward, but Fanon's perspective is based on the sheer military might of Gallieni's campaign and its quantitative effect on the Malagasy psyche, the flattening of Malagasy life by French force. What is clear to him is the destruction of local lived experience.

Mannoni is unabashedly Eurocentric. Europe's development explains non-European cultures. Africa is mainly in a "primitive" state of dependence and egalitarianism, or in some cases like the Malagasy (read Merina) at the feudal level of dependency, with lifelong pseudo-parents in the form of elders and ancestors. Faced with colonization, the Malagasy transfer their dependence onto the colonials, who become a type of father figure. Abandoned by their own parents, the colonials, on the other hand, are dominated by an inferiority complex and need to dominate the natives. This is the "psychology of colonization."

Despite his use of scare quotes, Mannoni cannot find another word for primitive "because the alternatives, such as "'isolated,' 'unevolved,' 'archaic,' 'stationary,' and 'backward,' are in fact no better" (1990: 22). All express the model of development from which he cannot escape. The linear progression from primitive to civilized of the Malagasy as a kind of recapitulation of an individual's development from dependency to independence (with the potential for inferiority) is absolutely central to his theoretical project, one aspect of which was the application of Kleinian ideas about infancy: "The wholly 'phantastic' world which Melanie Klein has found in infants, and has attributed to persecution, is also to be found in 'primitive peoples.'" One application was his belief that ancestor worship (which Mannoni calls the Cult of the Dead) was an act of protection against "persecution anxieties" (1990: 34).

Although the colonization of Madagascar was achieved only after 1895, the Merina empire (the dominant political unit on the island) had established a relationship with Britain in its attempt to counterbalance French influence. Britain recognized the Merina monarch's claim to the whole island (even if the Merina were far from physically dominating it), and as far back as 1817 British officers had helped train the Imperial army and the Imerina had allowed missionaries to establish an educational system (see Covell, 1987). Missionaries from London first arrived in Madagascar in 1817, and even though they were later expelled, in 1869 Merina Queen Ranavalona announced that Protestantism was the official state religion and alternate (indigenous) religious expressions were silenced.[15] Stephen Ellis contends that "Imerina [Merina society] after 1869 closely *resembled a colonial society* ruled by an indigenous élite but one so far distant from its citizens in taste, means of subsistence, and religion, as to be quite foreign" (1985: 156, emphasis added). The *menalamba* revolt (1896–1897) against the French in the 1890s was also a revolt against external and internal colonization couched in religious terms, namely a revivalist notion of a "pure" Merina identity (see Ellis, 1985). Such a claim expressed by the most Europeanized of its leaders betrayed internal contradictions that were exploited by the French colonial military commander, General Gallieni.[16] He knew that desecrating the royal tombs of the ancestors was an easier route to victory than entering into battle. However, Gallieni's pacification of the entire island, which did not end until 1905, included the French soldiers taking young *ramatoa* as "temporary wives." Although aware of the charged atmosphere of sexual excitement and unconscious notions of the black's sexual potency among Europeans (see Mannoni, 1990: 111n.1), Mannoni never asks why these unconscious tendencies are directed toward the Malagasy. Further, Mannoni claims that relations between soldiers and their "temporary wives" were "healthy" and unmarred by complexes. He adds, "this goes only to show that racial conflicts develop gradually and do not arise spontaneously" (1990: 122). However, the pacification campaign, the murdering, and the domination of the Malagasy by the French were in reality a fruitful site for racial conflicts to develop quickly and "spontaneously." Racial conflicts coexisted with the war: "Let us not exaggerate," counters Fanon, "when a soldier of the conquering army went to bed with a young Malagasy girl, there was undoubtedly no tendency on his part to respect her entity as another person. . . . The fact that Algerian colonists go to bed with fourteen-year-old housemaids in no way demonstrates a lack of racial conflicts in Algeria" (Fanon, 1967a: 46n.5).

Working in a phenomenological rather than a specific historical framework, Fanon employs notions of being and existence instead of a specific analysis of Malagasy culture, peoples, and social formation.[17] Can Merleau-

Ponty's concept of body in the world be of any analytical benefit in a totally different environment, where the dead also have a society that is central to lived social life?

According to Mannoni, the Malagasy *are* sealed into their own customs and become Malagasy only in relation to the white man. In contrast, Fanon argues for an essential Malagasy being. Fanon's phenomenology notes the contradictions of "being among one's own." Indeed, who were the Malagasy before colonization? For Fanon the Malagasy are Malagasy but don't know that because that is what they are. In other words, before colonialism the Malagasy were in-themselves and for-themselves Malagasy. Although the process of colonization may have been going on for some time, it was the pacification campaign that marked the real turning point. Gallieni's campaign interrupted Malagasy life and culture, sealing it and then attempting to petrify it into forms of local rule and customs.

One can see how Fanon's phenomenology works in the context of the black in Paris. It is understandable, although not acceptable, that *being* is reduced to the body. But how does this work when speaking of a national body or moving from the black's lived experience to that of a nation? This problem is partially addressed in Fanon's critique of negritude, but how does Fanon's phenomenology work? Fanon does not employ a sociology of Malagasy society or a critical history of Madagascar before French colonialism that would show the ways in which hierarchy (Merina monarchy, regional contestations, etc.) might problematize Malagasyhood. In fact, before the official declaration of Madagascar as a French colony, the Sakalava to the West developed, against the Merina's British connection, a "'French connection' that often involved trading recognition of a French protectorate [in 1841] for weapons and other supplies" (Covell, 1987: 17).

Unaware of these internal power divisions, which could raise problems in the political body of independent Madagascar, Fanon posits French colonialism as an absolute dividing line, an absolute shock to Malagasy life. The loss of Malagasyhood is a result of French colonialism: "Robbed . . . of all worth, all individuality," the Malagasy are told that they are only human in as far as they are in step with the white world. Who is told this? Who listens? This classic question is not really addressed in Fanon's critique of Mannoni. For those who do listen the logical move is to become French, to which Mannoni counters, but you cannot do it because in your depths there is a dependency complex (1990) (reminding us that those who had taken part in the revolt were not fully assimilated). Fanon's reply is that such attempts are doomed because the colonizer *qua* master who remains the subject of actions is also white. He posits Aimé Césaire's articulation of a new rebellious consciousness, an identity that finds its equivalent in the 1947 revolt (1967a). Perhaps this is Toussaint in place of Mannoni's bestial Prospero, who is in the end a betrayed and abandoned native (Mannoni, 1990: 108).

1947: 100,000 Massacred

Mannoni explains the 1947 rebellion as a reaction of the dependent natives to their apparent abandonment by the colonial master, which resulted from a liberalization of colonial rule. Ignoring what Malagasy nationalists were saying,[18] as well as rational causes for the revolt, Mannoni "searched instead only for unconscious causes" (Bloch, 1990: vii). The feeling of abandonment apparently provided Mannoni with an answer to how thousands of Malagasy could face death in such unfavorable circumstances. For Mannoni feelings of abandonment were evoked by colonial policies that granted greater liberties and ended forced labor (1990: 135). The weakening of the colonial father figure, exacerbated by World War II and Allies' rhetoric about self-determination and imminent independence,[19] was "intolerable" for the Malagasy and "aroused in them feelings of abandonment and guilt" (Mannoni, 1990: 136). These feelings engendered a massive (childish) rage against the colonial system (father figure) and a massive overreaction by the colonizers. Characterized by the inferiority/authority complex, the colonialists experienced the revolt as a threat exacerbating the complex. To regain their feeling of superiority, they slaughtered 100,000 Malagasies. Mannoni's psychological typology was quite akin to the structural functionalism of British social anthropology. In the penultimate chapter of his book, titled "What Is to Be Done?" Mannoni suggests that the solution to the problem lies in the proper education of the colonial administration. In place of the colonials, who are characterized by doubts about themselves, Mannoni proposed the development of a new enlightened colonial administration that would depend on the inclusion of modern, perhaps Mannonian psychology, in its education.

By eliding the political activities of the nationalist organizations and looking to the unconscious and the irrational for the "real" motives behind the rebellion, Mannoni made the mistake of not retranslating these unconscious feelings back into a discourse of political grievance. Since the repression of open political dissent in late nineteenth-century Madagascar, politics had been expressed in other forms. During the colonial period the various forms of deliberate refusal to obey colonial laws—not paying taxes or not being able to pay, advocating "traditional" practices or "retreating" into religion, in other words, being actively resistant or engaging in passive or inert resistance—were seen by the French as equal challenges to their authority. During 50 years of French colonial rule there had been periodic peasant revolts and open resistance to the administration, but a greater threat was posed by the possession of a written national language, giving the nationalist elite a vehicle not found in many colonies.[20] Just as they did in Algeria, the French countered with an *indigénat*, a censorship of newspapers in languages other than French, which included a ban on meetings other than those of family and "traditional" gatherings. It is no secret that nationalist meetings were held under "traditional" auspices or in Protestant parishes, which were considered by the French to be hotbeds of conspiracy.

The events leading up to the revolt did indeed include a brief period of liberalization during the popular front period of the late 1930s. The roots of the rebellion can also be found in the changes effected by World War II on the colonial system and on the character and goals of the nationalist movements. The local colonial administration aligned itself with the Vichy regime. The British invaded, occupied, and then handed the island over to the Free French. The Free French used the island as a war resource, creating disruption in the local economies, rationing, scarcity, and a black market. But of enormous importance across the colonial world were the hopes created at the end of the war along with the victors' pronouncements about self-determination. In Madagascar forced labor was abolished and laws forbidding political activities relaxed. Independence became the goal, with many of the returning veterans becoming hardened nationalist militants. The French response was to arrest the leadership of the Mouvement de la Rénovation Malagache (MDRM). In Paris the Fourth Republic rejected calls for independence and Madagascar remained a colony (with very limited self-government). On March 29, 1947, armed groups of Malagasies attacked French government houses, French properties, and French collaborators. The rebellion was not crushed until 18 months later, at which time the High Commissioner put the number of dead at over 100,000. Not until 1956 was the state of siege lifted, but by then France was deeply embroiled in a far more serious conflict in Algeria, a conflict that could be dated to another French reaction to revolt, the slaughter of 45,000 people at Setif in 1945.

The 100,000 massacred, according to Mannoni, were not a result of colonial policy but of a latent inferiority complex made manifest "by the colonial situation" (1990: 88). The colonialists expressed an inferiority complex exhibited through domination and superiority. The few Europeans "unaffected by the contagion" (perhaps latter-day Gallienis or Mannonis?) understood that their power lay not in force alone but in exploiting "a certain 'weakness' of personality on the part of the Malagasies." This "position of dominance was due to the fact that in their network of dependencies they occupied roughly the same position as the dead ancestors" (Mannoni, 1990: 87). The dependency complex (and fear of abandonment) meant that "what the immense majority of the Malagasies needed far more was to feel that they were not being abandoned" (1990). Mannoni's psychological typology was crucial to future colonial administrations. It is not economic riches but psychological domination, "the satisfaction of the master who owns a slave," (Mannoni, 1990: 204) that characterizes the European in the colonies:

> What keeps the real colonial tied to the colonial situation, then, is not primarily profit. No economist can explain it. Economics ... has very little to say about a man who uses his economic superiority simply for the pleasure of enslaving another man can tell us how a man can dominate. (Mannoni, 1990: 203, 204)

Fanon found this psychologizing problematic. What the white master wants from the black slave, he insists, is not recognition but work (1967a: 220n.8).

The "corvee system" of forced labor was central to French colonial policy in Madagascar. The French had "abolished" slavery with the emancipation decree of 1896, partly as a strategy to woo emancipated slaves to the French cause against the *menalamba* rebellion and partly to undermine the authority of the Merina monarchy. After pacification they introduced a system of forced labor taxing and taxation was almost feudal in structure and was accomplished through Gallieni's "revival of native institutions" (Roberts, 1929: 397). Like British "indirect rule" under Lugard in Nigeria, Gallieni's policy was a form of colonialism on the cheap. Thus, in contrast to Mannoni's assertions, successful economic exploitation was essential to the colonization of Madagascar. The "natives" had to be pacified for political and economic reasons just as they had to be recruited for forced labor. Communities paid tax in terms of labor, so slavery was abolished legally but not practically. Forced labor continued in times of drought and hunger, causing untold misery, hardship, dislocation, and death. In short, political and economic reasons were "behind" the systematic dehumanization of populations. In response to Mannoni's claim that colonial racism is different from other racisms, Fanon asks, is one form of racism better than another? "[Mannoni] speaks of phenomenology, of psychoanalysis, of human brotherhood, but we would be happier if these terms had taken on a more concrete quality for him" (Fanon 1967a: 88). From the point of view of concrete experience all forms of exploitation resemble each other. Fanon had in mind Karl Jaspers's concepts of metaphysical guilt and historicity; Fanon sketched a "historico-racial schema" insisting that it is a problem of systematic exploitation. Mannoni had begun with an assumption that colonial exploitation is not the same as other forms because "the colonizing peoples are among the most advanced in the world, while those which undergo colonization are among the most backward" (27). Fanon rejected such a precondition. The similarity of racisms was exploitation: "Blacks exploited, enslaved, despised by a colonialist capitalist society that is only accidentally white" (1967a: 202).

Although Fanon might agree with Mannoni that "North American Blacks . . . are ill-treated because they are treated as *Blacks*" (Mannoni, 1990: 32), Mannoni ignored the types of labor that define "Blacks" *qua* "Blacks." In other words, labor is the central characteristic of ill-treatment.[21] Alternatively, even if the colonials do betray properties of an "inferiority complex," with the attendant need to dominate on one hand and the fear of the native's sexuality on the other (see Mannoni, 1990: 110; Fanon, 1967a: 107), Mannoni's view that such neurosis is the *realization* of a type, rather than a result of specific social relations, means the situation is little scrutinized. Like Algeria, Madagascar was seen as an experiment. But "unlike its Mediterranean prototype, . . . it was successful from the beginning" and played a great role in molding French colonial policy (Roberts, 1929: 375). Although Gallieni's policies were praised for creating "freedom from native discontent," which "marked off Madagascar from every other French colony" (Roberts, 1929: 404), the history of Madagascar is just like other African colonies, full of revolts. It was the belief in the "native's" passivity that increased French fears about uprisings. These fears of revolt provided a rich seam for neurotic complexes.

Mannoni maintained that what keeps the *real* colonial tied to the colonial situation is not primarily profit. He uses his economic superiority simply for the pleasure of enslaving and dominating another man (Mannoni, 1990: 203, 204). Fanon admits that colonialism might attract people with neuroses, but he adds that the majority of Europeans go to the colonies to get rich as quickly as possible. If one concentrated on a socioeconomic type, the colonial would be a huckster and trafficker. Mannoni, Fanon insists, has not understood the "real coordinates" of the colonial situation (Fanon, 1967a: 84). But what are they?

Fanon agrees with Mannoni's claim that only a psychological analysis can "place and define . . . the colonial situation," was fruitful, but Fanon disagrees with Mannoni's argument that the inferiority complex is something that antedates colonization (Mannoni, 1990: 85). Fanon explores the logical conclusion of Mannoni's argument, namely that "the Malagasy has ceased to exist" (Mannoni, 1990: 94). Sealed into their own customs, the Malagasy are described by Mannoni as living within a closed circle. Such a static society characterizes dependency. Where Mannoni viewed French colonialism as breaking the circle positively, Fanon sees the arrival of the French as breaking the Malagasy and creating the circle. The "real" multi-ethnic history of the Malagasy is anything but a closed circle. The subjugation of the Malagasy by the French,[22] the subsequent colonization, and the economic expropriation of the island are not only the historical reality, but constitute the present reality (i.e., in 1947) that is under scrutiny:

> What M. Mannoni has forgotten is that the Malagasy alone no longer exists; he has forgotten that the Malagasy exists *with the European* [as a "triple person"]. The arrival of the white man in Madagascar shattered not only its horizons but its psychological mechanisms. As everyone has pointed out, alterity for the Black man is not the Black but the white man. (Fanon 1967a: 97)

Alterity is both absolute and situational. That is why "Bantu Philosophy" is not an adequate response to colonial discourse and being (Fanon 1967a: 184–186). Fanon's critique of Alioune Diop's introduction to Placide Tempels's *La philosophie bantoue* (the first book printed by *Présence Africaine* in 1949) illuminates situatedness in the *Présence Africaine* debates and indicates Fanon's refusal to bow to Manicheanism as a method or goal of a philosophy of liberation. He brings us instead back to "the real":

> Be careful! It is not a matter of finding Being in Bantu thought, when Bantu existence subsists on the level of non-being. . . . Now we know that Bantu society no longer exists. (1967a: 186)

Later Aimé Césaire put this view more materialistically: "Since Bantu thought is ontological, the Bantu only asks for satisfaction of an ontological nature. Decent wages! Comfortable housing! Food! These Bantu are pure spirits" (1972: 38). On the other hand, negritude had an important presence in Madagascar, as the title of Senghor's anthology attests (1948). Perhaps the most famous of the Malagasy poets was Jacques Rabémananjara, a cofounder of *Présence Africaine* and a leader of the nationalist movement who had been sentenced to death for his part in the 1947 uprising.[23] He had earlier befriended Diop during the war and from jail helped found *Présence Africaine*. He embraced negritude and *Présence Africaine* as vehicles to develop "new values for the African" and the "Black world" (interview with Jules-Rosette, 1992: 18) and viewed the Malagasy as part of that black world.

Rabémananjara's involvement in the uprising of 1947 indicates that neither negritude in general nor Césaire's poetry in particular were alien to the nationalist discourse in Madagascar. Negritude spoke to the meaning of the revolt even if it took an ambiguous form in Rabémananjara's "Song," which was both a declaration of national freedom and of his own innocence. Provocatively, he ended the poem "12, Juin 1947, Prison Civile—Tananarive." Mannoni was also no stranger to the Malagasy poetry included in Senghor's anthology, writing a preface to Flavien Ranaivo's 1947 *L'Ombre et le Vent*.

Finally, Fanon's emphasis on Césaire's, rather than Senghor's more essentialized negritude, indicates his involvement in the *Présence Africaine* debate about negritude, which had become heated since Sartre's "Orphée Noir." Fanon was rejecting the African essentialism of Tempels, Diop, and Senghor, underlining instead the lived experience of Césaire's rebel, who knows, just like the black sugar worker in the conclusion of *Black Skin*, the only solution: to fight.

Mannoni's Dreams and Fanon's Reality

The savage, as I have said, is identified in the unconscious with a certain image of the instinct—of the id.

Mannoni

For Fanon it is not simply the arrival of the colonizer but the violent pacification campaign that creates Malagasy "dependency." In *The Wretched*, Fanon's focus on violence is more dialectical and reciprocal; in *Black Skin* it might seem that Fanon has taken Malagasy dependency too seriously, as expressed in the "shattering" of the Malagasy's "psychological mechanisms." Where Mannoni finds the basis of a dependent character type in ancestor worship, Fanon reminds us that whatever argument is made in terms of "magical-totemic patterns . . . the fact remains that something new had come into being on that island. . . . A new element having been introduced, it became mandatory to seek to understand the new relationships" (1967a: 97). One aspect of this new element is ideological. The government functionaries, school inspectors, and missionaries play an important role in the effort to make the chosen (Merina) elite French: "In the end they dropped him and told him, 'You have an indisputable complex of dependence on the white man'" (1967a: 216). To be emptied and then refilled with the civilizing mission only to be "abandoned" might very well create the complexes described by Mannoni, but it also indicates that even if correct, Mannoni's descriptions might be applicable to a very small number and not, as he assumed, to everyone including his tennis coach.[24]

Fanon's assessment of Mannoni owes much to the critique of the idea of the unconscious by phenomenological existentialism, which claimed that the dream merely expresses, perhaps in a roundabout way, a wish. Thus, Fanon's approach to criticizing Mannoni is to view dream interpretation socially. It is a mistake, Fanon believes, to begin an analysis from the individual's unconscious rather than from the individual's social situation. What comes out strongly in Fanon's critique of Mannoni's use of the unconscious is the centrality of subjectivity. For Fanon, subjectivity is uncontaminated by unconscious motives, and he believed in the ability of the oppressed people's conscious activity to change the world and to realize their freedom as self-determining human beings.

Fanon's critique of Mannoni's dream analysis is the only part of Mannoni's "ethnographic material" that Fanon criticizes directly. Mannoni includes six dreams as an epilogue to part one of his book as evidence of his theory of dependency. In a footnote he informs us that the dreams have come from different sources, although "in the main they have been collected in schools in the form of French homework" (1990: 91n.2). Mannoni is not fazed by the fact that the dream recollections were written in a language foreign to the students even though he attached great importance to the choice of words. Mannoni's analysis is further problematized through translation; for example, he takes note of the use of the singular and plural nouns, whereas in Malagasy singular and plural are not indicated.

Before he records Mannoni's dream analysis, Fanon questions Mannoni's use of the unconscious as the basis to answer why the Malagasy was prone to colonization. For Mannoni, it is the unconscious that accounts for why the Malagasy welcomed the shipwrecked Europeans and strangers (*vazaha*). But could he just as easily given an answer in "terms of humanity, of good will or courtesy" rather than in unconscious desires? Fanon retorts, "Yes, the unconscious—we have got to that. But one must not extrapolate" (1967a: 99). Fanon describes a black man's dream of a long, exhausting walk:

> I had the impression that something was waiting for me I came into an empty hall, and behind a door I heard a noise. I hesitated before I went in, but finally I made up my mind and opened the door. In this second room there were white men, and I found that I too was white. (1967a: 99)

How do we understand this dream psychoanalytically, as a wish fulfillment? What is the significance of the long, tiring walk? Could the second room be a tomb of the dead? Could the white men be ancestors or father figures?

Mannoni does not engage in a thorough analysis and gives very little background to each dream, seeming to be content with dream symbolism, dominated by notions of protection and danger associated with the mother and the more symbolically rich father. For example, the mother is equated with security and symbolized by a tree; the father is associated with a lack of security and sexual danger symbolized by bull's horns, the phallus, and Senegalese troops. But what is particularly striking about Mannoni's interpretations is his insistence that even though the dreams "were recorded at the time of public disturbance ... their authors had seen nothing of the disorders and knew nothing of the them" (Mannoni, 1990: 89).

How easy it is to follow a Mannonian interpretation. But like any good psychoanalyst, we need more information. The dream has multiple meanings; we need to know who told it, how, and under what circumstances it was told. But we also want to get to its latent content. Fanon at least informs us that the analysand has problems in his career, so the dream fulfills an unconscious wish. But "outside my psychoanalytic office, I have to incorporate my conclusions into the context of the world" (1967a: 100). In Mannoni's world the informants knew nothing of the uprising and thus it was not the "uprising" that was fundamental but unconscious motivations lying deeper. For Mannoni the "real" was expressed in irrational terms and could only be read psychoanalytically. In contrast, Fanon advocates a humanist psychology: The black should no longer be confronted by the predicament "turn white or disappear" but "should be able to take cognizance of a possibility of existence." In other words, if society makes it difficult to exist because of color, then the psychoanalyst, whose task is to help the analysand become conscious of the unconscious, should not encourage the analysand to adjust to that difficulty but should "put him in a position to *choose* action (or passivity) with respect to the real source of the conflict—that is, toward the social structures" (1967a: 100). Later Fanon says that the colonized doesn't have time to make the racial drama unconscious, but inside his psychoanalytic office Fanon is more orthodox. He wouldn't disagree with Freud's comment that "where there was Id, ego shall be" nor with D.W. Winnicott's connection of the real to self-awareness. Winnicott argued that the main work of psychoanalytic treatment "comes about through bringing to consciousness that which is unconscious" (1988: 60). Yet Fanon is also aware of the limitation of this process. Citing Anna Freud, he notes that sometimes analysis makes the problem worse, sometimes "the result of analysis is to weaken the ego still further and to advance the pathological process" (1967a: 59). This observation can lead Fanon in only one direction: The point is not only to understand the world but to change it.

For Fanon, the dreams Mannoni records had everything to do with the rebellion: "What must be done is to restore this dream to its proper time, and this time is the period during which eighty thousand natives were killed" (1967a: 104) (only after 1956 was the number estimated at 100,000). Central to Mannoni's dream analysis is the Malagasy's supposed reversion to routine, which he equates with the Malagasy's childish need for security. He writes: "'To depart from routine is to wander in pathless woods; there you will meet the bull who will send you helter-skelter home again" (Mannoni, 1990: 70). For Fanon, routine is nothing but pacification: "[S]ettle down

Malagasies, and stay where you belong. . . . You better keep your place" (1967a: 34, 107), ventriloquizes Fanon, who then responds, "Certainly not! . . . I will tell him, 'The environment, that is society is responsible for your delusion'" (1967a: 216).

What then is the meaning of the dream imagery? For Fanon there is no ambiguity:

> The rifle of the Senegalese soldier is not a penis but a genuine rifle. . . . The Black bull and the robber are . . . [not] "reincarnated souls" but actually the irruption of real fantasies into sleep. (1967a: 106)

In the circumstance of the massacre of 1947 the *socius* is more important than the individual or the symbolic. The Senegalese soldier is not the smiling consumer of Banania, but rather part of the military intelligence terror machine. It is the reality of torture, and the Senegalese soldiers were often used as torturers, that haunts the dreams. Fanon records testimony at a trial where a witness spoke of torture at police headquarters. Prefiguring the French torture in Algeria, the Senegalese soldiers had been instructed in new methods: "When one read such things," Fanon comments, "it certainly seems that M. Mannoni allowed one aspect of the phenomena that he analyzes to escape him: The Black bull and the Black men are neither more nor less than the Senegalese police torturers. . . . The discoveries of Freud are of no use to us here." (1967a: 104, 106n.32)

What Fanon knows of colonial life in Madagascar is limited, limited also by his focus on Mannoni. His ability to speak of the Malagasy and Malagasyhood is as much indebted to Merleau-Ponty's notion of lived experience as it is to his own experience of Martinique. It is Césaire's expression of negritude and the rebel in which Fanon finds "inspiration" (1967a: 187) for an alternative history. But here it seems that this island—its history, African, Polynesian and other—lay ambivalently, precisely between. Is Madagascar part of Africa, an island in the Indian Ocean, or both? This sense of separation and islandness is also expressed in Césaire's negritude.

Fanon kept coming back to the quandary that the colonial world had sealed the blacks into their blackness, while insisting that he wanted to find a concrete way beyond such a confinement. Fanon rejected Sartre's intellectualized way out of the problem, looking instead to lived experience of revolt. The French drama would be best expressed by the colonial movement against the French and the revolt in Madagascar in 1947, just as the revolt in Setif in 1945 shook the sense of national consciousness on both continents. It is for this reason that Fanon's thought is itself a product limited by a situation, perhaps constructed in a contested terrain, but also contextualized within the terrain of his critique of French radical thought and his involvement in decolonization movements against France in the post–World War II period. It is a terrain Fanon himself crosses and challenges as Martinican, as Frenchman, and as Algerian revolutionary and in doing so finally finds more nuanced ways to speak of humanism and intersubjectivity.

There is quite a distance between the invocation of Césaire's rebel in the context of the massacre in Madagascar and diving into the histories of Sudan, Ghana, Mali, and Gao during his field trip of 1960. In other words, Fanon began to realize that "things are not simple" (Fanon, 1967b: 185). With his experiences in revolutionary Algeria, Fanon moves toward a concretion of his claims about "being among one's own." No longer defined by the other, "being among one's own" is not about race but about those human beings who want to share with him "the open door of every consciousness" (1967a: 232), a reciprocal relation. His notion of a multicultural Algeria was an expression of this project. Nonetheless, the move from negritude to national consciousness to an international dimension is not a linear progression. A product of his thinking through his own experiences, it is less a straight line than a deepening spiral. Fanon thus remains an original character and exemplar of the new Pan-African intellectual of the postwar years because of his ability to imbibe and reflect translucently the spirit of the times.

11
Contesting Terrains Over a Massacre
The Case of Wiriyamu

MUSTAFAH DHADA
Clark Atlanta University

The Walls of Aching Silence*

Life in exile, specially after a massacre, does things to you. It slams you against a wall of aching silence. You no longer have an active social matrix as a point of communal reference. In a sense exile is worse than death. The ground gives way. You free fall, body intact, but your land below vanishes. You can hear your land whimper or pulsate but can do nothing about it. It can no longer propel you to action, to fight, to reflect, to commune socially, or to cultivate on it cotton, maize, or manioc. You live animated by a cluster of memories and exposed to the core. You are never the same again.

Like Lear,[1] you confront two things: the essential you inside and the host elements outside. To paraphrase Byron, you live not in yourself.[2] You are forced to face the reality of the unfolding moment. The outside elements hang midair and over you. They stretch mortal pulses into eternities. You are poised all right, but ache in uprooted silence. You cannot wait to replant yourself with a new or revised construct, a new or reformed social matrix (set

---

*This chapter forms part of a much larger work.

of relational parameters) in which to contextualize both your identity in the past and the new social and other realities in exile.

Further, you no longer have discourses with your own kind, your compatriots in your own land. Discourses between you and others of your kind and intercourse between you and the hosts granting you leave to stay with them (host others) have to be re-initiated, networks, relationships, and trust built. Such discourses can prove successful only among the briefed and the receptive. Even then, these discourses are likely to be bereft of the continued sustenance that under non-exiled circumstances feeds commonalities of experiences, nurtures pluralism in culture, and allows social construction and reformation. These others or host others can hardly be expected to "walk the talk with you," that is, join you in the struggle to defeat tyranny afflicting your home. After all, it is your home and not theirs.

Exile has one other effect on your intellectual innards. It strips you raw. It denudes you of the bark holding together the contents of your baobab[3]—pots, pombe, and pans; jugs and beakers; m'ssingas and m'foias;[4] precepts, values, and hopes; ideas, images, masks, and altars—that as a collective centripetally converge to construct your identity, who you are in the context of where you come from and what you are at the very core of your being.

It is not easy to recraft a life in exile. For that matter, it is not easy to cover the denudation of the self within after a massacre with a new or reconstructed bark protective enough to ensure survival before a return home. I should know. I was nearly there once, not as a massacre survivor but as an exile. I shall never forget that Koestlerian[5] descent into darkness at noon of August 16, 1972, only to be interrogated by walls reverberating with a question to which I could only reply with an aching silence. Had I finally betrayed the struggle? Try as I might I could not purge the silence from semiotic existence. I had arrived at London's Heathrow from Mozambique via several continents with a one-way ticket, £1500 sterling in my pocket, and very little English. The little English I had, had picked off the streets[6] (to paraphrase Amílcar Lopes Cabral, the Cape Verdian agronomist then leading the fight to free Guinea and the adjacent Cape Verde Islands from Portuguese colonial rule in West Africa. He was alive then and had six more months to live.)

I remember the English sun most vividly. It was a tired sun, a mellow sun, as if crafted to fit an empire in decline, unlike what I was used to back home, a fireball fit to roast your back and that of your prey, a sun searing your soul to seek solace in discourses with others. But I was not alone. Others before me had gone through the exile mill. Some had survived to tell the tale. Others had prospered as nouveau de-exilé. Yet others had taken exile as an opportunity to recraft not only their own lives but a social matrix for their compatriots to fight for and live by.

Several come to mind as I write this. Cabral was one of these exiles.[7] Another was Agostinho Neto, then leading the fight to oust the Portuguese in Angola via the Popular Movement for the Liberation of Angola (MPLA).[8] Yet another was Eduardo Mondlane, who was by then dead, but who until 1969 had led the Frelimo—Front for the Liberation of Mozambique.[9] Whereas Cabral sought the recrafting of the self through a strategy of "re-Africanization" as a relational matrix on which the nurturing of identity and culture could rest (Etudiants d'Afriques Portugaise, 1952), Neto had opted for a different route.

Unlike Cabral, who also stressed the vitality of liberation diplomacy in the global context to educate the host others about Luso-Africa (Ginwala, 1965; Dhada, 1995),[10] Neto had engineered a two-track approach. He focused on healing: poetry as a vehicle for healing from within, and Marxism as a strategy for healing the Angolan collective wounded by colonialism (de Andrade, 1962, 1966). Mondlane had taken a very intricate, and perhaps too delicate, approach resting on charismatic pluralism. He was to deploy the force of his personality and his considerable persuasive skills to get disparate nationalist forces to coexist and thence work together toward one aim, a free Mozambique (Mondlane, 1970).

But Cabral and others like him were fueled by intellects on fire, a fire that burned with varying degrees of intensity and quality in each of the leaders mentioned above. Some were analytically agile; others were praxeologically swift to apply normative matrices to transcend the purely personal. They sought to transform the personal into a usable strategy of liberation for mainland Luso-Africa—Guinea-Bissau, Mozambique, and Angola. For lesser mortals of my ilk, the perspective was much narrower and the challenges harder to face with existential and intellectual handicaps.

It would have been easier for the Luso-African struggle to continue if the Western world in general had not stood by in mortal silence, and in particular if the major Euro-Atlantic powers had not helped Portugal by design or unknowingly through the supply of arms, ammunition, training in counterinsurgency, and above all diplomacy.[11] Instead Luso-Africa fought to free itself from imperial Portugal during the late 1950s, the 1960s, and the early 1970s despite the West's indifference.

This is not to say that there were not periodic rumbles of interest from the West. No. There were. A report or two on labor conditions, obtuse debates in the General Assembly of the United Nations, and articles in leading newspapers did appear, only to fade into a Conradian pool of Kurtzian horror.[12] On the whole, however, Luso-Africa inhabited the margins of the West's consciousness as a political fakir at best or as an anti-Richburgian,[13] quasi Shangri-la at worst.

Many of the people I met and discussed Luso-Africa with did not know where Mozambique was. One educated historian I once encountered thought it was in Albania. Another thought it was a British colony, which in some ways did make sense, given British economic interests in some parts of Mozambique. Yet others I spoke to thought its lingua franca was English, perhaps because of the fluency in English with which the issues under review were being tackled.

On many an occasion some knew the location of the two-pronged oblong colony kissing the fringe of Atlantic ocean breezes in East Africa. They could recall its pristine beaches, beaches that many were shooed off to make way for whites then ruling the colonial roost as administrators and allied officials. Amusingly, Mozambique was often mistaken for the adjacent island of Madagascar as an idyll clustered with colorful butterflies and collectable postage stamps. So much for the tectonic awareness of Mozambique, let alone knowledge of the struggle of its people and that of Luso-Africans elsewhere! I suppose this was more forgivable than Hugh Trevor Roper's pronouncement that Africa as an ontological void.[14]

The personal and the anecdotal aside, the problem of lack of global consciousness in matters Luso-African was real, and truly hurtful. Cabral and his fellow leaders repeatedly attempted to rectify this. They sought to establish solidarity committees in major European capitals. They wanted to make the struggle a deeply felt presence in Europe and North America, strong enough to catalyze a change of policy toward Portugal's African colonies. Perhaps more than any other leader of Luso-African fighters, Cabral understood the importance of public and private diplomacy to free Luso-Africa. In this he was an unparalleled master and a consummate practitioner. Between 1960 and 1973 he traveled to more than 20 countries, on more than 80 visits, which yielded new friends and donors for the cause and neutralized enemies in various quarters (Dhada, 1993: 172–181, tables 2–5).

The diplomatic struggle to gain the support of Western governments proved an uphill battle during the 1960s. The liberation leaders and the solidarity committees abroad had tried everything: publicity, alliance with some elements of the Labour opposition in the British Parliament, invitations to Westerners to travel and see for themselves demonstrable evidence of new social matrices and therefore of a new life in areas under Luso-African governance,[15] and above all evidence and more evidence of Portuguese abuse of human rights and of acceptable standards of conduct in war (Dhada, 1993: 55–125).

Nothing had worked to change the Western establishment's support of imperial Portugal, and for good reason. All other factors notwithstanding,[16] evidence from liberators, particularly evidence about Portugal's misconduct, was seen as at best suspect. At worst it was attacked as a lie. Portuguese missions abroad and Portugal's allies had the upper hand here given its statist diplomatic networks and financial strength. This is not to suggest that the solidarity committees did nothing for liberation. They did. They strengthened ties among its supporters. They won new converts from among the public, and facilitated the flow of non-state aid to Luso-African liberation movements.

As stated earlier, what they did not do was persuade Portugal's major allies to weaken their ties with Caetano's Lisbon to stem the flow of military supplies through Portugal's imperial jugular. Something more dramatic, more fundamental, more visceral was needed to break the walls of aching silence surrounding the Luso-African struggle. But what could that be? A credible strategy was called for, a strategy involving a broader and perhaps multilayered set of tactics, some of which were unacceptable to ideological purists involved in the struggle. Consorting with the enemy to influence its behavior was one tactic that came to mind. Even then there could be no guarantee that these tactics would work.

To some of us who were active in exile politics in London, albeit at its margins, several things became crystal clear with regard to the handling of information on Portugal. First, any evidence of this nature deployed in a strategy of persuasion had to be collected by a disinterested third party. Second, such evidence and the concomitant strategy had to be constructed by neutrals with no motive other than to further veracity. In short, materials tainted by the hands of Luso-African movements and their committees in the West were unlikely to "cut it." Finally, a publicity drive involving the press had to be handled by a newspaper with clout, a thunderer universally seen by the Western establishment as a trustworthy gatekeeper of truth.

Some of the solidarity committees in Europe, constituted as they were to deal essentially with elements outside the corridors of institutional power, had no visible role to speak of, at least not in this discourse advocating plurality in tactics. Nor was the tactical ball firmly on the Luso-African side of the net in Africa. The ball was somewhere in or outside the African court, the initiative in the hands of an entity or entities, structure or structures that no one could take at face value or control and/or influence. The catalysts for action were nowhere to be seen. All one could do was wait and see and let events dictate the next move.

But such a stance wrought havoc in the movement. Key questions of tactics and strategy arose. Could the cause of Luso-African liberation remain ideologically pure and yet accommodate a plurality of tactics—particularly from activists outside the organizational fold, waverers, and agents and freelancers working for Portugal disguised as activists in the fold—for dealing with the establishment in an effort to influence it? Could the cause be served by these tactics and survive penetration from Portuguese intelligence agents? In a way the Luso-African cause in exile was faced with the same dilemma that Cabral and others had confronted. Cabral had dealt with the dilemma successfully through a complex network of alliances and alignments to keep factions at bay (Dhada, 1995). Mondlane also encountered a similar dilemma when he sought and ultimately failed to contain several tactical strands of strategic operations being advocated by organizational subclusters within Frelimo (Mondlane, 1970).

The result of this dilemma was a brief period of paralysis. There were conflicts between ideological purists and tactical pluralists as tempers frayed. Friendships broke up. Loves and intemperate passions skidded on shifting alliances and broken promises. Tragically, these events achieved exactly the paralysis alluded to here in the wait and see strategy; but not as a conscious act of strategic transcendence; rather as acts by default, propelled by egos rather than visions for the greater good—Luso-African liberation.

At the level of dialectics the impact of considering such a strategy of tactical pluralism was even more profound. It foisted upon the exiles a "return to the source" (Cabral, 1973). It brought into question the theoretical underpinnings of the exiles' foundational ontology. Of these underpinnings, two focused on the supremacy of the individual over that of structures as sole determinants propelling liberation strategy and the ascendancy of a given process or a concatenation of events over any entity as a trigger to break down Western resistance to the Luso-African liberation in the West.

Perhaps the most difficult question focused on an essential: Must liberation diplomacy be viewed exclusively in terms of historical materialism per se, or could it embrace historical materialism subsumed by a heuristic proto-theology that allowed God and Marx to coexist?

In a different context, and faced with similar questions and reflections, Cabral had already resolved these issues in his own way.[17] However, for me these questions clung like a pair of Tiberian bats, fomenting intellectual discontent for nearly a decade. (My discontent was only resolved in part during the writing of the preface to *Warriors at Work*.)

In the end tactical deliverance came in the early 1970s in the form of two breakthroughs. The irony is that both breakthroughs were handled by men of God and not Karl Marx. Someone up High or closer to home in Highgate had a sense of humor it would appear! The first breakthrough took place in Rome, where the Luso-African leaders were received in the Vatican, then undergoing major doctrinal revisions under the Vatican II Council. This reception tacitly acknowledged the legitimacy of the Luso-African fight. It brought the Vatican into open diplomatic conflict with Caetano's Lisbon, and for the first time flung open prospects for state-level humanitarian aid from the Nordic nations and from Holland (Dhada, 1995).

The other breakthrough was exactly what Luso-Africans needed to smash the walls of aching silence: a story of Portuguese dastardly misconduct in an act of war, compiled by men of the cloth and published by a major newspaper as a true story, a story powerful enough to rattle Portugal's imperial cage and unnerve its allies. That story was the massacre at Wiriyamu (see Hastings, 1974).

Wiriyamu: Genesis

The massacre at Wiriyamu was revealed in the early summer of 1973. In July, *The Times* of London splashed its front page with the story, depicting murder, massacre, and mayhem in Tete, Mozambique. The paper subsequently stayed with the story as a gatekeeper for nearly five months. This is what it covered in essence.

On December 16, 1972, Portuguese paratroopers had gone into the village of Wiriyamu, located half an hour's drive south of Tete city in north central Mozambique. They had liquidated all humans. A few directly in the line of fire escaped, as did most of the chicken, cattle, goats, and pigs.[18]

Wiriyamu villagers and the people around them had apparently been reluctant to move to "strategic hamlets" constructed to isolate them from the "communist contagion." In addition, Wiriyamu and the villages surrounding it were suspected to be harboring Frelimo fighters. The paratroopers and their cohorts had been instructed to eradicate the villagers and to leave no survivors. "Aphani Wense!" ("Kill them all!") could be heard all over Wiriyamu. Wiriyamu was a contested terrain from the point of view of the Portuguese. It had be wiped off the face of the map.[19]

Both *The Times's* extensive coverage and its timing were remarkable. The paper was under the general editorship of William Rees-Mogg, a conservative pro-Tory, with Louis Heren, a "feisty" journalist,[20] working under him in charge of the foreign news desk. The British government, then headed by Tory Prime Minister Edward Heath[21] and backed by an influential clutch of Tory Members of Parliament (MPs), was about to host Caetano in London to celebrate the 600th anniversary of the Anglo-Portuguese Alliance.[22]

What is even more astonishing is that up to that point, the paper had remained for the most part neutral on all aspects of the wars of liberation in Luso-Africa. During the eight years between the onset of the war of liberation in Mozambique in 1964 and July 1973, *The Times* had published just under 535 articles related to Portuguese affairs inclusive of Luso-Africa, an average of 177 a year or an item of news every eight days.[23] During this period an occasional article did appear to side with Portugal on its views on communism and its measures of counterinsurgency in defense of empire in Africa.[24]

However, in early 1973 the paper's news reports on this area changed dramatically, becoming strongly critical of Portugal (see Howard, 1973; Perrott, 1973). Eighty-three articles related to Wiriyamu were published in July, an all-time peak. Subsequent months saw a decline, with 24 articles in August, 8 in September, 11 in October, and 14 in November, and 5 in December. During the period between 1973 and 1975, just after the April revolution that brought the demise of the Caetano regime, thus ushering in democracy in Portugal, *The Times* published an average of one article every two days on this issue, almost all critical of Portuguese rule in Luso-Africa.[25]

The Portuguese denied charges of wrongdoing.[26] Reactions from other quarters, including mobs hired by the Portuguese to protest, were intense (*The Times*, 1973).[27] Others were more derisive.[28] *The Times* stuck to its position: The story it had published was true; the priests as handlers of its sources and the sources themselves were solid.

Attempts at denial and deconstruction of the Wiriyamu massacre continued. Some contested the fact of the mass killings.[29] Others questioned the description of the massacre as Portugal's own "My Lai." The comparison between Wiriyamu and My Lai was first drawn by Father Adrian Hastings, who had brought the story to the attention of *The Times* and who wrote a book on the subject soon after the revelations. To this day, Father Hastings's book is the only publicly documented account of the massacre detailing the names of the killed and their numbers and the context of the events that brought Wiriyamu to extinction (Hastings, 1974).

The Portuguese focused at first on Wiriyamu's etymology and contextual hermeneutics—all contestable terrains, as we are about to see—by vigorously denying the very existence of Wiriyamu as a place, let alone a place where a massacre had taken place. According to their maps the coordinates, or "cartographic codes" for and of Wiriyamu, as spelled out and reported in *The Times*, were missing. Therefore Wiriyamu could not and did not exist (Derelius, 1973).

Proponents of Portugal's continued reign in Luso-Africa sharply criticized the portrayal of evil underscoring Portugal's role in the story. It seems that in the absence of King Leopold's ghost[30] this story had abstracted itself. The portrayal had stripped Portugal of its imperial complexity, reducing it to a venal essence, an abuser of colonial power in imperial Africa. *The Times* covered the rebuttals, reports, and epistemological retrenchments faithfully and extensively in more than 200 articles, all published in a six-month period beginning in July 1973.[31]

The Wiriyamu massacre was depicted not as an event but as written text, unfolded on contested grounds over a naked truth, on a rock bed of essentialism,[32] a seed of a larger imperial truth, most dreadful and deadly. In the middle stood Wiriyamu, its life drained of pulse, its geography a mortician's paradise. Its epiphany as an event was still at stake; its epistemonical value in the context of Mozambican liberation now in doubt; its hermeneutic taxonomy perilously close to self-abnegation.

Essentialism Defined

Essentialism strips entities, processes, or structures of constituents, complexities, contradictions, and behavioral disconsonants to unmask epistemonies. The result is truth revealed. In other words, essentialism is a context-specific tool to reach a kernel of truth, serving as a point of departure for construction of canons in the literature of a given field.[33]

However, like any theory seeking supremacy in the social sciences, essentialism as employed in this discourse on massacre has numerous mutually porous characteristics, and they come with attendant pitfalls. For example, binary essentialism focuses on veracities. It involves a contest between two arguments over an event or entity, each seeking to attest to a point in a reductionist or concatenated true/false continuum. A thing, entity, or event either is or is not, depending on the weight of evidence. Either a murder or massacre did take place, and here is the evidence to prove it, or it did not because the evidence is either untrue or inconclusive. Denial of evidence in binary essentialism, taken to its logical extreme, can easily become a parody of itself, *reductio ad absurdum*. Ultimately, if used with value-laden essentialism, it can act as fodder for constructing pure fiction, rendering facts as fiction, or transforming fiction into fact.

Value-laden essentialism, on the other hand, hones in on the social and existential worth of "the other." It distills human behavior and motivation into icons along a linear continuum of values: good and evil. Value-laden essentialism shows up in literary texts as overt myths. In social texts these appear as putative seeds of truths, substantiated by highly selective historical, manufactured, or anecdotal data. Value-laden essentialism, to use René Lemarchand's term, helps to demonize (Lemarchand, 1994)[34] "the others" and thus purge their social legitimacy and discourse in an *Ubermensch/Untermensch* continuum. Communists are evil and anti-communists are not; Hutus or Tutsis are demons or a variant thereof and non-Tutsi or non-Hutu are saintly or saved.

Value-laden essentialism is invariably terminal and predatory. It provides the ultimate raison d'etre to "finish 'the other' off." It acts as a corollary to reify either systemic existentialism and governance (hence dictatorships and authoritarian rule) or existential beingness and ultimately supremacy over "the other" (hence the phenomena of genocide, massacre, ethnic cleansing, or ethnocide in the Lemarchandian sense of discursive coinage).[35]

This is not to suggest that value-laden essentialism precludes transformational change or change in taxonomies. No, it does. Such transformation of value-laden essentialism can come about against its will through penetrative intrusion or consensualism. Further, the transformation is indicative of a process of de-essentialization, which can occur at two levels, applied and dialectical. In terms of application de-essentialization manifests itself in several ways: through revolutions, civil wars, and allied strategies for change, deploying through either orgiastic violence or violence in service of a set of prespecified objectives; through juridical binary essentialism, war crimes tribunals with teeth to punish; or through conciliation strategies, as in mediation and dialogue operating under the rubric of either forgiveness or give-and-take.

Dialectically, de-essentialization can emerge in either intellectual or popular form. Intellectually, it appears as a trans-Spivakian discourse aimed at a "full non-binary emergence" of ontology. In other words, it can lead to the construction of a truly post-colonial text,[36] methodologically crafted to push the envelope of post-colonial textuality that much farther. In a more popular form, de-essentialist transformation emerges because widely publicized revelations of an empirically driven truth over time have altered the social matrix of global awareness sufficiently for reassessing the normative value of "the other."

Consider how Luso-African leaders fighting to free African colonies were seen by the Portuguese establishment initially as communist-instigated terrorists, only to be hailed later by some elements in the new post-Caetanist government as liberators (De Carvalho, 1975). Better still, examine how the Truth and Reconciliation Commission in South Africa presided over by Bishop Tutu has sought to underpin its validation with public revelations to elicit veracity based on forgiveness and without fear of juridical retribution (Truth and Reconciliation Commission Report, 1999).

Attributive essentialism focuses on causality in social science phenomena. Current theories in attributive essentialism are memetics,[37] which Stephen Gould sees as a meaningless metaphor in Darwinian fundamentalism (Gould, 1997), and Edward Wilson's consilience (Wilson, 1998), which views collective human behavior as determinably sociobiological. Consilience attempts to carve a meta-theory in a field hewn with infinite uncontrollable variables, that is, the social sciences. Stylistically, the search for consilience is demonstrably akin to the search in pure science for a unified universal theory, a search that has bedeviled many a theoretical physicist, including the likes of Albert Einstein.[38] Consilience cuts against the methodological grain of its antithetical counterparts, which are numerous. They include postmodernism[39] and Gouldian conflationary analysis.[40]

Two other genres of attributive essentialism are worthy of discussion here, both likely to be familiar to readers of this text: structural determinism and variants thereof, including Braudelian, Althusserian, and Wallersteinian world system approaches to social science, and the less recognizably arcane field of classical Marxism.[41] Whereas the first perspective, Braudel's *la longue durée*, gives weight to structures as propellants for discourse on causality, the others examine processes as a complex web of normative causality underpinned by capitalism and concatenated variants thereof.

Binaries, Values, and Attributions at Work

As implied previously in the discussion of Portugal's initial responses to Wiriyamu's revelation in London, right from the start Lisbon had understood the dynamics of essentialism at work—and exploited it to the hilt. At first Portugal had denied the very existence of Wiriyamu as a place by pitting itself as an attestant of untruth in a contest of binary essentialism with others. But then something happened. A baobab tree had stood silent witness to the massacres. It was revealed with its girth intact, etched with the word *Wiriyamu*.

A photograph of a survivor was produced for the pages of *The Times*. Subsequently, the Portuguese denied any wrongdoing, then proceeded to debunk the story as an exaggeration, a product of the fertile imaginations of a clutch of subversive priests (*The Times*, 1973). As if to prove the point, journalists were invited on carefully constructed tours of the Tete region away from the massacre site, to a place the Portuguese had declared to be Wiriyamu and where no evidence of military misdeeds could be found.[42]

Whatever the truth, one thing was certain about Wiriyamu: As a tale of woes it was truly spellbinding, a story with fictional potency. It was at this stage that the Portuguese set about trying to deconstruct the story as value-laden essentialism, and to a point they were correct.

As a sepulchral text, Wiriyamu was steeped in value-laden essentialism and was thus vulnerable to parody. Every aspect of the story, from the characters, to the thematic drive, to the plot and outcome, was at face value linearly comfortable—theatrically predictable, familiar, with a certain Cartesian air driving the logic of the characters and their categorical features. The characters followed causal lines of consilience. They were bereft of untidy layers of nebulous emotional shades of complex greys. No behavior could be witnessed outside the box, that is, outside the parameter of sociobiological determinism. It would appear that the soldiers were driven to kill by instinct wrapped around a rational act of war.

Additionally, the characters were denuded of several features that underscored what Gould called "emergences," anti-consilience analyses and perspectives. The perspective rested more on heurism, disjuncture, and lack of comprehension (and was thus outside Wilson's consilience paradigm) than on social determinism, ontology as exclusion of plural discourses, and gonadal causality catapulting men on a binge to kill fellow humans *en masse*.

Consequently, Wiriyamu as revealed was bereft of features propelling textured reality: duplicity of nuances and purpose, frayed unstable psychosomatic edges, and fissures and flaws sullying pristine moral conduct. A gamut of cultural, social, psychological, and historical factors was left out of the Wiriyamu massacre in its Western genesis—and for good reason. The story was there to prove a point, not to provide nuances underpinning the massacre. The inclusion of such nuances, however, would have led to the portrayal of non-iconic characters, propelled to acts of confusing mercies in a pool of infernal destruction, capable of blurring this otherwise neo-digital portrayal of men-in-hyphenated-action in pursuit of a doggedly greater good, anti-communism.

The story as a text made little allowance for flawed lives inside Wiriyamu, either.[43] Instead, the thematic drive set the killers and the victims into rigid iconic clusters: the anti-Portuguese good versus its antithetical bad, the ugly and the irredeemable; the sublime versus its opposite. The news stories abounded with a plague of contesting "Vs"[44]—vengeance, vilification, vituperation, and violence versus victimhood—and innocent lives laid to waste.

Some glimpses of de-essentializing realism were shown: forbearance by the priests engaged in missionary work under war conditions, clashes with a Kafkaesque bureaucracy solidly chiseled out of a castle rock[45]; death versus shades of conscience among killers; and scholarly and apoliticized priestly conduct versus activism and compromised activism in collecting names, ages, and genders of the killed at Wiriyamu.

Others aspects of textured realism never surfaced. Notable among these were the voices of the survivors, killers, and the killed speaking directly or as reconstructed text; noncompliance through exploitation of weaknesses in the system; personal loves, divorces, cherished moments spent in gay mirth or social get-togethers over a drink; and betrayals of confidences in the face of a colonial will of iron bent on extermination of the village.

The plot also proved to be simple and straightforward—again essentialist and laden with values—and thus an easy target for Portuguese critical offensives. Because of this binary simplicity, it was difficult to mangle or distort such a plot beyond a point; even though by the time the story hit *The Times* it had gone through several hands. Among these were a variety of cataloguers, translators, and handlers: different fascist regimes, the Vatican, royal democracies, priests, subeditors with pugilistic temperaments, professors, and typesetters about to go on strike.

In the end the revelations about Wiriyamu proved essentially true when Portuguese complicity was eventually revealed by Lisbon after the fall of Caetano's regime. In the meantime, Wiriyamu's plot stayed virtually intact as a binary. It had a beginning of sorts when orders to decimate Wiriyamu were given and a four-hour intense and "real" middle, in which the bulk of the massacre took place, led by the "bad guys," with Wiriyamu villagers taking the full terminal brunt. It had a long-drawn-out end, miserable to many who died and many who lived to tell the tale or remain painfully silent.

The Portuguese were not the only ones to recognize Wiriyamu both as a story in need of empirical reification and as a tale potent with fictional possibilities. Several others did too. Among them were Lisbon-based Portuguese writers and African novelists. One such writer was Felicia Cabrita, whose postmortem account dug deeper into the old binary furrow, seeking and establishing the veracity of *The Times'* story some 20 years after the event. She held her fellow countrymen (the killers at Wiriyamu were all men) responsible, leaving the local villagers yet again mute, innocent, and free of attributable guilt (Cabrita, 1992, 1998).

A similar (but fictional) work pitting entities along both value-laden and attributive lines of essentialism was written by the West African author William Sassine (Sassine, 1976; Reed & Wake, 1976). His work appeared barely three years after the public revelations, a year after Mozambique achieved freedom from Portuguese colonial rule, and several years before the bones at the massacre site were collected for a burial of sorts.[46] As late as 1975 the massacre site had charred remains strewn on its grounds. These were given a burial in a ceremony under the guidance of Father Vincente Beringuer, a Burgos priest who at the time was in Changarha south of Tete and who had earlier played a small part in the Wiriyamu revelations.

Although Sassine's work was well intentioned, it shared some of the ailments afflicting essentialism and its variants. The colonized appeared bereft of residual proto-subaltern sentiments (Guha, 1997).[47] The little they could manifest fully complied with Spivak's rubric and reservations: that a full nonbinary discourse would be difficult to execute as a truly post-colonial text.[48]

Sassine, however, attempted to evoke "the personalities and the state of mind of a group . . . trapped by the colonial situation and drawn inexorably towards the appalling horror of the massacre" (Sassine, 1976: back cover). In other words, it was a work of interpretative essentialism in which structures as well as processes operating under colonial conditions drove and determined actions and outcomes.

To a point, Sassine was right in his exploration of Wiriyamu as an outcome of interpretative essentialism. Mozambique's colonial governance had not been in the hands of an imperial, Protestant democracy ruling its own racial kind in the metropolis in an all-inclusive, supra-dermal plurarchy. It was in the hands of an avowedly anti-democratic state with a state-crafted, state-sanctioned, and state-directed mission to civilize peoples with a denser pigmentation of skin than its own. That is why India had gained constitutional independence without a sustained and protracted armed struggle. Indians could do so by exploiting two democratic principles: the need for broader political and social inclusion of people in a democracy to ensure its viability as a credible process of governance and competitive allocation of resources to ensure (in theory) alternation of power.

Britain ultimately could not deny India either principle even if the Indian skin wasn't blanched enough for the latter to be pukka British. No sir, they could not; unless Britain was to propound for its own constitutional kind in the isles the colonial realities and structures governing its disenfranchised brown sahibs. That is why Satya Graha (peaceful resistance) worked in India. Satya Graha exploited contradictions in democracy-led Protestant imperialism by deploying channels demanding inclusive politics (i.e., enfranchisement) to make its voice heard.

Britain was prepared up to a point to hear de-essentializing voices of discontent before these crystallized into an armed force fighting from outside. That is why ultimately subaltern voices emerged as a seed of resistance in India, albeit at the periphery of the periphery in the Galtungian sense;[49] and that is why subaltern voices could be placed on record however imperfectly as a construct for scholarship later and as a fabric for presaging national consciousness in state-formation.

Portugal had no such principles, no such structures in place, no such processes for conflict resolution. It was in a league of its own. It could manufacture its own myths (such as Catholic corporatism,[50] and Lusotropicalism[51]) as realities for its government to live by and thus etiolate itself from de-essentializing intrusions from within and from outside, the latter in the form of global opinion contesting its raison d'etat as a dictatorship with an overseas empire. Nor was Portugal in the same imperial league as other empires in industrialized Europe. It never had been and never could be even if it wanted to because of its lack of a strong industrial base; an over-reliance on mercantile capitalism and labor as variable capital to fuel surrogate industrial imperialism elsewhere; a poor economic demography to fuel indigenous capitalism;[52] and an Erastian Catholicism that advocated the ideological supremacy of the state in matters ecclesiastical, which effectively smothered Weberian capitalist initiatives.[53]

Furthermore, Portugal's regime since the demise of the republican experiments just after the First World War had actively sought to excise all-inclusive pluralism from its discourse, politics, and deliberations. This pluralism, among other factors, could have underpinned responsive governance if it had been in force.[54] Instead, Portugal had essentialized in praxis its own national politics. That is what Salazarist dictatorship was all about.

As a consequence, Portugal could not but see the genesis of Wiriyamu from a pluralist London as colorful fiction. Therefore it excised liberation in Luso-Africa with preemptive and systematic alacrity.[55] Portugal had to react as it did for dear political life at home and in the colonies. That is how it had cultivated its own vision for governance at home: as a discourse for and among the rarified few headed by a recluse from Coimbra, and afterward his successor Caetano, both acting as trustees of self-constructed myths disguised as the only truth allowed political legitimacy in Portugal and in its colonies in Africa.

In short, Portugal had marginalized its own kind. Its periphery of the center, namely the rural countryside, the very guts of its society, was by then eviscerated of its own version of subalternity. It had one option: self-protection. Bereft of its center, the gutless rural voted with its feet by migrating abroad. Portugal responded to voices of opposition from two quarters: opposition from exile, targeted as a dialectic at its personified essence, Caetano and his cohorts, and opposition from within, at the very center of the rarified center.

The opposition from exile came from the Portuguese in exile, from Luso-Africans, or from both (Birmingham, 1995; Marcum, 1969, 1978; Mondlane, 1970; Coelho, 1989; Dhada, 1993; Chabal, 1980). But this opposition was wrapped in a revolutionary violence that was poignantly didactic in its Fannonist catharsis, purging Portugal's ideological insides of value-laden Salazarist essentialism. The opposition from within was more peaceful and would only emerge as a discourse of dissent, from Portugal's powerful men-at-arms, Caetano's enablers ensuring his rule in Africa by fiat (De Figueiredo, 1975).

The Grateful—and the Dead

But where did Wiriyamu fit in the context of the liberation struggle in Luso-Africa as fight-in-the-field and liberation as discourse? Key leaders within Frelimo saw the revelations as doing more for the revolution "than decades of fighting in Mozambique."[56] They were not exaggerating. Mozambique's struggle, which began in 1964, had been preceded half a decade earlier by the fight to oust the Portuguese from Guinea-Bissau and Angola, led by Cabral and his Luandan-based compatriots. As a tri-frontal attack on the Portuguese, the war had met with mixed success at all three levels of the struggle: reclamation, reformation, and public diplomacy.[57]

The broad dynamics behind these tripodal tactics was freedom-as-meaningfully-constructed-fact: Fight to claw back land, develop transformatively a nation-state in formation in the land reclaimed as the fight advances, and win friends and influence enemies. "Friends because we need them to support us morally and materially, enemies so as to weaken Portugal."[58]

It is in the arena of transnationalism that Wiriyamu outshone all other efforts by Luso-Africans to publicize their cause for freedom. One saving grace of Wiriyamu was its non-Frelimo origins of construction. The sources used to compile the text of the revelations were handled almost entirely by priests of various denominations and religious orders. Frelimo got nowhere near it. This is not to suggest that Frelimo leaders had not attempted to publicize massacres before. They had, but their efforts came to naught. The news was buried under other, more pressing headlines. Neither am I suggesting an absence of desire to take the initiative on the part of those active in the Wiriyamu story.[59] However, those involved were all avowedly neutral; some as priests stressed this point: "We were not serving both God and Marx."[60]

In addition, Frelimo leaders did not know the full story, nor could they. Communications between the field and headquarters via stringers and satellite posts in Zambia and Malawi were slow and proving slower south of the Zambezi River, where the fighting was becoming more intense as 1972 closed. Additionally, the Zambezi River was about to be flooded as the dam project Cabora Bassa drew close to completion. What is ironic is that the Frelimo leaders had as yet to grasp the full import of Wiriyamu as a weapon in the transnational struggle. They did so only after the story broke out in London in July, a full seven months after the event.

The commanders in the field knew the full extent of the killings. They may well have had a hand, however inadvertently, in bringing the wrath of the commandoes down on Wiriyamu.[61] Further, they were aware that the priests were active in gathering information for a report. They, like the priests collecting the data, had assumed the report was destined for the church hierarchy in Tete, Lourenço Marques, Lisbon, Madrid, and ultimately the Vatican. They, like the priests, never dreamed of its full and public disclosure in *The Times* on the eve of Caetano's visit.

It is as well that the Frelimo leaders did not get involved directly in the transmission of the report to *The Times*. Had they done so or been in a position to do so, Wiriyamu as text would have been assured the kiss of death as contaminated evidence. The dead were mercifully denied an opportunity to speak through Frelimo leaders, yet again leaving Wiriyamu's genesis in London to do the work for the leaders, albeit at the expense of gut-wrenching sorrow at home in Tete.

On the international front, and particularly to many in exile in London and Europe who at the time were desperate to see an end to imperial rule in Mozambique, the revelations about Wiriyamu were truly a satisfying moment in the Luso-African struggle. To some it did not matter that the veracity of the report had been questioned. What mattered was what the revelations had achieved for Luso-African liberation. Wiriyamu reached audiences beyond imagination and beyond the resources and reach of Frelimo and Luso-African nationalists.[62] It drew attention to events in the colonies previously ignored in the world press. In the end it shattered the walls of silence smothering Luso-Africa and helped air critical evaluations of Portuguese colonial realities in Africa. It was a kind of coming out, a subaltern spring of the dead, outward bound with a new life for all to see.

On the domestic front, the revelations on Wiriyamu shook Caetano's statist timbers, helping open fissures of discontent already in place in his innermost circles and thus bringing to the fore a process of de-essentializing the regime. Caetano admitted as much to himself in his deposition in exile, crafted under a warm Brazilian sun (Caetano, 1974). Six months after the revelations his government fell. Democracy was ushered in with tumultuous fragility. Mozambique was set free at last. In this sense Wiriyamu acted as a discourse in aiding pluralist de-essentialization of the Portuguese empire at its metropolitan core, a discourse by the dead in aid of a collective colonial and colonized life fighting to be free.

In the context of liberation-as-discourse, Wiriyamu as a text remained where it was, fettered by binaries. It began overseas as an epistemonical discourse, catalyzed by Father Adrian Hastings in the pages of *The Times* with the aid of the paper's foreign editor, who had already been sensitized to the horrors of the Vietnam War during a brief stint in Washington, D.C.[63] Its veracity as a valid epistemony was assured in the end for two reasons: first, because its publication on the eve of Caetano's visit was subsequently confirmed and reified as true by Lisbon-based authors and the military; and second, because of its "whiteness"; that is, because it was free of any imagined, real, or residual taints at the hands of the "other"—the Frelimo.

Once Portuguese complicity was revealed as it were from within its own camp, Wiriyamu's value in dialectical praxis was assured as a truth helping to catalyze transformational change within. Its "death (embodying a kernel of some truth) was denied," to paraphrase Flora Gomes, a filmographer from Guinea-Bissau.[64]

Decades have passed since Wiriyamu was exterminated and then brought to public attention. The dead are dead, some buried after the fact. Others remain pulverized by time. The communal graves are recumbent, silent witnesses to dust, scarce rain, scorching sun, grazing cattle, and goats with bells a-peeling. Baobabs dotting the perimeter of Wiriyamu still stand, one providing shelter to a speechless bone or two. The dead themselves could speak, although only at their killers' beck and call. Some of the killers are dead as well. The remainder are largely silent.

There is only a handful of survivors who fled the scene just before the massacre or who witnessed parts of it. These few did speak; once to priests and information gatherers culling the names and the numbers of the killed and on other occasions to confirm that Wiriyamu as a massacre had happened. Their sentiments, thoughts, and feelings remain locked, shut off from the world. On occasion they do share these feelings and thoughts, but only among themselves, as if in a communion with and for the dead.

What really happened at Wiriyamu on that fateful day, December 16, 1972? Put differently, is the story as revealed, or is there more to it than meets the eye?[65] What was Wiriyamu like before the killing? Are its causal roots structurally traceable, and were these roots perhaps more complex than described? What role did the priests, and the predators heading the kill, play in the massacre? How was the story put together and thence transported overseas?

These are questions worthy of methodical discourse, if only to push the envelope of post-colonial textuality[66] and thus bring Wiriyamu back into Mozambique's historical mainstream, not as a text on the dead for the living; but rather as a text with the dead vocalized. Until that happens, it is the world outside time that now stands where Luso-Africans stood, once—slambanged against a wall aching with ontological silence.

12
Negotiating Postwar Identities
Child Soldiers in Mozambique and Angola

ALCINDA HONWANA
Department of Social Anthropology
University of Cape Town

Introduction

Angola[1] and Mozambique were both Portuguese colonies that, after a long period of armed struggle for national liberation, acceded to independence in 1975. Both post-colonial governments adopted a Marxist orientation and socialist models of development. After independence opposition parties (Mozambique National Resistance—RENAMO in Mozambique—and United Front for the Total Liberation of Angola—UNITA in Angola) initiated a war against the Front for the Liberation of Mozambique (FRELIMO) and Popular Movement for the Liberation of Angola (MPLA) governments.[2] It is in the process of these wars, which lasted for several years (more than 15 years in Mozambique and more than 20 in Angola), that many children were drawn into armed conflict as active combatants. These children of the war are the subject of this chapter.

This chapter discusses the issue of postwar identity construction among children directly involved in armed conflict in Mozambique and Angola. It is based on ethnographic material resulting from research carried out in Mozambique and Angola with war-affected children, particularly child sol-

Map of Mozambique, Map No. 3706 R.2, UN Cartographic Section. Permission granted by the United Nations.

diers. The intention is to convey these children's experiences of war and the context of their involvement in political conflict. Contrary to some positions taken in the literature, I argue that the issue of child soldiers cannot be explained in terms of Africa's pre-colonial history or in terms of African "traditional" culture. Rather, it has to be understood in the context of the post-independence wars in Angola and Mozambique. I also pay particular attention

Map of Angola, Map No. 3727 R.2, UN Cartographic Section. Permission granted by the United Nations.

to the healing and reintegration mechanisms through which former child soldiers try to come to terms with their war experiences and reconstitute their identities in the aftermath of war. In this regard, I stress the importance of local cultural understandings of war trauma in post-conflict processes of healing, reconciliation, and social reintegration in Africa.

Child Soldiers: A Worldwide Phenomenon

The issue of child soldiers is not unique to Mozambique and Angola. Many African countries at war feature young combatants. This is the case in Uganda, Rwanda, Sierra Leone, Congo, Liberia, and Algeria, to mention just a few. Again, such a phenomenon is not peculiar to Africa. Historically, young people have been at the forefront of political conflict in many parts of the world. In Europe in the Middle Ages a boy who hoped to become a knight would, from about the age of 14, serve as a squire (Brett & McCallin, 1996). The children's crusade of 1212 featured many children, and it is known that boys of 12 years of age took an active role as soldiers in Napoleon's army. Nelson's navy included many young naval cadets and midshipmen of 15 or over, and more recently protests were expressed that the British army used youths of 17 on active service in the Gulf War (Furley, 1995). Youth and children continue to feature in armed conflicts in places such as Cambodia, Yugoslavia, Palestine, Northern Island, and Afghanistan. Due to its widespread character and to the terrible consequences it has for the future of these societies, the phenomenon of child soldiers merits careful attention and study.

Child Soldiers in Post-Colonial Conflicts in Africa

Various authors have discussed the phenomenon of child soldiers in post-colonial conflicts on the African continent. Psychological approaches have been used to explain the impact of political violence on the children's mental health (Boothby, 1990; Dawes, 1996; Junior, 1996; Wessells, 1997). The issue has also been studied from the point of view of human rights, analyzing international laws that protect children from participating in armed conflicts (Cohn, 1991; Goodwin-Gill & Cohn, 1994; Human Rights Watch, 1994). Anthropologists, sociologists, and historians have also examined children's involvement in wars as a social and cultural phenomenon (Geffray & Pedersen, 1988; Geffray, 1990; Furley, 1995; Abdullah & Bangura, 1996; Boyden & Gibbs, 1997). R. D. Kaplan's (1994) study in Sierra Leone has attempted to explain the phenomenon of child soldiers as an expression of cultural propensities and environmental breakdown. Others, like P. Richards (1996) and W. Reno (1995), look at it as the result of a crisis in patrimonial politics. The phenomenon has also been made intelligible from within traditional cultural forms of initiation and rites of adulthood (Richards, 1996).[3]

The issue of child soldiers cannot be explained in terms of Africa's pre-colonial military history, nor does it have roots in African traditional culture. Rather, the phenomenon is rooted in the crisis of the post-colonial state in

Africa. The crisis is reflected in ethnic conflicts over power sharing, identity, and access to resources; in the incapacity of the state to provide for and protect its citizens; and in the collapse of social and economic structures in rural areas and the massive migration to urban areas. The development of armed conflicts into which youth and children are drawn is a direct symptom of such crisis. In the case of Mozambique and Angola this crisis was exacerbated by external pressures, the South African apartheid regime's destabilization though direct support of rebel movements. During the war, many youths become vulnerable to recruitment due to lack of opportunities in the countryside. In addition, internal issues such as ethnic alliances and a general disenchantment with the state over rejection of "traditional" authorities and "traditional" cultural values determined the positions taken by some "traditional" chiefs, who helped to recruit youth and children to join the rebel forces. Many children and youth also volunteered to join either the government or the rebels as soldiers. For many the possession of an instrument of coercion was often the only access to food and to a sense of power. In the aftermath of the war [4] many of these youths continue to be vulnerable; they have no skills, no jobs, and no education (many had to go back to primary school next to small children half their age). The economic situation in the countryside did not improve: Extreme poverty, lack of infrastructure (hospitals, schools), and difficult environmental conditions such as El Niño continued.

This is the situation of the many villages to which the young soldiers return, communities physically devastated by the war and with profound social wounds. These are the dilemmas that face youth and children of war in the post-colonial state. It is within this framework that the issue of child soldiers is analyzed in this chapter, which tries to weave together threads of experiences of violence, terror, and survival by presenting children's testimonies. Emphasis is placed on local social and cultural understanding of childhood, psychological trauma, and mechanisms of healing and social reintegration of young soldiers.

Notions and Discourses About Childhood

What Is a Child? What Is a Child Soldier?

The dominant framework that still informs the understanding of childhood maintains that children are vulnerable, dependent, and innocent human beings who need to be protected by adults. Child development happens through the process of socialization and follows a predetermined path composed of several stages children go through on their way to a state of adulthood

(Gibbs, 1994). Thus, the notion of childhood stands in opposition to adulthood, and children are seen as "people in the process of becoming rather than being" (James, 1993). This concept of childhood and child development is generally taken to be a natural and universal phase of human existence, shaped more by biological and psychological than by social factors (Freeman, 1993).

This view is also predominant in international law regarding children. The need to establish global standards of childhood to protect children led to a universalization of what constitutes a child. Several international agreements define a child as anyone up to the age of 15. This is clearly stated in the UN Geneva Convention of 1949, which forbids the recruitment into the armed forces of children up to 15 years of age. This age limit is also laid down in the UN Convention of the Rights of the Child. The African Charter of Rights of the Child defines a child as a person up to 18 years of age, and its article 22, paragraph 2, forbids their recruitment or participation in armed hostilities.

In these conventions children appear as presocial and passive recipients of experience who need to be protected up to the age of 15 or 18. They need protection, nurture, and enlightenment, because they are vulnerable, immature, and incapable of assuming responsibilities. Thus, they should be excluded from work and other responsibilities and confined to the protection of home and school. This is a predominant concept of childhood among middle-class people, especially in Europe and North America, which has been universalized in such a way that children who do not follow this path are considered to be at risk. The age limits established in international law raise the issue, what is a child? Is a 15-year-old a child in the same sense as a 2- or 3-year-old? When do we use the term *youth*? Both in Mozambique and Angola many young soldiers started their military activities well before their teens, but when they returned home after the war they were 17, 18, or even in their twenties. For many families these young combatants come back as men, not as children. By embodying the image of the dependent child and the potential victim, international law has failed to look at childhood as a social and historical construction.

Childhood as a Social Construction

Various authors have stated the importance of understanding childhood as a social construction and as an analytical category: not focusing on children simply as proto-adults or future beings, but rather, and essentially, as beings-in-the-present, social actors with an active presence of their own (Fine & Sandstrom, 1988; Boyden, 1990; Dawes, 1996; James, 1993; Reynolds, 1996; Boyden & Gibbs, 1997). Notions of childhood cannot be understood in universal terms. They vary cross-culturally, and they are attached to culture, class, gender, and other variables.

Unlike middle-class Western children, whose parents can afford to provide for them up to 15 or 18 years of age, many children in different parts of the world are exposed to work at an early age. They participate actively in productive activities, household chores, and care of younger children. In these contexts children learn by participating in, rather than being protected from, social and economic processes. Mozambican and Angolan children are often portrayed as strong, as survivors, and as often actively growing in difficult conditions (Gibbs, 1994; Honwana, 1997). In many African societies, children are often synonymous with wealth because of the contribution they can make to the productive work of the family. Children are also valued as a source of security for the future.

In some contexts, the boundary between adulthood and childhood becomes ambiguous, as children actively create and recreate their roles according to the situations presented to them. Both in Angola and Mozambique, war and political violence favored a displacement of roles between adults and children. Many children were and are active soldiers, assuming roles that in "normal" circumstances would be fulfilled by adults. The shifting of roles in such a dramatic way, in which children become killers and commit the most horrific atrocities, is intrinsically linked to the breakdown of society's structures and morality in the context of the crisis of the post-colonial state. What kind of conditions made possible this massive participation of children in armed conflicts? How and why were they recruited? Why did they stay? What effect may this phenomenon have on their generation? What of their future? In the following sections I try to deal with some of these questions by looking at the ways in which young soldiers in the Mozambican and Angolan conflicts experienced war and violence.

Experiencing War and Violence

The number of children who have been directly exposed to the war as combatants in Angola and Mozambique is enormous. It is estimated that more than 9,000 children in Angola, and between 8,000 and 10,000 in Mozambique, participated in the conflicts as soldiers. Both RENAMO and UNITA were active in recruiting children to their armies. There are also accounts of the use of children in the government forces in the two countries, although to a lesser extent. Children were used to carry weapons and other equipment on the front lines, in reconnaissance missions, in mining, in espionage, and so forth. This systematic preference for children as soldiers was often based on assumptions that children are easier to control and manipulate, are easily programmed to feel little fear or revulsion for their actions, and are easily programmed to think of war and only war. Children are also believed to possess excessive energy that can be used; once trained they carried out attacks with greater enthusiasm and brutality than did adults (Furley, 1995; Human Rights Watch, 1992).

Recruitment into Violence

Child recruitment into the armed forces in Angola and Mozambique took many forms, as the following interviews reveal.

Dunga, an 18-year-old whom I interviewed in Lombe, province of Malanje, Angola, was captured by UNITA soldiers when he was on his way to visit his brother-in-law:

> They told me to go with them, later I managed to escape and returned home. But the UNITA soldiers asked the soba (traditional chief) to show them my house, and in the evening they came and took me for the second time.[5]

Astro was 12 years old when he started his military training with UNITA in Karilonge (Huambo). His recruitment took place when he was on the street:

> I was walking.... When I was near the railway line, the UNITA soldiers came and said "Hey boy, come with us we want you to do some work for us." It was a lie, they took me to N'gove ... and there I did my military training which lasted only five months due to an attack which we suffered from the government troops.... My training should have lasted eight months.[6]

Fernando was a 14-year-old from the district of Chokwe in Mozambique. Following is his story:

> I was kidnapped at my house by armed bandits in the night while sleeping together with my brothers.... They tied me up and took me away together with my two brothers. While doing this some [bandits] were burning down the village and after that they took us all to the base.... We walked to the base. ... Later I was sent for [military] training.... They taught me during four months to dismount and mount guns.[7]

Lopes was 12 years old in 1993, when he was selected at school to be sent to the UNITA forces. Lopes told me that:

[S]obas [traditional chiefs] had to provide UNITA with soldiers from their sobados [areas of jurisdiction of the sobas], so they would ask the teachers to give them children. I was taken from school straight to the UNITA base where I had military training for three months before starting to go on missions.[8]

Pitango was 15 years old when he joined the military in the province of Bie (Angola):

I started military service in 1994, I volunteered to join the government army because we were suffering a lot in my village.... I wanted to defend my province and help my family with the products that I could get from the military ambushes.[9]

When RENAMO soldiers attacked the neighborhood on 1st May in District no. 5 in Maputo they kidnapped a number of youngsters, among them Paulo, who was only nine years old. He was taken to Chinhangwanine military camp, where he was forced to drink water from a skull after days of walking. Unlike other recruits, Paulo managed to escape after nine months of captivity.[10]

These accounts make clear that forced recruitment of children was significant. Children were taken from school, from their homes, and from the street directly to military camps for training. Many were kidnapped during military attacks on villages as well as in road ambushes. Many children also joined the army (both the government and the rebel) for protection, food, opportunities to loot, and a sense of power with a gun in their hands (Furley, 1995).

In Mozambique, in certain areas of the country many youths became attracted to RENAMO, especially due to the crisis in the countryside. Many youths migrated to town and returned to the rural areas unable to find work. In 1984 the Operacao Producao returned back to the countryside those considered "unproductive." The state closed its doors to "parasites." These returned youths could no longer fit in with local structures (gerontocratic authority) and the unattractive life in the rural areas (lack of food, education, employment, etc.). To these discontented youth RENAMO offered a different purpose in life by putting a gun in their hands (Geffray, 1990; Geffray & Pedersen, 1988).

The situation was no different in Angola. Many children pointed to insecurity, vulnerability, boredom, and lack of food as some of the reasons that drove them to volunteer. Particularly important was the sense of security and power that the possession of a gun seems to provide: "[N]o one messes with you when you have a gun.... [Y]ou can defend yourself."[11]

In Angola there was direct involvement of the traditional authorities in the recruitment of child soldiers. In Malanje many people referred to the role of *sobas* in identifying and recruiting young soldiers. Some mentioned that the *sobas* were forced by UNITA to provide them with recruits and would go from village to village recruiting minors. There were cases in which parents had to give their young boys to the *soba*, who would then send them to UNITA:

> UNITA asked the sobas to give a certain number of boys. Parents were responsible for encouraging the boys to stay with UNITA, and to return them if they escaped. If the boys escaped and were not returned to the soba, the families would suffer.[12]

Mrs. Andrade, mother of a former young soldier, told us that her son was recruited and then sent back because he was ill. When the UNITA troops who recruited him found out that he was back home they blamed it on her and her husband. In her own words:

> They said that I prevented him to join the military. . . . I said no, the boy was very ill. My husband is a very religious person . . . and the UNITA soldiers harassed him, and he had to let them take our son.[13]

In these circumstance parents became unable to protect their own offspring and had to surrender to political pressures and the power of the guns, often manipulated by young soldiers. Political and ethnic alliances may also have played a role in this because not everyone was compelled to act in this way. Some *sobas,* some parents, and even some youths might have decided to take that course of action because, according to their own convictions, that was the right thing to do. In the province of Bie (Angola) there was a case in which the *soba* was recruiting young soldiers for the government army, not for UNITA.

These cases illustrate the different processes through which children joined the rebel groups in the recent conflicts in Angola and Mozambique. This process of becoming a soldier and part of the rebel movement happened through a direct encounter between the rebels and the children and their families or was mediated by local chiefs. In southern Mozambique the latter seems to have been less common, although there are accounts of local chiefs who supported the rebels or the government. However, the extent to which they had a direct hand in recruiting young combatants is not clear. In other areas of the country (especially in the central and northern regions) there are reports of a stronger link between "traditional" authorities and the rebels (see Geffray, 1990; Vines, 1991; Minter, 1972). Both processes seem to have occurred in Angola and Mozambique. Some recruitment strategies might be used more often in one country and others in another country, or they might have been more frequent in certain areas of the country than in other areas.

Such differences of degree and frequency have to do with the particularities of that specific context (for example, if it was a rebel-controlled or government-controlled area, etc.). My Mozambican research was mainly carried out in areas under government control in southern Mozambique. That might explain why there was less testimony of the direct involvement of "traditional" chiefs in the recruitment of young soldiers.

The repercussions of the breakdown of social and economic structures in the countryside and of ethnic divisions and conflicts illustrate some of the complexities that shape the politics of power and identity in the post-colonial state.

"Being in the War": Initiation to Violence and Terror

Military training started as soon as the youths arrived at the camps and lasted between three weeks and eight months. The process of training was aimed at preparing these children to fight a war and commit terrible atrocities. Heavy psychological pressure was placed on them. Military training in these particular conditions constituted a process of initiation to violence, marked by cutting the links of the children with society (family, friends, and "normal" life) and programming them to think of war and only war. There seems to have been a deliberate policy to dehumanize the children and turn them into killing machines.

Forced young recruits had often to endure long periods of darkness, severe beating, and deliberate terror to impress on them that there was no going back. Once under training, discipline was very harsh, and the penalty for failed escape was execution. Almost all ex–child soldiers that I met both in Angola and in Mozambique referred to "the parade." The parade happened every morning, and on many occasions those who were found trying to escape would be executed in the presence of the entire group. Sometimes recruits were given their first military assignment at the parade: to kill a colleague who had tried to escape. To save one's own life, that order had to be carried out:

> Whoever did not want to fight was killed. . . . They would slice the throat of those who did not want to fight. . . . I was trained for three days on how to march and run. Then they gave me my weapon and I got used to fighting. The orders were to kill anyone we caught and to bring back anything they had on them.[14]

Sometimes the child soldiers were urged to suck and drink the blood of the person they had just executed, as the following interview attests. This was aimed at making them be fearless and not feel remorse for the atrocity committed.

I saw many people being killed, many dead bodies.... My friend who tried to escape was killed in front of me.... [T]hey drunk his blood.... I saw it, they do it in front of everybody to discourage those who want to flee.[15]

When asked if he thought drinking the blood works, one youth replied "Yes, it works."[16]

Another youth elaborated: "I used to drink the blood of the people I killed. ... [T]oday I cannot look at red wine because I feel like killing and sucking blood again."[17]

Drinking of blood seems to have had the function of an initiation rite, as Eduardo, a 17-year-old from Kuito, recalls:

I drunk blood the day I finished my military training, in the swearing in ceremony. We all had to drink 2 spoons of blood each. They told us that this was important to prevent us from being haunted by the spirits of the people we might kill.

Some traditional treatments were also provided for the young recruits who were unable to cope with drinking blood or killing their colleagues in the parade. Treatments were also performed to make them fearless and give them protection during combats. There were references to healers who helped the soldiers in the camps:

[I]n order not to be afraid of fighting the war we had to kill a person at the parade.... [T]hose who cried in the evening [after having killed] were treated by the kimbandas [traditional healers].[18]

Some young soldiers pointed out that the commanders were also submitted to treatments by "kimbandas" to defend themselves against death. Antonio Sula from Cangumbe said that they used "mufuca" (a tail of an animal prepared with remedies). In situations of danger they had to shake the "mufuca" to protect them. However, not all commanders and soldiers had access to these special treatments: "I don't think all commanders were protected by the kimbanda.... I saw many commanders die in combat."[19]

Some had to hold in their suffering and could not have access to help. This was the case of a young man who witnessed the brutal killing of his own brother and could not do anything about it, not even cry:

My brother and I were together in the same camp.... [M]y brother was caught while trying to escape and was tied to a tree and killed. I was watching but I had to hold myself from crying because if they discovered that we were related I could be killed too.[20]

When talking about his training in a RENAMO camp, Fernando mentioned that:

> After four months of training they put me to a test. They put a person before me and ordered me to shoot him. I shot him. After the test they considered me good and they gave me a weapon and a gun and they told me that [from that] time on I was a chief of a group of other children.... My first task was to attack a village and steal cattle for the base. We burnt down the village. We killed cattle. We returned to the base. Some weeks after that, they ordered us to ambush a convoy which was passing by Maluana. We walked two weeks from Chockwe to Maluana.[21]

Some of them were forced to kill their own relatives, raid and loot their own villages, or kill their neighbors. This happened to 11-year-old Marula, from Gaza province in Mozambique, who was forced to kill his own father in a RENAMO military camp. Marula and his father were captured by RENAMO troops and taken to a military base, where they were separated. They would meet occasionally in the evening. Marula's father organized an escape plan and shared it with his son so that they could escape together. Eventually they were caught escaping and Marula, who had been training for some time, was given his first military mission: to kill his own father.

The suppression of close relatives seems to have been part of the strategy to create an insurgent force of youth. If the relatives of the kidnapped children were also in the camp they would be killed in the child's presence, precisely to cut the links and eliminate the desire to escape and join the family. In Angola there are also several cases of children who had to eliminate relatives. A young soldier in Huambo mentioned that during their long walk to the base the mother of one of his friends was unable to proceed with the march because they had been walking for four days and she was carrying a heavy load. The commander took his gun and gave it to the son, ordering him to kill his mother.

In other instances, RENAMO soldiers would go out and look for relatives of these children and kill them in their villages. This is what happened to Noel, a 12-year-old boy from Nhamatanda (Mozambique). Noel was forcibly recruited to join RENAMO when he was seven years of age. He happened to mention to his colleagues during training that his father was a captain in the government army, and that he would come and rescue him. When the information got to the RENAMO commanders, some soldiers were sent back to Noel's village to kill his father. The father was away from home, so they killed Noel's grandfather and made sure that Noel got the news, stating that they would find and kill his father also.[22]

It was common practice to give the children new war names. Most of them received new names and were forbidden to use their birth names, traditional names, or nicknames that were related to their past experiences with family, relatives, and neighbors. These new names were constructed to enhance their combative morale and performance, such as "the strong," "Rambo," "the invincible," "Russian," or "the powerful," or they were just ordinary names but different from the birth names.

Especially in Angola, many children mentioned the fact that on certain evenings they were forced to sing and dance non-stop the whole night through. This practice, according to some of the children, was aimed at not allowing them to think of home, their parents, brothers, sisters, or friends. They had to be busy all the time. Some children in both countries also reported the use of hallucinogenics. Many Angolan children said that *liamba* (marijuana) was used in some camps and that they also ate bullet powder to be strong.

Training consisted of hard physical exercise, manipulation of weapons, and the internalization of a very strict code of conduct. Most of the youths did not have proper military uniforms and boots, and food was very scarce because the "best" food was for the commanders and other chiefs. The children often ate the leftovers, the skin, and the bones. They lived in constant fear of being accused of treason or attempted escape, which could result in execution, so they were constantly watching their backs and trying not to give reasons for suspicion. It was a relationship built on fear and terror.

The hard military training to which these children were subjected, together with the elimination of close relatives or persons to whom they could relate; the use of hallucinogenics; and the changing of their birth names were a powerful initiation to violence and terror. They were brainwashed and subjected to the most violent psychological pressures to make them shed their previous identities and assume new ones, as merciless killers. They had become completely dependent on and subservient to their mentors. They appear to have committed the most cruel war atrocities. As Vines pointed out:

> [Y]oung RENAMO soldiers as little as 10 [years of age] seem to have been put through psychological trauma and deprivation, such as being hung upside down from trees until their individualism is broken, and encouraged and rewarded for killing. Some commentators believe that massacres in southern Mozambique are committed by these child combatants, who have been programmed to feel little fear or revulsion for such actions, and thereby carry out these attacks with greater enthusiasm and brutality than adults would. (Vines, 1991: 95-96)

This raises the question, what is the agency of these children in these processes? Should we consider them passive agents, empty vessels into which the capacity for violence has been poured? Many of the children were forced to join the military and were cut off from society. Many among them came from completely dispossessed and impoverished communities, which offered no hope for the future. As previously mentioned, during the war for many of them the possession of a gun was often the only access to the bare necessities of life, through looting and the capacity to threaten others and exercise some degree of power and control. Because they were so vulnerable, the children were instrumentalized and turned into killing machines. Nevertheless, some children might have exercised their own agency and consciously decided to commit atrocities that went well beyond their regular military assignments, out of vengeance, greed, immaturity, jealousy, and the like, or in the expectation of being rewarded or positively acknowledged by the commanders. Some might have also found some thrill from and enthusiastically participated in the process.

Michel de Certeau (1984) establishes an important distinction between strategies and tactics. He sees strategies as having long-term consequences or benefits, and tactics as means devised to cope with concrete circumstances even though those means are likely to have deleterious long-term consequences. Applying de Certeau's distinction, it seems that these young combatants exercised what could be called a "tactical agency"[23] to maximize the circumstances created by the constraints of the military environment in which they were forced to operate. Many had no prospect of returning home after raiding and burning villages, killing defenseless civilians, and looting food convoys. This was the life they were constrained to live, both in the present and for the future. Also, some of the children were as young as seven years of age when they were abducted from their families and initiated into violence and terror. A few years down the line, that was all they knew life to be about, and many have tried to make the best of it. In this sense they were conscious "tactical" agents who had to respond to the demands and pressures of their lives. The exercise of a "strategic" agency would imply a long-term consequence of seeing the results of their actions concretized in some form of political change, which does not seem to be the case for the majority of the child soldiers. Following are some of the young combatants' comments when they looked back at their involvement in the war:

> I lost my time in the military and now I don't manage to study to learn a profession. . . . When I think of all this my heart beats and becomes sore and I am unable to sleep at night. (Mario, 19 years old, Angola)

> My first task was to attack a village and still [steal] cattle. . . . We burnt down that village. . . . [W]ith my gun I killed the ammunition chief. . . . I am very sad about my story; but I had no choice. (Fernando, 14 years old, Mozambique)

If I could I would have told those who gave orders to start the war to talk among themselves and stop the war. Because of the war I cannot be a truck driver, I needed to have studied, but I lost my time in the war. When I came back I learned that my father died. Now I cannot study, I have to work to help my mother and my younger siblings. (Joao, 20 years old, Angola)

I want to have a wife and twelve children. But I don't want my children to go to war, there is a lot of suffering in the war. (Gito, 19 years old, Angola)

The Quest for Reconciliation and Healing

With the end of armed hostilities most child soldiers were taken to demobilization centers. Through the help of the Red Cross and other local and international organizations many were reunited with their relatives or placed in foster care. In Mozambique, the first group of child soldiers that came from the RENAMO camps was placed in a recuperation center in town (Languene), and a group of child psychologists (a few Mozambicans, but the majority were foreigners) worked with them. That experience proved to be unsuccessful because the children were completely removed from their community and cultural environment and were asked to talk about their painful memories as a way of healing. Such methods are common in Western psychological approaches. Western definitions and understandings of distress and trauma, of diagnosis and healing, and of childhood were applied to a society that possesses very different ontologies and social and cultural patterns.

Dominant Western psychotherapeutic models are often seen as universal and applicable everywhere. However, this assumption has been challenged because modern psychology is also a culturally constructed system. Modern psychology locates the causes of psychosocial distress within the individual and devises responses, which are primarily based on individual therapy (Boyden & Gibbs, 1997). Recovery is achieved through helping the individual "come to terms" with the traumatic experience, and healing is held in private sessions aimed at "talking out," externalizing feelings and afflictions. The treatment of post-traumatic stress disorder (PTSD), which appeared in the 1980s in the United States, is firmly grounded in these dominant Western psychological paradigms. Although modern psychotherapy can be useful in contexts other than the Western, it should take into account local understanding of mental health and local strategies to heal psychological problems.

In other sociocultural contexts a great deal of importance is placed on the role that the ancestral spirits and other spiritual forces play in the processes of causation and healing of mental health problems. Also, and unlike modern

Western psychology, the emphasis is placed not only on the person but on the collective body. In this context the exclusive focus on the individual would undermine family and community efforts to be part of the healing process (Honwana, 1997). Likewise, studies on healing war trauma in Mozambique (Marrato, 1996; Honwana & Pannizo, 1995) have shown that recalling the traumatic experience through verbal externalization as a means to heal it is not always effective. In many instances people would rather not talk about the past, not look back; they want to start afresh after certain ritual procedures, which do not necessarily involve verbal expression of the affliction, have been performed.

Beyond Post-Traumatic Stress Disorder

The PTSD approach was born out of trying to understand the problems faced by the U.S. soldiers who fought in the Vietnam War. In this regard it was conceived of as an instrument to deal with psychological distress in people who left a situation of relative "normality," went into a traumatic experience (the Vietnam War), then returned to "normality." In Mozambique and Angola, and in other conflict zones, especially in Africa, the vast majority of children we are dealing with today were born during the war. The armed conflict in Mozambique lasted more than 15 years, and in Angola more than 20 years (recent reports indicate that UNITA has reignited the war in certain areas of the country). Thus, for these children trauma is not *post*, but rather current and very much part of their everyday life. Carolyn Nordstrom's (1997) work on war and violence in Mozambique stresses the fact that there violence goes well beyond the military attacks, the land mines, and direct war situations, touching on spheres like poverty, hunger, and displacement. In line with this argument, one can say that most of the children we have been dealing with in the aftermath of the war in Angola are still living under violent and traumatic circumstances. Therefore, when applying such models there is a need to adapt them to the concrete situations of the children in question.

In Mozambique and Angola there are local ways of understanding war trauma. In both countries people believe that war-related psychological trauma is directly linked with the anger of the spirits of the dead killed during the war. In southern Mozambique these spirits are called *Mipfhukwa*, and they are believed to have the capacity to harm those that killed them or mistreated them in life. I have discussed this type of spirit at length elsewhere (see Honwana, 1994, 1997). In Angola this is also a common phenomenon. All over the country people mentioned that the spirits of the dead had to be appeased so that peace could follow.

Social pollution constitutes an important factor in the context of postwar healing both in Angola and Mozambique. Pollution may arise from being in contact with death and bloodshed. Individuals who have been in a war, who killed or saw people being killed, are believed to be polluted by the "wrongdoings of the war." They are seen as the vehicles through which the spirits of the dead of the war might enter and afflict the community. These spirits may afflict not only the individual who committed the offenses but also the entire family or group. After the war, when soldiers and refugees return home, they are believed to be potential contaminators of the social body. The spirits of the dead, which might haunt them, can disrupt life in their families and villages. Therefore, the cleansing process is seen as a fundamental condition for collective protection against pollution and for the social reintegration of war-affected people into society (Honwana, 1997).

In the following discussion I analyze three cases and examine how postwar identities are negotiated and constructed through ritual performance in these particular contexts. Not everybody performs cleansing and purification rituals or rituals to appease the spirits. Such practices are more common in the rural areas, although some people might still perform them in urban settings. The availability of health care alternatives and religious and political affiliations determine the ways in which people make decisions concerning treatment of war trauma.

Rituals performed for former child soldiers are aimed at dealing with what happened during the war. An acknowledgment of the atrocities committed and subsequent break from that past is articulated through ritual performance. There are different types of rituals. Some are addressed to those who have participated in the war but did not kill; others are particularly directed to those who killed other people. The latter are more complex and require the expertise of a traditional healer. It is believed that the spirits of the dead can make the killer become insane.

Case One

In Mozambique, a 14-year-old youth kidnapped by RENAMO and forced to be a soldier had to go through a cleansing ritual when, after the war, he was reunited with his relatives. On the day of his arrival his relatives took him to the *ndumba* (the house of the spirits). There he was presented to the ancestral spirits of the family. The boy's grandfather addressed the spirits, informing them that his grandchild had returned, and thanked them for their protection as his grandson was able to return alive. Then, the family elders talked to the boy to know how he was and what happened while he was away. A few days later a spirit medium was invited by the family to help them perform the cleansing rituals for the boy. The practitioner took the boy to the bush, and there a small hut covered with dry grass was built. The boy, dressed in the dirty clothes he brought from the RENAMO camp, entered the hut and undressed himself. The hut was set on fire, and an adult relative helped the boy get out. The hut, the clothes, and everything else that the boy brought from the camp had to be burned. This symbolized the rupture with that past.

A chicken was sacrificed for the spirits of the dead and the blood spread around the ritual place. The chicken was then cooked and offered to the spirits as a sacrificial meal. After that the boy had to inhale the smoke of some herbal remedies and bathe himself with water treated with medicine. In this way his body was cleansed both internally and externally. Finally, the spirit medium made some incisions in the boy's body and filled them with a paste made from herbal remedies, a practice called *ku thlavela*. The purpose of this procedure was to give strength to the boy. During this public ritual relatives and neighbors were present and assisted the practitioner by performing specific roles or just by observing, singing, and clapping.

Case Two

When Pitango from Cambandua in Angola returned home, his family organized a ritual for him. The ritual took place the day he returned, before he was allowed to socialize with relatives and friends. His body was washed with cassava meal, and chicken blood was placed on his forehead (the chicken was killed during the proceedings). Then his mother took some palm oil and rubbed it on Pitango's hands and feet. During these proceedings the ancestral spirits of the family were called on to protect the young man who was back from the war and had to start a new life. This was done through addresses made by elderly relatives. Pitango mentioned that the elderly in his family, who spoke to him on his arrival, explained that the performance of this ritual was necessary so that the spirits of those killed in the war would not harm him. This was necessary for him to start a new life. Pitango also said that because he did not kill anybody during the war he did not need to go through a ritual performed by a *kimbanda* (traditional healer).

Case Three

Nzinga is a 55-year-old traditional healer in Malanje in Angola. When her 19-year-old nephew Pedro returned after spending more than seven years fighting the war alongside UNITA she performed a ritual for him. When asked about it she said:

> I could not let him stay without the cleansing treatment. He needed it because there he might have done bad things like kill, beat and rob people. . . .

[W]ithout the treatment the spirits of the dead would harm him. I do not know what happened there, he said he did not do anything. ... [Y]oung people sometimes lie. ... I decided to go for full treatment because otherwise he could become crazy or even die.[24]

Traditional healers generally perform the full treatment Nzinga refers to. It lasted four days and took place in her house. It required a chicken, a *luando* (mat), and some wine or "traditional" beer. She put her nephew Pedro in a place of seclusion called *mwanza* (place of ritual treatment), and there she placed the mat for him to sleep on. She placed some powdered medicine (*ditondo* and *dikezo*) under the mat and in his food and drink. Pedro had to stay inside the *mwanza* for three consecutive days. At dawn on the fourth day he was taken to the river to be washed. After this he was not allowed to look back. He had to break with the past, and asking him not to look back at the river symbolized that break with the dirty war (the dirt of the war was washed from his body and left to go on the river stream). Back home Nzinga opened an egg, put some sugar and powdered medicine inside, and threw it away, saying: "[Y]ou malevolent spirits here is what you want . . . leave us now." The ritual chicken and drinks were prepared with medicine, and Pedro ate and drank them throughout the duration of his treatment. During the ritual family members were present and contributed food and drink, which they all shared during the proceedings.

In all these rituals is the idea of pollution that the children bring to their homes and villages. They have to be cleansed as soon as possible to be able to socialize freely with relatives and friends. In the case of Samuel, the cleansing ceremony happened a few days after his arrival and was performed by a specialist. In Pitango's case, he was "washed" with cassava meal, chicken blood, and palm oil the day of his arrival. Pedro's aunt decided to give him a full treatment because she was not sure about what he had done during the war. Another important issue that comes out of these cases is the idea of symbolically breaking with the past: the washing of the body in the river so that the dirt of the war would go away; the burning of the hut and the clothes brought from the war. It is interesting to see in all three cases the use of a chicken in the rituals (the blood for cleansing, and the meat for the sacrificial meal shared with the ancestors), and of herbal remedies to cleanse the body internally (inhaling and drinking) and externally (bathing and rubbing). In these cases the Cartesian dichotomy separating body and mind cannot be applied because individuals are seen as a whole body/mind composite and as part and parcel of a collective body (their wrongdoings can affect their families as well). This explains the direct involvement of the family (both the living and the dead, the ancestors) in the cleansing and healing processes. The ancestors are believed to play a powerful role in protecting their relatives against evil and misfortune. That is why Samuel's relatives took him to the hut of the ancestors and thanked them for the fact that he was alive and safe back home, Pitango's family also addressed the ancestors, and Nzinga put Pedro in the place of the ancestors for the duration of his ritual treatment.

The performance of these rituals and the politics that precede them transcend the particular individual(s) concerned and involve the collective body. The family and friends are involved, and the ancestral spirits are also implicated in mediating for a good outcome. These cases show how the living have to acknowledge the dead (the past), both the ancestors and the dead of the war, to carry on with their lives. The rituals were aimed at asking for forgiveness, appeasing the souls of the dead, and preventing any future afflictions (retaliations) from the spirits of the dead, in this way severing the links with that "bad" past.

Postwar identities are constructed with reference to the past. Through remembrance individuals and groups are linked with others: A person is represented as part and parcel of a chain of generations and a web of kinship relations that includes the ancestors. In this sense, memory becomes a "culturally mediated expression of the temporal dimension of experience, in particular of social commitments and identifications" (Lambek & Antze, 1996: 248). Remembrance constitutes also an act of identity building. Identities constructed through remembrance can be both "negative" and "positive" (Meyer, 1998). "Negative" identities are those from which the person wishes to escape and which originate in a past that he or she needs to control. This is clearly seen in the case of the child soldiers, who have to acknowledge and appease the dead of the war to avoid being haunted by them. Only through this unmasking and acknowledgment of the past can individuals in these circumstances create new identities. These new identities are not built on memories as such but rather on the rejection of all the links those memories reveal (Meyer, 1998). That is why the clothes and all the things that the child soldier brought from the war had to be burnt. A "positive" identity is one that links the individual to a past that he or she wishes to maintain and reinforce. This is seen in the veneration of the ancestral spirits, who are acknowledged and asked to protect the child who needs to start a new life. Here the effort is to regain and assert the connection with one's roots.

There is no doubt that these rituals are instrumental in building family cohesion and solidarity and in dealing with the psychological and emotional side of these children's problems. However, they return to a countryside that remains as poor as it was when they left, with no job opportunities and no vocational schools. Although in Mozambique the end of the armed hostilities gave rise to some degree of confidence and the economy is slowly showing signs of improvement, in Angola the war did not stop; UNITA troops continue to fight and recruit children in certain areas of the country. The situation of child soldiers in post-colonial conflicts on the African continent is intrinsically linked with the crisis in state politics of power, identity, and access to resources. Community mechanisms of healing, social rebuilding, and conflict resolution are important, but on their own they cannot be a solution to the basic problem.

Conclusion

This chapter discusses the problem of child soldiers within the context of the crisis of state politics of power, identity, and access to resources. It was precisely this crisis, which resulted from internal and external causes, that gave rise to political violence and armed conflicts into which children were drawn as soldiers. Forced recruitment was the most common process of entering the military. However, more complex incorporation processes took place, and these involved "traditional" leaders and sometimes relatives. Voluntary affiliation of minors with the armies also occurred in certain areas. Children's participation in these wars (especially in the rebel armies) involved a carefully devised process of initiation into violence and terror. During military training children were completely cut off from society and reborn with the new identity of merciless killers.

The children's tales of terror, violence, and survival are shared experiences that link all children involved in war, extending beyond local and regional communities (Nordstrom, 1997). The experiences of child soldiers in Mozambique are very similar to those of Angolan child combatants. Despite having been instrumentalized, these children were not empty vessels into which violence was poured. I argue that they exercised a "tactical agency" to make the most of the circumstances created by the constraints of the military environment to which they were confined. Children's experiences are related not just to war and violence but also to the processes of healing the "social wounds of war" in the aftermath of conflict. Both in Angola and Mozambique, and as society tries to reconstitute its social fabric, local rituals of healing and reconciliation and reintegration are organized and performed by families and communities to rehabilitate these children of war. It is important to take into consideration local understanding of childhood, war trauma, and the strategies people use to heal and reintegrate war-affected children.

13
Sex and the Politics of Space in Colonial Zimbabwe

The Story of Chibheura (Open Your Legs) Exams

LYNETTE JACKSON
University of Illinois at Chicago

This chapter explores an aspect in the lives of African women who traveled to urban areas in colonial Zimbabwe: compulsory venereal disease exams. The exams were imposed on mobile and "unattached" black women between roughly 1924 and 1958. They were popularly known as *Chibheura* (literally, open up) exams by the African inhabitants of Salisbury (Harare), Fort Victoria (Masvingo), and Shabani (Zvishavane). In Bulawayo, they were simply called Town Pass exams. Michel de Certeau's concept of the spatial story best describes this undertaking (1984: 115). This spatial story is about the surveillance, containment, regulation, exposure, and exclusion of the African female body; about how ideological and social divisions between public and private, safety and danger, good and bad women, were concretized spatially on African women's bodies. Chibheura was Southern Rhodesia's influx control (policy) for African women; those not formally incorporated into the capitalist wage labor economy were viewed as the extensions of men, in terms of their sexuality, genitals, and potential to infect.

The similarities between colonial and post-colonial constructions of black women led to the current inquiry into Chibheura in particular and how public health measures have been marshaled to regulate African women's sexual mobility in general. Sections of this chapter are devoted to the politics of space, of sex, and of memory. I discuss how Zimbabwean women remember these exams and argue that the ambivalence, ambiguity, and contradictions apparent in their memories express the multiple and mobile subject positions of African women under southern Rhodesian colonialism.

The Politics of Space

Southern Rhodesian colonialism was all about space. Once the British had subdued the majority of Ndebele and Shona communities following the 1896–1897 Native Rising, in which 10 percent of the entire European population was killed,[1] the Chief Native Commissioner (CNC), H. M. Barberer, instructed his Native Commissioners (NCs) to suspend their regular activity of collecting taxes and native labor, using their time to "gain a more thorough knowledge of their districts . . . making maps and drawing up statistics."[2] In other words, the colonizers set about the process of domesticating the newly conquered lands, demarcating boundaries and establishing mechanisms of surveillance and social control, with the NCs as mediators between the spaces of the colonizers and the colonized. African chiefs and headmen reported to the NCs, who reported to the CNC, who reported to the administrator, and so forth. The NCs located huts and laborers, mapped and taxed people, set up settlements and reserves, patrolled, and got to "know" the natives and their movements. Still, the settlers were anxious that, as Doris Lessing puts it in *The Grass Is Singing*, the bush would avenge itself.[3]

Benedict Anderson (1991) uses the spatial concept of mapping to represent the ways in which states and nations imagine and attempt to concretize human landscapes under their control, to make their domains visible. But although Anderson argues that "the condition of visibility was that everyone, everything had a serial number" (1991: 185), one finds that in Southern Rhodesia, African women were not formally charted onto the official maps/grids of public space. Instead, they were expected to be at a distance, in the reserves set aside for the habitation of Africans whenever they were not engaged in wage labor. This point is illustrated by the fact that African women were not incorporated into the official colonial measures of influx control. An example is the 1913 Native Pass Consolidation Ordinance, in which the term *native* referred exclusively to "any male native above the age of 14, both of whose parents are members of some aboriginal race or tribe of Africa."

Although African women were not formally incorporated or actively sought after for wage employment and were expected to remain in rural villages (reserves) under strict parental and patriarchal control, many preferred mobility.[4] The history of the Chibheura exams is the history of the colonial state's dealings with these women and this reality. Gayatri Spivak refers to the "unaccommodated female body," which, although "displaced from the empire/nation negotiation," ultimately contests this displacement by imposing herself bodily, by reinscribing space with her body (Spivak, 1992). This is precisely what happened in colonial Zimbabwe, and the battle against venereal disease was the discourse through which this spatial reinscription was combated.

As early as 1899, the town leaders and public health officials in Southern Rhodesia had expressed concern over what they believed was a rising incidence of venereal disease among the colony's Africans. Although this perception was never confirmed, and medical experts wavered about, for example, whether they were viewing venereal syphilis or non-venereal yaws, the belief in the problem continued to grow. The source of the problem was the skewed gender ratio in the towns and worker compounds. Because the colonial capitalist economy was based on a migratory labor system in which African men traveled from parts inside and outside Southern Rhodesia to work as "single" wage laborers on mines and farms, these were predominantly male spaces. Men were either prohibited from bringing their wives and families, could not afford to, or did not dare to because of fears for the safety and fidelity of wives and daughters. For these reasons, a steady demand existed for the sexual and domestic services provided by some of the "unattached" women who came anyway.

To combat the "problem," the authorities considered implementing Part Two of the Cape Colony's Contagious Diseases Act of 1882, the section that dealt with compulsory detention and treatment for those suffering from infectious diseases. However, there was only lukewarm support for this. No one, not the British South Africa Company (BSAC), the municipal ratepayers, or the mine owners, wanted to absorb the costs of constructing and maintaining lock hospitals.[5] Part One of the 1882 Act dealt with compulsory examinations. This section was not initially considered because it was deemed impolitic and unworkable.[6] However, although there was much foot dragging around how exactly to tackle the venereal disease issue, annual *Reports of the Medical Director and Principal Medical Officer of the British South Africa Police* and the *Reports on the Public Health* did not tire of announcing the existence of the problem, and NCs, District Surgeons, and Medical Officers of Health (MOHs) were sent circulars and asked to measure occurrences within their domains. In places like Fort Victoria (Masvingo), Shabani (Zvishavane), and other areas with a high density of mines, the infection rate was believed to be particularly high. Characteristic of the waffling on this issue is a 1906 report submitted by Medical Director Andrew Fleming in which he bemoaned the absence of "lock hospitals for the compulsory segregation and treatment in Rhodesia" in one sentence, then stated that "their establishment is quite impracticable at the moment" in the next.[7] The government did at least make "anti-syphilitic remedies with full instructions" available to NCs, missionaries, and others upon request. At the time, these remedies consisted of mercury and iodine or arsenic tablets.[8]

During the mid-1910s and into the First World War, concern over "the venereal native" and disease rates among Africans in employment grew. What is more, the majority of African cases that came to the attention of colonial authorities were already at the tertiary stage. In other words, they came to official attention because of the more conspicuous nature of tertiary sores. Once these sores cleared up, patients were unlikely to return for continued treatment. They remained infectious.[9] This fact convinced some within the colonial medical community to call for a system of regular examinations for all Africans employed and seeking employment.[10]

The MOH in Salisbury asked why Africans recruited through the Rhodesia Native Labor Bureau (RNLB) were checked for infectious diseases prior to employment but African domestic workers were not.[11] He was part of a growing chorus seeking some form of regular examination of any and all Africans likely to come into contact with Europeans. But it was not until the catastrophic Influenza Epidemic of 1918 that the administration took action. In that year, the Native Registration Act was amended to add the "compulsory vaccination and medical examination of natives applying for certificates of registration under the Native Registration Ordinance, 1901." The amendment also made it a crime for an employee to continue in employment while knowingly suffering from a venereal disease. Moreover, "any native refusing to allow himself to be vaccinated or examined in accordance with the regulations or to submit to such treatment as may be directed by the MOH, could be fined £10" or "sentenced to imprisonment with or without hard labor, for a period of not more than three months."[12]

Although this amendment dealt with one of the discrepancies in previous policy, it did not deal with another issue that was receiving attention: "the existence of unregulated native women, particularly unmarried women residing within or in the vicinity of mining compounds." According to Dr. Andrew Fleming, these women were a public health catastrophe just waiting to happen.[13] The Native Registration Ordinance of 1901 and subsequent amendments to that ordinance, such as the 1913 Act, excluded African women. Meanwhile, traveling African women were increasingly presented as the crux of the colony's venereal disease problem, as the key vectors of *Treponoma spirochaete* transmission.¹⁴ Dr. Andrew Fleming certainly believed this to be the case, as did delegations of "respectable" African men from the groups that historian Terrence Ranger has referred to as "the African Voice."¹⁵ In 1921, a group of African men calling themselves "leaders of the Christian missions at work on the Falcon Mine and the township of Umvuma" sent an appeal to both the Medical Director and the Loyal Women's Guild of Salisbury:

> For some time we have considered that there is something wrong with a people to give rise to the great amount of quarreling, fighting and burning of houses, and also the vast amount of venereal disease. All those happenings are interfering with the morals and welfare of the man in employment and the only cause of the trouble is the number of loose women who are permitted to roam about without hindrance. . . . Men have evil communication with them, the result is that the men are stricken with foul disease.¹⁶

To push both the point home and a colonial nerve, they stated that "many of these loose women are decaying the white people when taken on as nurses to white babies."¹⁷

These and other "African Voice" men were quite unambiguous. They wanted the state to assist them in preventing single African women from traveling from place to place. They wanted the state to require all African women to show valid marriage certificates or other documentation attesting to parental or spousal consent before entering towns and compounds. Government officials and industrial capitalists, on the other hand, resisted any form of total prohibition. They did this at the same time that they refused to permit African men to bring wives to the towns in which they worked and lived for months (sometimes years) at a time, *and* complained about the rising incidence of venereal disease. Many state and municipal authorities were candid about what they thought was the prophylactic benefit of single African women in town, even if they did consider them disease transmitters. According to one officer of the British South Africa Police, "the acknowledged prostitute is somewhat of a safeguard to native men's instincts."¹⁸ In other words, they were thought to protect white society against the Black Peril.¹⁹ The other recognized benefits were that these women kept the workers content, or at least made their lives more bearable by providing hot meals, sex, and other domestic services.²⁰ Thus, the mine managers continued to allow single women to live on compounds even though, or precisely because, they believed most to be prostitutes (van Onselen, 1977: 48).

Some officials and influential settlers wanted to tackle the Black Peril by employing more African women in European households, thereby taking the men away from temptation. Meanwhile, women's groups like the Rhodesian Women's Guild pressured the government to institute policies protecting the European household from venereal infection, something increasingly associated with the presence of single African women. An ordinance was issued in 1922 to the effect that African men and women were to be medically examined before the commencement of employment and at three-month intervals thereafter.[21] Not surprisingly, however, adequate funds were not provided to pay for additional healthcare workers or to build the additional isolation units and clinics. And again, the ordinance only applied to the very small minority of African women who were employed in European households, hotels, and restaurants, not the traveling ones about whom so many were complaining.

As long as the British South Africa Company administered the colony, public health measures remained oriented toward short-term expediency. It was not until after the granting of the Responsible Government and Settler Rule in 1923 that public health policies extended beyond the direct capital/labor framework. The issue of compulsory venereal disease examinations for African women surfaced and was hotly debated almost immediately after the gaining of settler self-rule. In the May 1923 meeting of the Legislative Council, a parliamentarian named Moffat moved that, "in view of the increases in VD among Natives," the government should institute "a system of compulsory medical examination on mines," and rather than simply sending those infected away, the government should treat "all native men and women found to be infected." This, he argued, would benefit both Africans and Europeans.[22] His proposal also bypassed employment as a criterion for examination and thus promised to net more African women.

At the same Legislative Council meeting, delegates from different mines reported on how they had addressed the problem on their compounds. At Falcon Mine, the incidence of venereal disease was said to have decreased after they instituted a policy whereby "all natives on engagement [were] medically inspected, and native women [were] similarly dealt with and compelled to carry a medical certificate." A similar system was instituted at Shamva Mine. African men were examined prior to employment and every six months thereafter. These exams were full pre-employment exams in which the man was checked for various infectious diseases. However, the African women were checked exclusively for venereal diseases when they sought "permission to live on compounds." According to the MOH at Shamva Mine, the women were examined by "a committee of native women" and did not mind this at all.[23] Perhaps it was statements like this that led historian Charles van Onselen, one of the only historians besides myself to discuss the compulsory exams, to attribute them to African initiative (van Onselen, 1977: 51). If one reads the various petitions and testimony from African townsmen during the period, it would indeed appear that they wanted the compulsory examination of single African women. However, as the memories section of this chapter reveals, the situation and African responses were far more complicated.

After gaining responsible government as a crown colony of Great Britain, Southern Rhodesia's hands were free to pass more sweeping legislation such as the Public Health Act of 1924, which gave authorities greater latitude in the apprehension of those deemed to be public health risks. The act provided the congealing settler social itinerary with more elaborate routes of expression. Section 52 authorized compulsory medical examinations of inhabitants in areas where venereal disease was believed to be prevalent, stating that "any person who refuses to comply with such order or with any lawful instructions shall be guilty of an offense." Further, section 53 specified that the examination of females should be done by female medical practitioners and nursing attendants if at all possible.[24] The exams were no longer confined to those in or seeking employment. Providing even more breadth to the campaign against venereal diseases, a government notice was issued to the effect that "no native female servant be allowed to accept a post as general servant, housemaid, nurse or children's attendant except she be in possession of a clean bill of health signed periodically by a suitable medical attendant."[25] Still, there was nothing to prevent unattached African women from moving from place to place, thereby circumventing apparatuses of inspection on the mine compounds.

The perceived "problem" of mobile, unattached, and unregulated African women grew. This was in no small measure due to the fact that the general mobility of African women had increased. Between 1929 and 1936, for example, the African female population of the Bulawayo Municipal African Location (later known as Makokoba) rose from 750 to 1,237. In other words, more women were traveling to towns.[26] The joining together of a series of growing colonial "problems"—mobile and unattached African woman, the venereal native, detribalization and the urban African—led to heightened anxiety over both public health and space. An elaborate discourse on how to regulate the bodies of mobile black women resulted. Other places were similarly mobilizing public health machinery to confront the perceived disorder of women out of place. Hazel Carby (1992) discusses how the state enacted policies of "policing black women's bodies" in the United States at around the same time.

The unease precipitated by the increased presence of African women and girls in the urban spaces of Southern Rhodesia reached new proportions in the late 1920s. In 1928, the Rhodesian Landowners' and Farmers' Association organized a conference of government officials and white community leaders to discuss the colonial venereal disease problem. Dr. Andrew M. Fleming attended the conference.[27] Although he stressed that the actual rate of venereal disease infection in Southern Rhodesia was low when compared to Britain, for example, he agreed with the general consensus of the meeting that something had to be done about "traveling prostitutes" and other mobile black women. During a follow-up meeting in 1929, Fleming presented the following chart, compiled in Bulawayo, to emphasize the fact that there was no public health crisis yet.

> Examination of Natives: Bulawayo
> Returns for Month Ended May 31, 1929
> number examined: 684
> number of cases of V.D. 4
> percentage: 0.5%

However, although he did not believe there was a venereal disease crisis, Fleming did want further steps taken to regulate the flow of unmarried African women into the vicinity of towns and mining compounds.[28] Indeed, he warned the colonial secretary that if more were not done to prevent the problem of "stray women . . . spreading disease all over the country, Southern Rhodesia would have a crisis on its hands."[29] Others used similarly colorful language and spatial metaphors to describe this danger. "Girls on the move," or "traveling prostitutes who changed their names" were all blamed for the host of fears encapsulated in the venereal African problem.[30]

The language, particularly Fleming's use of the adjective "stray" to refer to the comings and goings of African women, is revealing of African women's position in the colonial socioeconomic and political landscape: the lack of formal inclusion, the fact that they were "a space displaced," and so forth. "Stray" implies no social agency. It is as if these women were cattle or goats who, unbeknown to them, roamed outside the right place. Not only were their bodies displaced in this discourse, so were their voices. Indeed, the general representation of African women during this period can be illustrated by the fact that a Domestic Labor Committee was formed in 1932 to determine whether African women were suitable for domestic service in European households. The conclusion was that they were not, and evidence supplied by one Salisbury housewife reflected the popular sentiment. According to Mrs. Chataway:

> Our girls in Southern Rhodesia are mentally inferior to other natives. They are merely accustomed to being regarded as goods and chattels. It would take a long

time to develop sufficient self respect to enable them to be employed with safety.[31]

The depiction of African women as inferior even to African men, as the other's other, meant that very little effort was made to record what they felt, thought, and wanted. To combat this silence, I explore language of their movements, what Michel de Certeau describes as the "space of enunciation" or, more fancifully, "the rhetoric of walking." In this interpretation their movements from place to place and across boundaries, rather than being subintelligent actions of beasts of burden, were acts of agency, products of deliberation, and statements of desire (see de Certeau, 1984: 98). Their movement made many uneasy.

The issue of compulsory venereal disease exams was, at its core, an issue of influx control. As long as African women were an unregulated group as per the Native Registration Act of 1901 (amended in 1913), there were no foolproof methods of keeping them within what various groups considered to be their "right place," to regulate their sexuality and/or their alleged infectiousness. Because there were many loopholes in the public health and influx control laws, different municipalities and different locations developed their own mechanisms to combat the scourge. A woman who lived on the Harari African Location in the 1930s and 1940s remembers frequent raids in the middle of the night. African homes were searched for women suspected of being in town illegally, brewing beer or housing the *Trepenoma spirochaete* (syphillis).[32] According to the superintendent of the Bulawayo Location, Mr. Collier, sporadic raids for "unmarried women" were conducted there as well. He estimated that in 1931, 135 single women and girls were caught by the raiding method. These women were examined by "a coloured nurse" for venereal disease. Mr. Collier, like the MOH at Shamva Mine, said they did not mind.[33] If found to be free of venereal disease, the women were issued with certificates to this effect. This document functioned as a *situpa* (the authorizing document that African men were made to carry, i.e., their passbooks).

Contrary to the representations of Collier, there is reason to believe that many African women did indeed mind the exams. At the 1928 Venereal Disease conference, Mr. H. R. Barbour mentioned that "some time ago, well-known women workers . . . asked why native women should be forced to undergo an examination." Barbour may have been referring to a protest meeting held by Martha Ngano and the Rhodesia Bantu Voters Association Women's League in the mid-1920s. At this meeting, the women asked the white authorities why they did not compulsorily examine white women's genitals as their admission price to town.[34] Rather than take these women seriously, the sentiments were attributed to the meddling of one European woman named Mrs. McKeurtan. However, there was a willingness to concede that African women might have been genuinely offended when examined by white male doctors.[35]

The Land Apportionment Act of 1930 gave authorities greater power to group African women together, whether in or out of employment, and to subject them to greater controls. The 1936 Native Registration Act was even more effective in this aspect. Among other things, it was a formal effort to systematically deal with the "influx of young women who evaded parental control." This was part effort to appease an African patriarchy clamoring for control over the mobility of African women and part effort to appease a growing population of whites, economically marginalized during the Depression and likely to face competition from African petty-entrepreneurs. A serious blow was dealt to Africans operating in the "informal" economic sector as keepers of rooming houses, beer brewers, wood sellers, and food hawkers, many of whom were women. The 1936 Act made such activities illegal or so restrictive that they became economically unviable.[36] Additionally, all Africans in employment were to be compulsorily examined and, if necessary, vaccinated for smallpox. These were not full medical or bacteriological investigations. Their purpose was to bring to light obvious cases of contagious and infectious disease, which could then be referred for further treatment.[37]

The fact that venereal diseases were on the rise among Europeans may have also been a factor in the decision to place more controls on the influx of African women. Not only did those in the urban areas suffer by being turned into criminals just for trying to survive, they also suffered from the further entrenchment of the colonial representation of them as diseased. In the annual *Report on the Public Health* for 1936, the Medical Director issued a warning to all European men stating that "venereal disease contracted from a native is generally of intractable character and noticeably resistant to treatment." Trying to cover all bases, the doctor continued: "I do not mean that it is impossible to cure, the disease can quite definitely be cured, particularly if the patient seeks treatment early, but the process is slower [and the] damage greater."[38]

While the Second World War was still raging, the Southern Rhodesian government would once again revisit its so-called native policy, particularly what had become known as "the problem of the urban native." There were many reasons for this, including the growth in the size of both African and European urban populations, the rise of a secondary manufacturing industry, and the consequent desire to restructure the labor force. Tighter controls were placed on the urban African population in general, and African women became more formally incorporated into the colony's influx controls discourse in response to the fact that their numbers among the employed were growing, as the following chart indicates.

Africans in Employment
(Based on Annual Census Returns, S.R., 1947: 39)[39]

Year	Males	Females
1921	139,676	628
1926	171,970	1,628
1931	179,092	1,066
1936	252,482	1,815
1941	299,450	3,778
1946	363,344	13,524

In 1943, Percy Ibbotson, the Organizing Secretary of the Native Welfare Society in Southern Rhodesia, noted that, in the period since the passage of the Native Registration Act in 1936, the number of African women employed in Salisbury alone had risen from 196 to 400, more than 100 percent. In addition, if Salisbury was like the rest of the colony, its population of African women in employment must have risen by around 350 percent by 1946. But while the number of black women in employment was rising, Ibbotson complained that two-thirds of these women were without contracts of service in accordance with the act. This was a problem because it meant that the Department of Native Affairs could not develop an accurate picture of them and could not map them in detail, which was a problem "because of the associated medical examination." In other words, European employers hired African women "under the table" and thus without requiring medical examinations.

Ibbotson's concern for the intersecting issues of sexual hygiene and mobility led him to focus his attention on the question of housing. Employers were slow to provide adequate housing for their female employees. This meant that many parents did not allow their daughters to take service positions and that only women suspected of questionable morality were available for employment. According to Ibbotson, the Harari Location Superintendent "very wisely does not allow women to rent rooms in the Location or African Township. Unmarried women are not allowed to obtain accommodation unless this is provided by a relative. This is a wise precaution." However, this meant that the locations and townships were filled with people forced into performing sordid acts to survive. In the late and post-Second World War climate of labor stabilization and improved social hygiene, social reformers like Ibbotson sought solutions, such as the erection of a hostel for African women and girls.[40]

Under the Native Urban Areas Act of 1946, all African women "not in employment or seeking work," except those who were wives, were directed to submit to a medical exam. Moreover, the act made it more difficult for employers to avoid providing their African female employees with contracts of service complete with medical certification. Thus, unlike the Public Health Act of 1924 or the Native Registration Act of 1936, the 1946 Act netted the informal sector as well and, quite frankly, any African woman who was not known to be married by whomever was making the inquiry. Although it became more difficult, many women continued to avoid the exam. The mayor of Bulawayo speculated that the unpopularity of the exams among some African women may have been due to the focus of the exams. They were obviously designed for the benefit of others and with the assumption that all single African women were prostitutes. The mayor thought that "the scope of this examination should be widened and possibly more investigations undertaken."[41] In other words, he felt that the exams should be made more similar to those imposed on African men in employment. His advice was not taken.

The Politics of Sexuality

Chibheura exams should be viewed as influx control for African women, distinct from influx control for African men for one simple reason: African women were viewed as the other's other. Although the colonizers initially sought to "emancipate" African women from their positions as "cunnubial slaves"[42] and encouraged African women and girls to run to mission stations,[43] the tide soon changed. As part of Southern Rhodesia's development of an indirect rule policy, the state deemed it advisable to go slow on the native gender question. In fact, the Native Affairs Committee of 1910–1911 decreed that the management and control of African female productive and reproductive powers were best left to African men.[44] Although Frantz Fanon argues that "the Native" was always seen at a genital level by the colonizer, Megan Vaughan argues that this was really only the case with African men. According to Vaughan, when the colonial authorities were interested in African female sexuality, it was generally as a marker of "the effectiveness of an indirect rule policy in shoring up existing systems of social control" (1991: 130). Thus, when it came to questions on the surveillance of black female sexuality and mobility, black and white patriarchies agreed on many things, or appeared to at any rate. When we examine Chibheura within the context of the colonial politics of sexuality, we find different factions employing the notion of African female sexual danger for different reasons and toward different ends. Each employed the rhetoric of public health, constructed mobile

African women as a sexualized other, and felt that they should be under some form of regulation.

Colonial perils were the product of anxieties, stereotypes, and settler group/capitalist interests, rarely of objective reality. As a result, the so-called Black Peril, the fear of a black male as a sexual predator lurking in the wings and waiting to pounce on the innocence of white settler womanhood, could thrive even though actual occurrences were extremely rare. As both John Pape and Anne Stoler argue, the underlying ideological foundation of the Black Peril was the preservation of whiteness, particularly white male supremacy (Pape, 1990; Stoler, 1989: 634–636). One of the most notorious examples of the Black Peril phenomenon in Southern Rhodesia was the Umtali Rape Case of 1911. The African defendant was convicted and sentenced to death by hanging. The High Commissioner, having doubts that the state had actually proved the commission of rape, commuted this sentence to life in prison. This fact so outraged the white male citizenry throughout the region that some took the law into their own hands. One group from South Africa complained that no extenuating circumstances could be accepted in such a case, that "the native must be shewn [sic.] at all costs that the honour of the white woman is to be held sacred, and any attempt at rape must be punished with death." Another group said that the "Native must be taught at all costs, that the person of a white woman is to be held sacred and inviolable."[45]

Since the beginning of the European penetration of south central Africa in the 1890s, white men had had both consensual and nonconsensual (rape) sex with black women. Indeed, such cases occurred with much more regularity than did so-called Black Peril incidents.[46] However, no "peril" was attached to them. The inviolability of the black woman was not a battle cry among the lawmakers and politicians in this settler colonial society. On the rare occasions when "White Peril" did emerge as a consideration, it was still in reference to sex occurring between white women and black men. The difference between the White Peril and the Black Peril was not the actors involved but that one was with the consent of the white woman and the other was not.

The fact that white men and black women fell outside the laws of interracial sexual regulation frustrated both black men and white women. In a 1916 petition to the administrator, the Amandebele Patriotic Society (AP Society), a group of Ndebele nationalists, complained of "promiscuous sexual intercourse between male whites and female natives, and the neglect by the parents of the results of such miscegenation." They warned that "the racial danger is not the only one following on this intercourse of black and white," but that there was also "the risk of the spread of syphilis."[47]

In the same year, 1,600 white women signed a petition for the inclusion of white men in the 1916 Natives Adultery Act. They wanted white men who had sexual relations with married black women to be subject to this law as well. However, the all-white male Legislative Council would not agree to this, claiming that it would lead to the blackmail of white males. They were apparently not concerned about the potential blackmail of white females, however.[48] Direct challenges to white male authority, privilege, and heterosexual impunity, within the colonial context, were rarely successful. European women had to turn their attentions elsewhere: the question of African female domestic labor. As the earlier quotation from Mrs. Chattaways testimony shows, many of these white women seemed much more afraid of having unattached black women, whom they viewed from an almost purely sexual perspective, working in their homes. Indeed, they became the most vociferous opponents of the employment of African women in domestic service (Schmidt, 1992: 158–179). The proximity of African women to the European husbands for whom miscegenation was no crime was their concern. But the real power was contained in all-male legal and regulatory bodies like the Legislative Council and the Criminal Investigation Department (CID), and as far as they were concerned, White Peril was consensual sexual relations between white women and black men. According to CID Superintendent Brundell, White Peril could be summed up as the problem of the white female nymphomaniac.[49] The only "peril" in which white males were involved was "yellow peril," the potential or actual offspring of their miscegenation.[50]

White men, white women, and black men all had something to say about black women's sexuality. Black men and white women wanted it regulated or essentially banished from public view. White men wanted it regulated in the form of compulsory venereal disease exams. Some black men also wanted this because it was the best way to guard against being infected with a venereal disease. For some, black female sexual mobility represented pleasure, for others danger. Theirs were the bodies to contain, control, and in some cases, allow in to serve as buffers between black manhood and white womanhood. Their voices, however, were absent from this discourse. Today their voices are absent from the way that the Black Peril and other aspects of colonial oppression and everyday life are remembered.

The Politics of Memory

The institutionalization of access to and control over African men's bodies as laborers has been well examined, most recently by scholars like Alexander Butchart (1998) and Dunbar Moodie (1994). With the exception of

Vaughan's *Curing Their Ills* (1991) and the valuable if problematic discussions of the compulsory examination of Herero women in colonial Namibia (Poewe, 1985: 200–216) few have tackled comparable questions regarding African women. In what is to date the best known work on the subject of the black working class in colonial Zimbabwe, women are scripted as "parasites within the black working class," saps on the already depleted blood supply of the black working class (van Onselen, 1977: 179). They are called "purveyors of sex in a sexually deprived community . . . simply one more level of social control" (1977: 182) who owed their "only allegiance to the highest bidder [and] acted as the catalyst of conflict among poorer workers" (1977: 180). The compulsory examination of these women was, according to van Onselen, an unequivocal good.

Fortunately, there has been considerable progress in the area of gender sensitivity and inclusivity since van Onselen's book was published in 1977. Historians such as Teresa Barnes (1992), Diana Jeater (1993), and Elizabeth Schmidt (1990) have brought women's voices and issues of gender power into their analyses of colonial socioeconomic and cultural history. Much more is needed, however, to counteract the androcentric ways in which the collective/public memories of the colonial past have been framed. What follows is an attempt to uncover some of the thoughts of the women who knew *Chibheura* intimately, the women who could not travel to town without opening up their legs for inspection. Using a series of interviews conducted during two separate visits to Zimbabwe, one in 1991 and the other in 1998, I attempt to tell this spatial story from the perspectives of the women themselves.

Mrs. Gosa left Mozambique with her husband sometime during the Second World War, "Hitler's war." They left to escape from the husband's forced labor. They chose Southern Rhodesia because Mrs. Gosa had a brother in Salisbury whom she hoped could find her husband, a mechanic, a job. The couple crossed the border into Southern Rhodesia at Mt. Darwin. They were medically examined at the border police camp. After successfully passing this "test" as Mrs. Gosa called it, the couple received their passes, her husband a *situpa* or a pass to seek employment and Mrs. Gosa a medical certificate verifying that she had no venereal disease. Mrs. Gosa describes the experience[51]:

> Before one was given an identity card one had to undergo a medical examination. It was only after the examination that I knew that the doctors and nurses were checking whether we had any sexually transmitted diseases. What happened was men and women went into separate rooms where there was a doctor and a nurse who was African. The doctor was male and a white man. Can you

imagine they even touched, poked and looked at our private parts. It was very embarrassing.

I got into the room and I was asked to take off my skirt. Those days we did not wear any panties at all. So I was asked to lie on the bed and open my legs. Then, wonder of all wonders, this white man began touching and poking at my private parts. It was the worst experience that had ever happened to me. Even my husband had never looked at my private parts like that. I just wished the earth would open up and swallow me. The black nurse was just standing there mum. I had to close my eyes tight to stop myself from crying because of the shame that I felt. You see, I was still in that age where women gave birth to their children at home with traditional midwives attending, not a foreign male doctor like what you have in hospitals right now. So you can imagine how I felt when this white man was looking at me naked.

Asked whether the doctor had explained what he was doing and why, she responded:

No. Those were the days when you could never ask a white man anything for fear of being thrown into prison. I could not ask the black nurse either because she also looked like someone who was also afraid of the white doctor.

When asked whether she told her husband what had happened to her, she became philosophical, stating that:

In life there are things that those close to you are better off not knowing. Can you imagine what telling him about the rigorous examination would have done to him. I just told him I had been examined and I had passed the test and it ended there. He died without knowing, I thought we were better off without him knowing.

Mrs. Gosa experienced the examination only once. This may be because she was known to be a "respectable" married woman and did not travel much, or because she was already quite mature by the time she and her husband traveled to Southern Rhodesia. Others, however, were not so fortunate.

Ambuya Madzingirwa remembers chibheura as a regular feature of African town life in Shabani (Zvishavane), a place that she frequently visited during the 1940s. I interviewed Ambuya Madzingirwa twice, once in 1991 and once in 1998, each time with the assistance of a fluent Shona speaker.[52] The information elicited during these two interviews varied considerably in response to questions of passing judgment on the exams in particular and colonialism in general, culpability, and so forth. During the 1991 interview, Ambuya Madzingirwa seemed more willing to condemn the colonial practice than she was in 1998. The reason for this discrepancy is unknown. Like Mrs. Gosa, she first arrived in the Southern Rhodesia towns in the late 1930s or early 1940s. She and her husband lived on a reserve near Morgenster mission, where her husband received a certificate in teaching. Ambuya Madzingirwa sometimes traveled to the nearby Rhodesia and General Asbestos Corporation, Ltd. mine compound to conduct shopping. She described the compound as a tightly run ship with Superintendent John Bera at its helm. John Bera was a strong paternalist who instituted schools and training programs for women who lived at the mines. He encouraged them to learn crafts, cookery, sewing, and knitting. Madzingirwa associates not only these programs with Bera but also the compulsory venereal disease exams, of which Bera was a strong proponent. Although the director of the asbestos mine hospital, Dr. Ireland, was the official face behind the VD Campaign on the compound and throughout the Shabani district,[53] John Bera was reputed to be behind it. According to Madzingirwa, the place where chibheura was conducted was even called *kwa* John Bera. The nurses were referred to as John Bera's people.[54]

"When you arrived with luggage, first thing you did" was have a chibheura exam.[55] Madzingirwa explained the exam's purpose. She said that "outside women," women who did not have husbands on the compound, were feared to bring disease to the compound. They were sent into a shelter, a long shed-like room with cement floors. Madzingirwa remembers the place as overcrowded and messy. She remembers the nurses in gum boots and rubber gloves, and says that even the women "patients" wore boots because of the wet and dirty floors. The women were told to lie down on cement counters and to *chibheura*, open their legs. If the doctor detected signs of venereal disease, the women were either chased from the compound or sent to the mine hospital for treatment. It is not clear to me when or why one option was chosen over the other. If deemed free from venereal infection, the women were issued certificates that functioned as passes. These were good until the next month's raid or until the next time they attempted to enter the compound. Although the ostensible purpose of Chibheura was to protect the compound inhabitants from *mahure* (prostitutes) or "outside women," all women who were not "grown up women," that is, quite old, were examined. As Madzingirwa put it, they couldn't distinguish between prostitutes and married women. "John Bera wanted everyone to be checked."[56]

Ambuya Madzingirwa seemed less critical of the compulsory examination in our 1998 interview than she was in 1991. Whom she found guiltier, the colonizers for conducting the intrusive and grossly insensitive campaigns or the "outside women" who were feared to be infecting other women's husbands, is hard to tell. In general, when blame is assigned for the spread of sexually transmitted diseases in Africa, women are the targets. Southern Rhodesia/Zimbabwe, like many other African countries in the past and the present, referred to sexually transmitted diseases colloquially as "woman's diseases" (Gelfand, 1943; Wall, 1988). As recently as the early 1990s, AIDS and HIV transmission was also associated with women and was popularly associated with female to male transmission.[57]

It is perhaps not surprising that Madzingirwa said that she thought it was a good thing for women to be checked "so that our husbands wouldn't get sick."[58] She was referring to the fact that a wife who feared that her husband slept with other women wanted these women examined regularly. Meanwhile, as an "outside woman" on the Rhodesia and General Asbestos mine compound in the 1940s, Madzingirwa was also examined. When asked how it felt to be treated like a *mahure* who infected other women's husbands, like the women from whom she wanted protection, she said that she was happy with this at the time, adding something about how modernity had changed morals and how people wanted protection. She said that she wanted protection against the women who dressed against the grain. "I was so happy that they were tested."[59] In fact, Madzingirwa stated that the only ones who were unhappy about the exams were those who were infected with sexually transmitted diseases, the "guilty" ones.

Raids were often used to net these so-called guilty ones. Ambuya Madzingirwa recalled how embarrassed she felt when the African police would parade through the compounds and locations shouting: "Chibheura, chibheura, madzimai, chibheura."[60] This was a bit like yelling: "Open your legs, open your legs, come along women and open your legs." Still, she said of those who complained: "If you don't like it, don't come. . . . If you go to mines, you obey their rules." I probed and asked interpreters to probe for memories of resistance and expressions of outrage, but Ambuya Madzingirwa generally refused to accommodate, either endorsing the compulsory exams or saying things like: "There was no way out, if you protested, you would be sent to the hospital." "It's obvious women did not like being looked at, but there was nothing we could have done."[61] Associating colonialism with a state of war and being under occupation, Madzingirwa saw the exams as simply how things were, as part of the realities of life under colonialism. It was not easy, but neither was the general condition of being colonized. "It was a mistake to walk next to a man" because you would be suspected of prostitution and sent for inspection. Some women refused to travel to the compound as a result, preferring to send others to shop for them. "Others just wanted to do their own shopping, so they just dealt with the exam" as the price to be paid. "It was a bit ridiculous but there was nothing else."62

Mrs. Munyoni, who lived in Shabani during the 1940s and 1950s, recalls the inspections:

> [I]nspected once a month especially those who were [not?] married. . . . Young women used to bring disease from other neighbouring mines. . . . Married women traditionally got the disease from their husbands. . . . The single or the new neighbors, unmarried women, were inspected more often. . . . Us [married] women were at times happy of that because it lessened diseases from our husbands; although it was harassment.63

Another Shabani inhabitant, Mr. Phiri, originally from Malawi, remembers how many people were attracted to the mines in the 1930s because of the availability of food and how single Shona women went to the mines in search of husbands. According to Mr. Phiri, they knew that men from Zambia and Malawi had a reputation for staying with their women until death. He believes that VD became prevalent as a result of these and other attractions to the compounds. Mr. Phiri did not mind the policy of compulsory exams.64 But, having said this, he seemed more aware than most of the precarious position of women in colonial town and compound life. He described the position of the African women at the mine as indirect workers who were there to keep the husbands healthy by cooking good food. According to Phiri:

> Those without muchato we kwa mudzviti (marriage certificate) were more prone to chibheura. The single ladies were given a passbook and in the mine they had a register. The passbook was a record to show your progress or your record of health on chibheura. . . . If you had no VD and the record showed it, you were usually allowed into the mine. . . . This (passbook) was demanded on entry into each and every mine. You had to produce it to show that you were clean. Even men, those who hired prostitutes, asked for the passbook so as to see that the person they were dealing with was clean and to make sure that they were dealing with a clean person because this could make them lose their monthly allowance.65

It seems that the most galling aspect of the exams for everyone who had spent time at Shabani was the fact that older women were sometimes examined by younger women. According to Mrs. Munyoni, "in our tradition the opposite was normal, [but] we couldn't resist because of fear of being chased from the mine." According to Mr. Banda, "the only consoling thing was that women were looked at by women and not men."⁶⁶ But, as Mrs. Gosa's evidence suggests, this was not the case everywhere, and certainly not at border posts. Banda also felt that the exams were unfair to men because he said that their wives were often examined. "Women, especially those from rural areas, were resistant because they believed that it was an intrusion of privacy. But they didn't resist for a long time because if the bosses found out that they were resisting they could be chased out of the mine so they had no choice but to do what they were told."⁶⁷

The level of resentment toward these particular aspects of chibheura is rooted in a practice the Shona call *kuchenurwa*. It appears that many equated the compulsory venereal disease exams with this practice, probably as an aid to understanding or perhaps domesticating the practice. However, *kuchenurwa* exams were conducted by older women on younger, unmarried women and girls.⁶⁸ A variety of methods were used, but the object was always to ensure the "innocence" or the virginity of the unmarried woman or girl.

This notion of innocence and guilt was prevalent in the discourse on the exams, revealing how they functioned for public health, social control, and morals policing; how they represented different and often opposing agendas. For some, the compulsory VD exams had a purpose similar to that of traditional virginity tests.⁶⁹ However, the fact that chibheura was not performed by one's *vatete* (paternal aunt) or *ambuya* (grandmother) was found deeply insulting, even by those who claimed to otherwise support the exams. The fact that it was not even always performed by women, or was performed on married women were also resented by those who placed themselves on the side of the respectable.

Mrs. Scott lived at Harare African location from the 1930s. Unlike Ambuya Madzingirwa, she remembers protests against the exams having occurred at Harare Location, mainly led by husbands, men like Mr. Banda, resentful of the fact that their wives were being examined. She also remembers groups like the Rhodesian Bantu Voters Association's Women's League holding protests.⁷⁰ However, she concurs with the others about the general absence of organized resistance and about the fact that, because they were afraid of what the whites might do and could not afford to be thrown out of town, there was little that could be done. Life was hard. As Mrs. Scott recalls:

[C]hecking wasn't in proper clinics; just every several months, [black] police would walk on foot (no shoes). They would come early in morning, 3 A.M.⁷¹

If one wanted to visit the towns and was not a recognizably married woman, there was only one way to avoid the crasser aspects of the exam. That was to visit a nurse voluntarily. One nurse who provided the service and certification for a nominal fee was Mrs. Mudzodze of the Red Cross. Because so many women sought exams by Mrs. Mudzodze, however, she was often unable to meet the demand for her services. Mrs. Ndongo, currently matron at Zvishavane (previously Shabani) Mine Hospital, remembers other efforts at resisting the compulsory exams. She says that women would return to the rural areas a day or so before inspection roundups and then sneak back into the compound when they were over.

From the perspective of the colonial authorities, a combination of factors made the raiding approach to public health and influx control less tenable following the Second World War. Throughout the 1940s, various officials and social reformers complained of the "the urban African problem" and that both the previous method of influx control and economic development strategies were inconsistent with the changing needs of industry. Prime Minister Geoffrey Huggins, the architect of Southern Rhodesia's Two Pyramids policy (Rhodesia's version of apartheid), became an advocate for married African housing in the towns.[72] Percy Ibbotson augmented his appeal for single women's hostels with one for married housing, arguing that a married man was much less liable to develop deficiency diseases than a single man.[73] An investigation conducted by the Bulawayo City Council in 1949 determined that not only were the locations and townships seedbeds of vice and disease, they were also sites of "hopelessness, sullenness and desperation," which, they feared, could grow into "mass disaffection" (Gussman, 1962: 99). There was thus a growing interest in providing more sources of married accommodation and more opportunities for formal and informal employment for single and married African women.

The *mahure* and the *mapoto* wives (casual, town wives) were no longer necessary for the profitability of colonial capitalism. The colonizer broadened the discourse on African women in the urban areas beyond the view of their bodies as extensions of African male workers' bodies. In 1958, the Urban Affairs Commission went so far as to advocate the inclusion of African women in the term *native*, thus creating opportunities for African women to exist in the urban areas in their own right.[74] There was a long way to go, but at least the compulsory exams were discontinued.

Ambuya Madzingirwa and Mrs. Ndongo attribute the end of the Chibheura in the late 1950s to the growth in nationalist politics: "People were made aware that this was an invasion of privacy by the politicians."[75] Of course, these politicians were responding to the issues and grievances that the people brought to them. The use of compulsion in venereal disease campaigns had always been unpopular among some segments of the African population. It was discontinued in 1958 because of a growth in political sophistication and the changing needs of capital due to the post-Second World War rise of secondary industry. To paraphrase Frederick Cooper here, these campaigns and, more particularly, the working and living conditions that made them necessary, were less and less capable of producing the type of labor force desired (1996: 32). The discovery and extensive usage of penicillin and antibiotics, public health education campaigns conducted by groups like the Native Welfare Society, and the establishment of township clinics also created environments conducive to more voluntary modes of examination.

However, campaigns targeting single, mobile African women as transmitters of STDs did not cease; they continued into the early 1990s at least in Zimbabwe. AIDS and HIV have replaced syphilis, but mobile, single women are still the scapegoats. In both colonial and post-colonial Zimbabwe, one encounters the ways in which discourses of public health and social order, gender, space, and disease intersect. Moreover, that this was the case on a day-to-day basis, made it one of the realities of colonial life. African women's experiences were always a combination, always at the intersection, of various discourses of control and regulations, of various systems of oppression. This chapter has been an effort to recover some of the memories from this space.

14
Girls, Sex, and the Dangers of Urban Schooling in Coastal Madagascar

LESLEY A. SHARP
Barnard College

Introduction*

Social power and danger lace localized understandings of schooling in urban, coastal Madagascar. Simply put, peaceful daily survival often requires basic literacy in this former French colony, where the ability to exercise one's rights may ultimately require identity cards, land deeds, and taxation and voting documents. It is no wonder, then, that schooling is so highly prized where jobs remain scarce for the well educated. Schooling is also valued for pragmatic reasons, because basic math and writing skills are of quotidian importance. It also figures prominently in dreams of social advancement for both boys and girls.

---

*The material reported in this chapter is part of a book in press entitled *The Sacrificed Generation: Youth, History, and the Colonized Mind in Madagascar*. The research was made possible through generous support from the American Philosophical Society; several faculty grants from Butler University and Barnard College; the Joint Committee on African Studies of the Social Science Research Council and the American Council of Learned Societies with funds from the National Endowment for the Humanities and the Ford Foundation; and a Richard Carley Hunt Fellowship from the Wenner-Gren Foundation for Anthropological Research. An association with L'Institut des Civilizations in Antananarivo, under the superb guidance of its director, Jean-Aimeé Rakotoarisoa, has also proved invaluable.

321

The bureaucratization of everyday life—and, thus, the skills associated with schooling—is especially pronounced in the northwestern urban center of Ambanja. Established immediately after French conquest of the island in 1895–1896, today Ambanja is a prosperous community, serving as the administrative and mercantile hub for the expansive and fertile Sambirano Valley, a lush coastal region where large plantations of cocoa, coffee, and pungent ylang-ylang dominate many smaller peasant holdings of both cash and subsistence crops. This region stands in stark contrast to much of the remainder of this large tropical island; although many of the valley's residents are poor, very few suffer from serious or long-term hunger. Access to land and labor are key to survival in this region, which draws migrants from all areas of the island in search of work and wealth. Success as either a wage laborer or a landed peasant requires that one's papers be in order, because it is necessary to have an identity card to acquire work, gain access to healthcare, hold on to housing, or assert claims to arable land.

An education beyond basic literacy carries with it hope for other possibilities in life, and several categories of educated elite dominate the valley's most influential spheres of power. First are the managers and engineers of central highland and metropolitan origins, who control the valley's imposing plantations; second are locally born (and primarily Sakalava) inhabitants who run the city and county governments and courts, and who dominate the staff at the region's clinics and schools; and third are members of the indigenous royal Sakalava dynasty, who exert their presence in both sacred and political spheres of influence (Sharp, 1993). The majority of the valley's elite completed their schooling at the *lycée* or high school level, and many passed the difficult pre-college *baccalauréat*[1] exam; still others received advanced training under the French in specialized professional schools or, since gaining independence in 1960, have attended one of the nation's several university campuses. Advanced schooling signifies at least remote possibilities for social mobility, greater wealth, and political clout.

The potential for social power and prestige is assumed to be universal and equally possible for boys and girls. Many local inhabitants embrace the possibility that anyone who is intellectually capable might succeed through schooling (SAK: *mahay*), if a person works hard at his or her studies (*miasa/mianatra mafy*), and if the person's kin have the financial means to do without the full-time labor of one or more children enrolled in school. Everyone must also struggle against failure, which may result from laziness, apathy, a weak mind, poor schooling, or poverty. Schooling is fraught with danger: an adversary may use potent magic to undermine or destroy another student's success through physical injury, ill health, or madness (Sharp, 1990). Furthermore, the schoolyard is rife with other equally significant hazards. The most potent are circumscribed by assumptions about the sexual activities of school youth. In this context, the greatest attention is focused on independent school girls who have come to town on their own to complete their studies. School migrants more generally bear the double burden of being perceived as among the greatest threats to an idealized urban world *and* simultaneously its most vulnerable victims. In this context, girls are the focus of greatest concern. As I show in this chapter, however, ethnographic investigation uncovers other truths. The sexual potency and danger assigned to independent migrant school girls is framed by localized perceptions of the corrupting power of popular culture and associated media of foreign origin, especially in discotheques and video cinemas, venues wrongly assumed to attract these girls. Such misguided assumptions hinge upon localized perceptions of urban versus rural life, where urban sexual dangers are so often paired with the predatory nature of economic potency and power. This chapter explores local critiques of the gendered nature of urban schooling's dangers in Ambanja.

The assumptions that drive local misunderstandings are complex because they embody critiques that are formulated and expressed solely by town-based adults. As such, they levy judgments on migrant school youth who are allowed neither agency nor voice in such matters. An ethnographic approach enables students to articulate the true nature of their lives. By contrasting their tales with assumptions voiced by adult critics, this chapter unravels the complex tale of sexuality and danger in this coastal town. At the end of the chapter I turn to contemporary concerns about AIDS (*SIDA*), only recently perceived as a threat to the survival of youth on a previously isolated island nation.

Urban Danger and Scholastic Failure

Ambanja is an impressive educational center, the facilities of which rival those located throughout much of the island. This town, with a population of approximately 30,000, houses an astonishing array of schools that serve the local juvenile population as well as that of the valley beyond (which has a population of approximately 80,000). Within the town's limits are six state-run primary schools, one middle school, and two *lycées* or high schools, one offering a standard curriculum, the other serving as a specialized technical school. These institutions compete with an array of private institutions, including the elite and highly exclusive French Elementary School,[2] the far more affordable Catholic Academy (its offerings extend from primary through the *lycée* grades and also include a special track for seminarists preparing for the priesthood), and, finally, three remedial schools that offer classes at the primary and middle school levels to students who have failed elsewhere. In addition to these town-based schools, scattered throughout the valley are numerous other state-run primary and middle schools and another private Catholic academy.

Even though the town's pedagogical facilities and even examination scores may exceed those for the nation as a whole, possibilities for schooling success are dismal in Ambanja. A close examination of total school figures reveals that only slightly more than half of the valley's juvenile population is in fact enrolled in school, a figure that parallels a national trend reported more than two decades ago (Ratsiraka, 1975: 80). Nearly all students repeat one, if not several, grades, and most drop out altogether before they ever reach *lycée*. Dropout rates are highest in the years that terminate the primary, middle, and *lycée* years, when, following the French model of schooling, students must pass rigorous national exams if they wish to continue on to the next level. However, Ambanja's *lycée* students fare slightly better on these exams than do many of their counterparts living elsewhere on the island. Although only around 1 percent of all students who enter primary school in Ambanja will ever pass the *baccalauréat* exam (a trend that is true nationally; see Clignet & Ernst, 1995), the *baccalauréat* success rates for Ambanja's *lycée* students have ranged from as low as 1 to 7 percent to an impressive 23 percent or even 50 percent in the 1990s. Success on this difficult exam allows a student to apply for university training. Few do so, however, because their elder kin lack the resources to support them.

Schooling and Sacrifice

The fact that any students manage to complete their schooling at the *lycée* level in Ambanja is truly astonishing, because during the 1980s and 1990s the town (and much of the island) was devoid of teaching materials.[3] There are virtually no textbooks or teacher's guides and no library facilities; schools lack contemporary maps, adequate numbers of desks and chairs, chalkboards, and chalk; and students may even be unable to afford paper and pens for class notes and homework. Severe shortages are a way of life in this nation's schools, a trend that initially emerged during the socialist era and remains so today. Waves of pedagogical reforms that have characterized six political regimes over four decades have only further exacerbated school failure. Among the most significant shifts has been a linguistic one: until the mid-1970s, French was the language of instruction; by 1975, Official Malagasy had been created and introduced in schools; this was then discarded and replaced, once again, with French in the 1990s. In the face of such radical reforms, several generations of teachers have been ill prepared for the two most recent transitions, lacking even rudimentary retraining or adequate instructional materials necessary for preparing them—and their students—for the state examinations at the end of primary and middle school and, finally, *lycée*.

For most local students school success is thus an unattainable dream, particularly when financial, political, and social forces determine access to quality education in a nation with a bankrupt educational system. The failure is felt most keenly in the island's coastal provinces. Students in the central highlands, and especially the capital of Antananarivo, have fared better, because their dialects most closely approximate Official Malagasy, and local bookstores have always stocked textbooks and school supplies. The highland elite have long sent their children to private schools that have ensured fluency in French. Children in Ambanja, on the other hand, are reluctant to speak Official Malagasy because they perceive it as a poorly disguised version of a dialect spoken by highland oppressors who attempted, yet failed, to conquer their territory in the nineteenth century. Many also openly and bitterly shun the teacher's craft, declaring that advanced schooling is useless because in reality it reaps few financial rewards. As a result, many students return to peasant farming where they know, ironically, they have a greater chance of financial success. Parents nevertheless make great sacrifices to enable their most gifted children to attend school beyond the primary level. It is only the most driven of students—those who thirst for knowledge even in the face of fierce obstacles—who ever manage to make it through the *lycée* years and beyond. Parents value equally the potential abilities of daughters and sons, yet in reality girls' opportunities may be more limited because of elders' heightened concern for their safety and welfare.

School Migrants

Primary schools are scattered throughout the rural regions of Madagascar, yet advancement to middle school or *lycée* frequently requires that one leave home. As a result of Ambanja's status as an educational center, it is populated by students as young as 10 years old who have gone there to continue their schooling, leaving villages located as much as several hundred kilometers away. Ambanja's schools provide no dormitory facilities (except for a few Catholic seminarists), and because town residents are reluctant to house or rent rooms to strangers, many school migrants live alone or share extremely modest dwellings with siblings or schoolmates. Parents are especially wary of sending their daughters to town because they fear that they will soon fall prey to schoolboys or adult men seeking their sexual favors. Pregnancy ensures school failure because schoolgirls are dismissed when their condition becomes obvious; their male partners, however, go unpunished.

Townspeople in general do not trust school migrants, who are frequently stereotyped in a host of ways. As naïve, rural-born children who presumably live without any form of adult supervision, they are said to fall prey quickly and inevitably to the dangers associated with such local distractions (FR: *diversions*) as discotheques and video cinemas, where they are certain to waste their school fees and valuable study time. Once they find their coffers empty, they will then succumb to criminal activities, becoming thieves, drug dealers, and prostitutes to make ends meet. They are thus simultaneously the town's most vulnerable victims and its most dangerous members. Whereas boys threaten the economic well-being of the community as thieves, girls figure prominently in discussions of sexuality, where pregnancy and prostitution are key concerns.

Such is the mythology surrounding these assumed miscreant migrants. Although girls certainly run the risk of becoming pregnant, and although many migrant students—be they girls or boys—suffer terrible financial hardships to attend school in town, my own data expose other trends. I have found that rural schoolgirls are no more sexually active than are their town-based counterparts who live under the daily, watchful eye of adult kin. Furthermore, school migrants are often more serious about their studies than are town-based children, an observation confirmed repeatedly by their own teachers. They also bear significantly larger economic burdens than do their town-based counterparts, such that they shoulder heavier demands on their time and that thus potentially rob them of both valuable study hours and time for play (and get them into trouble). This is especially true on weekends. Many school migrants return each weekend to the countryside to provide adult kin with essential farm labor. In contrast, town-based children have far more free time on their hands. They may share chores with other siblings or have parents who see to such daily needs as shopping and cooking, or if they are from elite households, servants may relieve them of many tasks. Unlike town-based youth, school migrants shoulder constant burdens. Because they must fend for themselves in town, each day is consumed by domestic chores. As one astute schoolteacher, Mr. Prosper, explained:

> To do well they have to sit and read, but how can they do that when they must support themselves, too? The [students] from the country[side], they're the most serious of all. Think of it—to come here from the country—they [must] really [be] motivated. But they might sleep in class, simply because they're so tired. This is the paradox—the ones who want to work the most, who care the most, may in fact be the ones most likely to fail.[4]

Contrary to many adults' assumptions, few migrant youth have the time or economic means to visit video cinemas and discotheques. None I have encountered engage in prostitution, and drug use, although a focus of much concern, is hardly pervasive in Ambanja. What, then, are the factors that underlie such misinformed views of school migrants' lives and, more specifically, of schoolgirls of rural origin? These questions require a close examination of schoolgirls' daily lives. As the following case examples reveal, girls of rural versus urban and poorer versus elite backgrounds truly have radically different experiences with foreign popular culture, challenging, in the end, portraits of those forces assumed to endanger their lives.

Girls in Town: An Independent Sister

Dalia is a feisty yet modest 21-year-old, an age typical for a student in the final year at *lycée*. She lives with her younger sister on a quiet street in Ambanja in a house that belongs to a maternal aunt, who in turn lives nearby and who owns a great deal of neighborhood property. Their house is simple, placed on a concrete foundation and built primarily out of *ravinala* palm. It consists of two rooms, one rented to another tenant; Dalia and her sister share the other. Inside this room are two single beds, two small tables, and a squat, unstable bookshelf upon which these girls store some of their study materials. Other notebooks are stacked high on a large tin can with a touch of kerosene inside, designed to prevent insects and rodents from devouring these precious items. The house is always neat and tidy, the beds covered with hand-embroidered sheets. Cooking pots are stacked carefully in one corner, and the front courtyard always appears freshly swept. This room is dark but airy, especially when the two windows are open. They can ill afford electricity, so at night Dalia and her sister rely on feeble oil lamps when they do their homework assignments.

When I met Dalia in 1994, she had lived in various locations in the Sambirano Valley since 1979. She is the oldest of eight children, the youngest being three years old. Dalia's parents live in a village a few kilometers north of Ambanja, so Dalia and her sister turn to their aunt when they are in need of immediate guidance and emotional support. Together these sisters bear much of the economic burden associated with their schooling. Formally they pay no rent to their aunt for their small house, but they regularly bring her gifts as informal payments. These include such luxury goods as yogurt and soap or fresh produce bought locally at the market, a portion of which they keep for their own use. Over the course of any given month these expenses amount to approximately 15,000–20,000 Malagasy francs (fmg), a price that is strikingly high when viewed as a rent payment for their single room. Much of their food expenditure is on rice; each month they eat about one *daba* (a measurement made using an old kerosene can), which costs approximately 38,000 fmg.[5]

Water is drawn from a nearby well for free. Dalia's parents do not own the land upon which they currently live; they sharecrop about half an acre. Dalia and her sister go home on foot nearly every weekend to work their parents' fields.

Dalia is an articulate and serious student who is respected among her peers for her strong will, her clearly defined desires, and her wry sense of humor. She is driven and serious when it comes to her schoolwork, and she strives regularly to help others, evident in the fact that she organized an evening *lycée* study group in preparation for the *baccalauréat* exam. Unlike many students, Dalia is not easily discouraged. When asked, for example, what she did or did not like about school, she at first looked at me with a puzzled expression and then explained that the question's difficulty lay in the fact that she so greatly enjoyed all of her subjects. She is in many ways an extraordinary student; most striking is the fact that she opted to take the *baccalauréat* exam in French, rather than in Official Malagasy; her spoken French is superb.

By 1994, Dalia was preparing for her second attempt at the *baccalauréat*. She wished passionately to attend a university, where she hoped to be trained as a teacher of philosophy or of history and geography. If she succeeded she would continue a tradition in her family; both of her parents are retired primary school teachers who attended a prestigious training school. As I learned in 1995, Dalia did in fact pass her exams, and by mid-1996 she was working in the provincial capital of Diégo-Suarez. She had, however, been unable to afford the modest cost of attending the local university. In this way Dalia's experiences typify those of serious coastal students: Even after successfully completing the arduous curricula of primary and secondary schooling, she has been unable to attend a national university. Contrary to local prejudice, pregnancy has not prevented her from completing her studies; as a schoolgirl with a serious boyfriend, she is well versed in abortifacients drawn from the local pharmacopoeia, and she makes use of the pubic health clinic's family planning program. Furthermore, her world remains far removed from the criminal activities assumed to plague the young school migrant's life. It is economic hardship that has kept so successful a student away from the university.

Worldly Diversions

In spite of the evidence offered by such students as Dalia and by teachers with firsthand contact with students, other adults in town overwhelmingly express the opinion that independent migrant children of village origins are the worst in school. This springs largely from urban prejudices about "the bush" (FR: *la brusse*) or "the countryside" (FR: *de la compagne*, SAK: *an-ban-volo*, literally, from "near the forest") as opposed to "in town" (FR: *en ville*,

SAK: *an-tanambe*). Almost in defiance of French connotations, these expressions are not used to convey backwardness so much as to stress an assumed innocence of rural people and, therefore, their susceptibility to urban dangers. By drawing on these expressions, Ambanja's adult inhabitants underscore the pervasiveness of threats that town life poses to the social and intellectual well-being of youth. All children require protection from such forces, but independent children of rural origin are perceived as being the easiest prey because their previous rural lives were devoid of many of the pernicious forces associated with cosmopolitanism. A subtext at work is that rural youth are incapable of *ever* adjusting to town life, as though innocence were inherent in their characters (see Pomponio, 1992).

Town life is often described as being rife with tempting distractions (FR: *diversions*). The fact that a French term is used is important here, because it underscores the recurrent belief that the majority of urban dangers originate abroad (SAK: *an-dafy*, FR: *de l'extérieur*). Such assumptions, however, are blind to the economic realities that characterize the lives of migrant students like Dalia. Ironically, it is town-based elite youth who have greater opportunities to experience forms of town entertainment. With this in mind, I now turn to those arenas that are consistently identified as the most menacing to the students' well-being.

For over a decade, the movie house (or, now, the video cinema), discotheque, and television have surfaced repeatedly in discussions and interviews with urban adults whenever the topic shifts to schooling and parenting. (Other people's) children are imagined as flocking to these venues in droves. Such fears are reminiscent of parental concerns cross-culturally, yet it must be stressed that the tenor of concerns as voiced in Ambanja reflects *localized* understandings of social decorum and the proper socialization of children. These venues are not considered dangerous simply because they are sexually charged spaces but rather because they are a threat to individual and collective morality. At risk are students' scholastic productivity and psychic well-being as well as community stability, where school migrants are perceived of as harbingers of social danger.

Video cinemas and discotheques together do indeed pose a significant financial threat, because students who spend time in either setting regularly will most certainly be short of essential funds for school supplies and food. In turn, videos (and television as well) are said to endanger students because they offer examples of superficial concerns: Kung-fu heroes, obsessed with their desire to perfect their kickboxing skills, do not focus steadily and seriously on their schoolwork. Such well-known stars as Arnold Schwarzenegger, Sylvester Stallone, and a host of Italian-produced cowboys and American soldiers lost and abandoned in Vietnam are similarly considered inappropriate social models. After all, they are consumed by a passion for revenge (or justice) and as such are loners adrift in worlds often bereft of social relations.

At the heart of such fears is a concern that the social persona of school-aged youth may very well be transformed into one far distant from current adult understandings of social worth (understandings that are often conflated as if no variation exists across class, ethnic, or regional lines). Of particular note is that educated parents and school administrators are the most concerned, and their comments often quickly take on a paternalistic tone. Mr. Jaozara, a history teacher at the state-run *lycée*, expressed such sentiments in these terms:

> I believe that [exposure to these things ultimately] transforms the mentality [FR: *la mentalité*] ... [of our] students—they don't respect their [adult kin]—*this* is the crisis of our youth today.... They understand only the very [rudimentary aspects] of Malagasy culture.... The films, with Stallone and others—oh, I don't know, I can't keep up with them!—but what I see is this: they see a film and it affects them *internally*—I see a change in their comportment, in their self understanding. They have no desire to acquire knowledge—they don't want to understand, to comprehend, or to work at the things that affect their [immediate] lives.⁶

It would be naïve to deny that exposure to videos of foreign origin has no impact on the psyches of Ambanja's youth; after all, exposure to a greater world beyond lies at the very heart of schooling in Ambanja, a fact that, interestingly, remains unproblematic for town adults. Yet adults assume that town life by itself will transform students' dreams and desires so that they will ultimately stand in opposition to those embraced by a previous generation of adults. A further underlying assumption is that transformation is a unique threat to the *current* generation. Such critiques are fairly easy to embrace, especially if one finds comfort in romanticizing the past (SAK: *taloha*) and local "traditions" (SAK: *fomba*, or more specifically, *fombandrazaña*, "ancestral customs"). This vision of contemporary life, however, is bereft of subtlety; furthermore, it is based on misconceptions of who, in fact, frequents video cinemas and discotheques and what it is such participants take away with them.

Video Cinemas, Television, and Discos

Over the course of nearly a decade of research in Ambanja, the town's school administrators, teachers, and parents have consistently reiterated a theme when asked about problems facing local youth. Local video cinemas and discotheques are typically described as powerful forces of foreign origin that "destroy our children" or "their minds," "are responsible for school failure rates," "keep our children out of school," and "undermine their respect for local customs [*fombandrazaña*]" and "for one's parents." Another frequent assumption is that school migrants, lacking any adult supervision, are far more likely to succumb to the allure of these institutions, spending their study time and limited funds on such corrupting *diversions*. By mid-month they have nothing left with which to buy food or such essential school supplies as paper and pens. It is said that they stay out late, carousing and drinking heavily; then, being penniless, boys become petty thieves and girls turn to prostitution. All of these factors are said to contribute to the moral demise of students who fall asleep in school, fail their studies, or altogether disappear from the classroom.

Throughout my research I have found, however, that very few migrant school youth have, in fact, ever set foot inside a disco or video cinema. Those who do are from relatively well-off, town-based households. Material concerns figure prominently in determining such trends. Students like Dalia consider a video entrance fee of 500 fmg to be prohibitive; discotheques are even farther out of reach because they typically cost twice as much or more. To spend one's money in this way ensures that one will indeed go hungry; 500 fmg alone can be the price one must pay for several days of rice. Therefore, it is only students with extra pocket money who can afford such luxuries.

Dalia, for example, when asked, "what do you like to do for fun?" responded, "I love to listen to the radio." At first I assumed this meant that she liked French pop music, because of the posters of rock singers that decorate her walls. Instead, she surprised me by replying, "ahh, no, I love sentimental Malagasy music ... and I like to [FR:] *promenade*, that is, [SAK:] *mitsangantsangana* [walk about town with friends]." "Do you go to discos or the cinema?" I asked. "No, I hate discos. I go to maybe one a year. They're expensive, you know—during holidays they can be as much as 7,500 fmg, and they're regularly 3,000 or 1,500 fmg."

School migrants are free, however, to join other townsfolk in watching the public television set mounted outside City Hall. When this occurs, students typically do so with a small group of friends, but what might begin as a collective viewing eventually gives way to lively conversation on other topics, because the set itself is small and the reception poor, making it difficult to view it from the ground. Also, what they do in fact view is far different from what adults imagine. The majority of broadcasts shown throughout the course of my fieldwork were sports matches, because this was the pronounced preference of the agent who controlled the town's single channel satellite connection. I did encounter a few other students who had stepped into a discotheque, but they did so only because a much wealthier (and, inevitably, town-based) classmate paid their entrance fee.

Non-migrant, town-based youth who come from homes of at least moderate (and more likely, elite) incomes have much greater access to broadcasts of foreign origin. These are the offspring of upper-level civil servants and successful merchants and professionals. They have access to pocket money; they may have a television and VCR in their homes, so that they can view one of the many videos that make their way about town; and they have more spare time on their hands because they share household duties with other siblings, parents, or servants. They are also free on weekends, unlike migrant school youth, who return frequently to their villages to farm. During their school breaks many migrant school youth also desperately seek out wage labor or go home to the countryside for several months to assist with a series of harvests. Most striking of all, however, is that overall I have found that neither discotheques nor video cinemas are heavily frequently by school youth, regardless of their background. Instead, on any given night the vast majority of attendees are not students at all, but slightly older adults, ranging in age from the mid-twenties to late thirties, who are members of the urban proletariat or professionals, such as teachers and civil servants. Only on Saturday afternoons is one likely to encounter students in large numbers viewing videos at the Alliance Française, the majority of whom come specifically to improve their French. They may view popular Westerns imported from India, Italian-made "commando" films, or Asian-made marshal arts extravaganzas. Again, the vast majority are not school migrants, but town-based youth. When I asked one school migrant, who loved the cinema, why he did not attend the less-expensive shows hosted by the Alliance, he responded as follows: "Even [100 fmg] is high if you consider what you may need to spend on kerosene or charcoal the next day."

The imagined threat of these venues is driven in part by their political potential, a fear that is hinted at in the language used by the history teacher, Mr. Jaozara. As he explains, video viewing can warp the *mentalité* of Ambanja's youth. His concerns (and choice of terminology) are rooted in realities that are historically based. During the colonial era, cinema and theater productions were regularly scrutinized for subversive material, and Malagasy community leaders and elders often sat on town censorship boards to determine how their contents might affect a collective indigenous *mentalité* (CAOM, 1930: DS0422, 1932–1954: PM0014). Much later, under President Ratsiraka, a few daring political opponents used film as a means to raise the consciousness of the nation's peasantry, touring small villages in trucks loaded with generators and film equipment. These films and the discussions that followed operated as powerful forms of subversive propaganda designed to persuade small-scale farmers to vote against Ratsiraka. On the one hand, Mr. Jaozara's comments appear to champion the cause of youth, because on the surface his tone seems protective of their needs. On the other hand, however, they smack of condescension, because he assumes that school youth are unable to filter messages and images of foreign origin. Such a statement is made with little regard for the style of teaching that has characterized his own work over the last two decades, where the tone and content of his and other teachers' lectures have been dictated by the political agendas of the state. What appears to underlie his comments is a deep-seated concern that adults cannot control how students will interpret such visual media. As Paul Richards's (1994) work among child soldiers in Sierra Leone reveals, African youth do indeed draw upon what they see on film, yet they transform the associated imagery in surprising and original ways to make sense of the disparities that plague their daily lives.

Contrary to adults' assumptions, most school migrants cannot afford the town's threatening *diversions*. The supposed corruption of Ambanja's youth is not so much a matter of living independently as a process that is class-based and a sign of privilege. Whereas Dalia and others who saunter together at night can only view foreign broadcasts by watching the town's mediocre public television, the children of elite and middle income households experience far greater exposure to foreign media. The *diversions* of children of the poorest households consist primarily of outdoor, inventive forms of social play. The youngest children can often be seen running together outside in wild packs, playing energetically with whatever tools they might encounter in the street: sticks turned into arrows, spears, swords, and guns; abandoned car chassis converted into percussion instruments; and a *bricolage* of plant material, wire, and twine that they fold, twist, and bend into elaborately fashioned miniature cars and other toys (Cerny & Seriff, 1996). As a result, the poorer the child, the greater the demand placed on the imagination for daily distraction and games, and the more limited the exposure to media of foreign origin.

Town-Based Girls

Elite children form a radically different social category. They stand apart in that they are rarely permitted to venture into the street, confined instead to their own or each other's homes, where, cooped up and bored, they rely heavily on the distractions offered by privately owned televisions and VCRs. Such children often repeatedly watch bootleg music and film videos copied from

French television and smuggled into Madagascar. These videos slowly make their way about town, passed from one elite household to another. They are just as likely to contain dubbed reruns of such American television series as *Starsky and Hutch* or *Dallas* as they are other films far more violent or sexually explicit in their dialogue, lyrics, and visual displays. Elite children have the added advantage of being able to understand what is being said, because they are often fluent in French.

Such contrasts are illustrated by the life of little Rova, the precocious oldest daughter of highland elite parents who have lived in Ambanja for several years. In mid-1995 Rova had just turned seven. Rova's father is a powerful plantation director, her mother a housewife and part-time petty merchant. This family employs three full-time house servants, as well as a private chauffeur, and they inhabit a luxuriously furnished three-bedroom house that is partially air-conditioned and has two bathrooms with European plumbing. Their most prestigious possessions are two cars, a large color television, and a VCR. Little Rova attends the town's exclusive French Elementary School, where she is known as Rosalie and where she speaks only French (as she does at home with her parents). She never ventures outside unescorted by an adult, and she is allowed to travel the town's peaceful streets only when driven by the family chauffeur. Her playmates are handpicked by her mother and are always the offspring of other elite families that double as important business contacts for her father. Rova spends much of her time at home, her only regular companions being her younger brother and two family maids, to whom Rova feels little emotional attachment. In a word, Rova is bored: Although she loves to read, she has no books, and her toys are typically so expensive that they spend much of their time out of reach and on display in a tall glass case in the family parlor. When Rova has nothing else to do, she repeatedly watches her parents' rotating collection of borrowed videos, many of which contain frightening images of brutal murders and often lurid sex scenes that drastically counter modest Malagasy conceptions of public displays of affection. On many an afternoon I have found Rova sitting by herself on the sofa, her mouth agape as she stares in awe at the images displayed before her.

A Wayward Daughter

Older children of prosperous families are most likely to become involved in the town's night life because they, like Rova, have far more leisure time than Dalia and her sister ever will. They also have access to the necessary pocket money. Rova may very well escape the assumed outside dangers of the discotheque or video cinema simply because her parents will continue to keep her sequestered, sending her to boarding school in the central highlands as soon as she completes primary school. As explained above, however, by age seven she is more aware of things foreign than other girls twice her age.

The story of Yasmine, who grew up in Ambanja, exposes some of the possibilities that may lie in store for older town-based daughters from prosperous households like Rova. Yasmine is the 23-year-old daughter of Alida, a woman whose story I have followed closely since 1987 (Sharp, 1993: 214ff).[7] She exemplifies the life of a prosperous middle-income family. Yasmine's mother Alida is the widow of a highly respected school principal and is well-known in town for her expert nursing skills. As a result, Alida's name is practically a household word in town. When Alida's husband died, he had provided well for her; she now owns a large, five-room concrete house, furnished with comfortable and sturdy furniture, a color television and stereo, a gas stove, and a refrigerator. A side room houses an Italian sewing machine where she receives clients as a skilled part-time seamstress. Yasmine is the second child and oldest daughter in a family of six children. In 1987 Alida was deeply concerned for her children's futures. She longed for her oldest son to attend university and succeed in medicine, as had her own father, and thus she appealed repeatedly to a well-known spirit medium for powerful magic that would boost his chances for success. Yasmine, on the other hand, had become a source of much frustration and worry. She was often seen carousing with men close to or beyond her own mother's age. Alida feared her daughter would become pregnant before completing her studies, only to be thrown aside by a wealthy philanderer. The spirit medium threatened the daughter with spiritual wrath if she did not obey her mother and take her studies seriously. When I returned to Ambanja in the mid-1990s, I found that Yasmine's mother's fears had in part materialized: Yasmine had indeed failed her studies at the Catholic Academy and had since spent much of her time idle at home. At this point, she was the mistress of an older, wealthy married man who would pick her up each afternoon in his air-conditioned Peugeot. Although Alida knew the man would never marry her daughter, she was resigned to Yasmine's actions.

Town opinion was divided on this and similar affairs that cut across the categories of age and class. As some informants argued, Yasmine was capable of bearing the responsibilities of adult life. She should not be condemned for her actions because it was clear that her mother appreciated the additional wealth that now flowed regularly into her home as a result of her daughter's lucrative love interest. To others, however, Yasmine had clearly sacrificed her virtue to become a mistress or *deuxième bureau*[8] to a powerful married man. In their eyes she was reduced to nothing more than a prostitute or *makarely*

(SAK from FR: *maquereau*, "mackerel," or maquerelle, "Madam"). These latter sentiments could only be expressed in the slang of a foreign tongue, mistress and prostitute being introduced into northern Madagascar as lucrative roles for indigenous women by the agents of colonial power. All agreed that Yasmine had sealed her fate; in time her lover would probably abandon her, so that she would most likely drift from one man to another in search of the wealth and prestige that inevitably accompany such unbalanced relationships.

If we look back at Yasmine's experiences, we find that schooling imposes especially difficult hardships on this girl and others her age. The greatest burdens spring from the troubles associated with sexual awareness, where the most obvious hurdles arise when a girl suddenly finds herself pregnant. All of Ambanja's public and private schools enforce strict sanctions against such girls. When it is clear they are pregnant, they are immediately expelled from school and, typically, close kin are contacted by school officials so that they can care for the pregnant girl at home until she bears her child. In recent years the state-run *lycée* has begun to readmit girls once their babies are born (a practice that is not followed at the Catholic Academy). Few girls are able to juggle the demands of young motherhood while attending school full-time unless their own mothers or other older female kin are willing to assume the responsibility of child care. Nearly all mothers in Ambanja breast-feed exclusively, so they must remain in close and constant proximity to their babies throughout the first year of life. As a former school director argued at an education conference in the mid-1980s, Madagascar could not hope to make strides in controlling adolescent pregnancy as long as boys went unpunished and were allowed to remain in school (Sharp, 1990). His words, however, fell on deaf ears, and the burden of pregnancy (expressed by the SAK term *mavesatra* or, literally, "[to be] heavy") remains the responsibility of these young single mothers.

Ambanja's teachers argue that although a handful of girls each year are often among the best of their students, collectively girls show far less interest in completing their studies. The reasons that inform such impressions are complex. For one, many village-raised girls never even make it past primary school because their parents are often reluctant to send them on to school, particularly if this requires that they become school migrants. However, older brothers, once they finish their own schooling, may convince parents to allow their gifted younger sisters to come live under their care and protection. Under such circumstances, parents frequently acquiesce.

When schoolgirls do become pregnant, they may suffer from an extraordinary angst; they must face their parents' disapproval and, more important, great disappointment. Many of these girls are struck by disturbing forms of possession sickness through which they articulate their frustration, guilt, anger, and sorrow (Sharp, 1990). The average marriage age has climbed slowly for Malagasy boys over the course of the last two to three generations; their female peers, on the other hand, must withstand pressure exerted on them at a much younger age by older men, who may be local merchants, well-off travelers, or even their own schoolteachers.

The Immorality of Play: *Ny Soma*

How are we to analyze the current ethos regarding the corruption of Ambanja's school youth? Beneath prudish critiques of foreign media, discotheques, and other contexts that seemingly encourage sexualized forms of play lies an insidious array of moral values of colonial origin that have long since been internalized by adults. Judgments against Yasmine or the imagined activities of migrant school youth like Dalia reveal a double standard, especially when juxtaposed with the behavior of colonial men, many of whom took Malagasy women as mistresses or *deuxième bureaux*. If indigenous values are taken to be static things, defined by a reified sense of "culture" and "tradition" (SAK: *fomba*) then, indeed, discotheques and video cinemas are powerfully dangerous milieux, for they introduce exotic and newly eroticized forms of social interaction characterized by sexualized public displays, sanctioned promiscuity, machismo, and militarized violence. Such values may also impart an imbedded sense of inferiority and inevitable failure in the post-colonial mind (Fanon, 1963; Fisher, 1985). In Ambanja, hour-long sets of music videos that precede any feature showing are typically drawn from the Antilles, France, and the United States. These are generally opulent and eroticized displays of material consumption, where dark men escort light-skinned women in expensive cars, luxurious homes, or expensive boutiques, where the clothes are garish and the food consumed outlandish. As a viewer how can one hope to touch such luxuries when they remain unavailable even in the nation's metropole of Antananarivo? In the feature shows that follow one finds much of the inspiration for the repetitive themes of consumption that appear in the musical shorts. Clearly, the greatest social and economic power rests with the Anglo or Asian male, who is strong, single, and virile: Stallone and Schwarzenegger, Eastwood and other cowboys, and Bruce Lee and other kickboxers and kung-fu masters.

Objections are rooted in judgments inspired by a Western ideology in which the reified forces of mass media are considered inevitably destructive, particularly to the vulnerable minds of youth. As Sharon Stephens (1995a) and Amit-Talai and Wulff (1995) stress, social scientific paradigms of children assume an inherent vulnerability, where minors are essentially proto-adults, their provocative gestures signaling resistance but not cultural maturity. In other words, children may periodically attempt to challenge the status quo, but they are unable to critique culture or generate sustainable cultural forms.

Stephens's (1995b) emphasis on play provides a provocative alternative paradigm for challenging such assumptions. It is through inversions of cultural norms that the creative cultural imagination of youth emerges. The concept of play also allows for a reexamination of the value of cultural innovation over the assumed despoilment of a romanticized, static traditionalism. In this light, the discotheque exemplifies a milieu in which such *generative* (as opposed to *degenerate*) forces are at work. When considered within a framework of older cultural forms, the discotheque in fact appears not so much as a radical departure from social norms as a continuation of—albeit highly embellished—indigenous style of interaction and expression. More specifically, discotheques share much in common with festive, ritualized events familiar to indigenous Sakalava of the Sambirano Valley.

Nowhere is this more evident than during festivities hosted by local royalty. Within any large-scale royal ritual in the coastal northwest—a royal child's first haircutting, a prince's circumcision, a ruler's instatement ceremony, or the annual cleaning of royal tombs—much of the surrounding events are defined locally as valued moments of "play" (SAK: *misoma*) (cf. Camo, 1931, from the colonial period). These involve dances (especially the graceful *ribiky*); praise singing as well as bawdy songs; and possession ceremonies, during which both living subjects and ancient spiritual ancestors arrive to participate in such "games" (*ny soma*). Nighttime in particular is a liminal period of sexual intrigue, when adults *and* youth participate in group singing, dancing, and drinking; they also stroll about (*mitsangantsangana*), hoping for erotic encounters. In anticipation of such events, girls and women may spend significant amounts of money on new clothes. For large-scale royal events female attire most often consists of matching body and head wraps fashioned from commemorative cotton cloth (*lambahoany*) that has been designed and printed at the nation's textile mills for this specific event. Groups of young friends stick close together throughout the event, creating moving masses of bright colors as they sport their identical outfits.

Are such behaviors so different from what occurs in the discotheque? What are we to make of the specially organized disco party (*bal* or *boum*) held in the lobby of City Hall, a market center, the Catholic Mission, or a renovated royal palace (Sharp, 1997)? In such venues the night provides a veil behind which one may seek out new sexual partners and participate in eroticized play, where the female body is elaborately decorated with preordered and individually designed flashy garb, this time consisting of tailored dresses of bright satins or polyester silks. At these town events, a successful sexual encounter can involve pairing up with an anonymous single or married partner. In other words, the spirit with which one approaches the royal festival and disco events is similar; it is simply the milieu and attire that define where the most radical innovations occur. Implicit, however, is the understanding that whereas royal rituals collectively define an appropriate liminal space for such play, Ambanja's streets, video cinemas, and discotheques are dangerous milieux because they are so radically open and unbounded.

A certain prudishness of colonial origin also frames such judgments. Their paradoxical nature is best illustrated by the activities of the Catholic Mission (whose clergy and staff are overwhelmingly indigenous Sakalava). A highly celebrated all-night disco extravaganza—complete with a *salegy* band—serves as a significant fund-raiser for the local Catholic Mission. Even clergy participate in the Mission's lively atmosphere during these events; one nun in particular is well-known in town by the nickname "Sister Disco." Non-Sakalava Catholics and Protestants generally shun such events, publicly declaring them sacrilegious (although they might, in fact, attend them). Such attitudes toward the use of the animated body display a prudishness of foreign origin, one that collides with an indigenous sense of the joyfulness of social play. In other words, once the urban, Euro-Christian patina is penetrated, it is difficult to distinguish the spirit with which one participates in such festive events, be they staged at a village ceremony or on an urban disco dance floor.

SIDA and Sexual Danger

Here the discussion could close, were it not for the current complications that link sexual intimacy and infection. Sex in Africa is now fraught with danger, as the shadow of AIDS, or *SIDA* (*syndrome d'immuno-déficience acquise*), as it is known in the francophone world, lies dormant yet dangerous, infecting many young people in the prime of life. In Madagascar, concerns over *SIDA* have changed radically since the 1980s, when coastal prostitutes tested seronegative in a national health survey. By 1994, however, *SIDA* was openly recognized as a serious threat that had invaded Madagascar's borders, brought from abroad not so much by Malagasy travelers but by thrill-seeking foreign sailors and tourists drawn to this island by dreams of sexual encounters with exotic African women. This shift in perception stemmed in part from the fact that the newly elected president, Zafy Albert, was a doctor. His regime also marked the end of Ratsiraka's isolationalist stance, so that the Malagasy encountered far more foreigners than they had during the previous two decades. By 1994 health clinics displayed posters on *SIDA*, radio soap operas included stories about the infected, and public health materials were integrated into primary and middle school curricula, reinforcing the pervasive assumption that students' lives were fraught with sexual danger.[9] At home, children and parents began to debate the topic, with children usually being far more informed than their parents on biological modes of transmission. On this isolated island nation, the danger of encountering the disease is perceived to lie with foreigners, whose own history is driven by the colonial enterprise. In the world of the post-colony, assumptions about *SIDA* shape judgments of social interaction, necessitating the weeding out of prudish reactions levied against the expressive use of the body (see Parker, 1991). A number of these issues were altogether too clear to some of my more astute young informants.

On several occasions I discussed *SIDA* with urban school youth, and these conversations generated several common responses. Among the most pronounced involved contrasts between an assumed fast-paced, urban life versus village ignorance. Second was a pervasive concern that *SIDA* had finally invaded Madagascar's borders, brought by foreigners from overseas. Students identified lethal carriers as being of European, Comorean, or continental African origin, but not Malagasy. Third was a strong association between prostitution and infection. As one young man, named Foringa, explained, "[in school they tell us] *'tsy mijangajanga'*—'don't go sleeping around' like a prostitute, or *'tsy mañano makotipa'* ['don't go to bordellos']." These and other related expressions involve plays on words; for example, the diminutive of *mijanga*, literally, "to stand upright" or "to be healthy," implies danger. As Foringa explained, "You say *mijangajanga* because it is a person who is in great shape—and so they want to go out and about, they want to strut their stuff. . . . But in the end they aren't healthy. And so the message here is, 'don't be a prostitute.'"[10]

It was Dalia, however, who provided one of the most compelling critiques. As she explained in response to Foringa's statements:

> But you know, it's more complex than this. It's just a new form of exploitation: foreigners have imposed their *fomba* [customs], their ways on us from the beginning of colonial contact. They like to tell the Malagasy what to do, and what is wrong with our culture. They don't like our marriage practices, they don't like our royal customs [*fom-bandrazaña*]. And now, look what they are doing—they say, we have too many children, we have too much sex. And so now they impose the threat of *SIDA* upon us, too.[11]

These two students' statements offer complementary readings of the assumptions that plague localized perceptions of gender within the dangerous urban space of Ambanja. Whereas Foringa's statement rests squarely on dominant readings of the dangers of sexuality, Dalia offers a far more radical critique of its underpinnings.

SIDA *in the Post-Colony*

Paul Farmer (1992), in his study of Haiti, delineates three levels of analysis that make up what he has aptly labeled the "geography of blame" associated with *SIDA* (cf. Lindenbaum's earlier analysis of the "geography of fear," 1979: 137), where three circles of danger coexist. Within the village one confronts the first level of "accusation" as jealousy and sorcery; moving outward, accusation is shaped by racist sentiments; and, finally, the nation as a whole rests at the periphery of the world, where *SIDA*'s destruction is a manifestation of empire. Dalia's astute comments echo this final circle of blame. As such, she offers a compelling critique of *SIDA*, one not normally heard—and therefore, one that is often silenced—in the literature on this worldwide epidemic (see Treichler, 1989: 43 as cited in Farmer 1992: 235, as well as Harrison-Chirimuuta & Chirimuuta, 1997). As the nation emerges from long-term socialist isolation, *SIDA* itself is a virulent form of neo-imperialism, its lethal carriers being foreigners who arrive on the island for tourism and trade.

Such beliefs are shaped by an essential component of collective identity in Madagascar, that is, that Malagasy consider themselves inhabitants of a highly isolated island nation. As a result, Dalia and others raised during the socialist era are sensitive to an assumed impenetrability of their national boundary, where the ocean has long served as a barrier against invasion by foreign troops, goods, and cultural values. During the socialist era foreigners were, in fact, kept away from the island's shores. Air travel, radio transmission, and, more recently, television via satellite, however, had become more pervasive by the early 1990s, generating new forms of contact media against which the ocean's boundaries have proved impotent. Dalia, Foringa, Rova, and Jasmine can all watch the French television station RFO, transmitted to Ambanja via satellite, the first two in the town square, the other two at home. Meanwhile, with the end of the nation's isolationist policies, eco-tourists and other foreign pleasure seekers now flood the island. *SIDA* is among the invisible yet lethal forces that have made their recent appearance here.

By 1994, a great deal of folklore had been generated within Madagascar surrounding the mysterious and lethal quality of *SIDA*. These stories are reminiscent of the Latin American stories involving the snatching of children for adoption or for their body parts by North Americans (Campion-Vincent, 1997; Leventhal, 1994). Folklore surrounding *SIDA* in Madagascar is now a popular genre that reflects localized perceptions of foreign exploitation. As the following story reveals, the most susceptible victims are believed to be girls and young women. Yvetty, the mother of three children and a trader who travels frequently to Antananarivo, provided the following chilling tale:

> Outside Madagascar, a team of foreign scientists has discovered that the *SIDA* virus can be found clustered prominently in girl's brains. For this reason there is a clandestine trade, a black market, that involves acquiring their heads! A bus driver told me this story: A middle aged woman gets on a bus, and she's carrying a basket that is very heavy. She's really careful with the basket, and she won't let anyone touch it. It has to stay with her all the time, even though it's big and takes up a lot of room, because she refused to let the driver put it on the roof. When it comes time to pay the bus fare to the driver, however, she doesn't have any change, and so she sets off in search of some, leaving her basket behind. It is during her absence that the contents are discovered: the basket gets in someone's way, and so they disturb it, knocking it over and exposing what's inside. It is full of the severed heads of young women! She has killed them and cut off their heads to sell them to her contact overseas, who wants them for research purposes to develop a serum against *SIDA!*[12]

Farmer (1992) has assembled similar "conspiracy" tales surrounding *SIDA* in Haiti. As he argues, these stories are powerful critiques of the political economy of disease in a nation where greed and corruption may in fact lead to the marketing of blood and other body products to wealthy nations (1992: 230–231, 239ff). More important than our ability to verify such stories, however, is the manner in which they expose the raw feelings of the exploited. The political metaphors associated with AIDS/*SIDA* operate in *both* directions. S. Lindenbaum, for example, writes as follows of Western perceptions of world epidemics: "By the 1990's, our *security* was further undermined by the worldwide emergence of *new and resurgent* epidemic diseases [such as AIDS and other diseases]" (1997: 191; emphasis added; for a detailed discussion of the political aspects of such metaphors see Martin, 1994; Sontag 1989). From a Haitian or Malagasy point of view, such apocryphal tales may easily be interpreted as weapons that the weak direct at more powerful international targets (see Scott, 1985), whose government officials may in fact be compelled to respond to counteract their effects (see Leventhal, 1994). Yet from Ambanja such tales also reflect other sentiments, including a deep-seated anger at yet another invasion by foreign forces—first by highlanders, then French colonists, who in turn facilitated the arrival of non-Sakalava labor migrants and, now, foreign tourists. A tale I encountered several times in Ambanja identified an anonymous Frenchman as the town's first victim of *SIDA*, a man said to have fallen ill at a local hotel and who later died there alone and far from any loving kin.

As Paula Ebron (1997) reminds us, European tourist women remain invisible partners in the sex trades throughout Africa; as the story above shows, however, indigenous women are granted an altogether different fate. If we look closely at the gruesome tale told by the lively storyteller Yvetty, we find that it focuses on a social category of person identified repeatedly by town informants as both victim and villain: the young, sexually active female who inevitably emerges in local discourse as a *makarely* or prostitute. As the primary locus of social concern, the prostitute is, on the one hand, young, strong, healthy, and daring, but on the other hand she now, under the shadow of *SIDA*, may ultimately undermine the health of an entire nation because her actions cannot be controlled. As Foringa explains above, the dominant message is "don't be a prostitute." As such, it is the *makarely* who bears the potential of becoming a localized Malagasy Typhoid Mary.

In this context, Dalia's critique emerges as a sophisticated understanding of *SIDA*-as-epidemic, in which health lessons regarding *SIDA* expose yet another form of foreign imperialism. As Madagascar emerges from isolation, it draws heavily on the aid offered by wealthier countries. Africa is frequently regarded by foreign policymakers as a cite of "explosions," ranging from civil warfare, to droughts and famine, to epidemics. As Maryinez Lyons explains, responses may assume the form of "scientific imperialism" (1997: 136ff) as foreign advisors attempt to shape the trajectories of responses. In reference to AIDS/*SIDA* in particular, these research agendas are inevitably laced with racist sentiments about Africa (see Fleming, 1990; Harrison-Chirimuuta & Chirimuuta, 1997). In Dalia's words, "they say, we have too many children, we have too much sex. And so now they impose the threat of *SIDA* upon us, too." The question raised here is, how are Malagasy women the victims of *SIDA:* as objects of foreign desire, as infected patients, or as targets of foreign health campaigns? Dalia reminds us that, in fact, they are all of these.

From Yvetty we can glean yet other meanings. In the much-imagined international trade in human body parts (Scheper-Hughes, 2000), the most highly valued bodies (or, in Madagascar, heads and brains) may be those of young women and girls. Herein lie references to the political economy of scarce and precious commodities of a macabre nature, in which the bodies of African women can be harvested to serve the needs of the wealthy abroad (see Farmer, 1992: 230–231). Only once quality items are exhausted will they perhaps return home, serving the needs of the elite before the final dregs fall to the nation's poor in a dangerous and virulent form. To borrow Michael Taussig's phrasing, such are the realities of the "magic of [the] modern" (1987: 274–283).

Conclusion: Girls, Sex, and Urban Danger

Yvetty's story conveys, in nightmarish symbolic terms, the anger and fear that plague urban coastal sentiments shown to be so pervasive in Ambanja. During colonial occupation, Malagasy women were prime targets for very particular forms of attention, taken as mistresses by men of foreign origin and thrust into prostitution in ports and other towns. As this chapter shows, vulnerability, guilt, and danger are currently associated with the lives of school girls in ways unknown to their brothers and male partners. Their suffering is unique in that, first, their failure in school is so closely paired with pregnancy; second, they so often bear the local shame associated with assumed prostitution; and, third, they must now shoulder the responsibility of national death from *SIDA*. The bodies of urban women and, more specifically, migrant schoolgirls emerge as a contested terrain upon which local anxieties are played out, regardless of the actual innocence of these moral victims. Bluntly put, an inevitably destructive path is clearly mapped out for independent schoolgirls. Their quest for advanced education draws them away from their rural homes and into the dangers of urban life, where they are assumed to fall victim to foreign forms of popular culture in milieux that ruin them financially and that drive them toward dangerous sexual encounters. As localized narratives make abundantly clear, it is young, urban Malagasy women who must consistently bear the heavy and often lethal burden of sexual trespass as their community and nation repeatedly fall victim to the predatory nature of foreign desires.

15
The Moving Frontier of AIDS in Uganda

Contexts, Texts, and Concepts

GEORGE CLEMENT BOND AND JOAN VINCENT
*Teachers College and Barnard College,
Columbia University*

Introduction

The human immunodeficiency virus (HIV) and the acquired immunodeficiency syndrome (AIDS) have afflicted more than 24 million Africans. HIV/AIDS is a powerful reality that has affected the daily lives of Africans and drawn upon their meager resources and those of their domestic units, communities, and governments. Since the recognition of AIDS in 1981 it has become a major pandemic, generating its own historical and social domain. In its steady progression it has brought into its deadly wake a range of social agents from the individual afflicted with the disease to major international organizations. In this chapter we seek to map the physical and social progression of HIV/AIDS in Uganda and, through the examination of research projects and their texts, to represent the manner in which the disease has been framed since its recognition in 1983. We are thus concerned with the history and politics of the disease and the contradictions between knowledge and action that they formed.

Within the domain of this pandemic one may observe the importance of geographical locations for research and the making of policies. The reports, based on specific localities, are sometimes used to generalize about the pan-

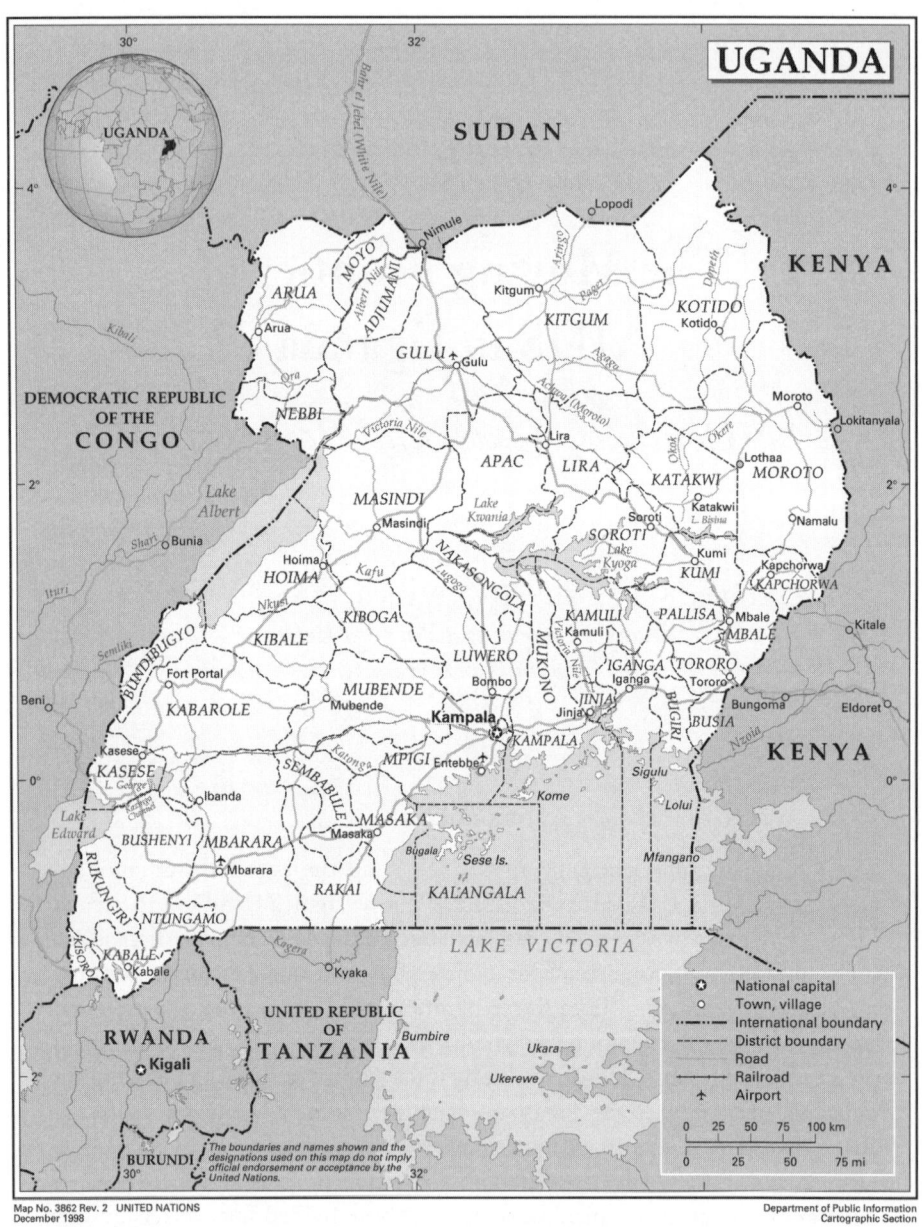

Map of Uganda, Map No. 3862 R.2, UN Cartographic Section. Permission granted by the United Nations.

demic for entire regions and countries, often obscuring political and social conditions as well as the effects of the disease. In the early stages of research, AIDS produced its own variety of African studies, one that was often insensitive to or possibly unaware of the complexities of African history, politics, and local beliefs, practices, and customs. In this chapter we intend to set the AIDS epidemic within the context of Ugandan history. The thrust of the argument is that much of the research on Uganda has been undertaken mainly in the south, but findings and paradigms have been generalized to all of Uganda.

The chapter seeks to map the physical, social, and intellectual geography of HIV/AIDS in Uganda. It situates the study of HIV/AIDS within the colonial and post-colonial history of Uganda and its social configurations and political upheavals. The physical point of reference for HIV/AIDS research has been the southern part of the country, in pre-colonial times the seat of powerful, expanding indigenous states, and under colonial rule, the center of agro-capitalist development.

The south, dominant in shaping Uganda's history, has become its center of knowledge on AIDS. Medical and social policies for monitoring and controlling the spread of the disease and treating its victims are based on information gathered primarily in the south. The north and northeast have remained at the margins, with much less known about the epidemic there.

The "security situation" has been a strong factor in locating AIDS research. Since the recognition of AIDS in 1983, Uganda has experienced a succession of political, ethnic, and religious conflicts. However, almost from the very beginning of AIDS research in Uganda, D. Serwadda and E. Katongole-Mbidde have deplored the quoting of data from small local surveys as representative of the entire country (1990: 843), as has occurred too frequently in descriptions of Uganda. Here, our point is the (unintended) complicity of AIDS research in obscuring the conditions in which HIV/AIDS is embedded in entire regions of Uganda. In considering these academic and popular representations of "Uganda," significant areas of the nation and numbers of its citizens are being, as it were, "written off." Unaccounted for in current AIDS research is territory that comprises the better part of 50 percent of the nation's land area and some 44 percent of its population.

The chapter is divided into four parts. The first examines HIV/AIDS as a moving frontier, mapping its steady progression. As a disease without a history, AIDS has involved an ongoing process of medical and social discovery of its attributes and social effects. In Uganda, the south became the main focus of study. The second part situates the epidemic within the context of social conflict and upheavals that have characterized much of the post-colonial history of Uganda. The third part explores the cultural or intellectual maps of researchers. It examines the types of texts that were generated through research, their relation to funding and political circumstances, and the shifts in focus that have occurred in HIV/AIDS research. The final part turns to the manner in which the central government has increasingly redefined the role of the international AIDS community in Uganda, its scope of activity, and its target populations. The government has steadily expanded its range of concern to include not only those afflicted with AIDS but also the weak and vulnerable.

The Moving Frontier: The Contextualization of a Pandemic

The idea of a "moving frontier," be it of knowledge, conquest, or of HIV/AIDS, emphasizes the importance of location and situation and the nature of time and space in the structuring of social and economic relationships, the production of knowledge such as in the form of generalized images and the making of history. The idea of a moving frontier combines two perspectives, one physical and the other intellectual. The first involves the cultural mapping of geographical distributions, whether of activities, events, or relationships. The second is the social and political concepts or conceptualizations that are used in constructing, representing, and explaining the "maps." As a point of departure, this type of formulation has been particularly useful in predicting the location and progression of HIV/AIDS in both Africa and Uganda. Now, a decade later, we use this approach to review reports and situate AIDS at one and the same time in both present-day Uganda and middle-range social theory.

East and Southern Africa

HIV/AIDS was first recognized in the United States in 1981 and first described in black Africans in 1983 (Serwadda & Katongole-Mbidde, 1990). An AIDS-related enteropathy had been identified in Uganda in autumn 1982, but AIDS in Africa was first confirmed in western Zaire and Rwanda in 1983–1984 (Grmek, 1990: 172–173, 177–179; Simmons, Farmer & Schoepf, 1996: 63–66). During this very early phase of the disease there was much discussion within epidemiology about the modes of transmission, the patterns of distribution, and the direction of progression of HIV/ AIDS in East and Southern Africa. It was a new disease without a history, with an unknown potential for human and social destruction. Teams of biomedical researchers were assembled, many of whom were unfamiliar with the cultural and social geography of Africa.

In 1988, as social anthropologists who had done research in East, Central, and West Africa, we were able to establish the general pattern of movement of the disease, to predict its progression, and to point to regions where rates would be, if they were not already, high. The technique was straightforward and could be done extemporaneously without new research. The disease was mapped onto or tracked into the main movements of goods, services, labor, and peoples. Having done this, we could readily predict the distribution of AIDS from southern Uganda to South Africa. At that time few researchers had focused on Zambia, Malawi, Zimbabwe, South Africa, Namibia, and Botswana. Today, with more than 19 percent of their populations infected by the virus, they are among the countries with the highest rates in Africa and the world. However, for Africanists the progression, if not the already established fact of HIV, was evident. In addition, there was every indication that the disease would be at a high rate, which was soon to become an established fact. The disease's progression followed the main routes of labor migration, population movements, trade, commerce, and tourism over land, water, and in the sky.

Among Africanists and within the social sciences the AIDS epidemic cannot be attributed to and understood solely in the context of individual sexual behaviors. It has been a disease deeply embedded in the expanding capitalist productive relations of most contemporary African countries, characterized by uneven development with rural poverty, of urban salaried employment, and the violent upheavals of post-colonial African states and societies. In many countries there is evidence that the epidemic is "striking disproportionately the groups with the highest level of productive skills, and human capital" (Ntozi et al., 1997: 209). A generation of highly skilled people may be in jeopardy, placing development at risk. HIV/AIDS is not confined to any one territory or social class. It has been a regional and an international disease that has recognized neither geographical nor social boundaries. Combined with civil wars, civil strife, and disasters such as drought and famine, it has become a formidable force in African history, with the potential of affecting the possibility of economic growth and development.

Uganda

Uganda has been one of the main African countries seriously affected by the AIDS epidemic and one of the first to take effective measures to control it. With an estimated population of 20 million people distributed over an area of some 236,860 square kilometers, preventing the spread of the disease has required planning, the cooperation of international NGOs, the use of scarce resources, and the active involvement of the Ugandan people. A comparatively extensive system of roads and waterways, especially in the south, has allowed for the movement of peoples, goods, and services as well as military combatants and diseases.

Population density is uneven throughout Uganda, with the lowest rates in the northern regions. It is highest (between 200 and 4,581 per square kilometer) in four clusters: (1) Kampala and Mpigi districts in the central region; (2) Jinja district and (3) Mbale, Tororo, and Pallisa districts in the eastern region; and (4) Kisoro, Kabale, and Rukunguri districts in the western region (Barton & Wamai, 1994: 27).

Uganda is one of the least-urbanized countries in Africa, with more than half of the urban population living in Kampala, the national capital, in the south. Other large urban populations are to be found in district headquarters and reflect (with one exception, Arua) the communications network of tarred major roads.

Some 89.6 percent of the population is rural (Uganda Government, 1991). Of this portion, 80 percent of what is described as "the economically active population" is said to be engaged in agriculture (Hunter, Bulirwa & Kisseka, 1993; Barton & Wamai, 1994: 173). In discourses on AIDS in Uganda, most agriculture is described as "subsistence" farming (in anthropology, a contested and dated designation); these discourses also tend to neglect commercial farming and non-agricultural rural enterprise. The agricultural systems found in Masaka and Rakai in the south, where most of the research on AIDS and agriculture has been conducted, are wrongly taken to represent Ugandan agriculture. In fact, with the development of capitalist agriculture in this colonial region of Buganda in the 1920s, Masaka became exceptional for its large landowners and commercial farming on vast estates. The southwest of the country in general fed the urban conglomerate that grew up around Mengo/Kampala, the capital, and Entebbe/Mpigi, the site of the colonial administrative headquarters (Powesland, 1957).

The south is also the center of commerce, higher education, and health services. The two universities are there, Makerere in Kampala and the other in Mbarara. Malago, the main hospital and AIDS research center in Uganda, is in Kampala, and most NGOs have their headquarters there. The south is thus the political, administrative, commercial, agricultural, and health center of Uganda. The centrality of the south is intimately related to British colonial rule and the recognition of the need to employ and extend the power of the Ganda state.

The very history of the founding of Uganda has been one of moving frontiers of conquest, domination, and differential incorporation. Colonial expansion was based on the collaboration of two imperial powers: the one foreign, the British, and the other indigenous and regional, the Ganda. By 1890 the British had established an administrative order using Ganda Agents that extended north, east, and west from Mengo, the royal Ganda capital, "for up to two hundred and fifty miles in each direction" (Vincent, 1999: 109). As the British extended their colonial frontier, small wars of conquest were fought against local peoples. By 1920 the peoples of the Protectorate had been conquered, and in the years that followed the north became increasingly subordinate and peripheral to the rapidly developing south as it became integrated into the world economy.

Colonial officials introduced agro-capitalist enterprises into southern Uganda from the very beginning. They fostered a cultural hegemony in which things associated with capitalism were valued, and those not associated with it were devalued. The south became the center of commercial farming, attracting large numbers of labor migrants from other parts of Uganda and surrounding colonial territories. The north received few benefits and remained peripheral to the commercial developments in the south. Given this uneven development within the protectorate, the population of the south thought of itself and was viewed by colonial officers as more modern and civilized, while the peoples of the north were seen to be less modern and somewhat uncivilized. The values associated with privilege and capitalist modernity "persisted into the postcolonial times" (Vincent, 1999; Reyna, 1999: 8) and heightened the sense of southern cultural hegemony over the north. This sense of cultural hegemony may well have intensified the violent conflagrations with the north referred to in this chapter. Although AIDS was known to have spread to the north by 1986, little AIDS research has been conducted there, let alone the AIDS prevention and intervention measures that have proved so successful in the south.

As agro-capitalism took hold and developed in the south it attracted an increasing number of labor migrants. From the late 1920s through the 1950s the three main immigrant routes into Uganda were "(a) the South-West Route from Tanganyika and Ruanda-Urundi; (b) the Northern Route from the West Nile and the Sudan; (c) the Eastern Route which carries the immigrants from the Eastern Province of Uganda and the Kavirondo district in Kenya" (Richards, 1955: 53). Audrey Richards also observes that "by far the heaviest traffic goes along the South-West Route" (Richards, 1955: 53). Labor migrants from northern Rwanda traveled from Mbarara to Masaka to Kampala, and those from northern Tanzania from Kyebe to Kalisizo to Masaka and then to Kampala. Masaka, a small commercial town, was the point of convergence for these two streams of labor migrants. Throughout much of the colonial period health officers tracked migrant laborers and the diseases they carried with them. They recognized that once the migrants reached Kampala they were difficult to trace and diseases difficult to control.

The "South-West Route" of the 1950s is almost identical with the one traveled by refugees fleeing from violence in Zaire and northern Rwanda in the 1960s and by labor migrants, traders, truck drivers, and soldiers in the 1970s and the 1980s. All gave rise to similar concerns about the spread of disease. However, with increasing periods of military activity and social upheavals from the 1960s through the 1980s, it became impossible for medical officers to either trace or control the spread of disease.

In 1987, the director of the AIDS Control Program speculated that AIDS had followed the trade routes from Rakai to Kyotera to Masaka and then exploded in Kampala, becoming almost invisible (Okware, 1987). There was thus a moving frontier of disease that could be tracked along the established southern routes of trade and labor migration as far as Kampala and then would be lost in the urban mix. In the late 1980s concerns about the diseases of the 1920–1980 period (malaria, relapsing fever, and enteritis) were set aside with the rapid spread of HIV/AIDS. Nonetheless, these diseases remain the main cause of morbidity in Uganda.

However, the same type of specific speculation about the passage of AIDS from the southwest to Kampala was not made to account for the spread of the disease in the north and east. It is certainly possible that the AIDS frontier was moving from the east at the same time as from the southwest. Given the security situation in northeast Uganda at the time, no inquiries could be made.

In the l980s the Kenya-Uganda-Sudan borders were fraught with international and Cold War tensions even as they had been earlier during the Tanzania-Uganda War of 1979 (Vincent, 1999). To obtain World Bank backing, Uganda tightened its regulation of long-distance truckers. In eastern Uganda the connection between trucking and *magendo* black-marketeering (Southall, 1985) and AIDS (Bond & Vincent, 1991) is comparable to that of the route from Tanzania to Kenya via the Ugandan southwest and Kampala. In 1991 it was estimated that 33 percent of the long-distance truck drivers in Uganda were infected. The month-to-month spread of HIV–1 along the Trans-African Highway was depicted graphically (Shannon, Pyle & Bashur, 1991: 69, 79–80). But whereas AIDS researchers have conducted extensive research into the sexual practices of target groups of truckers and sex workers along international highways in the south and southwest (from the Tanzanian border to Kampala in particular) no such studies have been carried out in the northeast and north—a point to which we will return. Nor has significance been attached to legislation passed in 1986 to limit foreign trucks in transit, on pain of arrest, to six stopover points at night. These were at Mulingire, Kampala, Emukaya, and Byantunda in the south, and Soroti and Gulu in the east and north.

AIDS: Civil War and Violence

In Uganda, research and programs dealing with the AIDS epidemic have been shaped by recent civil wars and violence. In February 1981 a guerrilla war was launched in Buganda against President Milton Obote's military government, and Uganda was immersed in a series of insurrections and civil wars that lasted until 1986 (Hooper & Pirouet, 1989). The World Health Organization's Bangui Conference arrived at a clinical case definition of AIDS in the same year that Obote's regime was overthrown in Uganda.[1]

In 1986, at the same time that it was establishing local units of administration throughout the war-torn Ugandan countryside, Museveni's victorious government (the National Resistance Movement/National Resistance Army, NRM/NRA) took three actions that would be critical to the transformation of HIV/AIDS research and intervention. The first step was the public recognition of HIV/AIDS in Uganda as a major health crisis, an action that won Museveni international renown and support and opened Uganda to international health organizations and aid. The second innovation was the establishment of a decentralized government framework throughout the Ugandan countryside, which had experienced a series of devastating conditions, including "famine; tyranny; widespread infringement of human rights, amounting to genocide; AIDS; malaria; cholera; typhoid, and a massive breakdown of government services; corruption, black marketeering, economic collapse; tribalism, civil war, state collapse"(Hansen & Twaddle, 1988: 1). The third critical innovation was the inauguration of a National AIDS Control Programme (NACP) within the Ministry of Health in May 1987 (Okware, 1987). The purpose of the NACP was to monitor the epidemic, establish a system of surveillance, and develop prevention protocols. At that time 25 to 30 AIDS deaths per month were being reported. Although AIDS had been "found" only in the south of Uganda at this time, it was recognized that "it" had "spread" to "the north" and "was probably being carried by the military conflict" (Economist Intelligence Unit (EIU), Uganda Country Report, 1986).

The NACP had seven principle components: mass public education and information; blood screening and the rehabilitation of its Blood Transfusion Service; the protection of the public, health workers, and children through supplying syringes, needles, gloves, aprons, boots, and disinfectants; condoms; an effective national surveillance system; supplying AIDS-drugs; training and reorienting health workers; and finally, operational research, Knowledge, Attitudes and Practices (KAP) studies for health education, and sero-epidemiology and risk factor research.

Violent opposition to the NRM government has challenged the success of all three innovations. It has seemed that at any moment since 1986 Uganda could again be plunged into chaos. During the 1980s and much of the 1990s in some regions the entire trajectory of research in Uganda, including AIDS research, was governed by what is euphemistically called the "Security Situation."

During the first half of 1983 security problems in the Luwero triangle (Mukono, Mpigi, and Mubende districts) and along the border with Sudan (Arua and Nebbi districts) constrained field research for a Social and Institutional Profile for the United States Agency for International Development (USAID). In the second half of the year conditions worsened in the north and northeast, with cattle raiding from Moroto to Kumi, Soroti, Lira, and Kitgum districts. In Mbarara and Rakai districts immigrants were driven out by youth "wingers," and refugees fled to Rwanda and Tanzania. Tax riots took the lives of several residents of Jinja and Kamulki districts in January 1984. But few details of security problems were noted in subsequent social science reports and virtually none in biomedical reports. In both, "silences" can be read to account for where the research being reported was—or more significantly was not—being done.

At the time of our first field trip to Rakai district in August 1988, *The New Vision* newspaper reported a total of 27 rebel organizations in operation within the national boundaries. By that time the northeast had become the testing zone of the conflict for the government forces, although insurrection had also broken out in the north (Vincent, 1999). Displacement camps were set up in Kumi district and in the North. Uganda as a whole was reported to have 100,000 displaced persons. A scorched earth policy had been adopted in both regions by both insurrectionary guerrilla forces and the NRA. We were informed that Kumi and Soroti districts were on the brink of civil war and were advised not to go there.

The long period of continuous fighting precipitated population movements on a very large scale, giving rise to resettlement camps, refugees, famine, and malnutrition; lowering resistance to infectious disease; and enhancing the spread of HIV. Although these conditions have ceased to be a prominent factor in the southern part of Uganda, they have provided the context of HIV/AIDS in the north, conditions that Museveni's government has sought to change.

In 1986, when the National Resistance Movement (NRM) assumed the reigns of government, it had to deal with the effects of years of warfare, state terror, and violence and a national economy that was in complete disarray. Government expenditures had been mainly on armaments and not on public services such as health. Thus, Museveni and the NRM confronted the great task of rebuilding or "rehabilitating" the south while, where necessary, containing dissent in the north. The embattled north remained peripheral, with a much slower pace of reconstruction.

The years of civil strife, high military expenditures, and now HIV/AIDS have had their effect on demographic, health, and social patterns in Uganda.

Health facilities have never been evenly distributed. About one-quarter of Uganda's 95 hospitals and health facilities are located in the three districts (Kampala, Mpigi, and Mukono) that make up Uganda's fertile crescent along the northern shore of Lake Victoria. Elsewhere there is considerable regional and district variation in the percentage of the population living within five kilometers of a health clinic (Barton & Wamai, 1994: 71, table).

Civil strife and the high prevalence of HIV/AIDS in Uganda have led to a projection of the expected lifespan of only 40 years by the end of the 1990s. The population of Uganda is rising rapidly. It stood at an estimated 18.5 million in 1994, and even with the so-called doomsday worst case scenario of HIV/AIDS, the population is expected to reach more than 22 million by 2010.

Cultural or Intellectual Maps

Medical and social researchers have cultural or intellectual maps that help to guide and shape their understandings of the physical and social world. In the first phases of the epidemic in Uganda the medical sciences took the lead. The South became the primary locus of medical activity and social science research. For social scientists and those trained in African studies the truncated delineation of "Uganda" that resulted was alarming. What is without question is that a new thrust in AIDS research by social scientists and others appeared at the beginning of the 1990s.

At the outset, such was the necessary focus on biomedical research at that time, and such was the concomitant concentration on the sexual behavior of individuals, that contemporary economic and social science sources of relevant information were ignored. Two examples may be given of neglected research texts. The first was a social and institutional profile (SIP) of Uganda and the second concerned AIDS-related mortality and orphans.

Text One: Uganda Social and Institutional Profile

One of the most neglected research texts (if frequency of citation is any indicator) is a social and institutional profile (SIP) of Uganda that appeared in August 1984 (Jaenson et al., 1984). Certain trends noted in this 1983–1984 profile are relevant to AIDS research:

1. A significant trend toward one-person households of widows and widowers.
2. An increasing proportion of single-parent, especially female-headed, households.

356 • GEORGE CLEMENT BOND AND JOAN VINCENT

3. An increase in the number of grandchildren living with heads of households.
4. A clear indication that polygamy accompanies wealth; in rural areas, the educated are more likely to be polygamous than the unschooled.
5. Continuing heavy investment in education both in terms of cash for school fees and labor foregone. Rural households expected education to provide them with an escape from poverty.
6. A marked decrease in the size of landholding per household since the Agricultural Census of 1982.
7. A substantial minority in all rural areas dependent on non-agricultural activities for their main source of income.
8. Decreased social welfare services everywhere.(For a fuller discussion of these trends, see Jaenson et al., 1984; Bond & Vincent, 1991: 114–116).

Attention should be drawn to the fact that Jaenson et al. (1984) pointed out that institutionalized religion plays a very important role in Ugandan society. In the four region studies (Busoga, Masaka, Teso, and Kigezi), in all but Teso more than 95 percent of the rural heads of households belonged to some organized religious group: Anglican (Church of Uganda), Roman Catholic, or Muslim. Even behavior-oriented AIDS research has tended to overlook this social fact (see Bond & Vincent, 2000).

The research team of the 1984 SIP study consisted of two anthropologists (Carol Jaenson and Josephine Harmsworth) along with Professors Tarsis Kabwegyere and P. Muzaale of Makerere University, Kampala.[2] The nine districts in the profile (here placed within the regions as classified by the 1991 Census for reasons that will become apparent) were

Central: Masaka, Rakai
Western: Kabale, Rukingiri
Eastern: Jinja, Iganga, Kamuli, Soroti, and Kumi.

Field research could not be carried out in the North for security reasons.

The reasons these districts were selected are stated with admirable, methodological rigor: "principal cropping patterns, a consideration of ethnic make-up and geographical location, the professional knowledge and background of team members, the known quality and quantity of earlier studies, financial constraints, and prevailing security conditions at the time of field research" (Jaenson et al., 1984: 2).

Comparative material on rural household composition in the profile provided a window through which the effects of immiseration, pauperization, and violence on the countryside were reflected. For us, after the fact as it were in 1988, the historically accumulated circumstances of HIV/AIDS dispersion and intervention loomed as "phantasmagoric representations" over our reading of the profile on Rakai and Masaka districts, where virtually all the biomedical AIDS field research was being done at that time (Bond & Vincent, 1991: 114–166; Reyna, 1999: 1).

In 1999, following the trajectory AIDS research had taken in the 15 years since the profile was written, it was apparent that household composition remained a crucial datum in AIDS research publications. But household composition has been decontextualized, removed from its specific ethnographic location in time and place. It has been replaced by little more than a minimal site specification that generates a number, just as the persons dwelling in the household have become little more than impersonal units that generate statistics. Thus, household composition has become no more than a quantitative artifact of social activities and relationships that structure the lived-in realities and experiences of the afflicted and those who may care for them. But AIDS is more than just a disease. It generates a way of life that mobilizes clusters of social relationships, informs and is informed by bodies of local knowledge and is as much a social and cultural condition as it is a medical one.

The more in-depth, theoretically informed field research that preceded the extensive western funding of AIDS research has tended to be bypassed in Ugandan AIDS research. As a result, the rich fabric of rural society and its institutional nucleations of sociability and illicit sexual behavior remain hidden or, worse, are pigeonholed as "traditional."

Text Two: Action Research and Orphans

A second text from the 1990s AIDS literature exemplifies not the neglect of social science contributions but the problem of getting action-oriented research projects funded in the first place. Susan Hunter's virtual coda to her report on a four-district study of AIDS-related mortality and orphans was published in 1990. It discloses facets of the arena in which action research operated in Uganda. Social scientists were then "still second string players in the eyes of their clinical colleagues" (Hunter, 1990a: 6). Hunter provides an 11-stage retrospective on the problems that had to be addressed to get orphan research funded. This included opposition from "other stakeholders who disagreed strongly with the need for systematic enumeration," among them World Vision, Uganda Women's Efforts to Save Orphans (UWESO), and The AIDS Support Organization (TASO). The World Bank refused to fund the project, which was then "rescued" (Akeroyd, 1990: 2) by a less-powerful donor, the Save the Children's Fund (SCF). Hunter's own participation was sponsored by the Rockefeller Foundation Population Sciences Division. A postscript to Hunter's report tells of events that occurred after her article was written in January 1990. Several NGOs committed funds to a bevy of orphan research projects to be undertaken solely in Rakai and Masaka districts.

A Biomedical Emphasis

At about the same time that the orphan project was encountering difficulties, the Rakai Study (Wawer et al, 1991; 1994) was approved by the AIDS Research Committee in Uganda and funded without local opposition. The Rakai Study has claimed pride of place as the first biomedical research project in Uganda to address social issues in its intervention procedures. Its long-term objectives were to collect descriptive epidemiologic data on HIV–1; determine the association between potential risk factors and HIV–1 in a study population; assess knowledge, attitudes, and behaviors related to HIV–1 transmission and prevention; and, on the basis of the data collected, design, implement, and evaluate intervention strategies with particular emphasis on preventive health education and, where appropriate, condom distribution (Wawer, 1991).

The Rakai Project and similar AIDS projects adopt "The Biomedical Paradigm" (Bond & Vincent, 1997b: 86–90) and variously involve, to a limited and controlled degree, social scientists. But as Hunter points out, the way in which researchers "define a problem and visualize solutions depends on our world view, our political and social belief systems, and our resulting purpose and motives" (Hunter, 1990a: 8). The biomedical paradigm is unlikely to be fully adequate in that it emphasizes clinical solutions to social problems.

The New Climate of Inclusion

The Ugandan government contributed to the creation of a wholly new climate for AIDS research at the beginning of the 1990s. This took the form of a new task force on AIDS called The Working Group on the Socioeconomic, Cultural and Legal Impact of AIDS (Republic of Uganda, 1990: 4). The dimensions enumerated, proposed, and consolidated the existing efforts of governmental agencies, NGO programs, the churches (a rare mention), and donor agencies. The dimensions set out were agriculture; the labor force; income and consumption; education; health; and psychological, cultural, and legal.

The task force recognized that "many current actors are not known, both within and outside the government, nor is the extent of their activities" (Uganda Government, 1990: 9). Among the best-known Ugandan organizations were TASO, UWESO, and Action for Development (ACFODE), a women's indigenous, charitable NGO based in Kampala. Among "the unknown" were individuals such as Rakai District Administrator Robinah Kasadha who, long before funded NGOs entered her district, offered personal fostering help to numerous orphaned children, and Nursing Sister Mary Eragu Asio, who on her own initiative pioneered the recording of AIDS mortality in Soroti General Hospital. Over a comparatively short time, the sheer scale of the epidemic began to generate its own social arrangements concerned with providing support for the most vulnerable: women, children, and the elderly.

The task force's final recommendation was that "an awareness/sensitization program be launched to the public on the importance and use of research in general in order to foster cooperation and *improve the quality* of information being collected" (Republic of Uganda, 1990: 9; emphasis in original).

Since the establishment of this task force at the beginning of the 1990s, Uganda has seen a considerable increase in the number of AIDS-related studies that fall under its rubric of socioeconomic, cultural, and legal. These include studies of AIDS in relation to orphans, women and children, and infant mortality (Chin, 1990; Hunter, 1990a; Anderson et al., 1990; Prebble, 1990); family and household (Ntozi, 1997; Ntozi & Nakanaabi, 1997; Seeley et al., 1993); and communities (Seeley et al., 1991), to name but a few. It is probably a fair observation that such research began to see the light of day only "when the [AIDS] epidemic was reported to be subsiding" (Ntozi & Nakanaabi, 1997: 189).

However, it was the "discovery" of the magnitude of the problem of AIDS orphans that opened a window onto research on women, adolescents, and children. This was systematized at the highest level in 1994 in *Equity and Vulnerability: A Situational Analysis of Women, Adolescents and Children in Uganda*, a project funded by UNICEF, sponsored by a newly created Uganda National Council for Children, and implemented by the Child Health and Development Centre of Makerere University, Uganda's national university. The project involved at the advisory level seven government ministries; a large contingent from UNICEF (including Carol Jaenson); the Save the Children Fund; World Learning, Inc.; Action for Development (ACFODE); Uganda Community-Based Health Care Association; and Child Health and Development Centre.

Involved in the situation analysis at the reviewing level were the Makerere Institute of Social Research (formerly the East African Institute of Social and Economic Research), SNV/NOVIS, Uganda Association for Women Lawyers (FIDA), and the United Nations Development Programme (UNDP). The document indicates a broad inclusiveness and a profound shift in focus toward the vulnerable and weak and the problems of the districts.

The Uganda Districts Speak Out

Much has changed since the late 1980s and the early 1990s. As the NRM has gained control of different regions, it has relied on a system of local government through decentralization, attempting to bring the people directly into the process of their own governance. Through its policies of decentralization and development it has sought to increase the political, administrative, financial, and planning authority of local government councils (Butegwa, 1998: 169), making them responsible for generating their own revenue, providing public services, and formulating development plans.

The central government is aware that the 39 districts differ and that health facilities and other public services are unevenly distributed. Since the enactment of the Local Government Act of 1997, it is responsible for providing districts with equivalent services. To do so, it is committed to making "equalization grants to local governments," especially to those districts "whose revenue-base has been eroded by conflict or natural disasters" (Butegwa, 1998: 196). The Ministry of Planning has been engaged in establishing national service delivery standards. The central government recognizes that its resources are limited and that it is unable to meet many of the basic demands of the districts. An assumption of the decentralization policy has been to expect financial support from international donors. In 1994, 40 percent of the formal health services in Uganda was provided by NGOs, including hospital beds and health centers (Barton & Wamai, 1994: 95). The policy has been to interest donors in directly supporting individual local governments in solving district problems and pursuing local projects (Butegwa, 1998: 193–194). The central government has sought to harness the resources of NGOs and bring them together with the districts to deal with local issues. As reported in the important volume on Uganda, *Equity and Vulnerability: A Situation Analysis of Women, Adolescents and Children in Uganda* (Barton & Wamai, 1994), AIDS does not seem to be considered the critical problem by most local governments.

This volume describes Uganda, reflects its current decentralization policies, and seeks to represent the voices of the people and their main concerns. As a document that has received the support of the government, it presents an interesting set of insights into Uganda's form of participatory democracy and the theoretical arguments related to the state and civil society. The NRM is lodged within both the state and civil society, and thus the personnel and policies of one are reflected in those of the other. There is a certain authority to the volume, so let us now turn to it.

Equity and Vulnerability, sponsored by the Uganda National Council for Children's Situation Analysis, carries a foreword from the president of the Republic, Yoweri Kaguta Museveni. Museveni's government, the NRM, has a history of taking matters to the people, providing a recurrent sense of involvement in the nation's trajectory or course of development. The situation analysis has built into it the requirement that "The Districts Speak Out." It bears witness to the dramatic change that has occurred in the assault on HIV/AIDS in the 1990s and is closely related to popular dissatisfaction with both the international and the national status quo. It is also fully in keeping with a policy of government decentralization. Museveni calls on the people of Uganda to read the document they have helped create: "Here are ideas from Ugandans, for Ugandans. Take them and use them instead of imposing ideas from elsewhere that do not fit our situation" (Barton & Wamai, 1994: v).

Museveni's paradoxically uninhibited two-sentence paragraph leaves a world unsaid. Note the transformation that has occurred since the 1980s when the "modern" "Western" clinical research paradigm was dominant. Ugandan critiques may have played a role in this shift (for example, Serwadda & Katongole-Mbidde, 1990), but the trajectory is wholly in keeping with Museveni's early vision of the dynamics of governmentality within the NRM. The districts speak out and, having solicited their voices, the centralizing organ of government returns the "data" to them for comparison. The 39 districts speak out severally, but from the compilation they are encouraged to learn from each other what can and cannot work. The extent to which the "quantitative" information, the statistics, are secondary to the "qualitative" is discussed in a section written for district planners and implementers (Barton & Wamai, 1994: 232–234, appendix F).

This is clearly a strategic document. It may also prove a dangerous strategy. The revelations on page after page of the advantaged central region, with its relatively impoverished periphery, will surely stir resentment among the excluded unless some form of catch-up is practiced. Concern has already been expressed at the local level about whether decentralization will make the districts disastrously competitive with each other (Butegwa, 1998) and at the global level whether "broad government support may not materialize and government be too weak to implement" certain World Bank funded programs (Dayton, 1998).

Statistics are given on nine health and well-being problems addressed by the districts. Approximately 25 program-level staff per district were interviewed in all 39 districts, a total of 906 interviews (Barton & Wamai, 1994: 76). Of the 39 districts, 15 named poverty as their leading "health and well-being" problem; eight (all in the northern and eastern regions) named lack of transport; seven (all in the northern and eastern regions) named war and crime; and six (in the central and western regions) named AIDS as their highest-ranking problem. The six districts were Bushenyi and Kabarole in the western region and Kampala, Masaka, Ntungamo, and Rakai in the central region. In the southern part of Uganda, encompassing the central and western regions, AIDS intervention strategies had been carried out over a period of several years; war lay in the past. In the northern and eastern regions the terror of both AIDS and violence was very much "in the making."

The views from the districts highlight local concerns with poverty, infrastructure, social services, and the general problems of rehabilitation and security. They reflect the fact that for the past 30 years Uganda has experienced a series of major upheavals in the form of state terror, civil wars, violence, famines, and major epidemics. This document and the others discussed in this chapter speak to the way in which these events have affected one another. One might say that Uganda has experienced a series of "complex emergencies" and that since the mid-1980s AIDS has been a crucial element, generating fields of medical and social activities.[3] It has engaged the 39 districts, but in different ways. The south has been the center of AIDS research and educational programs, involving local and international organizations and their resources. The north has received much less attention and remained at the periphery, retaining its marginal position in Uganda's history.

Conclusion

This chapter has traced the location and progression of a disease through the analysis of research projects and their texts. It has examined the manner in which the disease was framed since its recognition in 1983 as a product of historical and social circumstances. HIV/AIDS was itself a disease without a history and thus provided a new challenge to the biomedical and social science communities. Yet Uganda has its own history and it was the circumstances of history that led to the concentration of research in one region and not another.

The potential of the disease was first recognized in the southern regions of Uganda, and as the magnitude of the epidemic became apparent, a global "community" of AIDS workers was created in Kampala, representing a range of international and local organizations. In the initial phases of the epidemic biomedical paradigms were dominant, and social scientists trained in African studies were engaged only in a peripheral capacity. The disease was decontextualized and removed from the intricate social and political configurations of Ugandan history. It was reduced to the activities of high-risk groups, truck drivers, traders, and sexual workers.

As this chapter indicates, the rich tradition of social research in Uganda and the basic research findings of projects such as SIP were set aside. The most vulnerable and weak segments of Ugandan society—women, children, and the elderly—were not placed at the center of the analysis. As the disease continued to spread and available resources proved to be limited, social scientists and their paradigms received greater recognition. It became apparent that there was no immediate medical cure in sight and that community self-reliance was essential. As the NRM, under the leadership of President Museveni, has secured its position in Uganda, the problems of AIDS have been increasingly incorporated into government policies. Although still global, the Uganda "AIDS community" has now been brought into the domain of the NRM, with its present emphasis on working with the districts to solve their problems. As the districts of Uganda speak out and express their concerns, poverty, the weak, and the vulnerable are being brought into central focus.

There is a tragic irony here in that it has taken the AIDS epidemic to bring into full focus the plight of persons who are the most vulnerable and weak. Women, youth, children, orphans, and the elderly are now at the center of government concerns. The "AIDS community" has now shifted its focus to a more inclusive recognition that the epidemic is as much a medical problem as it is a social one. Marginalized regions and dependent classes of people should be recognized as central to any analysis of the AIDS pandemic.

16
Contested Claims and Individual Bodies

MEREDETH TURSHEN
Edward J. Bloustein School of Planning and Public Policy
Rutgers University

This chapter explores the broad topic of contested claims and individual bodies at the nexus of health and state policy. It focuses on three current interrelated issues—epidemic disease, population growth, and endemic wars—and pays particular attention to the impact of political and structural violence on health. These themes are universal and involve the world system, but the concern here is with how they play out in contemporary Africa.

International health policy has undergone as many permutations since World War II as has economic development policy. The changes are not indicative of the sorts of paradigm shifts that Thomas Kuhn (1970) wrote about but rather of attempts to salvage failed neoliberal policies. At present both the causes of ill health and the shape of biomedical health system responses to the sick and injured are under intense scrutiny. Researchers are asking such questions as: Does personal behavior explain illness and does education hold the key to better health? Or do rapid population growth, a poor environment, and poverty account for ill health, and does sustainable development (itself a contested concept) hold the prescription for longevity? Does either of these explanations account for the extreme inequalities in health status and health expenditures within and between countries? Do they explain political instability and conflict?

Explanations of illness that implicate personal behavior, which is said to dictate diet, hygiene, exercise, and sex practices, are common in discussions of communicable diseases such as cholera, AIDS, and sexually transmitted infections as well as conditions related to obesity, smoking, alcoholism, and drug addiction (Jamison, 1993: 3–34). The policies that flow from this analysis emphasize persuasive prevention, a combination of health education and use of the police powers of the state to enforce public health regulations.

Neo-Malthusian claims that rapid population growth, a poor environment, and poverty account for ill health inform the World Bank's approach to sustainable development (World Bank, 1996b: 8–10). The World Bank uses these claims to justify structural adjustment programs (SAPs), which are responsible for decreasing state health service budgets as well as the privatizing of health services (as exemplified by fees for the use of public facilities). Bilateral and multilateral aid agencies and international donors are urging nongovernmental organizations (NGOs), including church missions, to deliver health services in the private sector, and they are experimenting with a variety of insurance schemes to help people pay for personal health care.

One variant of neo-Malthusian theory is called "population health"; its promoters maintain that too much money is diverted to health services and that investment in economic development would better serve the health of peoples in the longer term (Evans & Stoddart, 1990: 1347–1363). Another variant claims that overpopulation and environmental degradation exhaust the fragile resource base of Africa and cause both disease and internal wars (Kaplan, 1994: 44–76).

Attempts to explain global divergences in health status and services focus on the role of political and structural violence in creating and maintaining health inequalities (Farmer et al., 1996). Some public health policymakers discuss the role of structural violence, but they mention political violence less often, although UNICEF criticized the violence done to maternal and child health by the wars in southern Africa and by the World Bank's SAPs (Cornia et al., 1987; UNICEF, 1989). Three economic dimensions of structural violence that impair health also reflect deepening poverty: unemployment, which paralyzes 20 to 50 percent of the labor force in most of Africa; labor migration, which is a central aspect of the global restructuring of economies; and labor market deregulation, which is a featured element of economic reforms and an impetus to labor migration.

While policymakers debate lifestyles, population growth, and the trade-offs of supposedly short-term costs and putative long-term gains in SAPs (the "contested claims" of the title of this chapter), health services are not able to meet the growing needs of ailing African communities. In the absence of any accountability, millions of individuals pay for the failed projects and false claims of the international community with their weakened bodies and lost lives.

Epidemic Disease

Public health planners sometimes consider diseases in clusters (for example, the respiratory diseases, the diseases of poverty), and sometimes they categorize them according to duration (the acute diseases, the chronic diseases) or by mode of transmission (the airborne or waterborne diseases). One theory notes that mortality in very poor communities is nonspecific; that is, if one disease such as measles is eradicated, the overall rate of death does not decrease because people will die of some other disease.[1] We discuss AIDS here as the highly controversial emblematic disease of Africa, the exemplar of epidemic disease today as smallpox was previously, and the current hog of scarce resources for health care.

There are a variety of contested claims about AIDS, a syndrome of many guises. AIDS, it is said, is the major health threat to African people; AIDS is a behavioral and medical problem; African sexuality—said to be the pivot of the epidemic—is so different from the Indo-European norm that it represents an alternative civilization; and health education and condoms are the only prevention currently available (Caldwell et al., 1989; Van de Walle, 1990; Ahlberg, 1994; Le Blanc et al., 1991; Turshen, 1991). The counterclaims are that the international community uses AIDS (an irreversible immune deficiency) as an excuse for inaction in building viable public health services capable of treating all diseases; that its policies regarding the arms trade, commodity prices, and debt repayment are indirectly responsible for the spread of HIV, and reversal of these policies is the real preventive measure; that donors undermine African health policies from "above" by cutting state budgets; that private health providers undermine health services from "below" by limiting access to care; and that condoms are a contraceptive (Lurie et al., 1995: 539–546; Turshen, 1999).

Because mathematical models of the AIDS epidemic project severe economic disruption, donors advise governments to reserve scarce health care resources for AIDS prevention. In accordance with the policy not to divert too much money to health services, donors prefer to single out HIV infection, separate it from other epidemic and nonepidemic diseases, and fund vertical projects at the ministerial level to deal with HIV as a sexually transmitted infection (Over & Piot, 1993: 455–527). Yet none of the 20 diseases listed as defining a case of AIDS is treated at STD clinics (World Health Organization, 1988: 1–7). Instead, donors advise home-based care because doctors consider these AIDS indicator diseases to be opportunistic infections secondary to an irreversibly impaired immune system. A survey of treatment (called "mitigation interventions") offered by NGOs in six African countries shows that counseling accounts for 50 percent of all help provided (Cohen & Trussell, 1996: 245–250). The World Bank advocates treating tuberculosis and the curable sexually transmitted infections:

> Governments in developing countries should reduce spending by about 50 percent on less-cost-effective interventions and instead double or triple spending on such basic public health programs as immunizations, AIDS prevention [15 percent in low-income countries], and essential clinical services. A minimum package of essential clinical services should include sick-child care, family planning, prenatal and delivery care, and treatment for tuberculosis and STDs. (World Bank, 1996a: 18)

One consequence of this approach, and indicative of growing global health inequities, is that AIDS is a chronic disease in the Northern hemisphere and an acute disease in sub-Saharan Africa. Another consequence is the facile way in which UN agencies can say that AIDS is causing health to decline in Africa (Crossette, 1998: A9), rather than SAPs, diminishing state health service budgets, the privatization of health services, or any of the other markers of political and structural violence.

The common depiction of AIDS as a personal, behavioral, and medical issue allows the state to project its responsibilities for public health onto individuals. The characterization of AIDS as a consequence of risky lifestyles, implying that individuals freely choose their addictions and that all sex is consensual, is false, and its rejection needs no elaboration because the arguments are well documented (Farmer et al., 1996). Africanists have thoroughly debunked the accusation that African sexuality is abnormal (Ahlberg, 1994: 220–242; Le Blanc et al., 1991: 497–505). AIDS is a grave health hazard for Africans, but the epidemiological data show that malaria and tuberculosis kill larger numbers of women, children, and men, and that war-related violence and land mines cause more deaths, dismemberment, and disability (Murray & Lopez 1997: 1269–1276). While policymakers dispute claims and counterclaims, thousands of individual bodies succumb for lack of health care.

Population Growth

Apparently the death rate from AIDS is not high enough for neo-Malthusians concerned with rapid population growth in Africa, or "excess fertility"

(Cochrane & Sai 1993: 333–361). From the very early stages of the AIDS epidemic, the United Nations has published demographic projections showing continued high rates of population growth; despite dire warnings of large numbers of deaths from AIDS, especially in the labor force, the UN agencies insist that now is not the time to stop family planning programs (United Nations, 1994).

The claims that revolve around population growth begin with the assertion that high birth rates are Africa's overriding problem and the cause of poverty, retarding progress in raising per capita income (World Bank, 1996b: 8–10). A related allegation blames the poor for land degradation and identifies the pressure of too many people on scarce physical resources as the cause of the environmental crisis. Emphasis on the relation between health and high birth rates waxes and wanes; since the International Conference on Population and Development, held in Cairo in 1994, health benefits are in ascendancy. The recommended solution to overpopulation is birth control, regulating reproduction in the individual bodies of millions of women.

The counterclaim is that high birth rates are symptoms of extensive poverty rather than the cause, that slower population growth does not necessarily lead to a fairer distribution of resources either within countries or between continents, and that smaller family size correlates with pension systems, social services, education for children, and remunerative work for women and men.

The debate between those for and against population control is important to women because the policy outcomes of the neo-Malthusian position are radically different from those of women-centered analyses.[2] Rather than slower rates of natural increase being their goal, women-centered family planning programs seek improved maternal and child health. Malika Ladjali of Algeria clarifies this distinction: "Family planning entails individual counseling; population control employs mass media campaigns, in which the health rationale is no longer primary. The difference between family planning and population control lies in the huge difference between contraceptive use and fertility control" (Ladjali, 1991).[3]

Population control programs have had tragic consequences for individual women. In their rush to market new contraceptives, pharmaceutical companies experimented on women in Mexico and Puerto Rico (usually unethically, without the subjects' informed consent), sold products such as high-dosage contraceptive pills that killed women, and distributed the Dalkon Shield, an intrauterine device that left many sterile (Corea, 1985). Demands for population control often incited governments to violate women's human rights—in Indian sterilization camps, by forced contraceptive injections at workplaces in apartheid South Africa and colonial Namibia, through Puerto Rican sterilization programs, and through forced abortions in China's one-child "family planning" program; the list is very long.

Behind these contested claims lie theories of how and why populations grow. The most popular, supporting the claim that high birth rates account for Africa's backwardness, is the theory of demographic transition. This theory holds that from prehistoric to pre-colonial times, Africans had high birth rates, which were balanced by high death rates that held population growth in check (stage one). With the advent of colonial rule and the introduction of biomedical services, death rates declined but birth rates remained high, causing the current population explosion (stage two). These theorists pronounce the desired state to be a new equilibrium—low birth rates to balance low death rates (stage three)—and point to the success of industrial countries as evidence of the felicity in completing the transition.

Progressive demographers contest demographic transition theory on a number of grounds. First, this theory is empirically inaccurate as regards the history of fertility rates in Africa, the impact of colonial biomedical services (which never reached more than 15 percent of the African population), and the so-called transition from stages one and two to three in Europe (O'Brien, 1994: 173–186). Second, the theory deals with only two parameters of demography—fertility and mortality—and ignores the third, migration. Yet clearly both emigration and immigration have played important roles in changing population levels and rates of growth at national and international levels and have far-reaching consequences for health. States have used emigration as a strategy to control unrest (the British transported political prisoners to their Australian and American colonies). Forced emigration is one way of describing the slave trade, which lowered the population in Africa but also lowered world totals because so many Africans died in transit and on New World plantations and in mines. And because men and women in their prime reproductive years constituted the age group most affected, the slave trade had long-term negative repercussions on population growth rates in Africa.

Demographic transition theory—which is applied indiscriminately worldwide—denies the intense cultural history of Africa's incredibly diverse population, which evolved a multitude of demographic regimes to respond to patterns of social organization in large and small societies living in a variety of ecological niches, and which employed an inventive array of social sanctions to enforce those regimes. Taboos on sexual relations during breast-feeding were effective in spacing out pregnancies; requirements of military service in age-regiments before marriage forced adolescent men to postpone marriage and fatherhood; and late age at first marriage for women combined with heavy social sanctions on pregnancy before wedlock limited the years of childbearing. And some nations relied on conquest rather than births to increase their size (Cordell et al., 1994: 14–32).

In addition, it is clear that colonialism—with its demands for laborers to serve in armies, as head porters, as road and rail construction workers, and as miners and plantations workers, as well as its insistence on taxes paid in cash—both placed pressure on families to have more children and decreased life expectancy (one estimate put the loss of life in the Congo during the rule of King Leopold II at 10 million) (Hochschild, 1998: 225–234). Colonialism also ended military age-regiments and enabled young men to marry earlier by providing them with the means of obtaining dowries that were independent of parental dispensation. Labor migration disrupted certain tribal relations of the obligation that sustained families in times of dearth and probably resulted in further loss of life to the synergies of malnutrition and disease.

Finally, it is well documented that African population growth fell from the onset of colonialism until well into the twentieth century as a result of the slave trade, wars of conquest, and the spread of old diseases that indigenous practices and practitioners could no longer keep under control (with the use of variolation against smallpox, for example, and hedged boundaries against trypanosomiasis), as well as new diseases against which Africans had no natural immunity and for which they had no experience of treatment (tuberculosis, syphilis, etc.) (Cordell & Gregory, 1994). Taken together, this evidence suggests that Africans in many parts of the continent enjoyed lower birth rates and lower death rates before the colonial period.

It is discouraging to note that however much evidence Africanists adduce to disprove demographic transition, it not only continues to inform mainstream international health and development projects but has expanded to encompass rising rates of noncommunicable diseases, a phenomenon referred to as the epidemiologic transition; the two together are referred to as the health transition (Mosley et al., 1993: 673–699). The result of the continued emphasis on reducing population growth, sometimes called the most important health measure a country can promote, is an assault on privacy, a diversion of attention away from inequities in the global distribution of resources, and a steady increase in poverty and the diseases of poverty. Once again, contested claims lead to individual deaths.

Endemic Wars

A third set of claims takes the neo-Malthusian argument a step further and describes overpopulation and environmental degradation as the causes of

Africa's internal wars; violence as endemic, institutionalized, and sanctioned by culture in Africa; African culture as essentially conflictual; social order as dependent on war and internal conflict; colonial rule as having suppressed these impulses; and the withdrawal of colonial powers as having unleashed long-pent-up coups, wars, and domestic and external conflicts.[4] Thus the Rwandan tragedy was simplistically summed up in the American media as a tribal war, majority Hutu against minority Tutsi, although some journalists noted the killings of moderate Hutu. This characterization fit the media's need to simplify a complex power struggle in a tiny nation far from the interests of the U.S. public. It also fit prevailing prejudices about the savagery of Africans, as in this report on the former Zaire: "It can be helpful to think of central Africa today as comparable to early-modern Europe—plagued by interminable tribal and religious wars, and crowded with corrupt despots, predatory élites, and a brutalized, illiterate, superstitious peasantry, festering with disease, stagnating in poverty, *and* laden with promise" (Gourevitch, 1997: 7–8).

The counterclaims are that the policies of Western powers, the interests of transnational corporations, and the demands of international financial institutions played central roles in civil conflicts; that many are the legacy of the Cold War and failed economic development policies; and that arms trading and armed interventions by foreign powers flooded the continent with the means of warfare.[5]

The bodies of countless individual women, children, and men are sacrificed to these claims, which are contested in the most brutal of ways. Millions of deaths have occurred since 1980 as a direct or indirect consequence of war: more than 1 million deaths in Sudan, 1 million in Ethiopia, over 1 million in Mozambique, and more than 1 million in Rwanda. Today nearly 90 percent of all war-related deaths are civilian. In more than 20 African countries during the past 30 to 40 years, war has destroyed housing, transport, and infrastructure and disrupted food production and distribution, causing hunger and malnutrition that exacerbate the effects of most infections. War has interrupted public health measures to control communicable diseases, and armed forces have spread disease, especially sexually transmitted diseases. Current military strategies use starvation as a weapon of war. And some guerrilla groups, like RENAMO in Mozambique during the civil war that ended in 1992, deliberately targeted health services and health personnel for destruction.

In the analytical framework adopted here, biology and culture are clearly entwined, just as economics and politics together shape health and state health policy. Indeed, the false categorization of disease-as-biological/war-as-political lies at the heart of the contested claims. The balance of this chapter is devoted to a discussion of violent conflicts and their aftermath.

Health and Political Violence

As a discipline public health is not given to high theory, and it has had little to say about the long-term health consequences of political violence in Africa. But beginning with the work of A. Zwi and A. Ugalde in the late 1980s (1989: 633–642), war and political violence have again appeared on public health conference agendas. The topics and approaches have changed; whereas the old work was about military medicine and disease epidemics, the new writing is about the health and social consequences of conflicts in which 90 percent of the victims are civilians (Levy & Sidel, 1997).

Increasingly privatized, contemporary conflicts are fought differently from conventional wars between states. The tactics of "dirty" wars are associated with authoritarian regimes, private armies, mercenaries, vigilantes, criminal gangs, paramilitary forces, death squads, and "tribal" militias. Guerrilla insurgents and dirty warriors do not abide by international protocols for war, and they disrespect international laws of warfare. Armed contenders for political power hold civilians ultimately responsible for actions carried out by those who represent them (with or without their consent): their governments, their religious and communal leaders, and their partisan fighters. Guerrillas attack civilians, particularly women, to an unprecedented extent (Littlewood, 1997). Often unpaid, rebels depend on the local population to feed them or they take what they want, not only food but also property and sex, usually violently. Armed combatants also interfere with international relief efforts to deliver food and medicines to civilians because they regard any form of support, even humanitarian assistance, as aid to the enemy. Their suspicions are often well founded: Relief agencies in Ethiopia and Mozambique, for example, played a strategic military role and helped government armies to secure contested areas.[6]

In the period since the end of the Cold War, deaths and injuries have been increasingly caused by the light weapons now found everywhere (because of the uncontrolled arms trade) and by the tens of millions of land mines yet to be removed (80 percent of all land mines are planted in Africa; Mozambique and Angola have the largest populations of amputees in the world). The United States undermines state health services from above by refusing to sign the 1997 universal ban on land mines, so the small budgets for health care (an average of $14 per person in Africa) must be diverted to clinical care and rehabilitation of the injured. The proliferation of guns makes it harder for women to resist rape and survive, yet there are few biomedical treatment services available to cope with the physical injuries of rape and virtually none to handle the mental health consequences, which are compounded by the grief and loss of war (Turshen & Twagiramariya, 1998).

War has churned up human settlements, creating the largest concentration of refugees in the world and an even larger number of internally displaced persons. Psychologists and psychiatrists are studying displacement and dislocation and the mental health consequences of civil war, about which so little is known. The number of people uprooted in Africa's civil wars is staggering: half the population of Liberia, half of Rwanda, 5 million Mozambicans, over 5 million Sudanese, 3 million Somalis, 1.5 million Ethiopians and Eritreans, over 1 million Angolans, 0.5 million Sierra Leoneans, 3 million forced relocations in South Africa, and more than 1 million people forced to flee their homes in KwaZulu.[7] The health consequences are counted in loss of place, family separation, poor nutrition, diarrhea, cholera epidemics, and limited access to health care, even in refugee camps. The physical, psychological, social, and economic effects of the violence from which people flee spill over into the refugee experience. Humanitarian agencies are finally paying attention to the plight of women refugees, who are vulnerable to rape and violence during flight from home, at borders, and in camps. And the reception that awaits returnees is only just now being studied (Marlin, 1998). The long-term social consequences are breakdown of the protective mechanisms of child rearing and disruption of the organizations of civil society, which have done so much to hold communities together and to find within them the resources and strength to confront local health problems.

The stress of political violence leads to health problems, both mental and physical, not just disease and injury but also diffuse malaise—nervousness, vague bodily pains, weakness, and fatigue—new conditions of ill health and disease that have no medical terms. Medical services can treat physical ills, war-related injuries, and the ghastly effects of land mine explosions. Rehabilitation services can fit the limbless with prostheses and bring victims of torture back to the community. Public health workers can stop the epidemics associated with massive population movements, such as cholera outbreaks in refugee camps, and can help restore sanitation and safe water supplies. But biomedical services have little experience in conflict resolution, violence reduction, prevention of alcoholism and drug addiction, or treatment of post-traumatic stress disorders. The human restoration project in war-torn Africa is enormous. It is too large for charities to handle alone; governments must aid them. But in this era of austerity, SAPs, and privatization, international donors deny aid for public social spending.

Gendered Violence

The claims that violence is gender-neutral and that violence against women is mainly a private, domestic matter dominated international conventions until the Vienna World Conference on Human Rights in 1993, when women succeeded in demanding recognition of women's rights as human rights. It now seems self-evident, at least to most women, that all violence is gendered and that rape is the most common form, one in which men assert their power over women and groups of men assert their power over other groups by overpowering "their" women. Feminists brought the use of rape as a strategy of war to international attention during the Yugoslav civil war, in which, it is estimated, between 20,000 and 50,000 women were raped. Just as many women were raped in the Rwandan civil war. In Africa the strategy of raping or forcibly abducting women was also used systematically in Mozambique, Uganda, and Zimbabwe.

In wartime there are gray areas in which it is not clear whether women are coerced or consent to have sex in exchange for food, clothing, shelter, or protection. One's standpoint defines the issue: Women may feel raped when they are coerced or have no choice but to submit if they are to survive, whereas society may brand even victims of forcible rape, including very young children, as collaborators, adulterers, provocative, or worse. How society responds conditions a woman's experience of rape; the rape experience is socially constructed.

Women also play a role in perpetrating violence. In the prisons of apartheid South Africa, women warders practiced institutionalized violence, inflicting torture on women prisoners, even pumping water into women's fallopian tubes and attaching electrodes to women's nipples. African women organized prostitution in men's single-sex hostels, and women caught up in township violence between rival political parties were central to the necklacing of informers. The fear and uncertainty of civil war affect family life and force some women to act even against members of their own family. Some, of course, were tricked or threatened into such behavior, sometimes by the state itself (Goldblatt & Meintjes, 1998: 27–61).

The feelings that women describe in response to their trauma—the fear, pain, grief, guilt, anxiety, revulsion, hatred, loss of dignity, and sadness—are associated with the breakdown of social life, the loss of language and cultural meanings, and the disruption of family, and community. These conditions cannot be treated by the biomedical rehabilitation or public health services available in Africa. For one thing, we know too little about them and almost nothing about how to treat them in non-Western cultural contexts. Few studies of mental health consequences of civil violence have been undertaken outside of Northern Ireland. We lack a conceptual framework to understand what happens to families and communities in places like Liberia and Somalia, where for a time the state ceased to exist. There is remarkably little literature on social and psychological aspects of violence in situations of prolonged civil unrest (Desjarlais et al., 1995).

Women's sense of responsibility and guilt for the trauma they have suffered seems to be heightened, rather than dispelled, when the sequelae of violence are treated on an individual basis. Violence must be addressed at a collective level, and the social forces that contribute to and legitimate such violence must be dealt with. If violence is political, if the context of that violence is a civil war, even when the violence has been called "random" or "meaningless," the health care response must also be a political act integral to a social context. Not only psychiatric symptoms but also social and moral harms must be attended to. The most helpful rehabilitation services are those that reintegrate members of a community in meaningful, durable, and politically valued ways.

For victims of torture, there is more hope, as centers open in South Africa and other countries with NGO assistance. But the specifics of gendered methods of torture are only beginning to surface because women are ashamed to speak of their experiences. The painful and moving interviews with torture victims make clear that there is no division between physical and psychological methods of torture; the torturers play upon women's fears for the well-being of family members as well as applying brutality aimed at their sexuality for the purpose of destroying their basic humanity. Although the physical symptoms of torture tend to lessen over time, psychological, behavioral, and social problems often persist for years. For women in particular, rape and sexual abuse suffered during detention often affect their sexual and emotional well-being for years after the abuse.

Intriguing new work comes from anthropologists who are beginning to etch an ethnography of violent zones. Carolyn Nordstrom contends that the vibrant African tradition of healing, which locates the cause of illness in the polity rather than in individuals, is working hard to heal the injuries and illnesses of political violence, to remove the violence and the war from survivors (Nordstrom, 1997). On the other hand, George Bond wonders about ideological assumptions of uniformity that assign disease to a polity, that fail to recognize illnesses as individual, and that obscure the role of the individual and variations in individualism in Africa.

Large areas remain to be examined: What are the social and demographic consequences of widowhood? In many African countries, data collected before the recent upsurge in civil conflict show high figures for widowhood.

There is talk now of increasing numbers of women-headed households in Africa but little connection to war as a cause. War creates widows. It can turn independent women into charity cases; women who before the war had access to land through their husbands are now destitute and dependent on relatives or social workers. War widows who were raped are stigmatized and find it hard to remarry; widowed rape victims who bear children are ostracized. The psychological toll is heavy: Women suffer from extreme depression, nightmares, and in some cases violent fantasies against the babies born of rape. In polygamous societies, the physical and financial insecurities of war may drive many women into subservient positions as third or fourth wives; for women who have fought against polygamy, this is a retreat. But some see it as preferable to dependence on grudging relatives or prostitution.

What are the long-term health effects of damaged dignity, of daily insecurity, of increased isolation, of entrenched violence? How does war change gender relations, and are the changes permanent? How do changed gender relations affect conceptions of disease? Does prolonged civil war engender creative responses to violence, as Nordstrom maintains? Can the techniques Mozambican healers use to remove the war and violence from its victims and from demobilized soldiers be replicated? Does civil war blur or destroy old ethnic distinctions and create new identities, or does it engender new social divisions?

A narrow economism usually dominates calculations of the scope of war damages and the costs of conflicts. The economic disruption is paramount: wrecked regional transportation networks, failed food production, marketing and trading, and foregone national and international investments. But war also causes child mortality to soar and results in decayed health systems, deteriorating health standards, and suspended education. These social consequences rarely figure in the balance sheets. The psychic costs of family breakup, of children witnessing the violent deaths of their parents, of children left traumatized and orphaned, of children forced to bear arms, may be incalculable. The lifelong price women and children pay for their abduction, rape, and forced prostitution may be unknowable. Clearly, the amount of money needed to reconstruct war-torn countries is enormous. The United States spent $700 million in Rwanda in the 18 months following the genocidal violence in 1994, roughly the same amount as was spent in 1994 in total bilateral development aid in sub-Saharan Africa. Meanwhile military spending continues, contributing to budget and foreign exchange imbalances and squeezing investment and social welfare. And the outcomes of these contested claims will be revealed on the scarred bodies of unknown individuals.

There is one last set of contested claims. If one accepts the neo-Malthusian explanation of the causes of Africa's internal wars, then the burden of the aftermath must fall on the cultures and social orders that institutionalize and sanction violence. International aid must be conditional on internal reforms that promote good governance and democracy. On the other hand, if one upholds the counterclaims—that the policies of Western powers, the interests of transnational corporations, and the demands of international financial institutions played key roles in these events; that Western economic policies brought these countries to the brink of war; and that arms trading and armed interventions by foreign powers flooded the continent with the means of warfare—then the Western powers, transnational corporations, and international financial institutions are responsible for the cleanup (including the removal of land mines), for a halt to geopolitical manipulation of the continent's conflicts and an end to the arms trade, for negotiations of GATT and World Trade Organization terms that will favor African producers, and for a cancellation of foreign debt.

This chapter is about accountability and transparency, about who pays for policies gone awry, and about the consequences of shifts in policy making from the national to the international level and of the privatization of social services. It uses the framework of contested terrains to examine the hegemony of neoliberal ideology in the post–Cold War period and to recount the fallout of that hegemony, as measured in body counts from epidemic disease, conditions related to maternity, and civil wars. Accountability and transparency are much more difficult to achieve in the private than the public sector, much less accessible when NGOs rather than national agencies deliver social services, and much less attainable when policy is made at the international rather than at the national level.

Notes

Introduction

1. Statistics on Africa today are revealing. In a recent report on life expectancy by the World Health Organization (WHO), 32 of the 33 countries with a Disability Adjusted Life Expectancy (the number of years expected to be lived in what might be termed the equivalent of "full health") of under 40 years were African. (WHO, 2000). Africa is the most war torn of the world's continents. Of the 25 major conflicts identified worldwide in 1997, all the new ones were located in Africa. One-third of sub-Saharan Africa is involved in war; of refugees worldwide, more than one-third live somewhere in Africa (Sahnooun, 2000: 6). Large numbers of people have been uprooted by civil wars: Half the population of Liberia, half of Rwanda, 5 million Mozambicans, 5 million Sudanese, and 3 million Somalis top the list (Turshen & Twagiramariya, 1998: 14). According to a UNAIDS report of June 2000, HIV is now deadlier than war in sub-Saharan Africa and has affected 10 percent of the population in some countries. Although the figures present a dire picture both African governments and the United Nations have recognized that steps must be taken to alleviate conditions of war, disease and poverty. Uganda (see Chapter 15) represents an example of successful local and creative approaches to the AIDS crisis and Mozambique (see Chapter 12) to postwar reconciliation.

2. We are using the globalized economy as the form of globalization that has developed in the world since 1975 and is linked to (1) post-Fordist structures of production and regulation, including technological change; (2) increasing concentration of private ownership and increasing inequality; and (3) a shift in activities of the state away from local control of the economy but not a decline in the economic role of the state.

Chapter 1

1. The need for record keeping is an essential piece of Wood's demonstration. Here one can recall the debate about the autonomous and autochthonous inventions of writing in Africa, a debate obscured for a long time by the assumed supe-

379

riority of writing (Europe) over orality (Africa). L. Vail and L. White (1991: 1–40) have launched a convincing attack on this assumption and on M. McLuhan's linking of print (including the map) with the triumph of individualism and the modern state (McLuhan, 1962).

2. "History begins when Man invented writing" is a punch line every elementary school student was taught to memorize until recently in most school systems. In addition, one was usually taught that the era before writing was developed was the "dark ages" of history (mostly in Africa or Pre-Columbian America), or "pre-history" (usually for Asia and Europe).

3. Although Conrad was referring to the history of European exploration, one can easily recognize the centrality of the map in his mind, not only through his writings and his personal interests, but also through the concepts he chose to order his chronology around. Overall, he used the map as the true reflection of the state of exploration in all of his writings.

4. For Conrad, Stanley represented this category of greedy and not-so-noble explorers.

5. Livingstone, Burton, and Speke belonged to this admirable group.

6. Africans' relations with Arabs or Europeans are well known and extensively written about, whereas those with the Chinese are almost ignored (see Snow, 1988; Filesi, 1972). This anomaly is more startling when one acknowledges that mapmaking existed in China from about 2100 B.C., well before it started in Greece.

7. Yoro Fall suggests that the first map to figure the kings of Mali and Nubia and Prester John dates from 1339, and was made by Angelino Dulcert (Fall, 1982: 183–185).

8. A. Godlewska (1994: 40–41) cites a report from 1802 by Maréchal Berthier, who counted 7,278 engraved maps, 207 manuscript maps, 51 atlases, and 600 descriptive memoirs in the course of one campaign.

9. Victor Levasseur's *Atlas national illustré des 86 départements et des possessions de la France* was published in 1847. Cited by Garson (1998: 105).

10. Félix Ansart (1838), *L'Afrique avec ses divisions d'après les découvertes les plus récentes. Dressée par Félix Ansart pour usage des collèges*, Paris. Cited by Garson (1998: 102–103).

11. See R. Girardet (1972); D. Figuier (1983); A. Godlewska and N. Smith (1994).

12. This change is also related to the triumph of photography in Western cultures in the late nineteenth century. Photography books and exhibitions "spoke" more to the masses and were more illustrative than maps. See James Ryan, *Picturing Empire: Photography and the Visualization of the British Empire* (Chicago: University of Chicago Press, 1997).

13. Colonial exhibitions regularly attracted more than 30 million visitors in France, where they had a much bigger success than in Britain (MacKenzie, 1984: 101).

14. For a description of this trend in the British Empire, see MacKenzie (1984: 173–197). There must be a special power assigned to the pink color; Benedict Anderson (1992: 175) states that on the British maps, British possessions were usually pink-red, French purple-blue, and Dutch yellow-brown. One should note the strong contrast effect created by the juxtaposition of brilliant and dull colors.

15. There is much historical work to be done in the detailed analysis of the imperialist components of the education system both in Europe and in Africa. However, the themes of nationalism and patriotism are well covered. On the French case, arguably the most systematic and longest lasting one, see M. Semidei (1966).

16. In 1992, 40 percent of the members of the Association of American Geographers were cartographers and remote sensing specialists (Kirby, 1994: 309).

17. The debate has sometimes been conducted as a an interdisciplinary issue, because Peters is a historian who assails what was once assumed to be part of hard science or visual art. To deflect his criticism, many state that the Mercator projection is no longer dominant. This may be true among scholars, but most of the maps produced for the public, and especially for students, are still overwhelmingly based on the Mercator projection (Wood, 1992: 51–66).

18. Few authors disagree about the Mercator projection's distortion of sizes, but many doubt that it is deliberately in favor of Europe, hence rejecting the idea of a Eurocentric bias. They claim that the distortion was merely caused by the obsession with itinerary, and thus distance ("How to get there?"). Many also point out that the Peters projection is basically the old orthographic (equal-area) projection invented by James Gall in 1885 (Thrower, 1996: 159).

19. The famous Fashoda incident of September 1898 in Sudan between France and Great Britain is a typical example of how maps help shape public opinions about faraway and unfamiliar lands.

Chapter 2

1. There is controversy about the origins of development theory and discourse. A few see it as the offspring of the Enlightenment and Hegelian and Marxist ideas of progress, but many see it largely as a construction of the post-Second World War era that has undergone several phases, first a period of international Keynesianism and state-mediated capitalism, then the era beginning in the 1970s of neoliberal, deregulated capitalism (Escobar, 1995; Moore, 1995; Leys, 1997; Shanin, 1997). All too often in deconstructing development as a discourse and tracing its evolution, inadequate attention is paid to the histories of struggle within and between the South and the North. I try to do the latter in *Manufacturing African Studies and Crises* (1997a: chapter 11) by showing that as an ideology of colonial and neo-colonial modernity, developmentalism was born during the Great Depression and bred into a hegemonic discourse in the immediate af-

termath of the Second World War, thanks to intensifying social and political struggles in the metropoles and the colonial and dependent world.

Chapter 3

1. The chapter goes well beyond an earlier critique that assigned a failing grade to SAP thus far (Schatz, 1994).
2. Some reasons for the dominance of this view are discussed later in this chapter.
3. The first phase may have begun before 1950; this was the first year for which World Bank data were available.
4. The low-income/middle-income classification is that of the World Bank.
5. I am using the simple average growth rate (unweighted average annual increase in gross national product) as the measure of growth. I calculated the averages from World Bank tables. Broad averages indicate continental trends but tend to mask differences in growth rate between countries and over time within countries.
6. The post-1977 slowdown was not simply an African phenomenon. A similar pattern generally prevailed throughout the Third World.
7. A similar view regarding World Bank–IMF responsibility has been expressed by the director of the Harvard Institute for International Development: "The IMF and World Bank would be absolved of shared responsibility for slow growth if Africa were structurally incapable of growth rates seen in other parts of the world or if the continent's low growth were an impenetrable mystery," but neither is the case; the problem has been poor policy (Sachs, 1996). It should be noted, however, that Professor Sachs's criticisms of World Bank and IMF policy and his recommendations are markedly different from my own.
8. An early seminal article on development is Paul Rosenstein-Rodan (1944). *Economic backwardness* is a more comprehensive term than those used currently. No pejorative connotation is intended.
9. All data in this section, unless otherwise noted, are from World Bank (1998d).
10. Once called the "least-developed" countries, but now dubbed simply "low-income" countries.
11. A less unfavorable comparison would match sub-Saharan Africa and other low-income countries but exclude the giants, China and India, which otherwise dominate the averages; still, other low-income nations experienced an average annual real income increase of 1 percent. (My approximation, given the form of the data available to me.)
12. Continuing the comparison, the growth rate divergence is such that 25 years after starting with the same real income, a hypothetical East Asian country would have a real income quadruple that of an African nation.
13. The IMF also plays an important role in formulating and urging implementation of the reform package, but for the sake of brevity I often refer to it as the World Bank package.

14. The report's grade for reform performance is based on its assessment of a country's improvement in overall macro-economic policies. Thus, a country's reform performance score is the summation of its *AIA*-assigned scores for implementation of monetary, fiscal, and exchange rate reforms (World Bank, 1994).

15. *AIA*'s major finding, stated above, is stated again as follows: that the growth data show that adjustment (i.e., positive reform performance)—even incomplete adjustment—can put African countries back on the road to development (World Bank, 1994: 16).

16. The fifth and sixth countries had equal growth ratings, as did the twelfth and thirteenth.

17. A combination of seigniorage and inflation.

18. Relevant countries are those for which *AIA* had sufficient data and that made significant changes in policy, that is, were assigned a reform performance score other than zero.

19. Of the IMF, the World Bank's partner but not a complete soul mate, Jeffrey Sachs declared that the organization has created a carefully constructed image of infallibility that hides a record of mediocrity punctuated by some truly costly blunders that almost never come to light (Sachs, 1998: 18–19).

20. In addition to *AIA*, other major examples of ideological marketing are the *World Development Reports* on outward orientation and price distortion.

21. Helleiner reminds us that the World Bank and IMF are committed by their articles of agreement to liberal, market-oriented approaches to international economic affairs (1990: 111).

22. Needless to say, the World Bank did not publicize this study, and until it was mentioned by *The Economist*, very few people had ever heard of it.

23. Unfortunately, almost any attempt to come up with a conclusive judgment on a major issue must resort to the use of information that is less than reliable.

24. For example, in its discussion and measurement of budget deficits, *AIA* had to choose between four different definitions of a budget deficit (overall and primary, each with or without grants) and consequent sets of data.

25. A graduate student who sought to visit the principal author of the *World Development Report* to talk about the deleterious effects of price distortions (i.e., deviations from free market pricing) and sought access to the detailed underlying data for use in a possible dissertation was turned down by the author. The student reported that he was told that there was no point in bothering with such an exercise, because one can get any result one wants from such econometric studies.

26. Following are two examples of subjective judgments that make the *AIA* case for SAP appear stronger. First, without explanation, *AIA* underweighted monetary policy relative to fiscal and exchange rate policy in arriving at its reform performance scores. This minimizes the dissonant impact of monetary policy contrariety. Second, *AIA* also chose to make no adjustment for the fact that *exogenously caused* variations in external income artificially bolstered the *AIA* position,

even though they agreed that this was the case, because the variations explain only part of the differences in growth (World Bank, 1994: 137).

27. In support of this assertion, see the description of playing with words in this list.

28. Nor was there any mention of the absence of correlation between growth performance scores on the one hand and both fiscal policy and overall macroeconomic policy scores on the other hand.

29. Certainly, not in any major publication on Africa or in any *World Development Report*.

30. What makes the Bank so powerful is that it has no real rival in research.

31. The IMF could also assist, but seems less likely to do so.

32. I plan to present this argument in a larger forthcoming work.

33. Only detailed evidence was able to shake the disbelief.

34. Ailments caused by medical treatment.

35. Many other scholars also sharply reject the public-choice, government-as-economic-disaster view. In place of what he calls the self-interest conception of the state, Paul Streeten offers a commonsense theory that allows for constructive government economic activism. Although government behavior may be damaging, governments are not impervious to forces making for socially beneficial policies. Nobel Prize winner Douglass North excoriates the myopic vision of many economists, who persist in modeling government as nothing more than a gigantic form of theft and income redistribution.

36. Thandika Mkandawire explicitly critiques public choice and argues that the African state can and sometimes does work for the general welfare.

37. If it is not possible to thrash out disagreements, Lance Taylor suggests resorting to mediation or arbitration by teams of independent economists with experience in developing countries.

38. For an example in a political dimension, see Sklar's idea of the complementary relationships among democratic participation, constitutional liberty, social pluralism, and economic efficiency (Sklar, 1987: 70).

Chapter 4

1. This is a revised and updated paper that was originally presented at the Conference on Information and Democratic Society: How to Represent and Convey Quantitative Data, Graduate School of Arts and Sciences, Columbia University, New York, March 31, 2000.

2. *Longevity* is measured by life expectancy; *knowledge* is measured by a combination of adult literacy (two-thirds weight) and mean years of schooling (one-third weight); *standard of living* is measured by purchasing power, based on real GDP per capita adjusted for the local cost of living (purchasing power parity, PPP).

3. Coefficient/income inequality is a summary measure of how unevenly incomes are spread in a given population. The coefficient ranges from 0, representing the perfect equality, to 1, representing perfect inequality.

Chapter 5

1. Jeffrey C. Isaac, personal communication with author (April 18, 2000).
2. See also Diamond (1994). Diamond's *Developing Democracy: Toward Consolidation* (Baltimore: The Johns Hopkins University Press, 1999) arrived during the writing of this chapter. In that volume, Diamond recapitulates and elaborates the basic thesis discussed in this chapter and provides an additional basis for disagreeing with his analysis, from his discussion of Chile (not a mention of the disgraceful Pinochet exit pact) and Portugal (Like Samuel Huntington in *The Third Wave*, he forgets that the overthrow of the dictatorship and the beginnings of democratization were rooted in the long and violent anti-colonial struggle), to that of Africa.
3. When H.R. 1432 reached the Senate, the Senate Finance Committee cut all references to debt relief and to targeted U.S. aid funding for Africa. This version kept demands that African nations remove restrictions on foreign investment and reduce allegedly "high" corporate taxes.
4. In the debates at the National Assembly, members of the opposition National Party (especially Dr. B. L. Geldenhuys) claimed that the U.S. Growth and Opportunity Bill offered "benefits" to African nations that "liberalize their economies and political systems." On the other hand, Deputy Minister of Foreign Affairs Aziz Pahad said: "We accept the positive features of this Act, but . . . we have indicated to the United States administration that there are certain elements of the Act that are not in the interest of its own vision for its new relationship with Africa. I am referring to the issue of conditionalities, which we think it is wrong to impose in an Act that is committed to trying to bring about better relations, economic and otherwise with the African continent" (Debates of the National Assembly [Hansard], Republic of South Africa, Second Session–Second Parliament, May 7, 1998: 1892). I am indebted to Tom Karis for this and other material on South Africa.
5. Progressive groups also continue to make the mistake of talking about "civil society" in the abstract, when they really mean particular interests. Pro-African church associations demand that U.S. programs require "broad consultation by giving African civil society groups a meaningful voice in policy planning and implementation." But by "civil society" they mean "African church, labor, human rights, and community groups," which they think are "often best placed to articulate the needs, interests, and aspirations of ordinary citizens." It is essential, they claim, that such groups be given a formal and continuing role in all the key structures responsible for implementing the legislation to "promote respect for labor rights and the environment" and assure African workers of substantially increased employment opportunities as well as to "provide a livable wage and humane working conditions." Talking about civil society in the abstract, however, does not aid these aims.
6. Most of the evidence about the human cost of the crisis was anecdotal, such as fieldworkers of Oxfam reporting that mothers could no longer afford milk and

were giving their babies tea. "The picture that emerges suggests increases in death rates, school dropouts and malnutrition" (Kristof 1998b, 1998d).

7. William I. Robinson (1996) argues that behind the façade of "democracy promotion," U.S. foreign policy supported an elite-based, undemocratic status quo rather than encouraging mass aspirations for democratization. For a discussion of the costs of the dams and of the plans of one Senegalese company to take advantage of the new opportunities provided, see the interview with Hamidou Sall, the executive vice president of OSBI. He tells us that the government of Senegal, in association with the governments of Mali and Mauritania, created an organization called the OMVS (Organisation de Mise en Valeur du Fleuve Sénégal). This organization for the last 10 years has worked at the construction of a number of hydro-agricultural works such as the Diamond Dam and other similar dams, which were designed not only for the production of energy but also to regulate the water in the river: And so, in this way the Government of Senegal came to control an area of 240,000 hectares, I believe, on the left bank of the river, for the management of these dams. We had thought that our project would have become perfectly integrated into the governments' post-dam program. In so far as it wasn't enough to simply build dams; they had to make these dams pay off, and to make these dams profitable, one had to do what? One had to create businesses, put in companies that would provide employment but at the same time produce added value. It's within these terms that our project would be a major producer of jobs, but also a major generator of value added. We would employ about 1000 employees. This is a project that would cost about fifteen million dollars. About 35% would come from our own funds. We have called upon regional providers of funds, especially the African Development Bank for the rest of the funds that are necessary to launch this project.

8. For a discussion of the differences among the Maurs see interview with Mamadou Djara, assistant to the director of planning at USAID, Senegal, April 30, 1990 in Markovitz (Interview tape 6:18). See the Djara interview also for his discussion of the impact of the Senegalese-Mauritanian impact on the continued construction of the USAID sponsored dams on the Senegalese river. Djara is also interesting because he talks about how many "Senegalese" protected Maurs when they were being assaulted and hid whole families until the riots abated. He discussed the plight of the "black" (his term) Maurs in particular. USAID had financed the studies in Dakar of seven or eight Mauritanian students who were caught up in the maelstrom and who had to go for a long period without knowing what had happened to their families.

9. The names of the Senegalese discussed in this section have been changed. See Markovitz (1990, 1991).

10. Interview with Aboubacar Fall, September 5, 1990.

11. Interview with Mr. Diouf, head of an association of small businessmen, Dakar, May 9, 1990.

12. Ibid.

13. Ibid.

14. See the caution offered by Frederic C. Schaffer (1998, esp. 146) on how fundamental terms like *democracy* can mean different things in different cultural and social contexts.

15. Anthony Marx, in his study of the United States, Brazil, and South Africa, tells us: "Certainly the cases explored in this book demonstrate that democracy neither is necessarily inclusive nor insures that the interests of all will be met" (1998: 277).

Chapter 7

1. See, for example, Gramsci (1971: 5–23).
2. Alan Thomas (1992: 122–132) provides a useful discussion of the category of the NGO.
3. See also Alan Fowler (1991); Ray Bush and Morris Szeftel (1996); and Sheelagh Stewart (1997).
4. Kate Crehan (1997b) explores how the category "tribe" was used in colonial Zambia.
5. The history of the term *coloured* in South Africa is a fascinating one. Under apartheid *coloured*, which defined a distinct position in the racial hierarchy between black and white, was an official category that was fiercely resisted by opponents of the regime and was never used by them without the obligatory prefix "so-called" or quotation marks. Steve Biko and the Black Consciousness Movement in the 1970s popularized the use of *black* as an inclusive term, which explicitly erased the distinction between black and *coloured*, for all those opposed to apartheid. In this chapter in general, *black* should be understood as including all those the apartheid regime categorized as non-white. Interestingly, in post-apartheid South Africa the category "coloured" has reemerged as a self-proclaimed political identity.
6. All except one of those we interviewed, and all those quoted in this chapter, had worked in their NGO as fieldworkers or as fieldworkers and administrators, rather than simply as administrators. Because all our interviewees spoke to us in their personal capacity, not as spokespeople for their organizations, exactly who said what and the NGO they worked for have not been explicitly identified. This decision was made all the easier because what I am primarily interested in here is certain underlying and shared threads running through the contradictory bundle of associations bound up in the term *community* and a certain shared uncomfortableness with this term.
7. The post-apartheid legislation governing land transfers to address historical injustices is very much based on the principle of righting wrong done to *communities* forcibly removed from their land or otherwise unfairly discriminated against, and the basic entity that can gain redress is a particular "community."
8. According to South Africa's *Mail and Guardian* for October 16–22, 1998, of the 26,000 claims received by the Land Claims Commission, only nine had actually been delivered.

9. See Cherryl Walker (1994) for a discussion of the marginalization of women in rural South Africa.

Chapter 8

1. South Africa has a population of approximately 37.5 million people, with Africans making up 75 percent, Coloureds 8 percent, Indians 3 percent, and whites 14 percent of the population.

2. Speech delivered on receiving the freedom of Tongaat, a town linked to the sugar industry in Natal with a significant Indian population, October 21, 1994.

3. The Freedom Charter was adopted at the Congress of the People in June 1955. Some 3,000 delegates from all regions of the country adopted the Freedom Charter as the document that articulated their basic demands for democratic rights in South Africa. The Charter was adopted by the ANC itself in 1956.

4. Reported in *Sechaba*, May 1985. *Sechaba* is the mouthpiece of the ANC.

5. President Nelson Mandela's Inaugural Address to the Nation on May 10, 1994. This speech is available at http://www.anc.org.za.

6. Reported in *The Weekend Argus*, April 23–24, 1994.

7. Reported in *The New York Times*, August 16, 1996. Betsie Verwoerd is the widow of Hendrik Verwoerd, one of the key architects of apartheid and the former prime minister who jailed Nelson Mandela for life. She is currently part of a group of right-wing Afrikaner nationalists calling for an independent Afrikaner republic in South Africa. Orania is a remote settlement in the northern cape that was established by right-wingers in 1991 trying to form the nucleus of a *Volkstaat* or Afrikaner state.

8. Reported in *The Electronic Weekly Mail and Guardian*, May 21, 1998; available at http://www. mg.co.za.

9. Editorial, "Rainbow Nation: Two Worlds in One", *City Press*, May 31, 1998.

10. Reported in *The Sunday Independent*, May 31, 1998.

11. The new political dispensation in South Africa was negotiated as the Convention for a Democratic South Africa (CODESA).

12. Statements made at King Shaka Day Celebrations, September 24, 1995.

13. Reported in *The New York Times*, February 26, 1990.

14. Reported in *The New York Times*, February 26, 1990.

15. Reported in *The New York Times*, September 21, 1990.

16. Buthelezi's decision to participate in the elections was based on a series of concessions he extracted at the last minute: (1) He obtained a promise of mediation over existing differences with the ANC; (2) he secured a special deal for the Zulu monarch that entrenched his position and granted powers no other traditional leader had; and (3) it was reported after the elections that the NP transferred some 3 million acres of land to the Zulu king as an inducement to participate in the election just two days before the new constitution ended white minority rule. This posed a major dilemma for the ANC: The deal deprives the

ANC of much-needed land to resettle displaced Africans and could generate resentment among other ethnic groups who were not favored with such deals. On the other hand, revoking the transfer and reclaiming the land could re-ignite the conflict in the volatile province. "What Buthelezi Gained by Joining the Elections," *Christian Science Monitor* April 21, 1994. See also *The New York Times*, May 25, 1994, for analysis of this issue.

17. Reported in *The Daily News (Durban)*, November 10, 1993.
18. Reported in *The Natal Post*, March 2–5, 1994.
19. Reported in *The Natal Post*, March 9–12, 1994.
20. Reported in *The Daily News (Durban)*, February 9, 1994.
21. Reported in *The Natal Post*, March 16–19, 1994.
22. Reported in *The Sunday Times (Extra)*, January 23, 1994.
23. Reported in *The Leader*, December 24, 1994.
24. Reported in *The Star*, July 18, 1991.
25. Statements made at a seminar on the changes in South Africa at Rutgers University, April 11, 1993.
26. Reported in *The Weekly Mail*, July 1–7, 1994.
27. Reported in *The Economist*, December 3, 1994.
28. Reported in *The New York Times*, December 5, 1997.
29. Reported in *The New York Times*, December 5, 1997. Murphy Morobe suggested that the UDF distance itself from Winnie Mandela in the 1980s in light of accusations of her involvement in murder and torture committed by her former bodyguards.
30. Reported in *The Weekly Mail*, May 11–17, 1994, Business Section.
31. Reported in *The Electronic Mail and Guardian*, March 7, 1997; available at http://www. mg.co.za.
32. Reported in *The Electronic Mail and Guardian*, October 1, 1997; available at http://www. mg.co.za.

Chapter 9

1. The determinative power of property rights is, of course, a central theme in both Marxist and liberal theories of political economy.
2. Most of the buyers were either foreign firms, whose capital and marketing skills eclipsed those of most domestic entrepreneurs, or members of the ruling elite, who obtained their new assets on credit from their political colleagues.
3. Variations on these themes have been urged, and praised, in nearly every major World Bank report on African development since the influential "Berg report" of 1981 (World Bank, 1981).
4. Wealth may, of course, consist of intangible goods—ideas, obligations, symbols—as well as material objects.
5. Marxist theory also considers property to be a fundamental condition for capitalist accumulation, but challenges the idea that the state is an independent

or disinterested agent. Under communism, property is abolished and, in theory, the problem of separating wealth and power disappears.

6. In a socialist economy, where the state both governs and owns the means of production, the logic of property rights implies that the state will police itself.

7. Important contributions to this literature include Hobsbawm and Ranger (1983), Martin Chanock (1985), and Leroy Vail (1987).

8. On the ambiguities and multiple directions of colonial and post-colonial debates over custom, see S. F. Moore (1986) and S. Berry (1992, 1993). On the contested nature of colonial rule in general, see F. Cooper (1994). In his richly documented study of nineteenth-century social transformation and conflict on the Swahili coast, J. Glassman (1995) argues that hegemony itself is never uncontested. Compare M. Lazarus-Black and S. Hirsch (1994).

9. See, for example, K. Firmin Sellers (1996). E. Ostrom (1990, 1995) argues that clear rules and consistent enforcement are both preconditions and consequences of flexibility.

10. Numerous examples are given in R. Downs and S. Reyna (1988) and T. Bassett and D. Crummey (1993). See also studies sponsored by the Land Tenure Center at the University of Wisconsin and reported in J. Bruce and S. Migot-Adholla (1994); see also M. Mamdani (1996). Compare the arguments for community titling in J. Galaty (1993).

11. S. Migot-Adholla et al. (1991); Bruce and Migot-Adholla (1996). Using opinion surveys to determine the incidence of different tenure rights among smallholders in selected rural areas in Kenya, Ghana, and Rwanda, these studies found that "land improvements" were not significantly related to the right to transfer land claims but were correlated with rights "to transfer without approval." In other words, where transfers of land rights were said to be least encumbered by land holders' obligations to others, land improvements appeared to have been more numerous. The authors' reliance on farmers' subjective assessments of "tenure security" and the absence of historical evidence on actual changes in land rights or agricultural production weaken the persuasiveness of their conclusions.

12. British forces occupied Asante in 1896 and annexed it to the Colony and Protectorate of the Gold Coast in 1901.

13. Chiefly office in Asante is designated by its principal symbol, the stool.

14. This assumption frequently underlies both the argument that common property means unrestricted access for all members of the "community" and the case, currently popular among some environmentalists, that community titling is an effective way to protect "local" rights in natural resources.

15. Crown land was excepted but accounted for a very small portion of the regional total. Compare West Africa Lands Commission (1916); A. Phillips (1989); B. Grier (1987); and R. Crook (1986).

16. Aspects of some of these cases are discussed in S. Berry (2001).

17. British efforts, after 1935, to treat the "restored" Asantehene as the definitive arbiter of customary knowledge did little to stem the production of varied

and conflicting interpretations of history (Berry, 1998). Compare J. Matson, writing in 1947: "[Land] disputes involve, not unnaturally, questions of historical fact . . . rather than Court decisions on legal principles. . . . For this reason it has not proved possible to abstract from the material used . . . any general principles of Akan land tenure" (quoted in Kyerematen, 1971: 36). See also Sutton (1984); Crook (1986); K. Mann and R. Roberts (1991); Gocking (1994); Berry (1992).

18. Contrast Janet Ewald's (1988) account of Taqali, a Sudanese kingdom (circa 1780–1884), whose rulers deliberately chose to conduct affairs of state and convey historical knowledge orally rather than in writing, partly to limit the power of Egypt's Ottoman rulers to intervene in the affairs of the kingdom.

19. This is, more or less, what happened. When I revisited Kumase in 1996, I learned that the judge had given a decision, but the ruling was overturned on appeal and the case had gone to the Supreme Court, a common trajectory in both land and chieftaincy disputes.

20. For a stimulating discussion of audiences in historical perspective and the role audiences play in the construction of meaning, see K. Barber (1997).

21. For a similar argument about the sociality and efficacy of prayer in Yoruba religious practice, see Barber (1981).

22. This argument, which I have made with reference to Yoruba society in Nigeria, is equally relevant in Asante (Berry, 1985).

23. Migot-Adholla (1991); Bruce and Migot-Adholla (1994). In the original draft report for this study, the authors pointed out that the actual exercise of various rights to land in Ghana has not always corresponded to farmers' stated opinions about what those rights are or ought to be. Not being readily quantifiable, however, most contextual information of this kind was omitted when the data were "cleaned" for purposes of analysis and publication. Compare Migot-Adholla et al. (1991).

24. Although she does not address the point directly, Guyer's critique is apposite to the treatment of knowledge as "intellectual property," a resource that may be represented analytically as homogeneous and countable, and whose value may be expressed in terms of a single standard.

25. For an example of how similar social processes may interact differently in different historical localities, see Berry (1993: ch. 7). Of course, the definition of historical localities or contexts is infinitely variable and has a major impact on how one identifies processes, their interactions, and the consequences. Comparative social history is more of an art than a science.

26. Compare Djeli Mamadou Kouyate's introduction to the Sundiata epic: "[Griots] teach to the vulgar just as much as we want to teach them," yet "my word is pure and free of all untruth. . . . I will give you my father's words just as I received them; royal griots do not know what lying is" (Niane, 1960: 1).

27. There is an extensive literature on Akan funerals, but more could be done to explore this rich source of performative evidence for insights into the constitu-

tive dynamics of economy and society. For example, there has been little explicit discussion of the point, which I learned only through fieldwork, that even if the deceased left no material possessions, the relatives will select an heir. In other words the heir, or "successor" as he or she is often denominated by English-speaking Asantes, inherits the persona as well as the property of the deceased, a potent reminder of the complex interconnection between property and personhood in Akan culture. On funerals see K. Arhin (1994); M. Gilbert (1988); R. S. Rattray (1923: ch. 11); R. Rathbone (1993); and McCaskie (1989).

28. Disputes over parts of the territory claimed by Kumawu in current litigation can be traced, in published and archival sources, to the mid-nineteenth century, or the early years of colonial rule (McCaskie, 1976; Berry, 1998).

29. This was also true in the colonial period. Questioning the applicability of Foucault's formulation to colonial Africa, Cooper has suggested that "power in colonial societies was more arterial than capillary—concentrated spatially and socially, not very nourishing beyond such domains, and in need of a pump to push it from moment to moment and place to place" (1994: 1533). In colonial Asante, I would argue, power was not so clearly confined to narrow, bounded channels, nor was it all moved by a single pump (Berry, 1998).

Chapter 10

1. In his periodization of *Présence Africaine*, Bernard Mouralis argues that during the second period (1950–1954) it became a symbol and voice of African resistance. Fanon was part of the *Présence Africaine* though never part of its inner circle. Invited to the First International Congress of Black Writers and Artists in 1956, Fanon hammered what he called the "culture of culture," the overvaluation of the artistic and literary rather than the political and socioeconomic, and argued the need for liberation to ground a new humanism (see Fanon, 1967c: 31–44). Fanon's position expressed an important tension found in many of the early *Présence Africaine* writers between the apparent essentialism of negritude (e.g., in Senghor's declarations of fixed black essences) and the lived existence of "the black" in an anti-black world, which reveals an essence that must be overcome.

2. DeBeauvoir adds that Fanon found him "distant" and rather cold (1992: 314).

3. Fanon also attended Trotskyist meetings in Lyons, which at the time was the scene of extensive working-class activity.

4. Merleau-Ponty was more sophisticated than Sartre in Marxian and Hegelian studies. Sartre recognized this and put him in charge of editing the political articles in *Les Temps*.

5. After 1950 Merleau-Ponty became less politically engaged and less supportive of anti-colonial movements. Overwhelmed by Cold War politics he went as far as to declare in 1958 that "I do not want Algeria, Black Africa, and Madagascar to become independent countries without delay" ("On Madagascar" in Merleau-

Ponty 1964a, 334), suggesting, like Mannoni, that a slow, negotiated process "with calculated delays and stages" was the best transition to independence. By the late 1950s Sartre had become the leading intellectual figure supporting Algerian freedom, and later wrote the introduction to *The Wretched of the Earth*. Sartre saw himself as an engaged intellectual, ridiculing Merleau-Ponty as an academic "professorial philosopher": "He accepted the university from the very beginning as a means of doing philosophy and I did not" (quoted by Stewart J. 1998 xxxvii n. 53).

6. This translation traces its philosophical pedigree to Merleau-Ponty's translation of the German "Erlebnis" (indicating a Husserlian influence) to the English "lived experience" (see Judy, 1996: 54).

7. Whereas the retranslation of "L'experience Vécue du Noir" emphasizes the existential lived experience, Charles Lam Markmann's mistranslation, "The Fact of Blackness," caught the facticity of blackness both as a social and historical construction and as a constructed fact that emphasizes not "the Black" *qua* being but blackness *qua* existence, as a lived fact. What Markmann's translation (Fanon, 1967a) signals (which could be lost in a mere accounting of lived experiences) is Fanon's concern to create a new fact and a new way of life. Such a conceptualization is attained by thinking of lived experience not only as a social construct reflecting reality but also dialectically (a subject/object in Merleau-Ponty's terms, of the body in the world, of touching and being touched, of seeing and doing (Merleau-Ponty, 1962: 94–95), embodying tensions and contradictions that necessitate struggles to shape new realities.

8. This is an awareness of the other's awareness of oneself, the third term that mediates and makes concrete "in-itself" and "for itself."

9. This is why Sartre writes the kind of introduction he does to *The Wretched of the Earth*.

10. A criticism that Jock McCulloch (1983) views as almost pathological. He believes Fanon is forced to violently separate himself from a position akin to his own.

11. Of the many different ethnic groups, Mannoni's principle investigation was of the Merina.

12. Ancestor worship was the object of much ethnographic study at the time but, Maurice Bloch informs us, it was "totally un-Merina" (1990: xx).

13. Jock McCulloch thinks that Fanon's critique of Mannoni is simply a mirror based on a kind of sibling rivalry (1983: 219): "There is nothing in Fanon's theory of colonial man which was not first suggested to him, in his encounter with *Prospero*" (1983: 214) and there is not much in Fanon's critique of post-independence that also hasn't already been suggested by Mannoni (1983: 234n.7). Although it is true that one can find a resonance between Mannoni and Fanon, not least the dehumanizing effect of colonialism on the European, McClulloch's assertion of an affinity between Fanon and Mannoni is mistaken. Mannoni's prediction that political independence would inevitably bring corruption, forced labor, arbitrari-

ness, and political oppression sprang from a political conservatism, not a critique of the pitfalls of national consciousness. In fact, Mannoni's belief in a slow decolonization based on the revival of the village councils soon became French colonial administration policy. Such a view of mixing the "traditional" and the "modern" was already a typically colonial form of rule in Madagascar (mapping the colonial administration on the top of perceived traditional forms of rule). Mannoni echoes the tradition/modernity binary. For example Mannoni uncritically celebrates the "modernizing" effects of issuing identification cards without seeing their more ominous side. He celebrates the transference of dependence to a "remote, abstract and almost imaginary object" as material for the creation of a different personality (Mannoni 152), while ignoring both the economic and political reasons for identifying Malagasy individuals as members of ethnic groups and units of taxation and labor. Finally, he ignores the larger structural, economic, military and political reasons for French colonization of Madagascar.

14. Madagascan history of this period is often considered a history of purges, repression, and civil war. No doubt it is, but it is also claimed that before French colonization, Madagascar began "modernizing" and in the early decades of the nineteenth century was producing scholars, officials, and civil servants along modern lines.

15. Representing, according to Mannoni, one of the "best minds," Gallieni was part of a new generation of radicals with regard to colonial policy. He was an intellectual freethinker and admirer of Herbert Spencer.

16. Jean Suret-Canale's *French Colonialism in Tropical Africa, 1900–1945*, published in 1964, is often cited as the first book to include in its analysis the lived experience of the colonial peoples.

17. We should remember that for Fanon a classic expression of the "dependent" native is the nationalist middle class, with organizations fashioned along the European model, which are always looking to the master for recognition.

18. Bloch thinks that Mannoni's belief that the revolt followed a liberalization of French policy is "at best a gross oversimplification and, at worst, a self-serving dissimulation of the situation, one much encouraged by the French at the time" (1990: vii).

19. The VVS (Vy, Vato, Sakelika—Iron, Stone, Branch), the first explicitly nationalist organization was suppressed in 1915. Later the French were so fearful of the Communist Party literati that they expelled them from the Island.

20. General Gallieni thought that the "native's" education should be above all utilitarian (quite different from French colonial practice in Martinique or Senegal, which adhered to traditional French literary methods).

21. Mannoni states that when Madagascar "was first conquered, the Malagasies fled at the first shots being fired." This is far from the truth. But he contrasts this with the revolt of 1947 to emphasize the different reactions of the dependency complex: first, the open-armed embrace of the white *qua* the

Malagasy's own ancestor; second, the feeling of abandonment by the whites' so-called liberalization (1990: 86).

22. The nationalist leadership said that they had tried to prevent the uprising, but the French scarcely believed them. Rabémananjara received an amnesty in 1960 and became a minister in the Madagascan government. Despite his early radical politics, he became a conservative politician, always willing to accommodate France, and served as an architect for a dialogue with apartheid South Africa. The accommodation with France over Algeria was noted by Fanon in *The Wretched* when Rabémananjara was still perceived as a radical (Fanon, 1968: 235).

23. Mannoni describes an experience with his tennis coach that he believes highlights the dependency complex. He gave the coach some antimalarial drugs, and instead of showing gratitude, the coach expected more presents (1990: 42). Fanon might immediately ask Mannoni for more information about the social context.

Chapter 11

1. William Shakespeare, Audio CD Edition, *King Lear (BBC Radio Presents)* (London: Bantam Books-Audio, 1994).

2. See Byron, "Childe Harold's Pilgrimage," in Alexander Leighton, ed., *The Poetical Works of Lord Byron* (London: William P. Nimmo, 1876), Canto the Third, verse lxxii, pg. 142.

3. For a visual snapshot of a baobab, see http://www.lpe.nt.gov.au/dlpe/ENVIRO/REGISTER/COMPLETE/BRADSHAW/snaps/large/brad12.jpg.

4. Waist beads and cloth wraparounds for women.

5. Arthur Koestler (1984).

6. Remark made by Cabral during his 1972 visit to the United States during a speech at Lincoln University.

7. For Cabral's life in exile see Patrick Chabal (1980) For a synopsis consult Mustafah Dhada (1993: 139–148).

8. For details of Neto's formative years, see Bishop R. E. Dodge (1967: 1–2).

9. For Mondlane's life see H. Shore (1983: xii-xxxi); and Barry Munslow (1983: 62, 66, 69, 81, 89, 98–104, 105, 107, 110, 111, 114–115, 119, 139).

10. As early as 1965, Cabral had already realized the importance of diplomacy in liberation. In an interview with the South African journalist Frene Ginwala of *The New African*, he said: "In this time of our struggle it is more important for us to get economic help than even weapons" (Liberating Portuguese Guinea," 1965: 85). Cabral's diplomacy is documented in Dhada (1995: 20–40).

11. The earliest and the best treatment of this subject of arms and ammunition from the West is William Minter (1972).

12. Joseph Conrad (1997). For recent discourses on the Internet about Western images of Africa consult the H-Africa Net archives, http://www.h-

net.msu.edu/~africa/threads/index.html, under "Africa in Fiction by Western Writers and under Africa in Western Writing."

13. The reference here is to the image of Africa as a continent in self-destructive decay, projected in Keith B. Richburg (1997).

14. "Perhaps, in the future, there will be some African history to teach. But at present there is none, or very little: there is only the history of the Europeans in Africa. The rest is largely darkness, like the history of pre-European, pre-Columbian America.... Please do not misunderstand me. I do not deny that men existed even in dark countries and dark centuries, nor that they had political life and culture, interesting to sociologists and anthropologists; but history, I believe, is essentially a form of movement, and purposive movement too." Hugh Trevor-Roper (1965: 9). Trevor-Roper's pronouncement is now a much quoted epigraph and follows close on the heels of attributions to Hegel (Fukuyama's *The End of History and the Last Man* comes to mind here) now so fashionable in academic and scholarly circles. Unlike attributions to Hegel, this one by Trevor-Roper encapsulates the simplistic perspectives focusing on Africa as a continental black hole in historical ontology; as such it is irresistibly quotable even at the risk of adding more fuel to maligning fire. For a teaser on the nature and validity of African historiography, see http://wings.buffalo.edu/academic/department/AandL/aas/faculty/ekeh/570fall98.htm.

15. In Guinea-Bissau alone more than 66 foreign travelers were recorded as having visited the areas under the control of the African Party for the Independence of Guinea-Bissau and Cape Verde Islands (PAIGC), the liberation movement led by Cabral. This information was compiled from numerous sources. For details see M. Dhada (1993: 264–267n.84).

16. I am alluding here to economic and cultural ties related to imperial interests between Portugal and its allies, multinationals operating from the latter, and mutual military interests between Portugal and NATO in the context of the Cold War strategy aimed at containing Soviet expansion outside its traditional sphere of interest in mainland Europe.

17. Cabral viewed his political and personal life as one: "I live life intensely and I draw from it experiences that have given me direction"; therefore nobody "is indispensable.... An achievement is worthwhile to the extent that it is an achievement of many ... even if one pair of hands is taken away" (Cabral, 1980: xxii, 96).

18. This summary is drawn from interviews I had with priests and survivors of the massacre when doing research on a Fulbright scholarship, January–July 1995. Additional material is from *The Times,* starting in June and July 1973.

19. Personal interview with Antonino Melo, Lisbon, 1995. Melo stated during the interview that he absolutely remembers these orders, which were at one point in dispute after the story was no longer being carried by *The Times*. Melo was the commander of the unit that carried out the offensive at Wiriyamu.

20. Personal interview with Michael Knipe, London, 1996. Knipe knew Louis Herren well.

21. Adrian Hastings, private diary entries, July and August 1973; Knipe, personal interview.

22. See the following issues of *The Times*: March 16, 1973: 8a; May 17, 1973: 18h; May 23, 1973: 6h. Additional information on the alliance and reactions to it is in, Staff, "Motions by Tory MPs support Caetano visit," *The Times*, July 12, 1973: 16a.

23. Figures compiled from the *Annual Index* for *The Times* for the years under review.

24. See, e.g., Staff, "Terrorists from Tanganyika," *The Times*, October 12, 1964: 11e; David Leigh (1973: 9c).

25. Figures culled from the *Annual Index* for *The Times*, July 1973.

26. *The Times*, June 27, 1973: 6h.

27. *The Times*, July 17, 1973: 1f.

28. For a glimpse of this type of derision particularly aimed at the priests who brought the story to light, see *The Times*, 11 July 1973, 6a.

29. Staff, "Massacre allegation not proved," *The Times*, July 26, 1973: 10e.

30. The allusion to Adam Hochschild (1998) is to illustrate how Congo was revealed 26 years later as a sort of Wiriyamu on a grander scale. Congo was demonstrably a colossus, driven at a slow, structured pace to collective death, albeit for a clearly identifiable economic purpose, the exploitation of rubber.

31. For details see *The Times Annual Index*(es) for July–December 1973. The complete set was consulted at the British Library, Newspaper Collection, Colindale.

32. For a brief feminist perspective see, Diana Fuss (1980).

33. A useful site for information on essentialism is http://www.emory.edu/ENGLISH/web.html.

34. I greatly benefited from discourses with René Lemarchand on this issue during a recent conference on Conflicts in Africa held at the Triangle Institute for Security Studies, Duke University, Durham. I take full responsibility for the use of the term here.

35. Lemarchand (1994: 17–34).

36. See Gayatri Chakrovorty Spivak, Donna Landry, and Gerald MacLean (1995). An alternative viewpoint is offered by Warren Montag (1998). This article is also available at http://eserver.org/clogic/i–2/montag.html.

37. Memetics is the theoretical construct in existential phenomenology that seeks to explain behavioral conduction through memes, informational clusters transmitted in bite/byte-sized units. See Richard Dawkins, (1990, 1998); Paul Weiner and Daniel C. Dennett (1992); Daniel C. Dennett (1996); and Susan J. Blackmore and Richard Dawkins (1999).

38. Barry Parker (1988).

39. Among expository works on postmodernism, the following have proved of use in constructing this discourse: Shadia B. Drury (1994); Colin Flack (1994); Pauline Marie Rosenau (1992); Charles Jencks (1999); F. F. Centore (1991).

40. Gould's rather elegant riposte to Wilson appeared in *Civilization* (1998: 86–88). See also Niles Eldridge (1998). See also Gould's other works seeking to debunk determinism in its mechanistic avatar: (1996a, 1996b).

41. Fernand Braudel (1995); Gregory Elliot (1994); Immanuel M. Wallerstein (1979).

42. Personal interview with Irmã Lucia, Tete, 1995 (a witness of the aftermath of the massacre); and personal interview with Father Beringuer, Maputo, 1995 (a witness of the aftermath of the massacre).

43. In-depth interviews with survivors and village elders suggest a much deeper and more complex tapestry of emotions and interests governing the events leading up to Wiriyamu, which ultimately compromised the integrity of the villages in the area as political neutrals in the conflict.

44. In light of autodidactic protests against such a proclivity made elsewhere in early 1998, let me hasten to apologize here for succumbing to such a plague of alliterative Vs. See Dhada (1997: 355–357).

45. Franz Kafka (1999).

46. Personal interview with Father Beringuer, Maputo, 1995.

47. Consult the following site for a brief overview of subaltern studies in postcolonial literature: http://www.upress.umn.edu/books/G/guha_subaltern.html.

48. See Spivak, Landry, and MacLean (1995). An alternative viewpoint is offered by Montag (1998). This article is also available at http://eserver.org/clogic/i–2/montag.html.

49. See the following site for an overview of Johann Galtung's center-periphery debate: http://www.moorhead.msus.edu/~gunarat/review.html.

50. For a study in corporatism, see Wiarda (1977).

51. A short bibliography of works by Gilberto Freyre, an advocate of Lusotropicalism, is included in Gerald J. Bender (1978: 250).

52. For a view of Portuguese imperialism by an economic determinist see Gervase Clarence-Smith (1985). For an alternative approach see R. J. Hammond (1966).

53. Max Weber (1996). The text of Weber's *The Protestant Ethic and the Spirit of Capitalism* is also available at http://www.ne.jp/asahi/moriyuki/abukuma/weber/world/ethic/pro_eth_frame.html.

54. By responsive government I mean a government open to constructive engagement with its own society in an all-inclusive discourse.

55. By liberation I mean liberation as discourse and liberation as a fight-in-the-field.

56. Personal interview with General Hama Tai, Maputo, 1995. Tai was at the time of the massacre active as a liberation commander in the area.

57. As stated elsewhere, the struggle to combat lack of interest in Luso-Africa was real. Nowhere is this more acutely pointed out than in Minter (1972).

58. Personal interview with General Hama Tai.

59. To name one who did take the initiative, Domingos Kansande, a seminary student, began compiling what was to become the first draft of a list of the names

of those killed. The draft was jotted down with charcoal on butcher's paper. Personal interview with Domingos Kansande, Changarha, 1995.

60. Interview with Father Sangalo, Madrid, 1995. Sangalo proved instrumental in getting the story out to Europe.

61. Some of these issues will be addressed in a forthcoming monograph.

62. It shared the fate of similar acts of advocacy for Luso-African liberation carried out by solidarity organizations in Cuba, England, Finland, France, Germany, Holland, Italy, the Nordic states, and even the United States, where some Luso-African liberation leaders were unwelcome before 1972. For an assessment of the role of diplomacy in Luso-African liberation focusing on Guinea-Bissau, see Dhada (1995: 20–40).

63. Personal interview with Michael Knipe

64. For a brief review see http://www.209.42.20.17/forms/guestbook-bissau/.

65. This is in no way to minimize the importance of Father Hastings's (1974) account cataloguing the names and numbers killed and the manner in which they died.

66. See Montag (1998); this article is also available at http://eserver.org/clogic/i-2/montag.html.

Chapter 12

1. My work in Angola was possible thanks to a Christian Children's Fund consultancy in 1997–1998. The Angolan data presented in this article were collected both by myself and by members of the CCF team in Angola.

2. In the case of Mozambique, RENAMO was created in 1977 by the Rhodesian Central Intelligence Organisation (CIO), which was interested in sponsoring a rebel force within Mozambique in retaliation for FRELIMO's support of the Zimbabwe National Liberation Army (ZANLA) and for its Marxist policies. RENAMO was later taken over by South African Security Forces in 1980, because FRELIMO was also a strong support base for the African National Congress (ANC) in the 1980s. In Angola, UNITA was one of the anti-colonial movements that, alongside the MPLA and UPA-FNLA, fought against colonial rule. However, after the Portuguese coup in 1974, these three movements fought each other for control of the country. The MPLA emerged victorious, the UPA-FNLA faded in importance, and UNITA reconstituted itself with mainly U.S. and South African support, continuing its fight against the MPLA government. See A. Vines (1991); W. Minter (1994).

3. On the Sierra Leone debate, see King's research proposal on children of war and post-colonial violence in Sierra Leone, Anthropology Department, Columbia University; Abdullah and Bangura (1996); and I. Abdullah and P. Muana (1998).

4. I started writing this chapter during the aftermath of war in Angola. Unfortunately, the armed conflict restarted in various areas of the country.

5. Interview conducted by the author in February 1998 in Lombe-Malange province.

6. Interview conducted by members of the CCF team in March 1998 in Huambo.

7. White (1988).

8. Interview conducted by author in July 1997 in Viana (Luanda) at the OIM Transit Center, where Lopes was waiting for his relatives to come and take him home.

9. Interview conducted by CCF team in March 1998 in Cambandua-Bie.

10. Interview with Paulo's father conducted by author April 1993 in urban district 5 (Bairro Primeiro de Maio).

11. Interview conducted by the CCF team with Miro, a former young soldier from Malange, Angola, in February, 1998.

12. Interview conducted by author with Ben, a 20-year-old youth from Malange who was a UNITA soldier, in February 1998.

13. Interview conducted by author and Carlinda Monteiro with Mrs. Andrade in February 1998 in Malange.

14. Calisto, in Junior (1996).

15. Interview conducted by members of the CCF team with Dunga, a former young soldier from Lombe-Malange, in December 1997.

16. Interview conducted by author with Domingo, from Malange, in February 1998.

17. Interview conducted by CCF provincial team with Jose from Malange, in June 1997.

18. Interview conducted by author with Sam, a former young soldier from Malange, in July 1997 in Viana.

19. Interview conducted by the CCF team with Eduardo, a 17-year-old from Kuito, Bie province in Angola, in June, 1997.

20. Interview conducted by members of the CCF team with Jose, an 18-year-old from Lombe, Malange (Angola), in June 1997.

21. Fernando, in White (1988).

22. Interview conducted by author with Noel and his father in September 1995 in Nhamatanda, Mozambique.

23. This idea of "tactical agency" came from a discussion on this issue with my colleague Mugsy Spiegel. I would like to thank Mugsy for the stimulating discussions we had and for his contributions to this chapter.

24. Interview conducted by the CCF team in March 1998 in Malanje.

Chapter 13

1. For thorough, if conflicting, discussion of the Native Rising, see D. N. Beach (1979: 395–420); Jullian Cobbing (1977); and T. O. Ranger (1967: chap. 2).

2. National Archives of Zimbabwe, DM 2/9/1. Native Commissioner of Melsettler to Magistrate of Melsetter, March 17, 1897.

3. Lessing (1991). In this novel, the settlers' anxiety about space and the need to maintain boundaries is almost palpable. The African bush signifies undomesti-

cated space and danger: "Often in the night she woke and thought of the small brick house, like a frail shell that might crush inwards under the presence of the hostile bush" (1991: 186). In other examples, the bush is imbued with the attitude of dangerous sexuality.

4. For detailed discussion of the politics of African women's mobility in Southern Rhodesia, see Teresa Barnes (1992); Elizabeth Schmidt (1990); and Lynette Jackson (1998).

5. Municipality of Bulawayo, *Minutes*, year ending 1899: 16.

6. NAZ A 3/12/7–10. Medical Director to Secretary of the Department of Administration, June 1, 1920.

7. *Report of the Medical Director and Principal Medical Officer of the BSAP, 1901–1919*. See 1906: 5.

8. Ibid., 1908: 12.

9. Ibid., 1914: 16.

10. Municipality of Salisbury, *Mayor's Minute*, 1914–1915.

11. NAZ H 2/9/2, Town Clerk's Office, Salisbury, to the Administrator, May 11, 1917.

12. NAZ H 2/9/2. Town Clerk's Office, Bulawayo, to Medical Director, Salisbury, September 7, 1920.

13. S.R., *Report of the Medical Director and Principal Medical Officer of the BSAP*, 1914: 16.

14. S.R., *Report on the Public Health*, 1914.

15. Ranger (1970). The "African Voice" is rendered as the seeds of African nationalism.

16. NAZ A 3/12/7, "Appeal from the Leaders of the Christian Mission at work at Falcon Mine and the Township of Umvuma" to the Medical Director, April 21, 1921.

17. Ibid.

18. NAZ S 12/27/1. "Immorality: Native Girls," 1931.

19. "Black Peril" in the colonial nomenclature refers to the perceived sexual threat that black males posed to white females. Black Peril was the rape or attempted rape of white women by black men. The rape or attempted rape of black women by white men was not considered a peril. For general discussion of the "Black Peril," see Dane Kennedy (1987); and John Pape (1990). An interesting yet problematic analysis of the Black Peril can be found in Charles van Onselen (1982). Van Onselen links Black Peril hysterias with periods of economic insecurity. He also, in my opinion, perpetuates the notion that the rape of the colonizer's/master's woman is an act of revolt against the system of oppression. Rape of the master's woman, although not presented as acceptable, is presented as manhood-reaffirming.

20. A very important literature developed in the early 1980s on the "reproductive labor," the "sexual and domestic services" that African women provided to African male workers on compounds and in urban locations. See George Chauncey (1981); Luise White (1980: 167–194); Janet Bujra (1975).

21. Government Notice no. 512, November 10, 1922.
22. NAZ A 3/18/34/35. Legislative Council Debates, May 19, 1921. Re: Motion as to legislation regarding intercourse between white men and native women.
23. Southern Rhodesia, Legislative Council Debates, May 30, 1923. Re: Venereal Diseases Among Natives.
24. Public Health Act 1924.
25. NAZ S 241/531, Office of Colonial Secretary, May 6, 1929. Re: Anti-Venereal Disease Clinics in Urban Areas.
26. NAZ S 235/394, *Commission of Inquiry on the Control and Welfare of Native Population of Bulawayo*, 1930: 3; and Percy Ibbotson (1946: 74).
27. NAZ S 1173/220, Minutes from the Conference on Venereal Diseases, Bulawayo, October 6, 1928.
28. S.R., *Report on the Public Health*, 1914.
29. NAZ S 1173/220, A. M. Fleming to Colonial Secretary, May 6, 1929. Re: Anti Venereal Clinics.
30. R. R. Willcox made these comments several years later in *Report on Venereal Diseases, Survey of the African in Southern Rhodesia*. S.R., Department of Public Health, 1949. This document is discussed further below.
31. National Archives of Zimbabwe, S 235/594. Notes of Evidence, Committee Appointed to Enquire into Employment of Native Female Domestic Labor, 1932: 112–116. By "insufficient self respect," Mrs. Chataway meant that African women could not be trusted to successfully fend off the sexual advances of their white employers', the madams', husbands.
32. Interview with Mrs. Johanna Scott, August 17, 1991.
33. NAZ S 235/594, Native Domestic Labour Commission Evidence, 1932. See also van Onselen & Ian Phimister (1979: 1–43).
34. NAZ S 138/37, Superintendent, Criminal Investigation Department, Bulawayo to Native Commissioner, Bulawayo, May 17, 1925.
35. NAZ S 1173/220, Venereal Diseases Conference, Bulawayo, October 6, 1928: 43, 44.
36. S.R., *Report of the Chief Native Commissioner*, 1936: 1.
37. NAZ S 51/5. Extracts from Mayor's Minutes, Salisbury, 1946.
38. S.R., *Report on the Public Health*, 1936: 23.
39. S.R., *Report of the Commissioner of Native Labour* for the year 1947, p. 39.
40. NAZ S 2805/FNWS/60, Internal Affairs, "Hostel for Native Women," 1942–1944.
41. NAZ S 51/5, Extracts from the Mayor's Minutes, Bulawayo, 1946.
42. The term is found in a letter to the editor in *The Rhodesia Herald*, March 1, 1902.
43. For examples see Reverend Cullen Reed, *Report of the London Missionary Society*, March 31, 1903. Special Collections Library, University of Zimbabwe.
44. National Archives of Zimbabwe, SRG/410, Native Affairs Committee, 1910–1911.

45. Bulawayo Records Center (BRO), Location 23/3/6R, Box 6435, January-February 1911. Re: Umtali Rape Case.

46. For a discussion of early sexual "outrages" perpetrated by white males against black females, see Stanlake Samkange (1969: 242); and Arthur Keppel-Jones (1983: 382). See also NAZ S 1222/2, "Immorality: Personal, 1913–1925." This file is full of examples of white males involved in sexual relations with black females.

47. NAZ N 3/21/1–10, Native Associations, September 20, 1916. Re: The Loyal Mandebele Society (AP Society) Petition to His Honour the Administrator. The AP Society complained about the lack of responsibility taken by the white fathers for their mixed-raced offspring.

48. NAZ A 3/18/34/35, Legislative Council Debates, May 19, 1921. Re: Motion as to legislation regarding intercourse between white men and native women.

49. NAZ S 1227/2, "Black and White Peril in Southern Rhodesia," compiled by Superintendent Brundell of the Criminal Investigation Department, n.d.

50. The term "yellow peril" connotes the result of interracial sexual intercourse. For a discussion of this colonial phenomenon, see Schmidt (1992: 178).

51. Interview with Mrs. Furiana Gosa, conducted by Joyce Chadya, Mbare, Harare, August 19, 1998.

52. Interviews with Ambuya Madzingirwa, conducted by Lynette Jackson and Elizabeth Ncube, Harare, July 16, 1991 and by Lynette Jackson and Isabel Mukonyora, Harare, September 10, 1998. .

53. S.R., *Report on the Public Health*, 1936: 25.

54. Interview with Ambuya Madzingirwa, 1998.

55. Interview with Ambuya Madzingirwa, 1991.

56. Ibid.

57. See, e.g., Never Gadaga (1991b). In this article, the "others" were single mothers living in growth points. These "others" were presented as synonymous with AIDS/HIV transmission. See also Gadaga (1991a). For a discussion of the scapegoating of women in Zimbabwe's early anti-AIDS campaign, see Mary Bassett and Marvelous Mhloyi (1991).

58. Interview with Ambuya Madzingirwa, 1998.

59. Ibid.

60. Interview with Ambuya Madzingirwa, 1991.

61. Interview with Ambuya Madzingirwa, 1998.

62. Ibid.

63. Interview with Mrs. Munyoni, conducted by Daphne Mpofu, Zvishavane, September 27, 1998.

64. In a chapter on colonial anti-syphilis campaigns in Buganda in the 1920s, Megan Vaughan observes that various village authorities seemed keen to have campaigns implemented. She also notes, however, that women were less excited by the prospects Vaughan (1991: 136–139). This was perhaps because it was woman's sexuality that was being regulated.

65. Interview with Mr. Phiri, conducted by Daphne Mpofu, Zvishavane, September 27, 1998.
66. Interview with Mr. Banda, conducted by Daphne Mpofu, Zvishavane, September 26, 1998.
67. Ibid.
68. I received this definition from Dr. Isabel Mukonyora. For more on this traditional virginity inspection, see S. Holland (1976: 219).
69. Interview with Mrs. Johanna Scott, August 1991.
70. Ibid.
71. Ibid.
72. S.R., *Debates of the Legislative Assembly*, November 23, 1944: cols. 2499–2506.
73. S.R., *Report of the Select Committee to Investigate Urban Conditions in Southern Rhodesia (Howman Commission)*, 1943: 11.
74. S.R., *Report of the Urban African Affairs Commission (Plewman Commission)*, 1958: 63.
75. Interview with Mrs. Ndongo, conducted by Daphne Mpofu, Zvishavane, September 27, 1998.

Chapter 14

1. The majority of foreign terms that appear throughout this article are drawn from northern Sakalava, a dialect of Malagasy. As a result of long-term contact with French missionaries, traders, and colonists, this dialect draws heavily on French vocabulary. Where it is necessary to specify the language cited, SAK and FR refer to Sakalava and French, respectively.
2. Following standard anthropological techniques, pseudonyms are employed for institutions and individual informants. At times I have also made use of composite case studies to protect identities.
3. The political trends that create such scarcity are complex and beyond the purview of this chapter. Briefly, the data reported here stem primarily from research conducted in 1993, 1994, and 1995, a period that marked the downfall of President Ratsiraka's socialist and isolationist state, which had been in power since 1975. The centerpiece of his reforms was Malagasization, a nationalist ideology that placed great significance on indigenous institutions and island-wide self-sufficiency over foreign (particularly French) institutions. Malagasization was the impetus for massive pedagogical reforms as well (see Sharp, 1990). Although youth were targeted as embodying the future of the nation, by the mid-1980s (when I first conducted research), the island's school system was virtually bankrupt, and schools were bereft of even the most basic supplies.
4. Interview with Mr. Prosper, schoolteacher, at Ambanja, June 1995.

5. The overall monthly costs of approximately 50,000 fmg that Dalia and her sister pay are indeed high, given that their rural-based parents have little income to spare. 50,000 fmg/month is only a little less than what a full-time plantation laborer earned in a month in the early 1990s. Schoolteachers fared better, making anywhere between 50,000 and 100,000 fmg per month, depending on their level of schooling and the institution in which they worked.

6. Interview with Mr. Jaozara, history teacher, at Ambanja, June 1995.

7. Elsewhere I have referred to Alida as Fatima; I have opted for a new pseudonym here to avoid confusion with another Madame Fatima who appears in Sharp (1996).

8. As I explain elsewhere (Sharp, 1993), this slang term is drawn from the French military: This was the office concerned with covert operations and sabotage.

9. One prominent icon for current nationally generated health and hygiene instructional materials is the comic book *Liza*, which first appeared in the form of the school publication *La Plume* in 1994 (see Madagascar, 1994). It tells the story of a young woman's rise to stardom as a pop singer, tracing her life from her village, to *lycée*, through a failed marriage, and to the stage. As a pop star she has sexual encounters with a number of men, and she is eventually diagnosed with *SIDA*. In the story she emerges as a heroine, because she is at heart a kind person, and in the end she donates her wealth to the national program responsible for combating *SIDA* in Madagascar.

10. Interview with Foringa, student, at Ambanja, July 1994.
11. Interview with Dalia, student, at Ambanja, July 1994.
12. Interview with Yvetty, trader, at Ambanja, July 1994.

Chapter 15

1. More detailed documentation of this embeddedness appears in "The First Decade: An AIDS-Related Calendar, Uganda 1981–1990," which accompanied a talk given at the Metropolitan Medical Anthropological Association meeting on 8 May 1991 (Bond & Vincent, 1991). A version of the talk, abbreviated and without the calendar, appears in Bond, Kreniske, Susser & Vincent (1997: 85–98).

2. The profile was funded by the U.S. Agency for International development, and its design reflected its preference that the study focus on five distinct agroecological zones. New districts were created out of old counties in response to political pressures on the Ugandan regime of that time.

3. That the physical distance between Entebbe, formerly the colonial administrative center of Uganda, and Kampala, its capital, was also a social distance is documented in Bond and Vincent (1997b: 101–102, 112n.5). In recent years, scholars and practitioners within the academic, humanitarian, and human rights communities have made use of the term *complex emergencies* (Bryant, 1998; Bryans, Jones & Stein, 1999) to describe a range of situations involving violence.

Chapter 16

1. For a full discussion of nonspecific mortality, see Turshen (1989).

2. It is an irony of history that Malthus, who opposed abortion and birth control on moral grounds, should have his name used for population control policies that rely in the first instance on artificial contraception.

3. Women's individual wishes and needs are usually subordinated to the goals of population control programs; this is illustrated by government policies that regulate women's fertility to control ethnic and racial diversity. In an extreme example, the apartheid government in South Africa employed natalist and antinatalist policies selectively; the policies worked to promote an increase in the white population but to limit fertility among blacks. And in Namibia, contraception was the only free health service provided for blacks by the South African government in the 1970s.

4. See R. D. Kaplan (1994: 44–76) for an exposition of the neo-Malthusian analysis of the causes of war in Africa, and see P. Richards (1996) for a critique of this analysis in the context of Sierra Leone's civil war. On culture and conflict see Adda Bozeman, quoted in J. P. Smaldone (1990: 5).

5. Establishing this connection between the relatively peaceful and prosperous industrial nations and the mayhem visited on many Africans in no way exonerates the leaders of the militias and armies for the havoc they have wrought.

6. A. de Waal and M. Duffield (1992: 390–396) state that relief centers were often the site of food aid diversion to militia forces, and they estimate that relief agencies in Ethiopia and Mozambique may have provided a 10 percent contribution to rural people's survival, but abetted the destruction of much of the other 90 percent. Some agencies deplore the fact that their hijacked aid has merely prolonged internal struggles.

7. Significant numbers in Burundi, Chad, Congo (Kinshasa), Kenya, Mali, Mauritania, Senegal, Uganda, and Western Sahara were also uprooted (U.S. Committee for Refugees, Washington, D.C. 1998).

References

Abdullah, I., and Bangura, Yusuf. 1996 (March 19). "Violence, Youth Culture and War: A Critical Reading of Paul Richards." *Lionenet: A Discussion of Sierra Leonean Issues*. Available at http://www.research.umbc.edu/~leoneadm.
Abdullah, I., and P. Muana. 1998. "The Revolutionary United Front of Sierra Leone: A Revolt of the Lumpenproletariat." In C. Clapham, ed. *African Guerrillas*. Oxford: James Currey.
Abu-Lughod, J. L. 1995. "The World-System Perspective in the Construction of Economic History." *History and Theory*, 34 (2): 86–98.
"Les Actes Infamants Des Fideles D'Allah." 1989 (Mai). *Promotion*, 50.
Adam, Heribert. 1995. "The Politics of Ethnic Identity: Comparing South Africa." *Ethnic and Racial Studies*, 19 (3): 457–475.
———. 1996. "The Mandela Cult Personality." *Indicator*, 13 (2): 7–12.
———. 1998 (April 1). Empowering the Black Fat Cats." *Electronic Mail and Guardian;* http://www.mg.co.za.
Adam, Heribert, and Kogila Moodley. 1986. *South Africa Without Apartheid*. Berkeley: University of California Press.
———. 1993. *The Opening of the Apartheid Mind: Options for a New South Africa*. Berkeley: University of California Press.
Adam, Heribert, Federick Van Zyl Slabbert, and Kogila Moodley. 1997. *Comrades in Business: Post-Liberation Politics in South Africa*. Cape Town: Talelberg Publishers.
Adams, W. H. 1992. *Green Development: Environment and Sustainability in the Third World*. London: Routledge.
Adejumobi, S. 1995. "Structural Reform and Its Impact on the Economy and Society." In S. Adejumobi and A. Momoh, eds. *The Political Economy of Nigeria under Military Rule*. Harare: SAPES Books, pp. 99–125.
Adelzadeh, Ashgar. 1996. "Growth and Development: Labor and Business Perspectives on Economic Development." In Jeremy Baskin, ed. *Against the Current: Labor and Economic Policy in South Africa*. Johannesburg: Ravan, pp. 41–60.
Adesina, Jimi. 1992. "Labor Movements and Policy Making in Africa." *CODESRIA Working Papers*, 1/92.

Adler, Glen. 1996. "New Social Movements: Democratic Struggles and Human Rights in Africa." In James H. Mittelman, ed. *Globalization: Critical Reflections.* Boulder, CO: Lynne Rienner, pp. 117–143.
Adler, Glenn, ed. 2000. *Engaging the State and Business.* Johannesburg: Witwatersrand University Press.
Adler, Glenn, and Eddie Webster. 1995. "Challenging Transition Theory: The Labor Movement, Radical Reform, and Transition to Democracy in South Africa." *Politics and Society,* 23 (1): 75–106.
Adler, Glenn, Judy Maller, and Eddie Webster. 1992. "Unions, Direct Action and Transition in South Africa." In Norman Etherington, ed. *Peace, Politics and Violence in the New South Africa.* London: Hans Zell, pp. 306–343.
Africa Recovery. 1996. New York: United Nations.
African National Congress (ANC). 1996. *The Reconstruction and Development Programme: A Policy Framework.* Johannesburg: Umanyano Publications.
_____. 1997 "Political Report of the President, Nelson Mandela to the 50th Conference of the African National Congress," Mafikeng, December 16. Available at http://www.anc.org.za/ancdocs/pr/1997/pr1216.html.
Aglietta, M. 1982. *A Theory of Capitalist Regulation: The U.S. Experience.* New York: Verso.
Ahlberg, Beth Maina. 1994. *Women, Sexuality, and the Changing Social Order: The Impact of Government Policies on Reproductive Behavior in Kenya.* Philadelphia: Gordon and Breach.
Aina, T. 1996. *Globalization and Social Policy in Africa.* Dakar: Codesria.
Ajayi, J. F. A., and M. Crowder, eds. 1976. *History of West Africa.* 2 vols. London: Longman.
Ake, Claude. 1997. *Democracy and Development in Africa.* Washington, DC: The Brookings Institution.
Akeroyd, Anne V. 1994. "HIV/AIDS in Eastern and Southern Africa." *ROAPE,* 60: 173–184.
Akwetey, Emmanuel. 1996. "Democratization and Labor Regime Reform in Post-Transitional Africa." Paper presented at the Workshop on "Labor Regimes and Liberalization: The Restructuring of State-Society Relations in Africa," University of Zimbabwe, Harare, May 16–18.
Akyeampong, Emmanuel, and Pashington Obeng. 1995. "Spirituality, Gender, and Power in Asante History." *International Journal of African Historical Studies,* 28 (3): 481–508.
Allen, R. B. 1997. "Review of *A Modern Economic History of Africa.*" *African Studies Review,* 40 (1): 189–190.
Altman, L. 2000. "U.N. Warning AIDS Imperils Africa's Youth." *New York Times,* June 28, pp. A1 and A22.
Amin, S. 1997. *Capitalism in the Age of Globalization.* London: Zed Books.
Amit-Talai, Vered, and Helena Wulff, eds. 1995. *Youth Cultures: A Cross-Cultural Perspective.* London and New York: Routledge.

Amsden, Alice. 1997 (April). "Bringing Production Back in: Understanding Government's Economic Role in Late Industrialization." *World Development*, 25 (4): 469–480.
Anderson, B. 1991. *Imagined Communities: Reflections on the Origin and Spread of Nationalism*. New York: Verso.
Anderson, Lisa, ed. 1999. *Democracy in Comparative Politics*. New York: Columbia University Press.
Anderson, M. 1992. "The History of Women and the History of Statistics." *Journal of Women's History*, 4 (1): 14–36.
Anderson, S. R., J. W. B. Bainbridge, A. Shah, P. El-Jassar, G. Schofield, H. Brook, and M. Kapila. 1990. "AIDS Education in Rural Uganda—A Way Forward. *International Journal of STD and AIDS*, 1: 335–339.
Andrae, Gunilla, and Bjorn Beckman. 1998. *Union Power in the Nigerian Textile Industry. Labor Regime and Adjustment*. Uppsala: Nordiska Afrikainstitutet.
Ankrah, E. Maxine. 1996. "AIDS, Socioeconomic Decline and Health: A Double Crisis for the African Woman." In Lorraine Sher, Catherine Hawkins, and Lydia Bennett, eds. *AIDS as a Gender Issue: Psycho-Social Perspectives*. London: Taylor & Francis, pp. 99–118.
Anunobi, Fredoline O. 1992. *The Implications of Conditionality: The International Monetary Fund and Africa*. Lanham, MD: University Press of America.
Appiah, Anthony K. 1992. *In My Fathers House*. New York: Oxford University Press.
Appiah, Kwame A. 1992 "Inventing an African Practice in Philosophy: Epistemological Issues." In V. Y. Mudimbe, ed. *The Surreptitious Speech: Présence Africaine and the Politics of Otherness. 1947–1987*. Chicago: University of Chicago Press, pp. 227–238.
Apple, R. W., Jr. 1998. "From Mandela, a Gentle Admonishment." *New York Times*, March 28.
Arens, W., and I. Karp, eds. 1989. *Creativity of Power: Cosmology and Action in African Societies*. Washington, DC: Smithsonian.
Arhin, K. 1994. "The Economic Implications of Transformations in Akan Funeral Rites," *Africa*, 64 (3): 307–322.
Arntzen, J., et al., eds. 1986. *Land Policy and Agriculture in Eastern and Southern Africa*. Tokyo: United Nations University Press.
Asad, T. 1973. *Anthropology and the Colonial Encounter*. London: Ithaca Press.
Asante, S. K. B. 1975. *Property Law and Social Goals in Ghana, 1844–1966*. Accra: Ghana Universities Press.
"Asia's Crisis Upsets Rising Effort to Confront Blight of Sweatshops." 1998. *New York Times*, June 15, p. A1
Asiwaju, A. I. 1990. *Artificial Boundaries*. New York: Civiletis International.
Austen, R. A. 1987. *African Economic History*. London: James Currey.
———. 1995. "Review of *A Modern Economic History of Africa*." *Africa*, 65 (1): 141–143.

Babawale, Tunde, Akin Fadahunsi, Abubakar Momoh, and Adebayo Olukoshi. 1996. "Nigeria Beyond Structural Adjustment: Towards a National Popular Alternative Development Strategy," *Africa Development*, 21 (2/3): 119–139.

Bagrow, L. 1966. *History of Cartography*, Chicago: Precedent.

Bangura, Yusuf. 1987. "The Recession and Workers' Struggles in the Vehicle Assembly Plants: Steyr-Nigeria." *Review of African Political Economy*, 14 (39): 4–22.

Bangura, Yusuf, and Bjorn Beckman. 1991. "African Workers and Structural Adjustment: The Nigerian Case." In Dharam Ghai, ed. *The IMF and the South: The Social Impact of Crisis and Adjustment.* London: Zed Books.

Barber, K. 1997. "Preliminary Notes on Audiences in Africa." *Africa*, 67 (3): 347–363.

Barber, K., et al. 1997. *West African Popular Theatre.* Bloomington: Indiana University Press.

Barber, T. 1981. "How Man Makes God in West Africa: Yoruba Attitudes Towards the *Orisa.*" *Africa*, 51 (5): 217–237.

Barchiesi, Franco. 1998. "Trade Unions and Organizational Restructuring in the South African Automobile Industry: A Critique of the Co-determination Thesis." *African Sociological Review*, 2 (2): 47–76.

Barker, T. C. 1985 (February). "What Is Economic History?" *History Today, 35 (2)*, 25–27.

Barnes, T. 1992. "The Fight for Control of African Women's Mobility in Colonial Zimbabwe, 1890–1939." *Signs*, 17 (3): 586–608.

Barnett, Tony. 1994. *The Effects of HIV/AIDS on Farming Systems and Rural Livelihoods in Uganda, Tanzania and Zambia.* Final Report, Executive Summary, ODA.

Barton, Tom, and Gimono Wamai. 1994. *Equity and Vulnerability: A Situation Analysis of Women, Adolescents and Children in Uganda.* Entebbe: Uganda National Council for Children.

Baskin, Jeremy. 1991. *Striking Back. A History of COSATU.* Johannesburg: Ravan.

———. 1993. "Corporatism: Some Obstacles Facing the South African Labor Movement," *CPS Research Reports*, 30. Johannesburg: Center for Policy Studies.

Bassett, M., and M. Mhloyi. 1991. "Women and AIDS in Zimbabwe: The Making of an Epidemic." *International Journal of Health Services*, 21 (1): 143–156.

Bassett, T. 1993. "Land Use Conflicts in Pastoral Development in Northern Cote d'Ivoire." In T. Bassett and D. Crummey, eds. *Land in African Agrarian Systems.* Madison: University of Wisconsin Press.

Bassett, T., and D. Crummey, eds. 1993. *Land in African Agrarian Systems.* Madison: University of Wisconsin Press.

Bates, B. 1981. *Markets and States in Tropical Africa.* Berkeley and Los Angeles: University of California Press.

Bates, R. 1983. *Essays in the Political Economy of Rural Africa.* Cambridge: Cambridge University Press.

———. 1989. *Beyond the Miracle of the Market: The Political Economy of Agrarian Development in Kenya.* Cambridge: Cambridge University Press.

Bates, R. F. 1987. *Essays in the Political Economy of Africa.* Berkeley: University of California Press.

Bayart, Jean-François, Stephen Ellis, and Béatrice Hibou. 1999. *The Criminalization of the State in Africa* Oxford: James Currey.

Baylies, Carolyn, and Janet Bujra. 1997. "Social Science Research on AIDS in Africa: Questions of Content, Methodology and Ethics." *ROAPE*, 73: 380–387.

Beach, D. N. 1979. "Chimurenga: The Shona Rising of 1896–97." *Journal of African History*, 20 (3): 395–420.

Becker, D., and R. Sklar. 1987. *Post Imperialism: International Capitalism and Development in the Late Twentieth Century.* Boulder: Lynne Rienner.

Beckman, Bjorn. 1993. "The Liberation of Civil Society: Neo-Liberal Ideology and Political Theory." *Review of African Political Economy*, 20 (58): 20–34.

Bell, Paul. 1998 (December). "Full Yellow Jacket." *Leadership*, 16 (4); http://www.leadership.co.za.

Bender, G. J. 1978. *Angola Under the Portuguese, the Myth and the Reality.* London: Heinemann.

Benjamin, Craig S., and Terisa E. Turner. 1992. "Counterplanning from the Commons: Labor, Capital and the New Social Movements." *Labor, Capital and Society*, 25: 2.

Bentley, Arthur Fisher. *The Process of Government.* Cambridge: Harvard University Press, 1967.

Berry, S. 1985. *Fathers Work for Their Sons: Accumulation, Mobility and Class Formation in an Extended Yoruba Community.* Berkeley and Los Angeles: University of California Press.

———. 1992. "Hegemony on a Shoestring: Indirect Rule and Access to Agricultural Land." *Africa*, 62 (3): 327–355.

———. 1993. *No Condition Is Permanent: The Social Dynamics of Agrarian Change in sub-Saharan Africa.* Madison: University of Wisconsin Press.

———. 1998. "Unsettled Accounts: Stool Debts, Chieftaincy Disputes, and the Question of Asante Constitutionalism." *Journal of African History*, 39 (1): 39–62.

Bhabha, Homi. 1999 "Remembering Fanon: Self, Psyche, and the Colonial Condition." in Nigel Gibson, ed. *Rethinking Fanon.* Amherst, NY : Prometheus Books.

Bhana, Surendra. 1991. *Indentured, Indian Immigrants to Natal 1860–1902*, New Delhi: Promilla and Co.

———. 1997. *The Natal Indian Congress: 1984–1994: Ghanda's Legacy.* Pietermaritzburg: University of Natal Press.

Biebuyck, D., ed. 1963. *African Agrarian Systems.* London: Oxford University Press.

Bienen, Henry, and Jeffrey Herbst. 1996. "The Relationship Between Political and Economic Reform in Africa." *Comparative Politics*, 29 (1): 23–42.

Biersteker, Thomas J. 1987. "Indigenization and the Nigerian Bourgeoisie: Dependent Development in an African Context." In Paul M. Lubeck, ed. *The African Bourgeoisie. Capitalist Development in Nigeria, Kenya, and the Ivory Coast*. Boulder, CO: Lynne Rienner, pp. 249–279.

Biko, Steve. 1978. *I Write What I Like*. London: The Bowerdean Press.

Birmingham, D. 1995. *The Decolonization of Africa*. Athens: Ohio University Press.

Birmingham, D., and P. Martin, eds. 1985. *History of Central Africa*. 2 vols. London: Longman.

Black, J. 1997. *Maps and History: Constructing Images of the Past*. New Haven and London: Yale University Press

Blackmore, S. J., and Richard Dawkins. 1999. *The Mean Machine*. Oxford: Oxford University Press.

Bledsoe, C. 1980. *Women and Marriage in Kpelle Society*. Stanford: Stanford University Press.

———. 1990. "'No Success Without Struggle': Social Mobility and Hardship for Foster Children in Sierra Leone." *Man*, 25 (1): 70–88.

Bloch, Maurice. 1990. "Introduction." In Octave Mannoni, *Prospero and Caliban: The Psychology of Colonialization (psychologie de la colonialization)*. Ann Arbor: University of Michigan Press.

———. 1995. *People into Places: Zafimaniry Concepts of Clarity*. In E. Hirsch and M. O'Hanlon, eds. *The Anthropology of Landscape: Perspectives on Place and Space*. Oxford: Clarendon Press, pp. 63–77.

Bohlen, Celestine. 1998. "Vatican Repents Failure to Save Jews from Nazis." *New York Times*, March 17.

Bohmke, Heinrich, and Ashwin Desai. 1996. "Everything Keeps Going Wrong . . . Toyota." *South African Labour Bulletin*, 20 (3): 52–58.

Bond, George C., and Angela Gilliam. 1994. *Social Construction of the Past*. New York: Routledge.

Bond, G. C., and Joan Vincent. 1990. "Politics and Methodology in Situating Multiple Contingent Risks (MRC) in AIDS Research." Paper presented at Assembling Knowledge to Address Human Problems Conference, Society for Applied Anthropology, University of York, March-April.

Bond, G. C., and Joan Vincent. 1991. "Living on the Edge: Changing Social Structures in the Context of AIDS." In H-B. Hansen and M. Twaddle, eds. *Uganda: Structural Adjustment and Change*. London: James Currey, pp. 113–129.

———. 1997a. "AIDS in Uganda: The First Decade." In George Bond, John Kreniske, Ida Susser, and Joan Vincent, eds. *AIDS in Africa and the Caribbean*. Boulder: Westview Press, pp. 85–99.

———. 1997b. "Community Based Organizations in Uganda." In G. C. Bond, J. Kreniski, I. Susser, and J. Vincent, eds. *AIDS in Africa and the Caribbean*. Boulder: Westview Press, pp. 99–113.

———. 2000. "AIDS in Uganda: A Medical and Moral Dilemma." Unpublished paper.
Bond, Patrick. 1998. *Elite Transition. Uneven Development, Neoliberalism and Globalization in South Africa.* London: Pluto Press.
Booth, D. 1993. "Development Research: From Impasse to a New Agenda." In F. J. Schuurman, ed. *Beyond the Impasse: New Directions in Development Theory.* London: Zed Books.
Boothby, N. 1990. "Working in the War Zone: A Look at Psychological Theory and Practice from the Field." *Mind and Human Interaction*, 2 (2): 34.
Boothby, N., P. Upton, and A. Sultan. 1992 (March). "Boy Soldiers of Mozambique." In *Refugee Children*. Oxford: Refugee Studies Programme.
Bourdieu, P. 1977. *Outline of a Theory of Practice*. R. Nice, trans. Cambridge: Cambridge University Press.
Boyden, J. 1990. "Childhood and the Policy Makers: A Comparative Perspective on the Globalisation of Childhood." In A. James and A. Prout, eds. *Constructing and Reconstructing Childhood: Contemporary Issues in the Sociological Study of Childhood*. London: The Falmer Press.
Boyden, J., and S. Gibbs. 1997. *Children and War: Understanding Psychological Distress in Cambodia*. Geneva: United Nations.
Bratton, B. 1989. "Beyond the State: Civil Society and Associational Life in Africa." *World Politics*, 41 (3): 407–430.
Bratton, Michael, and Nicolas Van de Walle. 1992 "Toward Governance in Africa." In G. Hyden and M. Bratton, eds. *Governance and Politics in Africa*. Boulder: Lynne Rienner.
Braudel, F. 1995. *A History of Civilizations*. New York: Penguin.
Brett, R., and M. McCallin. 1996. *Children, the Invisible Soldiers*. Stockholm: Radda Barnen (Swedish Save the Children).
Bromley, D. 1989. "Property Relations and Economic Development: The Other Land Reform." *World Development*, 17 (6): 867–877.
Brown, Lynn. 1999. "The Potential Impact of AIDS on Economic Growth Rates in Sub-Saharan Africa." Paper presented at symposium HIV/AIDS in Africa: Reviewing the Past, Understanding the Present, and Charting the Future symposium, University of Illinois at Urbana-Champaign, July 14–17.
Bruce, J., and S. Migot-Adholla, eds. 1994. *Searching for Land Tenure Security in Africa*. Dubuque, IA: Kendall Hunt.
Bryans, Michael, Bruce Jones, and Janice Stein. 1999. *Mean Times: Humanitarian Action in Complex Political Emergencies*. Toronto: Program in Conflict Management and Negotiation, Centre for International Studies, No. 3, pp. 1–45.
Bryant, Coralie. 1998. "Strategic Management of Humanitarian Assistance in Complex Emergencies: Possibilities and Prospects." Unpublished paper, Columbia University, pp. 1–25.
Buhlungu, Sakhela. 1996. *Trade Union Responses to Participatory Management: A Case Study*. Master's thesis, Department of Sociology, University of the Witwatersrand, Johannesburg.

Bujra, Janet. 1975. "Women Entrepreneurs of Early Nairobi." *Canadian Journal of African Studies*, 9 (2): 213–234.
Bulhan, Hussein A. 1999. "Revolutionary Psychiatry of Fanon." In Nigel Gibson, ed. *Rethinking Fanon*. Amherst, NY: Prometheus Books.
Bush, Ray, and Morris Szeftel. 1996 (June). "ROAPE Review of Books [Editorial]." *ROAPE*, 23 (68): 127–128.
Busia, K. A. 1951. *The Position of the Chief in the Modern Political System of Ashanti*. Oxford: Oxford University Press.
Butchart, A. 1998. *The Anatomy of Power: European Constructions of the African Body*. New York: St. Martin's Press.
Butegwa, Florence. 1991. "Women's Legal Right of Access to Agricultural Resources in Africa: A Preliminary Inquiry." *Third World Legal Studies*, 8:45–67.
———. 1998. "Uganda." In Gita Gopal and Maryam Salim, eds. *Gender and Law: Eastern Africa Speaks*. Washington, DC: World Bank, pp. 163–198.
Buttel, F., and P. MacMichael. 1991. "Reconsidering the Explanandum and Scope of Development Studies: Towards a Comparative Sociology of State-Economy Relations." Paper for the Hull Workshop on "Relevance, Realism and Choice in Social Development Research," Centre for Developing Area Studies, University of Hull, January 10–12.
Byrne, David. 1999. *Social Exclusion*. Milton Keynes: Open University.
Byron, Lord. "Childe Harold's Pilgrimage." 1876. In A. Leighton, ed. *The Poetical Works of Lord Byron*. London: William P. Nimmo, Canto the Third, verse lxxii, p. 142.
Cabral, A. 1973. *Return to the Source*. New York: Monthly Review Press.
———. 1980. *Unity and Struggle*. London: Heinemann.
Cabrita, F. 1992. "Os Mortos Não Sofrem." *Revista Expresso*, December 5.
———. 1998. "Wiriyamu, Viagem ao fundo do Terror." *Revista Expresso*, November 21.
Caetano, M. 1974. *Depoimento*. Rio de Janeiro: Distribuidora Record.
Caldwell, J., P. Caldwell, and P. Quiggin. 1989. *Disaster in an Alternative Civilization: The Social Dimensions of Aids in Sub-Saharan Africa*. Canberra: National Centre for Epidemiology and Population Health.
Cameron, V. L. 1877. *Across Africa*. London: Daldy, Isbister.
Camo, Pierre. 1931. *La protection de la vie locale a Madagascar*. Proceedings of the Congres International et Intercolonial de la société Indigène, Exposition Coloniale Internationale de Paris, October 5–10.
Campbell, Catherine., Gerhard Marè, and Cherryl Walker. 1985 (June)."Evidence of an Ethnic Identity in the Life Histories of Zulu-speaking Durban Township Residents." *Journal of Southern African Studies*, 21 (2): 287–301.
Campion-Vincent, Véronique. 1997. *La légende des vols d'organes*. Paris: Les Belles Lettres.
Candland, Christopher. 1995. "Trade Unionism and Industrial Restructuring in India and Pakistan." *Bulletin of Concerned Asian Scholars*, 27 (4): 63–78.

CAOM. 1930, 1932–1954. Centre des Archives l'Outre-Mer in Aix-Provence, France. Series MAD 4: DS0411, PM0014.
Carby, H. 1992. "Policing the Black Woman's Body in an Urban Context." *Critical Inquiry*, 18 (4): 738–757.
Carney, J. 1988. "Struggles over Crop Rights and Labor Within Contract Farming Households in a Gambian Irrigated Rice Farming Project." *Journal of Peasant Studies*, 15 (3): 334–349.
Carney, J., and M. Watts. 1990. "Manufacturing Dissent: Work, Gender and the Politics of Meaning in a Peasant Society." *Africa*, 60 (2): 207–241.
Centore, F. F. 1991. *Being and Becoming: A Critique of Post Modernism*. Newport: Greenwood Press.
Centre for Rural Legal Studies (CRLS). 1996. *Centre for Rural Legal Studies, 1991–1995: Five Years in Development*. Stellenbosch, South Africa: CRLS.
Cerny, Charlene, and Suzanne Seriff, eds. 1996. *Recycled Re-Seen: Folk Art from the Global Scrap Heap*. New York: Harry N. Abrams, Inc. in association with the Museum of International Folk Art, Santa Fe.
Césaire, Aimé. 1972. *Discourse on Colonialism*. New York: Monthly Review Press.
Chabal, P. 1980 (August). "Cabral as Revolutionary Leader." Ph.D. dissertation, Cambridge University.
Chandler, D. P. 1999. *Brother Number One: A Political Biography of Pol Pot*. New York: Westview Press.
Chanock, Martin. 1985. *Law, Custom and Social Order: The Colonial Experienece in Malawi and Zambia*. Cambridge: Cambridge University Press.
Charmé, Stuart. 1991. *Vulgarity and Authenticity*. Amherst: University of Massachusetts Press.
Chauncey, G. 1981. "The Locus of Reproduction: Women's Labor in the Zambian Copperbelt, 1927–1953." *Journal of Southern African Studies*, 7 (2): 135–164.
Chazan, Naomi. 1992 (Spring). "Africa's Democratic Challenge." *World Policy Journal*, 9 (2): 279–308.
Cheater, A. 1990. "The Ideology of 'Communal' Land Tenure in Zimbabwe: Mythogenesis Enacted?" *Africa*, 60 (2): 188–206..
Chege, Michael. 1997. "The Social Science Area Studies Controversy from the Continental African Standpoint." *Africa Today*, 44 (2): 133–142.
Chin, J. 1990 "Current and Future Dimensions of the HIV/AIDS Pandemic in Women and Children". *The Lancet*, 336: 221–224.
Clarence-Smith, G. 1985. *The Third Portuguese Empire, 1825–1975: A Study in Economic Imperialism*. Manchester, England: Manchester University Press.
Cleaver, K., and G. Schreiber. 1994. *Reversing the Spiral: The Population, Agriculture and Environment Nexus in Sub-Saharan Africa*. Washington, DC: World Bank.
Clignet, Rémi, and Bernard Ernst. 1995. *L'Ecole a Madagascar. Evaluation de la qualité de l'enseignement primaire public*. Paris: Karthala.
Coats, A. W. 1985 (February). "What Is Economic History?" *History Today*, 35 (2): 41–43.

Cobbing, J. 1977. "The Ndebele Under the Khumalos." Ph.D. dissertation, University of Lancaster.
Cochrane, S., and F. Sai. 1993. "Excess Fertility." In D. T. Jamison, W. H. Mosley, A. R. Measham, and J. L. Bobadilla, eds. *Disease Control Priorities in Developing Countries.* Oxford: Oxford University Press.
Coelho, João Paulo Borges. 1989. *O Início da Luta Armada Em Tete, 1968–1969.* Maputo: Archivo Histórico de Moçambique.
Cohen, B., and J. Trussell, eds. 1996. *Preventing and Mitigating AIDS in Sub-Saharan Africa: Research and Data Priorities for the Social and Behavioral Sciences.* Washington, DC: National Research Council.
Cohen, Jean, and Andrea Arato. 1992. *Civil Society and Political Theory.* Cambridge, MA: MIT Press.
Cohen, Robin. 1974. *Labor and Politics in Nigeria 1945–1971.* London: Heinemann.
Cohen, Robin, Peter C. W. Gutkind, and Jean Copans. 1978. "Introduction." In Robin Cohen, Peter C. W. Gutkind, and Jean Copans, eds. *African Labor History.* Beverly Hills: Sage Publications.
Cohen, Roger. 1998. "Redrawing the Free Market: Amid a Global Financial Crisis, Calls for Regulation Spread." *New York Times*, November 14, pp. B9.
Cohen, W. B. 1980, *The French Encounter with Africans: White Response to Blacks, 1530–1880.* Bloomington: Indiana University Press
Cohn, I. 1991. "The Convention on the Rights of the Child: What It Means for Children in War." *International Journal on Refugee Law*, 3: 100.
Coleman, D. C. 1985 (February). "What Is Economic History?" *History Today*, 35 (2): 23–25.
Collier, Ruth B., and James Mahoney. 1997. "Adding Collective Actors to Collective Outcomes. Labor and Recent Democratization in South America and Southern Europe." *Comparative Politics*, 29 (3): 285–303.
Colson, Elizabeth. 1971. "The Impact of the Colonial Period on the Definition of Land Rights." In Victor Turner, ed. *Colonialism in Africa, 1870–1960.* Cambridge: Cambridge University Press, pp. 193–216.
Comaroff, J. and J. Comaroff, eds. 1993. *Modernity and Its Malcontents: Ritual and Power in Postcolonial Africa.* Chicago: University of Chicago Press.
"Commerce de Detail: Les Jeunes Derriere Le Comptoir." 1989 (May 17). *Le Soleil.*
Compagnie d'Etudes Industrielles et d'Amenagement du Territoire. 1960. *Rapport general sur les perspectives de developpement du Senegal.* Dakar: Compagnie d'Etudes Industrielles et d'Amenagement du Territoire.
Congress of South African Trade Unions. 1996. *A Draft Program for the Alliance, Discussion Paper Presented to the Executive Committee.* Johannesburg: COSATU.
Conrad, J. 1926. "Geography and Some Explorers." In *Last Essays.* London: Dent.

———. 1995. *Heart of Darkness: Complete, Authoritative Text with Biographical and Historical Contexts, Critical History, and Essays from Five Contemporary Critics*. Ross C. Murfin, ed. New York: Bedford Books.
Cooper, F. 1983. "Urban Space, Industrial Time, and Wage Labor in Africa." In F. Cooper, ed. *Struggle for the City: Migrant Labor, Capital, and the State in Urban Africa*. Beverly Hills: Sage Publications.
———. 1994. "Conflict and Connection: Rethinking Colonial African History." *American Historical Review*, 99 (5): 1516–1545.
Cooper, F., F. E. Mallon, S. J. Stern, A. F. Isaacman, and W. Rosebury. 1993. *Confronting Historical Paradigms*. Madison: University of Illinois Press.
Cooper, Frederick. 1996. *Decolonization and African Society* Cambridge: Cambridge University Press.
———. 1997 (Fall). "Review of Mahmood Mamdani, *Citizen and Subject*." *International Labor and Working Class History*, 52: 156–160.
Cooper, Frederick, and Randall Packard. 1997. *International Development and the Social Sciences: Essays on the History and Politics of Knowledge*, Berkeley: University of California Press.
Cordell, D. D., and J. W. Gregory, eds. 1994. *African Population and Capitalism: Historical Perspectives*. Madison: University of Wisconsin Press.
Cordell, D. D., J. W. Gregory, and V. Piché. 1994. "African Historical Demography: The Search for a Theoretical Framework." In J. W. Gregory, ed. *African Population and Capialism: Historical Perspectives*. 2d ed. Madison: University of Wisconsin Press.
Corea, Gena. 1985. *The Mother Machine: Reproductive Technologies from Artificial Insemination to Artificial Wombs*. New York : Harper & Row.
Cornia, G. A., R. Jolly, and F. Stewart. 1987. *Adjustment with a Human Face: Protecting the Vulnerable and Promoting Growth*. New York: Oxford University Press.
Cotgrove, S. 1982. *Catastrophe or Cornucopia: The Environment, Policies and the Future*. Chichester: Wiley.
Covell, Maureen. 1987. *Madagascar: Politics, Economics and Society*. London: Frances Pinter.
Crafts, N. F. R. 1995. "Macroinventions, Economic Growth, and 'Industrial Revolution' in Britain and France." *Economic History Review*, 68 (3): 591–598.
Crehan, K. 1997a. *The Fractured Community: Landscapes of Power and Gender in Rural Zambia*. Berkeley and Los Angeles: University of California Press.
———. 1997b. "'Tribes' and the People Who Read Books: Managing History in Colonial Zambia." *Journal of Southern African Studies*, 23, (2): 203–218.
Crook, R. 1986. "Decolonization, the Colonial State and Chieftaincy in the Gold Coast." *African Affairs*, 85: 75–105.
Cross, Sholto, and A. Whiteside, eds. 1993. *Facing up to AIDS: The Socio-economic Impact in Southern Africa*. London: Macmillan.
Crossette, B. 1998. "AIDS Is Blamed for Reversing Health Gains in Poorest Countries." *New York Times*, December 1, p. A9.

Crouch, Colin. 1979. *The Politics of Industrial Relations*. London: Fontana.
Curtin, P. D. 1964. *The Image of Africa: British Ideas and Action, 1780–1850*. Madison: Wisconsin University Press.
Curtin, P. D., et al. 1995. *African History*. 2d ed. Boston: Little, Brown.
Curtin, Philip. 1969. *The Atlantic Slave Trade*. Madison: University of Wisconsin Press.
Dalby, D. 1986. *Africa and the Written Word*. Paris: Karthala.
Dalla Costa, Mariarosa, and Giovanna F. Dalla Costa. 1993. *Paying the Price. Women and the Politics of International Economic Strategy*. London: Zed Books.
Daly, H. E. 1977. *Steady-State Economics: The Economics of Biophysical Equilibrium and Natural Growth*. New York: W. H. Freeman.
———. 1993. "Introduction to *Essays Toward a Steady-State Economy*." In H. E. Daly and K. N. Townsend, eds. *Valuing the Earth: Economics, Ecology, Ethics*. Cambridge, MA: MIT Press.
Daunton, M. J. 1985 (February). "What Is Economic History?" *History Today*, 35 (2): 28–30.
Davidson, B. 1992. *The Black Man's Burden—Africa and the Curse of the Nation-State*, New York: Times Books
Davidson, Basil. 1994. *The Search for Africa*. New York: Random House.
Davies, Rob, Dan O'Meara, and Sipho Dlamini. 1988. *The Struggle for South Africa: A Reference Guide, Volume 2*. Atlantic Highlands, NJ: Zed Books.
Davis, John, ed. 1958 *Africa from the Point of View of American Negro Scholars*. Paris: Dijon Special Issue of *Présence Africaine*.
Davis, L., and R. Huttenback. 1986. *Mammon and the Pursuit of Empire: The Political Economy of Britain Imperialism 1860–1912*. Cambridge: Cambridge University Press.
Davis, T. C. 1993. "Reading for Economic History." *Theatre Journal*, 45: 487–503.
Dawes, A. 1996. "Helping, Coping and 'Cultural Healing.'" *Recovery: Research and Co-operation on Violence, Education and Rehabilitation of Young People*, 1 (5): 5–8.
Dawes, A., and A. Honwana. 1996. "Children, Culture and Mental Health: Interventions in Conditions of War." *Children, War and Prosecution—Rebuilding Hope*. Proceedings of the Congress in Maputo, December.
Dawkins, R. 1990. *The Selfish Gene*. Oxford: Oxford University Press.
Dawkins, Richard. 1998. *Unweaving The Rainbow: Science, Delusion, and the Appetite for Wonder*. Boston: Houghton Mifflin.
Day, Beth. 1972. *Sexual Life Between Blacks and Whites*. New York: World Publishing.
Dayton, Julia M. 1998. *World Bank HIV/AIDS Interventions: Ex-ante and Ex-post Evaluations*. Washington, DC: World Bank.
de Andrade, M. 1962. "Literature and Nationalism in Angola." *Présence Africaine* 13 (41): 115–122.
———. 1966. "Poesia Africana de Expressão Portugusa, Breve Notas Explicativas." *Présence Africaine* 80 (58): 433–500.

De Carvalho, O. S. 1975. *Insight on Portugal, the Year of the Captains.* London: Andre Deutsch.
De Certeau, M. 1984. *The Practice of Everyday Life.* Berkeley: University of California Press.
De Figueiredo, A. 1975. *Portugal: Fifty Years of Dictatorship.* Harmondsworth: Penguin Books.
"De La Republique Islamique A La Republique Sataneque." 1989. *Le Politician,* May 16, p. 249.
De Vroey, M. 1984. *Peasant Resettlement in Sri Lanka.* Louvain-la-Neuve: Tricontinental Centre.
de Waal, A., and M. Duffield. 1992. "Can Africa Conquer Famine?" *Dissent,* 39 (3): 390–396.
de Beauvoir, Simone. 1992. *Force of Circumstance, II.* New York: Paragon House.
Demery, Lionel, and Lyn Squire. 1996. "Macroeconomic Adjustment and Poverty in Africa: An Emerging Picture." *World Bank Research Observer,* 11: 39–59.
Dennett, D. C. 1996. *Darwin's Dangerous Idea, Evolution and the Meanings of Life.* New York: Touchstone Books.
Department of Finance. 1996. *Growth, Employment and Redistribution. A Macroeconomic Strategy.* Pretoria: Government Printer.
Derelius, H. 1973. "Wiriyamu 'Is Marked on Tete Mission Maps.'" *The Times,* July 16, p. 1d.
Desai, Ashwin, and Brij Maharaj. 1996. "Minorities in the Rainbow Nation: The Indian Vote in 1994." *South African Journal of Sociology,* 27 (4): 118–125.
Desjarlais, R., et al. 1995. *World Mental Health: Problems and Priorities in Low-Income Countries.* New York: Oxford University Press.
Desoto, Hernando. 1989. *The Other Path: The Invisible Revolution in the Third World.* New York: Harper & Row.
Development Action Group (DAG). 1996. *Annual Report.* Cape Town: DAG.
Dhada, M. 1993. *Warriors at Work, How Guinea Was Really Set Free.* Niwot: University Press of Colorado.
———. 1995 (Spring-Summer). "Guinea's Liberation Diplomacy." *Portuguese Studies Review,* 4 (1): 20–40.
———. 1997 (June). "Traditional Religion and Guerrilla Warfare in *Modern Africa* by Stephen L. Weigert" (Review). *The Journal of Modern African Studies,* 35 (2): 355–357.
Diamond, Larry. 1983. "Class, Ethnicity, and the Democratic State: Nigeria, 1950–1966." *Comparative Studies in Society and History,* 25 (3): 457–489.
———. 1994 (July). "Rethinking Civil Society: Toward Democratic Consolidation." *Journal of Democracy,* 5 (3): 4–17.
———. 1997. "Civil Society and Democratic Consolidation: Building a Culture of Democracy in a New South Africa." In Rukhsana A. Siddiqui, ed. *Subsaharan Africa in the 1990s: Challenges to Democracy and Development.* Westport, CT: Praeger, pp. 3–23.

Diamond, Larry, Juan J. Linz, and Seymour M. Lipset. 1995. *Politics in Developing Countries. Comparing Experiences with Democracy.* 2d ed. Boulder, CO: Lynne Rienner.

Dilbey, R., ed. 1992. *Contesting Markets: Analyses of Ideology, Discourse and Practice.* Edinburgh: Edinburgh University Press.

Dixon-Muller, R., and R. Anker. 1988. *Assessing Women's Economic Contribution to Development.* Geneva: ILO.

Dodge, C., and M. Raundalen. 1991. *Reaching Children in War: Sudan, Uganda and Mozambique.* Uppsala: Sigma Forlag.

Dodge, R. E. 1967. "Antonio Agostinho Neto, Some Biographic Notes." Unpublished manuscript, Kitwe, Zambia, pp. 1–2.

Douglas, Mary. 1966. *Purity and Danger.* New York: Pelican Books

Downs, R., and S. Reyna, eds. 1988. *Land and Society in Contemporary Africa.* Durham, NH: University Press of New England.

Drury, S. B. 1994. *Alexandre Kojeve: The Roots of Postmodern Politics.* New York: St. Martin's Press.

Du Toit, Darcy. 1997. "Industrial Democracy in South Africa's Transition." *Law, Democracy and Development,* 1 (1): 39–68.

Duignan, P., and L. Gann, eds. 1969–1975. *Colonialism in Africa 1870–1960.* Cambridge: Cambridge University Press.

Ebron, Paula. 1997. "Traffic in Men." In M. Grosz-Ngate and O. H. Kokole, eds., *Gendered Encounters: Challenging Cultural Boundaries and Social Hierarchies in Africa.* New York: Routledge, pp. 223–244.

Economist (London). 1994. March 25.

Economist Intelligence Unit (EIU). 1986. *Uganda Country Report.* London: The Unit.

Edwards, M. 1989. "The Irrelevance of Development Studies." *Third World Quarterly,* 11 (1): 116–136.

———. 1993. "How Relevant Is Development Studies?" In F. J. Schuurman, ed. *Beyond the Impasse: New Directions in Development Theory.* London: Zed Books.

Eidelberg, Phil G. 1997. "The Tripartite Alliance on the Eve of a New Millennium: The Congress of South African Trade Unions, the African National Congress, and the South African Communist Party." *Institute for Advanced Social Research Seminar Papers,* 413. Johannesburg: University of the Witwatersrand.

Ekeh, Peter P. 1992. "The Constitution of Civil Society in African History and Politics." In B. Caron, A. Gboyega, and E. Osaghae, eds. *Democratic Transition in Africa.* Ibadan: CREDU, pp. 187–213.

Eldridge, Niles. 1998 (October/November). "Cornets and Consilience." *Civilization,* 5: 84–86.

Elliot, G., ed. 1994. *Althusser: A Critical Reader.* Oxford: Blackwell.

Ellis, S. 1985. *The Rising of the Red Shawls: A Revolt in Madagascar 1895–1899.* African Studies Series, No 43. Cambrdige: Cambridge University Press.

Elson, D., ed. 1995. *Male Bias in the Development Process*. Manchester: Manchester University Press.

Ensminger, J. 1996. "Culture and Property Rights." In S. Hanna and M. Munasinghe, eds. *Rights to Nature: Ecological, Economic, Cultural, and Political Principles of Institutions for the Environment*. Washington, DC: Island Press.

———. 1997. "Changing Property Rights: Reconciling Formal and Informal Rights to Land in Africa." In J. Nye and J. Drobak, eds. *Frontiers of the New Institutional Economics*. London: Academic Press.

Erasmus, Z., and E. Pieterse. 1997. "Conceptualizing Coloured Identities: Prelimary Thoughts." Paper presented to the National Identity and Democracy Conference, Mayibuye Center, University of Western Cape, Bellville, March 14–16.

Escobar, A. 1995. *Encountering Development: The Making and Unmaking of the World*. Princeton, NJ: Princeton University Press.

"Et Quoi Demain?" 1989. *Wal Fadjri*, April 28, p. 160.

Etkind, Roger. 1995. "Rights and Power: Failings of the New Labor Relations Act." *South African Labor Bulletin*, 19 (2): 30–37.

Etudiants d'Afriques Portugaise. 1952 (November). "Situation des Etudiants Noirs Dans le Monde." *Presénce Africaine*, 13: 236.

Etukudo, Akanimo J. 1977. *Waging Industrial Peace in Nigeria*. Hicksville, NY: Exposition Books.

Evans, Peter. 1995. *Embedded Autonomy: States and Industrial Transformation*. Princeton: Princeton University Press.

Evans, R. G., and G. L. Stoddart. 1990. "Producing Health, Consuming Health Care." *Social Science & Medicine* 31 (12): 1347–1363.

Ewald, J. 1988. "Speaking, Writing and Authority: Explorations in and from the Kingdom of Taqali." *Comparative Studies in Society and History*, 30 (2): 199–224.

Eze, Emanuel, ed. 1997. *Post Colonial African Philosophy*. Cambridge, MA: Blackwell.

Fabian, J. 1983. *Time and the Other: How Anthropology Makes Its Object*. New York: Columbia University Press.

Fall, Y. K. 1982. *L'Afrique à la naissance de la cartographie moderne*. Paris: Karthala.

Fanon, Frantz. 1967a. *Black Skin White Masks*. Charles Lam Markmann, trans. New York: Grove Press.

———. 1967b. *Studies in a Dying Colonialism*. Haakon Chevalier, trans. New York: Monthly Review Press.

———. 1967c. *Toward the African Revolution: Political Essays*. Haakon Chevalier, trans. New York: Grove Press.

———. 1968 (1963). *The Wretched of the Earth*. Constance Farrington, trans. New York: Grove Press.

Farmer, P., M. Connors, and J. Simmons, eds. 1996. *Women, Poverty and AIDS: Sex, Drugs and Structural Violence*. Monroe, ME: Common Courage Press.

Farmer, Paul. 1992. *AIDS and Accusation: Haiti and the Geography of Blame*. Berkeley: University of California Press.
———. 1999. *Infections and Inequalities: The Modern Plagues*. Berkeley: University of California Press.
Farmer, Paul, Margaret Connors, and Janie Simmons, eds. 1996. *Women, Poverty and AIDS: Sex, Drugs and Structural Violence*. Monrow, ME: Common Courage Press.
Fashoyin, Tayo. 1980. *Industrial Relations in Nigeria: Development and Practice*. London: Longman.
———. 1990. "Nigerian Labor and the Military: Towards Exclusion?" *Labor, Capital and Society*, 23: 1.
Fatton, Robert, Jr. 1995. "Africa in the Age of Democratization: The Civic Limitations of the Civil Society." *African Studies Review*, 38: 2.
Feeley-Harnik, Gillian. 1991. *A Green Estate: Restoring Independence in Madagascar*. Washington, DC: Smithsonian Institution Press.
Feldman, G. D. 1986. "German Economic History." *Central European History*, 19: 174–185.
Ferguson, James. 1990. *The Anti-Politics Machine*. New York: Cambridge University Press.
Fieldhouse, D. K. 1986. "The Economics of French Empire." *Journal of African History*, 27: 169–172.
———. 1991. "French and British Colonialism." *Canadian Journal of African Studies*, 25 (1): 117–121.
Figuier, D. 1983. *Races imaginées et imaginaires*. Paris: Maspero.
Filesi, T. 1972. *China and Africa in the Middle Ages*. London: Frank Cass.
Fine, Gary Alan, and Kent L. Sandstrom. 1988. "Knowing Children: Participant Observation with Minors." *Qualitative Research Methods*, 15.
Firmin Sellers, K. 1996. *The Transformation of Property Rights in the Gold Coast*. Cambridge: Cambridge University Press.
Fisher, Lawrence E. 1985. *Colonial Madness: Mental Health in the Barbadian Social Order*. New Brunswick, NJ: Rutgers University Press.
Flack, C. Myth. 1994. *Truth and Literature: Towards a True Post-Modernism*. Cambridge: Cambridge University Press.
Fleming, Bruce E. 1990. "Another Way of Dying/African Perspectives of AIDS." *The Nation*, April 2, pp. 447–450.
Flieschman, Janet, and Lois Whitman. 1994. *Easy Prey: Child Soldiers in Liberia*. New York: Human Rights Watch.
Folbre, N. 1991. "The Unproductive Housewife: Her Evolution in Nineteenth Century Economic Thought." *Signs: Journal of Women, Culture and Society*, 16 (3): 463–484.
Fortes, M. 1948. "The Ashanti Social Survey: A Preliminary Report." *Rhodes-Livingstone Journal: Human Problems in British Central Africa*, 6: 1–36.
Fowler, A. 1992. "Distant Obligations: Speculations on NGO Funding and the Global Market." *ROAPE*, 55: 9–29.

Fowler, Alan. 1991 (March). "The Role of NGOs in Changing State-Society Relations: Perspectives from Eastern and Southern Africa." *Development Policy Review*, 9 (1): 53–84.
Francis, P. 1984. "'For the Use and Common Benefit of All Nigerians': The Land Use Decree of 1978." *Africa*, 54 (3): 5–28.
Frank, A. G. 1991. "The Underdevelopment of Development." Special issue of *Scandinavian Journal of Development Alternatives* 10 (3): 2–148.
Frederikse, Julie. 1990. *The Unbreakable Thread: Non Racialism in South Africa*. Bloomington: Indiana University Press.
Fredrickson, George M. 1995. *Black Liberation: A Comparative History of Black Ideologies in the United States and South Africa*. New York: Oxford University Press.
Freeman, M. 1993. *The Rights and Wrongs of Children*. London: Francis Printer Publishers.
French, Howard W. 1996. "Where Proud Moors Rule, Blacks Are Outcasts." *New York Times*, January 11, pp. A4.
———. 1998. "Africa Enduring Rebirth Awaits Clinton's Arrival." *New York Times*, March 21, p. 1.
Freund, B. 1984. *The Making of Contemporary Africa: The Development of African Society Since 1800*. London: Macmillan.
Freund, Bill. 1988. *The African Worker*. Cambridge: Cambridge University Press.
———. 1995. *Insiders and Outsiders: The Indian Working Class of Durban, 1910–1990*. Portsmouth, NH: Heinemann Press.
Frieden, J. 1987. "International Capital and National Development: Comments in Postimperialism." In D. Becker and R. Sklar, eds. *Postimperialism: International Capitalism and Development in Late Twentieth Century*. London: Lynne Rienner, pp. 179–193.
Friedman, Steven. 1987. *Building Tomorrow Today: African Workers in Trade Unions, 1970–1984*. Johannesburg: Ravan.
Fukuyama, F. 1992. *End of History and the Last Man*. New York: Free Press.
———. 1995. "Reflections on *The End of History*, Five Years Later." *History and Theory*, 34 (2): 28–43.
Furedi, F. 1997. *Population and Development: A Critical Introduction*. Cambridge: Politics Press.
Furley, O. 1995. "Child Soldiers in Africa." In O. Furley, ed. *Conflict in Africa*. London: Tauris.
Fuss, D. 1980. *Essentially Speaking: Feminism, Nature & Differences*. New York: Routledge Kegan & Paul.
Gadaga, N. 1991a. "AIDS: What Others Say." *Sunday Mail*, September 15.
———. 1991b. "Anatomy of AIDS in Mashonaland." *Sunday Mail*, September 8.
Galaty, J. 1993. "Rangeland Tenure and Pastoralism in Africa." *Session on Policy, Politics and the Crisis of Pastoral Property*. Mexico City: Proceedings of the International Congress on Anthropological and Ethnological Science.

Garson, Y. 1998. *Africa in Europe's Eyes: Maps of Africa in the Library of the Witswatersrand University.* Johannesburg: University of the Witswatersrand Library.
Gary, Ian. 1996. "Confrontation, Co-operation or Co-option: NGOs and the Ghanaian State During Structural Adjustment." *ROAPE*, 68: 149–168.
Geertz, C. 1973. *The Interpretation of Cultures.* New York: Basic Books.
Geertz, Clifford. 1968. "Thinking as a Moral Act: Dimensions of Anthropological Fieldwork in the New States." *Antioch Review,* 28: 39–58.
Geffray, C. 1990. *La Cause des Armes au Mozambique: Anthropologie d'une Guerre Civile.* Paris: Credu-Karthala.
Geffray, C., and M. Pedersen. 1986. "Sobre a Guerra na Provincia de Nampula." *Revista Internacional de Estudos Africanos,* 4–5: 303–318.
Geismar, Peter. 1971. *Frantz Fanon.* New York: Dial Press.
Gelb, Steven. 1998. "The Politics of Macroeconomic Policy Reform in South Africa." Paper presented at the Conference on Democracy and the Political Economy of Reform. University of Cape Town, January 16–18.
Gelfand, M. 1943. *The Sick African.* Cape Town: Juta and Company.
Gendzier, Irene. 1973. *Frantz Fanon: A Critical Study.* New York: Grove Press.
Georgescu-Roegen, N. 1971. *The Entropy Law and the Economic Process.* Cambridge, MA: Harvard University Press.
Geschiere, P. 1992. "Kinship, Witchcraft and the Market: Hybrid Patterns in Cameroonian Societies." In R. Dilbey, ed. *Contesting Markets: Analyses of Ideology, Discourse and Practice.* Edinburgh: Edinburgh University Press.
Geschiere, P., and C. Fisiy. 1994. "Domesticating Personal Violence: Witchcraft, Courts and Confessions in Cameroon." *Africa,* 64 (3): 323–341.
Ghana. 1962. Administration of Lands Act Cap 123.
———. 1992. *Constitution of the Republic of Ghana.* Accra: Government Printer.
Gibbs, S. 1994. "Post-War Reconstruction in Mozambique, Reframing Children's Experiences of War and Healing." *Disasters,* 18 (3): 268–300.
Gibson, Edward L. 1997. "The Populist Road to Market Reform. Policy and Electoral Coalitions in Mexico and Argentina." *World Politics,* 49 (3): 339–370.
Gibson, Nigel. 1988. "Black Consciousness in South Africa." *Africa Today,* 35 (1): 5–26.
———. 1990. "Why Participation Is a Dirty Word in South African Politics." *Africa Today,* 37 (4): 23–52.
———. 1999a. "Radical Mutations: Fanon's Untidy Dialectic of History." in Nigel Gibson, ed. *Rethinking Fanon.* Amherst, NY: Prometheus Books.
Gibson, Nigel, ed. 1999b. *Rethinking Fanon.* Amherst, NY: Prometheus Books.
———. 2001. "Ideology and the Pitfalls of South Africa's Transition from Apartheid." *Journal of Asian and African Studies.*
Giddens, A. 1990. *The Consequences of Modernity.* Stanford: Stanford University Press.
Gilbert, M. 1988. "The Sudden Death of a Millionaire: Conversion and Consensus in a Ghanaian Kingdom." *Africa,* 58 (3): 281–305.

Gills, Barry, Joel Rocamora, and Richard Wilson. 1993. "Low Intensity Democracy." In Barry Gills, Joel Rocamora, and Richard Wilson, eds. *Low Intensity Democracy. Political Power in the New World Order.* London: Pluto, pp. 3–34.
Ginwala, F. 1965 (June). "Liberating Portuguese Guinea from Within [interview with Amilcar Cabral]." *The New African,* 4 (4): 85.
Girardet, R. 1972. *L'idée coloniale en France de 1871 à 1962.* Paris: La Table Ronde.
Glassman, J. 1995. *Feasts and Riot: Revelry, Rebellion and Popular Consciousness on the Swahili Coast.* Portsmouth, NH: Heinemann.
Gocking, R. 1994. "Indirect Rule in the Gold Coast: Competition for Office and the Invention of Tradition." *Canadian Journal of African Studies,* 28: 421–445.
Godlewska, A. 1994, "Napoleon's Geographers, 1797–1815: Imperialists and Soldiers of Modernity." In A. Gadlewska and N. Smith, eds. *Geography and Empire.* Oxford: Blackwell.
Godlewska, A., and N. Smith, eds. 1994. *Geography and Empire.* Oxford: Blackwell.
Gogwilt, C. L. 1995. *The Invention of the West: Joseph Conrad and the Double-Mapping of Europe and Empire.* Stanford: Stanford University Press.
Goldblatt, B., and S. Meintjes. 1998. "South African Women Demand the Truth." In M. Turshen and C. Twagiramariya, eds. *What Women Do in Wartime: Gender and Conflict in Africa.* London: Zed Books.
Goldschmidt-Clermont, L. 1982. *Unpaid Work in the Household: A Review of Economic Evaluation Methods.* Geneva: ILO.
———. 1987. *Economic Evaluations of Unpaid Household Work: Africa, Asia, Latin America and Oceania.* Geneva: ILO.
———. 1990. "Economic Measurement of Non-Market Household Activities: Is It Useful and Feasible?" *International Labour Review,* 129: 279–299.
Goodwin-Gill, G., and I. Cohn. 1994. *Child Soldiers: The Role of Children in Armed Conflict.* Oxford: Clarendon Press.
Gopal, Gita, and Maryam Salim, eds. 1998. *Gender and Law: Eastern Africa Speaks: Proceedings of the Conference Organized by the World Bank and the Economic Commission for Africa.* Washington, DC: World Bank.
Gordon, A. A. 1996. *Transforming Capitalism and Patriarchy: Gender and Development in Africa.* Boulder, CO: Lynne Rienner.
Gordon, Lewis. 1995. *Bad Faith and Antiblack Racism.* Atlantic Highlands, NJ: Humanities Press.
Gordon, Lewis, et al., eds. 1996. *Fanon: A Critical Reader.* Oxford: Blackwell Publishers.
Gould, S. J. 1996a. *Full House: The Spread of Excellence from Plato to Darwin.* New York: Harmony Books.
———. 1996b. *The Mismeasure of Man.* New York: W.W. Norton & Company.
———. 1997. "Darwinian Fundamentalism." *New York Review of Books,* June 12, pp. 34–37.

———. 1998 (October/November). "Gratuitous Battle." *Civilization: The Magazine of the Library of Congress*, 5 (5): 86–88.

Gourevitch, P. 1997 (May 19). "Kabila's March: Zaire's Rebels Confront the West's Legacy." *New Yorker*, 73: 7–8.

Graf, William. 1986. "Nigerian 'Grassroots' Politics: Local Government, Traditional Rule and Class Domination." *Journal of Commonwealth and Comparative Politics*, 24: 2.

Gramsci, Antonio. 1971. *Selections from the Prison Notebooks*. Q. Hoare and G. N. Smith, eds. New York: International Publishing Co.

Green, W. A. 1995. "Periodizing World History." *History and Theory*, 34 (2): 99–111.

Grier, B. 1987. "Contradictions, Crises and Class Conflict: The State and Capitalist Development in Ghana Prior to 1948." In I. Markovitz, ed. *Studies in Class and Power in Africa*. New York: Oxford University Press.

Grindle, Merilee. 1997 (April). "Divergent Cultures? When Public Organizations Perform Well in Developing Countries." *World Development*, 25 (4): 481–495.

Grmek, Mirko D. 1990. *History of AIDS: Emergence and Origin of a Modern Pandemic*. Princeton: Princeton University Press.

Guha, Ranajit. ed. 1997. *A Subaltern Studies Reader, 1986–1995*. Minneapolis: University of Minnesota Press.

Gussman, B. 1962. *Out in the Mid-Day Sun*. New York: Oxford University Press.

Guyer, J. 1993. "Wealth in People and Self-Realization in Equatorial Africa." *Man*, 28 (2): 243–265.

Guyer, J., and S. Eno Belinga. 1995. "Wealth in People as Wealth in Knowledge: Accumulation and Composition in Equatorial Africa." *Journal of African History*, 36: 91–120.

Gyekye, K. 1987. *An Essay on African Philosophical Thought: The Akan Conceptual Scheme*. Cambridge: Cambridge University Press.

———. 1997. *Tradition and Modernity: Philosophical Reflections on the African Experience*. New York and Oxford: Oxford University Press.

Hailey, Lord. 1951. *Native Administration in the British African Territories. Part IV: A General Survey of the System of Native Administration*. London: His Majesty's Stationery Office.

Hall, Stuart. 1988. "Authoritarian Populism: A Reply to Jessop et al." In *The Hard Road to Renewal: Thatcherism and the Crisis of the Left*. London: Verso.

———. 1993. "Culture, Progressive Politics and Global Change" (interview). In *Common Purposes*. New Brunswick, NJ: Rutgers University.

Hammond, R. J. 1966. *Portugal and Africa 1815–1910: A Study in Uneconomic Imperialism*. Stanford: Stanford University Press.

Hanna, S., and M. Munasinghe, eds. 1996. *Rights to Nature: Ecological, Economic, Cultural and Political Principles of Institutions for the Environment*. Washington, DC: Island Press.

Hansen, Emmanuel. 1999. "Frantz Fanon: Portrait of a Revolutionary." In Nigel Gibson, ed. *Rethinking Fanon*. Amherst, NY: Prometheus Books.
Hansen, Holger B., and Michael Twaddle. 1988 "Introduction." In *Uganda Now: Between Decay and Development*. London: James Currey, pp. 1–25.
Hardt, Michael. 1995. "The Withering of Civil Society." *Social Text*, 14 (4): 45.
Harrington, Michael. 1962. *The Other America*. Baltimore: Penguin Books.
Harrison-Chirimuuta, Rosalind J., and Richard Chirimuuta. 1997. "AIDS from Africa: A Case of Racism vs. Science?" In G. Bond, J. Kreniske, I. Susser, and J. Vincent, eds. *AIDS in Africa and the Caribbean*. Boulder: Westview Press, pp. 165–180.
Harsch, Ernest. 2000 (April). "Privatization Shifts Gears in Africa." *Africa Recovery*, 14 (1). Available at http://www.un.org/ecosocdev/geninfo/afrec/vol14no1/privat1.htm.
Hartog, F. 1980. *Le miroir d'Hérodote: Essai sur la représentation de l'autre*. Paris: Gallimard.
Harvey, D. 1989. *The Urban Experience*. Baltimore: Johns Hopkins University Press.
———. 1991. *The Condition of Postmodernity*. Cambridge: Basil Blackwell.
Hashim, Yahaya. 1994. 'The State and Trade Unions in Africa: A Study in Macrocorporatism." Ph.D. dissertation, The Hague, Institute of Social Studies.
Hastings, A. 1974. *Wiriyamu: My Lai in Mozambique*. London: Search Press Limited.
Haugerud, A. 1989. "Land Tenure and Agrarian Change in Kenya." *Africa*, 59 (1): 61–90.
Hearn, Julie. 1998. "The NGO-isation of a Kenyan Society: USAID and the Restructuring of Health Care." *ROAPE*, 75: 89–100.
Helleiner, G. K. 1990. "Conventional Foolishness and Overall Ignorance: Current Approaches to Global Transformation and Development." *Canadian Journal of Development Studies*, 10 (1): 107–120.
Heller, Patrick. 1995. "From Class Struggle to Class Compromise: Redistribution and Growth in a South Indian State." *Journal of Development Studies*, 31 (5): 645–672.
Herbst, Jeffrey. 1990. "The Structural Adjustment of Politics in Africa." *World Development*, 18 (7): 949–958.
Heston, A. 1973 (March). "A Comparison of Some Short-Cut Methods of Estimating Real Product per Capita." *Review of Income and Wealth*, 19 (1): 79–104.
Hill, P. 1986. *Development Economics on Trial: The Anthropological Case for the Prosecution*. Cambridge: Cambridge University Press.
Hippler, Jochen. 1995. "Democratization of the Third World After the End of the Cold War." In *The Democratization of Disempowerment. The Problem of Democracy in the Third World*. London: Pluto Press, pp. 1–31.
Hirschman, Albert. 1982. *Shifting Involvement*. Princeton, NJ: Princeton University Press.

Hobsbawm, E. 1987. *The Age of Empire, 1875–1914*. New York: Pantheon.
Hobsbawm, E., and T. O. Ranger, eds. 1983. *The Invention of Tradition*. Cambridge: Cambridge University Press.
Hochschild, A. 1998. *King Leopold's Ghost*. Boston: Houghton Mifflin.
Hodge, I. 1995. *Environmental Economics*. New York: St. Martin's Press.
Holland, S. 1976. "Sexually Transmitted Diseases in Rhodesia, Part Two." *Central African Journal of Medicine*, 22 (11): 216–220.
Holmquist, Frank W., Frederick S. Weaver, and Michael D. Ford. 1994. "The Structural Development of Kenya's Political Economy." *African Studies Review*, 37: 1.
Honwana, A. 1994. "Traditional Religious Institutions and the Social Reintegration of Vulnerable Groups." Research Report for the Swiss Cooperation for Development in Mozambique.
_____. 1997. "Sealing the Past, Facing the Future: Trauma Healing in Mozambique." *Accord*, 3 (special edition on the Mozambican peace process).
Honwana, A., and E. Pannizo. 1995. "Evaluation of the Children and War Project in Mozambique." Research Report for Save the Children US and USAID.
Hoogvelt, A. 1997. *Globalization and the Postcolonial World: The New Political Economy*. Baltimore: Johns Hopkins University Press.
Hooper, E., and L. Pirouet. 1989. *Uganda*. Minority Rights Group Report No. 66. London: Minority Rights Group.
Hopkins, A. G. 1973. *An Economic History of West Africa*. London: Longman.
_____. 1980. "Africa's Age of Improvement." *History in Africa*, 7: 141–160.
Hountondji, Paulin J. 1992 "Recapturing." In V. J. Mudimbe, ed. *The Surreptitious Speech: Presence Africaine and the Politics of Otherness, 1947–1987*. Chicago: University of Chicago Press, pp. 238–246.
Howard, P. 1973. "Gangsters' Pact Has Lasted 600 Years." *The Times*, June 7, p. 18g.
Howes, C., and A. Singh. 1995. "Long-Term Trends in the World Economy: The Gender Dimension." *World Development*, 23 (11): 1895–1911.
Huang, P. C. 1991. "The Paradigmatic Crisis in Chinese Studies: Paradoxes in Social and Economic History." *Modern China*, 17 (3): 299–341.
Hubbard, W. H. 1990. "The New Inflation History." *Journal of Modern History*, 62: 552–569.
Hufton, O. 1986. "Fernand Braudel." *Past and Present*, 112: 208–213.
Hughes, David. 1999. "Refugees and Squatters: Immigration and the Politics of Territory on the Zimbabwe-Mozambique Border." *Journal of Southern African Studies*, 25 (4): 533–552.
Hull, J. P. 1996. "From Rostow to Chandler to You: How Revolutionary Was the Second Industrial Revolution?" *Journal of European Economic History*, 25: 191–208.
Hulme, David, and Michael Edwards, eds. 1997. *NGOs, States and Donors: Too Close for Comfort?* New York: St. Martin's Press.

Human Rights Watch. 1994. *Easy Pray: Children and War in Liberia.* London: Human Rights Watch Children's Project.
Hunt, C. 1994. "Some Notes on Indigenous Map-making in Africa." In J. C. Stone, ed. *Maps and Africa-Proceedings of a Colloquium.* Aberdeen: University of Aberdeen, pp. 32–35.
Hunter, Susan. 1990a. "Orphans as a Window on the AIDS Epidemic in Sub-Saharan Africa: Initial Results and Implications of a Study in Uganda." *Social Science and Medicine,* 31 (6): 681–690.
―――. 1990b. "An Update on the Orphan Situation in Uganda." Paper presented at the Conference on AIDS: Community Coping Mechanisms in the Face of Exceptional Demographic Change, Kampala.
Hunter, Susan, Elizabeth Bulirwa, and Edward Kisseka. 1993. "AIDS and Agricultural Production: Report of a Land Utilization Survey, Masaka and Rakai Districts of Uganda." *Land Use Policy,* 10: 241–258.
Huntington, Samuel. 1968. *Political Order in Changing Societies.* New Haven, CT: Yale University Press.
Hyden, Goran. 1988. "State and Nation Under Duress." In *Recovery in Africa.* Stockholm: Swedish Ministry for Foreign Affairs.
Hyman, Richard. 1997. "Trade Unions and Interest Representation in a Changing Europe." Unpublished document, Industrial Relations Research Unit, Coventry, University of Warwick.
Ibbotson, P. 1946. "Urbanization in Southern Rhodesia: Report on a Survey of Urban African Conditions in Southern Rhodesia." *Africa,* 16 (2): 73–82.
Ihonvbere, Julius O. 1992. "Resistance and Hidden Forms of Consciousness Amongst the Petroleum Proletariat in Nigeria." In Midnight Notes Collective, ed. *Midnight Oil: Work, Energy, War, 1973–1992.* Brooklyn, NY: Autonomedia, pp. 91–105.
Ihonvbere, Julius O., and Timothy M. Shaw. 1988. *Towards a Political Economy of Nigeria.* Aldershot: Gower.
―――. 1998. *Illusions of Power. Nigeria in Transition.* Trenton, NJ: Africa World Press.
Iliffe, John. 1995. *Africans: The History of a Continent.* Cambridge: Cambridge University Press.
Inikori, J. E. 1976. "Measuring the Atlantic Slave Trade: A Review of the Literature." *Journal of African History,* 17: 197–223.
International Labor Organization (ILO). 1993. *Report of the Conference: Fifteenth International Conference of Labour Statisticians.* Geneva: ILO.
―――. 1995. *World Labor Report 8.* Geneva: ILO.
―――. 1996. *Restructuring the Labor Market: The South African Challenge, Country Study.* Geneva: ILO.
―――. 1999. *Country Studies on the Social Impact of Globalisation: South Africa.* Geneva: ILO.
Isaac, Jeffrey. Personal communication with author, April 18, 2000.

Isaacs, Katherine. 1995 (June). "Nigeria: A Strike for Democracy." *Multinational Monitor*, 17 (1). Available at http://www.essential.org/monitor/hyper/issues/1995/06/mm0695_09.html.
Isichei, Elizabeth. 1997. *A History of African Societies to 1870*. Cambridge: Cambridge University Press.
Issawi, C. 1982. *An Economic History of the Middle East and North Africa*. New York: Columbia University Press.
IUCN. 1980. *The World Conservation Strategy*. Geneva: International Union for Conservation of Nature and Natural Resources, United Nations Environment Programme, World Wildlife Fund.
———. 1984. *National Conservation Strategies: A Framework for Sustainable Development*. Geneva: IUCN.
Jackson, Karl D., ed. 1992. *Cambodia 1975–1978: Rendezvous with Death*. Princetown, NJ: Princeton University Press.
Jackson, L. 1998. "'Stray Women' and 'Girls on the Move': Gender, Space and Disease in Colonial and Postcolonial Zimbabwe." In Paul Zeleza and Ezekel Kalipeni, eds. *Sacred Spaces and Public Quarrels: African Cultural and Economic Landscapes*. Lawrencesville, NJ: African World Press.
Jackson, M. 1978. "An Approach to Kuranko Divination." *Human Relations*, 31 (2): 117–138.
Jackson, M., and I. Karp, eds. 1990. *Personhood and Agency: The Experience of Self and Other in African Cultures*. Uppsala: Almqvist and Wicksell.
Jaenson, Carol, Josephine Harmsworth, T. Kabwegyere, and P. Muzaale. 1984. "The Uganda Social and Institutional Profile." Unpublished paper prepared for USAID/Uganda, 331pp.
James, A. 1993. *Childhood Identities: Self and Social Relationships in the Experience of Childhood*. Edinburgh: Edinburgh University Press.
Jamison, D. T. 1993. "Disease Control Priorities in Developing Countries: An Overview." In D. T. Jamison, W. H. Mosley, A. R. Measham, and J. L. Bobadilla, eds. *Disease Control Priorities in Developing Countries*. Oxford: Oxford University Press.
Jeater, Diane. 1993. *Marriage, Perversion and Power: The Construction of Moral Discourse in Southern Rhodesia, 1894–1930*. Oxford: Clarendon Press.
Jencks, C. 1999. *What Is Post-Modernism?* London: Academy Editions.
Jessop, B. 1989. *Thatcherism: The British Road to Postfordism?* Colchester, Essex: Department of Government, University of Essex.
Joffe, Avril, and Chris Lloyd. 1996. *Collective-Bargaining Agreements 1995. Volume One: Innovations and Trends*. Johannesburg: NEDLAC.
Joffe, R. 1984. *The Killing Field* (film).
Johnson, D. T., and Q. W. Ssekitoleko. 1989. *Current and Proposed Farming Schemes in Uganda*. Entebbe: Ministry of Agriculture.
Jordan, Pallo. 1988. "The South African Liberation Movement and the Making of a New Nation." In Maria van Diepen, ed. *The National Question in South Africa*. London: Zed Books, pp. 110–124.

Joseph, Richard A. 1984. "Class, State, and Prebendal Politics in Nigeria." In Nelson Kasfir, ed. *State and Class in Africa*. London: Frank Cass.
Judt, Tony. 1992. *Past Imperfect: French Intellectuals, 1944–1956*. Berkeley: University of California Press.
Judy, Ronald A. 1996. "Fanon's Body of Black Experience." In Lewis Gordon et al., eds. *Fanon: A Critical Reader*. Oxford: Blackwell Publishers.
Jules-Rosette, Bennetta. 1992. "Conjugating Cultural Realities; Présence Africaine." In V. Y. Mudimbe, ed. *The Surreptitious Speech. Presence Africaine and the Politics of Otherness, 1947–1987*. Chicago: University of Chicago Press.
July, Robert. 1995. *A History of the African People*. 4th ed. Prospect Heights, IL: Waveland.
Jung, Courtney, 1996. "Understanding Zulu Identity." *Indicator SA*, 13 (2): 47–54.
Junior, B. E. 1996. "The Psychic Reconstruction of Former Child Soldiers." In *Children, War and Prosecution—Rebuilding Hope*. Proceedings of the Congress in Maputo, December.
Kafka, F. 1999. *The Castle*. Mark Harman, trans. New York: Schocken Books.
Kaplan, R. D. 1994 (February). "The Coming Anarchy: How Scarcity, Crime, Overpopulation and Disease Are Rapidly Destroying the Social Fabric of Our Planet." *Atlantic Monthly*, pp. 44–76.
Kasfir, Nelson. 1998. "Introduction: The Conventional Notion of Civil Society: A Critique." Commonwealth and Comparative Politics, 36 (2): 1–20.
Kasfir, Nelson, ed. 1998. *Civil Society and Democracy in Africa: Critical Perspectives*. London: Frank Cass.
Kassimer, Ronald. 1996. "The Social Power of Religious Organization and Civil Society: The Catholic Church in Uganda." In N. Kasfir, ed. *Civil Society and Democracy in Africa: Critical Perspectives*. London: Frank Cass.
Kedourie, Elie. *Nationalism*. London, Hutchinson.
Kennedy, D. 1987. *Islands of White*. Durham, NC: Duke University Press.
Kenny, Bridget, and Andries Bezuidenhout. 1999. "Contracting, Complexity and Control: An Overview of the Changing Nature of Subcontracting in the South African Mining Industry." Paper presented at the Symposium on Leaner and Smarter Outsourcing in the Mining Industry, Johannesburg, South Africa.
Keppel-Jones, Arthur. 1983. *Rhodes and Rhodesia: The White Conquest of Zimbabwe, 1884–1902*. Kingston, Ontario: McGill University Press.
Kesteloot, Lilyan. 1974. *Black Writers in French: A Literary History of Negritude*. Philadelphia: Temple University Press.
Kester, Gerard. 1995. "Towards Effective Worker Participation in South Africa." In National Labor and Economic Development Institute, ed. *Opinions on the New Labor Relations Bill*. Johannesburg: Progress Press.
Kester, Gerhard, and Ousmane O. Sidibe', eds. 1997. *Syndicats africains: a vous maintenant!* Paris: L'Harmattan.
Khadiagala, G. M. 1999 (Fall). "Reflections on the Ethiopia-Eritrea Border Conflict." *The Fletcher Forum of World Affairs*, 23 (2): 38–56.

Ki-Zerbo, J. 1997. *General History of Africa from the Twelfth to the Sixteenth Century*. Berkeley: University of California Press.
Kirby, A. 1994, "What Did You Do in the War, Daddy?" In A. Godlewska and N. Smith, eds. *Geography and Empire*. Oxford: Blackwell.
Kleinman, A. 1989. *Patients and Healers in the Context of Culture*. Berkeley: University of California Press.
Klerck, Gilton. 1998. "Between Corporatism and Neo-Liberalism? Collective Bargaining and South Africa's New Labor Relations Act." *African Sociological Review*, 2 (1): 85–113.
Kodjo, E. 1985. *Et demain l'Afrique?* Paris: Stock.
Koestler, A. 1984. *Darkness at Noon*. New York: Bantam Books.
Konczacki, Z. A,. and J. M. Konczacki, eds. 1977. *An Economic History of Tropical Africa*. 2 vols. London: Frank Cass.
Konczacki, Z. A., J. L. Parpart, and T. M. Shaw, eds. 1990–1992. *Studies in the Economic History of Southern Africa*. 2 vols. London: Frank Cass.
Korten, David. 1990. *Getting to the 21st Century: Voluntary Action and the Global Agenda*. West Hartford, CT: Kumarin.
Kraak, Andre. 1996. "Transforming South Africa's Economy: From Racial Fordism to Neo-Fordism?" *Economic and Industrial Democracy*, 17 (1): 39–74.
Kraak, Gerald. 1993. *Breaking the Chains: Labor in South Africa in the 1970s and 1980s*. London: Pluto Press.
Kravis, I. B., Z. Kenessey, A. Heston, and R. Summers. 1975. *A System of International Comparisons of Gross Domestic Product and Purchasing Power*. Baltimore: Johns Hopkins University Press.
Kreps, D. M. 1997. "Economics—The Current Position." *Daedalus*, 126 (1): 59–85.
Kristof, Nicholas D. 1998a. "Asia Feels Strain Most at Society's Margins." *New York Times*. June 8.
———. 1998b. "Asia's Crisis Upsets Rising Effort to Confront Blight of Sweatshops." *New York Times*, June 15.
———. 1998c. "It's a Bad Time for Weak Leadership." *New York Times*, August 30, p. sec. 4, p. 1.
———. 1998d. "With Asia's Economies Shrinking, Women Are Being Squeezed Out." *New York Times*, June 11.
Kuhn, Thomas S. 1970. *The Structure of Scientific Revolutions*. Chicago: University of Chicago Press.
Kuklick, H. 1994. *The Savage Within: The Social History of British Anthropology, 1885–1945*. Cambridge: Cambridge University Press.
Kuznets, S. 1972. "The Gap: Concept, Measurement, Trends." In G. Ranis, ed. *The Gap Between Rich and Poor Nations*. London: Macmillan.
Kyerematen, A. A. Y. 1971. *Inter-state Boundary Litigation in Ashanti*. African Social Research Documents 4. Cambridge: African Studies Center, Cambridge University.

Laclau, E., and C. Mouffe. 1985. *Hegemony and Socialist Strategy: Towards a Radical Democratic Politics.* London: Verso Books.
Ladjali, M. 1991. "Conception, Contraception: So Algerian Women Really Have a Choice?" In M. Turshen, ed. *Women and Health in Africa.* Trenton, NJ: Africa World Press.
Lambek, M., and P. Antze, eds. 1996. *Tense Past: Cultural Essays in Trauma and Memory.* New York: Routledge.
Landes, D. S. 1995. "Some Further Thoughts on Accident in History: A Reply to Professor Crafts." *Economic History Review,* 68 (3): 599–601.
Landler, Mark. 1998. "Grim Assessment by U.N. of Asia Crisis." *New York Times,* December 3, sec. A. p. 20.
Langer, Monika. 1989. *Merleau-Ponty's Phenomenology of Perception: A Guide and Commentary.* Tallahassee: Florida State University Press.
Larby, P. M., ed. 1987. *Maps and Mapping of Africa.* London: SCOLMA.
Lazarus-Black, M., and S. Hirsch, eds. 1994. *Contested States: Law, Hegemony and Resistance.* New York and London: Routledge.
Le Blanc, M. N., D. Meintel, and V. Piché. 1991 (September). "The African Sexual System: Comment on Caldwell et al." *Population and Development Review,* 17 (3): 497–505.
Lee, Eddy. 1998. *The Asian Financial Crisis: The Challenge for Social Policy.* Geneva: International Labour Office.
Lehmbruch, Gerhard. 1979. "Consociational Democracy, Class Conflict, and the New Corporatism." In Philippe C. Schmitter and Gerhard Lehmbruch, eds. *Trends Towards Corporatist Intermediation.* Beverly Hills: Sage Publications, pp. 53–61.
Leigh, D. 1973. "War Against Frelimo 'Like Fight with IRA.'" *The Times,* July 18, p. 9c.
Lemarchand, R. 1994. *Burundi, Ethnocide as Discourse and Practice.* Cambridge: Cambridge University Press.
Lemarchand, Rene. 1992. "Uncivil States and Civil Societies: How Illusion Became Reality." *Journal of Modern African Studies,* 30 (2): 177–192.
Lemon, Anthony. 1996. "Ethnicity and Political Development in South Africa." In Denis Dwyer and David Drakakis-Smith, eds. *Ethnicity and Development: Geographic Perspectives.* New York: John Wiley & Sons, pp. 89–113.
Lessing, D. 1991. *The Grass Is Singing.* New York: Penguin Books.
[Letter to the editor]. 1902. *Rhodesia Herald,* March 1.
Leventhal, Todd. 1994. "The Child Organ Trafficking Rumor: A Modern 'Urban Legend.'" Report submitted to the United Nations Special Rapporteur on the sale of children, child prostitution, and child pornography. Washington, DC: United States Information Agency.
Levy, B. S. and V. W. Sidel. 1997. *War and Public Health.* Oxford: Oxford University Press.
Lewis, Peter M. 1994. "Endgame in Nigeria? The Politics of a Failed Democratic Transition." *African Affairs,* 93: 372.

Leys, C. 1997. *The Rise and Fall of Development Theory.* Bloomington: Indiana University Press.
"Liberating Portuguese Guinea from Within." 1965 (June). *The New African,* 4 (4): 85.
Lindblad, J. T. 1995. "Current Trends in the Economic History of Southeast Asia." *Journal of Southeast Asian Studies,* 26 (1): 159–168.
Lindenbaum, Shirley. 1979. *Kuru Sorcery. Disease and Danger in the New Guinea Highlands.* Palo Alto, CA: Mayfield Publishing Company.
Lindenfeld, D. F. 1993. "The Myth of the Older Historical School of Economics." *Central European History,* 26 (4): 405–416.
Lipietz, A. 1984. *Enchanted World: Inflation Credit and the World Crisis.* New York: Verso.
Lipset, Seymour Martin. 1983. *Political Man.* Expanded and revised ed. London: Heinemann.
Littlewood, R. 1997. "Military Rape." *Anthropology Today,* 13 (2): 7–16.
Livingston, J. 1987. "The Social Analysis of Economic History and Theory: Conjectures of Late Nineteenth-Century American Development." *American Historical Review,* 92: 69–95.
Long, N. 1990. "From Paradigm Lost to Paradigm Regained? The Case for an Actor-Oriented Sociology of Development." *European Review of Latin American and Caribbean Studies* 49: 3–24.
Low, Donald A. 1974–1975. "War Bands and Ground-Level Imperialism in Uganda, 1870–1900." *Historical Studies,* 16: 584–597.
Lummis, C. Douglas, 1996. *Radical Democracy,* Ithaca: Cornell University Press.
Lurie, P., P. Hintzen, and R. A. Loew. 1995. "Socioeconomic Obstacles to HIV Prevention and Treatment in Developing Countries: The Roles of the International Monetary Fund and the World Bank." *AIDS,* 9 (6): 539–546.
Lyons, M. 1999. "Uganda, an Island of Hope in a State of Risk? Mobile Populations and HIV/AIDS in East Africa." Paper presented at Symposium on HIV/AIDS in Africa: Reviewing the Past, Understanding the Present, Charting the Future, University of Illinois at Urbana-Champaign, July 14–18.
Lyons, Maryinez. 1997. "The Point of View: Perspectives on AIDS in Uganda." In G. Bond, J. Kreniske, I Susser, and J. Vincent, eds. *AIDS in Africa and the Caribbean.* Boulder: Westview Press, pp. 131–146.
Macdonald, M. 1995. "Feminist Economics: From Theory to Research." *Canadian Journal of Economics,* 28 (1): 159–176.
Mackenzie, F. 1989. "Land and Territory: The Interface Between Two Systems of Land Tenure, Murang'a District, Kenya." *Africa,* 59 (1): 91–109.
―――. 1993. "Perspectives on Land Tenure: Social Relations and the Definition of Territory in a Smallholding District, Kenya." In T. Bassett and D. Crummey, eds. *Land in African Agrarian Systems.* Madison: University of Wisconsin Press.
MacKenzie, J. M. 1984. *Propaganda and Empire—The Manipulation of British Public Opinion, 1880–1960.* Manchester: Manchester University Press.

Madagascar. 1994. "Liza." *La Plume*, 5. School publication, Mission Français de coopération, with Alliance Française, Programme de Renforcement du Système Éducatif Malgache and Programme National de Lutte Contre les MST/SIDA in collaboration with the ministère de la santé and le ministère de l'Éducation Nationale.

Magubane, Bernard M. 1996. *The Making of a Racist State*. Trenton, NJ: African World Press.

Maharaj, Brij. 1992. "Ethnicity, Class and Conflict: The Indian Question in Natal." Paper presented at the Conference on Ethnicity, Society and Conflict in Natal, Pietermaritzburg, University of Natal, September 14–16.

Mamdani, Mahmood. 1990. "A Glimpse at African Studies, Made in the USA." *CODESRIA Bulletin* 2: 7–11.

———. 1996a. *Citizen and Subject: Contemporary Africa and the Legacy of Late Colonialism*. Princeton, NJ: Princeton University Press.

———. 1996b (November-December). "Reconciliation Without Justice." *Southern African Review of Book*, 46: 3–5.

Mann, K., and R. Roberts, eds. 1991. *Law in Colonial Africa*. London and Portsmouth, NH: James Currey and Heinemann.

Manning, P. 1974. "Notes Toward a Theory of Ideology in Historical Writing on Modern Africa." *Canadian Journal of African Studies*, 7 (2): 235–253.

———. 1989. "The Prospects for African Economic History: Is Today Included in the Long Run?" *African Studies Review*, 32: 49–62.

———. 1994. "Escaping the Tyranny of Theory." *Journal of Africa Studies*, 36: 145–147.

———. 1996. "African Economic History, A View from the Continent." *Comparative Studies of South Asia, Africa and the Middle East* XVI (1): 117–121.

Mannoni, Octave. 1990. *Prospero and Caliban: The Psychology of Colonialization* (psychologie de la colonialization). Ann Arbor: University of Michigan Press.

Marais, Hein. 1998. *South Africa: Limits to Change, the Political Economy of Transformation*. London: Zed Books and Cape Town: University of Cape Town Press.

Marcum, J. 1969. *The Angolan Revolution, Volume I*. Cambridge: MIT Press.

———. 1978. *The Angolan Revolution, Volume II*. Cambridge: MIT Press.

Marcussen, Henrik Secher. 1996. "NGOs, the State, and Civil Society." *Review of African Political Economy*, 69: 405–423.

Marè, Gerhard, and Georgina Hamilton. 1987. *An Appetite for Power: Buthelezi's Inkatha and South Africa*. Johannesburg: Ravan Press.

Maree, Johann. 1998. "The COSATU Participatory Democratic Tradition and South Africa's New Parliament: Are They Reconcilable?" *African Affairs*, 386: 29–51.

Markovitz, I. ed. 1987. *Studies in Class and Power in Africa*. New York: Oxford University Press.

Markovitz, Irving Leonard. 1969/1970. *Léopold Sédar Senghor and the Politics of Négritude*, New York: Atheneum, and London: Heinemann Educational Books.

———. 1976. "Bureaucratic Development and Economic Growth." *Journal of Modern African Studies*, 14, (2): 1–18.

———. 1990. "African Capitalism in Comparative Perspective: African Entrepreneurship in Senegal." Paper presented at Annual Meeting of the American Political Science Association, San Francisco, September 1.

———. 1991. "Entrepreneurs and Development in Senegal." Paper presented at African Seminar, Center for International Affairs, Harvard University, Cambridge, MA, November 15.

———. 1998. "Uncivil Society, Capitalism, and the State, in Africa." In N. Kasfir, ed. *Civil Society and Democracy in Africa: Critical Perspectives*. London: Frank Cass.

———. 1999. "Constitutions, the Federalist Papers, and the Transition to Democracy." In Lisa Anderson, ed. *Democracy in Comparative Politics*. New York: Columbia University Press.

Marks, Shula, and Stanley Trapido. 1987. "The Politics of Race, Class and Nationalism." In Shula Marks and Stanley Trapido, eds. *The Politics of Race, Class and Nationalism in Twentieth Century South Africa*. London: Longman, pp. 1–70.

Marlin, R. P. 1998. "Violence, Gender and Illness in Post-War Mozambique." *Bulletin of the Association of Concerned Africa Scholars*, 50.

Marrato, J. 1996. "Superando os Efeitos Sociais da Guerra em Mocambique: mecanismos e Estrategias Locais." Paper presented at the fourth Congress of Lusophone Social Sciences, Rio de Janeiro, September.

Martin, Emily. 1994. *Flexible Bodies: Tracking Immunity in American Culture from the Days of Polio to the Age of AIDS*. Boston: Beacon Press.

Martin, G. 1995. "Definition and Subjectivity in the Writing of Imperial History." *Historical Journal*, 38 (3): 769–779.

Marx, Anthony W. 1992. *Lessons of Struggle: South African Internal Opposition, 1960–1990*. New York, Oxford University Press.

———. 1993. "Contested Images and Implications of South African Nationhood." In Kay. B. Warren ed. *The Violence Within: Cultural and Political Opposition in Divided Nations*. Boulder: Westview Press, pp. 157–179.

———. 1998. *Making Race and Nation: A Comparison of South Africa, United States, and Brazil*. Cambridge: Cambridge University Press.

———. 1993. "Contested Images and Implications of South African Nationhood." in Kay. B. Warren, ed. *The Violence Within: Cultural and Political Opposition in Divided Nations*. Boulder: Westview Press, pp. 157–179.

Mayer, T. 1993. *Truth Versus Precision in Economics*. Brookfield, VT: Edward Elgar.

Mbembe, Achille. 1992. "The Banality of Power and the Aesthetics of Vulgarity in the Postcolony." *Public Culture*, 4 (2): 1–30.

Mbodj, M. 1999, "L'invention d'une tradition: Anciens sites et nouvelle mémoire ou les ambiguités de la célebration de l'independence de la Gambie en 1965."

In Odile Goerg, ed. *Fêtes urbaines en Afrique: espaces, identités et pouvoirs*. Paris: Karthala, pp. 229–254.

McCaskie, T. C. 1976. "The History of the Manwere *nkoa* at Drabonso." *Asante Seminar*, 6: 33–38.

———. 1984. "*Ahyiamu*—'a Place of Meeting': An Essay on Process and Event in the History of the Asante State." *Journal of African History*, 25 (2): 169–188.

———. 1989. "Death and the Asantehene: A Historical Meditation." *Journal of African History*, 30: 417–444.

———. 1995. *State and Society in Precolonial Africa*. Cambridge: Cambridge University Press.

McCay, B., and J. M. Acheson. 1987. *The Question of the Commons: The Culture and Ecology of Common Resources*. Tuscon: University of Arizona Press.

McCloskey, D. N. 1985a. "The Problem of Audience in Historical Economics: Rhetorical Thoughts on a Text by Robert Fogel." *History and Theory*, 24 (1): 1–22.

———. 1985b. *The Rhetoric of Economics*. Madison: University of Wisconsin Press.

———. 1996. "The Economics of Choice: Neoclassical Supply and Demand." In T. Rawski et al., eds. *Economics and the Historian*. Berkeley: University of California Press.

McConnell, Grant. 1967. *Private Power and American Democracy*, New York: Knopf.

McCulloch, Jock. 1983. *Black Soul, White Artifact: Fanon's Clinical Psychology and Social Theory*. Cambridge: Cambridge University Press.

McKenzie, John. 1989 (October). *A Study with Strategy Recommendations Towards the Design of a Small Enterprise Credit Activity in Dakar as an Extension of the Community and Enterprise Development Project*. Dakar: USAID/Senegal.

McLuhan, M. 1962. *The Gutenberg Galaxy*. Toronto: University of Toronto Press.

McNeil, Donald G., Jr. 1998. "Aids Stalking Africa's Struggling Economies." *New York Times*, November 15, sec. 1, p. 1.

Merleau-Ponty, Maurice. 1948. "Le Manifeste Communiste a cent ans." *Le Figaro Littéraire*, April 3, pp. 30–31.

———. 1962. *Phenomenology of Perception*. Colin Smith, trans. London: Routledge.

———. 1964a. *Primacy of Perception*. Carlton Dallery, trans. Evanston, IL: Northwestern University Press.

———. 1964b. *Sense and Non-Sense*. Hubert L. Dreyfus and Patricia Allen Dreyfus, trans. Evanston, IL: Northwestern University Press.

———. 1964c. *Signs*. Richard C. McCleary, trans. Evanston, IL: Northwestern University Press.

———. 1973. *Consciousness and the Acquisition of Language*. Hugh Silverman, trans. Evanston, IL: Northwestern University Press.

Meyer, B. 1998. "Make a Complete Break with the Past: Memory and Post-colonial Modernity in Ghanaian Pentecostalist Discourse." *Journal of Religion in Africa,* 28 (3): 316–349.
Miers, S., and I. Kopytoff, eds. 1977. *Slavery in Africa.* Madison: University of Wisconsin Press.
Migot-Adholla, S. 1991. "Indigenous Land Rights Systems in Sub-Saharan Africa: A Constraint on Productivity." *World Bank Economic Review,* 5 (1): 155–175.
Migot-Adholla, S., et al. 1991. "Land, Security of Tenure and Productivity in Ghana." Paper prepared for conference on Rural Land Tenure, Investment and Agricultural Productivity in Africa, Nairobi.
Minchinton, W. E. 1988. "History Is Multifaceted." *William and Mary Quarterly,* 345: 560–568.
Ministerial Legal Task Team. 1995. "Explanatory Memorandum to the Draft Negotiating Document in the Form of a Labor Relations Bill." *Government Gazette,* 16259. Pretoria: Government Printer.
Minter, W. 1972. *Portuguese Africa and the West.* New York: Monthly Review Press.
———. 1994. *Apartheid's Contras: An Inquiry into the Roots of War in Angola and Mozambique.* London: Zed Books.
Mittelman, J. 1996. *Development: Critical Reflections.* Boulder, CO: Lynne Reiner.
Mkandawire, T. 1987. "Introductory Remarks." In T. Mkandawire and N. Bourenane, eds. *The State and Agriculture in Africa.* Dakar: Codesria Book Series, pp. 1–25.
———. 1995. "Beyond Crisis: Towards Democratic Developmental States in Africa." Paper presented at Eighth CODESRIA General Assembly, Dakar, June.
———. 1996. "Stylizing Accumulation in African Countries and the Role of the State in Policy Making." In M. Lundahl and B. J. Ndulu, eds. *New Directions in Development Economics.* London and New York: Routledge.
———. 1998. "Social Sciences and Democracy Debates in Africa." Claude Ake Lecture, Ninth CODESRIA General Assembly, Dakar, December.
Mkandawire, Thandika. 1997 (September). "The Social Sciences in Africa." *African Studies Review,* 40, (2): 15–36.
Mokaba, Peter. 1997. "The National Question." Paper presented at special parliamentary caucus of the ANC, July 24.
Momoh, Abubakar. 1996a. "Popular Struggles in Nigeria 1960–1982." *African Journal of Political Science,* 1 (2): 154–173.
———. 1996b. "The Structural Adjustment Program and the Transition to Civil Rule in Nigeria, 1986–1993." *Africa Development,* 21 (1): 19–37.
Mondlane, E. 1970. *The Struggle for Mozambique.* Penguin African Library ed. Harmondsworth. Penguin Books.
Monga, Celestin. 1996. *The Anthropology of Anger: Civil Society and Democracy in Africa.* Boulder, CO: Lynne Rienner.

Montag, W. 1998 (Spring). "Can the Subaltern Speak and Other Transcendental Questions.'" *Cultural Logic*, 1 (2). Available at http://www.eserver.org/clogic/1-2/1-2index.html.

Moodie, Dunbar. 1994. *Going for Gold: Men, Mines and Migration*. Berkeley: University of California Press.

Moodley, Kogila. 1980. "Structural Inequality and Minority Group Anxiety: Responses of Middle Groups in South Africa." In Robert Price and Carl G. Rosberg, eds. *The Apartheid Regime: Political Power and Racial Domination*. Berkeley: Institute for International Studies.

Moore, D. B. 1995. "Development Discourse as Hegemony: Towards an Ideological History—1945–1995." In D. B. Moore and G. J. Schmitz, eds. *Debating Development Discourse: Institutional and Popular Perspectives*. New York: St. Martin's Press.

Moore, S. F. 1986. *Social Facts and Fabrications*. Cambridge: Cambridge University Press.

Morris, M. D. 1979. *Measuring the Condition of the World's Poor: The Physical Quality of Life Index*. New York: Pergamon Press.

Mosley, W. H., J. L. Bobadilla, and D. T. Jamison. 1993. "The Health Transition: Implications for Health Policy in Developing Countries." In D. T. Jamison, W. H. Mosley, A. R. Measham, and J. L. Bobadilla, eds. *Disease Control Priorities in Developing Countries*. Oxford: Oxford University Press.

Mouralis, Bernard. 1984. *Littérature et développement*. Paris: Edition Silex.

———. 1992. "*Présence Africaine*: 'Geography of an Ideology.'" In V. Y. Mudimbe, ed. *The Surreptitious Speech:* Présence Africaine *and the Politics of Otherness 1947–1987*. Chicago: University of Chicago Press.

Mouzelis, N. 1988. "Sociology of Development: Reflections on the Present Crisis." *Sociology*, 22 (1): 23–44.

———. 1988. *The Invention of Africa: Gnosis, Philosophy, and the Order of Knowledge*. Bloomington: Indiana University Press.

———. 1994. *The Idea of Africa*. Bloomington: Indiana University Press.

Mudimbe V. Y., ed. 1992. *The Surreptitious Speech:* Présence Africaine *and the Politics of Otherness 1947–1987*. Chicago: University of Chicago Press.

Munro, J. F. 1976. *Africa and the International Economy*. London: J. M. Dent.

Munslow, B. 1983. *Mozambique, The Revolution and Its Origins*. Harlow: Longman.

Murphy, Robert. 1971. *The Dialectic of Social Life*. New York: Basic Books.

Murray, C., and A. Lopez. 1997 (May). "Mortality by Cause for Eight Regions of the World: Global Burden of Disease Study." *Lancet*, 3: 1269–1276.

Murray, Martin J. 1995. "Apartheid and the National Question in South Africa." In Berch Berberoglu, ed. *The National Question*. Philadelphia: Temple University Press, pp. 61–76.

Mustapha, Abdul R. 1991. "Structural Adjustment and Multiple Modes of Social Livelihood in Nigeria." *UNRISD Discussion Papers*, 26. Geneva: UNRISD.

———. 1998. "Son of the Soil or Sin of the Soil? Identity Politics and Democratization in Nigeria." Paper presented at the Workshop on Comparing Experiences of Democratization in Nigeria and South Africa, University of Cape Town, May 30–June 2.

Mzala. 1988. *Gatsha Buthelezi: Chief with a Double Agenda.* London: Zed Books.

Naidoo, Ravi. 1997. "Unions and Investments: Preliminary Assessment and Framework Development." *Discussion Papers,* RR 01/97. Johannesburg: NALEDI.

Nandy, A. 1995. "History's Forgotten Doubles." *History and Theory,* 34 (2): 45–66.

Nash, June. 1979. *We Eat the Mines and the Mines Eat Us. Dependency and Exploitation in Bolivian Tin Mines.* New York: Columbia University Press.

National Economic Development and Labor Council. 1995. *Discussion Document on a Framework for Social Partnership and Agreement Making in NEDLAC.* Johannesburg: NEDLAC.

National Economic Intelligence Committee. 1996. *Economic Recovery Program, 1996–1998: An Alternative to the Medium-Term Program of the World Bank/IMF.* Abuja: NEIC.

National Institute for Economic Policy. 1996. *From the RDP to GEAR: The Gradual Embracing of Neo-Liberalism in Economic Policy.* Johannesburg: NIEP.

———. 1999. *Poverty Elimination, Employment Creation and Sustainable Livelihood in South Africa.* Johannesburg: NIEP.

Nattrass, Nicoli, and Jeremy Seekings. 1996. "Citizenship and Welfare in a Labor-Surplus Economy: the Case of Post-Apartheid South Africa." Paper presented at the Australian Political Science Association Annual Conference, Perth, University of Western Australia, September.

Ndegwa, Stephen N. 1996. *The Two Faces of Civil Society: NGOs and Politics in Africa.* West Hartford, CT: Kumarian Press.

Netting, R. 1968. *Hill Farmers of Nigeria: Cultural Ecology of the Kofyar of the Jos Plateau.* Seattle: University of Washington Press.

———. 1993. *Smallholders, Householders: Farm Families and the Ecology of Intensive, Sustainable Agriculture.* Stanford, CA: Stanford University Press.

Niane, D. T. 1960. *Sundiata: An Epic of Old Mali.* London: Longman.

Nixon, Rob. 1992. "The Collapse of Communist-Anticommunist Condominium: Repercussions for South Africa." *Social Text,* 31 (2): 235–251.

———. 1993. "Of Balkans and Bantustans." *Transition,* 60: 4–26.

Nnoli, Okwudiba. 1993. "The Deteriorating Condition of the Nigerian Working Class." In Okwudiba Nnoli, ed. *Dead End to Nigerian Development: An Analysis of the Political Economy of Nigeria 1979–1989.* Dakar: Codesria: 154–179.

Nooter, M. 1990, "Secret Signs in Luba Sculpture Narrative: A Discourse on Power." In C. D. Roy, ed. *Art and Initiation in Zaire—Iowa Studies in African Art: The Stanley Conferences at the University of Iowa, Volume 3.* Iowa City: The School of Art and Art History, The University of Iowa, pp. 35–60.

Nordstrom, C. 1997. *A Different Kind of War Story.* Philadelphia: University of Pennsylvania Press.

North, D. 1981. *Structure and Change in Economic History*. New York: Norton.
Novak, Michael. 1997. *The Fire of Invention: Civil Society and the Future of the Corporation*. Lanham, MD: Rowman & Littlefield.
Ntozi, James 1997. "AIDS Morbidity and the Role of the Family in Patient Care in Uganda." *Health Transition Review*, Supplement to Vol. 7, pp. 1–27.
Ntozi, James, and Immaculate Nakanaabi. 1997. "The AIDS Epidemic and Infant and Child Mortality in Six Districts of Uganda." *Health Transition Review*, Vol. 7, 189–205.
Nyambara, P. 1999. "A History of Land Acquisition in Gokwe Northwestern Zimbabwe, 1945–1997." Ph.D. dissertation, Northwestern University.
Nye, J., and J. Drobak, eds. 1997. *Frontiers of the New Institutional Economics*. London: Academic Press.
Nzimande, Blade, and Jeremy Cronin. 1997. "ANC Thatcherites Want Black Boses." *Electronic Mail and Guardian*, October 1, http//www.mg.co.za.
Obbo, Christine. 1993a. "HIV Transmission: Men Are the Solution." *Population and Environment*, 14 (3): 211–243.
———. 1993b. "HIV Transmission Through Social and Geographical Networks in Uganda." *Social Science and Medicine*, 36 (7): 949–955.
Obi, Cyril I. 1997 (January). "Structural Adjustment, Oil and Popular Struggles. The Deepening Crisis of State Legitimacy in Nigeria." Dakar: *CODESRIA Monograph Series*.
O'Brien, J. 1994. "Differential High Fertility and Demographic Transitions: Peripheral Capitalism in Sudan." In D. D. Cordell and J. W. Gregory, eds. *African Population and Capitalism: Historical Perspectives*. Madison: University of Wisconsin Press.
O'Brien, Richard. 1992. *Global Finance Integration: The End of Geography*. London: Pinter Press.
O'Donnell, Guillermo, Philippe C. Schmitter, and Lawrence Whitehead, eds. 1986. *Transitions from Authoritarian Rule: Prospects for Democracy, Volumes 1–4*. Baltimore: Johns Hopkins University Press.
Ohiorhenuan, John F. E. 1989. *Capital and the State in Nigeria*. Westport, CT: Greenwood Press.
Okolie, Andrew C. 1995. "Oil Rents, International Loans and Agrarian Policies in Nigeria, 1970–1992." *Review of African Political Economy*, 22 (64): 199–212.
Okome, Mojubaulo O. 1997. *A Sapped Democracy: The Political Economy of the Structural Adjustment Program and the Political Transition in Nigeria*. Lanham, MD: University Press of America.
Okoth-Ogendo, H. W. O. 1986. "The Perils of Land Tenure Reform: The Case of Kenya." In J. Arntzen et al., eds. *Land Policy and Agriculture in Eastern and Southern Africa*. Tokyo: United Nations University Press.
Okware, S. I. 1987. "Towards a National AIDS-Control Program in Uganda." *The Western Journal of Medicine*, 146 (6): 726–729.
Oloyede, Olajide. 1992. "Surviving in an Economic Recession: 'Game Play' in a Nigerian Factory." *Review of African Political Economy*, 20 (55): 44–56.

Olukoshi, Adebayo. 1989. "Impact of IMF-World Bank Programs in Nigeria." In Bade Onimode, ed. *The IMF, the World Bank and the African Debt, Volume 1: The Economic Impact.* London: Zed Books.
Omotola, J. 1983. *Cases on the Land Use Act.* Lagos: Lagos University Press.
Onimode, B. 1985. *An Introduction to Marxist Political Economy.* London: Zed Books.
Osaghae, Eghosa. 1998. *Crippled Giant. Nigeria Since Independence.* London: Hurst.
Ostrom, E. 1990. *Governing the Commons: The Evolution of Institutions for Collective Action.* Cambridge: Cambridge University Press.
———. 1995. "Designing Complexity to Govern Complexity." In S. Hanna and M. Munasinghe, eds. *Rights to Nature: Ecological, Economic, Cultural and Political Principles of Institutions for the Environment.* Washington, DC: Island Press.
Othman, Shehu. 1984. "Classes, Crises and Coup: The Demise of Shagari's Regime." *African Affairs*, 83: 333.
Otobo, Dafe, ed. 1992. *Labor Relations in Nigeria, Volume One.* Lagos: Malthouse Press.
Over, M., and P. Piot. 1993. "HIV Infection and Sexually Transmitted Diseases." In D. T. Jamison, W. H. Mosley, A. R. Measham, and J. L. Bobadilla, eds. *Disease Control Priorities in Developing Countries.* Oxford: Oxford University Press.
Owomoyala, Oyekan. 1994. "With Friends Like These. A Critique of Pervasive Anti-Africanisms in Current African Studies Epistemology and Methodology." *African Studies Review*, 37 (3): 77–101.
Padayachee, Vishnu, S. Vawda, and Paul Tichmann. 1985. *Indian Workers and Trade Unions in Durban: 1930–1950.* Durban, Institute for Social and Economic Research.
Pahad, Essop. 1988. "South African Indians as a National Minority in the National Question." In Maria van Diepen, ed. *The National Question in South Africa.* London: Zed Books.
Panaf, A. 1972. *Great Lives, Eduardo Mondlane.* London: Panaf.
Panitch, Leo. 1996. "COSATU and Corporatism: A Response to Eddie Webster." *Southern Africa Report*, 11 (3): 6–8.
Pankhurst, R. 1989, "An Early Ethiopian manuscript of Tigre." *Proceedings of Eighth International Conference of Ethiopian Studies*, 2: 73–78.
Pape, J. 1990. "Black and White: The 'Perils of Sex' in Colonial Zimbabwe." *Journal of Southern African Studies*, 16 (4): 196–227.
Parekh, Bhikhu. 1993. *Some Reflections on the Indian Diaspora.* London: The British Organization of People of Indian Origin.
Parker, B. 1988. *Einstein's Dream: The Search for a Unified Theory of the Universe.* New York: Plenum Press.
Parker, J., and M. Slaughter. 1990. "Management by Stress." *Science as Culture*, 8: 71 90.
Parker, Richard G. 1991. *Bodies, Pleasures, and Passions: Sexual Culture in Contemporary Brazil.* Boston: Beacon Press.

Passé-Smith, J. T. 1993. "Could It Be That the Whole World Is Already Rich? A Comparison of RGDP/pc and GNP/pc Measures." In M. A. Seligson and J. T. Passé-Smith, eds. *Development and Underdevelopment: The Political Economy of Inequality*. Boulder, CO: Lynne Rienner.

Patterson, Amy S. 1996. *Participation and Democracy at the Grassroots: A Study of Development Associations in Rural Senegal*. Ann Arbor, MI: UMI Microfilm.

Peace, Adrian J. 1979. *Choice, Class and Conflict: A Study of Southern Nigeria Factory Workers*. Atlantic Highlands, NJ: Humanities Press.

Pebble, E. A. 1990. "Impact of HIV/AIDS on African Children." *Social Sciences and Medicine* 31 (6): 671–680.

Perham, Margery. 1958. *Lugard: The Years of Adventure, 1858–1898*. London: Collins.

Perlin, F. 1998. "Disarticulation of the World: Writing India's Economic History. A Review Article." *Society for Comparative Study of Society and History*, 30: 379–387.

Perrott, R. 1973. "What Prince Philip Will Find in Portugal after 600 years." *The Times*, June 3, p. 9a.

Peters, A. 1983, *The New Cartography*. New York: Friendship Press.

———. 1989. *Atlas of the World*. London: Harlow, England: Longman.

Peters, K., and P. Richards. 1998. "Voices of Youth: Why We Fight: Combatants in Sierra Leone. *Africa*, 68 (2): 183–199.

Peters, P. 1994. *Dividing the Commons: Politics and Culture in Botswana*. Charlottesville: University of Virginia Press.

Phillips, A. 1989. *The Enigma of Colonialism: British Policy in West Africa*. London: James Currey.

Phimister, I., and C. Van Onselen. 1979. "The Political Economy of Tribal Animosity: A Case Study of the 1929 Bulawayo Location 'Faction Fight.'" *Journal of Southern African Studies*, 6 (1): 1–43.

Pieterse, Jan Nederven. 1992. *White on Black: Images of Africa and Blacks in Western Popular Culture*. New Haven, CT: Yale University Press.

Poewe, K. 1985. *The Namibian Herero: A History of Their Psychological Disintegration and Survival*. Lewiston, NY: E. Mellen Press.

Pomper, P. 1995. "World History and Its Critics." *History and Theory*, 34 (2): 1–7.

Pomponio, Alice. 1992. *Seagulls Don't Fly into the Bush: Culture Identity and Development in Melanesia*. Belmont, CA: Wadsworth Publishing Company.

Poovey, Mary. 1998. *A History of the Modern Fact: Problems of Knowledge in the Sciences of Wealth and Society*. Chicago: University of Chicago Press.

Porter, A. 1988. "The Balance Sheet of Empire, 1850–1914." *The Historical Journal*, 31 (3): 685–699.

"Pour Une Offensive Diplomatique." 1989. *Sopi*, May 16.

Powesland, Philip G. 1957. *Economic Policy and Labour*. Kampala: East African Institute of Social Research.

Prebble, E.A. 1990." Impact of HIV/AIDS on African Children." *Soc. Sci. Med.* 31 (6): 671–680.

Pretorius, Louwrens. 1996. "Relations Between State, Capital and Labor in South Africa: Towards Corporatism?" *Journal of Theoretical Politics*, 8 (2): 255–281.
Przeworski, Adam. 1991. *Democracy and the Market: Political and Economic Reforms in Eastern Europe and Latin America.* Cambridge: Cambridge University Press.
Przeworski, Adam, et al. 1995. *Sustainable Democracy.* Cambridge: Cambridge University Press.
Putnam, Robert. 1993. *Making Democracy Work: Civic Traditions in Italy.* Princeton, NJ: Princeton University Press.
Raftopoulos, Brian. 1992. "Beyond the House of Hunger: Democratic Struggle in Zimbabwe." *Review of African Political Economy*, 54/55: 59–74.
Rahnema, M., and V. Bawtree, eds. 1997. *The Post-Development Reader.* London: Zed Books.
Raikes, P. 1988. *Modernizing Hunger. Famine, Food Surplus and Farm Policy in the EEC and Africa.* Portsmouth, NH: Heinemann.
Rakner, Lise. 1992. *Trade Unions in Processes of Democratization: A Study of Party-Labor Relations in Zambia.* Bergen: C. Michelsen Institute.
Ramsamy, Edward. 1996. "Post-Settlement South Africa and the National Question: The Case of the Indian Minority." *Critical Sociology*, 22 (3): 57–79.
Ranger, T. O. 1967. *Revolt in Southern Rhodesia.* London: Heinemann.
———. 1970. *The African Voice in Southern Rhodesia, 1898–1930.* Evanston: Northwestern University Press.
———. 1983. "The Invention of Tradition in Colonial Africa." In E. Hobsbawm and T. O. Ranger, eds. *The Invention of Tradition.* Cambridge: Cambridge University Press.
———. 1993a. "The Communal Areas of Zimbabwe." In T. Bassett and D. Crummey, eds. *Land in African Agrarian Systems.* Madison: University of Wisconsin Press.
———. 1993b. "The Invention of Tradition Revisited." In T. O. Ranger and A.O. Vaughan, eds. *Legitimacy and the State in Twentieth-Century Africa.* Oxford: St. Antony's College.
———. 1996. "Postscript to Richard Werbner and Terence Ranger." In *Postcolonial Identities in Africa.* London: Zed Books.
Ranger, T. O., and A.O. Vaughan, eds. 1993. *Legitimacy and the State in Twentieth-Century Africa.* Oxford: St. Antony's College.
Rathbone, R. 1993. *Murder and Politics in Colonial Ghana.* New Haven, CT: Yale University Press.
Ratsiraka, Didier. 1975. *Charte de la Révolution Socialiste Malgache tous Azimuts* [Ny Boky Mena]. Antananarivo: Imprimerie d'Ouvrages Éducatifs.
Rattray, R. S. 1923. *Ashanti.* Oxford: Clarendon Press.
Rawski, T. G. 1996. "Issues in the Study of Economic Trends." In T. Rawski et al., eds. *Economics and the Historian.* Berkeley: University of California Press.

Redclift, M. 1984. *Development and the Environmental Crisis: Red or Green Alternatives?* London: Methuen.
Reddy, E. S. 1986. "The Significance of African and Indian Joint Struggle." In *Struggle for Freedom in Southern Africa.* New Delhi: Mainstream, pp. 7–34.
———. 1991. *India and South Africa.* Occasional Paper Series, No. 1. Durban: University of Durban-Westville.
Reed, C. 1903 (March 31). *Report of the London Missionary Society.* Harare: Special Collections Library, University of Zimbabwe.
Reed, J., and C. Wake. 1976. *Wiriyamu.* London: Heinemann Educational Books Ltd.
Rees, Rob. 1997. *Organizing Downards, Preliminary Findings of a Research as Personal Communication.* Johannesburg: NALEDI.
Reid, Elizabeth. 1996. "HIV and Development: Learning from Others." In Lorraine Sher, Catherine Hawkins, and Lydia Bennett, eds. *AIDS as a Gender Issue: Psycho-Social Perspectives.* London: Taylor & Francis, pp. 235–253.
———. 1997. "Placing Women at the Center of Analysis." In George C. Bond, John Kreniske, Ida Susser, and Joan Vincent, eds. *AIDS in Africa and the Caribbean.* Boulder, CO and Oxford: Westview Press, pp. 159–164.
Reno, W. 1995. *Corruption and State Politics in Sierra Leone.* Cambridge: Cambridge University Press.
Reno, William. 1998. *Warlord Politics and African States* Boulder, CO: Lynne Rienner.
Republic of Uganda. 1990. *Report. The Working Group on the Socioeconomic, Cultural and Legal Impact of AIDS.* Entebbe: Government Printers.
Republic of Uganda. 1994. *The 1991 Population and Housing Census (National Summary) Uganda.* Entebbe: Ministry of Finance and Economic Planning.
Reyna, Steven P. 1999. "Introduction: War in Uganda, North and South." In S. P. and R. E. Downs, eds. *Deadly Developments: Capitalism, States and War.* Philadelphia: Gordon & Breach, pp. 1–22.
Reynolds, Andrew. 1994. *Election '94: South Africa.* New York: St Martin's Press.
Reynolds, P. 1996. *Traditional Healers and Childhood in Zimbabwe.* Athens: Ohio University Press.
Richards, Audrey I. 1955. "The Travel Routes and the Travelers." In Audrey Richards, ed. *Economic Development and Tribal Change.* Cambridge: W. Heffner & Sons, pp. 52–77.
Richards, P. 1996. *Fighting for the Rain Forest: War, Youth and Resources in Sierra Leone.* Oxford: The International African Institute, in association with James Currey.
Richards, Paul. 1994. "Videos and Violence on the Periphery: Rambo and War in the Forests of the Sierra Leone–Liberia Border." *IDS Bulletin,* 25 (2): 88–93.
Richburg, K. B. 1997. *Out of America, a Black Man Confronts Africa.* New York: Basic Books.

Riesman, P. 1986. "The Person and the Life Cycle in African Social Life and Thought." *African Studies Review*, 29 (2): 71–198.
Riley, Stephen P., and Trevor W. Parfitt. 1994. "Economic Adjustment and Democratization in Africa." In John Walton and David Seddon, eds. *Free Markets and Food Riots: The Politics of Global Adjustment*. Oxford: Blackwell.
Roberts, A. D. 1962. "The Sub-Imperialism of the Baganda." *Journal of African History*, 3 (3): 435–450.
Roberts, Stephen. 1929. *The History of French Colonial Policy 1870–1925*. London: P. S. King and Co.
Robinson, Randall. 1998. Letter-to-the Editor. *New York Times*, March 24.
Robinson, William I. 1996. *Promoting Polyarchy: Globalization, US Intervention and Hegemony*. New York: Cambridge University Press.
Rosaldo, Renato. 1989. *Culture and Truth*. Boston: Beacon Press.
Rose, C. 1994. *Property and Persuasion: Essays on the History, Theory and Rhetoric of Ownership*. Boulder, CO: Westview Press.
Rosenau, P. M. 1992. *Post-Modernism and the Social Sciences: Insights, Inroads, and Intrusions*. Princeton, NJ: Princeton University Press.
Rosenstein-Rodan, P. 1944. "The International Development of Economically Backward Areas." *International Affairs*, 20 (2): 157–165.
Roudinesco, Elisabeth. 1990. *Jacques Lacan & Co*. Geoffrey Mehlman, trans. Chicago: University of Chicago Press.
Ryan, J. R. 1997, *Picturing Empire: Photography and the Visualization of the British Empire*. Chicago: University of Chicago Press.
Sachs, J. 1996. "Growth in Africa: It Can Be Done." *The Economist* (London), June 29, pp. 19–21.
Sachs, J. (1998, March-April). "The IMF and the Asian Flu." *American Prospect*, 37: 18–19.
Sahnooun, Mohamed. 2000. "The Humanitarian Challenge of Small Arms Violence." Statement to the ECA/APIC Electronic Roundtable on Peace and Security, March; www.un.org/depts/eca.
Said, Edward. 1991. "Identity, Authority and Freedom: The Potentate and the Traveler." *Transition*, 54: 4–18.
———. 1993. *Culture and Imperialism*. New York: Alfred A. Knopf.
Samkange, S. 1969. *Origins of Rhodesia*. New York: Frederick A. Praeger.
Sandberg, Eve, ed. 1994. *The Changing Politics of Non-Governmental Organisations and African States*. Westport, CT: Praeger.
Sandbrook, R. 1986. "State and Economic Stagnation in Tropical Africa." *World Development*, 14 (3): 319–332.
Sartre, Jean-Paul. 1957. *Being and Nothingness*. Hazel Barnes, trans. London: Methuen.
———. 1963. "Orphée noir" (preface). In *Anthologie de La Nouvelle Poésie Nègre et Malagache*. S. W. Allen, trans. Paris: Présence Africaine.
———. 1965. *Situations*. Benita Eisler, trans. New York: Braziller.

Sassine, W. 1976. *Wiriyamu*. Paris: Presénce Africaine and London: Heinemann Educational Books Ltd.
Saul, John. 1991 (July-August)."South Africa: Between Barbarism and Structural Reform." *New Left Review*, 188: 3–44.
Schaffer, Frederic C. 1998. *Democracy in Translation: Understanding Politics in an Unfamiliar Culture*, Ithaca: Cornell University Press.
Schatz. Sayre. 1994. "Structural Adjustment in Africa: A Failing Grade So Far," *Journal of Modern African Studies*, 32 (4): 679–692.
⸺. 1996 "The World Bank's Fundamental Misconception in Africa." *Journal of Modern African Studies*, 34 (2): 239–247.
Scheikart, L. 1991. "U.S. Commercial Banking: A Historiographical Survey." *Business History Review*, 65: 606–661.
Scheper-Hughes, Nancy. 2000. "The Global Traffic in Human Organs." *Current Anthropology*, 41 (2): 191–211.
Schiller, Nina Glick. 1992. "What's Wrong with This Picture? The Hegemonic Construction of Culture in AIDS Research in the United States." *Medical Anthropological Quarterly*, 63 (3): 237–254.
⸺. 1993. "The Invisible Women: Care-Giving and Construction of AIDS Health Services." *Culture, Medicine and Psychiatry*, 17 (4): 487–512.
Schmidt, E. 1990. "Negotiated Spaces and Contested Terrain: Men, Women and the Law in Colonial Zimbabwe, 1890–1939." *Journal of Southern African Studies*, 16 (4): 622–648.
⸺. 1992. *Peasants, Traders and Wives: Shona Women in the History of Zimbabwe, 1870–1939*. Portsmouth, NH: Heinemann.
Schmitz, G. J. 1995. "Democratization and Demystification: Deconstructing 'Governance' as Development Paradigm." In D. B. Moore and G. J. Schmitz, eds. *Debating Development Discourse: Institutional and Popular Perspectives*. New York: St. Martin's Press.
Schneider, W. H. 1982. *An Empire for the Masses: The French Popular Image of Africa, 1870–1900*. Westport, CT: Greenwood Press.
Schoepf, Brooke G. 1988. "Women, AIDS and Economic Crisis in Zaire." *Canadian Journal of African Studies* 22 (3 : 625–644).
⸺. 1992a. "Gender Relations and Development: Political Economy and Culture." In Ann Seidman and Frederick Anang, eds. *Twenty-First Century Africa: Toward a New Vision of Self-Sustainable Development*. Trenton, NJ: Africa World Press, pp. 203–241.
⸺. 1992b. "Women at Risk: Case Studies from Zaire." In Gilbert Herdt and Shirley Lindenbaum, eds. *Social Analysis in the Time of AIDS*. Newbury Park, CA: Sage, pp. 259–286.
⸺. 1993. "AIDS-Action Research with Women in Kinshasha, Zaire." *Social Science and Medicine*, 37 (11): 1401–1413.
⸺. 1995a. "Action-Research and Empowerment in Africa." In Beth E. Schneider and Nancy E. Stoller, eds. *Feminist Strategies of Empowerment*. Philadelphia: Temple University Press, pp. 246–269.

_____. 1995b. "Culture, Sex Research and AIDS Prevention in Africa." In Han ten Brummelhuis and Gilbert Herdt, eds. *Culture and Sexual Risk: Anthropological Perspectives on AIDS.* New York: Gordon & Breach, pp. 29–51.
Schuurman, F. J. 1993a. "Modernity, Post-modernity and the New Social Movements." In F. J. Schuurman, ed. *Beyond the Impasse: New Directions in Development Theory.* London: Zed Books.
_____. 1993b. "Introduction: Development Theory in the 1990s." In F. J. Schuurman, ed. *Beyond the Impasse: New Directions in Development Theory.* London: Zed Books.
Schweikart, L. 1991. *Banking in the American West from the Gold Rush to Deregulation.* Norman: University of Oklahoma Press.
Scott, C. V. 1995. *Gender and Development. Rethinking Modernization and Dependency Theory.* Boulder, CO: Lynne Rienner.
Scott, James. 1985. *Weapons of the Weak: Everyday Forms of Peasant Resistance.* New Haven, CT: Yale University Press.
Scott, James C. 1990. *Domination and the Arts of Resistance: The Hidden Transcripts.* New Haven, CT: Yale University Press.
Secher Marcussen, Henrik. 1996. "NGOs, the State and Civil Society." *Review of African Political Economy*, 69: 405–423.
Seeley, J., U. Wagner, J. Mulemwa, J. Kengeya-Kayondo, and D. Mulder. 1991. "The Development of a Community-based HIV/AIDS Counseling Service in a Rural Area in Uganda." *AIDS Care*, 3: 207–217.
Seeley, J., E. Kajura, C. Bachengama, M. Okongo, V. Wagner, and D. Mulder. 1993. "The Extended Family and Support for People with AIDS in a Rural Population in South West Uganda: A Safety Net with Holes?" *AIDS Care*, 5 (1): 117–122.
Seligson, M. A., and J. T. Passé-Smith, eds. 1993. *Development and Underdevelopment: The Political Economy of Inequality.* Boulder, CO: Lynne Rienner.
Semboja, Joseph, and Ole Therkildsen. 1995. *Service Provision Under Stress in East Africa: The State, NGOs and People's Organizations in Kenya, Tanzania and Uganda.* London: J. Currey.
Semidei, M. 1966, "De l'Empire à la décolonisation à travers les manuels scolaires français." *Revue française de Science Politique*, 16 (1): 56–86.
"Senegal-Mauritanie, Union Sacree Dans La Vallee." 1989. *Le Soleil*, May 16.
Senghor, Leopold. 1948. *Anthologie de La Nouvelle Poésie Nègre et Malgache de langue Française.* Paris: Presses Universitaires de France.
_____. 1991. *The Collected Poetry.* Melvin Dixon, trans. Charlottesville: Caraf Books.
September Commission—COSATU. 1997. *Report of the September Commission on the Future of the Trade Unions.* Johannesburg: COSATU.
Serote, Wally. 1997. "A Question of the National Question." Paper presented at a Special ANC Parliamentary Caucus on the National Question, May 24.
Serwadda, D., and E. Katongole-Mbidde. 1990. "Viewpoint: AIDS in Africa, Problems for Research and Researchers." *The Lancet*, 35: 842–843.

Shakespeare, W. 1994. *Audio CD Edition, King Lear.* BBC Radio Presents. London: Bantam Books–Audio.

Shanin, T. 1997. "The Idea of Progress." In M. Rahnema and V. Bawtree, eds. *The Post-Development Reader.* London: Zed Books.

Shannon, Gary W., Gerald F. Pyle, and Rashid L. Bashur. 1991. *The Geography of AIDS: Origins and Course of an Epidemic.* New York/London: The Guilford Press.

Sharp, Lesley A. 1990. "Possessed and Dispossessed Youth. Spirit Possession of School Children in Northwest Madagascar." *Culture, Medicine and Psychiatry,* 14 (3): 339–364.

―――. 1993. *The Possessed and Dispossessed: Spirits, Identity, and Power in a Madagascar Migrant Town.* Berkeley: University of California Press.

―――. 1996. "The Work Ideology of Malagasy Children: Schooling and Survival in Urban Madagascar." *Anthropology of Work Review,* 17 (1): 35–42.

―――. 1997. Royal Difficulties: A Question of Succession in an Urbanized Sakalava Kingdom." *Journal of Religion in Africa,* 27 (3): 270–307.

Shipton, P., and M. Goheen, eds. 1992. "Introduction: Land and Its Contested Meanings in Rural Africa." *Africa,* 62 (3): 307–325.

Shore, H. 1983. "Mondlane: A Biographical Sketch." In E. Mondlane, ed. *The Struggle for Mozambique.* London: Zed Press, pp. xii–xxxi.

Simmons, Janie, Paul Farmer, and Brooke G. Schoepf. 1996. "A Global Perspective." In Paul Farmer, Margaret Connors, and Janie Simmons, eds. *Women, Poverty and AIDS.* Monrow, ME: Common Courage Press, pp. 39–90.

Simon, David, Wim Van Spengen, Chris Dixon, and Anders Narman, eds. 1995. *Structurally Adjusted Africa: Poverty, Debt and Basic Needs.* London: Pluto Press.

Simutanyi, Neo R. 1996. "Organized Labor, Economic Crisis and Structural Adjustment in Africa: The Case of Zambia." In Owen Sichone and Bornwell Chikulo, eds. *Democracy in Zambia: Challenges for the Third Republic.* Harare: Sapes Books, pp. 151–172.

Singh, Ratnamala, and Shahid Vawda. 1988. "What Is in a Name: Some Reflections on the Natal Indian Congress." *Transformation,* 6: 1 21.

Sklair, L. 1988. "Transcending the Impasse: Metatheory, Theory, and Empirical Research in Sociology of Development and Underdevelopment." *World Development* 16 (6): 697–709.

Sklar, R. L. 1987. "Developmental Democracy." *Comparative Duties in Society and History,* 29 (4): 686–714.

Slater, D. 1990. "Fading Paradigms and New Agendas—Crisis and Controversy in Development Studies." *European Review of Latin American and Caribbean Studies* 49: 25–32.

Slater, D. 1993. "The Political Meanings of Development: In Search of a New Horizon." In F. J. Schuurman, ed. *Beyond the Impasse: New Directions in Development Theory.* London: Zed Books.

Slater-Thomas, B. 1985. *Politics, Participation and Poverty: Development Through Self-Help in Kenya.* Boulder, CO: Westview Press.

Smaldone, J. P. 1990. "Militarization in Africa: Methodology, Measurement & Mystery." Paper presented at the 33rd meeting of the African Studies Association, Baltimore, MD.

Smith, D. 1993. "Business and the Environment: Towards a Paradigm Shift?" In D. Smith, ed. *Business and the Environment: Implications of the New Environmentalism.* New York: St. Martin's Press.

Snow, P. 1988. *The Star Raft: China's Encounter with Africa.* London: Weidenfeld & Nicolson.

Solow, R. M. 1997. "How Did Economics Get That Way and What Way Did it Get?" *Daedalus,* 126 (1): 39–57.

Sontag, Susan. 1989. *Illness as Metaphor and AIDS and its Metaphors.* New York: Doubleday.

Southall, A. 1985. "Social Disorganization in Uganda: Before, During and After Amin." *Journal of Modern African Studies,* 18 (4): 627–656.

Spivak, G. C. 1990. "Woman in Difference: Mahasweta Devi's 'Douloti the Bountiful.'" In A. Parker et al., eds. *Nationalisms and Sexualities.* New York: Routledge.

Spivak, G. C., Donna Landry, and Gerald MacLean, eds. 1995. *The Spivak Reader: Selected Works of Gayatri Chakravorty Spivak.* New York: Routledge.

Spivak, Gayatri C. 1990. *The Post-Colonial Critic: Interviews, Strategies, Dialogues.* New York: Routledge.

Standing, Guy. 1997. "Labor Market Dynamics in South African Industrial Firms: The South African Labor Flexibility Survey." Paper presented at the Conference on Labor Markets and Enterprise Performance in South Africa, Pretoria, Department of Labor, January 30.

Stephens, Sharon, ed. 1995a. *Children and the Politics of Culture.* Princeton, NJ: Princeton University Press.

Stephens, Sharon. 1995b. "Introduction: Children and the Politics of Culture in 'Late Capitalism.'" In S. Stephens, ed. *Children and the Politics of Culture* Princeton, NJ: Princeton University Press, pp. 3–48.

Stevenson, Richard W. 1998. "Europe Sharpening Its Challenge to the U.S. Over Economic Crisis." *New York Times,* October 7, p. A1.

Stewart, Jon. 1998. *The Debate Between Sartre and Merleau-Ponty.* Evanston, IL: Northwestern University Press.

Stewart, Sheelagh. 1997. "Happy Ever After in the Marketplace: Non-governmental Organisations and Uncivil Society." *Review of African Political Economy,* 71: 11–34.

Stocking, G., ed. 1984. *Functionalism Historicized: Essays on British Social Anthropology.* Madison: University of Wisconsin Press.

Stoler, A. 1989. "Making Empire Respectable: the Politics of Race and Sexual Morality in 20th Century Colonial Cultures." *American Ethnologist,* 16 (4): 634–660.

Stone, J. C. 1995. *A Short History of the Cartography of Africa.* Lewiston, PA: E. Mellen.

_____. 1997. *Norwich's Maps of Africa—An Illustrated and Annotated Carto-Bibliography.* Norwich, VT: Terra Nova Press.
Stone, J. C., ed. 1994. *Maps and Africa—Proceedings of a Colloquium.* Aberdeen: University of Aberdeen.
Summers, R., and A. Heston. 1984 (September). "Improved International Comparisons of Real Product and Its Composition: 1950–1980." *The Review of Income and Wealth,* 3: 207–259.
_____. 1988 (March). "A New Set of International Comparisons of Real Product and Prices: Estimates for 130 Countries, 1950–1985." *The Review of Income and Wealth,* 34 (1): 1–25.
Sutcliffe, Michael, and Paul Wellings. 1988. "Inkatha Versus the Rest." *African Affairs,* 87 (348): 325–360.
Suret-Canale, Jean. 1971. *French Colonialism in Tropical Africa,* 1900–1945. Till Gottheiner, trans. New York: Pica Press.
Surplus People Project. 1995. *SPP Funding Proposal 1996–1998.* Cape Town: SPP.
Sutton, L. 1984. "Law, Chieftaincy and Conflict in Colonial Ghana: The Ada Case." *African Affairs,* 83 (330): 41–62.
Swift, J. 1733. *On Poetry—A Rapsody.* London: J. Huggonson.
Taiwo, O. 1998. "Exorcizing Hegel's Ghost: Africa's Challenge to Philosophy." *African Studies Quarterly,* 1 (4); http://web.africa.ufl.edu/asq/.
Taussig, Michael. 1987. *Shamanism, Colonialism, and the Wild Man. A Study in Terror and Healing.* Chicago: University of ChicagoPress.
Taylor, Rupert. 1991 (October-December). "The Myth of Ethnic Division: Township Conflict on the Reef." *Race and Class,* 33 (2): 1–14.
Theron, Jan. 1996. "On Homeworker." *Institute of Development and Labor Law Occasional Papers.* Cape Town: University of Cape Town.
Thomas, Alan. 1992. "Non-governmental Organisations and the Limits to Empowerment." In Marc Wuyts, Maureen Mackintosh, and Tom Hewitt, eds. *Development Policy and Public Action.* Oxford: Oxford University Press.
Thompson, R. F. 1984. *Flash of the Spirit: African and Afro-American Art and Philosophy.* New York: Vintage.
Thompson, R. F., and J. Cornet. 1981. *The Four Moments of the Sun: Kongo Art in Two Worlds.* Washington, DC: National Gallery of Art.
Thornton, Robert, and Mamphela Ramphele. 1988. "The Quest for Community." In Emile Boonzaier and John Sharp, eds. *South African Keywords: The Uses and Abuses of Political Concepts.* Cape Town: D. Philip.
Thrower, N. J. W. 1996. *Maps & Civilization: Cartography in Culture and Society.* Chicago: University of Chicago Press.
Tilly, C., L. A. Tilly, and R. Tilly. 1991. "European Economic and Social History in the 1990s." *Journal of European Economic History,* 20: 645–671.
Tilly, Charles. 1990. *Coercion, Capital and European States.* Cambridge, MA: B. Blackwell.

Tilton, J. 1983. *Material Substitution: Lessons from the Tin-Using Industries.* Washington, DC: Resources for the Future.
Timár, L. 1992. "Regional Economic and Social History or Historical Geography?" *Journal of European Economic History*, 21: 391–406.
The Times (London). 1964. "Terrorists from Tanganyika." October 12, p. 11e.
The Times (London). 1973. "Missionary Work Viewed in Mozambique as Subversive," August 3, p. 6f.
The Times Annual Index. 1973 (July-December). Colindale, London: The British Library, Newspaper Collection.
Tooley, R. V. 1980. *Maps and Map-Makers.* New York: Dorset.
Touval, S. 1972. *The Boundary Politics of Independent Africa.* Cambridge, MA: Harvard University Press.
Toye, J. 1987. *Dilemmas of Development: Reflections on the Counter-Revolution in Development Theory and Policy.* Oxford: Blackwell.
Treichler, Paula. 1989. "AIDS and HIV Infection in the Third World: A First World Chronicle." In B. Kruger and P. Mariani, eds. *Remaking History.* Seattle: Bay Press, pp. 31–86.
Trevor-Roper, H. 1965. *The Rise of Christian Europe.* New York: Harcourt, Brace & World.
Tripp, Aili Mari. 1996. "Urban Women's Movements and Political Liberalization in East Africa." In Kathleen Sheldon, ed. *Courtyards, Markets, City Streets: Urban Women in Africa.* Boulder, CO: Westview Press, pp. 285–308.
———. 1998. "Expanding Civil Society: Women and Political Space in Contemporary Uganda." In N. Kasfir, ed. *Civil Society and Democracy in Africa: Critical Perspectives.* London: Frank Cass, pp. 84–108.
Truman, David, 1951. *The Governmental Process.* New York: Knopf.
Truth and Reconciliation Commission of South Africa Report. 1999. Vols 1–5, book and CD-Rom eds. New York: Groves Dictionaries of Music.
Turner, Terisa E. 1997. "Oil Workers and Oil Communities in Africa: Nigerian Women and Grassroots Environmentalism." *Labor, Capital and Society*, 30 (1): 66–89.
Turner, V., ed. 1971. *Profiles of Change: African Society and Colonial Rule.* Volume 3 of P. Duignan, P. Gann, and L. Gann, eds. *Colonialism in Africa.* Cambridge: Cambridge University Press.
Turshen, M. 1989. *The Politics of Public Health.* New Brunswick, NJ: Rutgers University Press.
———. 1991. "Gender and Health in Africa." In M. Turshen, ed. *Women and Health in Africa.* Trenton, NJ: Africa World Press.
———. 1999. *Privatizing Health Services in Africa.* New Brunswick, NJ: Rutgers University Press.
Turshen, M., and C. Twagiramariya, eds. 1998. *What Women Do in Wartime: Gender and Conflict in Africa.* London: Zed Books.
Turshen, Meredeth, ed. 1991. *Women and Health in Africa.* Trenton, NJ: Africa World Press.

Tutu, Desmond. 1994. *The Rainbow People of God: The Making of a Peaceful Revolution.* New York: Doubleday.
Umzamo. n.d. *Resume.* Cape Town: Umzamo.
UNAIDS. 2000. *Report on the Global HIV/AIDS Epidemic.* New York: United Nations.
UNCTAD. 1988. *Trade and Development Report 1988.* New York: United Nations.
———. 1989. *Trade and Development Report 1989.* New York: United Nations.
———. 1997. *Trade and Development Report 1997.* New York: United Nations.
UNDP. 1990–1998. *Human Development Report.* New York: Oxford University Press. Available at http://www.undp.org/hdro.
UNICEF. 1989. *Children on the Front Line: The Impact of Apartheid, Destabilization, and Warfare on Children in Southern and South Africa.* New York: UNICEF.
———. 1998. *Statistical Data,* http://www.unicef.org/statis/index.html.
United Nations. 1994. *AIDS and the Demography of Africa.* New York: United Nations.
———. 1999. *The Human Development Report of 1999.* New York: Oxford University Press.
Uvin, Peter. 1998. *Aiding Violence: The Development Enterprise in Rwanda.* West Hartford, CT: Kumarian Press.
Vail, L., ed. 1987. *The Creation of Tribalism in Southern Africa.* Berkeley: University of California Press.
Vail, L., and L. White. 1991. *Power and the Praise Poem: Southern African Voices in History.* London: James Currey.
Valenzuela, J. Samuel. 1989. "Labor Movements in Transition to Democracy: A Framework for Analysis." *Comparative Politics,* 21 (4): 445–472.
Van de Walle, E. 1990. "The Social Impact of AIDS in Sub-Saharan Africa." *Milbank Quarterly* 68, supplement vol. 1.
Van Driel, Maria. 1998. "Local Government Privatization Through the Back Door." *South African Labor Bulletin,* 22 (3): 14–17.
Van Onselen, C. 1977. *Chibaro: African Mine Labour in Southern Rhodesia 1900–1933.* Johannesburg: Ravan Press.
———. 1982. *Studies in the Social and Economic History of the Witwatersrand.* Johannesburg: Ravan Press.
Vandergeest, P and F. Buttel. 1988. "Marx, Weber, and Development Sociology: Beyond the Impasse." *World Development* 16 (6): 683–695.
Vaughan, M. 1991. *Curing Their Ills: Colonial Power and African Illness.* London: Stanford University Press.
Vilakazi, Herbert. 1991 (June). "Isolating Inkatha: A Strategic Error." *Work in Progress,* 75: 21–23.
Vincent, Joan. 1999. "War in Uganda, North and South." In S. P. Reyna and R. E. Downs, eds. *Deadly Developments: Capitalism, States and War.* Philadelphia: Gordon & Breach, pp. 107–132.

Vines, A. 1991. *RENAMO: Terrorism in Mozambique.* London: Centre for Southern African Studies, University of York and Indiana University Press.
Von Bulow, D. 1992. "Bigger Than Men? Gender Relations and Their Changing Meaning in Kipsigis Society, Kenya." *Africa,* 62 (4): 523–546.
Von Freyhold, Michaela. 1987. "Labor Movements or Popular Struggles in Africa." *Review of African Political Economy,* 14 (39): 23–32.
Von Holdt, Karl. 1995. "The LRA Agreement: 'Worker Victory' or 'Miserable Compromise?'" *South African Labor Bulletin,* 19 (4): 16–26.
Vujakovic, P. 1989. "Mapping for World Development." *Geography,* 74 (2): 97–105.
Walker, Cherryl. 1994. "Women, 'Tradition,' and Reconstruction." *ROAPE,* 61: 347–358.
Wall, Lewis. 1988. *Hausa Medicine: Illness and Well-being in a West African Culture.* Durham, NC: Duke University Press.
Wallerstein, I. M. 1979. *The Capitalist World-Economy: Essays.* Cambridge: Cambridge University Press.
Wallerstein, Immanuel. 1997. "The National and the Universal: Can There Be Such a Thing as World Culture?" In Anthony King, ed. *Culture, Globalization and the World System.* Minneapolis: Minnesota University Press.
Wallis, H., and D. Middleton. 1987. "The Mapping and Exploitation of Africa and George Banks." In P. M. Larby, ed. *Maps and Mapping of Africa.* London: SCOLMA, pp. 47–54.
Walter, E. 1981. *The Immorality of Limiting Growth.* Albany, NY: State University of New York Press.
Walters, Ronald. 1993. *Pan Africanism in the African Diaspora: An Analysis of Modern Afrocentric Political Movements.* Detroit: Wayne State.
Walton, John, and David Seddon, eds. 1994. *Free Markets and Food Riots: The Politics of Global Adjustment.* Oxford: Blackwell.
Ward, M. 1985. *Purchasing Power Parities and Real Expenditures in the OECD.* Paris: OECD Press.
Waring, M. 1990. *If Women Counted: A New Feminist Economics.* San Francisco: HarperCollins.
Wawer, M., D. Serwadda, S. Musgrave, and K. Konde-Lule. 1991. "Dynamics and Spread of HIV–1 Infection in a Rural District of Uganda." *British Medical Journal,* 303: 1303–1306.
Wawer, M., et. al. 1994. "Incidence of HIV–1 in a Rural Region of Uganda." *British Medical Journal,* 308: 171–173.
Webb, Douglas. 1997. *HIV and AIDS in Africa.* London: Pluto Press.
Weber, M. 1996. *The Protestant Ethic and the Spirit of Capitalism.* Talcot Parson, trans. Los Angeles: Roxbury Publishing Company.
Webster, Eddie. 1988. "The Rise of Social Movement Unionism: The Two Faces of the Black Trade Union Movement in South Africa." In Philip Frenkel,

Noam Pines, and Mark Swilling, eds. *State, Resistance and Change in South Africa*. London: Croom Helm, pp. 174–196.

Webster, Eddie, and Karl Von Holdt. 1991. "Toward a Socialist Theory of Radical Reform: From Resistance to Reconstruction in the Labour Movement." Paper presented at the Ruth First Memorial Symposium, Bellville, University of Western Cape.

Webster, J. B., and A. A. Boahen. 1967. *The Revolutionary Years. West Africa Since 1800*. London: Longman.

Weiner, A. 1992. *Inalienable Possessions: The Paradox of Keeping While Giving*. Berkeley and Los Angeles: University of California Press.

Weiner, P., illus., and D. C. Dennett. 1992. *Consciousness Explained*. New York: Little, Brown.

Wessells, M. 1997 (November/December). "Child Soldiers." *Bulletin of the Atomic Scientists*, 53 (6): 32–39.

West African Lands Committee. 1916. *Report*. London: Printed for the Colonial Office.

Weyland, Kurt. 1996. "Neopopulism and Neoliberalism in Latin American: Unexpected Affinities." *Studies in Comparative International Development*, 31 (3): 3–31.

White, E. 1988. *Voices of Blood*. Maputo: INLD.

White, L. 1983. "A Colonial State and an African Petty-Bourgeoisie." In F. Cooper, ed. *Struggle for the City: Migrant Labor, Capital, and the State in Urban Africa*. Beverly Hills: Sage Publications, pp. 167–194.

Whiteside, Kerry. 1988. *Merleau-Ponty and the Foundation of an Existential Politics*. Princeton, NJ: Princeton University Press.

Whitfield, P. 1994. *The Image of the World–20 Centuries of World Maps*. San Francisco: Pomegranate.

Whitford, Margaret. 1982. *Merleau-Ponty's Critique of Sartre's Philosophy*. Lexington, KY: French Forum Publishers.

Whyte, Susan. R. 1997. *Questioning Misfortune: The Pragmatics of Uncertainty in Eastern Uganda*. New York: Cambridge University Press.

Wiarda, H. J. 1977. *Corporatism and Development*. Amherst: The University of Massachusetts Press

Widner, J., and A. Mundt. 1998. "Researching Social Capital in Africa." *Africa*, 68 (1):1–24.

Wilford, J. N. 1982. *The Mapmakers*. New York: Vintage.

Wilks, I. 1993. *Forests of Gold*. Athens: Ohio University Press.

Willcox, R. R. 1949. *Report on Venereal Diseases, Survey of the African in Southern Rhodesia*. Salisbury: Southern Rhodesia: Department of Public Health.

Williams, Raymond. 1983. *Keywords*. London: Fontana.

Wilson, E. O. 1998. *Consilience: The Unity of Knowledge*. New York: Knopf.

Winnicott, D. W. 1988. *Human Nature*. London: Free Association Books.

Winter-Nelson, A. 1995a. "Natural Resources, National Income, and Economic Growth in Africa." *World Development*, 23 (9): 1507–1519.

_____. 1995b. "Discount Rates, Natural Resources, and the Measurement of Aggregate Economic Growth in Africa." *Ecological Economics*, 17: 21–32.

Wiredu, K. 1996. *Cultural Universals and Particulars: An African Perspective.* Bloomington: Indiana University Press.

"With Asia's Economies Shrinking, Women Are Being Squeezed Out." 1998. *New York Times,* June 11, p. A12

Wolfensohn, J. D. 1999. *The World Bank Group Publications: 1999 Highlights.* Washington, DC: World Bank.

Wood, D. 1992. *The Power of Maps.* New York: Guilford Press.

World Bank. 1981. *Towards Accelerated Development in Sub-Saharan Africa.* Washington, DC: World Bank.

_____. 1989. *Sub-Saharan Africa: From Crisis to Sustainable Growth.* Washington, DC. The World Bank.

_____. 1990. *World Development Report 1990.* New York: Oxford University Press.

_____. 1994. *Adjustment in Africa: Reforms, Results and the Road Ahead.* New York: Oxford University Press.

_____. 1996a. *AIDS Prevention and Mitigation in Sub-Saharan Africa: An Updated World Bank Strategy.* Washington, DC: World Back Report No. 15569-AFR.

_____. 1996b. *Taking Action for Poverty Reduction in Sub-Sahahan Africa: Report of an Africa Religion Task Force.* Washington, DC: World Bank Report No. 15575-AFR.

_____. 1996c. *Towards Environmentally Sustainable Growth in Sub-Saharan Africa.* Washington, DC: World Bank.

World Bank. 1997a. *Confronting AIDS: Public Priorities in a Global Epidemic.* New York: Oxford University Press.

_____. 1997b. *World Development Report 1997.* Washington, DC: World Bank.

_____. 1998a. *Global Economic Prospect 1998/99.* Washington, DC: World Bank.

_____. 1998b. *The World Bank Annual Report 1998.* Washington, DC: World Bank.

_____. 1998c (December 2). "World Bank Predicts Lowest Growth Rates for Developing Countries Since Eighties' Debt Crisis? Outlook to Improve by 2000, Washington" (press release). Washington, DC: World Bank.

_____. 1998d. *World Development Indicators 1998.* Washington, DC: World Bank.

_____. 1998e. *Statement of World Bank President James D. Wolfensohn on the 1998–1999 Global Economic Prospects, December 3, 1998.* Washington, DC: World Bank, pp. 1 and 2.

_____. 1999a. *World Bank Atlas.* Washington, DC: World Bank.

———. 1999b. *The World Bank Group Publications: 1999 Highlights*. Washington, DC: World Bank.
World Health Organization (WHO). 2000. "WHO Issues New Health Expectancy Ratings. Press release, Washington, DC, June 4.
———. 1988. "Acquired Immunodeficiency Syndrome. AIDS 1987. Revision of CDC/WHO Case Definition for IADS." *WHO Weekly Epidemiological Record*, 63: 1–8.
Wurgaft, L. D. 1995. "Identity in World History: A Postmodern Perspective." *History and Theory*, 34 (2): 67–85.
Yoshikuni, T. 1991. "Black Migrants in a White City: A History of African Harare, 1890–1925." Ph.D. dissertation, University of Zimbabwe.
Zambia Central Statistical Office (CSO), http://www.finance.gov:zm/cos.htm.
Zarour, Charbel. 1989 (August). *La Reorganisation du Secteur De La Distribution De Detail*. Dakar: USAID/Senegal.
Zartman, William, ed. 1995. *Collapsed States: The Disintegration and Restoration of Legitimate Authority*. Boulder, CO: Lynne Rienner.
Zeleza, P. T. 1993. *A Modern Economic History of Africa. Volume 1: The Nineteenth Century*. Dakar: CODESRIA Book Series.
———. 1997a. *Manufacturing African Studies and Crises*. Dakar: CODESRIA Book Series.
———. 1997b. "Fictions of the Postcolonial." *The Toronto Review*, 15 (2): 19–29.
Zeleza, P. T. 2001. *Globalizing Africa: From Epistemology to Economy*. Trenton, NJ: Africa World Press.
Zwanenberg R. M. A., and A. King. 1975. *An Economic History of Kenya and Uganda 1800–1970*. London: Macmillan.
Zwi, A., and A. Ugalde. 1989. "Towards an Epidemiology of Political Violence in the Third World." *Social Science & Medicine*, 28 (7): 649–657.

Contributors

Franco Barchiesi is a lecturer in the Department of Sociology and a Ph.D. candidate at the University of the Witwatersrand, Johannesburg. He is currently researching welfare and social citizenship in the context of changes in work and employment in post-apartheid South Africa. He has published in the *Review of African Political Economy*, *Critical Sociology*, and *Rethinking Marxism*.

Sara Berry is Professor of History and Anthropology at Johns Hopkins University. For more than 25 years she has specialized in the study of African social and economic history, economic development, and agrarian change, with particular emphasis on West Africa. She is the author of *Cocoa, Custom and Socio-economic Change in Rural Western Nigeria*, *Fathers Work for Their Sons: Accumulation, Mobility and Class Formation in an Extended Yoruba Community*, and *No Condition is Permanent: The Social Dynamics of Agrarian Change in Sub-Saharan Africa*.

George Clement Bond, the William F. Russell Professor of Anthropology and Education, is Professor of Anthropology and Education at Teachers College and formerly the Director of the Institute of African Studies at Columbia University. He has published extensively on central Africa, and his latest books include *The Social Construction of the Past*, co-edited with Angela Gilliam; *AIDS in Africa and the Caribbean*, co-edited with John Kreniske, Ida Susser, and Joan Vincent; and *Witchcraft Dialogues*, co-edited with Diane Ciekawy.

Kate Crehan is an Assistant Professor in the Department of Psychology, Sociology, and Anthropology at the College of Staten Island, and the Anthropology Program of the Graduate Center, City University of New York. She is the author of *The Fractured Community: Landscapes of Power and Gender in Rural Zambia*. She is currently working on a manuscript that examines how anthropologists have used the work of Antonio Gramsci and how they might most fruitfully use it.

Mustafah Dhada is Associate Professor of International Affairs and Coordinator of the African Studies Area Concentration at the Graduate School of International Affairs and Development, Clark Atlanta University, and teaches as an adjunct in fine arts at the Atlanta College of Art. Among his published works are *Warriors at Work*, which focuses on the liberation struggle in Guinea-Bissau, and critical review essays on Lusophone cinema and art. His next monograph delves into the Wiriyamu massacres in Mozambique, the subject of his chapter in this volume. Dhada is an avid calligrapher and sculptor.

Nigel C. Gibson teaches at Emerson College, Boston. Formerly the Assistant Director of the Institute of African Studies, Columbia University, he is presently a research associate in Africana studies at Brown University and at the Department of Afro-American Studies at Harvard University. He is editor of *Rethinking Fanon* and co-editor of *Adorno: A Critical Reader*, and is currently finishing a monograph on Frantz Fanon.

Alcinda Honwana is a senior lecturer in the department of Social Anthropology at the University of Cape Town in South Africa. Her research interests cover topics such as spirit possession and traditional healing in Mozambique, cultural politics, and local mechanisms of healing and reconciliation in the aftermath of war in Mozambique. Having done extensive research on child soldiers in Mozambique and Angola, Dr. Honwana is currently studying the impact of the war on women in Mozambique. She is also working on a project on new age and alternative healing among white South Africans in Cape Town. Dr. Honwana has published several articles about the war, politics of culture, and processes of reconciliation and social reintegration in Mozambique.

Lynette Jackson is Assistant Professor of Women's Studies at the University of Illinois, Chicago. She is the author of numerous articles, and her forthcoming book is entitled *From Regime to Regime: The Social History of Ingutsheni Mental Hospital in Colonial Zimbabwe*.

Irving Leonard Markovitz is Professor of Political Science at Queens College, New York, and specializes in the politics and economics of development, especially in Africa. His books include *Leopold Sedar Senghor and the Politics of Negritude*, *African Politics and Society: Basic Issues of Government and Development* (co-author and editor), *Power and Class in Africa*, and *Studies in Power and Class in Africa* (co-author and editor). He is Co-Editor in Chief of *Comparative Politics*. During January 1995 he acted as a consultant to the Constitutional Commission of Eritrea in Asmara, Eritrea.

Mohamed Mbodj is Professor of History and Director of African Studies at Manhattanville College. His research interests center on the economic and social history of Africa, Islam, and nationalism. He has published numerous articles on these topics. His forthcoming books include *The Emergence of a National Identity, 1817–1965* and *Economic and Social Change in Senegal, 1887–1960*.

Edward Ramsamy is Assistant Professor of Africana Studies at Rutgers University. He obtained his doctorate in urban planning and policy development at Rutgers University. His research examined trends in the World Bank's Urban Development policy in Zimbabwe. He is also interested in the political economy of transition in post-colonial societies and has published several articles on regional integration and nation-building in South Africa.

Oliver S. Saasa is Professor of International Economic Relations and Director of the Institute of Economic and Social Research at the University of Zambia. He is author of a number of books and monographs, including *Aid Relationship in Zambia: A Conflict Scenario* (with Jerker Carlsson) and *Joining the Future: Economic Integration and Cooperation in Africa*.

Sayre P. Schatz is Professor Emeritus, Temple University, and formerly Visiting Professor of Economics at the Institute of African Studies, Columbia University. He is the author of *Nigerian Capitalism, Economics, Politics and Administration in Government Lending: The Regional Loans Boards of Nigeria*, and *Development Bank Lending in Nigeria: The Federal Loans Board*; co-author of *Postimperialism: International Capitalism and Development in the Late Twentieth Century*; and editor and co-author of *South of the Sahara: Development in African Economies*. He has published approximately five dozen journal articles and contributions to books. He has done research in Africa mainly in Nigeria, and has been an advisor to the government of Nigeria on the Third National Development Plan.

Lesley A. Sharp is Assistant Professor of Anthropology at Barnard College, Columbia University. She is the author of *The Possessed and the Dispossessed: Spirits, Identity, and Power in a Madagascar Migrant Town*. The chapter that appears in this volume is drawn from a larger work in progress, entitled *The Sacrificed Generation*, which explores historical consciousness and the significance of political activism in the lives of secondary school youth in Madagascar.

Meredeth Turshen teaches gender and development and Third World social policy at the Edward J. Bloustein School of Planning and Public Policy, Rutgers University. She is the author of *The Political Ecology of Disease in Tanzania*, *The Politics of Public Health*, and *Privatizing Health Services in Africa*, and the editor of *Women and Health in Africa*, *Women's Lives and Public Policy: The International Experience*, *What Women Do in Wartime: Gender and Conflict in Africa*, and *African Women's Health*. She serves as Political Co-Chair of the

Association of Concerned Africa Scholars and as contributing editor of the *Review of African Political Economy*.

Joan Vincent is Emeritus Professor of Anthropology at Barnard College, Columbia University. Her research has been in Africa and Northern Ireland and she has published widely concerning the historical emergence of political conflict and ethnicity. Her most recent books are *Anthropology and Politics* and *AIDS in Africa and the Caribbean*, co-edited with George C. Bond, John Kreniske, and Ida Susser.

Paul Zeleza is Professor of History and Director of African Studies at the University of Illinois at Urbana-Champaign. He is the author of *Modern Economic History of Africa* and *Manufacturing African Studies and Crises* and co-editor of *Sacred Spaces and Public Quarrels: African Cultural and Economic Landscapes*. He is also the author of a novel, *Smouldering Charcoal*, and a collection of stories, *Night of Darkness*. He is currently completing the *Modern Economic History of Africa: Volume 2*.

Index

Abacha, General, 157, 158
Abiola, Moshood, 157, 158
Abubakar, Abdulsalam, 159
Abu–Lughod, J. L., 63
Abyssinia, 45
Academic Staff Union of Universities (ASUU), 158
Acquired Immunodeficiency Syndrome (AIDS), 30–31, 367–368
   civil war/violence and, 352–355
   Madagascar, 339–344
   moving frontier, 348–352
   Uganda, 345–363
Action for Development (ACFODE), 359
AD. *See* Alliance for Democracy 159
Adam, Heribert, 212
Adesina, Jimi, 156, 159
Adjustment in Africa: Reforms, Results, and the Road Ahead, 91–95
Adler, Glenn, 162–163
Africa
   contemporary context, 9–11
   historical configurations, 6–9
   population growth, 368–371
   resources, 6–9
   wars, 371–373
African Charter of Rights of the Child, 282
African Growth and Opportunity Act, 118–119, 130–131
Africanists, 76, 122, 349
African National Congress (ANC), 15–20, 124, 130–131, 161, 163–164, 167–169

Charterists, 197–198
IFP and, 200–204
Indian community and, 205–209
50th Conference, 182, 196
Zulus and, 200–204
African Recovery (United Nations), 14
African Voice, 303
Africa Structural Adjustment Program (World Bank), 9
AIDS. *See* Acquired Immunodeficiency Syndrome
AIDS Control Program, 352
AIDS Research Committee (Uganda), 358
AIDS Support Organization (TASO), 358, 359
Aina, Tade, 75–76
Akan cosmology, 227–228
Akwetey, Emmanuel, 152
Akyeampong, Emmanuel, 227–228
Albert, Zafy, 339–340
Alexander, Neville, 208
Algeria, 250, 258
al–Idrisi, 44
Allen, R. B., 60
Alliance for Democracy (AD), 159
All People's Party (APP), 159
Amandebele Patriotic Society (AP Society), 311
Ambanja. *See* Madagascar
Amin, Samir, 74
ANC. *See* African National Congress
Anderson, Benedict, 50, 300
Andrae, Gunilla, 154
Anglo–Portuguese Alliance, 265

Angola, 108, 261, 264
  See also child soldiers
Anthropology of Anger, The (Monga), 128
anti–colonial African studies, 235–236
Anville, Jean Baptiste d', 46
APP. *See* All People's Party
AP Society. *See* Amandebele Patriotic Society
Arabia, 44
Asante, 38, 213–215
  negotiable property, 220–226
  property as exclusion, 215–217
  See also Ghana
Asantehene, 223, 225–226
Asia, financial crisis, 132–134
Asio, Mary Eragu, 359
Asmal, Kader, 196
ASUU. *See* Academic Staff Union of Universities
Austen, R. A., 61
Azmi, Shabana, 208

Babangida, General, 155, 156, 159
Banania, 239, 240, 257
Bangui Conference, 353
Bantu philosophy, 253
Bantustans, 203
Barberer, H. M., 300
Barker, T. C., 76
Bates, Robert, 70
Beauvoir, Simone de, 236, 241
Beckman, Bjorn, 154
Being and Nothingness (Sartre), 237, 239
Bera, John, 315
Beringuer, Vincente, 271
Berlin conference (1884–1885), 7, 49, 64
Bernal, Martin, 61
bias, 95–99
Bienen, Henry, 157–158
binaries, 269–273
Black Athena (Bernal), 61
Black Consciousness Movement, 180, 198
Black Peril, 303, 311
Black Skin, White Masks (Fanon), 237, 243–244, 254
blame, 315–316, 320, 341
Bledsoe, Caroline, 228

body, 238, 239, 241–242
  contested claims, 365–378
  spatial control of, 299–320
Boesak, Allan, 208
Bond, George Clement, 376
Bond, Patrick, 163–164
Book of Roger, The (al–Idrisi), 44
Booth, David, 69
Botswana, 108, 220
Braudel, Fernand, 65
Britain, 7–9, 220–222, 262, 272
British South Africa Company (BSAC), 301, 304
BSAC. *See* British South Africa Company
Buganda, 352–353
Buhari, General, 155
Buhlungu, Sakhela, 163
Bulawayo Municipal African Location, 305, 307, 310
Burundi, 107
Bush, George, 75
Buthelezi, Gatsha, 196, 200–204, 207
Buttel, F., 69

Cabora Bassa project, 274
Cabral, Amílcar Lopes, 260–262, 274
Cabrita, Felicia, 271
Caetano regime, 265, 266, 271, 273–276
Cambridge series, 60–61
Cameron, V. L., 49
Cape Colony's Contagious Diseases Act of 1882, 301
Cape of Good Hope, 45
capitalism, 121, 122, 211, 213–214, 351
Carby, Hazel, 305
Carrim, Yunus, 205
cartography, 300–301
  accuracy, 52–56
  cultural/intellectual maps, 355–360
  decoding, 39–42
  development of scientific, 43–46
  European expansion and, 47–52
  geography and, 46–47
  history, 38–43
  imperialism and, 47–52
  military, 50–51
  moving frontier, 348–352

murals, 51–52
projections, 41, 51, 53
territorial disputes and, 54–56
Casamance independence movement (MFDC), 56
Catholic Academy, 323–324, 336
Catholic Mission, 338, 339
Central Statistical Office (Zambia), 115
Centre for Rural Legal Studies (CRLS), 174
Certeau, Michel de, 291, 299
Césaire, Aimé, 248, 253–254, 258
Chege, Michael, 2
Chibheura exams, 299–320
Chief Native Commissioner (CNC), 300
Child Health and Development Centre, 359
child soldiers, 277–298
　discourses of childhood, 281–283
　exposure to war and violence, 283–287
　initiation to violence and terror, 287–292
　in post–colonial conflicts, 280–281
　reconciliation and healing, 292–298
China, 44, 78–79
Christians, 226
civil society, 15–16, 117–121, 136–142, 146, 166
　conceptions of, 121–130
　definitions, 118–119
　neoliberalism and, 129–130
　pro–democracy advocates of, 121–122
　radical, 123–124
　transition studies, 147–148
class issues, 151–160
Clinton, Bill, 131
CNC. *See* Chief Native Commissioner
CODESA, 201
CODESRIA. *See* Council for the Development of Social Science Research in Africa
Cohen, W. B., 37–38
Cold War, 352
Coleman, D. C., 71
colonial rule, 7–9, 20–22, 220–222, 245–249, 371

Colson, Elizabeth, 218
community, 18
　historical context, 189–192
　Indian community, 205–209
　NGOs and, 174, 175, 177–180
　as term, 177–179
　women and, 187–189
　working with, 182–189
Congress, U.S., 134
Congress of South African Trade Unions (COSATU), 16–17, 160–164, 168–169
Conrad, Joseph, 41–43, 48
consilience, 268–269, 270
consumption, 114–115
contested claims, 365–378
contrariety test, 93–95, 96
Convention on the Rights of the Child, 282
Cooper, Frederick, 320
corporatism, 166–167
corvee system, 251–252
COSATU. *See* Congress of South African Trade Union
Council for the Development of Social Science Research in Africa (CODESRIA), 3
Crafts, N. F. R., 80
Crane, Philip, 130
CRLS. *See* Centre for Rural Legal Studies
Curtin, Philip, 37–38

DA. *See* developmental activism
DAG. *See* Development Action Group
Dasgupta, Dipak, 123
data, bias, 95–99
decoding, 39–42
De Klerk, F. W., 205, 206
de Kock, Eugene, 199
Dell, Daniel, 123
democracy, 118, 126–127, 166–168
dependency, 23–24, 66, 243–246, 254–258
development, as discourse, 174–175
Development Action Group (DAG), 174, 178, 181
developmental activism (DA), 87, 90, 100–104
developmentalism, 66–70, 174–175

Diagne, Lamine, 138
Diamond, Larry, 124–130, 144
Diop, Alioune, 253–254
Diouf, 135
Domestic Labor Committee (Southern Rhodesia), 306–307
Dormaa, 225
Duase (Asante), 224–225
Durban (South Africa), 205–207

Eastern Europe, 120
Ebron, Paula, 343
Economic Commission for Africa (ECA), 81
economic growth, 79–83, 87–90, 93, 110–111
economic history, 59–60
  comparisons and connections, 72–83
  data, 79–82
  social history and, 76–77
  spatial and temporal scales, 60–65
  themes and theories, 65–72
economic policies, 129–130
economic reversal, 88–90
Economic Stabilization Act of 1982, 155
Economist, The, 97
Egypt, 43–44
Eidelberg, Phil, 164
Ejisu, queen mother of, 221–222
Ellis, Stephen, 247
Emergency Powers Decree 22 of 1985, 155
empowerment, 174, 177
End of Ideology (Bell), 123
entertainment, 329–333
Equity and Vulnerability: A Situational Analysis of Women, Adolescents and Children in Uganda, 359–361
Erasmus, Z., 205
1844 Essays (Marx), 236
essentialism, 267–269, 272
establishment civil society, 121, 124–128
Ethiopia, 45, 56, 372, 373
ethnic identity, 19–20, 196–201
exclusion, 105, 215–217
exile, 259–262
existentialism, 241–242
expansionism, 47–52

experience, 237–240
exploitation, 251–252
Eze, Emmanuel, 3

Falae, Olu, 159
Fall, Aboubacar, 138–139
Fall, Yoro, 39
Fanon, Frantz, 210, 227, 235–238, 245–248, 254–258, 310
Farmer, Paul, 341–342
Federalist Papers, 120, 122, 127–128
Fifteenth International Conference of Labor Statisticians, 81
Fire of Invention, The: Civil Society and the Future of the Corporation (Novak), 122
Fleischman Corporation, 141
Fleming, Andrew M., 301–303, 306
Fort Victoria (Southern Rhodesia), 301
France, 30, 136, 245–251
  cartography, 48, 49, 51–52
Freedom Charter (South Africa), 15, 197–198
Free French, 250
Frelimo. *See* Front for the Liberation of Mozambique
French Elementary School, 323
Freud, Anna, 256
Freund, Bill, 206–207
Front for the Liberation of Mozambique (Frelimo), 25, 261, 265, 274–276, 277
Fukuyama, Francis, 69
Furedi, Frank, 75

Gallieni, General, 246–248, 251–252
Ganda Agents, 350
Gary, Ian, 175
gaze, 238–239, 241
GDI. *See* Gender–Related Development Index
GEAR. *See* Growth Employment and Redistribution
Gelb, Steven, 169
GEM. *See* Gender Empowerment Measure
Gender Empowerment Measure (GEM), 113

INDEX • 467

gender issues
   health and violence, 375–378
   South Africa, 113, 186–189
   See also women
Gender–Related Development Index (GDI), 113
Geneva convention (1949), 282
geography, 46–47, 60–65
Germany, 141
Ghana, 38, 221, 231–232
   See also Asante
Giddens, Anthony, 73
Gills, Barry, 169–170
Global Economic Prospect 1998/99, 133
globalization, 74–76
Gold Coast Colony, 220–222
Goldilocks society, 119–120
Gomes, Flora, 276
Gosa, Furiana, 313–314, 318
Gould, Stephen, 268
Gramsci, Antonio, 118, 141, 173–174, 193
Greeks, 43, 57
Green, William, 64
Grindle, Merilee, 104
Growth Employment and Redistribution (GEAR), 15, 164, 167, 169
Guinea–Bissau, 56, 261, 274
Guyer, Jane, 228–229
Gyedifo, 226

Haggard, Rider, 244
Haiti, 341–342
Hall, Stuart, 210
Harari African Location, 307, 309, 318
Hardt, Michael, 149–150
Harvey, David, 73
Hastings, Adrian, 266, 275
Hausa, 61
HDI. *See* Human Development Index
health issues, 32–33
   biomedical emphasis, 358, 363
   epidemic disease, 367–368
   explanations of illness, 365–367
   gendered violence and, 375–378
   political violence and, 373–374
   population growth, 368–371
   wars and, 371–373

Heart of Darkness (Conrad), 41, 48
Heath, Edward, 265
Heavily Indebted Poor Countries (HIPC) Initiative, 112
Hegel, G. W. F., 60
hegemony, 173–174
Herbst, Jeffrey, 157–158
Heren, Louis, 265
High Court (Asante), 224–225
History and Class Consciousness (Lukács), 236
HIV. *See* Acquired Immunodeficiency Syndrome
Hopkins, Anthony, 76
HPI. *See* Human Poverty Index
Huang, Philip, 78–79
Hubbard, William, 77
Huggins, Geoffrey, 319
Hull, James, 77
Human Development Index (HDI), 15, 83, 112–114
Human Development Reports (UNDP), 83, 112, 118
Humanism and Terror (Merleau–Ponty), 236
Human Poverty Index (HPI), 113
Hunter, Susan, 357–358

Ibbotson, Percy, 309, 319
IBM Senegal, 139
identity, 195–212, 197–200, 297
IFP. *See* Inkatha Freedom Party
ILO. *See* International Labor Organization
IMF. *See* International Monetary Fund
India, 272
Indian–African riot of 1949, 206, 207
Indian community (South Africa), 204–209
individualism, 216–217, 227
Influenza Epidemic of 1918, 302
Inkatha Freedom Party (IFP), 200–204, 207
intellectuals, 173–174, 193
interest group, community as, 189–192
International Comparison Project, 82
International Conference on Population and Development (1994), 369

468 • INDEX

International Labor Organization (ILO), 80, 81, 164
International Monetary Fund (IMF), 4, 21, 87, 111–112, 131–132, 145, 154–155, 176
intersubjectivity, 238–243

Jacques Lacan & Co. (Roudinesco), 244
Jaenson, Carol, 359
Jaspers, Karl, 252
Johannesburg Star, 200

Kampala (Uganda), 350–352
Kasadha, Robinah, 359
Katongole–Mbidde, E., 347
Kenya, 213, 214, 217–218, 351
Keywords (Williams), 178
Kgatleng district (Botswana), 220
Ki–Zerbo, Joseph, 68
Klein, Melanie, 247
Knowledge, Attitudes and Practices (KAP), 353
knowledge production, 173–174, 193
Kojève, Alexandre, 236
Korten, David, 176
Kramer, Gerhard (Mercator), 46–47, 57
Kreps, David, 72
Kuhn, Thomas, 365
Kumase (Asante), 223
Kumase Traditional Council, 225
Kumawu (Asante), 226
Kumawuhene (Asante), 230
KwaZulu Natal (South Africa), 196, 202–204, 207
  labor, 16–17, 145–171
  marginalization of, 165–170
  regimes, 152–154
  SAPs and, 160–164
  transition studies, 147–151

Labor Department (South Africa), 165
Labor Relations Act (LRA) (South Africa), 162, 163, 165
Lacan, Jacques, 244
Ladjali, Malika, 369
Land Apportionment Act of 1930, 308

Landes, David, 80
Land Use Act (Nigeria), 218
Land Use Decree of 1978 (Nigeria), 159
Langer, Monika, 241
Latin America, 167
Lemarchand, René, 267
Lemon, Anthony, 204
Leon, Tony, 200
Leopold II, 371
Leys, Colin, 69–70
Libya, 43
Lindblad, Thomas, 78
Lindenbaum, S., 342
Lipset, Seymour, 123
lived experience, 237–238, 245, 257
Livingston, James, 78
Local Government Act of 1997 (Uganda), 360
LRA. *See* Labor Relations Act
Luba, 39, 40, 57
Lugar, Richard, 130
Lugard, Lord, 244, 251
Lummis, C. Douglas, 123–124
Luso–Africa, 261–265
  Wiriyamu massacre, 265–267, 269–276
  See also Angola; Guinea–Bissau; Mozambique
Luthuli, Albert, 203
Lyons, Maryinez, 343

Macdonald, Martha, 82
MacKenzie, J. M., 38, 51
Madagascar, 29–30, 241, 243–244, 247, 258
  labor camps, 236, 251–252
Madison, James, 127
Madzingirwa, Ambuya, 314–316, 319
Makerere Institute of Social Research, 360
Makerere University (Uganda), 359, 360
Malagasies, 245–249, 253–258, 339, 340–341
  massacre of, 244, 249–254
  poverty, 106–107
  schooling, 321–344
Malagasy, Official, 324–325
Malawi, 64, 107, 274

INDEX • 469

Mali, 44
Mamdani, Mahmood, 2
Mandela, Nelson, 131, 182, 196–197, 199–204, 208, 211
Mandela, Winnie, 208–209, 211
Manicheanism, 238–243
Manning, Patrick, 71, 79
Mannoni, Octave, 235–237, 243–257
Manufacturing African Studies and Crises (Zeleza), 59–60, 64, 66
mapmaking. *See* cartography
Marcusson, Henrik Secher, 176
Markovits, Irving, 120–121
Marx, Karl, 236
Marxism, 66–69
Masaka (Uganda), 350, 351
Mauritania, 121, 134–144
Mauritius, 107
Maurs, 124–135, 136, 138, 140
Mbeki, Thabo, 167–168, 197, 200
McMichael, P., 69
MDRM. *See* Mouvement de la Rénovation Malagache
Medical Officers of Health (MOHs), 301, 302
Mediterranean Sea, 44
Medium Term Program (Nigeria), 158
Meer, Fatima, 207
memory, 312–320
Mengo (Uganda), 350
Mercator (Gerhard Kramer), 46–47, 57
Merina empire, 247, 251
Merleau-Ponty, Maurice, 235, 236–243, 247–248, 257
Mfayela, Senzo, 201
MFDC. *See* Casamance independence movement
Ministry of Home Affairs (South Africa), 204
Mkandawire, Thandika, 80–81
Mlambo-Nguka, Phumzile, 211
Modern Economic History of Africa, A (Zeleza), 59, 61, 64, 65–66, 79
MOHs. *See* Medical Officers of Health
Mokaba, Peter, 210, 211
Mondlane, Eduardo, 261, 264

Monga, Celestin, 128
Morobe, Murphy, 209
Mouvement de la Rénovation Malagache (MDRM), 250
moving frontier, 348–352
Mozambique, 25–26, 372, 373
  war of liberation, 265–266, 274
  See also child soldiers
Mozambique National Resistance (RENAMO), 277, 283, 285, 289, 292, 372
MPLA. *See* Popular Movement for the Liberation of Angola
Mudimbe, Valentin, 43
Museveni, Yoweri Kaguta, 353, 354, 361, 363
Mustapha, Abdul, 171
My Lai massacre, 266
Mzala, 202

Namibia, 107
Napoleon I, 48
Nash, June, 160
Natal Indian Congress, 198, 205
National AIDS Control Programme (Uganda), 353
National Archives (Kumase), 224
National Economic Development and Labor Council (NED–LAC), 162, 166–167
National Labor Congress (NLC), 153–154, 156
National Oceanographic and Atmospheric Administration (NOAA), 13
National Party (NP), 15, 19–20, 179–180, 196, 203, 205–208
National Resistance Movement/National Resistance Army (NRM/NRA), 353, 354, 360, 363
Native Adultery Act of 1916, 310
Native Affairs Committee of 1910–1911, 310
Native Affairs Department, 309
Native Commissioners (NCs), 300
Native Pass Consolidation Ordinance, 300
Native Registration Act of 1918, 302
Native Registration Act of 1936, 308, 310

Native Registration Ordinance, 1901, 302, 307
Native Rising (Southern Rhodesia), 300
Native Urban Areas Act of 1946, 310
Native Welfare Society, 309, 320
Nazi Germany, 141, 144
NCs. *See* Native Commissioners
Ndebele, S'bu, 203
Ndebele community, 300, 311
Ndegwa, Stephen N., 127
NED–LAC. *See* National Economic Development and Labor Council
neoliberalism, 68–70, 129–130, 145–146, 169–170
Neto, Agostinho, 261
New Imperialism, 72
newly industrialized countries (NICs), 68
New Vision, The, 354
New World Order, 75
Ngano, Martha, 307
NGOs. *See* nongovernmental organizations
NICs. *See* newly industrialized countries
Nigeria, 16–17, 218, 231
   labor movement, 151–160
   militarized economic adjustment, 155–160
   oil boom, 152–154
   structural adjustment, 145–160, 171
Nile River, 44, 47
Nixon, Rob, 198, 202
Nkrumah, Kwame, 221
NLC. *See* National Labor Congress
nongovernmental organizations (NGOs), 10–11, 19, 127, 174, 181–182
   AIDS and, 30–31
   community and, 177–180
   space of, 175–176
Nordstrom, Carolyn, 293, 376
North, Douglas, 70, 71–72
North Africa, 60
North–South comparison, 73–79
Novak, Michael, 122
NRM/NRA. *See* National Resistance Movement/National Resistance Army
NUPENG, 158

OAU. *See* Organization of African Unity
Obasanjo, Olusegun, 159
Obeng, Pashington, 227–228
Obote, Milton, 353
OCSs. *See* Organizations of Civil Society
Ogoni, 158
Ombre et le Vent, L' (Ranaivo), 253
Operacao Producao, 285
oral transmission, 224, 226
Organization of African Unity (OAU), 54, 55
Organizations of Civil Society (OCSs), 16
"Orphée Noir" (Fanon), 241, 243, 254
Other, 43, 241–242, 253
Owomoyela, Oyekan, 2

Pan African Congress, 198
Panitch, Leo, 169
Pankhurst, Richard, 40
Pape, John, 311
PDP. *See* People's Democratic Party
PENGASSAN, 158
People's Democratic Party (PDP), 159
periodization, 42, 63–65
Peters, Arno, 53
Peters, Pauline, 220
Philosophie bantoue, La (Tempels), 253
Pieterse, E., 205
play, 337–339
pluralism, 120–121, 124–128, 273
Pomper, Philip, 63
Popular Movement for the Liberation of Angola (MPLA), 261, 277
population growth, 368–371
Portugal, 56, 261–276
post–colonialism, 37, 64–65
postmodernism, 37, 68
post–traumatic stress disorder, 292–294
poverty, 14–15, 90, 105, 167
   causes, 109–112
   measurement, 112–115
Poverty Reduction Growth Facility, 111, 112
Poverty Reduction Strategy Paper (PRSP), 111–112
Présence Africaine, 235–236, 245, 253–254
"Présence Noir" (Sartre), 235
Prester John, 44–45
primitive, concept of, 246–247

property, 213–215, 230–232
  custom and, 215, 218–219, 220–223
  as exclusion, 215–217
  negotiable, 220–226
  as participation, 226–230
  reforms, 20–22, 217–220
Prospero and Caliban: The Psychology of Colonialization (Mannoni), 243–249
PRSP. *See* Poverty Reduction Strategy Paper
Psychologie de colonization (Mannoni), 235
psychology, 244–250, 254–258, 292–294
Public Health Act of 1924, 305, 310

Rabémananjara, Jacques, 253
Raikes, Philip, 80
Rajah, D. S., 206
Rajbansi, Amichand, 205
Rakai Project, 358
Ramaphosa, Cyril, 208
Ramphele, Mamphela, 179–180, 184
Ranaivo, Flavien, 253
Ranavalona, Queen, 247
Ranger, T. O., 218–219, 303
rape, 373–376
Ratsiraka, President, 332–333, 340
Rawlings, Jerry, 225, 231
Rawski, Thomas, 79–80
Reconstruction and Development Program (RDP), 162, 164
Reddy, J. N., 206
Rees–Mogg, William, 265
reform performance groups, 91–95
RENAMO. *See* Mozambique National Resistance
rent–seeking, 222–225, 232
Reports of the Medical Director and Principal Medical Officer, 301
Reports on the Public Health, 301, 308
Responsible Government and Settler Rule (1923), 304
Reynolds, Andrew, 205
Rhodesia. *See* Southern Rhodesia; Zimbabwe
Rhodesia and General Asbestos Corporation, 315–317
Rhodesia Bantu Voters Association Women's League, 307–308, 318

Rhodesia Native Labor Bureau (RNLB), 302
Rhodesian Landowners' and Farmers' Association, 305–306
Rhodesian Women's Guild, 304
Richards, Audrey, 351
RNLB. *See* Rhodesia Native Labor Bureau
Robinson, Randall, 131
Rocamora, Joel, 169–170
Rockefeller Foundation Population Sciences Division, 358
Roudinesco, Elisabeth, 244
Rowaski, Thomas, 72
Rwanda, 26, 33, 107, 351, 354, 372, 377

SACP. *See* South African Communist Party
Said, Edward, 210
Sakalava dynasty, 322, 339
Sambirano Valley, 322
Samuel, John, 208
Sandberg, Eve, 176
SAPs. *See* structural adjustment programs
Sartre, Jean–Paul, 235, 236, 237–243, 254
Sassine, William, 271–272
Saul, John, 202
Save the Children's Fund, 358, 359
Schneider, W. H., 38
schooling
  dangers, 322–323, 339–344
  diversions, 328–337
  play and morality, 337–339
  sacrifice and, 324–325
  school migrants, 325–327
  town–based girls, 333–336
  urban danger and scholastic failure, 323–327
Schuurman, Frans, 69
Schweikart, Larry, 78
Scott, Johanna, 318–319
Senegal, 117, 121, 134–144
Senghor, Léopold, 254
Serote, Wally, 209–210
Serwadda, D., 347
sexuality, 335–337, 367
  dangers, 322–323, 339–344
  politics of, 310–312

schooling and, 322–323
Zimbabwe, 299–320
sexually transmitted diseases (STDs), 301–309
  Chibheura exams, 299–320
  See also Acquired Immunodeficiency Syndrome
Seychelles, 107
Shagari administration, 155, 157
Shapiro, Julia, 174
Shona community, 300, 317, 318
SIDA. See AIDS
Sierra Leone, 228
SIP. See social and institutional profile
Slovo, Joe, 198
social and institutional profile (SIP), 355–357, 363
social capital, 228–229
social categories, 17–19
social history, 76–77
social policy making, 165–170
social pollution, 293–296
Solow, Robert, 71
"Song" (Rabémananjara), 253
South Africa, 15–21, 55
  Africanization, 204–211
  apartheid, 179–180, 181
  Dutch settlement, 179–180
  economy, 210–211
  ethnic groups, 196–201
  gender differences, 113, 186–189
  identity, 195–212
  Indian community, 204–209
  industrial relations, 160–161, 165–170
  NGOs in, 181–182
  social terrain, 173–193
  structural adjustment, 160–170
  Zulu nationalism, 196–197, 200–204
South African Communist Party (SACP), 161, 201
Southern Rhodesia
  Chibheura exams, 299–320
  Legislative Counsel, 304, 312
South–North comparison, 73–79
South–West Route, 351
Soviet Union, 68

space
  control of, 299–320
  politics of, 300–310
  spatial and temporal scales, 60–65
Spear of the Nation, 200
spiritual power, 227–228, 293–297, 338
Spivak, Gayatri, 272, 301
SPP. See Surplus People Project
Stephens, Sharon, 337–338
Stoler, Anne, 311
Stone, Jeffrey, 40–41
Strategic Management Committee (ANC), 208
structural adjustment programs (SAPs), 14–15, 70, 76, 81, 176, 366
  Asante, 217–218
  failure of, 87–95
  homegrown structural adjustment, 163–164, 166, 170
  labor and, 146–147, 149, 154, 156–160
  Nigeria, 145–160, 171
  South Africa, 160–170
  World Bank and, 87, 91–92, 102, 106
sub–Saharan Africa
  African Growth and Opportunity Act, 118–119, 130–131
  economic reversal, 88–91
  poverty, 105–116
Sudan, 372
Superior Court (Accra), 230
Surplus People Project (SPP), 174, 178, 181
Swift, Jonathan, 45–46
Swynnerton Plan, 214

Taiwo, Olufemi, 60
Tano Kwabena, 225
Tanzania, 352
Tanzania–Uganda War of 1979, 352
TASO. See AIDS Support Organization
Tempels, Placide, 253
Temps Modernes, Les, 236
Thatcher, Margaret, 15
Third National Development Plan (Nigeria), 101
third person, 239, 253
Third World, 66–68, 73–76

Thornton, Robert, 179–180, 184
Thrower, Norman, 40
Tilly, Charles, 77
Timbuktu, 44
Times, The, 265–267, 269, 271, 275–276
TINA (there is no alternative), 15, 18–19, 76
Trade and Development Report (UNCTAD), 111
Trade and Tariff Act of 1988, 130
TransAfrica, 131
Trans–African Highway, 352
transition studies, 147–151, 370–371
Transkei, 203
TRC. *See* Truth and Reconciliation Commission
Tripartite Alliance (South Africa), 161–162
Truth and Reconciliation Commission (TRC), 208, 268
Turner, Terisa, 158
Tutu, Desmond, 197, 199, 268
Tutu, Osei, 223, 225
Two Faces of Civil Society, The (Ndegwa), 127

UDF. *See* United Democratic Front
Ugalde, A., 373
Uganda, 31–32, 107
  action research, 357–358
  AIDS, 345–363
  civil war and violence, 352–355
  colonization, 350–351
  districts, 360–362
  household composition, 355–357
  inclusion efforts, 358–360
  Mbarara district, 350, 354, 358
  orphans, 357–358
  population density, 349–350
  Rakai district, 350, 352, 354, 358
  security situation, 347, 353–355
  social and institutional profile, 355–357, 363
Uganda Community–Based Health Care Association, 359
Uganda National Council for Children's Situation Analysis, 361

Uganda Women's Efforts to Save Orphans (UWESO), 357, 359
Umtali Rape Case of 1911, 311
Umzamo, 174, 178, 181
UNCTAD. *See* United Nations Conference on Trade and Development
UNDP. *See* United Nations Development Programme
unemployment, 14–15, 80, 105
UNESCO series, 60–61
UNICEF, 359
Union Investment Funds (South Africa), 163
UNITA. *See* United Front for the Total Liberation of Angola
United Democratic Front (UDF), 201, 209
United Front for the Total Liberation of Angola (UNITA), 277, 283–286, 293
United Nations, 81, 261, 282, 369
United Nations Conference on Trade and Development (UNCTAD), 81, 111
United Nations Development Programme (UNDP), 81, 107, 108, 110
United States, 76–78, 130–134, 135
United States Agency for International Development (USAID), 134–136, 141, 220, 354
University of Durban–Westville, 207
Urban Affairs Commission (Southern Rhodesia), 319
USAID. *See* United States Agency for International Development
UWESO. *See* Uganda Women's Efforts to Save Orphans

values, 269–273
van Onselen, Charles, 304, 313
Vatican, 264–265
Vaughan, Megan, 310
Venereal Disease conference (1928), 307
Vilakazi, Herbert, 203
violence, 22–33, 373–375
  AIDS and, 352–355
  as gendered, 375–378
  torture, 241, 257
  See also child soldiers

wars, 371–373
wealth-in-people, 227–229
Webster, Eddie, 162–163
Weiner, Annette, 222
Whitford, Margaret, 241–242
WHO. *See* World Health Organization
Wilks, Ivor, 38
Williams, Raymond, 178
Wilson, Edward, 268
Wilson, Richard, 169–170
Winichakul, Thongchai, 15
Winnicott, D. W., 256
Winter–Nelson, Alex, 82
Wiriyamu massacre, 265–267, 269–276
Witch's Head (Haggard), 244
Wiwa, Ken–Saro, 158
Wolfensohn, James D., 103, 132
women
    Chibheura exams, 299–320
    community and, 187–189
    exclusion of, 300–303
    population control and, 368–371
    rape and, 373–376
    spatial control of, 305–306
    See also gender issues
Wood, D., 39
Workers' Organization for Socialist Action (WOSA), 208
Working Group on the Socioeconomic, Cultural and Legal Impact of AIDS, The, 358
Work in Progress, 203
World Bank, 4, 9, 13, 21, 22, 81, 103, 131, 145, 177, 352, 366
    Asian financial crisis and, 132–134
    bias, 95–99
    data, 91–95, 108
    health issues and, 368
    property rights and, 214, 228
    publications, 97–98, 102–103
    structural adjustment and, 87, 91–92, 102, 106
    success, 99–100
World Development Report (World Bank), 102–103
World Health Organization (WHO), 353
World Learning, Inc., 359
World War I, 302
WOSA. *See* Workers Organization for Socialist Action
Wretched of the Earth, The (Fanon), 210, 237, 241

Xhosas, 200, 203

Youth League (ANC), 208, 211

Zambezi River, 274
Zambia, 106, 107, 110, 113, 115, 274
Zeleza, P. T., 13, 59, 61, 64, 65–66, 79
Zimbabwe, 20–21, 107, 218, 299–320
    See Also Southern Rhodesia
Zulu nationalism, 196–197, 200–204, 206
Zulus, 61, 203
Zweliyhini, Goodwill, 201
Zwi, A., 373